# CONSPECTUS

JuraLaw™

*an imprint of*

TellerBooks™

ISBN (13) (paperback): 978-1-68109-040-5
ISBN (10) (paperback): 1-68109-040-6



2012 Edition

Published by TellerBooks™
Manufactured in the U.S.A.
First printing August, 2008.

# TABLE OF CONTENTS

# ABBREVIATIONS

A ...................... Grantee (for present estate/ future interest hypotheticals)
AGI .................. Adjusted gross income
AP.................... Adverse possession
A/R .................. Assumption of the risk
B ...................... Buyer
BFP ................. Bona fide purchaser or bona fide purchase
C ...................... Constitution
CIF................... Cause-in-fact
Cl. .................... Clause
CLEO............... State Chief Law Enforcement Officer
Court (cap.) ..... United States Supreme Court
CP ................... Court of Pleas (UK)
CR ................... Contingent remainder
CSD................. Common Scheme of Development
CSI .................. Compelling state interest
Ct. .................... Court
Ct. App. ........... Court of Appeals
Ct. Chan. ........ Court of Chancery (England)
ED ................... Emotional distress
EI .................... Executory interest
Eng. ................. England
ES.................... Equitable Servitude
FI ..................... false imprisonment
FLSA ............... Fair Labor Standards Act
FMLA............... Family and Medical Leave Act
FQJ.................. Federal question jurisdiction
FRAP............... Federal Rules of Appellate Procedure
FRCP............... Federal Rules of Civil Procedure
FRCrP ............. Federal Rules of Criminal Procedure
FRE ................. Federal Rules of Evidence
FS.................... Fee simple absolute (fee simple)
FSCS............... Fee simple on condition subsequent
FSD ................. Fee simple determinable
FS EL .............. Fee simple on executory limitation
FT ................... Fee tail
H.L. ................. House of Lords (England)
IIED................. Intentional infliction of emotional distress
IT..................... Intentional tort
JMOL .............. Judgment as a matter of law
JNOV .............. Judgment non obstante veredicto
J/SL ................ Joint and several liability, or jointly and severally liable
JT.................... Joint tenant/tenancy
K ..................... Knowledge (criminal law) or Contract (all other law)
K.B. ................. King's Bench (UK)
KSC ................ Knowledge to a substantial certainty
L...................... Loss in value
L1.................... First landlord
Lat. .................. Latin
LE ................... Life estate
LED................. Life estate determinable
LLC ................. Limited liability company
LLP ................. Limited liability partnership
LRM ................ Least restrictive means
MPC................ Model Penal Code
MSAJ .............. Motion to set aside the judgment
N ..................... Negligence
N.B. ................. Nota bene
NIED ............... Negligent infliction of emotional distress
O ..................... Original owner, or grantor (in present estates and future interests)
OLQ ................ Owner of the *locus in quo*
OO .................. Original owner
P ..................... Purpose or purchaser
PJ.................... Personal jurisdiction
PJI................... Pattern Criminal Jury Instruction
Q.B. ................ Queen's Bench (UK)
R ..................... Recklessness
RAP ................ Rule against perpetuities
RC................... Real Covenant

Restatement.... Restatement (of Contracts, Torts, Judgments, etc.)
RFRA............... Religious Freedom Restoration Act of 1993
RIL.................. Res ipsa loquitur
RPP................. Reasonable prudent person
Rule................. Federal Rule of Evidence or Federal Rule of Civil Procedure
§ ...................... Section
S ...................... Sublessee or seller
S.Ct. ................ Supreme Court or U.S. Supreme Court Reporter
SJ .................... Summary judgment
SL .................... Strict liability
SMJ ................. Subject matter jurisdiction
SP.................... Specific performance
T1.................... First tenant
TE ................... Tenant/tenancy by the entireties
TO.................... True owner
UCC................ Uniform Commercial Code
US.................... United States of America or United States Reports (compilation of U.S. Supreme Court opinions)
USC ................ United States Code
VR.................... Vested remainder
VR SD............ Vested remainder subject to divestment

## Chapter I. Contracts and Sales

# 1 Introduction

## 1.1 Defining Contracts

1.1.1 The Restatement (Second) of Contracts § 2 establishes the following definitions:

(a) *Promise*: a manifestation of intention to act or refrain from acting so made as to justify a *promisee* in understanding that a commitment has been made.

(b) *Promisor*: the party making the promise.

(c) *Promisee*: the party receiving the promise.

(d) *Beneficiary*: the party that will benefit from a performance, when this person is not the promisee.

1.1.2 "A contract is a promise or set of promises, for breach of which the law gives remedy, the fulfillment of which is a legal duty" (§ 1 Restatement).

1.1.3 "An agreement is a manifestation of mutual assent by two or more persons. A bargain is an agreement to exchange promises or exchange a promise for a performance or to exchange performances" (§ 3 Restatement).

1.1.4 A contract can be made orally or in writing, or inferred from conduct (§ 4 Restatement).

## 1.2 Sources of the Law on Contracts

1.2.1 The case law, which can vary from state to state.

1.2.2 In the sales of goods, the Uniform Commercial Code (UCC).

(a) This is a uniform law that all of the states have adopted.

(b) However, Louisiana has not adopted the UCC in all of the ways suggested its drafters.

(c) The UCC applies to contracts for the sale of goods (art. 2) and for leases (art. 2A).

(d) The UCC also deals with negotiable instruments (art. 3), bank deposits (art. 4), letters of credit (art. 5), investment securities (art. 8).

(e) The present text will limit itself to discussing sales of goods and will make some mention of the UCC provisions with respecto to leases.

1.2.3 Furthermore, secondary sources such as the Restatement (Second) of Contracts, legal treatises, and scholarly articles may apply.

## 1.3 Classes of Contracts

1.3.1 Bilateral contracts are accepted by return promise.

(a) Example: a contract in which A promises to sell B land at a particular price if B promises to purchase the land at that price.

1.3.2 Unilateral contracts are accepted by performance.

(a) Example: A promises to pay $10 to whoever finds and brings him his lost dog.

(b) The person who finds and brings the dog, without notifying A of his acceptance or promising to bring A the lost dog, is entitled to the $5 at the time he brings the lost dog.

# 2 Mutual Assent

## 2.1 The Objective Theory of Assent

2.1.1 An Objective Meeting of the Minds: the Reasonable Person Standard

(a) For there to be a valid contract, there must be a "meeting of the minds."

(b) *Actual mutual assent* is not required; it is the *expression* of assent through behavior that matters.

(c) What is important in the objective theory of assent is not the inner motives of the parties, but rather, their outward expressions.

(d) Determining the "secrets of the mind" is thus not necessary in determining mutual assent.

(i) *See Embry v. Hargadine, McKittrick Dry Goods* Co. (Mo. Ct. App. 1907), where the defendant acted as though the plaintiff had his job contract back, but then fired him after two months. The court ruled in favor of the plaintiff, since the defendant expressed his assent through behavior and whether he intended to renew the contract was irrelevant.

(e) One must determine whether a *reasonable person* in the offeree's position would come to conclude that an offer or assent to an offer is being made.

(f) Even if the offeror is joking or intoxicated, if his outer conduct would lead a reasonable person to conclude that there was an agreement, then the promise is enforceable.

(i) *See Lucy v. Zehmer* (Va. 1954), where a court held that if the defendant were sober enough to spend forty minutes discussing the terms of an agreement, then regardless of whether he was intoxicated, that promise was enforceable because of the manifestation of assent.

2.1.2 A Written Contract

(a) The commitment does not need to be memorialized as a written contract.

(b) A contract is enforceable as soon as there is a meeting of the minds.

(i) *See Sanders v. Pottlitzer Fruit Co.* (N.Y. l894), where after much negotiation, the plaintiff sends a letter offering apples, the defendant says it will take apples only if conditions are met, and the plaintiff accepts. The defendant then asks for the written contract to be sent, which it tries to change. The plaintiff refuses to change it and sues to enforce the original contract. The court held that there was an agreement in the prior correspondences; a formally written contract was not required. Judgment for the plaintiff.

## 2.2 The Offer

### 2.2.1 Definition

(a) An offer is a manifestation of willingness to enter into a bargain, so made as to justify another person in understanding that his *assent* to that bargain is invited and will conclude it (§ 24 Restatement).

### 2.2.2 The Four Elements of an Offer

(a) A Commitment

(i) There must be a promise to enter into a contract, not an invitation to negotiate.

(ii) Language such as "I offer" or "I promise" tends to indicate commitment; language such as "I consider" or "I quote" tends to indicate an invitation for offers.

(iii) If offeror did not intend to make the offer, the objective test will be used: "would a reasonable person in the offeree's position know or should he have known that there was an offer?"

(iv) To answer this question, the following will be considered:

(1) Industry practices and prior practices between the parties.

(2) Circumstances: was the offer made in jest? If so, would a reasonable person have construed it to be an offer?

(aa) *See Zehmer*, where the defendant said he was joking about selling his land, but the court held there was a commitment because a reasonable person would not have understood that he was joking.

(b) Communicated

(i) The offeree must have knowledge of the offer before being able to accept it.

(ii) Example: A offers to buy B's car for $5,000. B, before he finds out about the offer, says that he will give A his car for the same price. Since A's offer was not communicated to B, B's communication is merely another offer; it does not constitution acceptance.

(c) To an Identified Offeree

(i) An offer is always personal; it cannot be transferred to a third party.

(ii) The broader the medium for communicating the offer, the more likely the courts will construe the communication to be an advertisement.

(iii) Advertisements are not offers, but rather, invitations to negotiate or make offers.

(1) *See Nebraska Seed Co. v. Harsh* (Neb. 1915), where a farmer invited a company to buy about 1,800 bushels of seeds for $2.25 each, and the company accepted. When the farmer did not deliver, the company sued for breach of contract. The

court held that there was never an offer, since the communication was not made to an identified offeree, but rather, to several. Furthermore, the delivery time and subject matter ("about" 1800 bushels) was indefinite.

(2) *See also Leonard v. Pepsico* (S.D.N.Y. 1999), where an advertisement was held not to be an offer, and furthermore, tested by the reasonable person standard, the content of the advertisement was an obvious joke, not a real offer.

(iv) However, the Restatement (Second) of Contracts allows offers to be made to more than one person (§ 29 Restatement). The communication would be a valid offer if it can only be construed as being open to a single offeree.

(1) For example, if a subject offers a reward to whoever finds and returns his lost dog, a court would treat the communication as an offer, since it is implicitly being communicated to an identified offeree: the first and only person to return the dog.

(d) With Definite Terms

(i) The rules requiring definiteness in a contract's terms are based on the concept that a party cannot accept an offer unless the terms of that offer are definite (certain).

(ii) The essential terms of an agreement must therefore be agreed upon before a contract is formed. If the terms of an agreement are so indefinite as to make it impossible for the court to determine them, it is not an enforceable contract.

(iii) Each category of contracts calls for different terms to be defined.

(1) For contracts of realty, the ***price*** and the ***land to be sold*** (the amount and location) must be specified.[1]

(aa) The land must be identified as to both the amount and the location to be sold.

(2) For employment contracts, the ***duration*** must be determined.

(aa) The duration may be manifested as a period of time (*e.g.*, a one year employment contract) or as a task (*e.g.*, a contract to repair a computer).

(bb) If the duration is not specified, the offeree is considered hired at will and can quit or be fired at anytime without being able to enforce any time provision.

(3) For loans or other financial instruments, the amount loaned, the maturity date (or "redemption date") of the loan, the interest rate (if any), and the repayment terms are generally required. *See T.O. Stanley Boot Co., Inc. v. Bank of El Paso* (Tex.1992).

---

[1] With respect to the description of the land, the test turns on whether a court can identify the land to be sold in order to enforce the contract.

(aa) However, the maturity date is only essential for financial instruments under which the loan is to be repaid on a fixed date.

(bb) If the financial instrument has no fixed maturity date, it continues indefinitely (unless repayment is agreed between the parties at some later point). An example of such an instrument is a "perpetual stock."

(cc) Other instruments have a range of possible maturity dates, any of which may be chosen by the borrower for repayment.

(4) For contracts for the sale of goods under the UCC, only the ***quantity*** must described (UCC Official Comment 1, § 2-201).

(aa) The indicated quantity need not be accurate, but the contract cannot be enforced beyond this quantity.

(bb) Other terms, such as the price, place of delivery, or time of delivery, can be determined by the UCC gapfillers.[2]

(cc) There are two exceptions to this rule:

(I) Requirements contracts (*e.g.*, "I will buy as many units as I need"); and

(II) Output contracts (*e.g.*, "I will buy as many units as you produce").

(dd) If terms, such as place of delivery and time of delivery, are left unspecified, the court can fill these in with what is reasonable.

(ee) If the price is unspecified, the court can fill it in when: (i) there is no mention of price in the negotiation; (ii) the price was left to the parties to agree upon but they did not; or (iii) the price was left to be determined by the market.

(I) For example, if A offers to sell B ten widgets "for the price we agree to," the price can be determined by the court, since the price was left to the parties to agree upon.

(II) However, if A offers to sell B ten widgets "for a reasonable price," a court cannot fill in the price because the offer does not fit into one of the three circumstances defined above.

(III) Since price is not determined, it is not a valid offer and the agreement is unenforceable; the court is not going to try to determine what a reasonable price is.

### 2.2.3 Terminating an Offer

---

[2] In the case of an open price term, see § 2-305 UCC; for the absence of a specified place of delivery, see § 2-308 UCC; for the absence of specific time provisions, see §2-309 UCC.

(a) The offeree's power of acceptance is terminated in the following circumstances (§ 36 Restatement):

(i) The offeree ***rejects*** the offer or makes a ***counteroffer***;

(ii) There is a ***lapse of time*** (must be reasonable);

(iii) The offeror directly or indirectly ***revokes*** the offer:

(1) The offer is considered to be indirectly revoked if the offeree receives reliable information that would lead a reasonable person to conclude that it has been revoked (*e.g.*, when the offeree learns that the offeror is searching for other purchasers).

(2) *See Dickinson v. Dodds* (Ct. App. U.K. 1876), where Dodds, the defendant, gave the plaintiff an option not bearing consideration that would remain open for two days to buy his house for 700 pounds. The plaintiff heard of Dodd's intent to sell the land to another purchaser, even though he never communicated a formal, direct revocation. The plaintiff then accepted the offer and sued for specific performance when the land was not delivered. Held: although Dodd's revocation was not directly communicated to the plaintiff, the offer was terminated the moment that the plaintiff heard about it indirectly.

(aa) *N.B.*: if there had been any consideration on the option, real or recited, the offer would have been irrevocable until the agreed-to termination.

(iv) The offeror or offeree ***dies*** or is ***incapacitated***.

(1) If the offeror dies before the offeree accepts the offer, the offeree's power of acceptance is terminated and no contract is formed.

(2) However, if the offerree accepts just prior to the offeror's death, an enforceable contract is formed. Once there is a meeting of the minds, the death of either party does not invalidate the contract.

(b) Exception: Options Contracts

(i) If an options contract is supported by consideration (or, in many courts, by recital thereof), the offeree's power of acceptance is not terminated through his rejection of the offer, counteroffer, death or incapacity, or through the direct or indirect revocation by offeror.

(ii) However, if there is no consideration, an options contract can be terminated in the same way that a regular offer can be terminated (rejection, lapse of time, revocation or death or incapacity).

(c) Revocation of Unilateral Contracts

(i) In the case of unilateral contracts, where the offer is accepted by performance, the offeror may revoke the offer at any time before the offeree completes performance.

(ii) However, where there is a ***tender*** (unconditioned willingness to perform immediately coupled with a manifest ability to perform) or a ***beginning of performance*** (more than just preparation to begin performance), a binding option contract is formed that the offeror is unable to revoke.

(iii) The offer expires on its own if the offeree leaves the job uncompleted and a reasonable time lapses.

(iv) Examples

(1) Suppose A offers to pay B $50 to shovel his driveway. If B shows up at A's home with a shovel and indicates that he is ready to begin performance, has a contract been formed?

(aa) Since B tendered performance, a valid option contract is formed.

(2) If B arrives at A's home and begins performing without informing A, has a contract been formed?

(aa) A valid options contract is formed from the moment that B begins performance until he completes it.

(3) If, without completing the job, B takes off, leaving the job incomplete, can A sue for breach of contract?

(aa) No; since B can only accept A's offer by complete performance, no acceptance was ever made, and therefore, no contract exists.

(4) What if B arrives at A's home, and, just before tendering performance, A shouts out that he revokes the offer. Is there nevertheless a contract?

(aa) No; B's power of acceptance expires if A revokes before B tenders or begins performance.

(bb) *See Petterson v. Pattberg* (N.Y. 1928), where the defendant offered the plaintiff the opportunity to obtain full title to the plaintiff's home by selling the plaintiff the mortgage to the home in exchange for $4,850 to be paid to the defendant before a certain date. The plaintiff sold the title to third party, expecting to use the funds obtained to pay the defendant $4,850 to purchase the mortgage. The plaintiff went to the defendant's home, but before he could accept the offer and tender payment, the defendant revoked the offer. The court held that no contract was formed, since the defendant had revoked his offer just before tender had been made.

(v) Thus, the defendant's obligations depend on whether the plaintiff has prepared for, tendered, begun, or completed performance.

| **Time** | ***Preparation of Performance*** | ***Tender or Beginning of Performance*** | ***Completion of Performance*** |
|---|---|---|---|

| | | | |
|---|---|---|---|
| **The Contract Formed** | There is no contract. | There is a valid option contract from this moment to the moment in which performance is completed. The offer is irrevocable. | There is a valid contract; the offeree must fulfill his contractual obligation. |
| **The Offeror's Duties** | Specific performance, if there is an options contract.<br>If there is no options contract, the offeror may be liable for damages through promissory estoppel if his revocation causes detrimental reliance on the offeree. | The offeror may not revoke the offer at any time. The offeree may, however, decide not to complete performance, at which point the option contract expires after reasonable time. | The offeror is obligated to pay the offeree. |

## 2.3 Acceptance

### 2.3.1 Introduction

(a) There are three kinds of contracts, each of which requires a different kind of acceptance:

(i) Unilateral contracts, which are constituted through performance by the offeree;

(ii) Bilateral contracts, which are created through a return promise;

(iii) Contracts for the sale of goods, which are governed by the UCC, whether they are unilateral or bilateral.

### 2.3.2 The Four Elements of Acceptance

(a) Commitment

(i) As with offers, acceptance must involve a commitment.

(ii) The primary issues raised involve the objectivity test.

(b) Communicated

(i) For determining if an acceptance is communicated, an objective standard is applied; the subjective state of mind of the parties is irrelevant.

(ii) The Mailbox Rule

(1) An acceptance is effective upon *proper dispatch* (when it is *sent*, not received), unless:

(aa) The offer stipulates that acceptance is effective when received; or

(bb) There is a valid option contract (having real or recited consideration), in which case there is acceptance only through receipt (§ 63(b) Restatement).

(2) Suppose A offers to sell B his car on January 1. On January 2, B sends a properly addressed letter accepting the offer, but revokes on January 3. On January 4, A receives the letter. Is there a contract?

(aa) A valid contract is formed the moment B sent the letter on January 2. At that moment, revocation was no longer possible.

(3) Since it is the dispatch of the acceptance, not its receipt that matters, an offer is properly accepted even if the acceptance is lost in the mail and is never received by the offeror.

(iii) Acceptance by Silence (§ 69 Restatement)

(1) When an offer is made, the offeree's silence cannot be construed as acceptance, *unless*:

(aa) The offeree puts himself within the duty of needing to speak up in order to reject an offer (*e.g.*, if he states, "unless I say something by Friday at noon, I accept this offer," *not* when the offeror puts the offeree in this position, by stating, for example, "unless you say something by Friday, you will have accepted").

(2) When industry standards or prior dealings establish acceptance by silence.

(aa) *See Hobbs v. Massasoit Whip Co.* (Mass. 1893), where the plaintif, Hobbs, sues Massasoit for failing to have paid for eel skins that the plaintiff had shipped. The defendant argues that it had never accepted the offer, an argument rejected by the court, which holds that, given trade practices and prior dealings, it was reasonable to conclude that the defendant had in fact accepted the plaintiff's offer.

(3) When the offeree silently accepts the offered benefits.

(aa) The offeree's benefiting from the proposed services are enough to constitute acceptance and create a contract.

(bb) For example, if a book club mails the offeree a book of the month, which the offeree reads, he will be considered to have accepted it. If he does nothing with it or throws it away, acceptance by silence will not be presumed.

(c) Communicated in the Right Way

(i) The offeror is the "master of the offer" sets the terms under which acceptance can be properly made.

(ii) If he asks for for acceptance by mail, acceptance cannot be transmitted fax, for example. If he states acceptance is rendered by performance, a return *promise* will not suffice.

(iii) If the way in which communication should be made is not stipulated by the offeror, the courts will presume it to be any method that is not slower or less legally reliable than the way that the offer was made.

(d) Unequivocal Acceptance that Does Not Vary the Terms

(i) Minority Approach

(1) This is the older common law approach known as the "Mirror Image Rule."

(2) To be valid, the acceptance must be *identical* to the offer.

(3) Any response varying the terms of the offer would be a counteroffer, not acceptance.

(ii) Modern Restatement Approach

(1) Some slight changes of the offer are tolerated if they do not set up a condition to the acceptance. Otherwise, they will be construed as counteroffers.

(2) *See Ardente v. Horan* (R.I. 1976), where the plaintiff made a bid to buy the defendant's house for $250,000. The defendant accepted and sent the plaintiff a purchase and sales agreement, which the plaintiff signed and sent back with a letter asking for the furniture in addition to the house. The court held that the offer was the purchase and sales agreement. The plaintiff's signing it did not constitute acceptance, since the letter sent along with it constituted a condition and therefore, a counteroffer.

(iii) UCC Approach

(1) Change or modification does not constitute rejection and counteroffer, but rather, it is an acceptance (unless it is made expressly contingent on the offeror's acceptance of the new terms) (UCC § 2-207(1)).

(2) Assuming that a contract is formed and the acceptance is not expressly conditional on offeror's acceptance of new or different terms, the following happens to the new terms in the acceptance:

(aa) When *both parties are merchants*, the new terms become part of the accepted offer *unless*:

(I) The original offer limited itself to its terms;

(II) The new terms materially alter the original offer; or

(III) The offeror already has rejected or rejects the new trems within reasonable time (UCC § 2-207(2)).

(bb) When one or both parties are *non-merchants*, the terms common to the offer and acceptance become part of the contract and the new terms become "proposals for addition to the contract." (UCC § 2-207(2)).

(iv) Last Shot Rule

(1) The last shot rule is used to determine which terms to apply when there is a contract in which the terms of the offer were different from those of the acceptance.

(2) Under the last shot rule, the terms of the "last shot" or last counteroffer apply whenever it is determined that there is a contract.

2.3.3 Acceptance by Performance in Unilateral Contracts

(a) A unilateral contract is contemplated when language in the contract or custom, trade practices, or tradition require acceptance via performance.

(b) Interpreting Ambiguities in a Contract

(i) When it is ambiguous whether the offeror intended acceptance by performance or by return promise, the courts will read the offer as creating a bilateral contract, inviting acceptance via return promise or performance (Restatement § 32, UCC § 2-206)

(ii) If the offeror states, for example, that B may purchase his car *only* if he comes to the offeror's home on a particular day and pays him, a unilateral contract is contemplated and acceptance can only be made if if the offeree shows up in person and pays. A return promise will have no effect.

(iii) However, if the word "only" is removed, it will no longer be unequivocally clear that acceptance can be made only by performance. A court will therefore interpret the contract to be bilateral and inviting acceptance via promise or performance.

(c) It may be easy to confuse acceptance in a bilateral contract with performance in a unilateral contract. In a unilateral contract, after the offeree accepts, he has no other obligations to discharge. In a bilateral contract, however, he has not yet performend, even though he has accepted.

(i) For example, if one party offers to sell his car for $5,000 and stipulates that the only way the offeree can accept is by doing a cartwheel, the offeree has not performed until he has paid the $5,000. The cartwheel is merely a way of manifesting acceptance.

(ii) In contrast, if the first party offers to give to the second his car, with the only way of acceptance being doing a cartwheel, there would be a unilateral contract where the offer is accepted by performance, since doing the cartwheel is the only duty mentioned.

(d) In unilateral contracts, there is no duty to give notice of acceptance.

(i) *See Carlill v. Carbolic Smoke Ball Co.* (Ct. App. U.K. 1892), where Carbolic offered a reward to any users of its product who might become ill. The court held that the offer was to be accepted by performance and did not require notice of acceptance. A contract was therefore formed upon Carlill's using the product, becoming sick, and thereafter notifying Carbolic and demanding 100 pounds. Carbolic was obligated to pay her.

(ii) Thus, although in bilateral contracts, notification of acceptance is required to create the contract, in unilateral contracts, no such notice is required, *unless:*

(1) The offeror requests notice of performance. Restatement § 54(1); or

(2) The offeree knows that the offeror will not have knowledge of his performance in reasonable time. In this case, if the offeror does not find out, his obligations are dismissed, *unless*:

(aa) The offeree, under due diligence, tried to inform him;

(bb) The offeror finds out about the offeree's performance on his own in due time; or

(cc) The offer indicates that notification of acceptance is not required. Restatement § 54(2).

(iii) For example, if A offers B $20 to shovel his driveway over the weekend, and then indicates that he will be out of town for a week, notification of B's performance will be required, since A will not find out about B's performance in reasonable time.

(e) Acceptance by performance to an offer done in jest does not create a contract if a reasonable person, in the place of the offeree, would have known that an offer was made in jest.

(i) *See Leonard v. Pepsico* (S.D.N.Y. 1999), where the court held that a valid offer was never made and therefore, no contract was formed by acceptance via performance.

## 2.4 E-Commerce and Mutual Assent

### 2.4.1 Rules Applied

(a) The same rules that apply to traditional cases also apply to e-commerce cases.

(b) However, courts are challenged as to how to *apply* traditional rules to cases involving the internet and other new phenomena.

(c) In some cases, opening up a package constituted acceptance to terms and conditions of an agreement when a notification was included on the package.

### 2.4.2 End User License Agreements (EULA's)

(a) In e-commerce, acceptance can be made by agreeing to the terms of a pop-up window from a web-site publisher warning end-users that entering a web-site or purchasing a program constitutes acceptance of a contract.

(i) *See Caspi v. Microsoft* (N.J. App. Div. 1999), where the plaintiff brings a class action lawsuit against Microsoft for breach of contract and fraud. The defendant moves to dismiss the action, on the basis that the plaintiffs signed a EULA and thereby agreed that the courts of Washington would have personal jurisdiction and venue. The court held that the forum selection clause that the plaintiffs agreed to when downloading the software was valid, since it was not fraudulent or based on undue bargaining power or forced litigation in a forum inconvenient to the parties. Motion to dismiss granted.

(ii) *Compare Ticketmaster v. Tickets.com* (C.D. Cal. 2003), where the plaintiff sued the defendant for having violated the EULA on the plaintiff's homepage by copying information onto the defendant's web site. The court held that the EULA was not enforceable as it was, since: (i) agreeing to the EULA was never required by users of the web site (as it was in *Caspi*); and (ii) the EULA was located in a part of the page that could be overlooked by users. Motion to dismiss granted, with a chance to amend the complaint in case there was evidence that the defendants saw the EULA.

(b) Thus, for a EULA to be binding, the parties that accept it must have seen and agreed to it before proceeding.

(c) Mere notification of the existence of a EULA on a different web page, or "browse wrap," does not constitute the necessary notification to end-users.

(d) Rather, there must be a "shrink wrap" or "click" wrap that forms a unilateral contract when opened or clicked by the end-user. Otherwise, no contract is formed.

(i) *See* Specht v. Netscape Communications (S.D.N.Y. 2001) and *Specht v. Netscape Communications* on appeal, where the defendant objected to the plaintiffs' suit by pointing out to the EULA, which required that disputes be resolved by arbitration. The court held that the EULA, tucked away on a distant page that required clicking several times to be viewed, gave insufficient notice to end-users, and therefore did not create a valid contract.

(ii) Shrink wrap or "click wrap" forms a unilateral contract when opened (or clicked); "browse wrap" is insufficient.

## 3 Enforceability

### 3.1 Consideration

#### 3.1.1 The Bargain Theory of Consideration

(a) Introduction

(i) Consideration is the concept of legal value in connection with contracts. It can be anything of value, including money, services, or any action or abstinence from a future action that is promised to another when making a contract.

(ii) As a general rule, in order for a promise to be enforceable, it must be supported by consideration (§ 17 Restatement).

(iii) For there to be consideration, there must be a *bargained for exchange*:

(1) The promisor's promise must induce the detriment of the promisee; *and*

(2) The detriment of the promisee must induce the promisor's promise.

(iv) In other words, the promisor makes the promise in exchange for the promisee's giving up of value and the promisee gives up something of value to induce the promise (§ 71 Restatement).

(1) In minority jurisdictions, in order to establish consideration, in addition to promisee's detriment, the promisor must be benefited.

(v) For example:

(1) A promisee and promisor sign an agreement whereby the promisee loans the promisor $1,000 in exchange for the promisor's promise to replay the $1,000 within six months.

(2) This forms an enforceable contract if the promise to repay induced the promisee's giving up of the $1,000 during six months and giving up the $1,000 during six months induced the promise.

(b) Distinguishing Bargains from Gratuitous Promises (Gifts)

(i) In a gift, on the other hand, a promise is made, but the promisee does not undergo any detriment. Furthermore, the promisor was not inducing an exchange.

(ii) Thus, gifts are not binding because of the absence of consideration.

(1) *See Johnson v. Otterbein University* (Ohio 1885), where the court refused to enforce Johnson's promise of a $100 gift to the university, since gifts lack consideration.

(iii) Even if a gift is conditioned, it is still a gift and is therefore not enforceable.

(1) A condition is not to be confused with consideration.

(2) If the gift is made on a condition, it is not enforceable. If it is made in exchange for consideration, then it is not truly a gift, but rather, a bargain, and is enforceable.

(3) To be enforceable, it is not enough that the promise be performable on a certain contingency (§ 24). There must be consideration.

(4) For example, if A promises to pay $100 to B to go to college, there is consideration if A is inducing B to go to college and B does.

(5) However, if B understands that A is offering him a gratuity conditioned on his going to college, then there is no consideration.

(c) Promise Exchanged for Performance that Benefits a Promisee

(i) If a promise is exchanged for performance, the promise is enforceable even if the performance benefits the promisee.

(ii) In *Hamer v. Sidway* (N.Y. 1891), the defendant promised to pay the plaintiff $5,000 if the plaintiff refrained from drugs, alcohol, and gambling. The plaintiff performed and dued when the defendant failed to pay. The defendant argued that because the plaintiff's performance benefited him, it did not constitute consideration. The court, reasoning that a forbearance of legal rights always constitutes bargained for consideration, ruled in favor of the plaintiff.

(d) Exceptions to the Bargain Requirement

(1) The exceptions to the requirement of a bargain are outlined in §§ 82 – 94 of the Restatement (§ 17 Restatement), among which we highlight:

(ii) Promise to Pay Indebtedness Discharged in Bankruptcy

(1) An express promise to pay all or part of an indebtedness of the promisor, discharged or dischargeable in bankruptcy proceedings begun before the promise is made, is binding (§ 83).

(iii) Promise to Perform a Duty in Spite of Non-occurrence of a Condition

(1) A promise to perform a conditional duty under an antecedent contract in spite of the non-occurrence of the condition is generally binding, whether the promise is made before or after the time for the condition to occur, unless (a) occurrence of the condition was a material part of the exchange for the performance of the duty and the promisee was under no duty that it occur; or (b) uncertainty of the occurrence of the condition was an element of the risk assumed by the promisor (§ 84).

(iv) Promise for Benefit Received (Moral Consideration)

(1) See "Promise for Past Benefit Received," *infra.*

(v) Option Contract

(1) An offer is binding as an option contract if it: (a) is in writing and signed by the offeror, recites consideration for the offer, and proposes an exchange on fair terms within a reasonable time; or (b) is made irrevocable by statute (§ 87).

(vi) Modification of Executory Contract

(1) See "Contractual Modification in Which Consideration is not Needed (§ 89 Restatement)," *infra*.

(vii) Promise Reasonably Inducing Action or Forbearance

(1) A promise which the promisor should reasonably expect to induce action or forbearance on the part of the promisee or a third person and which does induce such action or forbearance is binding if injustice can be avoided only by enforcement of the promise.

(2) A charitable subscription (promise to give money to a charity) or a marriage settlement is binding without proof that the promise induced action or forbearance (§ 90).

### 3.1.2 Promise for Past Benefit Received (Moral Consideration) (§ 86 Restatement)

(a) Traditional Approach

(i) A past benefit received has traditionally been held to be insufficient as consideration.

(ii) Therefore, a promise made for a past benefit received has traditionally been held to be not binding and thus unenforceable.

(iii) Courts have generally held such a promise to not have been bargained for; past consideration is no consideration.

(1) *See Moore v. Elmer* (Mass. 1901), where Moore predicted that Elmer would die, and Elmer *later* promised to pay Moore his mortgage if he died as predicted. Valid consideration was not made since the prediction (the alleged consideration) was made before the promise.

(2) If Elmer had promised to pay Moore for the correct prediction *before it was made*, the prediction would serve as consideration and a court would have enforced Elmer's promise to pay.

(b) Modern Approach (§ 86 Restatement)

(i) In the modern approach, however, under the doctrine of "moral consideration," a past benefit received is considered sufficient consideration to the extent necessary to prevent injustice.

(ii) This is made clear in the Restatement, § 86(1): "A promise made in recognition of a benefit previously received by the promisor from the promisee is binding to the extent necessary to prevent injustice."

(iii) Such a benefit previously received is always good consideration if the promisor has been unjustly enriched by the benefit received.

(iv) The benefit received will not however constitute good consideration and the promise made in exchange for the benefit will not be binding in the following cases (§86(2) Restatement):

(1) The promisee conferred the benefit as a gift;

(2) The promisor has *not* been unjustly enriched; or

(3) To the extent that its value is disproportionate to (*i.e.*, much greater than) the benefit (*e.g.*, if X promised to pay Y $1,000 for a raisin, the promise to pay $1,000 would not be binding because the value of the promise is disproportionate to that of the raisin).

(v) In cases in which past acts substantially benefited the promisor and detrimented the promisee, moral consideration nearly always applies. In these cases, although the past services are not strictly consideration, the courts construe them as such.

(1) *See Webb v. McGowin* (Ct. App. Ala. 1935) (Supr. Ct.), where Webb, in protecting his boss from a falling object, became crippled. Although McGowin promised to pay Webb for the rest of his life, his executor failed to make the disbursements to Web from McGowin's estate. The court conceded that McGowin's promise did not induce Webb's fall, and that there was therefore no consideration. However, given McGowin's benefit and Webb's detriment, the court enforced the promise by substituting consideration with "moral consideration."

(aa) This court represents the majority view, which not all courts adopt.

(2) *Compare Mills v. Wyman* (Mass. 1825), where the defendant offered to pay the plaintiff for the expenses of having taken care of the defendant's son during the defendant's son's illness, but never paid. The court held that the plaintiff did not act in consideration of the defendant's later promise to pay. Moral consideration would apply if the son were an infant or of a well-disposed son, but he was instead a major who did not consider himself to be part of the father's family. The defendant is not morally obligated to his estranged son and is thus not obligated to his (implied) moral contracts.

(aa) Note the difference in this case from *Webb*. Whereas in *Webb*, there is a material benefit to the promisor (McGowin), whose life was saved, in *Mills*, the promisor (father) received no direct benefit.

(vi) Example

(1) X promises to pay $1,000 to Y for a car that Y gave to X one year ago.

(2) If the car was worth $50,000, but Y did not know this at the time, and Y is now deeply in financial need, a Court would likely hold the promise to pay Y $1,000 to be binding in order to prevent injustice.

(3) However, the promise to pay $1,000 would not be binding if:

(aa) The car received was a gift;

(bb) The promisor has not been unjustly enriched; or

(cc) The value of the promise ($1,000) is greater than the benefit.

3.1.3 Contractual Modification

(a) Traditional Rule: Consideration is Needed

(i) Under the traditional common law, all contractual modifications require consideration to be binding.

(ii) If one party promises the other extra compensation for the same performance, the promise is unenforceable, since there is no consideration for the new promise.

(iii) This rule is based on the ***preexisting duty rule***, which holds that a promise to compensate for performance that was already within a preexisting duty is not enforceable.

(1) *See Stilk v. Myrick* (Ct. Common Pleas 1809), where a captain agrees to distribute wages of two deserters to the remaining crew members in order to compensate them for their work. When the promised extra wages are never paid, a crew member sues. The court held that a subsequent promise offering more compensation for the same performance is not enforceable. Since the crew members had a preexisting duty to work until the ship arrived safely, even if, as the contract foresaw, some of the crewmembers deserted, the promise of extra compensation is unenforceable.

(iv) This is currently the majority rule for contracts, outside of those governed by the UCC (see *infra.*).

(b) Modern Approach: Foreseeability Test

(i) In some jurisdictions, actual consideration is not needed for contractual modifications undertaken when unforeseeable circumstances cause the costs of performance of one of the parties to rise substantially.

(ii) Under these circumstances, the extra costs serve as consideration for the contractual modification.

(1) *See Brian Construction and Development Co. v. Brighenti* (Conn. 1978), where a contractor hired a subcontractor and furnished him with plans and information on what the job requires. The subcontractor agreed to complete "all requisite work," but later discovered that there is much more work than either party foresaw. The parties agreed for all the work to be done for 10% more. When subcontractor failed to perform, the contractor successfully enforced the new contract, which was held to be supported by consideration.

(2) *Compare Stilk v. Myrick* (Ct. Common Pleas 1809), where *it was foreseen* in the contract that sailors might desert the ship. In *Brighenti*, on the other hand, because the quantity of work required was not foreseen by either party, the new contract was binding and does not merely grant more compensation for the same performance.

(iii) This rule reflects the approach of those few states that have abrogated the preexisting duty rule.

(c) Contractual Modification in Which Consideration is not Needed (§ 89 Restatement)

(i) As an exception to the general rule, a modification of a contract with a preexisting duty is enforceable even if it has no consideration, under the following circumstances (§ 89 Restatement):

(1) It is fair and equitable in light of circumstances not anticipated by the parties when the contract was made.

(aa) This rule reflects the modern approach of those states that do not follow the preexisting duty rule.

(bb) Example: the modification of a contract will be enforceable, even if unforeseen costs significantly increase the costs of performance by one of the parties.

(2) It is provided for by statute.

(aa) This would be the case, for example, of the UCC: an agreement modifying a contract for the sale of goods needs no consideration to be binding (UCC § 2-209(1)).

(bb) The foreseeability test is not applicable; the parties only need to show they were modifying the contract in good faith.

(cc) A party would be considered to have acted in good faith, even if he foresees the possibility of prices going up, but is not certain, and prices actually do later go up.

(3) It is required by justice in light of a material change of position in reliance on it.

3.1.4 Discerning the Agreement: Illusory Promises

(a) Introduction

(i) An illusory promise is one that appears on its face to be so insubstantial as to impose no obligation on the promisor.

(ii) When an illusory promise is made, the promisor is not really bound to do anything; there is no bargain or exchange.

(iii) As a general rule, a conditional promise is unenforceable when the condition is entirely within the promisor's control. In such a case, the promisor's promise is illusory and lacks consideration.

(b) Conditions of Satisfaction

(i) Many courts therefore consider *conditions of satisfaction* based on taste (*e.g.*, "I will pay you to pay my portrait *if I like the result*") to be illusory, since there is no objective standard.

(ii) Others, however, consider them to be valid by employing a good faith standard (if it can be shown that the promisor did not pay because he was genuinely not satisfied, there will be no breach; otherwise, there will be a breach).

(c) Examples of Illusory Promises Lacking Consideration

(i) "I promise to buy your laptop for $2000 *if I feel like it* when the time comes."

(ii) A and B agree that B will buy as many widgets *as she wants* from A over the month at $1 each.

(1) B's promise is illusory and unenforceable, since she has not committed to doing anything.

(iii) "I will give you the exclusive right to use and license my name if you give me 50% of all your profits."

(1) *See Wood v. Lucy, Lady Duff-Gorden* (N.Y. 1917), where the defendant (Lucy) gave the plaintiff (Wood) an exclusive license to her name. When the Wood sued for breach of contract, Lucy argued that there was no contract because Wood assumed no obligations and was not required to earn any profits; the promise was illusory. The court held that although it was not explicitly stated, Wood implicitly promised to use his best efforts to sell Lucy's name to clothing licensees, he had indeed assumed obligations. The contract was thus binding.

(iv) "I will buy your strip mall for $1,000,000 if I can find satisfactory lessees in the market."

(1) This is not an illusory promise because fulfilling it is not entirely within the promisor's control, but rather, depends on external conditions that can be objectively tested by the market.

## 3.2 Adequacy of Consideration

3.2.1 Courts do not inquire as to adequacy of consideration or whether the values exchanged between parties are comparable. They are only concerned that *something of value* induced the promise forming the contract.

3.2.2 Under § 79 of the Restatement (Second) of Contracts, if there is consideration, there need not be:

(a) A benefit to the promisor or a detriment to the promisee (the Restatement's language is slightly different from the case law here; focus on the language of the Restatement);

(b) Equivalence of values exchanged;

(c) Mutuality of obligation (it does not matter whose duty is greater).

3.2.3 Inadequacy of consideration is thus no defense to the creation of an otherwise valid contract; all that is required for valid consideration is a "peppercorn's worth of value," as long as it is a good faith bargained-for exchange.

3.2.4 Thus, if a party purchases a good that has considerably less value than that party anticipated, an enforceable contract is nevertheless created. It is not for the courts to determine whether the prices in a contract was fair.

(a) *See Hardesty v. Smith* (Ind. 1851), where the defendant purchases from the plaintiff the ability to use an improvement to a lamp. When the plaintiff sues to force the defendant to pay, the defendant claims that he did not get what he was paying for. The court held that there was an enforceable contract, regardless of the value and insufficiency of the consideration.

(b) *N.B.:* had the defendant returned the product, he may have been able to get his money back; but rather, he sought to invalidate the contract while keeping the product.

### 3.3 Formalities Manifesting an Intention to be Legally Bound

3.3.1 Introduction

(a) Formalities have several functions. In the first place, they serve as evidence that a transaction took place.

(b) Additionally, they serve a cautionary function: the promisor is warned that he is engaging in an enforceable act of volition. He is made aware that the device being used will attain a certain result.

(c) Historically, formalities have either taken the place of or "imported" consideration. The modern trend has been to abandon such practices and to look to the substance of the bargain to determine whethere there was in fact an exchange.

3.3.2 The Seal (Restatement § 95)

(a) Under the common law, an agreement made under seal was considered to be binding even if it was not supported by consideration because the seal makes it clear that the parties were meant to be bound.

(b) The seal was said to "import" consideration.

(c) In the modern law, however, seals are rarely considered to import or serve as a substitute for consideration.

(i) For promises involving the sales of good, the UCC does not recognize seals.

(ii) At least thirty four states have abolished seals or treat sealed written promises as unsealed; most others modify the effect of seals.

(iii) Even in those states that do or did recognize the seal, it imports only a *rebuttable presumption of consideration*.

(1) *See In re Conrad's Estate* (Pa. 1938), where the court showed suspicion of a plaintiff who sought payments for judgment notes after the defendant died. Although the judgment note included a seal that, at the time, imported consideration at that time, the court does not recognize the note as binding, because it was presented so late after it was written.

(2) *Compare Aller v. Aller (N.J. Sup. Ct. 1878)* , where the court did enforce a sealed note.

3.3.3 Nominal Consideration

(a) Although the courts will not look into the adequacy of consideration, a disparity in value sometimes indicates that the consideration was not in fact bargained for but was a mere pretense. Such consideration is said to be "nominal consideration" (in name only) and does not satisfy the requirements of a bargain (Comment *d*, § 79 Restatement).

(b) Something of indeterminate value can be validly exchanged as consideration for a sum of money. However, something of nominal determinate value, such as a penny, cannot be considered to be consideration in exchange for something else of a much greater value.

(c) Such an exchange is no bargain, but rather, an unenforceable contract.

(i) *See Schnell v. Nell* (Ind. 1861), where the husband promises to give money to three parties stipulated by his wife. He exchanges his promise to pay later for one cent, his wife's love, friendship, and affection, and her wish to have the money paid. The court rules that this nominal consideration is not valid consideration. This promise is really no more than a gift, for there is no bargain, and it is therefore unenforceable.

3.3.4 Recitals

(a) When consideration is not exchanged, but is recited in the contract, there is a rebuttable presumption of consideration (just as with seals).

(b) This is like nominal consideration, except that, rather than being exchanged, it is simply written down.

(c) Recital of consideration may be contradicted by parol evidence (oral or written evidence of the bargain that occurred before the final terms of the contract were laid down and were not made part of the final contract).

(i) *See Allen v. Allen* (D.C. Ct. App. 1957), where the court ruled that the consideration of $1 in a promise by a mother to her son and daughter regarding the proceeds of the sale of the house was just a pretense. The parties never intended for the consideration to be paid and the lower court did in fact find that it was not paid. The agreement was therefore not enforceable.

(d) However, the fact that consideration is not delivered does not automatically void a contract. Many courts will enforce an options contract even when the recited consideration is never delivered.

(i) *See, e.g., Smith v. Wheeler* (Ga. 1974), where the defendant, in exchange for $1, gave the plaintiff one year to decide whether he wanted to purchase property for $30,000. The defendant rescinded the option on the basis that $1 was recital of nominal consideration that was never paid. The court nevertheless enforced the options contract, holding that the recital of consideration was sufficient for options contracts.

(ii) This view is reinforced by § 87 of the Restatement (Second) of Constracts, which states that an *options contract* is enforceable if it merely recites consideration, as long as it is:

(1) in writing;

(2) signed by the offeror;

(3) for a reasonable duration; and

(4) fair.

(iii) The recital of consideration needs to *look* like a bargain; this formality is essential.

(e) The UCC goes even further, by establishing the enforceability of firm offers (options contracts), even when they are exchanged for neither real nor recited consideration (UCC § 2-205). Options contracts are legally binding and cannot be revoked for the time stated or a reasonable time not exceeding three months if no time is stated, if:

(i) They are made by a merchant;

(ii) To buy or sell goods;

(iii) In a *signed writing* (this serves as a formality that can be said to have "replaced" the need for real or recited consideration); and

(iv) Gives assurance that it will be held open.

## 3.4 Promissory Estoppel (Restatement § 90)

### 3.4.1 Definition and Elements

(a) Promissory estoppel, or "detrimental reliance," is yet another means by which a party may argue for the enforceability of a contract that lacks consideration. It can be thought of as a form of protection in situations of detrimental reliance.

(b) A promise may be enforced to prevent injustice, even if it lacks consideration, if the promisor should have expected the promisee to have relied on the promise and if the promisee did in fact rely on it to his detriment.

(c) There are thus four elements:

(i) There is a promise;

(ii) The promisor reasonably expects that the promise will induce the promisee's action or forbearance (this can be shown deductively—"it is natural that ..."—or inductively, "the facts show that ...");

(iii) The promise does in fact induce such action or forbearance;

(iv) The detriment resulting from the promise requires enforcement of the promise in order to avoid injustice.

(d) It is the same as equitable estoppel, except that equitable estoppel requires not a promise, but a representation of facts that lead to detriment.

(e) Not all jurisdictions recognize promissory estoppel, and many will struggle to find consideration before going to this doctrine.

### 3.4.2 Promissory Estoppel as a Substitute for Consideration

(a) If a promise is made that induces the promisee to act in a way that detriments him, then even if the promise was not bargained for, it can be enforced under the doctrine of promissory estoppel.

(i) *See Ricketts v. Scothorn* (Neb. 1898), where the plaintiff successfully sues her grandfather's estate, requiring it to pay her the promissory note which induced her to leave her job to her detriment.

(b) A promise to make a gift may be enforceable, if the promise induces the promisee to act to his detriment.

(i) *See Allegheny College v. National Chautauqua County Bank of Jamestown* (N.Y. 1927), where the court "created" consideration for Johnston's promise to pay $5,000 after she dies. Although Johnston considered the school's work in promoting Christian education as consideration for her promise, there was no bargain because her promise did not induce the Christian education. The court nonetheless found consideration in the detriment the school faced in relying on hre promise and in setting up Johnston's memorial fund.

(c) A pension that normally would be considered to be a gift can similarly become enforceable under the doctrine of promisory estoppel.

(i) *See Feinberg v. Pfeiffer Co.* (Mo. 1959), where Feinberg, in reliance of a promise to pay a pension of $200 per month for the rest of her life, left her job when she was ill with cancer. When that pension was later cut, she sued, claiming that she and her husband had relied on this income.

## 3.5 The Writing Requirement and the Statute of Frauds

3.5.1 The Statute of Frauds was an English statute whose purpose was to avoid fraud and perjury.

3.5.2 Today, the Statute of Frauds imposes the following requirements on certain contracts in order for them to be enforceable:

(a) To be evidenced in a ***writing***;

(b) That is ***signed*** by the party to be charged; and

(c) That sufficiently describes the ***essential terms of the contract***.

3.5.3 The Statute of Frauds is an *affirmative defense*. Thus, if the defendant fails to plead that the oral contract on which the plaintiff is suing falls within the Statute of Frauds writing requirement, he waives the defense and the contract may be enforced.

3.5.4 The following contracts fall within the Statute of Frauds and therefore can only be enforced if evidenced by a writing:

(a) Contracts Made upon Consideration of Marriage

(i) These fall within the statute and must be written and signed.

(ii) In order to induce B to accept his offer to get married, A orally offers to purchase her a car. B accepts, but A never delivers. Can B enforce the contract?

(1) Since it was not made in writing. It cannot be enforced.

(iii) However, an agreement consisting only of "mutual promises of two persons to marry each other" *that does not include ancillary promises to transfer property* does not fall within the statute and is enforceable even when not written and signed (§ 124 Restatement (Second) of Contracts).

(b) The One-Year Provision

(i) *Service contracts that cannot be performed within one year* from the making of the contract are only enforceable if in a signed writing.

(ii) *See Boone v. Coe* (Ky. 1913), where Coe, the defendant farm owner, promised the plaintiff that the plaintiff could lease Coe's land for one year as soon as the plaintiff arrived to the defendant's land. The court held that the contract was within the Statute of Frauds, since its completion could *only* happen *after* one year from the date that the contract was formed. Since the contract was not in writing, the plaintiff was not entitled to damages.

(c) Contracts for the Sale of Land Interests

(i) Contracts conveying the following land interests fall within the Statute of Frauds and must be in signed writings:

(1) Land *sale contracts*;

(2) Real estate *mortgages*;

(3) *Leases* of land[3];

(4) *Easements* (the right to make use of another's property); and

(5) Life *estates*.

(ii) Although *construction contracts* relate to land, they are not interests in land and therefore do not fall within the Statute of Frauds.

(d) Sales of Goods

(i) Contracts for *sales of goods for more than $500* ($5,000 under amended art. 2 UCC) fall within the Statute of Frauds.

(ii) *Exception*: if B keeps the good for more than ten days, the writing requirement is waived.

(e) Suretyship/Guarantyship

(i) This refers to contracts where a second party is answering for the duty of another (*e.g.*, a surety answering for the duties of a debtor).

(ii) The contract must have three elements to fall within the Statute of Frauds:

(1) There must be three parties (the creditor, the debtor and the surety);

[3] However, in the majority of jurisdictions, when a lease lasts for less than one year, it is not within the Statute of Frauds.

(2) There must be two promises (the debt obligation promise and the collateral promise); and

(3) The collateral promise must be secondary to the first; it must not take effect until there is breach of the first promise. That is, the surety will only pay the debt if the debtor fails to do so.

3.5.5 The following ***exceptions*** allow for oral contracts to be enforced despite the violation of the Statute of Frauds:

(a) Realty and Service Contracts

(i) *Complete Performance*: when there has been complete performance by either side.

(1) For example, B offers to pay C to write a memo that can only be completed in eighteen months, but never signs a contract. C writes it and seeks payment. Normally, C would be unable to enforce the contract. However, the Statute of Frauds writing requirement does not apply, since performance was complete.

(ii) *Part Performance*: when there has been part performance by either side that *unequivocally* evidences a contract.

(1) For example, A takes possession and improves or begins payment of land sold to him by B, but B repudiates the contract. Even in the absence of a written contract, the sale can be enforced because of A's part performance.

(iii) *Preparation for Performance*: when there has been preparation for performance that evidences the existence of a contract, the promisee may invoke promissory estoppel (§ 129 for land; § 139 generally).

(1) When the promisor expects the promise to induce actions of the promisee, the promise does induce these actions, and the promisee is detrimented, the promise can be enforced even if it does not comply with the Statute of Frauds requirements.

(2) Hypo: the lessee arrives to Texas and the lessor revokes the offer. The lessee sues. Is the contract enforceable without a contract signed by Coe?

(aa) Normally, no, since the contract could only have been performed more than one year after the agreement and since it does not fall within the two exceptions: *complete performance* or *part performance* (coming to Texas is not the beginning performance; moving in and beginning to erect the barn is).

(bb) However, the lessee may invoke *promissory estoppel* for damages against the promisor for revoking his offer, to the extent that the lessee's preparations induced damages.

(b) Sales of Goods

(i) This section applies to the sale of goods for over $500 ($5,000 in amended art. 2) (UCC § 2-201).

(ii) Between Merchants (UCC § 2-201(2))

(1) The Statute of Frauds writing requirement does not apply to contracts when the purchaser receives an invoice and does not protest for over ten days. The seller may enforce the contract, even without a writing signed by the purchaser.

(2) For example, purchaser P purchases ten computers from seller S. S sends an invoice for one hundred computers. P neither signs the invoice, protests, nor pays. S tries to enforce the contract and B defends on the basis that there was no written contract.

(aa) A court will hold that because B never protested, the Statute of Frauds does not apply.

(bb) The contract will be enforced.

(iii) Between Non-Merchants (UCC § 2-201(3))

(1) Specially Manufactured Goods (UCC § 2-201(3)(a))

(aa) The Statute of Frauds writing requirement does not apply when the offeree orders *specially manufactured goods*.

(bb) For example, if the plaintiff orders ten customized coffee mugs, but never pays, the seller S can enforce the contract, even if P never signed a written document. The Statute of Frauds does not apply because the goods were custom made.

(2) Estoppel (UCC § 2-201(3)(b))

(aa) Estoppel applies when the party against whom the contract is being enforced admits to there having been a contract. He becomes "estopped" from asserting the Statute of Frauds defense.

(bb) One cannot admit that he made a promise while simultaneously invoking the Statute of Frauds defense on the basis that the promise was not in writing. The admission prohibits the Statute of Frauds defense.

(3) Part Performance (UCC § 2-201(3)(c))

(aa) The Statute of Frauds defense similarly does not apply when payment is sent to and accepted by the seller, or goods are sent to and received by the purchaser.

(bb) For example, if S sends P two computers, which P accepts without protesting. The contract is enforceable, even absent a signed contract, through the plaintiff's part performance by accepting, thereby waiving his Statute of Frauds defense.

(cc) This exception is similar to that offered to merchants, except that the exception for merchants would apply *even if only the invoice were received*.

3.5.6 Satisfying the Writing Requirement

(a) When an offer to sell property is made in writing, the mailed title and deed cannot become a binding contract upon oral acceptance of the offer. Written acceptance is necessary.

(i) *See Schwedes v. Romain* (Mont. 1978), where the court did not accept as binding the plaintiff's oral acceptance of the defendant's written offer to sell property.

(b) Satisfying the writing requirement does not mean satisfying a strict, rigid standard; the contract can be evidenced in *any* writing, even by a note written to oneself in a journal.

(c) The writing must identify the subject matter of the contract and must be signed by the party against whom it is being enforced.

(i) If the subject matter is not identified in the writing of a journal entry, then another journal entry from the same journal, whose subject matter can reasonably traced to the one where there was acceptance, can be used to create the necessary writing.

(d) Many questions have arisen with respect to whether emails and other electronic texts can be construed as satisfying the writing requirement.

(i) *See In re RealNetworks* (N.D. Ill. 2000), where a digital EULA was considered to be a written contract for the purposes of the Statute of Frauds. Contrary to the plaintiffs' arguments, it can easily be saved to one's hard drive and printed.

3.5.7 Satisfying the Signature Requirement

(a) The party being charged must have signed the writing in order for it to be enforced.

(b) For example, if A sues to enforce B's payment of $10,000 for a car sold to him, and all A can produce is an invoice with his own signature, the courts will not enforce.

(c) However, there are no strict, rigid rules for satisfying the signature requirement.

(i) *See Parma Tile Mosaic and Marble Co. v. Estate of Fred Short* (N.Y. 1992), where MRLS Construction Corp. sent a written notice that indicated "MRLS" but was not signed. MRLS argued that this did not satisfy the Statute of Frauds signature requirement. The court disagreed, holding that any symbol written or stamped on the document may constitute a signature, as long as the intent to be bound is manifested.

(ii) With this broad definition of "signature," one can argue as to whether an email, or a voicemail can also constitute a signature.

3.5.8 Interpreting a Writing: the Parol Evidence Rule

(a) Common Law Approach

(i) Under the parol evidence rule, supplementary oral or written evidence of any agreement prior to or contemporaneous with the laying down of the final terms of the contract cannot be used to contradict or vary the final agreement.

(ii) However, such supplementary oral or written evidence can be used to clarify incomplete or vague contractual terms, even if the parol evidence is oral and the contract is written.

(iii) If the terms of a contract are neither vague nor incomplete, parol evidence is inadmissible.

(1) *See Thompson v. Libbey* (Minn. 1885), where the plaintiff sued when the logs that he ordered turned out to be of poor quality. During the trial, the defendant submitted parol evidence regarding the warranty that was not in the written agreement, which the lower court admitted. On appeal, the court reversed, excluding the parol evidence, since the terms of the written agreement were neither *incomplete* nor *vague*. The parol evidence was not necessary to clarify or determine the terms of the agreement.

(iv) Under the parol evidence rule, collateral agreements that deal with issues not addressed in the final agreement are admissible, since they do not contradict or vary the terms of the final agreement.

(b) UCC Approach for the Sale of Goods

(i) The UCC does not allow written or oral evidence prior to the written *final expression of the agreement* to contradict that agreement or to contradict the terms "to which the confirmatory memoranda of the parties agree" (UCC § 2-202).

(ii) Evidence of *consistent additional terms*, however, may be used to explain or supplement the final expression of the agreement, *unless the court finds the written agreement to be the complete, final, and exclusive statement of the terms* (usually through a merger clause).

(iii) However, even if there is a merger clause, the final agreement may be *explained or supplemented* by course of performance, course of dealing, and usage of trade.

(c) Compared

(i) Both the common law and the UCC are based the idea that outside terms may not be used to contradict a fully integrated agreement.

(ii) However, the UCC allows evidence of course of performance, course of dealing, and usage of trade *even if there is a fully integrated agreement*.

## 4 Conditions and the Absolute Duty to Perform

### 4.1 Introduction to Conditions

#### 4.1.1 Definition

(a) A condition is an uncertain future event on which an obligation depends.

(b) When performance is based on an unsatisfied condition, nonperformance is not a breach of contract.

(c) Suppose, for example, that an insurance company promises to indemnify a client if (i) his home burns down; and (ii) he files a claim without thirty day. The insurance company's failure to pay would not constitute breach of contract if either of the conditions were not met.

4.1.2 Classification of Conditions

(a) Classification by Time of Occurrence

(i) Condition Precedent

(1) A condition precedent is an event whose occurrence or non occurrence triggers the obligation to perform.

(2) For example, if the promise is to shovel a driveway if it snows, the fact of snowing is a condition precedent that triggers the duty to shovel.

(ii) Condition Subsequent

(1) A condition subsequent excuses the duty to perform after the performance has begun.

(2) For example, if the promisor agrees to "work for you for one year, unless I am accepted to graduate school," the occurrence of admission to graduate school discharges the duty to continue working for a full year.

(iii) Condition Concurrent

(1) A condition concurrent is an occurrence that must occur at the same time as other occurrences.

(2) The parties may, for example, agree to exchange payment and a deed at a closing. The conditions in this case would be "I will give you the payment if you give me the deed" and vice versa.

(b) Express, Implied-in-Fact, and Constructive (Implied-in-Law) Conditions

(i) Express Conditions

(1) Express conditions are mentioned in the contract.

(2) No special language is necessary, but courts will more likely enforce express conditions if phrases such as "provided that" or "if" are included.

(3) When a condition relates to time, the best way would be to include the phrase, "time is of the essence."

(4) There are two kinds of express conditions:

(aa) *Simple express conditions*, where the event is outside the control of either party (*e.g.*, whether it will rain); and

(bb) *Promissory express conditions*, where one of the parties has some control over the occurrence of the event (*e.g.*, "I will buy the computer subject to my getting the finances").

(ii) Implied-in-Fact Conditions

(1) Implied-in-fact conditions are deduced by the facts in a case that make it reasonable that they were intended.

(2) For example, it is implied that a fire insurance company will pay only for damage caused by a fire and not by a flood, even if this condition is not expressly made in the contract.

(iii) Constructive (Implied-in-Law) Conditions

(1) A constructive condition is a legal fiction invented by the courts.

(2) It is not derived from a contract, as in the case of an express condition, or from the intent of the parties or facts of a case, as in the case of an implied-in-fact condition.

4.1.3 Other Conditions

(a) Conditions of Satisfaction

(i) Two standards can be used in measuring satisfaction.

(ii) When the satisfaction involves utility or marketability (construction, manufacturing, etc.), an *objective standard* based on a reasonable person is employed.

(iii) When the satisfaction relates to purely subjective tastes, a *subjective standard* based on *good faith* seen in the discussion on illusory promises is employed.

(b) Certificates of approval

(i) A party's paying another may be contingent on a certificate by a third party expert attesting that the work is in accordance with specifications.

(ii) This would be the case of a condition that a contractor's improvements on a home are subject to the inspection and approval of an architect who indicates that the work is of adequate quality.

(c) Conditions of time

(i) The best way to make a time condition express would be to state "time is of the essence" (or similar terms such as "provided that" or "if") or to create an options contract.

(ii) Without these "magic phrases," time is neither a condition nor a promise and therefore, if performance is late, the contract is not considered to have been breached, as long as performance is rendered in reasonable time.

4.1.4 The Effect of a Condition

(a) When a condition is not met, the party protected by the condition is not obligated to perform.

(b) However, conditions will be ignored by the courts when they are prohibited by public policy.

(i) *See Inman v. Clyde Hall Drilling Co.* (Alaska 1962), where the plaintiff Inman signed a contract agreeing that he would give the defendant thirty days notice if he made any claims against him. When he was fired, Inman sued for wrongful discharge. The defendant argued that Inman could not sue because he did not meet the notice provision. Held: because the defendant's requirement was not contrary to public policy, and since courts should not alter the contracts of parties who are sufficiently capable of drafting them, the provision is a valid condition.

## 4.2 Satisfying a Condition

4.2.1 Introduction

(a) This section applies when one party's performance is *expressly* or *constructively* a condition precedent to the other party's counter-performance.

(b) The standard of performance required depends on whether the condition is *express* or *constructive* (implied-in-law).

4.2.2 Express Conditions

(a) Perfect Performance

(i) Perfect performance is full, not necessarily perfect performance, within the bounds of reasonable expectations.

(ii) One party's perfect performance *satisfies the condition precedent* and triggers the other side's duty to counter-perform.

(b) Substantial Performance

(i) Substantial performance is slightly below reasonable expectations.

(ii) Generally courts consider substantial performance to give rise to a non-material breach and *not to satisfy an express condition;* otherwise, the intent of the parties may be defeated.

(c) Inferior Performance

(i) Inferior performance is far below reasonable expectations.

(ii) It is the equivalent of a material breach that does *not satisfy express conditions*.

4.2.3 Constructive (Implied-in-Law) Conditions

(a) Perfect or substantial performance satisfies the condition.

(b) Inferior performance does not satisfy the condition.

**4.3 Excusing Conditions**

4.3.1 Interpretation of an Event as a Promise or Condition

(a) When it is ambiguous whether an event is a condition or a promise, a court will interpret the event as a promise in order to avoid the forfeiture of a contract.

(i) *See Howard v. Federal Crop Insurance Corp.* (4th Cir. 1976), where the court held that because the plaintiff Howard's duty to not destroy the crops before the defendant inspected them was described as a condition precedent in one place in the contract but in another place not, the event will be considered to be a promise.

(b) Sometimes, a court will see an event as neither a condition nor a promise, but rather, as a convenient way of fulfilling a contract.

(i) *See Chirichella v. Erwin* (Md. 1973), where the court held that the settlement on the defendants' new home in approximately October of 1971 was *not a condition precedent* to their sale of their old home to the plaintiffs, but rather, an agreement of a convenient time to settle.

4.3.2 Excuse to Prevent Forfeiture

(a) When the non-occurrence of a condition would lead to a *disproportionate forfeiture*, courts often excuse a condition precedent, treating it as though it had occurred.

(b) If a court were to strictly require the condition to be met, the counter-performing party would be unjustly enriched, since he would have received nearly full performance while being discharged from his duty to perform.

(c) Courts tend to excuse conditions in these circumstances when their occurrence is not a material term of the contract.

(i) *See J.N.A. Realty Corp. v. Cross Bay Chelsea* (N.Y. 1977), where the plaintiff J.N.A. granted the defendant an option as an express condition to renew its lease within six months notice. The defendant failed to renew and the plaintiff's duty to continue to lease the property was discharged. The plaintiff sued to recover possession. Held: where failure of a condition is caused by a party's negligence, and that failure does not harm the other party, equity will excuse the condition. Here, the defendant invested $15,000 on the property and equity demands that the condition be excused.

4.3.3 Divisibility of Contract

(a) Divisibility of contract is meant to avoid the harsh effects of forfeiture when one side has substantially performed.

(b) A contract is divisible when:

(i) The performance of each party *may be divided* into two or more parts;

(ii) The parties agree on the *equivalence* of one party's unit of performance in relation to that of the other party; and

(iii) The *number of units* of each side's performance is the *same*.

(c) The condition of complete performance is excused when one party performs some of the units of a divisible contract. That party receives compensation for the parts performed.

(d) For example, if A agrees to mow ten lawns but only mows nine of them, he will receive the payment proportional to the work he did, even if mowing all ten lawns was a condition precedent to his being paid.

(e) Similarly, *installment contracts*, where goods are delivered in separate lots, are divisible contracts that permit the seller to demand payment for each lot delivered.

4.3.4 Minor Breach

(a) When one party's performance is a condition precedent to a second party's counter-performance, the failure to meet the condition prevents the second party's duty to perform from becoming absolute.

(b) However, when the breach is minor, the condition is excused and the duty to counter-perform becomes absolute.

(i) Exception: when ***perfect performance*** is an ***express condition*** to the second party's counter-performance, courts will generally not excuse its occurrence.

(ii) Exception to the exception: when enforcing the express condition of perfect performance causes ***forfeiture***, courts will generally excuse the condition.

4.3.5 Anticipatory Repudiation

(a) If a party whose duty to perform is contingent on the occurrence of a condition repudiates the contract, the benefit of the condition is extinguished and treated as though it has occurred.

(b) The breaching party may not assert the failure of the condition as a reason for nonperformance.

(c) For example, suppose that a purchaser, before he goes to the bank to get the financing to buy a computer, repudiates the purchase agreement. If the seller sues, the purchaser may not assert as a defense the non-occurrence of the condition precedent that he obtain financing. Because the purchaser anticipatorily repudiated the contract, the condition is treated as though it occurred.

4.3.6 Wrongful Interference

(a) The elements to a wrongful interference (failure to cooperate) are as follow:

(i) There must be a party whose duty to perform becomes absolute upon the occurrence of a condition.

(ii) A party must wrongly interfere with the occurrence of the condition in one of the following ways:

(1) ***Passive non-cooperation*** that would not have been anticipated by the other party in the contract;

(2) ***Active non-cooperation***; or

(3) ***Malice***/bad faith.

(iii) Finally, it must be clear that the condition would have occurred, but for the wrongful interference.

(b) When these elements are met, the duty to perform becomes absolute, even though the condition did not occur.

(c) For example, if a purchaser agrees to buy a car if he is able to get the financing, but then fails to cooperate with a lender by giving his requisite credit history, the condition precedent that he acquire financing will be treated as though it occurred.

4.3.7 Waiver and Estoppel

(a) Waiver

(i) Waiver occurs when the party having the benefit of a condition indicates by words or action that he will perform, regardless of whether the condition occurs.

(ii) Some waivers are treated as unenforceable gifts.

(1) For example, if one party waives the requirement that the other party substantially perform, in essence he is giving a gift by agreeing to pay or perform without requiring the other party to do the same.

(2) Because there is no bargained for exchange, the waiver is unenforceable.

(b) Estoppel

(i) Once a party has waived a condition, he is estopped from later raising its nonoccurrence as a defense.

(1) *See Clark v. West* (N.Y. 1908), where the court held that if the defendant waived the condition that the plaintiff Clark abstain from alcohol in order to be paid $6 per page of law books written, the non-occurrence of the condition could not be raised as a defense and the defendant would be obligated to pay $6 per page, even if Clark did not abstain from alcohol.

(ii) Elements of estoppel:

(1) The party benefiting from a condition indicates that he is waiving the condition; and

(2) The other party detrimentally relies on this indication.

4.3.8 Impossibility, Impracticability, Frustration

(a) *See infra.*, "Defenses to Contractual Obligation" for rules and tests.

## 4.4 Constructive Conditions

4.4.1 Introduction

(a) Constructive conditions have the effect of conditions but are not expressed in the contract.

(b) Courts create them based on the facts of the case for the sake of equity.

(c) They are not *implied* from the facts, as implied-in-fact conditions are; nonetheless; courts often refer to and treat implied-in-fact conditions as constructive contracts.

4.4.2 The Three Classes of Contracts under the Old Common Law

(a) Mutually Independent Covenants

(i) One party's breach does not excuse the other party's nonperformance; each party is required to perform, regardless of the other party's failure to perform.

(ii) Either party may recover damages from the other party for breach.

(b) Dependent Covenants

(i) These are covenants conditioned on the other side's performance; a party is not required to perform until a condition requiring the other side's performance is met.

(ii) A party's duty to perform is excused if the other party does not perform.

(c) Concurrent Covenants

(i) In a concurrent covenant, each party has a concurrent duty to perform that is dependent on the other side's performance.

(ii) These are therefore a kind of dependent covenant.

(iii) An example would be a purchase where the seller is obligated to deliver the good at the same time that the purchaser is obligated to tender payment.

4.4.3 Construing Dependency and Independency of Covenants Based on Timing (§ 234 Restatement)

(a) Default rule: when both performances can be exchanged simultaneously, they are due simultaneously.

(i) A court may look to whether the performances *can be exchanged simultaneously.*

(ii) If so, a constructive condition is created whereby dependant covenants are formed and the duties to perform are concurrent.

(iii) Each side must tender performance before declaring the other side to have breached.

(1) *See Kingston v. Preston* (K.B. 1773), where the court held that, because giving sufficient security for payments was to be performed at or before the delivery of the deeds of the business, it was a condition precedent to the sale. Thus, the plaintiff Kingston must first show that he obtained the requisite security before being able to sue for SP.

(iv) Many courts further require that the parties aver in the pleadings that they tendered performance.

(1) *See Morton v. Lamb* (U.K. 1797), where the plaintiff was to pay the defendant at the time that the defendant was to deliver corn. The court concluded that the covenants were concurrent and hence dependent. However, in a suit to recover for damages for breach, the suing party must have been ***ready and willing to tender performance*** and aver the same in his pleadings. Here, the plaintiff failed to make such an averment.

(b) When, however, only one party requires a period of time to perform, *that party should perform earlier.*

(i) A constructive condition is created whereby this first performance is a condition precedent to the second performance.

(ii) The first performance is thus an independent promise; the second promise is dependent on performance of the first (unless the language or circumstances require otherwise).

## 5 When the Duty to Perform is Discharged

### 5.1 Satisfaction of Duty by Performance

5.1.1 Introduction

(a) Performance is the most common way of discharging a duty to perform.

(b) There are several standards through which to measure performance.

5.1.2 Standards of Performance

(a) Perfect Performance

(i) Perfect performance is full performance within the bounds of reasonable expectations.

(ii) It ***always satisfies*** the duty to perform.

(b) Inferior Performance

(i) Inferior performance is far below reasonable expectations and constitutes a material breach.

(ii) It ***always discharges*** the second party's duty to counter-perform.

(c) Substantial Performance

(i) This is performance with a minor breach that is slightly below reasonable expectations.

(ii) It generally satisfies a party's duty to perform.

(iii) However, when there is an ***express condition*** that a party's performance be perfect, courts are hesitant to allow substantial performance satisfy the condition, *unless strict adherence to the condition leads to forfeiture*, in which case the condition will be excused.

(1) *See Jacob & Youngs v. Kent* (N.Y. 1921), where the contract expressly required Reading pipe, but the plaintiff used another kind of pipe. Held: when the breach is slight, the condition should be treated as an independent promise leading to damages rather than an express condition precedent leading to unjust forfeiture. Here, the departure from the contract was trivial and the plaintiff acted in good faith. To avoid injustice, the condition will be considered met. Thus, substantial performance of an independent covenant is satisfaction of a constructive condition and triggers the dependent covenant to make payment.

(2) *N.B.*: factors that courts look to when allowing a condition to be met through substantial performance include ***good faith*** on the part of the performer (no intent to breach) and the ***functional equivalence*** of the substantial performance.

(iv) Some contracts specifically state that if performance deviates from perfect performance, there must be replacement. Even in these circumstances, courts will only reward damages.

(1) *See Jacob & Youngs v. Kent* (N.Y. 1921) on motion for reargument, where the defendant, pointed out that a contractual provision required the plaintiff to replace all of the plumbing if he did not use the Reading pipe. Held: since substitution of the Reading pipe with another pipe is of such a trivial difference and the promise to perfectly perform is independent of the promise to pay, the plaintiff is liable only for damages in the form of ***the difference between*** the ***perfect performance*** and the ***actual performance.***

## 5.2 Agreements Discharging the Duty to Perform

### 5.2.1 Mutual Rescission

(a) Mutual rescission causes the duty of each party to perform to be discharged.

(b) The parties must expressly and mutually agree to be discharged from the agreement.

### 5.2.2 Accord and Satisfaction

(a) This applies when there is a dispute and the parties disagree on the content of the original contract (*e.g.*, the price in a sale of goods).

(b) The parties may come to a compromise through accord and satisfaction.

(c) An ***accord*** is an agreement that a debt obligation be settled for less than the creditor is entitled.

(d) ***Satisfaction*** refers to the satisfactory fulfillment of the debt obligation through the rendering of the agreed-to lesser performance.

(e) If, in a dispute on price, one side sends partial payment in a check with "payment in full" indicated thereon, accord and satisfaction will be presumed if the receiving party cashes the check.

(f) This is true even if the receiving party ***crosses out "payment in full"*** when cashing the check.

(g) The obligee is thereafter barred from seeking to enforce the full contract price.

(h) Under the UCC, however, the check can be cashed without the presumption of accord and satisfaction if the receiving party writes "without prejudice" or "cashed under protest" on the back of the check. UCC § 1-308.

5.2.3 Novation and Substitute Agreements

(a) Novation is the substitution of a party or parties in a contract.

(b) The following elements are required:

(i) A previous ***valid contract***; and

(ii) A new ***valid contract*** that, with the agreement of all the parties:

(1) Revokes the former contract; and

(2) Names different parties.

(c) A substitute agreement is a form of novation that requires:

(i) A previous ***valid contract***;

(ii) A ***valid substitute agreement*** that, with the *agreement of all the same parties*:

(1) Expressly or impliedly revokes the former contract; and

(aa) If the new contract does not expressly revoke the old contract, the old contract will be impliedly revoked when the new contract contains terms that are inconsistent with the former.

(2) Includes *new terms*.

## 5.3 Prospective Nonperformance and Material Breach of Contract

5.3.1 Prospective Nonperformance

(a) Anticipatory Repudiation

(i) There are two interests in any contract:

(1) The actual performance;

(2) The assurance in knowing that there is a deal.

(ii) Even when a party does not breach his duty to perform, the second interest may be breached if he repudiates his promise to perform.

(iii) In such a case, the other party need not wait until the anticipated or agreed to time of performing before suing to recover damages.

(1) *See Albert Hochster v. Edgar De La Tour* (Q.B. 1853), where the defendant Edgar De La Tour argued that the plaintiff should not be able to bring suit against him, since he had not yet breached his duty to hire the plaintiff, but had only repudiated the contract. The court held that a non-breaching party may *immediately sue* when the other party anticipatorily repudiates.

(iv) Repudiation must be ***unequivocal***.

(1) A request or inquiry is not the same as anticipatory repudiation.

(2) *See Harrell v. Sea Colony, Inc.* (Md. 1977), where the court held that a conditional inquiry regarding the cancellation of a contract was not enough to constitute anticipatory repudiation.

(v) Retraction of Repudiation

(1) Under the common law approach, once a party repudiates a contract, he cannot retract it; the other party is discharged of his duty.

(2) Under the UCC and Restatement approaches, a party may retract the repudiation if the following conditions are met:

(aa) The retraction is done in ***reasonable time*** (under the circumstances);

(bb) The non-breaching party has ***actual notice*** (through either the retracting party or another party); and

(cc) The non-breaching party has ***assurances*** that the retracting party will perform.

(vi) Prospective Inability to Perform

(1) The anticipatory repudiation may also be by conduct.

(2) This would be the case when a purchaser learns that the seller has sold the object of the sale to another party.

(b) Adequate Assurances of Performance

(i) In some cases, it is not clear whether a party has repudiated.

(ii) In such situations, the second party may demand adequate assurances of performance in writing.

(iii) If the second party does not receive the assurances, he may withhold performance.

(iv) However, in sales under the UCC, the request for adequate assurances of performance *must be made in writing*.

(1) *See Scott v. Crown* (Colo. Ct. App. 1988), where the plaintiff Scott entered into a contract to sell the defendant wheat, and later entered into identical contracts with him. The plaintiff, later hearing about the defendant's trade practices, became worried about being paid, and demanded adequate assurances of performance. The defendant never responded but sent trucks to pick up wheat, which the plaintiff refused to load. When the defendant failed to make April payments, the plaintiff sued for breach of contract. The defendant counterclaimed, arguing the plaintiff's breach for not loading the wheat. Held: the plaintiff did not in fact have adequate assurance of performance, but because the plaintiff did not request assurances in writing as required by the UCC, the plaintiff was not discharged of his duty to deliver the wheat.

5.3.2 Material Breach (Inferior Performance)

(a) A party's ***material breach*** resulting from ***inferior performance*** discharges the other party's duty to perform.

(b) In determining whether a breach was material or immaterial, the courts will consider:

(i) Whether the breach is *intentional* or *negligent*;

(ii) Whether the breaching party *gains from the breach*;

(iii) Whether the breach was *outside of the breaching party's control*;

(iv) The extent to which the *non-breaching party will obtain substantial benefits*;

(v) The extent to which *damages make non-breaching party whole*;

(vi) The likelihood that the *breaching party will perform the remainder* of contract.

(c) Several of these factors together considered will usually shape the court's decision.

(i) *See Continental Grain Co. v. Simpson Feed Co.* (E.D. Ark. 1951) where the defendant Simpson Feed Co. agreed to sell 10,000 bushels of soybeans to the plaintiff. In the second shipment, the defendant did not receive the plaintiff's instructions, and, considering that to be a material breach, did not deliver the bushels. Held: a delay in sending shipping instructions is not sufficiently material to discharge the defendant of his duty to perform when ***time was not of the essence***. The defendant was not materially injured by the delay and the plaintiff did not delay the instructions in intentionally.

(d) Failure to pay only a slight percent of a contract price is not sufficiently material to discharge the non-breaching party of the duty to perform.

(i) *See Lane Enterprises v. L.B. Foster Co.* (Pa. Super. 1997), where the plaintiff, a general contractor, subcontracted a job to the defendant to treat bridge steel components. When the defendant's performance was inadequate, the plaintiff demanded that it be redone and requested assurance that the second batch would be done correctly. When the defendant failed to make assurances, the plaintiff sued for breach of contract. The defendant counterclaimed that the plaintiff materially breached by not giving full payment on part performance. Held: the plaintiff's withholding of 5% payment is not a material breach under the Restatement § 241. The defendant's failure to give adequate assurances of performance is anticipatory repudiation and discharges the plaintiff of the duty to perform.

### 5.4 Other Ways of Discharging the Duty to Perform

5.4.1 Unilateral Rescission

(a) One party may sue under equity to rescind a contract unilaterally, even when the second party does not want to rescind.

(b) A party generally seeks unilateral rescission when he may assert a defense, such as improper obtainment of assent, or a failure of a basic assumption (*see infra.*).

5.4.2 Occurrence of a Condition Subsequent

(a) When a condition subsequent occurs, the party whose duty to perform was contingent on the nonoccurrence of that condition is discharged of that duty.

5.4.3 Discharge by Illegality

(a) This applies when the parties enter into a contract and the performance of a contractual obligation later becomes illegal.

(b) *See* "Changed Circumstances," *infra*.

## 6 Defenses to Contractual Obligation

### 6.1 Legal Incapacity

6.1.1 Infancy

(a) Anyone under the age of eighteen is considered by the law to be an infant.

(b) Generally, a contract between an infant and an adult is voidable by the infant, but binding on the adult.

(c) The infant may disaffirm the contract at anytime before he reaches majority (eighteen years of age).

(i) Upon disaffirming, the infant gets restoration, not restitution.

(1) For example, if an infant purchases a bike that he later destroys in an accident, by later disaffirming the contract, he would be entitled to a full refund, regardless of the condition of the bike.

(d) After reaching majority, he may only void the contract *after a reasonable time*.

(e) Exceptions

(i) Misrepresentation

(1) The infant's power to disaffirm the contract may terminate if the he lies about his age.

(2) A clause in the contract including the minor's misrepresentation of his age could be used to prove the misrepresentation.

(ii) Necessities

(1) Infants are bound by contracts involving necessities and are responsible for the fair market value of the goods.

(2) Necessities are determined relatively according to the child's economic class; rich and poor children will have different necessities.

6.1.2 Mental Incapacity

(a) Mental incapacity applies when a party is adjudicated as incompetent.

(b) It serves as a defense to a contractual obligation by making the contract voidable.

(c) If a mentally incompetent person enters into a contract, he may disaffirm it when he is lucid or have it disaffirmed by a legal representative.

(d) He may similarly affirm the contract when lucid or when restored to normal mental capacity (with or without judicial action).

(e) There is quasi-contractual recovery for necessities furnished during incapacity.

6.1.3 Intoxication

(a) Contracts entered into by intoxicated persons are voidable when a reasonable person would have known that the person was intoxicated.

(b) The intoxicated party may disaffirm the contract upon becoming sober.

(c) There is quasi-contractual recovery for necessities furnished during the intoxication.

**6.2 Obtaining Assent by Improper Means**

6.2.1 Misrepresentation

(a) A misrepresentation is any statement "not in accord with the facts." Restatement § 159.

(b) It may be ***innocent*** or ***fraudulent***.

(c) Misrepresentation serves as a defense to a contractual obligation that makes a contract voidable when:

(i) The misrepresentation is *material* (it is "*likely to induce a reasonable person*" into the contract, or the maker knows that the misrepresentation would be likely to do so. Restatement § 162); and

(ii) The victim *justifiably relies* on it.

(d) The remedy for material misrepresentation, whether it is innocent or fraudulent, is ***rescission***.

(i) *See Halpert v. Rosenthal* (R.I. 1970), where the plaintiff Halpert represented that a home was termite-free and agreed to sell it to the defendant. After learning that the home was infested with termites, the defendant sought to rescind the contract and his deposit. The plaintiff sued for SP and damages. Held: even if the plaintiff's misrepresentation was innocent, it was material and rescission is therefore available to the defendant.

(e) However, the representation must be as to present, existing ***facts***, not opinions.

(i) *See Byers v. Federal Land Co.* (8th Cir. 1924) where the plaintiff entered into a contract to purchase the defendant Federal Land Co.'s 3,200 acres based on the defendant's promise that each acre was worth $35 and that the plaintiff would obtain immediate possession. When the plaintiff later found out that the defendant was not the actual owner and that each acre was worth substantially less, the plaintiff demanded rescission. Held: since the defendant's representation of the value of each acre was an opinion made innocently, the plaintiff was not justified in relying on it. However, the misrepresentation regarding the possession constitute a material breach, since the defendant never had possession of property.

(f) Although generally, recipients of opinions are not justified in relying on those opinions, there are exceptions under the Restatement § 169:

(i) When the parties are in a ***fiduciary relationship***;

(ii) When the party receiving the opinion is ***particularly susceptible*** to misrepresentation;

(iii) When the party making the opinion has ***superior knowledge***.

(1) *See Vokes v. Arthur Murray, Inc.* (Fla. 1968) (defendant), where the plaintiff claims that the defendant intentionally misrepresented the plaintiff's potential to succeed in dance in order to induce her to purchase substantial hours of dance lessons. Held: when an opinion is made by one having superior knowledge, that opinion will be treated as a fact and material misrepresentation through that opinion will allow contract rescission.

### 6.2.2 Fraud

(a) Fraud in the *Factum*

(i) This occurs when one party induces a second party to sign a contract without the second party's understanding of what he is signing.

(ii) Example: an employee signs a contract when misleadingly told by his employer that it merely allows the company to publish the employee's email address on the directory. In reality, the employee transferred title to his car.

(iii) Fraud in the *factum* is a defense that voids a contract and discharges the victim of his contractual obligation to perform.

(iv) It is a defense that is rarely invoked in comparison to fraud in the inducement.

(b) Fraud in the Inducement

(i) In referring to fraud, the courts generally are making reference to fraud in the inducement, which is a misrepresentation made whenever:

(1) The inducer intends his assertions to induce a second party to enter into the agreement; and

(2) The inducer knows that his assertions are false or does not have the confidence that he states or implies in the truth of the assertions or knows that he does not have the basis that he states or implies for the assertion. Restatement § 162.

(ii) Fraudulent misrepresentation is a defense that voids a contract and discharges the victim's contractual obligation to perform.

6.2.3 Duress

(a) Duress excuses contractual obligations when the following elements are met:

(i) There is a threat;

(ii) That is improper;

(iii) That induces a party to enter into a contract.

(b) A threat is improper when:

(i) The threatened act is *illegal*;

(ii) The threat is of *death* or *bodily harm*;

(iii) The threat is of *criminal prosecution* for personal gain;

(iv) The threat is a *breach of good faith* and fair dealing that hurts the victim without benefiting the party making the threat.

(v) The victim is *left without a choice* in entering the contract.

(1) *See Silsbee v. Webber* (Mass. 1898), where the plaintiff entered into contract to pay a $1,500 settlement agreement to the defendant Webber for her son who was accused of embezzling from the defendant, his employer. The plaintiff signed a settlement agreement with the defendant when he threatened to tell the plaintiff's deeply troubled and melancholy husband, who would be greatly

disturbed if he found out about the accusation. The plaintiff later sued for duress to recover the money paid. Held: the defendant's acts were improper because they left the plaintiff ***without the ability to exercise independent judgment***. The fact that the transaction was handled by the defendant's former attorney further supports this thesis.

(c) The standard applied does not look to "a person of ordinary sensibilities"; it is subjective.

6.2.4 Undue Influence

(a) Undue influence leads to rescission whenever:

(i) The victim is ***particularly vulnerable*** at the time he is broached by the other party; and

(ii) The other party exercises ***unfair persuasion*** over the victim through ***domination***.

(b) Several factors are looked at in determining whether there was undue influence:

(i) Broaching a subject at an *improper time* or *place*;

(ii) Placing undue pressure on the victim through *limiting the victim's time to decide*;

(iii) Having *many parties* influence a sole victim at the *same time*;

(iv) Giving the victim *no opportunity to consult third party advisors*.

(v) *See Odorizzi v. Bloomfield School District* (defendant), where the plaintiff was charged for homosexual activity and the defendant employer, in the plaintiff's vulnerability and exhaustion, offered to not allow any publicity (and thus the possibility of another job) in exchange for the plaintiff's resignation. The plaintiff assented, but later, realizing that the offer was made with undue influence, sought to rescind his resignation. Held: because the plaintiff was *particularly vulnerable* at the time of the offer, which was made at an *improper place* and *time* (at home outside of work hours) and had *no opportunity to consult any advisors*, he pleaded sufficient facts to reverse the trial court's dismissal.

6.2.5 Unconscionability

(a) Courts consider a contract unconscionable when its terms are ***shocking to the conscience***. The following factors are considered:

(i) There was ***undue bargaining power*** between the party that dictated the terms of the contract and the party that accepted them;

(ii) There is ***unfair surprise*** and the weaker party did not understand or notice some of the hidden provisions of the contract;

(iii) The terms of the contract are ***oppressive***;

(iv) The clauses are ***one-sided***, deprive the party with inferior bargaining power of reasonable choice, and unduly favor the party with superior bargaining power.

(1) Example: an adhesion contract that permits a seller to repossess *all previously sold goods* if the buyer fails to make even a single payment on time. *Williams v. Walker-Thomas Furniture Co.* (D.C. Cir. 1965).

(b) A contract may be:

(i) ***Procedurally unconscionable*****:** where unfair terms are inconspicuous (*e.g.*, in the fine print) or incomprehensible (*i.e.*, written so that an average person would not understand them); or

(ii) ***Substantively unconscionable*****:** the terms of the contract themselves are unfair or one sided.

(c) Price unconscionability applies to two situations:

(i) A purchaser is charged a price without being aware of the actual price he was agreeing to (courts will void the contract); or

(ii) He is charged a much higher price than other purchasers because he is in a state of particular need and is taken advantage of.

(1) Example: a driver comes to the only rest stop on a long, abandoned road. The clerk, aware of the driver's need, charges him triple the normal price of a bottle of water.

(2) Since courts are reluctant to intervene when the parties have come to an agreement, they would be unlikely to rescind the contract.

### 6.3 Mistakes of Present Existing Facts

#### 6.3.1 Introduction

(a) This section deals with mistakes made about *basic assumptions at the time the contract was made*.

(b) Some, but *not all mistakes*, rise to the level required to *void a contract*.

#### 6.3.2 Mutual Mistake

(a) "A mistake is a belief that is not in accord with the facts" (§ 151).

(i) A mistake cannot deal with *value judgments* or *future predictions*.

(ii) Rather, it must be about ascertainable knowledge in the present.

(b) The elements for making a *prima facie* case for mutual mistake are as follow (§ 152):

(i) Both parties must be ***mistaken***;

(ii) About a ***presently existing fact***;

(iii) That is a ***basic assumption*** going to the heart of the deal;

(1) *See Sherwood v. Walker* (Mich. 1887), where the court allowed rescission of a contract when the parties, according to the majority, mistakenly believed that the cow being traded was barren, since the cow's being barren was a *basic assumption* going to the heart of what was a "beef contract," not a "breeding cow contract."

(iv) That has a ***material effect on the agreed-to exchange*** (one of the parties is gaining more than expected and the other party less); and

(v) The adversely effected party ***did not assume the risk*** through:

(1) The *allocation of the assumption of the risk* in the contract;

(2) *Conscious ignorance* (knowing that he has limited knowledge, he treats his knowledge as sufficient); or

(3) *Allocation of the risk to him by the court* on the grounds of equity.

6.3.3 Unilateral Mistake

(a) This is the mistake of only one party.

(b) The elements of unilateral mistake are as follow:

(i) One of the parties to a contract is ***mistaken***;

(ii) As to a ***presently existing fact***;

(iii) That is a ***basic assumption*** going to the heart of the deal;

(iv) That has a ***material effect*** as to the agreed-to exchange (one of the parties is gaining more than expected and the other party less);

(v) For which he did not assume the risk through either:

(1) The *allocation of the assumption of the risk* in the contract;

(2) *Conscious ignorance* (knowing that his knowledge was limited but treating it as sufficient); or

(3) *Allocation of the risk to him by the court* because the circumstances make doing so reasonable; and

(vi) The other party ***had reason to know of the mistake*** or was ***at fault for it***, *or*, it ***would be unconscionable to enforce the contract.***

(1) The other party has a duty to disclose information when she knows that the other party "is mistaken as to a basic assumption" regarding that information.

(2) This does not, however, mean that she is obligated to disclose the other party's *every mistake*.

(3) Rather, she must act "in accordance with reasonable standards of fair dealing" (§ 161, Comment *d*).

### 6.4 Changed Circumstances

6.4.1 Introduction

(a) Changed circumstances do not excuse a party's performance *unless* they render the performance ***impossible*** or ***impracticable*** or ***frustrate the purpose*** behind the contract.

6.4.2 Impossibility

(a) This defense applies when a *supervening event* renders a party's performance *objectively impossible*.

(b) Elements:

(i) The parties must have entered into a contract with a ***basic assumption that the event would not occur;***

(ii) The event ***does occur;***

(iii) The event renders performance ***objectively impossible*** (*i.e.*, impossible for *anyone* to perform);

(iv) The adversely affected party ***is not at fault*** for the event; and

(v) The adversely affected party ***did not contract to perform*** in case the event occurred.

(c) Subjective Impossibility

(i) For the duties to be discharged under impossibility, performance ***must not be possible for anyone*** (objective impossibility).

(ii) If they can be performed by *someone*, albeit not the party adversely effected, the impossibility is said to be subjective and does not discharge the duty to perform.

(1) *See Paradine v. Jane* (K.B. 1647), where a tenant was not discharged of his duty to pay rent to a landlord even though he was ousted from the property by an invading German army, preventing him from farming the land in order to pay the rent. Held: judgment for landlord affirmed because the defendant's performance is not objectively impossible (he can secure the payment using other means).

(d) Rather, the impossibility must be objective: no one would be able to perform.

(i) *See Taylor v. Caldwell* (K.B. 1863), where the defendant lessor was excused from performance to the plaintiff lessee when his theatre was burned down. There was an implied condition that where the subject matter of a transaction was destroyed, the parties are discharged from their duties because it has become impossible to perform.

(e) Supervening Illegality

(i) One common category of impossibility occurs when the parties enter into a contract for the performance of an act, and that act *later becomes illegal*.

(ii) For example, if the defendant agrees to deliver twenty bottles of French wine each week to the plaintiff's restaurant, but then an embargo is imposed against France, the defendant will have a valid defense for nonperformance.

6.4.3 Impracticability

(a) Impracticability is a defense when performance becomes extremely and unreasonably difficult and/or burdensome.

(b) It represents a level of difficulty between impractical and impossible.

(c) Elements:

(i) The parties entered into contract with the ***basic assumption*** that a supervening event would not occur;

(1) The event may be an act of God or of a third party.

(2) Examples: natural disaster, war, embargo, currency devaluation, etc.

(ii) The supervening event ***does occur;***

(iii) The ***event*** made the performance ***impracticable;***

(iv) The party seeking rescission is ***not at fault*** for the resulting impracticability; and

(v) The party did ***not agree to perform*** despite the event's occurrence.

6.4.4 Frustration of Purpose

(a) Frustration of purpose applies when supervening events render the *value* of a contract to a party worthless or virtually worthless.

(b) The party is *deprived of the benefit* of the contract because her *purpose* for making the contract *is "frustrated."*

(c) The elements are virtually identical to those of impracticability:

(i) The parties entered into contract with the ***basic assumption*** that a supervening event would not occur;

(ii) The supervening event ***does occur;***

(iii) The event completely or substantially ***destroys the party's primary purpose*** in entering the contract;

(1) *See Krell v. Henry* (K.B. 1903), where the defendant was discharged of his duty to pay for an apartment when Edward VII's coronation's date was rescheduled,

since the central purpose behind the contract, the viewing of the coronation, was frustrated.

(iv) The party seeking rescission is ***not at fault*** for the supervening event; and

(v) The party ***did not agree to perform despite the occurrence*** of the event.

(d) Discharge of performance through impracticability and frustration of purpose

(i) ***Impracticability*** generally applies to lessors, service providers, and sellers.

(ii) ***Frustration of purpose*** generally applies to lessees and purchasers.

## 7 Warranties for Sales of Goods

### 7.1 Overview

7.1.1 Introduction

(a) When parties to a contract for the sale of goods do not specifically agree to the terms of a warranty, the UCC applies as a "gap filler."

(b) The UCC gap fillers are found in UCC Article 2, Part 3.

(c) The two main gap fillers are the Implied Warranty of Merchantability (§ 2-314) and the Implied Warranty of Fitness for a Particular Purpose (§ 2-315).

(i) *NB:* there are other implied warranties as well (*e.g.*, trade custom).

(d) Unless the provisions of § 2-316 are used to disclaim or modify these warranties, they automatically become part of the contract if the seller is a "merchant with respect to goods of that kind."

(e) In order to recover for breach of warranty, the plaintiff must prove:

(i) The existence of a contract;

(ii) A term existed (warranty);

(iii) The obligation was breached;

(iv) Damages.

7.1.2 The Implied Warranty of Merchantability. UCC § 2-314.

(a) In order for the Implied Warranty of Merchantability to arise, the following elements must be met:

(i) There was a ***contract for sale***;

(ii) The seller must be a ***merchant*** with respect to goods of that kind; and

(iii) It is not disclaimed.

(1) The plaintiff does not need to prove that the warranty was not disclaimed, excluded, or modified under § 2-316; this is an affirmative defense to be raised by the defendant.

(b) To determine whether the Warranty had been violated, consult UCC § 2-314(2) for a list of factors. Two key provisions to § 2-314 are as follow:

(i) The goods would pass without objection in the trade according to the contract description. § 2-314(2)(a); and

(ii) The goods are fit for the ***ordinary purposes*** for which "goods of that description are used" or in their ***foreseeable misuse.*** § 2-314(2)(c).

(c) ***Note:*** if the plaintiff can show that any single provision of § 2-214(2) has not been met, then the Implied Warranty of Merchantability would be considered breached.

(d) Example → plaintiff sues a beer company after contracting illness after decades of heavy drinking.

(i) The plaintiff will argue that because it is foreseeable that occasional drinking of the defendant's beer could in some cases lead to alcoholism, which could lead to serious health problems, the defendant's product was not fit for the ordinary purpose for which it is used. Some courts in fact are accepting this controversial line of reasoning and ruling in favor of plaintiffs.

(ii) The defendant will argue that ruling in the plaintiff's favor would implicate not only the beer company, but the entire alcohol industry and that decisions that would have such vast consequences should be made not by courts, but by legislatures.

7.1.3 The Implied Warranty of Fitness for a Particular Purpose. UCC § 3-315.

(a) The Implied Warranty of Fitness for a Particular Purpose warrants that the goods ***will be fit for any particular purpose*** for which the goods are required when the seller has reason to know of such purpose at the time of contracting.

(b) The implied warranty of fitness for a particular purpose arises under the following elements according to the circumstances of the contract:

(i) The buyer has a ***particular purpose***;

(ii) The seller ***has reason to know*** of that purpose;

(iii) The buyer ***relies*** on the seller to select a suitable good;

(iv) The seller has reason to know that the buyer is relying on him.

(c) ***Note:*** the ***seller needs to be neither a merchant*** with respect to goods of that kind nor a merchant at all.

(d) ***Note:*** the plaintiff does not have to prove that the implied warrant for a particular purpose was not disclaimed. This is an affirmative defense to be raised by the defendant.

(e) Example →

(i) A purchaser goes into a greenhouse that has an annual sale for the equipment that it no longer uses. He tells an employee that he needs a space heater for his 10' x 12' garage and that he did not know which one to purchase. The employee tells him that he has just the right heater, which the the purchaser buys. Within 15 minutes of turning it on, the room was warmed up. The purchaser then went to put his hand on it and burned his palm. The purchaser sued.

(ii) Does the purchase have a cause of action for breach of an implied warranty?

(1) Implied Warranty of Merchantability

(aa) Here, this warranty would not arise because the greenhouse is not a merchant with respect to goods of that kind. Rather, it is a greenhouse, which deals with plants.

(bb) The sale of the space heater was part of an annual sale that is outside of the scope of the greenhouse's normal sales. The implied warranty of merchantability does not arise.

(cc) However, if the implied warranty of merchantability would have arisen, then it would have been breached, since placing one's hand on a space heater is a foreseeable misuse.

(2) Implied Warranty for a Particular Use

(aa) Does the warranty arise?

(I) The purchaser had a particular purpose (to heat his 10' x 12' garage);

(II) The employee had reason to know of this purpose, since the purchaser had told him;

(III) The purchaser relied on the employee's selection of a suitable good (admitting that he did not know which one he needed;

(IV) The defendant had reason to know of this;

(V) The warranty was never disclaimed.

(VI) Therefore, the warranty arose.

(bb) Was the warranty breached?

(I) The space heater did in fact heat the room according to the purchaser's purpose.

(II) Therefore, the warranty was never breached.

7.1.4 Express Warranties. UCC § 2-313 – § 2-313B.

(a) Express warranties can be made by affirmation, promise, description, or sample.

(b) Elements. The seller must make:

(i) "Any affirmation of ***fact or promise***" (UCC § 2-313(2)(a));

(1) The words "warranty," "guarantee," "promise," etc. do not have to be used.

(2) Example → a can of V8 states "100% of Vitamin C." That is an express warranty.

(ii) ***Relating*** to goods;

(iii) That is the ***basis of the bargain.***

(1) This element does not require a "but-for" analysis (*i.e.*, but for this warranty, B would not have purchased the good).

(2) Rather, a mere writing, even if never read by B, is sufficient for meeting this element.

(3) Example → S warrants in a certificate that the diamonds are of a certain cut, color, carat, and clarity. Even if B never reads the certificate, the warranty is breached if the diamonds do not conform to the certificate.

(c) The content of the warranty is whatever was affirmed or promised.

(d) The "affirmation of fact or promise" can at times be difficult to distinguish from "puffery."

(i) Example 1 → S says, "this car is great."

(1) This is likely to be "puffery," since it is difficult to quantify "great."

(2) If this were a promise, it would be ***difficult to prove*** that the warranty was breached.

(3) Words such as "good," "excellent," and "great" generally refer only to sales talk, not to warranties.

(4) In contrast, descriptions that are easy to measure (*e.g.* this car gives 30 miles to the gallon) can lead to warranties.

(ii) Example 2 → B tells S that he needs a car with good gas mileage. S tells him "I know just the car for you."

(1) Although S did not make a promise, courts would find that a promise was made.

(2) It would not be necessary that the words come out of S's mouth; S's words, taken in conjunction with B's words, could form a representation.

(3) However, a problem here is that B never stated a purpose. Had he stated, "I need a car to drive across the mountains with no gas stops," there would have been a purpose.

(e) ***Note:*** revised § 2-313 limits remedies for breaches of express warranties to "immediate buyers," or those who enter into a contract with a seller.

(i) Example → B purchases a John Deere lawnmower from Home Depot. B is an immediate buyer of Home Depot, not of John Deere.

(ii) Under § 2-313, if John Deere makes any express warranties, only Home Depot, the immediate buyer, will have privity to sue.

(iii) ***However,*** under § 2-313A and 2-313B, John Deere may have obligations to even remote purchasers (in our example, B) based on (i) records packaged with or accompanying goods and promises or affirmations made on the product's box itself (§ 2-313A) and (ii) advertisements or other public communications (§ 2-313B). John Deere must stand behind the promises and affirmations of fact made to remote purchasers.

(iv) Although remote purchasers may not recover under § 2-313 (where no affirmations or promises were made with a record, advertisement, or other public communication), the warranty of merchantability still applies.

(v) §§ 2-313A-B include language about disclaiming warranties and remedies that remote purchasers may pursue.

(f) Thus, in the above example, B could sue John Deere under § 2-313A or 2-313B for advertisements and promises on and in the box and can also sue Home Depot under § 2-313.

## 7.2 Reducing or Eliminating Warranty Liability: Basics

### 7.2.1 § 2-316 Under the Current (Unrevised) Code

(a) Disclaiming express warranties (UCC § 2-316(1)):

(i) Words disclaiming and words creating warranties will be read to the extent possible as being consistent with one another.

(ii) In the event that the words contradict one another, the words creating warranties trump.

(b) Disclaiming the ***implied warranty of merchantability*** (UCC §2-316(2)):

(i) May be in ***writing*** or ***oral*** (but if it is in writing, it must be ***conspicuous***);

(ii) It must mention "merchantability."

(c) Disclaiming the ***implied warranty for a particular purpose*** (UCC § 2-316(2)):

(i) Must be in ***writing***;

(ii) Must be ***conspicuous***;

(iii) An example of language that would suffice if in writing and conspicuous: "There are no warranties which extend beyond the description on the face hereof."

(d) Otherwise, implied warranties may be excluded by UCC § 2-316(3):

(i) Language

(1) "As is," "with all faults," or other language which in ***common understanding*** calls the buyer's attention to the exclusion of warranties and makes plain that there is no implied warranty.

(2) "There are no warranties" does not do the trick. That is legalese. If it were sufficient, the rest of § 2-316 would be rendered meaningless.

(3) There is no writing requirement.

(4) There is no difference between consumer and non-consumer requirements.

(ii) Inspection (***note Comment 8***)

(1) Before entering into a contract, the seller may demand that the buyer inspect, at which point the buyer may either inspect or refuse to do so.

(2) According to Comment 8 of the UCC, the seller's demanding that the buyer inspect is equivalent to his putting the buyer on notice that the buyer is responsible for an inspection of the goods, but if he refuses to inspect, he is assuming the risk.

(3) Whether this would exclude the implied warranties would depend in part on what, under the circumstances, the examination should have revealed.

(4) It is also important to note that the comments are not law; the statute, not the comments, is the law enacted by the legislature.

(iii) The "Golden Three":

(1) Course of performance;

(2) Course of dealing;

(3) Usage of trade.

7.2.2 § 2-316 Under the Revised Code

(a) Disclaiming the Implied Warranty of Merchantability (§ 2-316(2)):

(i) A record is required; and

(ii) One of the following:

(1) Consumer contracts (a higher standard than that of the current (unrevised) code)

(aa) It must state, "The seller undertakes no responsibility for the quality of the goods except as otherwise provided in this contract";

(bb) Must be in a ***record;*** and

(cc) Be ***conspicuous.***

(2) Non-consumer contracts (merchants) (same as the current (unrevised) code):

(aa) May be in **writing** or **oral** (but if it is in writing, it must be **conspicuous**);

(bb) It must mention "merchantability."

(b) Disclaiming the Implied Warranty for a Particular Purpose (§ 2-316(2)):

(i) Consumer contracts, which have a higher standard than that of the current (unrevised) code), require:

(1) A record;

(2) That is conspicuous; and

(3) The following language: "The seller assumes no responsibility that the goods will be fit for any particular purpose for which you may be buying these goods, except as otherwise provided in the contract."

(4) NOTE: in the unrevised version, there was safe harbor language, but no required language.

(ii) For non-consumer (merchant) contracts (same requirements as the current (unrevised) code):

(1) Must be in writing;

(2) Must be conspicuous;

(3) Having the safe harbor language: "There are no warranties which extend beyond the description on the face hereof" (this language in a conspicuous writing would pass).

(c) § 2-316 (3) Exceptions to the § 2-316(2) Exclusion or Modification of Warranties Provisions:

(i) The revised code is the same as the unrevised except that in revised § 2-316(3)(a), if the language appears in a record, that record must be conspicuous.

(d) Disclaiming express warranties: (§ 2-316(1)): there are no changes.

## 8 Remedies for Breach of Contract

### 8.1 Damages for Breach of Contract

#### 8.1.1 The Common Law

(a) The Three Damage Interests that a Promisee may Choose Between

(i) The Expectation Interest

(1) The expectation interest puts the ***promisee*** back in the position that he would have been in if the promisor had not breached the contract.

(2) The plaintiff's damages are thus equal to the value of profits he would have obtained had the promisor performed (the plaintiff's loss of value, "L") plus incidental and consequential losses and costs (spent in reliance of the contract) minus costs saved. Restatement § 347.

(aa) The formula is: (L + I/C) – CS = EI.

(3) *See Hawkins v. McGee* (N.H. 1929), where the court held that the plaintiff's damage interests should be limited to the difference in value between the promised, 100% cured hand and the actual hand that the plaintiff got. Pain and suffering should *not* be taken into account.

(aa) *N.B.*: when the plaintiff enters into surgery knowing that there will be pain, this pain is part of the consideration that the plaintiff is putting up in order to get better. The plaintiff cannot collect damages on pain.

(4) Incidentals and consequential costs may exponentially increase the plaintiff's loss in value

(aa) *See Nurse v. Barnes* (K.B. 1664), where the court allowed the jury to reward 500 £ of "special" damages, even though the actual damages were only 10 £.

(ii) The Reliance Interest

(1) The reliance interest puts the ***promisee*** in the position that he would have been in had there been no contract.

(2) The promisee is compensated for any detriment suffered in performance or preparation for performance undertaken in reliance on the breaching party's promise.

(iii) The Restitution Interest

(1) The restitution interest puts the ***promisor*** back into the position that he would have been in had there been no contract.

(2) The promisor must disgorge any benefit received because of the existence of the contract.

(b) Pain and suffering

(i) Contract law is coldly commercial: if the plaintiff can only recover those damages that correspond to a commercial loss, *not to pain and suffering*.

(ii) Regardless of the defendant's culpability, damages are given for economic, not emotional, losses.

(iii) The plaintiff is also unable to recover for hassle.

8.1.2 Sales Contracts under the UCC

(a) Buyer's Remedies

(i) If the seller breaches, the buyer may recover the difference in value between the market price of an item at the time that he learned of the breach and the contract price (the buyer's loss), plus incidental and consequential costs minus costs avoided (similar to the expectation interest described above).

(ii) He may recover the difference between the amount paid for the good that he was forced to obtain from another seller and the original price he would have paid under the contract.

(iii) This remedy is referred to as "cover." UCC § 2-712.

(b) Seller's Remedies

(i) General Rule

(1) If the buyer breaches, the seller may recover the difference between the contract price and the market price at the time of the breach. UCC § 2-708.

(2) The seller may also sell the goods to another buyer and may recover the ***difference between the contract price and the resale price*** (referred to as "Seller's Cover"). UCC § 2-706.

(ii) Exception: the "Lost Volume" Seller

(1) Under the "lost volume" doctrine, if the seller has a virtually unlimited supply of the goods, the court will allow him to make a double profit, awarding profit damages from first breaching buyer on top of profit received from the second buyer to whom the goods were actually sold.

(c) When UCC Provisions Conflict

(i) The UCC has both general and specific provisions.

(ii) When the two seemingly conflict, the more specific provision applies. *Tongish v. Thomas* (Kan. 1992).

**8.2 Three Limitations on Damages**

8.2.1 Remoteness of Foreseeability of Harm

(a) The defendant is liable to the plaintiff for (i) all general damages that naturally arise from the breach of contract; and (ii) any damages resulting from special circumstances ***that he has reason to know about***.

(b) This second group of damages is referred to as "consequential damages," and is limited to only those damages that are foreseeable.

(c) If the defendant has no reason to know about special circumstances that could lead to consequential damages, he will not be held liable for consequential damages.

(i) *See Hadley v. Baxendale* (Ct. of Exchequer 1854), where the plaintiff's employee brought a mill shaft to the defendant, explained that it was broken, and requested that it be repaired for the next day, without explaining that the mill would be shut down until the shaft was repaired. The defendant failed to ship the shaft overnight as agreed and as a result, the mill was shut down for five days. The plaintiff sued to recover both his ***loss in value*** (the difference between overnight and five day delivery) and the ***consequential damages*** resulting from the breach (five days of lost profits), or about 300 £. Held: the plaintiff cannot recover for the consequential damages because the defendant had no way of foreseeing the special circumstances leading to the consequential damages.

(1) This case establishes an ***objective test*** for determining whether the defendant is liable for *general damages*; it does not matter whether the defendant actually foresaw the general damages.

(2) However, with respect to the special circumstances leading to consequential damages, the court employs a partially subjective test: the special damages are equal to what one would "reasonably contemplate would be the amount of injury which would ordinarily follow from a breach of contract under these special circumstances so *known and communicated*."

(aa) On the one hand, the special circumstances must be "known" by the defendant (subjective prong);

(bb) On the other hand, the amount of damages for which the defendant is liable is equal to the injury that one would "reasonably contemplate" to follow from such special circumstances (objective prong).

(d) The Restatement (Second) of Contracts § 351 establishes an objective, reasonable person test to ***both general as well as special damages***.

(i) General damages: the defendant is not liable for damages (loss in value) when he "did not have reason to foresee" the damages as a result of his breach.

(ii) Special damages: the defendant is not liable for damages resulting from special circumstances that he did not have "reason to know."

(e) Under the common law, when the defendant is put on notice of potential consequential and incidental damages arising out of his breach, he becomes liable for these damages.

(i) The common law duty may be modified by contract. Such agreements are usually enforced by the courts, unless they are unconscionable, illegal, or against public policy.

(ii) For example, many courier services, such as UPS, require their clients to sign a waiver whereby they agree not to hold the courier responsible for any consequential damages that may arise as a result of non-delivery of a parcel. Courts generally uphold such contracts.

8.2.2 Proving Damages with Certainty

(a) The second limitation on recovering damages requires that the damages be proven with certainty.

(b) In order to recover expectation, reliance, or restitution damages, there must be sufficient evidence to establish with *relative certainty* the amount of harm resulting from the defendant's breach. Restatement § 352.

(c) It is especially difficult to determine expectation damages when large profits are expected from a one-time event and there are no former regular practices that could reasonably establish expected profits. In these cases, expectation damages will not be rewarded.

(i) *See Chicago Coliseum Club v. Dempsey* (Ill. Ct. App. 1932), where the court held that the plaintiff Chicago Coliseum Club could not recover for the defendant's anticipatory repudiation because there was no way of calculating lost profits with certainty. The plaintiff could, however, recover the reliance damages that were directly related to the contract.

(d) Under these circumstances, non-breaching parties will often seek reliance damages.

(i) Courts are divided as to whether reliance damages include only those expenditures made *after* the contract was entered into, or those preceding the contract as well.

(ii) Under the ***American rule***, plaintiffs may recover reliance damages for costs incurred as a result of "preparation of performance or in performance," Restatement § 349, but these costs do not include the costs incurred from before the contract was made.

(iii) Under the ***English rule***, plaintiffs may recover reliance damages for costs incurrent as a result of performance or of preparation of performance, and these costs include the costs incurred from before the contract was made *when both parties had reason to know that those damages would result* from the breach.

(1) *See Anglia Television Ltd. v. Reed* (Q.B. 1972), where the plaintiff Anglia Television Ltd. hired the defendant to act in a show. Because the defendant's agent double-booked him, he breached the contract and the plaintiff sued. The plaintiff sought reliance damages, since expectation interests could not be established with reasonable certainty. The defendant argued that the plaintiff should only be allowed to recover for expenditures made *after the contract with the defendant was formed*. Held: the plaintiff may recover for *all expenditures* made from before or after the contract was agreed to, since *both parties could have reasonably foreseen* that the breach would have led to such damages.

(e) When expectation damages are uncertain (or when they are certain but the plaintiff was not expecting to turn a profit), the plaintiff will often sue for reliance damages.

(i) *See Mistletoe Express Service v. Locke* (Tx. Ct. App. 1988), where the defendant contracted the plaintiff Locke to build a ramp over twelve months. At the ninth month, the defendant notified the plaintiff that it was going to breach. The plaintiff sued the defendant and opted for reliance damages (since money was being lost on the contract and there was a net loss at the time of the defendant's breach), seeking all costs expended on the project (loans taken out, vehicles purchased, etc.). The defendant argued that the plaintiff should not be entitled to all those costs, but rather, *should only be put back into position she would have been in had the contract not been breached* (which would have been at lost profits). Held: although expectation interests are the general measure of damages, the plaintiff may elect to sue for reliance damages.

8.2.3 Mitigation of Damages

(a) The third limitation on damages is avoidability of harm (this is the Restatement language), commonly known as the "duty to mitigate."

(b) Once the plaintiff knows that a breach of contract has occurred and nevertheless continues accruing damages, the plaintiff may not recover those damages sustained after the time the plaintiff knew of the breach. The plaintiff has a duty to mitigate.

(i) *See Rockingham County v. Luten Bridge Co.* (4th Cir. 1929), where the defendant Rockingham County contracted the plaintiff to build a bridge and later notified the plaintiff that it would breach the contract, since it had no use for the bridge. The plaintiff continued to build, and at the end of the process, claimed $18,000 in damages. The defendant contended that the plaintiff should only be entitled to $1,900, which is what was spent before the plaintiff received notice of the breach. Held: according to the American rule, the plaintiff has a duty to mitigate. There is no use for a bridge built in the middle of a forest. The plaintiff cannot recover for losses accrued after receiving notice that the defendant would breach.

(c) When an employment contract is breached by an employer, the non-breaching party must mitigate by either: (i) making reasonable efforts to find new work; or (ii) accepting new work when offered by the employer.

(i) Searching for New Work

(1) The non-breaching party must search for new work, but if after a reasonable effort, he is unable to find comparable work, he may sue for damages equivalent to his expectation interest.

(2) If the non-breaching party finds comparable work that pays less, he may sue for the difference.

(ii) Accepting New Work Offered by the Employer

(1) If new work is offered by the employer as a replacement for the work to be performed in the new contract, the non-breaching party should accept it.

(2) However, if the new work is not substantially similar to the original work, the non-breaching party is not required to accept it. § 350.

(aa) *See Parker v. Twentieth Century-Fox Film Corp.* (Cal. 1970), where the defendant hired the plaintiff Parker to play lead role in a musical for $750,000. The defendant breached the contract and instead offered the plaintiff the chance to play a lead role in a Western style movie to be filmed in Australia under similar terms. The plaintiff refused the new contract and sued for damages. The defendant argued that accepting the new job was required mitigation. Held: the plaintiff is not required to accept the new job as mitigation because the new job is substantially different from the old and cannot substitute it. The plaintiff is entitled to the $750,000.

(bb) *N.B.*: the court never discussed the plaintiff's duty to make reasonable efforts to find work. It may have been because these kinds of jobs come around so rarely that it may not have been practical to have required her to make such efforts.

(d) Mitigation in the Sale of Goods under the UCC

(i) General rule when the buyer breaches:

(1) If the seller resells the good, he is entitled to the difference between the purchase price and the contract price.

(2) If the seller does not resell, he is entitled to the difference between market price and contract price plus incidental and consequential damages minus costs avoided.

(ii) If the seller withholds delivery because of the buyer's breach, he must refund the defendant all the money that the defendant gave him less either $500 or 20% of contract price, whichever is less. UCC § 2-718(2).

(iii) However, this rule is subject to another damage-measuring formula under UCC § 2-708:

(1) Damages for the seller are the difference between the market price and the contract price at the time and place of tender, plus incidental and consequential costs, minus costs saved.

(2) If § 2-708(1) does not offer a reasonable result, then the seller may collect the profit (including reasonable overhead) that he would have made, plus incidentals, due allowance for costs, and due credit for payments.

**8.3 Liquidated Damages v. Penalty Clauses**

8.3.1 Introduction

(a) Generally, damages for breach of contract are equal to expectation damages, reliance damages or restitution damages.

(b) However, when calculating damages would be too difficult, the parties may elect to include liquidated (stipulated) damages clauses in the contract itself, to be applied in case of breach.

(c) However, courts are hesitant in enforcing stipulated damages clauses that appear to be penalties.

(i) Rationale: contracts must be seen in terms of economic realities. When damages could be calculated, the non-breaching party should be able to recover only monetary damages. When exorbitant damages are claimed, they are seen by the courts as penalties, which contract law does not recognize.

8.3.2 Stipulated damages clauses will generally not be enforced when:

(a) Actual damages can be calculated; and

(b) The stipulated damages are significantly greater than the actual damages (this indicates that the stipulated damages are really a penalty).

(i) Courts are especially reluctant to enforce stipulated damages clauses when they apply to all breaches, including immaterial ones.

(ii) *See Kemble v. Farren* (C.P. 1829), where the defendant Farren had a contract to be a comedian at the Royal theatre. The contract had a 1,000 £ liquidated damages clause. When the defendant breached after the second season, the plaintiff sued to recover the full 1,000 £. Held: because this contract allows the plaintiff to collect 1,000 £ in damages for even slight breach, it functions as a penalty clause and will not be enforced.

8.3.3 On the other hand, courts will enforce liquidated damage clauses when they are ***reasonable***, as determined by three factors:

(a) There is *no intent to create a penalty clause.*

(b) The damages *would be difficult for a court to ascertain* at the time the contract was made.

(i) *N.B.*: under the minority approach, courts look to see if the damages would be difficult to ascertain *at the time the suit is brought.*

(c) The damages *accurately predict* the damages at the time they arise.

(i) *See Wassenaar v. Towne Hotel* (Wis. 1983)., where the plaintiff employee Wassenaar entered into an employment contract with the defendant. Under a stipulated damages clause, the defendant was responsible for its entire three year financial obligation to pay the plaintiff in the event that the defendant terminated the contract prematurely. With twenty one months remaining, the defendant terminated the contract. On the issue of whether the liquidated damages clause was valid, the court held that the damages for breaching the employment contract comprised more than just the amount of money owed; it also included harm to reputation and other incalculable factors. The clause was therefore applied.

(ii) *N.B.*: this court ***did not require the plaintiff to mitigate damages*** because when a stipulated damages clause is found to be reasonable, the non-breaching party is not required to mitigate. However, although courts do not formally require mitigation, in practice mitigation is factored into courts' decision through the ***reasonableness*** analysis. If in *Wassenaar*, the defendant was able to submit evidence that the plaintiff had in fact gotten a job just after leaving the defendant's employment, the court, in evaluating the accuracy of the stipulated damages clause in predicting actual damages, would have likely held that the stipulated damages were inaccurate, and the liquidated damages clause to have been unreasonable. Rather than applying it, the court would have required the plaintiff to prove expectation damages. Thus, mitigation may be indirectly factored into the analysis.

## 8.4 Other Remedies and Causes of Action

### 8.4.1 Specific Performance and Injunctions

(a) General Rule

(i) Specific performance (SP) and injunctions will not be ordered by a court unless there is *no adequate remedy at law* (*i.e.*, money damages).

(ii) It is an exceptional remedy that tends to be applied in only real estate transactions.

(b) Contracts for Land

(i) For real estate transactions, SP is granted as a matter of course.

(1) *See Loveless v. Diehl* (Ark. 1963), where the defendant leased his farm to the plaintiff Diehl for three years with an option to purchase it for $21,000. The plaintiff found a buyer who would buy the land, allowing the plaintiff to make a $1,000 profit, but when the defendant found out about this, he repudiated the options contract. The plaintiff sued for SP. The defendant counterclaimed for a $1,440 promissory note. The courts originally held that the plaintiff was entitled to $1,000 and the defendant was entitled to the payment of the promissory note. On rehearing, it was held that there was no reason to deny SP. The general rule is that for realty, SP is granted as a matter of course. The plaintiffs spent much more on improving the property than the meager $1,000 awarded as damages. To refuse SP would be to unjustly enrich the sellers for breaching their own options contract.

(ii) But if it can be shown that there really is no difference between two pieces of real estate, then only damages will be rewarded (this would be exceptional).

(c) Contracts for Goods

(i) Under the common law, courts only order SP when the goods are scarce, rare, irreplaceable, or of sentimental value.

(1) *See Cumbest v. Harris* (Miss. 1978), where the defendant Harris loaned the plaintiff money and the plaintiff gave the defendant hi-fi equipment as collateral, with an option to purchase the equipment at any time before 5 pm on a specified date. When the day arrived, the plaintiff did everything he could to purchase the goods, but the defendant avoided him. The plaintiff sued for SP. The court held that the test for determining whether SP should be rewarded requires the court to consider whether damages are adequate. Here, some parts of the equipment were irreplaceable and other parts were replaceable only with much effort and time. Because the equipment was rare, unique, and difficult to acquire, SP was rewarded.

(ii) UCC § 2-716 similarly awards SP when the good is unique or in other proper circumstances (*e.g.*, it is not commercially feasible for the plaintiff to obtain the good).

(1) *See Sedmak v. Charlie's Chevrolet* (Mo. App. 1981), where the plaintiff ordered a limited edition Corvette from the defendant for $15,000. When the time came to tender purchase, the value rose and the defendant reneged on its promise and required the plaintiff to bid on the car. The plaintiff sued for SP. Held: although

this Corvette is not unique, it is so rare and finding the equivalent would be so difficult that under UCC § 2-716(1), judgment for SP is affirmed.

(d) Contracts for Personal Services

(i) Originally, SP was offered for contracts for personal services.

(ii) However, courts later became unwilling to order SP, finding such orders impractical and unjust.

(1) *See The Case of Mary Clark, A Woman of Colour* (Ind. 1821), where Mary Clark sued to be freed from Johnston, to whom she voluntarily indentured herself. Johnston called for SP, arguing that Clark should be bound by a contract she voluntarily signed. Held: to enforce this contract and require SP would be to put Clark in a state of ***involuntary servitude***. She should be discharged.

(iii) Just as courts were reluctant to enforce SP, they also were reluctant to enforce *negative injunctions*, which prohibit the breaching party from taking on similar work. Many courts consider negative injunctions to be an indirect form of SP.

(1) *See Ford v. Jermon* (Pa. 1865), where the defendant Jermon breached her contract to act in a theatre. The plaintiff sued for a negative injunction. Held: forbidding the defendant from acting in any other play would have the effect of enforcing SP through the "backdoor," which the court refused to do. SP within the context of employment contracts is a mitigated form of slavery. Judgment for the defendant was affirmed.

(iv) Later, courts began allowing negative injunctions, even when they were not expressly provided for in the contract.

(1) *See Duff v. Russell* (N.Y. 1891), where the plaintiff Duff sued the defendant performer for breaching her acting contract. The court awarded a negative injunction against her, since the contract implied that she would not work for competitors.

(v) Today, negative injunctions are permitted in personal service contracts for employment of unique individuals, where *the breaching party is unique* or *when finding a replacement is unusually burdensome*.

(1) Rationale: there is an implied warranty by employees offering rare or unique services not to work for competitors during the employment period.

(2) Furthermore, courts are more willing to enforce negative injunctions than SP because negative injunctions are easier to enforce.

(3) *See Dallas Cowboys Football Club v. Harris* (Tex. Civ. App.1961), where the court held that the plaintiff Dallas Cowboys Football Club was entitled to a negative injunction against the defendant's working for competing football teams because the defendant's skills were sufficiently unique and exceptional, regardless of the fact that it was never shown that he was the best.

(vi) Although today, SP is not enforced in personal service contracts, this rule is limited to *personal service contracts*, not *corporate service contracts*. When there is no adequate remedy at law, corporate service contracts may be enforced through SP.

(1) Rationale: the policy of not wanting to force a defendant to work does not apply when the defendant is a large corporation with many employees working at an hourly rate.

(2) In personal services contract, then, the only SP that a party can obtain is a negative injunction in certain circumstances (the defendant has rare or unique services).

8.4.2 Restitution – Damage Interest and Cause of Action

(a) Restitution for Breach of Contract

(i) One of the alternative damage interests that a party may seek for breach of contract is restitution.

(ii) Generally, restitution is sought by non-breaching parties to collect damages for breach of contract when expectation damages cannot be calculated.

(iii) It is available when the contract between the parties has been rescinded; however, some ***courts allow restitution even when a contract has not been rescinded***.

(1) *See Bush v. Canfield* (Conn. 1818), where the defendant Canfield breached his contract after the plaintiff paid the first $5,000 of the $14,000 owed for a shipment of 2,000 barrels of flour. Because the price of the flour dropped between the time the contract was made and the time of the breach, the plaintiff did not seek expectation damages, which would have been negative. The court allowed the plaintiff to collect $5,000 of restitution damages without first rescinding the contract.

(aa) *Dissent*: for the plaintiff to collect restitution damages, it must first rescind the contract. Here, the plaintiff did not first rescind.

(bb) *Concurring opinion responding to the dissent*: the dissent is simply dwelling on a technicality. Whether the plaintiff was to start the case all over again after rescinding the contract or pursue restitution by skipping that step, the same result will transpire.

(b) Restitution to the Party in Breach

(i) Under the old common law, restitution was not available to the breaching party.

(ii) Under the modern law, the breaching party is still unable to collect damages under the contract, since he breached it.

(iii) However, in support of the ***public policy discouraging forfeiture***, the breaching party may collect restitution when the non-breaching party receives a benefit from the breaching party.

(1) *See Britton v. Turner* (N.H. 1834), where the defendant Turner agreed to pay the plaintiff $120 upon the plaintiff's completing a one year labor contract. The plaintiff quit work after nine months and sued to recover the nine months of labor. Held: the plaintiff may recover *quantum meruit* ("as much as he deserves") the market value of the benefit he conferred on the defendant.

(2) *N.B.*: it may seem unusually harsh that a person be held liable for restitution damages by a party that breaches a contract. It would seem that such a rule would discourage parties from keeping contracts and fully performing. However, most cases do not work out like *Britton*; usually, the non-breaching party's injury will be mitigated:

(aa) He can repudiate whatever benefit the breaching party has given to him, and thus not be liable for restitution damages (because he will have nothing to disgorge); and

(bb) Even if he keeps the benefit, he may be able to sue the breaching party for damages if he can prove them.

(3) *N.B.*: breaching parties, as in this case, are not required to rescind the contract before collecting restitution, since their breach is in a sense already a rescission.

(iv) The restitution collected is to equal ***the market value*** of the benefit that the breaching party transferred to the non-breaching party.

(v) Thus, if the plaintiff breaches contract and then sues the defendant for restitution, and if the contract price was higher than market price, a court will only reward market price.

(vi) However, the plaintiff is entitled only to contract price when the market value would afford him greater recovery than the contract price.

(1) The rationale is not to encourage the plaintiffs to breach their contracts when they realize they made a bad deal.

(c) A valid liquidated damages clause may prevent a breaching party from collecting restitution damages. However, if the breaching party shows that the damages clause is invalid (*i.e.*, the other party would be unjustly enriched), he may be able to collect restitution.

(i) *See Vines v. Orchard Hills* (Conn. 1980), where the plaintiff Vines entered into a contract with the defendant to buy a condominium. The contract had a stipulated damages clause that established the 10% down payment ($7,880) as damages in the event of the plaintiff's breach. The plaintiff informed the defendant that he would not go through with the deal, since he would be moving to NJ, and demanded the deposit. When the defendant refused, the plaintiff sued for restitution, arguing that as a result of the appreciation of the condo, the defendant benefited from the breach, since he could sell the condo for more. Held: stipulated damages clauses will not be upheld when they lead to the unjust enrichment of the non-breaching party, who ***suffers no damages***. If the breaching party seeks restitution, the burden of proof is on him to show that the liquidated damages clause leads to unjust enrichment. The case is remanded with a new opportunity given to the plaintiff to bring forward evidence showing that the damages clause is unreasonable and its enforcement would lead to unjust enrichment.

(d) Restitution and "Quasi Contract"

(i) ***Quasi contracts*** are implied contracts that are created by the courts to avoid unjust enrichment when the elements of a contract are not met.

(ii) There are two kinds:

(1) Implied in Fact Contracts

(aa) Contracts may be implied by the conduct of the parties.

(bb) Example: if a party finds a man shoveling his driveway and then greets him, a court may hold that he is obliged to pay him for the service rendered under an implied contract, even if he never expressly contracted the man to mow his lawn.

(2) Implied in Law Contracts

(aa) Implied in law contracts, also known as constructive contracts, have no basis in the facts of a case.

(bb) These are created by the courts in order to avoid injustice when there is neither an express nor an implied in fact contract.

(cc) Courts, in creating implied in law contracts, may order that a party that is enriched by the service of another restitute the benefit received, in order to avoid unjust enrichment.

*(I)* *See Cotnam v. Wisdom* (Ark. 1907), where the defendant Cotnam was knocked unconscious from his street car and the plaintiff performed medical services upon him. The plaintiff sued to recover for the medical procedures performed on the defendant. Held: although no express contract was entered into, the law will construct a contract for the medical services delivered. This will encourage doctors to help those who are in need and will avoid the unjust enrichment of those receiving the benefits. The plaintiff is thus entitled to restitution equal to the value of his services.

8.4.3 Reformation

(a) When a written contract fails to reflect the meeting of the minds of the parties when they come to an agreement, the equitable remedy of reformation is used to change the document in order to reflect the agreement reached.

(b) Situations in which reformation may arise include: (i) when both parties are mistaken; and (ii) when one party is mistaken and the other acted fraudulently.

**Summary Chart for Determining**
**When the Duty to Perform Has Become Absolute**

| Question | | |
|---|---|---|
| 1. Are there any conditions precedent to a party's performance? | Yes | Go to question 2 |
| | No | The duty to perform has become absolute. Go to question 4. |
| 2. Have the conditions been met? | Yes | The duty to perform has become absolute. Go to question 4. |
| | No | Go to question 3. |
| 3. Has the condition been excused (treated as though it occurred, in order to avoid forfeiture)? | Yes | The condition to perform has become absolute. |
| | No | The duty to perform has become absolute. Go to question 4. |
| 4. Has the contractual obligation been discharged through (i) substantial/perfect performance; (ii) material breach; or (iii) agreement of the parties (rescission; accord and satisfaction; novation; substitute agreement)? | Yes | There is no absolute duty to perform. |
| | No | Go to question 5. |
| 5. Are there any defenses to contractual obligation (*e.g.*, legal incapacity, the improper obtainment of consent, mistake, changed future circumstances)? | Yes | The duty to perform may be voided. |
| | No | The party is contractually obligated to perform. |

## Chapter II. Real and Personal Property

# 1 The Acquisition of Unowned Property

## 1.1 The Acquisition of Wild Animals and Unowned Property

### 1.1.1 The Acquisition of Unowned Personal Property

(a) *Ad Coelum* Doctrine

(i) Under the *ad coelum* doctrine, for the purpose of immovable minerals, "to whomever the soil belongs, he also owns to the sky and to the depths."

(ii) *See Edwards v. Sims* (Ky. 1929), where the plaintiff Edwards owned and excavated a cave that Lee claimed ran under his property. The plaintiff asserted that he should be the owner because it was the result of his hard labor, he owned the entrance, he paid for it to be explored (*first occupant theory*). However, the court, applying the *ad coelum* doctrine, ordered an excavation of the plaintiff's cave to determine whether it did in fact run under Lee's property. The plaintiff sued to stop the defendant judge Sims from enforcing the order. Judgment for the defendant: the court order is to be enforced in order to determine whether the plaintiff trespassed on Lee's property.

(1) Dissent (minority view): the *ad coelum* doctrine is an outdated theory that should not be applied; the ownership by *first occupant theory* would make more sense. The plaintiff excavated the cave through his own funds and labor; he alone is able to use and exploit it; he owns the entrance. Preventing his enjoyment of it hurts the plaintiff and does not help Lee, who cannot take dominion.

(b) *Ratione Soli* Doctrine

(i) Under the *ratione soli* doctrine, also known as "*ad coelum* minor," the owner of the soil *is the first occupant* and owner of whatever is found on the soil, including minerals and *ferae naturae*, regardless of who the finder is.

(1) *See Goddard v. Winchell* (Iowa 1892), where Winchell found a meteor on Goddard's property. Because the court applies the *ratione soli* doctrine, Goddard is able to replevy it.

(ii) This doctrine is not recognized by all states and even in those states that do recognize it, it is not always applied.

(iii) As we will explore later on, the more general rule allows finders to keep what they have found; the law grants finders better title than all the world except for the true owner, with some exceptions.

### 1.1.2 First Occupancy Theory

(a) Under the first occupancy theory, the first occupant becomes the owner. The doctrine applies to the acquisition of *ferae naturae* (wild animals).

(b) However, the *ratione soli* doctrine continues to apply when an animal is captured and killed on someone's property.

(c) When not captured and killed on another's property, *ferae naturae* belongs to the first occupant, regardless of whether the animal was originally on another's property.

(d) The first occupant is the one who:

(i) Intends to possess and control an animal; and

(ii) Injures or traps it in a way that makes its escape either impossible or improbable, depending on the state's approach.

(1) Impossible (Strict Occupancy approach under *Pierson*)

(aa) The animal's escape must be ***impossible***.

(bb) *Mere pursuit* of an animal does not constitute ownership.

(cc) Rather, one of the following must occur:

(I) The animal must b trapped *and* escape must be impossible; or

(II) The animal must be mortally wounded *and* there is continued pursuit.

(dd) *See Pierson v. Post* (N.Y. 1805), where the defendant was charged with unlawfully killing and capturing a fox that was under pursuit by the plaintiff. Held: mere pursuit of an animal does not constitute ownership. The animal would have had to be put into a situation where escape was impossible.

(2) Improbable (Law of the Chase approach under *Liesner*).

(aa) The animal's escape must be ***improbable***.

(bb) If an animal is so badly wounded that escape will be made improbable, then the animal belongs to the party that wounded it.

(cc) *See Leisner v. Wainie* (Wis. 1914), where Leisner mortally wounded a fox, then Wainie delivered shot that killed it and took it away. The court ruled that Leisner was the first occupant and that the fox belonged to him.

**1.2 Acquisition of Volatile Minerals (Oil and Gas)**

1.2.1 The general rule regarding minerals can be summarized by the *ad coelum* doctrine: the owner of a parcel of property has a right to the property as it extends "to the sky" and "to the depths." He becomes owner of all minerals beneath his land.

(a) *See Hammonds v. Central Kentucky Natural Gas Co.* (Ky.1934), where the court held that the defendant was not liable for using a reservoir under the plantiff's land to store gas. Once the minerals, through their natural volatile tendencies, migrate under the plaintiff's land, the defendant cannot be liable because he no longer controls and possesses them.

1.2.2 However, once volatile minerals are captured and stored, title to them is not lost, even if they migrate underneath another's land. The landowner may not exploit the stored mineral. *Lone Star Gas Co. v. Murchison* (Tex. Civ. App. 1962).

1.2.3 In summary, with respect to acquiring unowned property, courts apply:

(a) The *ad coelum* doctrine to the acquisition of fixed minerals and imbedded objects; and

(b) The *first occupant theory* to the acquisition of volatile minerals and *ferae naturae* (unless the *ferae naturae* is caught while on another's land).

### 1.3 Acquisition by Conquest

1.3.1 General rule: when Europeans came to the Native Americans' land, the applicable rule was that the discoverer's government gained title to the land by conquest, despite the Native Americans' occupancy.

1.3.2 Thus, courts held that one who was granted land by a Native American does not have good title, since the Native Americans did no have good title to give.

(a) *See Johnson v. McIntosh* (U.S. 1823), where the Court held that the plaintiff, who claimed land through deeds granted to him by the Native Americans, did not in fact have title because full title was never passed on. Because the land was conquered by the early settlers, the Indians have a right to occupancy, but they do not have transferable title. Rather, transferable title belongs to the U.S. government, to which England gave title after it relinquished title after the Revolution. Because of the savage habits of the Native Americans, they have no claim to their land's title.

## 2 Personal Property

### 2.1 Bailment

2.1.1 Bailment can be defined as a legally recognized property relationship between a bailor, who gives personalty to another to be held for a particular purpose, and a bailee, the party that receives the property. Bailment and bailment.

2.1.2 The agreement between the bailor and the bailee can be written or oral, gratuitous or for consideration.

2.1.3 For there to be a bailment relationship, the following five elements must be met:

(a) The object of the bailment must be ***personal property***;

(b) There must be actual or constructive ***delivery*** to the bailee[4];

(c) The bailee must expressly or impliedly ***consent*** to accepting the personal property;

(d) The bailee must have the ***right of possession and actual possession***; and

(e) The bailee must agree to ***return*** the personal property back to the bailor, who keeps title.

---

[4] An example of constructive delivery would be giving to another the keys to a car.

2.1.4 Conditions under which the bailee becomes liable to the bailor:

(a) If he fails to return the item, he becomes strictly liable.

(b) If he fails to exercise requisite care as bailee, the following standards of care apply:

(i) The Modern Law Approach

(1) An ordinary standard of care under the circumstances is *always required*.

(2) The bailee is thus liable for ordinary negligence.

(ii) The Three Approaches of the Common Law

(1) Gratuitous Bailment

(aa) Gratuitous bailment is solely beneficial to the bailor.

(bb) The bailee has a minimum standard of care; he is only liable for gross negligence;

(2) Mutually Beneficial Bailment

(aa) When the bailment is mutually beneficial to the bailor and bailee, an ordinary standard of care is required.

(bb) The bailee is liable for ordinary negligence;

(cc) *See Hanes v. Shapiro and Smith* (N.C. 1915), where Shapiro is held to the ordinary standard of care for bailment of a sideboard destroyed in a fire, since both parties had a stake in the bailment.

(3) Bailment Solely Beneficial to the Bailee

(aa) When the bailment only benefits the bailee, a high standard of care is required.

(bb) The bailee is liable for even slight negligence.

(c) Example: a store clerk finds in his store a mislaid wallet, which he intends to return to its rightful owner. If he loses the wallet, his standard of care will be:

(i) Under the common law approach, he is subject to a slight duty of care (he is liable only for gross negligence).

(ii) Under the modern law approach, he has an ordinary standard of care under the circumstances; he is liable for ordinary negligence.

2.1.5 In trial, the burden of proving negligence in bailment cases falls on the plaintiff bailor.

(a) The plaintiff's *prima facie* case consists in proving: (i) he gave the personalty to the defendant in good condition; and (ii) the bailee did not return the personalty or return it back in a damaged condition.

(b) When the problem was caused by abnormal causes, the burden is on the defendant to show that he was not at fault.

(c) If he is able to show he was not at fault, the burden shifts back to the plaintiff to show that the defendant was negligent in exposing the personalty to the risk of harm.

## 2.2 Findings

### 2.2.1 Introduction to the Findings Law

(a) The overarching goal of findings law is to get the item back to the original owner (OO) or to preserve the rights of the OO.

(b) At the same time, in order to promote honesty, finders are generally permitted to keep their findings. with the exceptions of the following circumstances, in which constructive possession is applied:

(i) Mislaid, imbedded property;

(ii) Trespass;

(iii) In other cases where the courts reserve the right to apply constructive possession.

### 2.2.2 Lost Items

(a) The general rule of findings is that the finder obtains the right to possession against all of the world but the true owner.

(b) *See Bridges v. Hawkesworth* (Q.B. 1851), where a man found a box of bank notes on the floor of a public section of a store and told the owner to hold it for the rightful owner. When the rightful owner never showed up, the finder asked for them back. The court held that the finder had the rightful title for the bank notes, since they were found in a public part of the store.

### 2.2.3 Mislaid Items

(a) An item is mislaid when its owner intentionally places it in some place and then forgets about it.

(b) An object will usually be considered to be mislaid when it is located on a table or a counter; it will be considered lost when found on the ground or some other area where it is unlikely to have been intentionally placed.

(c) Possession of mislaid items is granted to the owner of the *locus in quo* (OLQ) (*Lat.*, "place in which").

(d) *See McAvoy v. Medina* (Mass. 1866), where a wallet left on a table in a store was considered mislaid, not lost. The difference is between someone deliberately placing an object on a table and saying they will come to it later, but forgetting, and dropping it on the ground without any intention. When it is the former, the owner of the OLQ, not the finder, obtains title.

### 2.2.4 Treasure Trove

(a) Treasure trove is gold, silver, bullion, money, or coins found hidden under the ground when the true owner (TO) is unknown.

(b) For the purposes of possession, treasure trove can be treated as a ***lost item***, in that the true owner keeps title, and the finder is given possession until the true owner appears. This is perhaps to encourage finders to make their findings known.

(c) However, not all courts recognize treasure trove. When a state does not recognize treasure trove, it will treat the question as an ordinary ***finding***, and will determine whether the object was *lost* or *mislaid*.

(i) *See Schley v. Couch* (Tex. 1955), where workers on the plaintiff's land discovered a bottle filled with money buried in the ground. However, the court in Texas did not recognize treasure trove and simply applied the doctrine of mislaid and lost property. Because the money was buried recently (within the last few years), it was concluded that it was not lost, but rather, mislaid, and therefore belonged to the OLQ.

### 2.2.5 Imbedded Property

(a) Imbedded property belongs to the OLQ

(b) *See South Staffordshire Water Co. v. Sharman* (Q.B. 1896), where the defendant, while working for the plaintiff, found rings imbedded in the plaintiff's cesspool, which the defendant surrendered to the police and then kept when the TO was not found. The plaintiff filed for detinue to recover the property or its value from the defendant. The court held that through *constructive possession*, the chattel should belong to the OLQ rather than to the finder because it was found on private property.

(i) This case makes a distinction with *Bridges*; the *Bridges* rule about lost property only applies if it is in the public or in the public part of a private store.

(c) *See also Goddard v. Winchell* (Iowa 1892), where possession of a meteor imbedded in the soil is granted to the OLQ; ownership is not granted to the finder.

### 2.2.6 Constructive Possession

(a) Constructive possession is control or dominion of property, as opposed to actual possession (physical occupancy).

(b) Under the doctrine of constructive possession, control or dominion of property is granted to the owner of the OLQ, in situations in which it would otherwise go to the finder (*e.g.*, in cases of treasure trove and findings generally).

(c) There are no hard, fast rules as to when courts would apply this doctrine.

(i) When an object lost in the public part of a store, a court probably *would not apply this doctrine*; the finder would obtain possession.

(ii) When an object is lost in a home or the private part of a store, a court would usually apply this doctrine; the OLQ would get possession.

2.2.7 Abandoned items

(a) First occupants of abandoned items acquire *full title*, even against the TO.

(i) *See Eads v. Brazelton* (Ark. 1861), where Eads claimed that cargo of a shipwreck was rightfully his, since he found it first and laid markers around it. Held: the possession of abandoned items is like the possession of wild animals: the first occupant acquires ownership.

(b) The occupant of an abandoned item must manifest the intent to exercise dominion and control and evidence that he is able to do so. In the example of *Eads v. Brazelton*, this would mean having a boat over the shipwreck that shows the intent to recover the cargo and the ability to do so.

2.2.8 Trespassing Finders

(a) Trespassing finders relinquish control of found items to the OLQ.

(b) *See Favorite v. Miller* (Conn. 1978), where the OLQ was able to keep the parts of a statue of King George that was found buried on his property, not only because it was imbedded in his soil, but also because it was taken by a trespasser.

**Summary of Findings***

| *Category* | *Finder* | *OLQ* | *Definitions*[5] |
|---|---|---|---|
| Lost | ✓ | | The object is not intentionally set down; the TO never intends to part with the good, but is separated from it through negligence. |
| Mislaid | | ✓ | The TO intends to temporarily part with the good but later forgets to retrieve it. |
| Treasure Trove | ✓ | | An unknown owner intends to hide coin, money, gold, silver, plate or bullion found under the ground or otherwise hidden. |
| Imbedded | | ✓ | When something is imbedded in the soil, even when the OLQ is unaware of its presence, he acquires possession. |
| Abandoned | ✓ | | The relinquishing of a right or interest with the intention of never again claiming it. The TO does not transfer title to any specific third party.<br>The finder acquires *ownership* of the article. |

*** However, regardless of whether an object was lost, treasure trove, etc., the OLQ will obtain possession when: (i) the court applies the doctrine of constructive possession, which deprives the finder of possession; and (ii) when the finder had been trespassing when he occupied the object.**

2.2.9 Legislation Regulating Findings

(a) Many states have adopted statutes regulating findings.

[5] Note that these often hinge on intent of TO.

(b) Generally speaking, the statutes are different from the common law in that they:

(i) Tend to lump together lost and mislaid items;

(ii) Require finders to turn in lost articles to police or face punishment; and

(iii) Give a time limit after which items are returned to finders and another limit after which finders become owners.

**2.3 Prior (Unauthorized) Possession**

2.3.1 Prior possession concerns when a prior wrongful possessor is able to replevy against a subsequent wrongful possessor.

2.3.2 There are two approaches as to prior (unauthorized) possession:

2.3.3 Majority Approach

(a) Under the majority approach, prior wrongful possessors are always allowed to recover the property, whether it is through trover (damages) or replevin of the property.

(i) *See Anderson v. Gouldberg* (Minn. 1892), where the plaintiff sued the defendant, who took pine logs from the plaintiff, who himself wrongfully took the pine logs. The court held that the plaintiff was entitled to possession, even though he was a wrongful possessor, because he was a *prior* wrongful possessor.

(ii) *See also Clark v. Maloney* (Del. Super. Ct. 1840), where the plaintiff found logs floating in a stream and took them up. The defendant later took possession of the logs, claiming that they had been loosened from the plaintiff's fastening and were adrift in the creek. Both the plaintiff and the defendant claimed that they had good finder's title. Held: because the plaintiff was a prior possessor, possession is given to he plaintiff. Trover (damages) is given to the plaintiff for the value of the logs that were converted by the defendant.

2.3.4 Minority Approach

(a) Under the minority approach, prior (unauthorized) possessors are always allowed to seek to replevy the property.

(b) Prior possessors are also allowed to seek trover (damages) of the property as a general rule.

(c) However, if the TO is known, the prior possessor may not seek trover (damages); he may only replevy the property.

(d) This is because it is presumed that the TO will ultimately try to recover the property through replevy.

(i) Thus, if the subsequent unauthorized possessor is required to pay damages to the prior unauthorized possessor, the subsequent possessor will risk a double penalty if the TO later seeks to replevy the property from him.

(ii) He will have a double net loss, first having paid damages through trover to the prior possessor, and later giving up the property itself to the TO through replevy.

(e) To avoid this prejudicial treatment of the subsequent possessor, the courts in the minority approach only permit the prior possessor to seek replevin of the property from the subsequent possessor.

(i) It is presumed that if the TO later tries to recover the property, he will replevy it against the prior possessor.

(ii) Thus, a double penalty will be imposed on neither the prior nor the subsequent possessor.

(f) Thus, under the minority approach, the prior possessor is only allowed to obtain trover *when the TO is unknown*. Otherwise, the only possible recourse is replevin.

(i) *See Russell v. Hill* (N.C. 1899), where the plaintiff purchased timber from McCoy, who did not have rightful title to the land because of an error in the deed. When the defendant took possession of the timber, the plaintiff brought sued for trover. The court held that because the plaintiff did not have title to the timber and the TO was known, he could not obtain trover.

## 2.4 Adverse Possession

2.4.1 If a party takes possession of property of which he is not the lawful owner and maintains possession for a period prescribed by the statute of limitations in the local jurisdiction, he acquires rightful title if the lawful owner fails to oppose the wrongful possession.

(a) The statute of limitations varies between jurisdictions, but can be as little as two years.

(b) With respect to real property, the possession should be a non-permissive use of the land with a claim of right by the adverse possessor.

2.4.2 The courts incrementally established that in order for the statute of limitations to run, the possession and use of the land must be:

(a) *Open* – the possession and use must not be hidden;

(b) *Continuous* – the defendant must have continuous possession throughout the running of the statute of limitations;

(c) *Exclusive* – the defendant must not share the possession with the TO;

(d) *Adverse* – the wrongful possessor must claim and act as though he has title to the property; the claim must be adverse to the TO's rights;

(e) *Notorious* – the use must suffice to put the TO on notice that the adverse possessor is using the good and claiming title to it.

(i) This element is virtually the same as the *open* element.

(ii) To meet the open and notorious elements, one must use the chattel in a way that it is normally used.

(iii) Examples: a store will openly display a wrongfully possessed ring; however, the owner of a ring may only wear it once per year if it is of great value.

2.4.3 Meeting the Statute of Limitations

(a) Tacking

(i) Many jurisdictions permit "tacking," which allows an adverse possessor to meet an adverse possession statute of limitations by adding together the periods in which previous possessors held the chattel.

(ii) The majority approach is to allow tacking; the minority approach is to require the adverse possessor claiming title to have possessed the property throughout the statute of limitations.

(b) Tolling

(i) Tolling, on the other hand, refers to the temporary stopping of the statute of limitations whenever one of the elements of adverse possession is not met.

(c) The Discovery Rule

(i) Sometimes, the statute of limitations begins to run not when the TO is deprived of possession of his property, but rather, when he discovered or reasonably should have discovered the whereabouts of the chattel.

(ii) This rule, referred to as the "discovery rule," works to the benefit of the TO.

(iii) Courts often apply this rule when meeting the adverse possession elements, to the disadvantage of the TO, would be relatively easy for a possessor. *See O'Keeffe v. Snyder* (N.J. 1980).

2.4.4 Two Approaches to Good Faith

(a) Majority Approach

(i) Under the majority approach, merely possessing the property throughout the statute of limitations will confer title to the adverse possessor, when the possession is open, continuous, exclusive, adverse, and notorious.

(b) Minority Approach

(i) However, under the minority approach, in addition to meeting these elements, the possession must be with *good faith*.

(ii) *See Riesinger's Jewelers, Inc. v. Roberson* (Okla.App.1978), where the plaintiff Riesinger's Jewelers lost a ring in an armed robbery. In order to determine whether or not the plaintiff had title to ring, the court applied the minority approach by requiring the previous owners to have held the ring in *good faith*, and remanded the case back to trial to determine the same.

(1) *N.B.*: *Riesinger's Jewelers* also establishes that, in order for the statute to run for a stolen chattel, whether in a majority or minority jurisdiction, the good must be held *within the vicinity* (*i.e.*, in-state) in order to give the true owner of an opportunity to find and reclaim it. The statute of limitations is tolled anytime the item is taken out of the vicinity of the plaintiff, where dispossession begins with a theft.

2.4.5 Elements of Adverse Possession

(a) In order for an adverse possessor to win in a claim for a good, he must prove:

(i) His possession was open, continuous, exclusive, adverse, and continuous;

(ii) He possessed the property throughout the statute of limitations;

(1) In the majority of jurisdictions, he may add on the periods in which the property was held by other possessors through tacking.

(iii) He possessed in good faith (in minority jurisdictions);

(1) If tacking is permitted, the other possessors similarly must have possessed in good faith.

(iv) The possession was within the *vicinity* (in the case of stolen chattels under *Riesinger's Jewelers v. Roberson*).

(b) When all of these elements are met, the TO loses his right to the property.

(c) Furthermore, under the "shelter principle," if one possessor can show that he became the owner under adverse possession (or some other ownership theory), then any subsequent possessor can claim that good title was also passed to him.

## 2.5 Accession

2.5.1 Introduction

(a) Accession is the acquisition of title to a thing through labor that transforms it into another thing.

(b) General rule: an innocent trespasser does not gain title to a chattel through making improvements to it (the TO can replevy the chattel), *unless* (i) the chattel is acquired in good faith; and (ii) *substantial* improvements are made to it.

(c) If both of these elements are met, title is transferred to the innocent trespasser and the TO cannot replevy the chattel.

2.5.2 Elements

(a) The object must be taken in ***good faith*** by the later improver.

(i) Thus, if the object is taken by a thief, no amount of improvement will cause title to transfer (this is the American approach, which follows the civil law, not the common law approach).

(ii) This does not require that *all* prior possessors have good faith.

(1) Example: if a good faith possessor purchases a chattel from a thief, and later makes substantial improvements to it, he may acquire title.

(2) *See Capitol Chevrolet Co. v. Earhart* (Tenn. Ct. App. 1981), where the court ruled that the innocent purchaser of the stripped down hull of a Corvette, who later made substantial changes to it, had good title to pass to Capitol Chevrolet, even though it was originally stolen from a previous possessor. When the stolen hull was recovered on the accessed vehicle, the TO had only the right to the value of the hull.

(b) The chattel must be transformed into a new chattel of ***substantially greater value*** from the time it comes into the later improver's hands.

(i) The improvements made to the chattel must not be easily separable from it.

(ii) Normally, the improvements must be so substantial that the value of the chattel increases by a factor of fifteen or more (depending on what the item is).

(1) Example: a later improver will acquire title to timber that was originally valued at $25, when, with good faith, he transformed it into hoops valued at $700. *Wetherbee v. Green* (Mich. 1871).

(iii) Note that this element does not require that a fifteen-factor improvement of the property is measured from the time that the property leaves the TO's hands to the time that the improvements are made; rather, it is measured from the time that the property is delivered to the later improver to the time that the improvements are made.

(1) Example: a thief steals a car valued at $15,000 and strips it down to a value of $1,000. A good faith purchaser purchases the car for $1,000 and makes improvements that bring the value of the car back up to $15,000.

(2) Although the improvements did not increase the value of the car from its *original* value, the later improver will obtain title, since substantial improvements were made from the time the car was delivered to him.

2.5.3 The True Owner's Remedies

(a) If either of the elements of accession are not met—the later improver fails to act in good faith or he fails to make *substantial* improvements to the chattel—the TO may ***replevy*** the chattel.

(i) When the later improver lacks good faith, the TO may replevy the chattel, no matter much labor and value the improver put into the good.

(ii) However, if he acts in good faith but fails to make *substantial* improvements, he may keep the improvements if they are separable from the original object. If they are not, the TO acquires them when he replevies the chattel.

(b) If a later improver acts in good faith *and* makes substantial improvements, although the TO may not replevy the chattel, he may obtain ***damages*** equal to the value of the chattel at the time that it was delivered to the later improver (*e.g.*, $25 in the case of *Wetherbee*).

## 2.6 *Bona Fide* Purchase

2.6.1 We have already examined two theories of ownership in which an owner may be deprived of property without his consent—adverse possession and accession).

2.6.2 We now turn our attention to a third theory where an owner may similarly be deprived of property without his consent—*bona fide* purchase (BFP).

2.6.3 Elements of BFP:

(a) Purchases in good faith;

(b) Without notice of fraud;

(i) Notice of fraud is knowledge that someone else owns a chattel.

(ii) This element requires that the plaintiff ask questions that would give notice of fraud. *Porter v. Wertz* (N.Y. App. Div. 1979).

(c) For value.

(i) The property may not be given as a gift or at a price that is so substantially below the market value that it is considered to be a gift.

(ii) It must be purchased at the market value or the appropriate value under the circumstances.

2.6.4 General Principle

(a) The general principle of BFP is *caveat emptor* ("buyer beware").

(b) The BFP does not acquire title to a good when the seller did not have title to transfer.

(c) A seller may not transfer better title than he has.

2.6.5 Exceptions

(a) The following exceptions to the *caveat emptor* ruling principle are recognized by the common law and statutes:

(i) Under ***equitable estoppel***, which is governed by the common law, there are two exceptions to *caveat emptor*.

(1) Voidable title; and

(2) Apparent authority.

(ii) Under ***statutory estoppel***, which applies to the sale of goods and is governed by the UCC,[6] there are two exceptions to *caveat emptor*:

(1) Voidable title; and

(2) Entrustment.

(iii) All of these exceptions permit the BFP to keep title because of some action of the OO that prohibits him from later replevying the chattel.

(b) Common Law Voidable Title

(i) When the OO has the intent to transfer title, voidable title passes, even if title is obtained through fraud. *Phelps v. McQuade* (N.Y. 1917).

(1) Rationale: when the OO had some intent to transfer title, the result can be to some extent imputed to his neglect or other conduct.

(2) *N.B.*: title is not passed when a party fraudulently represents himself to be an agent of another.

(ii) However, when the OO had no intention of transferring title, *no title* passes.

(iii) The sale must be face to face; voidable title does not pass when it is done through letter or by agent.

(iv) Since there is no intent to transfer title when a chattel is stolen, thieves do not obtain voidable title or any other transferable title.

(1) *See Lieber v. Mohawk Arms* (N.Y. 1970), where the defendant purchased the plaintiff's Hitler uniform, which was stolen by the plaintiff's chauffeur. The defendant obtained no title, since the title that the chauffeur purported to transfer was void.

(v) Even when the thief makes improvements to the stolen good, he obtain neither full nor voidable title.

(1) *See National Retailers Mut. Ins. Co. v. Gambino* (N.J. Sup. Ct. App. Div. 1948), where title to a stolen vehicle was held not to be transferable, even though the thief substituted the engine with one from another vehicle.

(vi) Since bailors have no intent to transfer title, bailees do not obtain voidable title and therefore have no title to pass.[7] *Baehr v. Clark* (Iowa 1891).

---

[6] The Uniform Commercial Code (UCC), which is enacted with some variations in all fifty states, governs the statutory estoppel exceptions to the principle of *caveat emptor*.

[7] However, under the entrustment exception of the UCC, discussed *infra.*, a merchant may pass voidable title of bailed chattel entrusted to him when he sells them to a buyer in the ordinary course of business.

(vii) Voidable title becomes full title when it is transferred to a BFP *for value*. However, because the title of a thief is void, it remains void, even if transferred to a BFP.

(c) Common Law Apparent Authority

(i) Under this second exception, even if an OO has no intent to sell a good, voidable title passes if the OO, through some level of conduct, clothes the possessor with the apparent authority to sell.

(ii) Under this exception, the OO's intent to sell is "imported" to the possessor.

(1) *See O'Connor v. Clark* (Pa. 1895), where the OO of a wagon painted the name of his new employee on the wagon. When the employee transferred the wagon to a third party, the court granted title to the defendant BFP through the employee's apparent authority to transfer title. The OO was estopped from denying that his employee was the owner.

(d) Voidable Title under the UCC

(i) "A purchaser of goods acquires all title that the purchaser's transferor had or had power to transfer." UCC § 2-403(1).

(1) Example: if a thief steals a chattel from an OO and later sells it, the later purchaser does not receive title, since the thief had no title to transfer.

(ii) However, a seller sometimes has power to transfer more title than he actually had: holders of voidable title may transfer good title to ***good faith purchasers*** for ***value***. UCC § 2-403(1).

(iii) Voidable title is passed when the OO has the intention to pass title (generally, the OO owner somehow acts negligently).

(iv) As long as goods are delivered under a transaction, voidable title passes, even if:

(1) The purchaser ***deceives the seller*** as to his identity;

(2) The goods are procured through a ***bounced check***;

(3) The transaction was by a "***cash sale***" (*e.g.*, the buyer promises to later deliver cash for a chattel that the seller immediately delivers); or

(4) The original owner is induced to sell to a wrongful possessor through "***fraud punishable as larcenous*** under the criminal law" (*e.g.*, stealing and using another's credit card, using counterfeit money, etc.). UCC § 2-403(1).

(v) Under the UCC, voidable title may pass by letter or face to face.

(e) Entrustment under the UCC

(i) The above-mentioned voidable title and apparent authority exceptions discuss when voidable title may pass to a BFP.

(ii) The entrustment exception under the UCC, in contrast, deals with when voidable title may pass to a buyer in ordinary course of business (BOC).

(iii) A BOC may obtain good title from a merchant who sells bailed chattel entrusted to him for repair, improvement, etc., when the merchant deals in goods of that kind. UCC § 2-403(2).

(iv) A BOC must:

(1) Purchase with good faith;

(2) Without notice of fraud;

(3) From a business establishment in the ordinary course of business.

(aa) *N.B.*: a purchase would *not be in the ordinary course of business* if a merchant over his lunch hour takes his client to his home to sell him a chattel.

(v) Note that, unlike the voidable title exceptions to BFP, it is not necessary to show that the purchase was "for value"; since the chattel is being purchased from a business, it is assumed that the BOC paid market value.

## 2.7 Gifts

2.7.1 A gift, or donative transfer, is a present, voluntary transfer of title without consideration.

2.7.2 Classes

(a) *Inter Vivos* Gifts

(i) *Inter vivos* gifts are given while donor is living.

(ii) They are not revocable.

(b) *Mortis Causa* Gifts

(i) *Mortis causa* gifts are given in anticipation of the donor's death.

(ii) They can be revoked if:

(1) The donee dies before the donor;

(2) The donor does not die from the anticipated illness and does not decide to give the gift *inter vivos*;

(3) The donor revokes the gift before he dies but while he is still ill.

2.7.3 Elements

(a) Donative Intent

(i) The donor must *intend* to *presently transfer* title to the donee.

(ii) If the transfer will take place in the future, it is not a gift, but rather, a promise that is unenforceable if it lacks consideration.

(b) Delivery

(i) The donor must deliver the chattel.

(ii) The delivery may take on any of the following forms:

(1) *Actual delivery*: the donee physically takes possession of the chattel.

(2) *Constructive delivery*: where the donor that which is necessary for possessing the chattel (*e.g.*, the keys to a car).

(3) *Delivery by written instrument*: the instrument must show the intent to transfer, be signed by the donor, describe the subject matter of the gift, and be delivered;

(4) *Symbolic delivery*: the donor delivers some object that symbolizes the gift (*e.g.*, a cow could symbolize one's entire herd).

(c) Acceptance

(i) The donee must accept the chattel.

(ii) Acceptance is often presumed if a gift is unconditional and beneficial.

2.7.4 Courts require the best possible delivery under the circumstances.

(a) Generally, a signed, executed deed is sufficient.

(i) Some courts have held that such a document comprised delivery *even when it was not actually delivered*.

(1) *See In re Cohn* (N.Y. 1919), where the court held that a signed, executed agreement granting the decedent's wife a donative transfer of stocks was held valid, even though it was never actually delivered.

(ii) *N.B.*: this case holding is exceptional; courts generally require actual delivery, unless precluded by the circumstances.

(b) Symbolic delivery in the form of a written instrument has also been held to be sufficient.

(c) Others courts have held that clear and unequivocal intent on its own is sufficient when delivery is impossible.

(i) In *Scherer v. Hyland* (N.J. 1977), Wagner committed suicide, leaving a check and letter for Scherer to recover. Since the letter and the fact that only Wagner had access to that space gave adequate evidence that Wagner intended to give check as gift, the court "imported" delivery, even though there was no actual delivery.

# 3 Conveyances and Acquiring Title

## 3.1 Financing Arrangements

### 3.1.1 Introduction

(a) There are two ways in which a vendee may purchase land without paying at once: through mortgages and through installment land contracts.

### 3.1.2 Mortgages

(a) A mortgage is essentially a security for a debt. The mortgagee, or lender, receives the mortgage, which usually looks like a deed.

(b) If the mortgagor, or borrower, defaults on a payment, the mortgage allows the mortgagee to obtain possession of the property, usually after a hearing with proof of default in payments by the mortgagor.

(c) Mortgages have *defeasance clauses* that recognize that, once the debt has been paid, the mortgage is no longer of any effect.

(d) Documents involved in a deed:

(i) The *deed of trust*, which conveys title of the property; and

(ii) The *note*, which makes mortgagors personally liable in case a property sale or foreclosure does not raise all of the funds.

(e) Default and Title

(i) At common law, the mortgage operates as a conveyance of title to the mortgagee, who holds the mortgage.

(1) However, *the title only becomes active* if the mortgagor defaults on his payments.

(2) Even a single default payment at common law allowed the mortgagee to keep all past payments, possess the land, and sell it to recover the money due.

(3) In many other states, a mortgage was not considered to grant title to the mortgagee. Rather, it is viewed as a *mere lien*.

(ii) To offset the harsh effects of the common law, the ***equitable right of redemption*** developed to allow the mortgagor to redeem his property (this doctrine is recognized in all states).

(1) Generally, the mortgagor may redeem the property by paying the amount due, plus interest.

(2) If he has defaulted on a mortgage note requiring the full balance in the event of a default, then he must *pay the entire balance to redeem* the property.

(iii) In about half the states, the mortgagor's right of redemption continues even ***after the foreclosure*** sale.

(1) The redemption period is set by statute and usually lasts from six to twelve months.

(2) The mortgagor may usually redeem the property by paying the foreclosure sale price.

(iv) Today, most states view the mortgage not as ***title*** to the property, but as a mere ***lien***.

(v) There are two approaches to foreclosure that correspond to the views states have adopted with respect to the mortgage and the title-bearer of the mortgaged property:

(1) Foreclosure by Sale

(aa) This is the approach in ***lien theory states***, which treat the mortgage as a lien on the land to repay a loan.

(bb) After the redemption period expires, the property is sold and the mortgagee returns to the mortgagor monies raised beyond the original debt.

(cc) Today, most states view the mortgage as a lien. Foreclosure by sale is therefore the *majority approach*.

(2) Strict Foreclosure

(aa) This is the approach in ***title theory states***, which treat the mortgage as an instantaneous, actual transfer of title.

(bb) Once an action is brought and the statutory period passes, the title actually changes hands and is transferred to the mortgagee (lender), who becomes the owner of the property.

(cc) Strict foreclosure follows the common law, which today is the minority approach.

3.1.3 Installment Land Contracts

(a) In installment land contracts, also known as "land contracts" or "conditional land contracts," the purchaser is granted possession, but the vendor retains title, in contrast to the mortgage, where in most states today, title passes to the mortgagor.

(b) The purchaser pays the vendor in periodic installments and, when he completes the requisite payments, he receives title.

(c) Installment land contracts are typically used when a buyer is unable to acquire a mortgage to purchase the land.

(d) Traditionally, courts enforce ***forfeitures*** (strict foreclosures) in installment land contracts in a summary manner.

(i) Thus, if purchaser defaults, the vendor may keep the land, as in a "summary," or "strict" foreclosure (forfeiture).

(ii) Exception: when the forfeiture is unequivocally unjust.

(e) Some states, however, by statute, allow the purchaser to pay off the accelerated full balance of the contract and keep the land (this parallels the equitable right of redemption for mortgages).

(f) Some states have also passed statutes that impose grace periods, allowing the purchasers to redeem the land.

(g) Courts consider a series of factors in determining whether to allow forfeiture in installment land contracts, including whether the purchaser has made most of the payments, whether he has made substantial improvements to the property, and whether the forfeiture provision allows the creditor to keep all monies paid as well as the defaulted land.

(i) *See Skendzel v. Marshall* (Ind. 1973), where the plaintiff sued the defendant Marshall to enforce the forfeiture provision in an installment land contract when the defendant failed to make a payment. A liquidated damages clause allowed the plaintiff to recover possession of the land while keeping all monies paid in the event of the defendant's default. Held: this liquidated damages clause is invalid because it leads to an ***unjust forfeiture***. Judgment for the plaintiff reversed.

## 3.2 Merchantable Title

### 3.2.1 Introduction

(a) Merchantable title is title that is not subject to such reasonable doubt that it would create a just apprehension of its validity in the mind of a reasonable prudent person.

(b) Title that would be subject to a substantial risk of litigation is not considered merchantable.

(c) However, merchantable title is not necessarily good title; it may have *slight defects* do not invalidate the title (*e.g.*, a missing signature in one of the preceding title holders' deeds; an unaccounted for period in the history of land ownership; etc).

### 3.2.2 The Implied Warranty of Merchantable Title

(a) In every land sale contract, an implied warranty of merchantable title guarantees that the seller will present and pass merchantable title to the purchaser *at the closing* ("law day"), unless the parties have contracted otherwise.

(b) If the seller does not have merchantable title at the time that the land sale contract is formed, he may acquire it during the executory period (the period between the formation of the contract and the closing).

(c) If there are outstanding liens that would breach the warranty of merchantable title, the seller may rely on a portion of the sale proceeds in escrow to remove the liens, as long as the purchaser is assured that the escrow funds will not be released until after the removal of the liens.

(d) If the seller fails to obtain merchantable title before law day, the purchaser may rescind the contract and seek restitution.

(i) Until then, a buyer may not sue for rescission and restitution.

(1) *See Luette v. Bank of Italy Nat. Trust and Savings Association* (9th Cir. 1930), where the plaintiffs were to purchase a parcel of land that they later realized was claimed by a third party. The defendant Bank refused to show good title or refund the price. The plaintiffs sued for either rescission and restitution or for an injunction preventing the defendant from canceling the contract. Held: the defendant has until law day to present merchantable title. In an installment land contract, that may mean several years after the contract was formed, when the last payment was made. Until then, rescission and restitution will not be granted. Judgment for the defendant is affirmed.

(ii) *Exception*: when property is so badly encumbered that the plaintiff may reasonably assume that the defendant will not have the merchantable title at the time that the last payment is due, the defendant may be required to offer merchantable title before law day.

(e) The parties may, however, limit the implied warranty of merchantable title. Very specific language is required.

(i) The language, "buyer agrees to purchase *all of the seller's interest in his premises*," or, "*all of the seller's interest, whether or not he has full title*," is sufficient in overcoming the implied warranty of merchantable title.

(1) *N.B.*: under this contract, if the buyer later discovers that the seller did not have merchantable title, he *may not rescind* the contract before or after law day.

(ii) However, if the contract states that the buyer "agrees to accept the land located at X location" or "all of the seller's premises," the implied warranty is not overcome. If the seller fails to present merchantable title at the closing, the buyer may rescind the contract.

(iii) If the contract states that the buyer "agrees to accept all of the seller's premises by *quitclaim deed*," the implied warranty is not overcome, and the buyer has the right to *rescind the contract* if he finds that the seller did not have merchantable title.

(1) *See Wallach v. Riverside Bank* (N.Y. 1912), where the court allowed the plaintiff to rescind a land sale contract and recover his deposit when he discovered that the *seller did not have merchantable title*, even though the seller was conveying only a quitclaim deed. Rule: between the land sale contract and the closing, the buyer has the opportunity to research the seller's title. If the seller does not possess merchantable title, the buyer may rescind the contract under the ***implied warranty of merchantable title***, even if only a quitclaim deed is offered. If, however, *after the closing*, the plaintiff discovered that he does not have merchantable title, then under the quitclaim deed, he is required to accept the title "as is."

3.2.3 Two Remedies for Breach of the Implied Warranty of Merchantable Title

(a) Specific Performance

(i) A court may require the seller to acquire merchantable title before law day, when doing so is practical.

(ii) For example, if there is a lien on the property, a court may require the seller to clear it with the money received from the sale.

(b) Rescission and Restitution

(i) This is awarded when (i) specific performance (SP) is neither practical nor possible; or (ii) the contract does not provide for SP.

(ii) *See Bartos v. Czerwinski* (Mich. 1948), where the plaintiff entered into a contract to purchase land from the defendant Czerwinski. The contract allowed the plaintiff to be released from the contract if the title was not merchantable. When the plaintiff discovered that the defendant may not have had good title to as much as half of the property, he sued for SP to force the defendant to clear title before proceeding. Held: SP will not be granted when the contract does not allow for it. The remedy would be to release the plaintiff from the contract, as provided by the contract, and to allow him to recover the monies paid.

### 3.3 Equitable Conversion and Risk of Loss

3.3.1 The Doctrine of Equitable Conversion

(a) There are three steps in the process of transferring title to property: (i) the *land sale contract*; (ii) the delivery of *merchantable (marketable) title*; and (iii) the *closing*.

(b) There is always a question as to who "owns" the land in the executory period between the formation of the contract and the closing and who bears the risk of loss.

(c) Under the ***doctrine of equitable conversion***, the purchaser is the owner of the property and bears the risk of loss from the moment the contract is executed.

(d) This doctrine is based on the equity rationale that "what ought to be done is considered done." Since a contract ought to be followed, the buyer is considered to be the title-holder, even when he does not yet have the deed or possession of the land.

(e) However, the doctrine of equitable conversion does not apply in the following circumstances:

(i) *Contractual provisions that state otherwise* (*e.g.*, "title shall remain with the seller");

(ii) *Vendor's negligence*, where the seller damages the property during the executory period and the buyer only finds out when he takes the property;

(iii) *Misrepresentation* or *fraud* by a party;

(iv) The *inexistence of a binding contract;*

(v) The *inexistence of marketable title;* or

(vi) *Changed circumstances* that frustrate the purchaser's purpose.

(1) *See Clay v. Landreth* (Va. 1948), where after the contract was formed, an ordinance was passed that prohibited the defendant from using the plaintiff seller Clay's land for the business for which he intended to use it. When the defendant tried to get out of the contract, the plaintiff sued for SP, arguing that the defendant was already bound to the land through the doctrine of equitable conversion: from the moment the contract was signed, the seller was only a trustee of the property and the buyer was only a trustee of the money to be paid. Held: because outside circumstances frustrated the buyer's purpose, equitable conversion does not apply.

3.3.2 The Three Approaches to the Effect of the Risk of Loss

(a) Majority Approach

(i) Under the majority approach, title is transferred to the buyer at the execution of the contract and the buyer bears the risks of loss during the executory period (in the absence of the above-described exceptions).

(ii) *See Bleckley v. Langston*, where the vendee Bleckley sued the defendant vendor for rescission of a land sale contract and restitution of the deposit when a frost destroyed pecan trees on the land. Held: the equitable owner, who in this case is the plaintiff, bears the risk of loss.

(b) Minority Approach

(i) Under the minority approach, the seller keeps title upon execution of the contract and retains the risk of loss during the executory period; he may collect damages if, after loss, the plaintiff decides not to go forward with the closing.

(ii) This is the approach adopted in Massachusetts.

(c) Uniform Vendor and Purchaser Risk Act

(i) If the Uniform Vendor and Purchaser Risk Act has been adopted, the doctrine of equitable conversion will not be applied when unanticipated damages occur.

(ii) Instead, the contract will be rescinded and any money paid by the purchaser will be restituted to him. The vendor will not be entitled to damages.

(iii) However, the purchaser assumes the risk of loss when either legal title or possession is transferred to him.

## 3.4 The Modern Deed

3.4.1 Introduction

(a) A deed has the following elements:

(i) It must be written;

(ii) It must contain:

(1) The names of the parties;

(2) A granting clause;

(3) A legal description of the property (the subject matter conveyed); and

(4) A signature (for the Statute of Frauds).

(iii) It must be delivered.

(1) Delivery refers to the mental state of the grantor, not to the physical custody of the deed.

(2) Thus, even if the deed is not physically delivered to the purchaser, the deed is deemed to be delivered if the grantor evidences an intent to presently transfer title.

(3) An undelivered deed is completely void and can pass no interest in the land, even if it is later recorded. *Stone v. French* (Kan. 1887).

(b) Other parts of the deed

(i) Some deeds also tend to include, but do not require: (i) the *stated consideration*; (ii) a *habendum clause* limiting the rights being conveyed (*e.g.*, a right to possess but not to disposed of the property); and (iii) a *redendum clause* reserving any interest in the property to the seller (*e.g.*, easements).

(ii) In the old common law, a deed required a seal to be valid. In most states today, this requirement has been abolished.

3.4.2 Construing Deeds

(a) Inconsistent parts within a deed must be reconciled by the courts.

(b) When all else is equal, a ***granting clause*** trumps an ***inconsistent* habendum *clause***.

(i) *See First Nat'l Bank of Oregon v. Townsend* (Or. 1976), where the defendant Townsend granted a deed called a "Warranty timber and mineral deed" to the plaintiff. There was ambiguity in the interest conveyed because the *granting clause* stated "grant and convey," but the *habendum clause* transferred only limited rights, such as the "right to enter upon said land, cut and remove trees, mine and remove minerals." The plaintiff, claiming that a fee simple was transferred, sued to quiet title. Since the land would escheat to the state absent a clear deed, the State of Oregon challenged the plaintiff's claim. Held: granting clauses trump inconsistent *habendum* clauses and courts disfavor escheat, they construe ambiguities in favor of the grantee. Judgment for the plaintiff affirmed.

(c) Although the granting clause trumps the *habendum* clause, the *intent of the parties* may rebut the granting clause.

(i) *See Grayson v. Holloway* (Tenn. 1958), where the intent of a land grant to the defendant and her husband trumped the granting clause, which mentioned only the husband.

## 3.5 The Recording System

### 3.5.1 Introduction

(a) The purpose of recording a deed is to protect present owners from subsequent BFP's.

(b) If a BFP purchases property in good faith for value without notice from a seller who is not the TO of the property being sold, he may acquire title to the land ***if the TO failed to record his deed***.

(c) If, however, the TO recorded the deed, the BFP would be charged with constructive notice and no title would pass.

(d) Although recording a deed is not an essential element to the validity of the deed, recording the deed is an important step towards protecting one's property interest.

### 3.5.2 Four Approaches to Recordings

(a) The Common Law Approach

(i) Under the common law, the party with the ***earlier deed*** obtains title and possession to the property conveyed.

(b) The Three Statutory Approaches

(i) Notice Approach

(1) A subsequent grantee wins if he is a BFP who purchases in ***good faith*** for ***value without notice***, regardless of when he actually records.

(2) *See Earle v. Fiske* (Mass. 1870), where decedent Nancy Fiske conveys land to Benjamin and Elizabeth Fiske as a life estate, with the remainder to Mary Fiske, but does not record the transaction. Upon Nancy's death, her only heir Benjamin sold the land to the plaintiff Earle, who ***purchased the property in good faith without notice for value***. The plaintiff sued for a writ of entry. Held: since Massachusetts is a notice state, the ***only requirement*** for passing title is that ***the plaintiff have no*** *actual or constructive* **notice** of the other property interest and that the plaintiff pay value. These elements are met, since the plaintiff was on neither actual nor constructive notice that Benjamin did not have fee title to transfer. Title is vested in the plaintiff.

(ii) Race/Notice Approach

(1) A subsequent grantee wins only if he (i) is a ***BFP***; and (ii) ***records first***.

(2) A BPF will thus not win against another purchaser who recorded first.

(aa) *See Simmons v. Stum* (Ill. 1882), where a grantor mortgaged property to the plaintiff Stum and later granted it to a party who had notice of the mortgage. That party later conveyed it to the defendant, who claimed to have no notice of the mortgage. The plaintiff sued to foreclose the mortgage. The defendant claimed that the plaintiff should have *no property interest* since she was a BFP. Held: since the plaintiff recorded his mortgage just two days after the property was transferred to the defendant, and since the defendant has never presented evidence showing when she recorded, the mortgage stands, since the mortgagor recorded his interest before the defendant, even if the defendant was a BFP.

(iii) Pure Race

(1) The grantee who ***records first*** wins title.

3.5.3 There are two systems for searching for records on one's property:

(a) The ***grantor/grantee index***, which is a list of all previous owners of a tract; and

(b) The ***tract index****,* which is a list of every tract and its particular owner and all recorded instruments affecting it. This index greatly facilitates the ability of prospective purchases to find if there is good title and to discover restrictions on the property.

3.5.4 Records of Easements

(a) Parties are on ***constructive notice*** of easements on land that they are purchasing when those easements are ***in the original deeds of record***.

(b) ***Contractors*** do not have this same duty to examine those records.

(i) *See Mountain States Telephone and Telegraph Co. v. Kelton* (Ariz. 1955), where the defendant contractor Kelton, while digging land, destroyed some of the plaintiff's buried cables. The plaintiff sued for damages, claiming that the defendant was on *constructive notice* of the underground cables and had a duty to examine the records. Held: contractors do not have the same duty of potential land purchasers and others with an interest in land in checking for easements in the records.

**3.6 Title Assurance and Warranties**

3.6.1 The Methods of Title Assurance

(a) Buyers need a way to assure that they are getting what they bargained for.

(b) Although personal covenants were developed in order to promise buyers they were getting good title, they were inadequate.

(c) This led to the recording system discussed above and to modern title assurance and title searches.

(d) In addition, buyers may insure themselves against defective title by obtaining *covenants for title*.

3.6.2 The Six Covenants in Warranty Deeds

(a) Covenant of Seisin

(i) The grantor covenants that he *owns* the estate that he purports to transfer.

(b) Covenant of the Right to Convey

(i) The grantor covenants that he has the *right to convey* the estate.

(c) Covenant Against Encumbrances

(i) The grantor covenants that there are *no undisclosed encumbrances*, including easements, covenants, servitudes, mortgages or liens, on the land.

(ii) If an encumbrance is open and notorious, it is not considered "undisclosed" for the purpose of the covenant against encumbrances.

(iii) However, even an open, adverse, and notorious irrevocable license violates the covenant, if it is not a *permanent, public encumbrance*. If it is a permanent, public encumbrance, the covenant is not violated when it would be inconceivable that the vendor would remove it. *Leach v. Gunnarson* (Or. 1980).

(d) Covenant of Warranty of Title

(i) The grantor covenants that the title is good and promises to defend the grantee against any paramount claims of title existing at the time of conveyance.

(ii) If the grantee is ever evicted, the grantor may take the steps necessary to secure good title for the grantee or the grantee may claim damages from the grantor.

(e) Covenant of Quiet Enjoyment

(i) The grantor covenants that there is *no third party with better title* to all or part of the property who may *evict* the grantee or otherwise disturb his possession and enjoyment of the property.

(f) Covenant for Further Assurances

(i) The grantor agrees to perform any reasonable, necessary acts in order to perfect the grantee's title.

3.6.3 Present and Future Covenants

(a) Present Covenants

(i) Present covenants do not run with the land under the *majority approach* and thus may *not* be enforced by remote parties.

(ii) They do, however, run with the land under the minority approach, subject to the statute of limitations.

(iii) The present covenants are: (i) the covenant of seisin; (ii) the covenant of the right to convey; and (iii) the covenant against encumbrances.

(iv) They may only be breached at the time of the conveyance, at which point the statute of limitations begins to run.

(b) Future Covenants

(i) Introduction

(1) Future covenants run with the land and may thus be enforced by remote parties.

(2) The future covenants are the covenant of warranty of title, the covenant of quiet enjoyment, and the covenant for further assurances.

(3) A purchaser's cause of action for breach of a future covenant is not limited to the party that conveyed his deed. Rather, he may sue all the way up the chain of title, if the statute of limitations has not expired.

(ii) Breach

(1) Future covenants may be breached any time a grantee or a remote party is evicted or disturbed in his ownership of the property.[8] The statute of limitations begins to run at that moment.

(2) Future covenants thus allow more leeway to grantees who may have missed the statute of limitations for the present covenants.

(3) If it becomes clear that a third party holds better title, but the grantee has not yet been evicted or disturbed in his possession, most courts will not grant damages.

(aa) *See Brown v. Lober* (Ill. 1979), where the plaintiffs (Brown) purchased land but later discovered that they owned only a partial interest in the subsurface coal rights. They sued the seller for breach of the covenant of seisin and of the covenant of the right to convey, but since it had been more than ten years since the plaintiffs purchased the land, the statute of limitations had expired. The plaintiffs then tried to sue on a covenant of quiet enjoyment theory, which was not barred by the statute of limitations, but which was inapplicable, since the mere existence of superior title absent a disturbance of the ownership does not constitute breach.

(bb) *N.B.*: the plaintiffs' recourse would have been to grant the coal option, and if the TO sued to quiet title, to show that the covenant of quiet enjoyment was breached.

---

[8] Under the old common law, only an actual eviction constituted breach of the future covenants. Today, the future covenants are also breached by "constructive eviction," (*e.g.*, a disturbance that prevents the grantee from obtaining complete possession of the property).

(iii) In the majority of states, damages for the breach of future covenants equal the *purchase price* at the time of the sale plus *interest* (*not* the current value of the property). *See, e.g., Davis v. Smith* (Ga. 1848).

3.6.4 Warranty Deeds

(a) The extent of a seller's liability is covered in the ***deed***.

(b) The seller may convey any of the following:

(i) ***General warranty deed***, where all of the warranties are included.

(ii) ***Special warranty deed***, which includes all of the warranties, but only during the *period in which the seller was in possession*.

(iii) ***Quitclaim deed***, where no warranty is provided.

(c) The seller may also expressly provide for some warranties or limit others in the deed.

## 3.7 Adverse Possession of Realty and After Acquired Title

3.7.1 Statutes of Limitation and Related Legislation as Aids to Title Assurance

(a) There are three approaches to adverse possession statutes: title assurance

(i) Objective Approach

(1) The objective approach involves an ***exclusive claim of right***.

(2) All that matters is that the possessor have a claim that is adverse and inconsistent with the TO's claim (*i.e.*, full title); his state of is irrelevant.

(ii) Subjective Approach

(1) The subjective approach takes into account the later possessor's ***state of mind*** in addition to a ***pure claim of right***.

(2) This generally means that the possessor must have *good faith* in order for the statute of limitations to run; in some states, however, the adverse possessor must actually have *bad faith*.

(3) In these latter states, if a person acquired possession through a mistake or good faith, the statute of limitations does not run.

(iii) Short Term Statute Approach

(1) While the other approaches require a statute of limitations range of about twenty years, the short term statutory approach involves a statute of limitations of as little as ***five to ten years***, when the possession is:

(aa) Under ***color of title***; and

(bb) Including the ***payment of taxes***.

(b) For a party to successfully acquire title to land by adverse possession, the possession must be:

(i) Open

(1) The use of the land must be of the kind of use that the normal owner would make of the land.

(2) It must be sufficient to put the owner on notice.

(ii) Continuous

(1) Continuous is *not synonymous with uninterrupted*, as long as the use is consistent with the nature of the property.

(2) *See Howard v. Kunto* (Wash. 1970), where the court held that summer occupancy of a summer home was sufficient to meet the *continuous* element of adverse possession.

(iii) Exclusive

(1) The adverse possessor must not share possession with the TO.

(iv) Adverse

(1) Under a claim of right against the TO.

(v) Notorious

(1) This element is virtually identical to the "open" element.

(c) Tacking

(i) If the adverse possessor does not meet the statutory period, he may reach it through *tacking*, or adding periods of prior adverse possession to the period of time in which he personally was in possession.

(ii) The elements of tacking are as follow:

(1) The former possessor must have transferred the same land through either:

(2) ***Deed*** (sale/conveyance), ***devise*** (gift or will), or ***inheritance*** (by law).

(iii) The transfer may be oral even when the deed refers to a ***different plot of land***. In meeting this ***privity requirement***, a court will not elevate form over substance.

(1) *See Howard v. Kunto*, where the court allowed tacking even though there was never a transfer on the adversely possessed land from the preceding possessor, since what was transferred in the deed was an entirely different plot of land. Because both the current and previous owners thought that their deeds

referred to the land they occupied, the substance of privity was met when the preceding owner transferred his interest.

(d) An owner may not claim adverse possession of subsurface minerals unless he actually exploits or occupies them, even if he possesses the surface rights.

(i) *See Failoni v. Chicago and North Western Railway Co.* (Ill. 1964), where the court held that leasing oil and gas rights to subsurface minerals was insufficient to establish the elements for adverse possession. The plaintiff Failoni failed to obtain adverse possession of the minerals because: (i) there was no color of title; (ii) she did not pay taxes on the severed minerals; and (iii) she did not try to mine or possess them. Judgment for the plaintiff reversed.

(e) For a tenant in common to claim adverse possession against another tenant in common, more than mere occupancy is required to meet the elements of adverse possession. Rather, an actual ouster must take place before the statute of limitations begins to run.

(i) *See Mercer v. Wayman* (Ill. 1956), where property was inherited as a tenancy in common by several family members. They all (including two minors through the actions of their father) agreed to quitclaim the property to one the plaintiffs, Mercer, who took possession. When one of the children reached majority, he disaffirmed his father's transfer and made a claim against the property, suggesting he was a part owner. The plaintiffs sued to quiet title under adverse possession. Held: the elements of the plaintiffs are met under neither the short term nor the long term Illinois statute of limitations. The short term statute of limitations is not met because there is no color of title, since the deed conveying property to the plaintiffs was not valid. The long term statute of limitations did not run because there was never an actual ouster of the defendants.

3.7.2 After-Acquired Title

(a) According to the ***after-acquired-title doctrine***, when a seller not having title to property purports to sell that property to a buyer, title vests in that buyer as soon as the seller acquires title.

(b) A purchaser thus acquires title when the following sequence takes place:

(i) A seller ***purports to sell*** the property;

(ii) A buyer ***purchases the property*** from the seller; and

(iii) The seller later acquires good or full title.

## 4 The Integrity of the Land

### 4.1 Trespass and Nuisance; Support of Land

4.1.1 Trespass and Nuisance

(a) A nuisance is a condition or activity on another's land that unreasonably affects the other's right to enjoy and use his land. The standard is one of a *person of ordinary sensibility*.

(b) Factors considered in determining whether a condition is a nuisance include whether:

(i) The condition begins or occurs after the plaintiff has been occupying the land;

(ii) The condition has little value to the one causing it;

(iii) The activity has little social value; and

(iv) The activity lowers the value of the owner's property.

4.1.2 Burdens of Proof

(a) If the owner of the land meets his burden of proving (i) ***causation;*** and (ii) ***damages***, an injunction will be granted.

(b) However, the defendant may raise a defense and avoid an injunction by showing that either: (i) the damage is unavoidable; or (ii) the cost of avoiding the damage is so high that it would deprive the defendant of the use of the land.

(i) *See Renken v. Harvey Aluminum* (D. Or. 1963), where the plaintiff Renken sought an injunction against the defendant, an aluminum plant that employed hundreds of workers and had a gross annual payroll of $3.5 million. There was undisputed evidence showing that the defendant's escaping fluoride caused damages to the plaintiff's apricot and peach trees. The plaintiff therefore met the burden of proving nuisance. The defendant had the burden of showing that either (i) the nuisance was *unavoidable*; or (ii) the costs of avoiding the damage would *deprive the defendant from the use of the land*. The defendant proved neither, since the problem was (i) avoidable and (ii) not cost-prohibitive. Therefore, a ***future*** injunction was awarded, even though the costs were substantial.

(c) If either of these elements are met by the defendant, a court will ***balance the equities*** by looking to each side's interests in order to determine whether to award damages or an injunction.

(i) Example: if granting an injunction against the activities of a major factory would cause a substantial loss of profits and the loss of thousands of jobs, a court may instead grant money damages to the plaintiff, especially when it appears that such a remedy would make the plaintiff whole.

(d) Furthermore, courts will not grant injunctions when doing so would entangle the judiciary in national policy areas generally reserved for legislatures.

(i) *See Boomer v. Atlantic Cement Co.* (N.Y. 1970), where the plant of the defendant Atlantic Cement Co. caused damages to the plaintiff's land. The plaintiff sued for an injunction. Recognizing that granting an injunction would cause a commercially important business to close down, the court held that where there is much substantial benefit from an activity, as in this case, it will grant monetary damages instead of an injunction.

4.1.3 Public and Private Nuisances

(a) Private Nuisance

(i) A nuisance is private when the party whose property interest is being disturbed is one individual or a few individuals, as opposed to an entire neighborhood or community.

(ii) The owner of the land being disturbed may recover for any nuisances against the defendant when he can prove causation and damages. He will obtain at least money damages, and possibly an injunction.

(iii) However, when the nuisance existed when the owner purchased the land ("*coming to the nuisance*"), the owner will not recover, unless the nuisance has become greater in degree since the land purchase.

(b) Public Nuisance

(i) A nuisance is public when the parties whose property interest is being disturbed are large groups of individuals or an entire community.

(ii) The plaintiffs may recover from the defendant for any nuisances when they can prove causation and damages, *including when they "come to the nuisance.*"

(1) *See Spur Industries, Inc. v. Del E. Webb Development Co.* (Ariz. 1972), where the plaintiff Del E. Webb Development Co.continued developing a rural housing project until it reached the defendant's feeding lot. The plaintiff sued for an injunction for flies and odors from the defendant's property. Held: because this is a public nuisance effecting not only the defendant but all of those in the defendant's housing, the injunction against the defendant is affirmed. However, the plaintiff is required to indemnify the defendant for his damages.

## 4.2 Zoning

### 4.2.1 Introduction

(a) Zoning occurs when a legislature limits the permitted uses of the land.

(i) Example: a ban on easily ignitable building materials in a part of town that is susceptible to fires.

(b) Among the purposes of zoning are aesthetic values, health, safety, and welfare.

### 4.2.2 Constitutionality

(a) All zoning laws, to be valid, must be deemed constitutional. The following two-part test is applied:

(i) The law must have a ***proper purpose*** (*i.e.*, a purpose within the police power of the state (morality, health, safety, welfare);

(1) A proper purpose may be aesthetic value.

(2) However, the zoning standard is unconstitutional when arbitrarily applied. *Nectow v. City of Cambridge* (U.S. 1928).

(ii) The law must reasonably promote that purpose.

(b) When these elements are met, the law is deemed *constitutional*, *even if it causes a decrease in the value* of the property affected.

(i) *See Village of Euclid v. Ambler Realty Co.* (U.S. 1926), where an ordinance that restricted land use caused the plaintiff's parcel to significantly lose value (from $10,000 to $2,500). The plaintiff sued to enjoin enforcement of the ordinance on the basis that it was facially unconstitutional, since it substantially violated the due process ***right to property*** (loss of value) and ***right to liberty*** (use of land). Held: the fact that an ordinance causes loss of value will not on its own invalidate the ordinance, particularly when it has other beneficial effects, such as promoting health, safety, and welfare, by providing a safer environment in which to rear one's children.

## 4.3 Takings

### 4.3.1 Introduction

(a) A taking is an appropriation of private property by the state for the common good.

(b) Property is considered to be "taken" when it is *actually taken* (*i.e.*, *physically invaded* and *appropriated*) or so *heavily regulated* that the owner has been deprived of all economic use.

### 4.3.2 Actual Takings

(a) Under the Fifth Amendment Takings Clause, private property shall not "be taken for public use, without just compensation."

(b) There are thus two requirements for valid public takings:

(i) "Just compensation" must be paid.

(1) Just compensation must be a "full and perfect equivalent" of the value of the property.

(ii) They must be done for a legitimate "public use."

(1) Today, however, the inquiry no longer looks into whether a taking is based on a legitimate public use; rather, the courts search for *any legitimate public purpose*, which may include:

(aa) Land redistribution from a small oligarchy to the general public; and

(bb) The development of a blighted sector.

(2) The purpose need not benefit all of the public; it is sufficient if only some benefit.

(3) Furthermore, a taking need not transfer ownership to the government; it may transfer ownership ***to private interests***.

(aa) *See Hawaii Housing Authority v. Midkiff* (U.S. 1984), where Hawaiian legislation that redistributed land by transferring title from lessors to lessees was held to be constitutional, since the redistribution of title that was previously predominantly held by a small oligarchy to the rest of the population was a legitimate "public purpose" affecting health, safety, and welfare.

(bb) *See also Kelo v. City of New London* (U.S. 2005) (Stevens, J.), where the Court held that the transfer of waterfront property to other private interests was constitutional when the purpose was to build hotels, offices, and restaurants in order to *develop the sector* and *benefit the public*.

(4) However, where the government's transfer of interests between private interests is done *for the sole purpose of transferring ownership*, the taking is *unconstitutional*, even if just compensation is paid.

4.3.3 Regulatory Takings

(a) As mentioned above, property is considered to be "taken" not only when it is *actually appropriated*, but also when it is so *heavily regulated* that the owner has been deprived of all economic use of his land.

(b) When property is "taken" through burdensome regulation, just compensation must be paid.

(c) There are two kinds of regulatory takings that require just compensation:

(i) Physical Invasions

(1) *See, e.g., Loretto v. Teleprompter Manhattan CATV Corp.* (U.S. 1982), where the installations of cables in apartment buildings constituted a taking, even though only an insignificant space in the apartments was occupied. The taking was imputed to the government, since a local law required certain property owners to permit the installations.

(ii) Regulations Denying All Economically Beneficial Use of the Land

(1) *See Lucas v. South Carolina Coastal Council* (U.S. 1992), where the Beachfront Management Act barred the plaintiff from any economically profitable use of land that he purchased for $975,000. Held (Scalia, J.): the act's effect on the plaintiff's ability to economically benefit from his land was a key factor for determining whether just compensation was required.

(2) *N.B.*: a distinction is to be made between: (i) regulatory takings, where the land is so burdened by regulations that it is deprived of all economic use, and where just compensation is required; and (ii) regulations preventing nuisances, where compensation is not required, since the government's rights are based on the common law.

# 5 Landlord / Tenant Law

## 5.1 Introduction to Non-Freehold Estates

### 5.1.1 The Two Kinds of Estates

(a) Freehold Estates

(i) In a freehold estates, the possessor is the owner of the property (at least for a temporary period of time).

(b) Leasehold Estates

(i) A leasehold estate is one where the possessor (tenant) has only possession, and full title will spring back to the owner (landlord).

(ii) Historical origins

(1) In feudal times, the king owned all of the land. Nobles that were loyal to him were able to use parts of the land. They then were able to parcel land out to serfs and peasants.

(aa) Today, this many-layered system of tenancy continues to exist. For example, in commercial shopping centers, sections of a store may be parceled out to merchants many times over.

(2) Later, leaseholds were established as collateral for loans. The tenant would "lend" the landlord the money in exchange for the use of the land. Rather than pay the loan back with interest, the landlord would simply grant the tenant use of the land.

(3) Eventually, the law began to recognize leaseholds as interests in land in and of themselves.

### 5.1.2 Three Kinds of Leaseholds

(a) Tenancy for Years

(i) Characteristics

(1) A tenancy for years is a discreet lease with a determined beginning and end date.

(2) If there is a provision clause in the lease, then a second, separate one-time renewal lease may be established.

(3) When there is a renewal clause in the lease, it is evidence of a tenancy for years, since periodic tenancies and at-will tenancies require no renewal to continue.

(ii) How It Is Created

(1) A tenancy for years is created formally.

(2) It requires a clear end date.

(aa) The end date need not be explicitly expressed, if the expiration of the lease could be determined.

(bb) The following clause, for example, would be sufficient: "the lease will begin on Jan 1, 2000 and will expire three years later."

(3) According to some authorities, there must also be a set start date.

(aa) Under the majority view, however, it does not need to be fixed.

(bb) The clause "the lease begins when the construction has ended" would be sufficient.

(4) Statute of Frauds: under the modern law, any lease for more than one year must be in writing to be enforced.

(iii) How It Is Terminated

(1) A tenancy for years ends automatically at the end of the term.

(2) The lease may provide the possibility of renewal.

(3) In such a case, a court would allow the new lease.

(4) Except for when a provision of the original contract (lease) is illegal, unclear or for some other reason against public policy, the original contract controls all matters in the new lease.

(b) Periodic Tenancy

(i) Characteristics

(1) A periodic tenancy is an indefinite lease.

(2) There is no need for renewal.

(ii) How It Is Created

(1) A periodic tenancy may be created by the parties in an express agreement (*e.g.*, "This lease is from month-to-month.").

(2) In addition, it may be created by law.

(aa) If the parties attempt to create a tenancy for years, but a period is mentioned (*e.g.*, "rent will be paid each month") and no end date is determined, then a periodic tenancy is presumed.

(iii) How It Is Terminated

(1) Either party may end a periodic tenancy with *proper notice* (unlike tenancies at will, which do not require proper notice).

(aa) For periods of one or more years, six months of notice is usually required.

(bb) For periods of less than one year, notice equal to one full period (generally measured by payment periods) is required.

(2) Generally, notice of termination must be in writing and delivered.

(3) Example: the tenant rents from a landlord in a monthly periodic tenancy. The tenant gives notice to the landlord on July 15 that he wishes to leave. Until when must the tenant pay rent?

(aa) Since the tenant must have one full month of rent paid before vacating, all of August must be paid before leaving. Thus, the tenant is responsible for rent up until August 31.

(c) Tenancy at Will

(i) Characteristics

(1) A tenancy at will may be terminated at any time.

(ii) How It Is Created

(1) It is usually created by operation of law; if a tenancy for years is attempted, but there is no clear end date and no basis for ascertaining a period, then a tenancy at will is presumed.

(2) Examples of tenancies where there is no basis for ascertaining a period:

(aa) The landlord agrees to allow his tenant to live on the property on the condition that the tenant keeps up the property and pays the taxes and insurance.

(bb) The tenant is an employee-at-will of a landlord who furnishes a home as part of the compensation.

(3) *See Womack v. Hyche* (Ala. 1987), where the parties disputed a tenancy "for $300 per year with the option to renew so long as the camp is run as a business." The landlord argued that there was no fixed end date and that the lease was therefore a tenancy at will that would allow him to evict the defendant. The defendant argued that the end date was the end of the year. Held: a tenancy at will is created, since the end date is not clear. Remanded to determine a reasonable time required to vacate.

(aa) N.B.: a court could have interpreted this to be a periodic tenancy based on the one year payment period.

(iii) How It Is Terminated

(1) Under the common law, a tenancy at will could be ended at any time.

(2) Today, many state statutes protect tenants, by requiring, for example, at least ten days of notice prior to the landlord's termination of the tenancy.

## 5.2 Discriminatory Preferences and Religious Liberty Issues

### 5.2.1 The Evolution of Regulations on Landlords

(a) Under the common law, a landlord could select whichever tenants or purchasers he wanted for his housing or land.

(b) Later, statutes prohibited landlords or sellers from discriminating on the basis of race, color, religion, sex, familial status, age, handicap or national origin.

(c) One example of such a statute is the federal Fair Housing Act.

(i) The Fair Housing Act prohibits:

(1) Discrimination on the basis of race, color, religion, sex, familial status, age, handicap or national origin for the basis of choosing a tenant or buyer; and

(2) The *publication* or *indication* of a preference as to any of the above categories in choosing a buyer or tenant.

(ii) The subjective intent of the owner or landlord is irrelevant; what is controlling is whether a reasonable person from one of the protected groups would interpret an indication as expressing a preference.

(1) *See Jancik v. Department of Housing and Urban Development* (7th Cir. 1995), where the Seventh Circuit held that the landlord violated the Fair Housing Act by indicating his preference for a "mature person," which a reasonable person would take to mean a middle-aged tenant without small children, thus violating the statute on familial status. He also violated the statute by saying that he did not want any teenagers and by inquiring as to race with a discriminatory purpose. Damages and an injunction were affirmed.

(aa) *N.B.*: a landlord could refuse to rent on an individualized basis to persons with children who were disruptive or would damage property, but a class-based exclusion is invalid.

(bb) *N.B.*: this court did not deal with the issue of whether inquiries as to race on their own are enough to violate the Fair Housing Act. The Second Circuit, however, in *dicta* stated that they were sufficient.

(d) Many states have adopted stricter versions of this federal act. Massachusetts, for example, has adopted statutes that also prohibit discrimination on the basis of sexual orientation.

(e) Regulations are usually more lax for the rental of rooms attached to the owner's abode (*e.g.*, a landlord may chose a tenant based on gender).

5.2.2 Modern Statutes and Religious Liberty

(a) Many state and federal statutes prohibit familial status discrimination.

(b) Such statutes do not necessarily prohibit landlords from discriminating against unmarried cohabitants.

(i) *See State v. French* (Minn. 1990), where the defendant French, a religious landlord, discriminated against unmarried cohabitant tenants. The Minnesota Human Rights Acts forbade the discrimination of tenants based on age, race, religion, and marital status. Because the Minnesota Constitution did not define "marital status," the court looked to the legislative history and found that the legislature excluded the language, "and other like categories" that would have protected unmarried cohabitants. Additionally, the Minnesota Constitution protects freedom of religion, with the exception of that which poses a threat to the safety of the state. Since the defendant landlord's discrimination did not threaten public safety, his right to follow his conscience outweighed the plaintiffs' right to live in his apartment.

(c) Since there is no federal law protecting against marital status discrimination, claims for marital status discrimination fall to the states, whose regulations vary widely.

(i) Most states have either: (i) not passed statutes prohibiting discrimination based on marital status; or (ii) passed legislation prohibiting discrimination based on marital status, but explicitly exclude unmarried couples from protection.

(ii) Other states have passed legislation protecting against marital status discrimination, but not specifically protecting unmarried cohabitants.

**5.3 Tenant's Rights and Remedies**

5.3.1 Introduction

(a) A tenant has four basic rights:

(i) Legal possession;

(ii) Actual possession;

(iii) The covenant of quiet enjoyment / constructive eviction; and

(iv) The implied warranty of habitability.

(b) Furthermore, he has certain remedies if the lease violates housing regulations.

5.3.2 Legal Possession

(a) All states recognize tenants' right to legal possession.

(b) The landlord must have title in order to enter into a lease.

5.3.3 Actual Possession

(a) The landlord has a duty to deliver the actual possession of the premises to the tenant.

(b) This duty prevents *third parties*, such as holdover tenants, from preventing new tenants from taking actual possession of the rented property.

(c) ***English (majority) rule***: the *landlord has the duty of delivering the actual possession* of the property and of preventing third parties from interfering with it.

(i) Some states that have adopted the English rule apply it only to *residential*, not *commercial*, leases).

(ii) In states that have adopted the English rule, the tenant's remedy for the landlord's failure to deliver actual possession is *expectation damages*.

(1) *See Adrian v. Rabinowitz* (N.J. 1936), where the plaintiff successfully sued the defendant landlord Rabinowitz for failing to vacate a building to be used in a commercial lease for a shoe store on the beginning day of the lease. Although NJ recognized the *universal rule* that *tenants are entitled to legal possession*, and though this lease imposed the *covenant of quiet enjoyment* (which otherwise would not have been recognized in NJ), the issue was whether the landlord had a *duty of delivering actual possession* to the tenant against holdover tenants. Held: NJ applies the English rule, which imposes the duty on landlords. The plaintiff is therefore awarded *expectation damages* equal to lost profits.

(d) ***American (minority) rule***: the *new tenant is responsible for obtaining possession* of the property and for evicting holdover tenants; the landlord is merely a title holder.

(i) In states that have adopted the American rule, the tenant has no remedy for the landlord's failure to deliver actual possession.

5.3.4 The Covenant of Quiet Enjoyment and Constructive Eviction

(a) The covenant of quiet enjoyment and constructive eviction deals with the tenant's *actual and constructive continued possession* of the property after delivery.

(b) It is implied in all states except NJ.

(c) There are two kinds of violations:

(i) Actual (Full or Partial) Eviction

(1) There are two kinds of actual eviction:

(aa) *Eviction for lack of title:* a third party with superior title evicts the tenant from the property.

(bb) *Wrongful eviction:* the landlord evicts the tenant without cause.

(2) The promises in a landlord-tenant relationship are independent from one another.

(aa) Thus, even if a lease is violated by a landlord, the tenant is generally not relieved of the duty to pay rent.

(bb) However, a violation of the covenant of quiet enjoyment is the exception.

(cc) Thus, if a tenant is evicted from the property, he is excused of the duty to pay rent.

(3) Full and Partial eviction

(aa) Full eviction applies when a tenant is evicted from *all* of the property.

(bb) An eviction is partial when the tenant is evicted from only *part* of the property.

(cc) In either case, the covenant of quiet enjoyment protects the tenant.

(dd) Since the lease is seen at common law as a transfer of *all* the property, *exclusion from any of the property* is seen to be an eviction.

(ee) Thus, the *remedy for partial eviction is similar to that for full eviction*: the obligation to pay rent is entirely excused until the tenant's full possession is restored.

(I) *See Smith v. McEnany* (Mass. 1897), where the court held that a lessor's putting up of a wall slightly encroaching upon his lessee's property was enough of an infringement of the lessee's right to enjoy all of the land that the lessee was entirely absolved of the duty to pay rent.

(ff) However, the restatement and many states take a different approach: partial eviction proportionally reduces the rent that the tenant must pay, but he is still obligated to pay rent for the *portion of the land from which he has not been evicted*.

(ii) Constructive Eviction

(1) Some violations of the lease may be so material that the tenant can be considered to have been *constructively evicted*, even if he continues to hold actual possession of the land.

(2) The elements of constructive eviction are as follow:

(aa) A material breach of the lease;

(bb) That is chargeable to the landlord;

(cc) Of which the landlord is given notice;

(dd) With the opportunity to cure; and

(ee) The tenant vacates the premises after a reasonable time.

(3) Violations of peace and quiet can constitute violations of the covenant of quiet enjoyment.

(aa) Example: the landlord leases a store to one tenant who opens a bookstore. The landlord then leases adjacent space to a second tenant, who opens up a gym that is always playing loud music. If the music is so loud that it alienates all of the first tenant's clients, the first tenant may have a claim for constructive eviction.

(4) Constructive eviction places a burden on the tenant to vacate the premises and then bring an action to *terminate the lease and the duty to pay*.

(aa) The problem with this is that it is possible that the tenant vacate the premises, sue, and lose.

(bb) He will then be required to pay the rent, even though he has vacated the premises.

(cc) *N.B.*: in some jurisdictions, constructive eviction is an affirmative defense and the burden is on the landlord to sue the tenant.

(d) Remedies for Violations of the Covenant of Quiet Enjoyment

(i) At common law, the tenant is *excused of the duty to pay rent* (in some states, if it is a partial eviction, he may do so while remaining in possession of the property).

(ii) In other states, the tenant is entitled to money damages.

5.3.5 The Implied Warranty of Habitability

(a) Because of the problems involving constructive eviction, some states have recognized the *implied warranty of habitability*.

(i) This warranty makes it easier for the tenant to recover damages when the condition of the premises is so poor that the tenant is *virtually constructively evicted*, whether the eviction be partial or full.

(ii) In a minority of jurisdictions, for commercial leases, some states recognize an "implied covenant of suitability" in place of an implied warranty of habitability.

(b) The implied warranty of habitability makes it possible to *recover the damages* that one would have recovered for constructive eviction (as well as other remedies, see *infra.*), but without the requirement that the tenant vacate the premises.

(c) The implied warranty of habitability is breached when there is:

(i) A violation of a housing standard that is based on either (i) local laws providing *standards*; (ii) statutes providing *specific terms*; or (iii) statutes providing *general terms* (as in New York).

(ii) That is chargeable to the landlord;

(iii) With notice given to the landlord; and

(iv) A reasonable opportunity to cure is given to the landlord.

(d) At common law, the only thing that justified not paying rent was the violation of the covenant of quiet enjoyment. It later came to be seen that some violations of the warranty of habitability could be so gross that the defendant could be considered to have been evicted.

(e) When the warranty is violated, the tenant has several possible remedies:

(i) To move out and terminate lease;

(ii) To abate the rent;

(iii) To remain in possession of the property, pay rent, and sue for damages;

(iv) To repair the property and recover the money spent; or

(v) To remain on the property and withhold the rent.

(1) *See Richard Barton Enterprises, Inc. v. Tsern* (Utah 1996), where the lease provided that the plaintiff tenant accepted the premises "as is" but that the landlord would put the elevator in good working order. Although the landlord put the elevator in working order, it failed city inspections. The tenant considered himself constructively evicted from part of complex and sued for a judgment declaring the landlord's duty to repair the elevator. Held: this lease will be considered a contract in which there is dependence of covenants. By breaching the lease, ***the landlord absolves the tenant of duty to pay full rent***.

(2) *N.B.*: many courts require the tenant to put the rent in escrow.

5.3.6 Illegal Leases

(a) The Common Law

(i) At common law, the landlord did not have the duty to maintain the property, unless specifically provided in the lease.

(ii) However, he had a duty to *make the premises safe*.

(iii) If he failed, the tenant still had the duty to pay rent, based on the independence of covenants, but he could ***recover damages***.

(b) The Modern Law

(i) Today, if a lease is invalid because of a housing law violation, the tenant's options include:

(1) Moving out of the apartment and asking that the courts declare the lease invalid, thereby absolving him of the duty to pay rent; or

(2) Remaining in the apartment and:

(aa) Asking a court to order the landlord to conform the apartment to housing laws;

(bb) Conforming the housing to local laws and asking the court to reward damages equal to the funds spent;

(cc) Remaining in the housing with an abatement of the rent equivalent to the difference in the value between what the tenant *bargained for* (property in conformity with the law) and what he *received* (property not in conformity with the law). This is the Restatement § 6.1 approach; or

(dd) Remaining in the housing rent-free (accepted in a few jurisdictions).

## 5.4 Duration and Use of the Premises

### 5.4.1 Duration of the Tenancy

(a) The Holdover Tenant

(i) A holdover tenant is one who ***keeps possession of the property*** beyond the expiration of the lease.

(ii) Landlords have a choice as to whether to (i) declare holdover tenants to be ***trespassers*** (and thus evict them); or (ii) declare a ***new periodic tenancy*** (equal to the length of the previous term), and thus to charge them. They may do this within reasonable time.

(iii) The period between the end of a lease and the landlord's deciding as to whether he will declare the holdover tenant to be a trespasser or a periodic tenant is known as a ***tenancy at sufferance***.

(iv) In order for a landlord to declare a new tenancy and to charge a tenant for another period, the holdover tenant must ***voluntarily remain*** on the premises.

(1) *See Commonwealth Building Corp. v. Hirschfield* (Ill. 1940), where the court held that the defendant tenant at sufferance Hirschfield was *not liable* to the landlord for rent for a new period, since the defendant's remaining on the premises beyond the end of the lease was *not voluntary*. Rather, he was forced to remain on the premises for one day because the building's elevator was down. When the plaintiff sued to recover double the value of the monthly rent for a one year period (as stipulated in the contract), the court held that, because it was not the defendant's voluntary act to remain on the property, and since the plaintiff had notice of this (the plaintiff's employees helped the defendant to

move out), the plaintiff was only entitled to rent for the one extra day for which the defendant remained on the property.

(b) The Right to the Extended Occupancy of Certain Housing

(i) Normally, a landlord has the right to terminate the tenant's right of occupancy at the expiration of the lease.

(ii) There are, however, exceptions when occupants are living in ***federally subsidized housing***.

(1) In such situations, tenants are constitutionally entitled to occupancy for life.

(2) However, eviction may occur if there is good cause (*e.g.*, illegal drug use on the premises by the tenant).

(iii) Similarly, there are statutes that protect the rights of ***mobile home owners***. Since the costs of relocating are relatively high compared to the cost of the mobile home, some states require park owners to extend leases of at least one-year.

(iv) There is also a law regulating ***rental units*** being converted into ***condominiums***. The purpose of these regulations is to *protect tenants who would be unable to purchase a condominium.*

(v) Finally, there is legislation, such as the Senior Citizens and Disabled Protected Tenancy Act, NJSA 2A:18-61.22 et seq., that protects the ***rights of senior citizens and the disabled***.

(1) If rental housing is converted into condominiums, some tenants are allowed a *forty year protected tenancy period.*

(2) To qualify, one must be:

(aa) *Disabled* to the point of being unable to engage in gainful activity; or

(bb) A *senior citizen* of over sixty two years of age, or a widow of more than fifty years of age who was married to a spouse who was sixty two years of age; and

(cc) Must have lived in the unit continuously for at least one year.

(3) When a landlord converts a housing unit to a condominium, he must inform the agency, which then contacts the tenants to inquire whether there is anyone *eligible for the protected status.*

5.4.2 Restrictions on the Uses of the Premises

(a) The hallmark of a lease is the tenant's *unrestricted possession.* This does not, however, mean *unrestricted use.*

(b) The uses of the property may be implied by the law or restricted by the landlord.

(c) The following are the only *implied* restrictions on use:

(i) Waste;

(ii) Illegal or immoral uses; and

(iii) Misrepresentation on the part of the lessee.

(d) The landlord may also impose restrictions. He may, for example, restrict which businesses may rent the premises (*e.g.*, to avoid competitors in a strip mall).

(e) In order for the landlord to restrict the tenant's use of the premises, one of following elements must be met:

(i) The intentions of the parties must be clear; or

(ii) Explicit restrictive language must be present in the lease, such as, "the tenant is to use the premises only as a restaurant."

(1) *N.B.*: without the word "only," this phrase would be considered to be ***permissive, not restrictive***.

5.4.3 The Duty of Continuous Operations

(a) There is ***no implied duty of continuous operations***, unless one of the following elements are met:

(i) The lease includes a *specific provision* requiring continuous use; or

(ii) There is an *implied covenant of continued use* based on the lease's implicit language or other circumstances.

(1) *See Lippman v. Sears* (Cal. 1955), where the court held that there was an implied covenant of continuous use if the following three elements were met: (i) there was *no express provision* in the lease calling for continuous use; (ii) the *intention of the parties* to enter into such a lease was so *clearly in their understanding* that they did not think that it was necessary to include it in the lease (correspondence between the parties may demonstrate this); and (iii) the implied covenant of continued use is *necessary to effectuate this intent.*

(b) To determine whether an implied covenant of continued use is applicable in a case, courts may implement a balancing test that looks to the following factors (*Thompson Dev., Inc. v. Kroger Co.*):

(i) Whether the lease contains an *inconsistent provision*;

(ii) Whether the lease grants *free assignability* to a tenant;

(iii) Whether the lease was *freely negotiated* by all the parties; and

(iv) Whether the lease contains a *non-competition provision.*

(c) When the ***base rent is token or nonexistent***, but the share of the profits is substantial, a court could infer continued operation as being within the parties' intent.

(d) When there is a ***substantial base rent***, courts usually will not recognize an implied covenant of continued use.

(i) *See Piggly Wiggly Southern, Inc. v. Heard* (Ga. 1991), where the defendant supermarket tenant Piggly Wiggly was purchased by another company and moved to a new location. The property it originally occupied, which was owned by the plaintiff, was kept vacant. The original lease required the defendant to pay $29,000 per month, plus a share of any profits over $2 million. The plaintiff sued for specific performance (SP), requiring the defendant to either *occupy the property* or *rent it out*. Held: since there is a substantial base rent, and since the lease states that the premises could be used for a supermarket or "any other lawful business," and there was thus free assignability, there is a strong presumption that the lease does not create an implied covenant of continued use.

## 5.5 Fixtures

### 5.5.1 Common Law

(a) At common law, fixtures remained with the landlord of the property.

### 5.5.2 Modern Law

(a) The traditional modern law view is that fixtures remain with the landlord, but if they are installed by the tenant, they could be taken by the tenant, as long as (i) their removal would not damage the property; and (ii) they were removed *before expiration of the lease*.

(b) However, the *general modern law rule* allows fixtures to be removed by tenants if the removal would not damage the property, *even if it is done after the expiration of the lease*, as long as it is done before possession of the property is yielded.

(i) *See Handler v. Horns* (N.J. 1949), where the defendant lessee Horns and the plaintiff were one third interest tenants in common of property. The defendant installed refrigerator units and the plaintiff later sued for partition. The defendant sought to remove the refrigerators from the property and the plaintiff objected, arguing that such fixtures form a part of the property and, since the defendant did not include a provision in the lease allowing him to take fixtures, he had forfeited the right by failing to remove them upon expiration of the first lease. The court criticized this rule and applied the *general modern law rule*: unless anything in the lease is contrary, the tenant has the right to remove trade fixtures, as long as doing so *does not damage the property* and removal is effected *before yielding possession of property.*

## *5.6* Lessor's Remedies Against Defaulting Tenants

### 5.6.1 Termination of the Lease

(a) A landlord may terminate a lease against a tenant who (i) ***fails to pay*** rent; (ii) ***wrongfully possesses*** the premises after the right has terminated; or (iii) ***abandons the premises*** before the end of the lease.

(b) However, landlords may not terminate leases for ***immaterial breaches***.

(i) *See Foundation Development Corp. v. Loehmann's, Inc.* (Ariz. 1990), where the court held that it would be inequitable to allow the plaintiff to terminate a lease with the defendant, whose rent arrived three days late because of the defendant's inquiry on his bill. The plaintiff relied on a statute that gives landlords the right to terminate leases *for any reason whatsoever*, but this statute must be read by its intent, which is to create a *modern day right of lease termination* (a right not possessed at common law absent a contractual provision). Since the breach is immaterial, the lease should not be terminated, despite the fact that the lease stated that "time is of the essence."

5.6.2 Eviction

(a) General rule: given adequate notice, month-to-month leases may be terminated at any time for *any reason whatsoever*.

(b) Exception: when allowing landlords to evict tenants jeopardizes a public policy.

(i) *See Edwards v. Habib* (D.C. Cir. 1968), where the plaintiff landlord Habib sued the defendant tenant for eviction after the defendant had reported the plaintiff's violations of housing codes. Held: allowing landlords to evict tenants who report housing code violations ***jeopardizes the public policy*** of keeping housing safe for tenants. Judgment for the plaintiff reversed.

(c) Retaliatory Eviction

(i) Retaliatory eviction refers to a landlord's eviction of a tenant based on the tenant's invocation of a protected right, reporting of a housing code violation, or some other act relating to the property.

(ii) There are three approaches to retaliatory eviction:

(1) ***Restrictive approach***: a tenant may only use the retaliatory eviction defense when the following occurs:

(aa) The property *violates housing standards;*

(bb) The tenant *reports* this to the housing authority; and

(cc) Immediately afterwards, *the landlord tries to evict* the tenant.

(2) ***Intermediate approach***: a tenant may use the retaliatory eviction defense when the landlord tries to evict the tenant for any action that the tenant takes that is *related to the property*, such as his joining of a tenants union.

(3) ***Permissive approach***: tenant may use the retaliatory eviction defense for an eviction resulting from tenant's exercise of *any legal or constitutional right*.

5.6.3 Damages

(a) Expectation damages are awarded for the breach of a lease.

(b) If the tenant leaves the property prematurely and stops paying rent, the landlord is entitled to the *difference* between what the landlord would have received under the original lease and any new lease that he obtains.

(c) Thus, if the breached lease leads to the landlord's higher profits, he may not collect damages. *United States Nat'l Bank of Oregon v. Homeland, Inc.* (Or. 1981).

5.6.4 Limits on the Lessor's Actions

(a) A landlord may not recover unpaid rents from a tenant when the lease is ***illegal***.

(i) *See Brown v. Southall Realty Co.* (D.C. App. 1968), where the defendant Brown failed to make certain rental payments and abandoned the apartment. The plaintiff lessor Southall sued for *possession and termination* of the lease. The defendant argued that the lease was illegal as against hygiene regulations and if a court granted the termination of the lease, it would make the lease valid *res judicata* in a future proceeding if the plaintiff sued to recover unpaid rent. Held: the lease, being in violation of housing regulations in place *before* the execution of the lease, is invalid. It may not be terminated or used by the landlord as the grounds for collecting unpaid rent.

(ii) *N.B.*: in order for the defendant's case to have succeeded, she had to show that laws that were violated were in place *before the lease was made*. Otherwise, the lease would have been valid. However, even if the laws were enacted after the lease was formed, the tenant could have argued that the *implied warranty of habitability*, which warrants that the leased property would continue to be fit to live in, was violated.

(iii) *N.B.*: the court could have also ordered the plaintiff to conform the property to the required standards. The plaintiff would have then been able to evict the defendant since the contract would not have been voided. However, the defendant would have then been able to sue for damages, since the housing did not conform to the housing standards.

(b) When a lease is invalid as against housing regulations, before evicting a tenant, a landlord may be required to either (i) make the necessary repairs and show a non-retaliatory reason to evict the defendant; or (ii) prove that he was going to take the housing off of the market.

(i) *See also Robinson v. Diamond Housing Corp.* (D.C. Cir. 1972), where the plaintiff sought to evict the defendant, who was not paying rent. The defendant invoked the *Brown v. Southall Realty Co.* defense: the lease was illegal because it was not in conformity with housing standards. The plaintiff then tried to evict the defendant, arguing that because there was no lease, the defendant should not be on the premises. The defendant invoked the thirty day notice defense. The plaintiff then gave the defendant sufficient notice and tried to evict her. The defendant invoked the *Edwards v. Habib* defense of retaliatory discharge. Held: perhaps because the court feared that if it allowed the plaintiff to evict the defendant, the plaintiff would simply rent it out to another tenant, it required the plaintiff to first show that he had either (i) made the necessary repairs and showed a non-retaliatory reason for evicting the defendant; or (ii) not made the repairs but was going to take the housing off of the market. In retaliatory discharge cases, then, in some states, the tenant can go on living in the housing unit indefinitely until the repairs are made.

## 5.7 Assignments and Subleases

### 5.7.1 Introduction

(a) A transfer of property shifts the possession from one possessor to another.

(b) There are two kinds of transfers:

(i) A ***sublease*** grants possession of the land to a new tenant for *part of the duration of a lease period*, even if it is as little as one minute.

(ii) An ***assignment*** grants the possession of land for the *entire period of the lease*.

(1) By default, an assignment grants *all of the property* for the lease period.

(2) A *partial assignment* may however, be granted for only *part of the property* for the lease period.

### 5.7.2 Determining Whether a Sublease or an Assignment has been Created

(a) Common Law

(i) Under the common law, if the first tenant has any reversion, even for one minute, a sublease has been created.

(b) Modern Law

(i) Under the modern law, the ***intent*** of the parties is *dispositive*.

(ii) *See Jaber v. Miller* (Ark. 1951), where the landlord leased property to the defendant tenant Jaber, who subleased the property to a second party, who in turn subleased it to the plaintiff second sublessee Miller. The lease between the landlord and the defendant stipulated that *if there was a fire, the lease would be terminated.* There was a fire and the plaintiff sought cancellation of promissory notes he owed to the defendant under the agreement, arguing that his sublease was terminated because it was based on a sublease between the defendant and a second party, which terminated when the underlying lease between the landlord and the defendant was terminated. Held: the plaintiff's sublease was not cancelled because it is not carved out of a sublease between the defendant tenant and the second party; rather, it was carved out of an assignment. Under the modern law, we know that it is an assignment because the *intent of the parties is clear*. Thus, *the plaintiff has a continuing obligation to pay the defendant* because the assignment did not terminate, even though the lease between the landlord and the defendant expired. Judgment for the plaintiff reversed.

### 5.7.3 Privity

(a) Suppose landlord 1 (L1) is in privity with this tenant (T1). L1 then sells the property to landlord 2 (L2). According to many sources, L2 and T1 are not in *privity of contract.*

(b) However, they are in privity of estate, since L2 owns the reversion.

(c) To have privity of contract between T1 and L2, there must be ***attornment***, where a party to a contract recognizes a new third party as a former party's valid successor to the contract. Here: it would be the tenant's recognition of the new owner and his agreement to pay rent to him.

(d) Examples

(i) L1 and T1 are in privity of contract and privity of estate.

(ii) If T1 assigns his lease to T2, the resulting relationships are as follow:

(1) L1-T1: privity of contract. L1 may look to T1 to continue to pay the rent. However, they are no longer in privity of estate.

(2) T1-T2: privity of contract. They would no longer be in privity of estate, since T1 no longer holds the estate.

(3) L1-T2: privity of estate. They are not in privity of contract, unless a lease is signed between them.

(aa) Privity of estate carries with it all of the lease provisions between L1 and T1 that ***run with the land***, including the payment of rent.

(bb) As a result, L1 may look to T1 or T2 to pay rent.

(iii) In the alternative, if T1 subleases the property to S2, the following relationships result:

(1) L1-T1: privity of contract, privity of estate

(2) T1-S2: privity of contract, privity of estate

(3) L1-S2: no relationship

(aa) A sublessee is not liable to pay L1 for rent.

(bb) However, since S2's lease is dependant on the L1-T1 lease, *S2 may not engage in activities prohibited by that lease*.

(I) Rationale: T1 cannot give away that which he does not have.

(II) Thus, if he owns only a limited possessory interest in the land, he may only give away that right to a sublessee.

(cc) Furthermore, when the L1-T1 lease is terminated, so too is the T1-S2 sublease, which is dependent on the former.

(dd) Thus, both T2's and S2's are obligated by at least some of the provisions in the L1-T1 lease, even though neither one is privy to it.

(I) T2s are required in as much as those provisions ***run with the land***.

(II) S2s are required in that they may not do that which T1 did not do.

(iv) Suppose L1 releases T1, and T2 agrees to assume T1's position with respect to L1 (this would be a case of *novation*). What are the relationships?

(1) L1-T1: no privity

(2) T1-T2: no privity

(3) T2-L1: privity of contract, privity of estate

(v) Suppose L1 leases to T1 who transfers the property to T2 who transfers the property to T3. T3 defaults. Who may L1 go after?

(1) Can go after T1 (privity of contract);

(2) T2 for the rent in the period in which L1 was in privity of estate with T2; or

(3) T3 (privity of estate).

5.7.4 Landlord's Rights

(a) Restrictions of Transfers by Landlords

(i) Provisions in which a landlord restricts transfers of the property are generally disfavored by the courts.

(ii) For the landlord to make a restriction, it must be explicit.

(iii) Courts will read such a restriction narrowly. For example, a *restriction on assignments does not restrict subleases*, unless the broad term "transfers" is used.

(iv) If there is such a provision, but a tenant nonetheless assigns or subleases the property, courts treat the landlord's acceptance of rent from the transferee as a waiver of the provision.

(b) When the landlord makes a restriction, he may limit who his tenant transfers his lease to.

(i) When there is a clause requiring the landlord's approval before the tenant subleases or assigns the property, the landlord's approval to the first transfer ***does not mean that he waives his right to disapprove future transfers***.

(ii) According to the ***Rule in Dumpor's Case***, however, once the landlord approves one transfer, he has *waived his right to disapprove others*.

(iii) However, when the lease ***makes it clear*** that the landlord has the right to approve multiple transfers, the landlord retains the right, even after the first approval. *Childs v. Warner Brothers Southern Theatres* (N.C. 1931).

(c) The landlord ***may act unreasonably*** (for any reason or for no reason at all) in deciding who his tenant may transfer the property to.

(i) *See 21 Merchants Row Corp. v. Merchants Row, Inc.* (Mass. 1992), where the defendant landlord Merchants Row, Inc. had a lease with the plaintiff lessee Merchants

Row, Corp. that prevented the lessee from assigning the lease without the defendant's consent. The plaintiff wanted to sell the business, but required the defendant's approval of the assignee. The plaintiff found an assignee that the defendant approved, but that assignee needed the plaintiff to approve an assignment to a bank that was going to finance the purchase. The defendant refused to grant it, since all the terms of the assignment would favor the bank. The plaintiff sued the defendant for breaching the contract in not allowing the assignment. Held: the court will not imply a reasonableness restriction on the defendant's right to reject potential assignees. Judgment for the defendant.

## 6 Easements

### 6.1 Distinguishing Easements, Profits à Prendre, and Licenses

#### 6.1.1 Easements

(a) An easement is the right to use part of land owned by another for a special purpose.

(b) There are two tenements created by an easement:

(i) The ***dominant tenement*** refers to the estate and the tenant using the easement.

(ii) The ***servient tenement*** refers to the estate and tenant burdened by the easement.

(c) Easements may be positive or negative.

(i) In a ***positive easement***, the grantee may use the property in a certain way.

(ii) In a ***negative easement***, the grantor must *refrain* from using the property in a certain way (*e.g.*, from building a wall that blocks an ocean view from the grantee's land).

(d) Easements can be classified based on how they are *created:*

(i) ***Express easements*** are created and conveyed by volition in a deed;

(ii) ***Implied easements*** are created by legal implication. There are two kinds:

(1) Easements implied (by law) *by necessity* (*e.g.*, the grantee needs the easement in order to enter and exit his land);

(2) Easements implied (by law) *by prior use* (*e.g.*, the grantee has always used the land in a certain way).

(iii) ***Prescriptive easements*** are created by continual use of the property without the plaintiff's protest (analogue to adverse possession).

(e) Easements Appurtenant and Easements In Gross

(i) ***Easements appurtenant*** benefit the grantee's land.

(1) They may thus make the grantee's land more valuable.

(2) When there is an easement appurtenant, there are ***both*** *dominant* and *servient tenements*.

(3) Easements appurtenant transfer with the title, whether or not the transferor of the servient tenant mentions its existence to the transferee.

(4) The creation of easements appurtenant does not require common law words of inheritance. *Mitchell v. Castellaw* (Tex. 1952).

(ii) ***Easements in gross*** do not benefit the grantee's land.

(1) Example: a utility company's right to enter the servient estate for cable work. Although this easement benefits the company, it does not benefit the company's land.

(2) There is a servient estate, but there is no *dominant estate*.

(3) Easements in gross do not necessarily transfer with the title.

6.1.2 *Profits à Prendre*

(a) A *profit à prendre* is an easement that grants the right to enter and remove timber, minerals, oil, gas, game, and other substances from another's land.

(b) Virtually all of the law that governs profits à prendre is the same as that governing easements.

6.1.3 Licenses

(a) A license is a right to use another's property that is terminable at the will of the owner of the land.

(i) Example: admission tickets to a racetrack.

(b) However, the revocation of a license could lead to a cause of action for damages.

(i) *See Marrone v. Washington Jockey Club* (U.S. 1913), where, although the plaintiff Marrone purchased tickets to a racetrack, he was denied entry. Held: the defendant had the full right to deny the entry, since the plaintiff's ticket represented only a license. The plaintiff may, however, sue for breach of contract.

(c) A license can only be created by a contract. Since the Statute of Frauds does not apply, the contract may be oral, as long as it can be *proven*.

**Summary Chart of Easements and Other Interests:**

| ***Name of Interest*** | ***Lease*** | ***Easement (and most profits à prendre)*** | ***License*** |
|---|---|---|---|
| *How Created* | By contract and conveyance. | Expressly by deed; also by implication or prescription. | By contract only (written or oral). |
| *Right / Interest Possessed* | Exclusive possession (the owner retains the right to enter in some circumstances). | Right to use (not to possess). | Right to use (not to possess). |
| *Nature of Right / Interest* | Estate in land. | Interest in land (but not an estate). | Mere permission. |
| *Application of Statute of Frauds* | Statute of Frauds applies. | Statute of Frauds applies (no parole easements). | Statute of Frauds does not apply. |
| *Revocable?* | Irrevocable. | Irrevocable (but it may be terminated). | Freely revocable. |

## 6.2 Express Creation of Easements

### 6.2.1 The Two Ways that Easements May Be Expressly Created

(a) ***Express creation by grant**:* since easements are property interests, they must comply with the requirements of deeds (a delivered writing that contains the names of the parties, a granting clause, a legal description of the property; and a signature), unless they are for less than one year.

(b) ***Express creation by reservation**:* these are created when a grantor reserves an easement interest in the deed of a land conveyance (typically, in the *redendum* clause).

(i) Under the common law and the American ***majority approach***, easements for third parties could not be reserved.

(ii) However, under a growing **minority approach**, they could be reserved in title transfers. *Willard v. First Church of Christ, Scientist, Pacifica* (Cal. 1972).

### 6.2.2 The Language Used

(a) The language "right of way" or "right to use land" conveys no more than an easement.

(b) However, coupled with intent, these words may create a fee simple.

(i) *See Urbaitis v. Commonwealth Edison* (Ill. 1991), where the plaintiffs sued to quiet title on property possessed by the defendant. The plaintiffs argued that the transfer was only for an easement good for use *as long as the defendant used it as a "right of way,"* and since that use had ended, the plaintiff was entitled to the property. Held: "right of way" was the language used *merely to reference the land*, not to describe the interest created. The language "*convey and warrant*" indicates the parties' *intent to create a fee simple*. Therefore, the defendant has a right to continued possession, even though the property is no longer used as a right of way.

(c) Such language does not, however, create a lease that entitles the holder to possession.

(i) *See Baseball Publishing Co. v. Bruton*, where the defendant entered into a contract to allow the plaintiff Baseball Publishing Co. to *use the defendant's wall for advertising*. The defendant never cashed any of the plaintiff's checks, repudiated the contract, and eventually took down the plaintiff's posters. The plaintiff sued for SP. Held: the trial court erred in declaring this contract to be a license and at the same time allowing for SP, since, *under a license, revocation is always permitted*. To enforce SP would be to limit that right. However, in this case, SP is appropriate because the instrument created was an *easement* that granted the plaintiff the *exclusive right to use the defendant's wall*. The plaintiff had an *irrevocable easement*. Judgment for the plaintiff affirmed.

(ii) *N.B.*: the court took the holding to where it wanted it, even though the facts of the case were inconsistent with that holding. ***Easements are generally created by deed***, but here, there was no deed. This interest was more likely a ***revocable license***.

6.2.3 The Interpretation of the Deed

(a) According to the ***rule of reason***, when the deed for an easement is silent on a question, a court, in interpreting the deed, may import *reasonable terms*.

(b) *See Sakansky v. Wein* (N.H. 1933), where the court refused to allow the defendant to force the plaintiff to accept a new easement in place of his old one, even though doing so would not inconvenience the plaintiff, since *the plaintiff's deed clearly laid out where the easement would be located*. However, because the height of the plaintiff's easement was not laid out, the defendant was permitted to build over the easement, leaving reasonable clearance for vehicles.

## 6.3 Implied Easements by Necessity and Prior Use

6.3.1 Introduction

(a) An implied easement is a property right that is in its essentials an easement.

(b) It may be created by necessity, by prior use, or by he creation of an irrevocable license.

6.3.2 Implied Easements by Necessity

(a) The elements of an implied easement by necessity are as follow:

(i) The ***prior common ownership*** of two parcels, which are divided when one (usually the dominant estate) is sold; and

(ii) The ***necessity*** that results when the dominant estate becomes landlocked as a result of the severance and sale (if the only ingress and egress is a revocable license, it is considered landlocked).

(b) Implied easements by necessity are created at the time of the conveyance that leads to their being landlocked.

(i) Even if at that time, the dominant tenant has other means of ingress and egress (such as a license), he still has the right to use the implied easement.

(ii) Implied easements by necessity ***may lie dormant*** for many years and only be exercised at the time ***when the need arises*** (*e.g.*, when a license that had been in use is revoked).

(1) *See Finn v. Williams* (Ill. 1941), where the plaintiff Finn received a land grant from several grantors, including the defendant. At the time of the grant, the plaintiff's only means of ingress and egress was through a license that was later revoked. The plaintiff sued for a judgment declaring the plaintiff's implied easement by necessity over the defendant's land in order to get to a public roadway. Held: an easement by necessity is created *at the time a conveyance depriving a parcel from ingress and egress is made*. Here, one was *created when the conveyance of land having no ingress and egress was made*. It lay dormant until actual necessity arose.

6.3.3 Implied Easements by Prior Use

(a) An implied easement by prior use is an easement that comes into being when an owner of two parcels of land uses one of them, the servient estate, to benefit the other in such a way that when he sells one of them, the purchaser can *reasonably expect* that the servient estate will continue to be used in a way that is consistent with its prior use.

(b) An implied easement by prior use is formed when the following elements are met:

(i) The ***prior common ownership*** of two parcels, which are divided when one is sold (this same element is required in implied easements by necessity);

(ii) A ***reasonable, not strict, necessity*** of continued use. The alternatives to the easement must either be impractical or dangerous (a higher standard is required for grantors than for grantees).

(iii) The ***prior use*** must be continuous, open and permanent.

(c) Thus, even when the dominant tenant's use of the servient estate is *not strictly necessary*, he may be entitled to an implied easement by prior use.

(i) *See Granite Properties Limited Partnership v. Manns*, where the plaintiff Granite Properties Limited Partnership sold a parcel to the defendant, but continued using two driveways sold to the defendant, in order to access the plaintiff's apartment complex and shopping center. The plaintiff sued to enjoin interference with the purported easement. Held: the plaintiff was the common owner of the two parcels before the sale and he used the servient estate continuously, openly and permanently before the transfer. Since an alternate means of accessing to the apartment building and shopping center was dangerous or impractical, an implied easement for prior use is recognized.

6.3.4 Creation by Irrevocable License

(a) An implied easement may also be created through an ***irrevocable license***, which is created by estoppel when a licensee spends large sums of money in reliance on a license.

(b) *See Stoner v. Zucker* (Cal. 1906), where the defendant spent more than $7,000 in constructing a ditch in reliance on the plaintiff's license. The plaintiff revoked the license and sued for an injunction. Held: where a licensee expends large sums of money or labor in reliance on a license, estoppel applies and the licensor may not revoke the license; an *irrevocable license* is created.

## 6.4 Prescriptive Easements

6.4.1 In addition to the express and implied creation of easements, easements may be created by prescription (adverse possession).

6.4.2 An easement is formed by prescription when it is held over the statutory period in an open, continuous, exclusive, adverse, notorious way.

(a) Open

(i) Any use that is consistent with the nature of the property is ***presumed to be open***, as long as it is not concealed and the owner would be able to discover it through inspection.

(ii) This requirement is therefore different from that of adverse possession of realty and personalty.

(b) Continuous

(i) The use need not be *strictly* continuous, but must be continuous in a way that is consistent with the user's requirements.

(1) Example: a path across a servient land owner's property used every summer to tow out a boat would be considered "continuous."

(ii) It is the same requirement as that for the adverse possession of *realty*.

(c) Exclusive

(i) Possession need not be *strictly* exclusive.

(ii) The TO may share possession with the owner, as long as he does not interfere with the adverse use.

(iii) This requirement is thus different from that of the adverse possession of personalty and realty.

(d) Adverse

(i) Introduction

(1) In most states, the servient tenant has the burden of rebutting the presumption that *the dominant tenant's use of the land was adverse* (in adverse states) or that it was *with the servient tenant's passive consent* (in acquiescence states).

(2) In a few states, no presumptions are applied.

(3) This requirement is thus different from that of the adverse possession of personalty and realty.

(ii) Adverse Approach States

(1) In adverse approach states, the use of the easement must be *hostile to the TO's use and enjoyment* of the property.

(2) The possessor must claim that and act like he has title, and that claim must be adverse to the TO's rights.

(3) The general presumption that the use of the land is adverse may be overcome by showing that the use was with either:

(aa) The express ***approval*** of the TO (*e.g.*, as in a license); or

(bb) There was ***no interference*** with the servient tenant's use.

(4) *See Beebe v. DeMarco* (Or. App. 1998), where the court held that the adverse element was met since (i) an open and notorious use during more than ten years is presumed to be adverse and (ii) the defendant failed to rebut this presumption by showing that either he granted the plaintiff Beebe's express permission to use his land; or the plaintiff's use of the land did not interfere with his use of it. Judgment for the plaintiff affirmed.

(iii) Acquiescence Approach States

(1) In acquiescence approach states, adversity is established through the servient tenant's passive consent.

(2) A general presumption that the dominant tenant has an easement inherited from sometime in the past is made (Lost Grant Theory).

(3) Exceptions to this presumption:

(aa) When the servient tenant opens up access to his property allowing others to use it in a way that does not interfere with his own use

(I) Example: the servient tenant opens up to the dominant tenant use of the servient tenant's driveway out of kindness.

(II) The presumption of adversity does not arise; the dominant tenant would have the burden of proving that his use was adverse to that of the servient tenant.

(bb) When the servient tenant allows use by a neighbor, a special relationship is established.

(I) The presumption is that the use was with the servient landowner's permission.

(II) No presumption of adversity arises; the burden of proving that the use was adverse shifts to the dominant landowner.

(4) The presumption of passive consent in acquiescence states is rebutted by the TO's showing of one of the following:

(aa) ***Affirmative consent***, in which case the dominant tenant is said to have had a license; or

(bb) ***Express protest***, where the servient tenant sends a letter or otherwise communicates his opposition to the dominant tenant's use of the property.

(iv) The No Presumption States

(1) A few states, such as California, have abolished the use of presumptions.

(2) These states treat adversity as an *issue of fact* to which presumptions are not applied.

(e) Notorious

(i) This is virtually identical to the open element: the use must be sufficient in putting the servient land owner on notice that the adverse possessor is using and claiming an easement on the servient estate.

**Summary chart of adverse possession and prescriptive easements**

| ***Element*** | ***Adverse Possession of Realty*** | ***Prescriptive Easements*** |
|---|---|---|
| *Open* | The use must be consistent with the normal use of the property and must be enough to put the owner on notice. | Any use consistent with the nature of the property is ***presumed to be open***, as long as an owner would be able to discover it. |
| *Continuous* | ***Need not be strictly continuous***, as long as use is consistent with nature of the property. | ***Need not be strictly continuous***, as long as use is consistent with the nature of the property. |
| *Exclusive* | TO must not share in the possession of the land with the adverse possessor. | ***Need not be strictly exclusive***; owner may share the land, as long as he does not interfere with the adverse use. |
| *Adverse* | - In ***objective approach*** states: an exclusive claim of right is required;<br>- In ***subjective approach*** states: an exclusive claim of right plus good faith is required.<br>- In ***short term statute states***: possession under color of title and the | Use of easement is ***presumed to be adverse*** and presumption must be rebutted by the owner of the burdened land. |

| | payment of taxes is required. | |
|---|---|---|
| *Notorious* | *See* the open element. | *See* the open element. |

**6.5 Scope**

6.5.1 The scope of an easement is limited by the nature of the easement and, in the case of an express easement, by the language of the deed defining it.

6.5.2 The following rules apply:

(a) Express Easements

(i) When the use of an express easement is defined in a deed, the easement holder may only use the easement according to what is stated therein.

(ii) If the use of the easement exceeds that scope, the servient tenant may obtain injunctive relief against the activities of the dominant tenant.

(iii) When the use is not defined in the deed or is unclearly defined therein, the easement is subject to growth over time.

(b) Implied Easements (by Necessity and Prior Use)

(i) The use of implied easements may change over time, according to the circumstances.

(ii) For example, if originally, an easement was used as a right of way to and from a farm, and the farm later grew, requiring greater traffic over the easement, the dominant tenant would acquire the right to the new, increased uses of the servient estate.

(c) Prescriptive Easements

(i) The holder of a prescriptive easement may only benefit from uses of the easement that gave way to the easement at its origin.

6.5.3 Where the easement is used to benefit a dominant estate, *it may not be used to benefit extensions, expansions, or annexations* of that estate.

(a) *S.S. Kresge Co. v. Winkelman Realty Co.* (Wis. 1952), where the defendant used a prescriptive easement over the plaintiff S.S. Kresge's lot to get deliveries to lot 3. The easement was later expanded to benefit lots 2 and 4 as well. The plaintiff complained over the increased traffic over its property and sued to quiet title and restrict use to the first parcel. Held: an easement holder may not use an easement to benefit non-dominant property, unless the use puts no extra burden on the servient estate. Here, this exception is not met: the burden is greater. Judgment for the plaintiff affirmed.

***6.6* Transfer of Easements**

6.6.1 Easements Appurtenant

(a) The burden and benefit of easements appurtenant pass automatically to subsequent owners of the dominant (benefited) estate.

6.6.2 Easements in Gross

(a) The burden of an easement in gross passes automatically with the transfer of the servient estate.

(b) The benefit in *easements for personal benefit* is presumed not transferable, absent clear evidence to the contrary. The benefit in *easements for commercial purposes* is presumed transferable, absent clear evidence to contrary. Finally, *profits in gross* are freely alienable, absent evidence to contrary.

## 6.7 The Termination of Easements

6.7.1 An easement may be terminated in any of the following ways:

(a) Natural Expiration

(i) An easement expires when it is for a specific use and it is *impossible for that use to continue*.

(ii) Example: an easement to mine coal expires if the coal is exhausted.

(b) Release

(i) The owner of an easement may release the servient tenant from it when both parties agree.

(ii) This is typically done through a deed granting the easement back to the servient tenant.

(c) Estoppel

(i) An easement is terminated by estoppel when the following elements are met:

(1) The servient tenant *detrimentally relies* on the dominant tenant's nonuse; and

(2) There is *no convenient way* for the servient tenant to know that the easement was not terminated and he must be ignorant if it was not terminated.

(d) Abandonment

(i) An easement is terminated by abandonment when it is: (i) no longer used; and (ii) the holder of the easement has the intent to abandon it.

(ii) The servient tenant has the burden of proving both elements.

(iii) Mere disuse without the intent to abandon does not bring about the termination of the easement.

(1) *See Lindsey v. Clark* (Va. 1952), where the plaintiff Lindsey sought an injunction preventing the defendant from using an easement over the plaintiff's land, claiming that the defendant had abandoned it because of its disuse. In reality, the defendant was ignorant of the location of the easement on the southern end of the plaintiff's property, and continued to use land to the north.

Held: because the defendant's disuse of the easement was not accompanied by the intent to abandon, the easement was not terminated.

(e) Merger

(i) An easement terminates when the dominant and servient estates come under the control of the same tenant.

(f) *Bona Fide* Purchase

(i) When a BFP purchases an estate and the BFP has no actual or visual notice of an unrecorded easement, the easement terminates.

(g) Destruction of the Servient Estate

(i) When the servient estate is a building or some other destructible property, the easement ends if the property is destroyed.

(h) Prescription

(i) Just as easements may be created by prescription, so too may they be terminated.

## 7 Real Covenants and Equitable Servitudes

### 7.1 Covenants Running with the Land at Law

7.1.1 In general terms, a real covenant (RC) is a promise relating to land use that runs with the land at law and is enforceable at law between the original covenanting parties as a contract.

7.1.2 The four elements of RC's (assuming that they are binding between the original covenanters) are as follow:

(a) A Writing

(i) Although covenants need not be recorded in a deed, they must be in a writing.

(ii) The writing is required for the Statute of Frauds.

(b) Intent

(i) The original parties must intend for the promise to run with the land.

(ii) Usually, this intent is expressed in the writing that conveys the covenant (*e.g.*, "this covenant shall run with the land…").

(iii) The intent may also be inferred from the circumstances.

(c) Touch and Concern the Land

(i) The RC must "touch and concern the land." That is to say, it must affect the use, enjoyment, or value of the land.

(ii) A covenant to supply water during a portion of the year would not qualify.

(1) *See Eagle Enterprises, Inc. v. Gross* (N.Y. 1976), where the court held that a covenant to supply water failed the *Neponsit Property Owners' Association* test (see *infra.*) because: (i) a covenant does not touch and concern the land when it only applies for half of the year; and (ii) the land would have been able to supply its own water, and its legal rights were thus not affected, since the land would have been no different without the covenant in the deed.

(d) Privity of Estate

(i) The Three Privities

(1) Horizontal Privity

(aa) Horizontal privity is between the original parties (the covenantor and the covenantee).

(bb) Horizontal privity is created when the covenant is in the deed conveying land between covenanting parties.

(2) Mutual Privity

(aa) Mutual privity exists between the covenantee and the party plaintiff.

(bb) When a covenantor and covenantee have a mutual and continuing interest in same land that is subject of covenant.

(cc) There must be mutual interest in burdened land.

(dd) The burdened land is the land of the covenantor who is being sued.

(ee) The mutual and continuing interest is generally an easement.

(I) However, it can also be a leasehold, though this leads to certain complications.

(II) It may not be a license, because a license is not an interest, but rather, an unenforceable right.

(III) Note: for ownership, possession, or the right to use to be a legal interest, there should be a ***written deed***.

(3) Vertical Privity

(aa) Vertical privity refers to the relationship between one of original covenanting parties with a subsequent owner.

(ii) The Three Approaches to Privity

(1) Under the ***traditional approach*** to privity, both *horizontal privity* between the original covenanting parties and *vertical privity* between an original party and any successor in interest are required.

(2) Under the ***minority approach*** (adopted in Massachusetts), both *mutual privity* between the original covenanting parties and *vertical privity* between an original party and any successor in interest are required.

(3) Under the ***modern approach***, only vertical privity is required.

(aa) *See Gallagher v. Bell* (Md. 1986), where the court held that there was privity in a 1961 agreement between the plaintiffs (the Bells) and the defendants in a covenant for sharing costs for constructing a road, even though at the time that it was made, there was no property interest transfer (and thus no horizontal privity). Furthermore, there was no mutual privity, since it would be necessary that the subject of the covenant also be of mutual and continuing interest, which did not exist in the covenant of the shared costs of a road. Nevertheless, although ***there was only vertical privity***, this was sufficient.

7.1.3 Transfers and Liability

(a) When a covenant runs with the land, the original covenanting party is not liable for its breach when he transfers the property to another party; rather, the subsequent purchaser is liable.

(b) This is true even when the subsequent party successfully bargains for indemnity against the obligation to follow the covenant at the time that he purchased the land.

(i) *See Gallagher v. Bell* (Md. 1986), where the plaintiffs (the Bells) and the defendants entered into a covenant to split the costs of a road to be built between the defendant's property and a public way. Camalier bought property from the defendants and insisted on an indemnity agreement. When she refused to contribute to the costs of the road, the plaintiffs sued the defendants. Held: because this covenant runs with the land, the defendants are absolved of liability for breach by the current owner.

(c) The subsequent party is thus bound by covenants running with the land whenever he is in vertical privity with the original covenanting party.

(i) *See Neponsit Property Owners' Association v. Emigrant Industrial Savings Bank* (N.Y. 1938), where Neponsit Realty Co., the plaintiff's assignor, conveyed lots with a RC requiring a yearly maintenance fee to be paid to the plaintiff. The defendant subsequently purchased land, but ***refused to pay the maintenance fee***, claiming that the covenant was not binding. The plaintiff sued to recover the fees. Held: there is a valid real covenant that runs with the land. There is vertical privity, even though the land was never transferred to the plaintiff by the Neponsit Realty Co. This is because the plaintiff was an agent of the original owners. Thus, because the plaintiff represents all of the owners, vertical privity was established. Judgment for the plaintiff is affirmed, and the defendant is required to pay the fees in accordance with the covenant.

## 7.2 Equitable Servitudes

7.2.1 Introduction

(a) Equitable servitudes (ES) are covenants restricting the use of land.

(b) They run with the land at equity and thus offer remedies at equity (*e.g.*, injunctions).

(c) The major difference between a RC and an ES is that while the former has remedies at law (monetary damages), the former has remedies at equity (injunctions).

7.2.2 The elements of ES's are as follow:

(a) Intent

(i) The original parties must *intend* that the promise run with the land.

(ii) This intent need not be expressed by common law words of inheritance; it may be inferred from the circumstances.

(b) Writing

(i) An original deed, or any other writing (*e.g.*, brochures) is required.

(ii) In the majority of states, no writing required when there is a common scheme of development (CSD, see *infra.*).

(c) Touch and Concern

(i) The covenant must affect:

(1) The *use or enjoyment* of both the benefited and the burdened land; and/or

(2) The *value* of both the benefited and the burdened land.

(ii) However, if there is a CSD, this rule only needs to be true of the burdened land (there need not be a benefited land within the strict meaning of the rule when a CSD exists).

(d) Privity

(i) As with RC's, only vertical privity is required.

(ii) For there to be vertical privity, the party to whom the property was transferred must be in the *same chain of title* as the original covenanting party.

(iii) *N.B.*: there need not be a transfer of the entire property interest.

(1) Mere ***possession*** is sufficient (*i.e.*, a fee owner who transfers a leasehold to another party would be in vertical privity with that party).

(2) Even if a holder of a fee interest in all of the land ***transferred only a portion*** thereof, there would still be vertical privity for the purpose of ES's.

(e) Notice

(i) A latter purchaser is only bound by an ES if there is:

(1) *Actual notice*;

(2) *Constructive notice*, where a possessor would be expected to run a title search and will be bound by any knowledge he might have; or

(3) *Inquiry notice* (permitted in some jurisdictions), where notice attributed to a person when the information available to him would cause a *reasonable prudent person* to investigate further into the matter (*e.g.*, a purchaser sees a row of homes all with the same design and shape).

(f) Common Scheme of Development

(i) The elements of a common scheme of development (CSD) are as follow:

(1) The plaintiff and the defendant must own lots within the *same scheme*; and

(2) There must be *substantial similarities* in the deeds of the properties in the scheme (exact uniformity is not required).

(ii) Only in Virginia is a CSD an affirmative element of ES's. *See, e.g., Sloan v. Johnson* (Va. 1997).

7.2.3 When these elements are met, both affirmative as well as negative covenants may run at equity. *See, e.g., Tulk v. Moxhay* (Ct. Chan. 1848).

7.2.4 The Touch and Concern Requirement

(a) As with RC's, the touch and concern element in ES's requires that the ***covenant affect the value, use, or enjoyment*** of both the benefited and the burdened land.

(b) Note the similarity between RC's, ES's, and easements appurtenant: in all of these categories, there must be benefited land and burdened land, which, in the case of easements, correspond to the dominant estate and the servient estate, respectively.

(i) *See London County Council v. Allen* (Eng. Ct. App. 1914), where the plaintiff London County Council was unable to enforce an ES against the defendant because the plaintiff had no benefited land. The plaintiff would only have been able to enforce the covenant with the defendant through customary contract law, since the covenant that the plaintiff made with the defendant was a valid contract. Thus, although the covenant was written, with the intent to run with the land, and though there was privity, an ES could not be recognized.

(c) The touch and concern element is met when a covenant establishes an anti-competition policy that limits the kinds of businesses that may be hosted on the land.

(i) *See Whitinsville Plaza, Inc. v. Kotseas* (Mass. 1979), where an anti-competition policy was considered to run with the land because (i) the burdened land's value was affected by the restriction; and (ii) the value of the benefited shopping center increased (the shopping center businesses more harmoniously worked together and more profits were generated).

7.2.5 Implied Equitable Servitudes Benefiting Third Parties

(a) A court may imply an ES even if all of the ES elements are not strictly met, when there is a CSD.

(b) The elements of a CSD are as follow:

(i) Both the plaintiff and the defendant must own lots within a common scheme;

(ii) The scheme must be apparent from the outset (*i.e.*, when sale of the lots begins);

(iii) There must be *substantial uniformity* between the restrictions in the deeds of the various lots in the scheme (*exact* uniformity not required).

(c) Majority View

(i) If there is a common scheme of development, ***it is not required that there be a writing or benefited land***.

(ii) The benefited land is implied through the common scheme of development.

(iii) Thus, even when the writing and benefited land (touch and concern) elements are not met, an ES may be formed through a showing of a CSD.

(1) *See Sanborn v. McLean* (Mich. 1925), where an ES is enforced, even though it is not recorded in the defendant McLean's chain of title, because the CSD put the defendant on inquiry notice that only residential uses of the property were permitted and the CSD did away with the writing requirement and the requirement that land be benefited (since the other properties were impliedly benefited through the CSD). The defendant was therefore enjoined from constructing a gas station.

(d) Minority View

(i) Under the minority view (adopted in Massachusetts), ***a writing is always required***, even if there is a common scheme of development.

(ii) Under this view, all of the elements of ESs must be met. When a covenant is not written, or when it does not touch and concern, an ES will not be recognized. *See Sprague v. Kimball* (Mass. 1913).

(iii) However, even if the strict requirements of touch and concern are not met (*e.g.*, there may be land by a covenant, but the covenant may not be reciprocal and there may be no benefited land), a court may imply the benefit.

(1) *See Snow v. Van Dam* (Mass. 1935), where a covenant restricting land to residential use was created, but there was no benefited land, since it was the

last piece of land to acquire such a covenant. However, because of the CSD, the court implied that the other lands would be benefited by the restriction, and the touch and concern element was met.

### *7.3* Construction of Covenants

7.3.1 In construing covenants, some states will only enforce what is ***expressly written***.

7.3.2 Other states, however, will also consider what the actual restrictions ***imply*** (*i.e.*, they consider intent in addition to the writing).

(a) *See Joslin v. Pine River Development Corp.* (N.H. 1976), where the plaintiffs sued to enjoin the defendant Pine River Development Corp. from using one of its shorefront lots as a common beach area for residents of all of its 161 non-shore lots. Held: it is clear from all relevant circumstances that the defendant's shorefront lot was not intended to serve as a common recreational area, even though this restriction is not expressly in writing. Injunction affirmed.

(b) *N.B.*: there are two inquires required when analyzing whether a covenant has been violated: (i) are all of the required elements of the covenant met; and (ii) has the covenant been violated? For the latter inquiry, both the writing as well as the parties' intent must be analyzed.

### *7.4* Modifications

7.4.1 Parties may modify covenants and servitudes by bringing all of the parties together to create a new agreements superseding previous agreements.

7.4.2 There may be provisions in a covenant that provide for how modifications may be made.

7.4.3 When a developer reserves the right to unilaterally modify a covenant, courts may find the covenant not to run with the land.

(a) *See Suttle v. Bailey* (N.M. 1961), where the plaintiff Suttle sued to enforce a covenant on the defendant when, in the covenant, the grantor retained the right to modify the restriction, and did in fact modify it by excepting the defendant from a requirement. Held: because the grantor retained the right to modify the restriction, it cannot be said to run with the land, since it does not touch and concern the land. Rather, ***it is a personal benefit*** that the plaintiffs may not enforce. Judgment for the plaintiff reversed.

(b) *N.B.*: not all courts have followed this approach. Some consider all lots to be benefited when the grantor acts reasonably.

7.4.4 When provisions in a covenant allow for modifications by an ***objective standard*** or a ***subjective standard plus good faith*** (as opposed to by the grantor's arbitrarily will), the covenant may be enforced.

(a) *See Rhue v. Cheyenne Homes, Inc.* (Colo. 1969), where the defendant Rhue tried to move an old-style Spanish home into a neighborhood having a covenant requiring plans for all homes to first be approved by a committee. The plaintiff sued to enjoin the defendant from moving into the neighborhood. The defendant argued that because the committee was not guided by any specific, written guidelines, its decisions were arbitrary and the restriction did not run with the land. Held: because the committee was governed by the general intent of protecting the value of the properties, the covenant is upheld, even though the criteria used were not objective.

### *7.5* Termination

7.5.1 Real covenants and equitable servitudes may be terminated in any of the following manners:

(a) When a promisee ***releases*** the promisor from a covenant or servitude through a written release;

(b) Through ***merger***, when a fee simple interest comes into the hands of a single owner;

(c) Through ***expiration***, in the case of a covenant or servitude that exists for a specific purpose, when that purpose is ended;

(d) By ***condemnation***, when the government acquires property by eminent domain (the government must pay damages to the owner of the benefited land that equal the difference of the land with and without the covenant or servitude);

(e) When a later ***BFP*** buys property without notice of the property's covenants, when there is no practical way for him to find out about the covenant;

(f) By ***legislation***;

(g) Through ***estoppel*** in changed conditions.

(i) When changed circumstances might discharge a party from compliance with an otherwise valid covenant, a court will ***balance the effects*** of not enforcing the covenant on both the burdened as well as benefited land.

(ii) *See Cowling v. Colligan* (Tex. 1958), where a covenant on the defendant Colligan's land restricted the land use to residential purposes. However, when surrounding land started to become developed and a country road became a thoroughfare, the defendant began to develop his land for commercial purposes, in violation of the covenant. The plaintiffs sued to enforce the covenant. Held: the equity of not enforcing the covenant outweighed the equity of enforcing it, since allowing the development of the property would cause the value to rise fourfold. Judgment for the defendant affirmed.

## 8 Estates in Land and Future Interests

### 8.1 Introduction to Estates in Land

8.1.1 Definitions

(a) An estate is the amount and nature of a person's present interest in land or other property.

(b) A future interest is a property interest where the possession and use of land is aimed at some future time.

8.1.2 The Five Present, Possessory Estates

(a) Fee Simple Absolute

(i) A fee simple absolute, or "fee simple" (FS), confers full title and is represented by the formula: "O → A and his heirs," where "O" represents the original owner, and "A" represents the party to whom the estate is transferred.

(ii) The grantee is entitled to possess and use the property throughout his life and his heirs may inherit it.

(1) To be fully inheritable, the word "heir" must be included in the deed.

(2) *See Cole v. Steinlauf* (Conn. 1957), where a court ruled that the formula "O → A and his assigns forever" was insufficient.

(iii) The fee simple has the following characteristics:

(1) It is *alienable*, since the grantee may sell it;

(2) It is *devisable*, since the grantee may transfer it to his non-heirs through a will;

(3) As mentioned, it is *inheritable;* and

(4) It has *no expiration;* even after direct line dies out, there is always an heir.

(b) Fee Simple Determinable

(i) A fee simple determinable (FSD), or "determinable fee," is represented by the formula "O → A and his heirs if ..."

(ii) It is essentially a fee simple, but with a condition, the breach of which automatically transfers the fee back to the grantor.

(iii) It is *self-executing*; the statute of limitations begins once the grantee breaches the condition.

(iv) It has the following characteristics:

(1) It is *alienable;*

(2) It is *devisable;*

(3) It is *inheritable;* and

(4) It is *not expirable;* however, since it terminates when the condition is breached, it is said to be "defeasible."

(v) The language must be precise by including, "if," "until," "while," or a comparable equivalent. The word "only" does not suffice.

(1) *See Roberts v. Rhodes* (Kan. 1982), where a deed transferring property to a local school district specified that the land was to be used "only" for school or cemetery purposes. The condition was later breached and the plaintiff, an heir to original owners, claimed he has a reversion through breach of the FSD. The

court held that the necessary language for creating a FSD was deficient; the word "only" did not suffice.

(c) Fee Simple on Condition Subsequent

(i) A fee simple on condition subsequent (FSCS) is characterized by a condition subsequent, the breach of which allows the grantor to go on land and reclaim it.

(ii) It is represented by the formula "O → A and heirs, but if [any particular condition] is not met, O and heirs may reclaim it."

(iii) The statute of limitations starts only when the grantor demands the land and the grantee refuses to surrender it.

(iv) A FSCS is like a FSD, except that unlike a FSD, in which the transfer is automatic when the condition is breached, in a FSCS, the grantor has the option of going on the land and reclaiming the estate (the transfer is not automatic).

(1) Where there is ambiguity and it is not clear if an estate is a FSD or a FSCS, courts will prefer to interpret the estate to be a FSCS, since courts prefer not to allow for the forfeiture of estates.

(2) *See Oldfield v. Stoeco Homes, Inc.*, where plaintiff taxpayer Oldfield sued to have Stoeco give title of land back to his city, since Stoeco breached the condition (filling the marshes within one year) of what the plaintiff argued was a FSD. The court held that the interpretation of the estate should be based on more than just the language; especially when the language is ambiguous, the intent of the parties and extrinsic circumstances may be used to determine the true nature of an estate granted by a deed. Here, given that the defendant and the city agreed to an extension to the fulfilling of the condition, the court ruled that the estate was a FSCS. Since the city did not enter and reclaim the estate, the defendant was able to keep it.

(v) The FSCS has the following characteristics:

(1) It is *alienable;*

(2) It is *devisable;*

(3) It is *inheritable;* and

(4) It is *not expirable;* however, since it terminates when the condition is breached, it is said to be "defeasible."

(d) Fee Tail

(i) A fee tail (FT) is represented by the formula: "O → A and the heirs of his body."

(ii) The grantee is entitled to the property his life.

(iii) A fee tail can be modified so that only the grantee's male heirs or his bodily heirs by his wife, for example, may inherit it.

(iv) The fee tail has the following characteristics:

(1) The property is *not fully alienable*, although the grantee may alienate it in his lifetime;

(2) It is *not devisable*, since the grantee may not pass it on to his non-heirs through a will;

(3) It is *inheritable*, but only to the grantee's bodily heirs; and

(4) The interest *expires* when the grantee's direct line is terminated.

(e) Life Estate

(i) A life estate (LE) is represented by the formula "O → A," "O → A for life," "O → A forever," or "O → A in fee simple absolute."

(1) *N.B.*: "O → A in fee simple absolute" does not create a fee simple interest because it fails to mention the word "heir."

(ii) The grantee is entitled to an estate throughout his life.

(1) A life tenant is obligated to take good care of the present estate for the holder of the future interest.

(2) Otherwise, the future estate holder may sue the life estate holder's estate to recover damages. *Moore v. Phillips* (Kan. 1981).

(iii) The life estate is the default estate at common law.

(iv) It has the following characteristics:

(1) It is *alienable*, but only during the grantee's life;

(aa) If the grantee sells it to B, B inherits a life estate pur autre vie (for the life of the grantee).

(bb) For B, it is inheritable and devisable if B dies before the grantee.

(2) It is *not devisable;*

(3) It is *not inheritable;* and

(4) The interest *expires* when the grantee dies.

**8.2 Introduction to Future Interests**

8.2.1 There are two kinds of future interests: (i) those that revert to the grantor of the estate; and (ii) those that revert to a third party, known as the "remainderman."

8.2.2 The Future Interest of the Grantor

(a) There are five possibilities with respect to the future interests of the grantor of an estate:

(i) If he grants a FS, he reserves ***no future interest*** (the grantee receives full title);

(ii) If he grants a FSD, he reserves the possibility of ***reverter*** (if the condition is breached);

(iii) If he grants a FSCS, he reserves a ***right of entry*** (if the condition is breached).

(iv) If he grants an expirable estate (a FT of LE), he reserves a ***reversion***.

8.2.3 The Future Interest of the Remainderman

(a) Introduction

(i) It is possible to indicate that the reversion of an expirable estate (the FT and LE) revert back not to the original grantor, but rather, to some third party.

(ii) The third party is known as a "remainderman," and he receives a "remainder."

(iii) Under the common law, the reversion of a defeasible estate (FSD or FSCS) could not be transferred to a third party as a remainder. However, later developments in the law made this possible in what is now termed a "fee simple in executory limitation" (*see infra.*).

(b) Two rules are worth highlighting:

(i) The future interest must not cut short the life of the present estate.

(1) For example, "O → A, then to B and his heirs if B is married" would be permitted.

(2) "O → A, but if B marries, then immediately transfer to B and his heirs" would *not* be permitted.

(ii) The future interest must take hold immediately upon the present interest's expiration.

(1) For example, "O → A, then to B and his heirs" would be permitted.

(2) "O → A, then one year after the death of A, to B and his heirs" would *not* be permited.

(c) There are two kinds of interests that the remainderman may receive: the vested remainder and a contingent remainder.

(d) Vested Remainder

(i) In order to receive a vested remainder (VR), the grantee must be born and ascertainable.

(1) *E.g.*, "O → A, then to B."

(2) However, the formula "O → A, then to B's oldest surviving son" would not be permitted, since it is not known who will be B's oldest surviving son at the expiration of A's interest.

(ii) Furthermore, there must be no conditions (besides the expiration of A's estate).

(1) Consider, for example, "O → A, then to B's children," where B has one son (S).

(2) S has a VR in LE subject to open (it is open to members of a class, *all* of B's children, who may enter if they are born before the expiration of the LE).

(3) There are two ways for the class to close:

(aa) A dies, which makes the VR subject to open a FS, and closes the class; or,

(bb) B dies, since B can have no more children who could enter the class.

(iii) Example: O → A, then to B's children who reach 18. If B has two children, S1 (19) and S2 (16), what is the state of the title?

(1) S1 has a VR in LE; S2 has an ***expectancy***.

(e) Contingent Remainder

(i) A contingent remainder (CR) arises when either:

(1) The grantee is not ascertainable; or

(2) There is a condition for the transfer (*e.g.*, "O → A, then to B and heirs if B is married").

(ii) Under the ***destructibility of contingent remainders doctrine***, a CR can be destroyed if it has not vested and any of the following have occurred:

(1) Expiration

(aa) A's estate has expired.

(2) Merger

(aa) The estate has merged.

(bb) Merger will occur if, for example, A sells his expirable estate (FT or LE) to O; O will then own both the present interest and the reversion, which together create a FS. The same will occur if O sells his reversion to A.

(cc) In order for merger to occur, the two interests that are merged together must be consecutive (*e.g.*, if "O → A, then to B, then to C for life," if B sells his LE to O, the LE and O's reversion will not merge into a FS).

(dd) However, in merger, the CR is no longer destroyed when the two consecutive estates are created by the same grant.

(3) Forfeiture

(aa) B forfeits his FT or LE, which means that the expirable estate, rather than expire, prematurely terminates.

(bb) This can occur through B's:

(I) Commission of a felony; or

(II) Refusal of or renunciation of the estate.

**Characteristics of Future Interests**

| | ***Future interest*** | ***Alienable*** | ***Devisable*** | ***Inheritable*** |
|---|---|---|---|---|
| ***Future Interests that Revert to the Grantor*** | Possibility of Reverter | ✓ | ×* | ✓ |
| | Right of Entry | ✓ | ×* | ✓ |
| | Reversion | ✓ | ✓ | ✓ |
| ***Future Interests that Revert to a Remainderman*** | Vested Remainder | ✓ | ✓ | ✓ |
| | Contingent Remainder | × | ✓ | ✓ |

*** This is because the Statute of Wills provided for devise of only estates "in possession, reversion or remainder."**

**8.3 Executory Interests and Fees Simple on Executory Limitation**

8.3.1 Whereas before, strict rules applied to the granting of future interests, today, equity enters the equation.

8.3.2 A new kind of future interest in the transferee was developed: the executory interest.

8.3.3 This is like a remainder, but it can break the rules required of remainders by cutting short the life of the present estate or failing to begin immediately upon the present interest's expiration.

8.3.4 Classes

(a) Shifting Executory Interests

(i) Shifting executory interests cut back the life of the preceding estates.

(ii) They either:

(1) Immediately follow a defeasible fee (FSD, FSCS, FS EL);

(2) Cut short a FS;

(aa) For example, if "O → A and his heirs, but if B marries C, to B and his bodily heirs," B has a shifting EI in FT and O has a FS EL.

(3) Cut short an expirable estate (FT, LE) or VR.

(aa) For example, if "O → A, but if B marries C, to B and his heirs," then B has a shifting executory interest in fee simple (EI FS).

(b) Springing Executory Interests

(i) Springing executory interests do not begin immediately after the preceding estate's expiration.

(ii) They either:

(1) Follow expirable estates (FT, LE) but do not become immediately possessory.

(aa) For example, if "O → A, then one year after A's death, to B and his heirs," then B has a springing EI FS.

(2) Are created by the grantor to take effect in the future, with no other interest given to any other grantee.

(aa) For example, if "O → A and his heirs upon his marriage," then A has a springing EI FS and O has a fee simple on executory limitation (FS EL).

8.3.5 After the Statute of Uses, a VR can become lost in two ways:

(a) Possession of the VR can become lost *after* the grantee has been granted possession (he therefore has a ***VR on executory limitation***).

(b) The remainder can be cut off *before the grantee acquires possession*.

(i) He therefore has a ***VR subject to divestment***.

(ii) For example, if "O → A and his heirs, then to B and heirs, but if A farms land, to C and his heirs," then B has a VR subject to divestment in FS (VR SD FS).

(iii) Distinguishing VR's Subject to Divestment from CR's

(1) If the condition is a condition subsequent, it is a VR SD; if it is a precondition, it is a CR.

(2) Preconditions tend to begin with "if."

(3) Conditions subsequent tend to have the following characteristics:

(aa) The language "but if" is indicated;

(bb) The clause introducing the condition is separated by commas; and

(cc) The condition follows a grant.

(4) If the condition is a condition subsequent, you must decide if the condition can be met before or only after B gets possession.

(aa) If the condition can be met *before* B gets possession, then it is ***subject to divestment***.

(I) For example, if "O → A, then to B and his heirs, but if B gets married, then to C and his heirs,"

(II) B has a VR SD FS.

(bb) If the condition *must happen after* B's possession, then it is on ***executory limitation***.

(I) For example, if "O → A, then to B and his heirs, but if B farms the land, then to C and his heirs."

(II) B has a VR FS EL.

## 8.4 The Rule Against Perpetuities

8.4.1 As earlier mentioned, CR's are destructible through expiration, merger, or forfeiture.

8.4.2 In the early days of EI's, courts were not certain whether they were destructible.

(a) In *Pells v. Brown* (K.B. 1620), the court held that they *were indestructible*.

(b) *Purefoy v. Rogers* (K.B. 1670) held that, in cases where there is ambiguity, a future interest will be construed as an EI, not a CR.

(c) In the *Duke of Norfolk's Case* (Ch. 1682) , the courts eventually decided that EIs are in fact destructible.

8.4.3 The Rule Against Perpetuities

(a) Under the Rule Against Perpetuities (RAP), "no executory interest is good unless it must vest, if ever, within 21 years following the lives in being at the time of the creation of the interest."

(b) In other words, no EI is valid if it is possible that it may vest more than twenty one years after the last "life in being." A "life in being" is any person mentioned in the grant who was living at the time of the grant.

(c) Thus, the rule requires both that the interest vest and that it vest soon enough (within twenty one years of the lives in being at the time of the creation of the interest).

(d) For our purposes, all present interests and future interests are vested, with the exception of only EI's and CR's. The RAP therefore applies only to EI's and CR's.

(e) A CR becomes vested if the condition is fulfilled or if the grantee becomes born or ascertainable. An EI vests by becoming possessory.

(f) Examples:

(i) O → A, then to B and his heirs, but if the well on Blackacre ever runs dry, then to C and his heirs.

(1) B acquires a VR FS.

(2) C does not have a valid EI under the grant because the well may go dry more than twenty one years after the last life in being.

(ii) O → A and the heirs of his body, then if the well on Blackacre runs dry, to B and his heirs.

(1) B has an invalid CR FS, since it is possible that the well run dry twenty one years after the last life in being.

(2) Thus, A has a FT and O has a reversion.

(iii) O → A for life, then if prayer has returned to the schools, to B and his heirs.

(1) A acquires a LE.

(2) B acquires a valid CR FS, since, if the CR were ever to vest, it would have to vest within twenty one years of A's life (since A has a LE).

(3) O has a reversion.

(iv) O → A for life, then if prayer returns to the schools, to B and his heirs.

(1) Under the common law, this scenario would have the same result as above.

(2) However, under the modern law, because of the RAP; B would not acquire a valid CR. Since the condition is within the present tense "*returns*," it is implied that there can be a gap between A's death and the vesting of B's interest. Therefore, B is granted a springing EI. However, because it is possible that prayer return to the schools more than twenty one years after the lives in being, the EI is invalid. B receives nothing.

**8.5 Defeasible Life Estates**

8.5.1 Life Estate Determinable

(a) The following are examples of life estates determinable (LED):

(i) "O → A, as long as the land is farmed."

(1) O has a reversion and a PR, but the PR is "swallowed" by the reversion.

(2) O thus simply has a reversion.

(ii) "O → A, as long as the land is farmed, then to B and heirs."

(1) It is not clear that O wanted to keep the reversion, so it is presumed he did not.

(2) B thus receives the reversion and the PR.

(3) The PR is swallowed by the remainder, giving B a VR FS.

(iii) "O → A, as long as the land is farmed, then to B upon A's death."

(1) A has a LED.

(2) B has a VR.

(3) O has a PR.

8.5.2 Life Estate on Executory Limitation

(a) "O → A, but if the land is farmed, then to B and heirs."

(i) A as a LE EL, since his interest is followed by an EI (it is an EI because it uses "but if" language).

(ii) O keeps the reversion; B gets only a PR.

8.5.3 There are five different scenarios that come out of *defeasible life estates*:

| | Who takes at expiration | Who takes on breach of condition | Name of present estate | Name of future interest |
|---|---|---|---|---|
| (i) O → A as long as A remains unmarried | O | O | LED | Remainder |
| (ii) O → A as long as A remains unmarried, then to B | B | B | LED | VR |
| (iii) O → A, but if A marries, then to B | O | B | LE EL | Shifting EI (B)<br>Rev. FS EL (O) |
| (iv) O → A as long as A remains unmarried, then to B upon A's death | B | O | LED | VR (B)<br>PR (O) |
| (v) O → A, then to B, but if A marries, then to C | B | C | LE EL | VR (B)<br>EI (C)<br>Rev. FS EL (O) |

8.5.4 When the future interest is split, and a grantee takes a PR (EI), then it is a LE EL, or another way of saying it:

(a) The only time when there is a LE EL is when the reversion is split from the EI, and the grantee takes only the EI, or

(b) The only time a defeasible LE is a LE EL is when an EI is formed.

**8.6 Modern Legal Approaches**

8.6.1 Life Estates

(a) Under the common law, "O → A" and "O → A in fee," like all estate transfers that did not include the word "heirs," were presumed to be LE's.

(b) Modern American statutes have changed this, and presume that O meant to transfer as much as he could to his grantees. The fee simple is thus default estate under the modern law.

(i) Thus, "O → A" and "O → A in fee" are seen as fees simple.

(c) The rule for creating LEs is now constructive, whereas earlier, it operated under a system of law. Now, an estate is seen to be a fee simple, unless otherwise indicated.

(i) *See Lewis v. Searles* (Mo. 1970), where the court read an estate that did not mention the words "heirs" as being a FS, since state statute eliminated the required words, and held that absent some evidence or indication showing otherwise (such as the mention of a remainderman), an estate will be read and considered to be a FS.

8.6.2 Fee Tails

(a) Many states have abolished FT's or changed their application.

(b) The California rule is exemplary:

(i) The FT is abolished.

(1) The formula "O → A and his bodily heirs" is equivalent to a FS.

(ii) However, where there is a remainder, the FT operates in a special way.

(1) The formula "O → A and his bodily heirs, then to B and his heirs" = is the equivalent of "O → A and his heirs as long as A dies with a bodily heir, then to B and heirs."

(2) In this case, A acquires a FS EL;

(3) B acquires a shifting EI FS.

(4) O reserves no interest.

8.6.3 Fees Simple Determinable and Fees Simple on Condition Subsequent

(a) These defeasible estates place two new conditions on the PR and right of entry:

(i) Many were given a statute of limitations (typically thirty years), after which the estate could no longer become terminated;

(ii) For the right of entry, there was a limit put upon O from the time that the condition was breached to the time that he could exercise his right of entry.

8.6.4 Inalienable or Undevisable Interests

(a) Interests that were inalienable or not devisable (such as CR's or EI's) became fully alienable and devisable.

(b) However, one still could not pass on more than what he had.

8.6.5 Destructibility of Contingent Remainders

(a) Under the majority approach of the modern law, CR's remain even if preceding estates have expired, merged, or been forfeited before the CRs have vested.

(b) The CR's continue and become possessory when they vest.

(c) Consider, for example, "O → A for life, then to B in fee simple if B marries C," and B is unmarried when A dies.

(i) Under the common law, B's CR terminates and O acquires a reversion.

(ii) Under modern law, however, O acquires has a reversion in FS EL, but B's CR continues to exist. If and when B marries C, B's CR vests, granting B a FS, and terminating O's reversion. B therefore is said to have a springing EI FS.

8.6.6 The Rule Against Perpetuities

(a) The RAP continues to apply to unvested interests (CR's and EI's), just as it did under the common law, by requiring them to vest within twenty one years of the lives in being at the time of the creation of the interest.

# 9 Concurrent Estates

## 9.1 Tenancy in Common

9.1.1 Introduction

(a) A tenancy in common is an estate conveyed to two grantees and to their heirs as co-tenants.

(b) Each co-tenant has a right to possess all of the property and to share in the rents.

(c) However, each co-tenant's share of the property is separate and distinct. Thus, each co-tenant may dispose of his undivided share, by deed or by will.

9.1.2 Creation

(a) Under the modern law, the tenancy in common is the presumed estate.

(b) Therefore, under the formula "O → A and B and their heirs," A and B hold a tenancy in common (under the common law, they held a JT).

9.1.3 Right of Survivorship

(a) Unlike joint tenancies, the tenancy in common does not carry a ***right of survivorship***; a co-tenant's share passes on to his devisees and heirs at his death, *not to his co-tenant(s)*.

(b) The tenancy in common, unlike joint tenancies, is thus both devisable and inheritable.

9.1.4 A tenancy in common is terminated when either of the following occur:

(a) The interests ***merge*** in one person; or

(b) One of the joint tenants files for a ***partition***, where the court physically divides the estate among the owners (*partition in kind*) or sells the interest and divides the profits (*partition by sale*).

(i) This usually occurs when the co-tenants cannot agree on how to share or split their interests.

(ii) *N.B.*: the concurrent owners may limit their ability to seek a partition if they sign an agreement that they will not partition the estate (this applies in joint tenancies and tenancies by the entirety as well).

## 9.2 Joint Tenancy

### 9.2.1 Introduction

(a) In a joint tenancy (JT), an estate is conveyed to grantees and their heirs as co-tenants.

(b) Each co-tenant owns an undivided share in all of the property.

### 9.2.2 Classes

(a) A joint tenancy can be made in FS or in LE.

(b) What the joint tenancy is based on will affect what interests the joint tenants may transfer.

(c) Note the difference between:

(i) "O → A and B for their joint lives, remainder to the survivor and his heirs."

(1) A and B each acquire a joint LE with a CR FS.

(aa) A's remainder is contingent on B's dying before him; B's remainder is contingent on A's dying before him.

(2) O will acquire a reversion if the CR does not vest within twenty one years of the lives in being at the creation of the interest, as required by the RAP.

(ii) "O → A and B as joint tenants, with a right of survivorship, and not as tenants in common."

(1) A and B each acquire a JT FS with a right of survivorship.

(2) O will retain no interest in the estate.

### 9.2.3 Creation

(a) As we have seen, the formula "O → A and B and their heirs" creates not a tenancy in common, but rather, a joint tenancy under the common law and under the modern law.

(b) However, under the modern law, this formula constitutes a *joint tenancy* under the following circumstances:

(i) Under the majority approach, the four unities (***time***, ***title***, ***interest***, and ***possession***) *and* clear intent are required.

(1) *N.B.*: under this approach, if A had a FS in land that he wanted to share with B in JT, he would need to go convey the estate to a strawman, who would reconvey the property to A and B, in order to assure that the conveyance satisfied the time unity.

(ii) Under the minority approach, *clear intent on its own* is sufficient to overcome the presumption of a tenancy in common.

(1) *N.B.*: under this approach, the intervention of a strawman would be unnecessary.

(iii) In some states, such as Texas, the JT is abolished, and language creating a JT (*e.g.*, "to A and B as joint tenants, and not as tenants in common, with the right of survivorship") is construed as a tenancy in common in LE with an indestructible CR to the survivor.

(c) When there is ambiguity, courts will sometimes overlook common law rules of construction and look to the grantor's ***intent***. *Palmer v. Flint* (Me. 1960).

(i) *See Miller v. Riegler* (Ark. 1967), where Mrs. Wager, before her death, devised her property to her two nieces. She left $45,000 worth of stocks to her niece, Mary Riegler, with whom she lived, through a right of survivorship of a joint tenancy. The other niece, the plaintiff, initiated a suit to set aside the joint tenancy, arguing that (i) there was no ***unity of time*** in the conveyance of the stocks, since Mrs. Wagar held the stocks before she granted them to her daughter; (ii) there was *no* ***unity of title***, since Mary received the stocks from a grant from her aunt and Mrs. Reigler had possession from an earlier title; and (iii) there was no ***joint possession***, since all of the dividends of the stocks continued to go to Mrs. Riegler throughout her life. The court placed heavier weight on Mrs. Riegler's intent than on the common law rules, holding that joint tenants may come to agree upon how revenues and possession would be split and shared; it is important only that the joint tenants would have a right to evenly split revenues.

(d) Language such as, "to A and B as joint tenants, with a right of survivorship and not as tenants in common" is ideal in creating a joint tenancy.

(e) In most states, including the word "survivor" simply clarifies the JT. In fact, in Virginia, not mentioning "survivor" creates the presumption of a tenancy in common and prevents the creating of a JT. *Hoover v. Smith* (Va. 1994).

(f) However, in some states, mentioning the word "survivor" prevents A and B from partitioning the land or severing the interest.

(i) *See Jones v. Green* (Mich. Ct. App. 1983), where the court held that the language, "joint tenants with full rights of survivorship" automatically precluded the right of partition, since a Michigan law stated that mentioning the word "survivor" indicates the grantor's intent to give the survivor an indestructible CR FS. Thus, while mentioning "survivor" is required in some states to create a JT FS, mentioning it in Michigan creates a joint LE with an indestructible CR FS to the survivor.

9.2.4 Right of Survivorship

(a) Each joint tenant holds a ***right of survivorship***; if one of the joint tenants die, the other tenant or tenants receive his share of the property.

(b) Nothing passes on to the decedent's devisees or heirs; the joint tenancy is neither devisable nor inheritable.

9.2.5 Termination

(a) A joint tenancy is terminated when one joint tenant ***conveys*** his interest to a third party.

(i) Suppose for example, the formula "O → A and B and their heirs," where the four unities and clear intent to create a joint tenancy are present.

(ii) If A transferred his interest to C, then B and C would own the estate as tenants in common.

(iii) However, if A alienated merely a portion of his undivided interest to C, the conveyance would destroy the joint tenancy only with respect to the portion conveyed.

(iv) In this same manner, if A is a joint tenant with two other co-tenants, the transfer of A's interest does not destroy the entire joint tenancy. Rather, B and C continue to hold a joint tenancy with a right of survivorship with one another. The grantee of A's interest would thereafter hold a tenancy in common with B and C. *See, e.g., Jackson v. O'Connell* (Ill. 1961).

(b) A joint tenancy is similarly terminated when one of the joint tenants files for a ***partition***.

(c) Termination also occurs if the joint tenants enter into an ***agreement*** to permit one join tenant to devise his share. The agreement, not the devise, is what severs the joint tenancy.

(d) Normally, a divorce does not destroy a JT, but the parties, through manifesting clear intent, may convert a JT into a tenancy in common.

(i) *See Mann v. Bradley* (Colo. 1975), where the defendant divorced his wife, and in the divorce decree, they agreed that, upon the wife's remarriage or the couple's oldest child's turning twenty one years of age, the property would be sold and the interest split between them. Mrs. Mann died and the defendant, claimed that none of the four unities were destroyed, that there was a JT, and he had full title through his right of survivorship. The children sued for one half of the interest, claiming that the interest was a tenancy in common. The court held that it was not necessary to destroy any of the 4 unities or sever the interest and convert it to a tenancy in common; it became a tenancy in common as soon as intent to end the right of survivorship was manifested through the JTs' plans to sell the property and split the proceeds. Therefore, a tenancy in common was created, and the children were entitled to one half of the interest.

(e) Finally, joint tenancies are terminated at the death of the joint tenant(s), leaving one joint tenant, whose right of survivorship is activated.

(i) Many states have adopted Slayer Statutes, which deal with the result on a joint tenancy when one joint tenant murders another.

(ii) States have adopted varying approaches:

(1) The murderer acquires nothing and the murdered joint tenant's heirs or devisees acquire the property;

(2) The murderer acquires everything through his right of survivorship;

(3) The murderer gets a LE, with the remainder to the heirs of the murdered joint tenant;

(4) The joint tenancy becomes a tenancy in common, one half of which is taken by the murderer, and the other half of which is passed to the murdered joint tenant's heirs and devisees.

## 9.3 Tenancy by the Entirety

### 9.3.1 Introduction

(a) The tenancy by the entirety (TE), which is recognized in only twenty states, is essentially a JT that includes a fifth unity: marriage.

(b) It is thus typically only used when there is an interest in land shared by a married couple.

### 9.3.2 Right of Survivorship

(a) Tenancies by the entirety, like joint tenancies, grant each tenant a right of survivorship.

(b) Tenancies by the entirety are therefore neither devisable nor inheritable; the survivor spouse takes the decedent's entire share of the property.

### 9.3.3 Termination

(a) Like a joint tenancy, a tenancy by the entirety gives way to a tenancy in common when it is severed.

(b) A tenancy by the entirety is severed when any of the following occur:

(i) The spouses ***agree to jointly convey*** a share of the property (one spouse may not do so without the agreement of the other);

(ii) The spouses jointly ***agree to destroy*** the tenancy;

(iii) The spouses ***agree to partition*** the tenancy (the agreement is essential; involuntary partition is not possible);

(iv) The spouses ***divorce***; or

(v) Either ***spouse dies***.

**Summary Chart of the Concurrent Estates**

| | ***Tenancy in Common*** | ***Joint Tenancy*** | ***Tenancy by the Entirety*** |
|---|---|---|---|
| *Alienable* | ✓ | ✓ | ✓* |
| *Devisable* | ✓ | × | × |
| *Inheritable* | ✓ | × | × |

*** A tenancy by the entirety is only alienable when jointly transferred by both spouses.**

### 9.4 Fiduciary duties

9.4.1 Accounting

(a) An accounting is a detailed statement of the debits and credits between parties to a contract.

(b) If one tenant in common rents out part of the estate and makes rental income, he is required to make an accounting and to distribute the profit to the other tenant in common, absent an agreement stating otherwise.

9.4.2 Contribution

(a) When one concurrent owner spends money on the property, he is doing it on behalf of all of the concurrent owners, and is thus entitled to contribution.

(b) However, if the funds are spent on something unnecessary, such as a swimming pool, the concurrent owner is only entitled to what would be the increased added value at the time of a sale.

(c) On the contrary, when one tenant in common spends money to save a property, the other tenants in common must contribute to his costs or lose their title.

### 9.5 Adverse Possession

9.5.1 One concurrent tenant may obtain full ownership of an estate through adverse possession when the following elements are met:

(a) The concurrent owner exclusively possesses the estate; and

(b) He makes an open claim to full ownership (*i.e.*, makes an "ouster").

## Chapter III. Torts

# 1 Introduction to Tort Law

## 1.1 Introduction

### 1.1.1 Definition

(a) A tort a civil wrong, other than a breach of contract, for which the law provides a remedy.

### 1.1.2 General Overview

(a) Seventy to eighty percent of torts fall under the classification of "negligence torts," a group of torts in which the civil wrong was not intentional.[9]

(b) The other torts fall into a smaller group known as "intentional torts," where the requisite *mens rea* is intent.

### 1.1.3 Purpose of the Tort System

(a) While the criminal law seeks as its principle objective the punishment of the offender, in the civil law, of which the tort law is one branch, restitution to the victim is the primary objective.

- (i) In the civil law, retribution also plays a limited role, since courts will at times award punitive damages, which are based on a theory of retribution.
- (ii) The restitution in the tort law aims to return innocent parties back to their original position through compensation.
- (iii) This is done through awarding them money damages, which the tortfeasor is required to pay.
- (iv) In the criminal law, in contrast, the criminal pays his debt to society through paying fines to the government or through serving prison sentences.

(b) Among the other purposes of the tort system are as follow:

- (i) To discourage negligence and civil wrongs;
- (ii) To protect innocent victims; and
- (iii) To avoid private revenge.

### 1.1.4 Sources

(a) The tort law is derived from the common law.

(b) However, in some states, the tort law is, to a certain extent, based on statute.

(c) In other states, such as California, it has been largely codified.

---

[9] The majority of these torts are automobile-related.

### 1.2 Development of Liability Based on Fault

1.2.1 Traditional approach: the "strict liability rule."

(a) There was a time when fault was not even considered for the purpose of ascertaining liability.

(b) Determining liability was *only about asking whether the defendant cause the injury*.

(i) If so, the defendant was liable.

(ii) If not, he was not liable.

(c) Intent, recklessness and negligence were not a part of the analysis.

1.2.2 Later developments

(a) Later, the idea of fault began to creep into the system.

(b) Under the earliest fault rule, the defendant was liable, *unless he was able to prove that he was **utterly without fault***.

(i) *See Weaver v. Ward* (K.B. 1616), where the plaintiff sued the defendant for an injury caused by the defendant when his musket accidentally discharged during a military exercise. The court held that the defendant was liable when he was unable to prove that he was utterly without fault. He would not have been liable if, for example, the plaintiff ran into the traveling bullet after the defendant pulled the trigger.

(ii) *N.B.*: this is perhaps the earliest case where fault was discussed.

(c) Eventually, the common law developed the notion that the burden was on the plaintiff to prove fault (intent for intentional torts, recklessness or intent for IIED, breach of duty for negligence), *not* on the defendant to prove that he acted with care. *See, e.g., Brown v. Kendall* (Mass. 1850).

(d) There is no fault when injury is caused by sudden, unforeseeable illness.

(i) *See Cohen v. Petty* (D.C. Ct. App. 1933), where the defendant caused a car crash when, while driving, he suddenly passed out. Since his passing out was unforeseeable and it was the first time it had happened, he was not held liable.

(e) Nevertheless, the traditional common law rule of strict liability still applies to some situations.

(i) *See Spano v. Perini* (N.Y. 1969), where the defendant's blasting caused damages on the plaintiff's land. Held: unless the plaintiff was trespassing or there was contributory negligence, the defendant is strictly liable. The plaintiff is therefore required to prove only causation, not fault (intent, recklessness, or negligence).

## 2 Strict Liability

### 2.1 Introduction and Background

2.1.1 Strict liability (SL) applies in cases involving: (i) ***animals****;* (ii) ***abnormally dangerous activities****;* and (iii) ***products liability***.

2.1.2 Unlike negligence, the plaintiff must not prove that the defendant violated a *duty to exercise reasonable care*.

2.1.3 Elements of a *prima facie* case:

(a) An absolute duty to protect the plaintiff from risks associated with the act;

(b) The breach of this duty;

(c) Causation in fact and proximate cause;

(i) Causation in fact is actual causation (*e.g.*, "but for X, Y would not have occurred").

(ii) Proximate cause is legal causation.

(1) This serves as a limitation on actual cause.

(2) All acts can be connected to a result; the law draws a limit with those acts which are closely enough connected to the consequence that the law will impose liability in a particular case.

(3) Proximate cause is the legal principle that courts apply in determining where to draw the line.

(d) Damage to the plaintiff's person or property.

## 2.2 Animals

2.2.1 Wild Animals

(a) There is no-fault liability for injuries caused by wild animals with vicious temperaments.

(b) One keeps such animals "at his peril."

2.2.2 Domestic Animals

(a) Under the common law, a domestic animal is entitled to one bite free of liability.

(b) However, if the domestic animal has a dangerous propensity known by the owner, he would not be entitled to any bites free of liability.

(c) The statutory approach in most states imposes *strict liability* for dog bites.

(d) Exception: there is no liability when the plaintiff was trespassing or committing some tort.

(e) Other states create other exceptions, such as when a sign is posted warning of a dangerous dog.

(f) Many states have passed statutes requiring muzzles or leashes.

(i) If a person is injured due to the violation of such a statute, he will be held guilty of negligence *per se* (negligence as a matter of law), such that breach of duty is not a jury question; the plaintiff only needs to prove that the violation of the statute caused damages.

(ii) However, if the violation of the statute was not the cause of the injury (*e.g.*, in the case of a statute requiring the use of a muzzle, abiding by the statute would not have prevented the dog from knocking over a child), the burden is on the plaintiff to prove the violation of a duty owed by the defendant.

2.3 Abnormally Dangerous Activities

2.3.1 There is strict liability for damages arising out of abnormally dangerous activities. To prove SL, the plaintiff must prove both of the following elements:

(a) The activity was abnormally dangerous.

(i) A weighing test that balances the following factors is used to determine whether an activity is abnormally dangerous:

(1) Whether the activity carries a high risk of serious injury;

(2) Whether the activity is infrequently engaged in within the community and whether it is inappropriate there;

(3) Whether it is impossible to perform the activity in a way that eliminates the risk, no matter how great the burden; and

(4) Whether the activity's social utility outweigh the risks. § 520 Restatement.

(ii) Activities that have been held to be abnormally dangerous include: blasting, the testing of rockets, the storage of water and of toxic chemicals, fireworks displays, and oil drilling.

(iii) Among the activities that have been held *not* to be abnormally dangerous include: the use of firearms and the use of fire.

(b) The abnormal activity was the actual and proximate cause of the plaintiff's damages.

2.3.2 The care exercised is immaterial in determining SL.

(a) *See Rylands v. Fletcher* (H.L. 1868), where the defendant Rylands constructed a reservoir on his land, which burst and caused damage on the neighbor's land. The court held that when the defendant brings unnatural substances on land (here, the unnatural substance being the great amount of water), he does so at his own peril; regarding of the amount of care he exercises, he will be liable for damages caused by his act. Judgment for the plaintiff.

2.3.3 There is no strict liability for activities that are not abnormally dangerous. The duty to exercise reasonable care is applied.

(a) *See Miller v. Civil Constructors, Inc.* (Ill. App. Ct. 1995), where a court held that the discharge of firearms was not an abnormally dangerous activity, but rather, the duty was of reasonable care under the circumstances.

## 2.4 Limitations (Defenses)

### 2.4.1 Superseding Cause

(a) The defendant will not be held guilty if the damage arose not from that which made the activity abnormally dangerous, but rather, from a superseding cause.

(b) *See Foster v. Preston Mill Co.* (Wash. 1954), where the plaintiff sued the defendant for blasting that caused the plaintiff's mink to kill its young. Held: what makes blasting dangerous is the damage it may cause to persons or property. The plaintiff's damages arose not from this dangerous quality, but rather, from the minks' nervous disposition, a superseding intervening cause that caused the mink to kill their young. The defendant is not strictly liable.

### 2.4.2 Unforeseeable Intervening Cause

(a) An intervening cause is an act that intervenes in the series of events after an act, such that it alters the resulting consequence.

(b) When an intervening cause is strong enough to relieve a wrongdoer of liability, it becomes a superseding cause.

(c) However, the defendant will not be liable when the intervening cause is unforeseeable.

(i) *See Golden v. Amory* (Mass. 1952), where the plaintiff, relying on *Rylands v. Fletcher* (H.L. 1868) , sought compensation when water being stored in a dike on the defendant's property caused damage on the plaintiff's property as a result of an unforeseeable act of God—a hurricane. Held: the defendant is not liable, since the intervening cause was unforeseeable.

(ii) *N.B.*: the defendant would have been strictly liable if he had reason to believe that an act of God would come to bear.

### 2.4.3 Contributory Negligence

(a) Contributory negligence is generally not a defense when a defendant is strictly liable.

(b) However, *knowing contributory negligence* may be a defense.

### 2.4.4 Assumption of the Risk

(a) Assumption of the risk is an affirmative defense for strict liability.

(b) *See Sandy v. Bushey* (Me. 1925), where the plaintiff was injured by the defendant's horse and sued. The defendant argued that the injury was caused by *contributory negligence*. Held: when the owner of an animal is aware of the animal's vicious propensity, the owner is strictly liable for injuries caused by the animal, regardless of whether there was contributory negligence. However, assumption of the risk *is* an affirmative defense. If the plaintiff unnecessarily puts himself in a situation where he knows of the probability of injury, the defendant is not liable. However, the facts in the present case do not support such a conclusion. Judgment for the plaintiff affirmed.

(i) *N.B*: assumption of the risk *and* contributory negligence are defenses in ordinary negligence cases, but only assumption of the risk is a defense in SL cases.

# 3 Intentional Torts

## 3.1 Introduction

### 3.1.1 Characteristics

(a) Intentional torts (IT's) are those that involve the most fault.

(b) They require actual intent, or, in the case of the intentional infliction of emotional distress (IIED), recklessness.

### 3.1.2 Elements of the Plaintiff's *Prima Facie* Case

(a) A Volitional Act

(i) A volitional act, or an external manifestation of the inner will, is always required.

(ii) Volition is an act of the will that indicates that a tortfeasor's action resulted from a conscious choice.

(iii) An action lacks volition if it was committed while the actor was sleepwalking or forced by some outside compelling force or circumstance (*i.e.*, *force majeure*).

(iv) If the plaintiff wants something to come about, his omission to make it materialize cannot constitute an IT, since such an omission would not be a volitional act.

(b) Intent

(i) All of the IT's require intent.

(ii) Intent is formed when the defendant possesses either:

(1) Purpose (a wanting or desiring) that a certain result come about; or

(2) Knowledge to a substantial certainty (KSC) of an extremely high risk that a particular consequence will materialize as a result of one's act (based on knowledge or belief).

(aa) *See Garratt v. Dailey* (Wash. 1955), where an infant was held liable for battery when, with knowledge to a substantial certainty that the plaintiff would try to sit in a chair, he moved it, causing the plaintiff to fall when she attempted to sit on it. Although the defendant did not have purpose, his KSC provided the requisite intent.[10]

(c) The Resulting Tort

[10] Infants are liable for their torts, just as adults (although in negligence cases, they are held to a different standard of care).

(i) Finally, the plaintiff must prove that a resulting tort (assault, false imprisonment, etc.) came about.

3.2 The Seven Intentional Torts

3.2.1 Assault

(a) The elements of assault are as follow:

(i) A volitional act (an act of the will; see definition, *supra.*, for fuller treatment);

(ii) With the intent (purpose or KSC) to cause an *offensive or harmful contact* or a *reasonable fear* of an immediate offensive or harmful contact; and

(iii) A resulting immediate fear of imminent offensive or harmful contact.

(b) Words alone, no matter how threatening, do not constitute assault.

(c) If the defendant unsuccessfully attempts battery on the plaintiff, he may be liable for assault.

(i) *See I de S et ux. v. W de S* (Assizes 1348), where the defendant came to the plaintiff's home to buy wine, but the door was shut. The defendant banged the door with a hatchet and when the plaintiff looked out the window to tell him to stop, the defendant threw the hatchet at her and missed. Held: the intent to offensively or harmfully contact the plaintiff is transferred to the intent to cause an immediate fear of an offensive or harmful contact. The defendant is liable for assault.

(ii) *N.B.*: this may be the first case that has come to recognize assault as a tort.

(d) Present ability to carry out offensive or harmful contact *not* necessary to establish assault, as long as there is an intent to cause an offensive or harmful contact and this causes the fear of such a contact.

(i) *See Western Union Telegraph Co. v. Hill* (Ct. App. Ala. 1933), where the plaintiff sued the defendant for assault when he attempted to offensively contact her by reaching across a counter and telling her he wanted to "love and pet" her. The defendant argued that he lacked the ability to reach across the table and touch the plaintiff. Held: the ability to make an offensive or harmful contact is unnecessary, as long as the defendant intends to effect the contact and he has the apparent ability to do so.

3.2.2 Battery

(a) The elements of battery are as follow:

(i) Volition (an act of the will, as in all intentional torts);

(ii) Intent (purpose or KSC);

(1) In some states, there must be intent to cause an *offensive or harmful contact;*

(2) In other states, the intent to cause *any contact at all* suffices.

(aa) Example: tortfeasor innocently intends to pat V on the shoulder, but, not realizing that V recently underwent surgery on her shoulder, he causes a harmful contact. The requisite intent would be met and the tortfeasor would be liable for battery.

(iii) A resulting offensive or harmful contact.

(1) The test for determining whether a contact is offensive or harmful is an objective test based on what a *reasonable person not unduly sensitive as to his personal dignity* would find harmful or offensive.

(2) However, there is an exception to the objective test when the defendant knows that the plaintiff would or would *not* find a contact offensive, based on past history, special sensitivities, or their relationship.

(aa) For example, if the plaintiff was the defendant's old wrestling partner, the defendant could reasonably expect a bear hug not to be offensive to the plaintiff, given their relationship.

(b) The victim need not be aware of the offensive or harmful contact at the time that it is done.

(i) Example: the tortfeasor, in a voluntary act, kisses a girl while she is sleeping. When the girl later finds out what happened, is is offended. If only the intent to cause *any contact at all* is necessary, the defendant will be held liable for battery.

(c) An offensive or harmful contact on the plaintiff's person need not transpire in order for there to be a battery; a rude or offensive contact with any object connected to the plaintiff's person suffices in establishing battery.

(i) *See Fisher v. Carrousel Motor Hotel, Inc.* (Tex. 1967), where the defendant snatched the plaintiff's plate and yelled that "Negroes can't eat here!" Held: the intent to cause offensive contact not only with the plaintiff's person, but to the plaintiff's clothing or objects attached to the his person, is sufficient in establishing battery. The defendant is liable.

(d) Proving insanity does not exculpate tortfeasors from their batteries or other IT's.

(i) *See McGuire v. Almy* (Mass. 1937), where the tortfeasor Almy battered a nurse with a furniture leg while having a psychological episode. Held: the tortfeasor is liable for battery because she *intended* to batter the nurse. Rationale: public policy seeks to make the insane liable for their actions (even though they cannot be at fault when there is no volition) in order to (i) give those responsible for the insane incentive to be more watchful; (ii) discourage tortfeasors from claiming insanity and (iii) to restitute the innocent, who should be allowed recovery for damages.

(ii) Exception: when the insanity precludes the requisite intent.

(1) Example: the tortfeasor thought that it was a disappearing furniture leg that could cause no contact. There would be no liability.

(2) Example: the tortfeasor, believing a nurse to be an alien trying to kidnap him, battered her in self-defense. There would be liability because *he had the intent to batter her.*

### 3.2.3 False Imprisonment

(a) Several acts can give rise to false imprisonment (FI), including: confining the plaintiff to a space; taking possession of the plaintiff's chattel such that the plaintiff will not leave until it is released; placing the plaintiff in a room where the only escape risks life or limb; or confining the plaintiff to a space where the exit is hidden.

(b) The elements of FI are as follow:

(i) A ***volitional act*** (an act of the will, as in all intentional torts);

(ii) Executed with ***intent*** (purpose or KSC) to confine the victim;

(iii) In an ***unlawful manner*** (not under the authority of a law permitting confinement);

(1) *See Enright v. Grove* (Colo. Ct. App. 1977), where the plaintiff sued the defendant for FI when the defendant arrested the plaintiff after the plaintiff refused to show him her drivers license after he interrogated her about a dog in violation of a dog-lease ordinance. Held: since no law permitted the arrest of a citizen for violation of the dog lease ordinance, or for the refusal of a citizen to hand over her license while in a non-moving vehicle, the defendant's confinement of the plaintiff was unlawful.

(iv) With the ***victim's consciousness*** of the confinement, or, if this is lacking, with a resulting harm. *Parvi v. City of Kingston* (N.Y. 1977) (police would not be liable for FI if the plaintiff were not conscious of the confinement);

(v) ***Against the plaintiff's will***. *Hardy v. LaBelle's Distrib. Co.* (Mont. 1983) (there is no FI when the plaintiff implies consent to an interrogation and states that she wants to stay to clear up a problem); and

(vi) A ***resulting confinement*** within boundaries (a room, moving car, city, state, etc.).

(1) This confinement requires that the plaintiff be deprived of the means to exit a space; it does not require the defendant to lay a hand on the plaintiff.

(2) *See, e.g., Whittaker v. Sandford* (Me. 1912), where the plaintiff was falsely imprisoned on a boat when the defendant refused to allow the plaintiff to use the rowboat to get to shore.

### 3.2.4 Intentional Infliction of Emotional Distress

(a) The elements for the intentional infliction of emotional distress (IIED) are as follow:

(i) A ***volitional act*** (an act of the will, as in all intentional torts);

(ii) Extreme and ***outrageous conduct***;

(1) The conduct must be shocking to the community.

(2) Under the Restatement, it must be "atrocious and intolerable in a civilized society."

(3) The test for the IIED, like that of battery, is based on an objective reasonable person of ordinary sensibilities standard.

(aa) *See Slocum v. Food Fair Stores of Florida* (Fla. 1958), where the plaintiff suffered a heart attack after an employee insulted her. Since a person of *normal sensibilities* would not have been so offended by the comment ("you stink to me") that he would have suffered a heart attack. The plaintiff's shock and outrage is not enough to establish that the conduct was extreme and outrageous, since the plaintiff may have been unduly sensitive. Since the conduct would not have been shocking to the community as a whole, the defendant is not liable.

(bb) *Compare State Rubbish Collectors Association v. Siliznoff* (Cal. 1952), where the court held that words threatening physical injury, and the destruction of one's property and business were sufficiently extreme.

(iii) A ***causal connection*** between the conduct and the emotional harm;

(1) *N.B.*: as in all the intentional torts, when we refer to the "resulting" harm, we are implying the causal relationship.

(iv) A resulting ***severe and disabling emotional distress*** that, in some jurisdictions, must be accompanied by bodily harm.

(1) *See State Rubbish Collectors Association v. Siliznoff* (Cal. 1952), where physical threats that lead to emotional distress, vomiting, and sleeping problems met this requirement.

(2) *Compare Harris v. Jones* (Md. 1977), where the exacerbation of one's speech impediment and increased nervousness failed this element.

3.2.5 Trespass to Land

(a) The elements of trespass to land are as follow:

(i) A volitional act (an act of the will, as in all intentional torts);

(ii) Intent (purpose or KSC) to enter a plot of land;

(iii) A resulting trespass.

(b) Neither knowledge of trespass nor damage to the land are necessary elements of trespass. If there is no damage, a court may infer nominal damages.

(c) The plaintiff may win damages if the defendant merely possesses the intent to enter the plaintiff's land, whether or not he knows that he is trespassing.

(i) *See Dougherty v. Stepp* (N.C. 1835), where the plaintiff sued the defendant for trespass to land and the defendant had no knowledge that the land belonged to the plaintiff, and did not intend to trespass or cause any damage to the land. Held: subjective intent to trespass is not necessary in establishing trespass, as long as there was an intention to enter the land; damages are not required.

(d) Failure to remove objects from the plaintiff's land after the plaintiff's consent has expired also constitutes trespass.

(i) *See Rogers v. Board of Road Commissioners* (Mich. 1948), where the plaintiff agreed to allow the defendant to put up a snow fence on the plaintiff's property with the understanding that the defendant would later remove it. The defendant failed to remove one post, which led to an accident in which the plaintiff's husband was killed. Held: trespass is the presence of a person *or* object on the plaintiff's land without the plaintiff's consent. If the plaintiff consents to presence of object for a limited period, and that period has passed, then the object is in trespass of the plaintiff's land and the defendant is liable for any damages arising out of the trespass.

(e) Trespass may occur without the defendant's actual setting foot on property; the defendant only needs to threaten the plaintiff's right to enjoy the property or violate the space above or below the surface of the property.

(i) *See Herrin v. Sutherland* (Mont. 1925), where the defendant was firing shots above the plaintiff's land from other property. The plaintiff claimed that this violated his right to enjoy the property. Held: the defendant is liable for trespass because his acts violate the integrity of the air space above the plaintiff's land.

3.2.6 Trespass to Chattels

(a) Trespass to chattels is defined as an act, without justification, of physical interference with a chattel that belongs to another person.

(b) The elements of trespass to chattels are as follow:

(i) A volitional act (an act of the will, as in all intentional torts);

(ii) The intent to physically interfere with a chattel belonging to another person; and

(iii) An act whereby the defendant either:

(1) *Dispossesses the possessor* of the chattel;

(2) *Impairs* the condition or value of the chattel;

(3) *Deprives the possessor of the use* of the chattel for a substantial period of time (can be through dispossessing him, impairing the value of the chattel, etc.); or

(4) *Causes bodily harm* to the possessor or harm to persons or property in which the possessor has a legally protected interest.

(c) Damages for harmless intermeddling are not rewarded.

(i) *See Glidden v. Szybiak*, where court held that a girl who played on a dog's back and pulled his ears was not liable for trespass to chattels, since she did not *impair* the dog's condition or value or *deprive the owner of use* of the dog for a substantial period of time.

(d) Damages *are* rewarded for *impairing the value of a chattel* or *causing harm to persons* in whom the owner has a legally protected interest, even when no dispossession takes place.

(i) *See CompuServe Inc. v. Cyber Promotions, Inc.* (S.D. Ohio 1997), where the defendant was found liable for trespass to chattels in sending spam through the plaintiff's server, since he (i) impaired the value of the services provided by the plaintiff to its clients; and (ii) harmed the plaintiff's clients, in whom the plaintiff had a legally protected interest.

3.2.7 Conversion

(a) Conversion is an act of willful interference with the property of another without lawful justification, in a way that *deprives the owner of the use of his property*.

(b) Examples of conversion include illegal takings, the assumption of ownership, and the destruction of the property of another.

(c) The elements of conversion are as follow (Restatement § 222A):

(i) A volitional act (an act of the will, as in all intentional torts);

(ii) The intent to exercise dominion over a chattel;

(1) In so doing, the interferer need not know that he is interfering with a chattel of another (the BFP of a stolen vehicle, for example, could be liable for conversion).

(iii) That results in such a serious interference with the true owner's right to control the chattel that the defendant may be required to pay the true owner the full value of the chattel.

(1) In determining whether the interference was sufficiently serious, the following factors are considered:

(aa) The intent to assert a dominion control incompatible with that of the true owner;

(bb) The duration of the dominion control;

(cc) Bad faith;

(dd) Harm to the chattel; and

(ee) Inconvenience to the owner.

(2) Use of a chattel for a short period is not considered sufficiently serious to meet the interference element.

(aa) *See Pearson v. Dodd* (D.C. Cir. 1969), where the plaintiff sued for conversion when the defendant broke into the plaintiff's office, took some documents, photocopied them, and returned them unharmed. Held: there is no conversion when the defendant has not been deprived of the documents for a substantial period and when the documents have not been substantially harmed.

(d) Damages for Conversion

(i) The plaintiff may ask the court to treat the conversion as a sale of the chattel to the defendant, and thus require the defendant to pay the full value of the chattel to the plaintiff.

(ii) Compare with damages in trespass to chattels, where the plaintiff is entitled only to damages equal to the diminished value of the chattel resulting from the trespass.

3.2.8 Person-to-Person Transferred Intent

(a) A tortfeasor intends to batter B, but instead, batters C.

(b) The tortfeasor will be liable for the battery of C; although he did not intend to cause an offensive or harmful contact with him, his intent to batter B is transferred to his battery against C.

3.2.9 Tort to Tort Transferred Intent

(a) Five of the IT's arose from the old common law tort of trespass: assault, battery, false imprisonment, trespass to land, and trespass to chattels.

(b) In all of these torts, the tortfeasor trespasses on the victim's *person* (assault, battery, false imprisonment), *land* (trespass to land), or *chattels* (trespass to chattels).

(c) Accordingly, these five torts all allow for what is called, "tort to tort transferred intent": if one tort is intended, but another results, the tortfeasor will be liable for the resulting tort, regardless if he did not intend it.

(d) This principle can be combined with the effects of person-to-person transferred intent, transforming the nature of a tortfeasor's act.

(i) Example: a tortfeasor intends to assault B, but instead, batters C. The tortfeasor will be liable for the assault of B (and possibly of C, if he caused C a fear of proximate harm) and the battery of C. The fact that there was intent to batter neither B nor C is immaterial; the tortfeasor will be liable for battery.

**3.3** Privileges (Defenses)

3.3.1 Introduction

(a) A privilege is a legal right, immunity, or exemption to a duty.

(b) Privileges are affirmative defenses where the defendant is not liable, even if the plaintiff's *prima facie* case is met.

3.3.2 Consensual Privilege: Consent

(a) There is no liability for IT's if the plaintiff consents.

(b) There are two kinds of consent: (i) express (actual) consent; and (ii) implied consent.

(i) Consent is express when a party declares orally or in writing that the defendant may engage in some act.

(ii) Implied Consent may be implied-in-law or implied-in-fact (apparent consent).

(c) Implied-In-Law

(i) The law "constructs," or "imports" the consent of certain actors when the following elements are met:

(1) The actor is in an emergency situation (the threat of life or limb);

(2) The actor is unable to consent (*e.g.*, because he is unconscious);

(3) A reasonable person would consent under similar circumstances; and

(4) There is no indication that the patient would *not* consent if he could.

(ii) The key is that there be a threat to life or limb, and, unless acts are taken to save the patient, substantial damage would result;

(iii) In non-emergency situations, doctors do not have implied-in-law consent to perform elective surgeries.

(iv) A doctor who performs surgery on a patient without his express or implied-by-law consent, or who performs surgery in a way that is contrary to the patient's consent, can be held liable for battery.

(1) *See Mohr v. Williams* (Minn. 1905), where a doctor, having the patient's consent to perform surgery on one ear, was liable when he performed surgery on the other ear without patient's consent.

(v) If the patient is mentally incapacitated, and tells the doctor that he does not want him to perform a procedure that doctor believes is necessary for preservation of the patient's life or limb, the law will construct the patient's consent.

(d) Implied-in-Fact (Apparent) Consent

(i) When the circumstances would lead the defendant to believe that the plaintiff has consented, the defendant is said to have the plaintiff's "implied-in-fact" consent.

(ii) The plaintiff's subjective state of mind is immaterial; what matters is whether a ***reasonable person*** would consider the plaintiff's conduct to imply consent.

(1) *See O'Brien v. Cunard Steamship Co.* (Mass. 1891), where the plaintiff sued a ship's physician for battery when he administered a vaccination to her. Held: the doctor is not liable, since the context (a boat where a sign was posted everywhere stating that all passengers needed a shot before disembarking)

coupled with the plaintiff's waiting on line and holding out her arm would cause a *reasonable person* to believe that she had consented.

(e) Consent is invalid under the following circumstances:

(i) When obtained through duress;

(ii) When obtained through fraud or mistake induced by fraud;

(1) *See De May v. Roberts* (Mich. 1881), where an obstetrician/gynecologist was found liable for assault, battery, and deceit when he brought a non-physician into a delivery room and introduced him to a patient as his "assistant." Held: there is no consent when it is based on the consenter's mistake obtained through the defendant's fraud.

(iii) When the person consenting lacks capacity (*e.g.*, infants, the mentally insane, etc.);

(1) When the subject lacks capacity, a parent, caretaker, or guardian must give consent on his behalf.

(iv) When consent is given to an activity prohibited by statute (*e.g.*, consenting to a statutorily-prohibited fistfight).

(1) Many courts will not allow the defense of consent under this circumstance.

3.3.3 Non-Consensual Privilege

(a) Introduction

(i) Non-consensual privilege is similarly an affirmative defense, but it is not based on the plaintiff's consent.

(ii) Examples of non-consensual privilege include: self-defense, defense of others, defense of property, and shopkeeper's privilege.

(b) Self Defense

(i) One is privileged to use reasonable force in defending himself if it ***appears reasonable*** that such force is necessary to protect himself. The privilege applies even when there is in fact no such necessity.

(ii) Two Approaches

(1) Majority View

(aa) One may use reasonable force in defending himself and standing his ground in *any situation*.

(bb) He may only use deadly (likely to cause death or serious bodily harm) force when threatened with the same.

(2) Minority View

(aa) Under the minority view, which is embraced by the Model Penal Code and the Restatement (Second) of Torts, one may stand his ground and defend himself using reasonable force.

(bb) However, when required to use deadly force, he first must "flee to the wall," *unless*:

(I) There is the *slightest* reason to believe that he cannot make a safe retreat (*e.g.*, he is threatened with a firearm at close range); or

(II) When he is threatened in his home, he may use deadly force when threatened with deadly force (the *"Castle" Exception*).

(3) Because guns have made much of retreat impractical, the distinction between the majority and minority (Restatement) views has decreased, since the plaintiffs will not be required to retreat when threatened with a gun under either approach.

(iii) Self-defense applies only to *threats to one's physical safety*, not to mere insults. The privilege expires when the threat retreats; it does not apply to retaliation.

(c) Defense of Others

(i) The self-defense privilege to use *reasonable force* when doing so appears necessary (or, in some states, *is* necessary) extends to defending others, including family and servants.

(ii) Reasonable Mistake

(1) Minority (Restatement) Approach

(aa) Under the minority approach, which is embraced by the Restatement, .one is privileged to use reasonable force when a ***reasonable person would have concluded that such force was necessary*** to defend others

(bb) *Reasonable mistake* applies in the same way that it applies under *self defense*: the privilege applies even if the actor is reasonably mistaken as to the threat.

(2) Majority Approach

(aa) Under the majority approach, the defendant is *only entitled to use reasonable force when* ***the party he is defending would have had that privilege***.

(bb) Thus, if the party being defended is in fact under no threat, the defendant would be liable for his tort, even if the mistake was reasonable.

(cc) Under the majority approach, one therefore must be *certain* that there is a threat to the third party before intervening.

(3) Example

(aa) B perceives that his family member C is being threatened by D. In the **interest**s of defending C, B batters D, but later finds out that C and D were only rehearsing for a play.

(bb) Under the minority approach, B would not be liable if the court concludes that his mistake was reasonable.

(cc) Under the majority approach, B would be liable, since C did not have the privilege to act in self defense.

(d) Defense of Property

(i) General Overview

(1) The owner of property is privileged to use ***reasonable force*** in defending this property when it appears that such force is necessary for the protection of his property.

(2) The ***reasonable force*** standard of self-defense and defense of others applies to the defense of property; the force employed must be proportionate to the threat detected.

(3) The defense of property privilege does not permit the defendant to use ***deadly force*** in protecting a home that is not a dwelling.

(aa) *See Katko v. Briney* (Iowa 1971) (Iowa 1971), where the court held that the blowing off of a petty thief's leg with a shotgun when the petty thief posed no threat to anyone's life in an abandoned home was *not* a reasonable use of force. The dignity of life outweighs the right to protect property.

(4) Under a traditional common law doctrine, the defendant may, however, use deadly force in his own home against trespassers based on the reasonable belief that such force is necessary to prevent certain felonies.

(5) A minority of jurisdictions have even gone as far as permitting defendants to use deadly force against trespassers *who do not commit felonies* within the home but who the occupant believes may use *even slight physical force* against the occupant (*see, e.g., Colorado Revised Statutes*).

(6) Other states have limited this use of deadly force, requiring, for example, that deadly force be used only against trespassers who threaten the occupant's *life or limb*.

(ii) Recovery of Property

(1) One is granted privilege of using reasonable force in recovering a chattel taken from him through fraud if (Restatement §§ 101-106):

(aa) He is entitled to the immediate recovery of the property;

(bb) He has demanded for the chattel to be returned and the other party has refused;

(cc) The force is proportionate to the threat;

(dd) There has been reasonable diligence in discovering the loss and attempting recovery;

(ee) The party against whom force is being exercised is a wrongdoer, not one who purchased in good faith from a wrongdoer;

(ff) He has not breached the peace.

(2) *See Hodgeden v. Hubbard* (Vt. 1846), where the plaintiff accused the defendant of using force in recovering a stove that the plaintiff had fraudulently induced the defendant to sell. Held: because the defendant used proportionate and reasonable force that was necessary (since the plaintiff drew a knife), the defendant is not liable.

(iii) Shopkeeper's Privilege

(1) A storeowner is entitled to detain shoppers in potential cases of shoplifting when the following elements are met:

(aa) The storeowner has a *reasonable belief* that the shopper is a shoplifter;

(bb) The detention is *in the store or within the immediate vicinity*;

(cc) The detention is conducted in a *reasonable manner* (the storeowner may not publicly embarrass the shopper) and over a reasonable *period of time* (generally, no more than ten to fifteen minutes); and

(dd) Reasonable, non-deadly force is used.

(2) *See Bonkowski v. Arlan's Dept. Store* (Mich. Ct. App. 1968), where a store owner was held not to be liable for false arrest and slander against a customer, since the store owner's detention of the customer was based on a reasonable belief of the shoplifting of costume jewelry and the detention was reasonable in duration.

(e) Necessity

(i) Public Necessity

(1) Trespass is privileged as a public necessity when the actor ***reasonably believes*** it to be necessary to avoid an imminent public disaster.

(2) The defendant not only has a privilege for his trespass, but he is also *not liable* for any damage to property incurred during the trespass.

(3) Example: A breaks into a private building in order to defuse a bomb that he has been informed is about to go off.

(ii) Private Necessity

(1) Trespass is privileged as a private necessity when the actor ***reasonably believes*** it to be necessary to avoid a grave risk of harm to his person, land, or chattels.

(2) Although the trespass is privileged, the trespasser is liable for any damage to property incurred during the trespass.

(3) Example: A is wandering about a forest when a lion spies him. A may break into B's log cabin to take shelter until the threat retreats.

(4) *N.B.*: the privilege of necessity does *not* permit one to trespass on another's land in order to recover a domestic animal that strayed off due to the owner's own negligence.

## 4 Negligence

### 4.1 Introduction

4.1.1 Negligence (N) arose as a tort of its own in the 1800s, as distinct from intentional torts (IT's), in that it does *not* require a volitional act; an ***omission*** would be sufficient in proving the plaintiff's *prima facie* case.[11]

4.1.2 The elements of the plaintiff's *prima facie* negligence case are as follow:

(a) The duty to protect persons and property from foreseeable, unreasonable risks;

(b) A breach of this duty;

(c) Actual and proximate cause; and

(d) Damages to a third party's person or property interests.

**4.2** The Duty to Exercise Reasonable Care

4.2.1 Introduction

(a) One has a duty to protect third parties from foreseeable, unreasonable risks.

(b) When an act is either unforeseeable or reasonable, the defendant does not have a duty to protect the plaintiff from the associated risks of the act.

4.2.2 Unforeseeability

(a) A defendant is liable for failing to protect others from *foreseeable risks.*

---

[11] However, as we will see, some N cases also involve a volitional act.

(i) *See Gulf Refining Co. v. Williams* (Miss. 1938), where the plaintiff Williams sued the defendant for giving him a gas drum whose bung cap was jagged, causing a spark when being opened that lead to a fire and injury to the plaintiff. The defendant's witnesses testified that the possibility of a fire was so unlikely that it was unforeseeable. The defendant therefore testified that he did not have a duty to prevent unforeseeable risks. The court, however, held that the defendant was liable because the condition of the bung attracted the attention of one of the defendant's employees and would have notified a reasonable prudent person of the foreseeable danger.

(b) He is not liable for failing to prevent damages resulting from unforeseeable risks.

(i) *See Lubitz v. Wells*, where the plaintiff sued the defendant for negligently leaving a golf club lying in his back yard, allowing the defendant's son to pick it up and hurt the plaintiff. Held: although there is a duty to exercise reasonable care and to prevent unreasonable risks, the risk of one's son's picking up a club lying in the yard and injuring a person is so slight that a reasonable person would not have taken actions to prevent it. The defendant is not liable.

(ii) *See also Blyth v. Birmingham Waterworks Co.* (Exch. 1856), where a company took measures to prevent damages resulting from foreseeable storms. However, when one highly unusual frost came to past, a fire hydrant burst, causing damages. Since the frost was so extraordinary, it was not foreseeable and the defendant was held not to be liable.

4.2.3 Unreasonable Risks

(a) Introduction to Risk-Utility Analysis

(i) One has a duty to protect third parties not from *all* foreseeable risks, but from all *unreasonable* foreseeable risks.

(ii) When a risk is reasonable, the defendant is not necessarily held liable for all resulting injuries.

(iii) Determining whether a risk is reasonable requires applying risk-utility analysis.

(iv) When the activity is of great public utility (*e.g.*, railroads, roads, shipping), society must be prepared to tolerate some degree of unreasonable risk in order to be productive.

(v) In these cases, defendants are less likely to be held liable for the resulting risks.

(b) When the burden of reducing unreasonable risks costs less than the damages that may otherwise result, there is a duty to protect others.

(c) However, when the burden is cost-prohibitive, no such duty exists.

(i) *See Davison v. Snohomish County* (Wash. 1928), where the court held that the defendant was not liable for not making stronger guard rails in order to prevent injuries on the roads, since making all roads safe would be cost-prohibitive.

(d) When the burden to prevent damage to third persons is low, there is liability despite an activity's high utility

(i) *See Chicago, B. and Q.R. Co v. Krayenbuhl* (Neb. 1902), where the plaintiff Krayenbuhl sued the defendant for negligence when his foot was severed while she was playing on a turntable. Held: society tolerates some of the unreasonable risks associated with trains because of the high utility of trains. However, *when the burden of prevention* is much *slighter than the risk of damage*, there is liability. Here, the burden of putting a padlock on the turntable is much slighter than the risk of injury to children. The defendant is therefore liable.

(e) The Learned Hand Formula

(i) According to Judge Learned Hand, one is negligent when the probability of ***damage*** (P), multiplied by the ***magnitude of the potential damage*** (L) is greater than the ***burden*** (B) of preventing the risk.

(ii) There is thus negligence when (P)(L) > B

(iii) *See United States v. Carroll Towing Co.* (1st Cir. 1988), where the plaintiff sued the defendant for negligently allowing the plaintiff's barge to sink. Because the probability of harm multiplied by the magnitude of potential harm being was greater than the burden of prevention (having an attendee on board), the defendant was held to be liable.

(f) Traditional Common Law View

(i) Judge Learned Hand's formula ignores an important factor that most courts include in their analysis: the degree to which an activity is useful to society (utility).

(ii) Under the traditional common law view, there is thus negligence when the ***risk*** (R) is greater than the ***utility*** (U) plus the ***burden*** (B).

(iii) There is thus negligence when R > U + B.

(iv) When the risk is great and unreasonable, there is negligence, unless the utility and the burden are very high and outweigh the risk (*e.g.*, *Davison v. Snohomish County*).

(v) When there is great risk, but greater utility, there will generally not be negligence, unless the burden is slight.

(g) The View of the Restatement of the Law (Second) of Torts

(i) The Restatement view summarizes the common law view and add precisions to the definitions of risk and utility.

(ii) Factors determining risk include the probability of the harm, the magnitude of the harm, and the number of people who would be harmed.

(iii) Factors determining utility include the social value of the activity and the extent to which this value can be met with other, less dangerous activities.

(iv) Under the Restatement, there is unreasonableness from which the defendant has a duty to protect third parties when:

(1) The ***risk*** (the probability of damage times the magnitude of the potential damage times the number of people (N) who would be harmed) is greater than the ***social utility*** plus the ***burden***.

(2) There is thus negligence when R (P x L x N) > U + B.

## 4.3 The Standard of Care

### 4.3.1 The Standard Objective Test

(a) In negligence cases, tortfeasors are generally held to an objective, reasonable prudent person standard.[12]

(b) It is an objective standard that does not take into consideration a party's lack of skill, thoughtfulness, or intelligence.

(i) *See Vaughan v. Menlove* (Ct. Common Pleas 1837), where the court applied an objective standard when it held the defendant liable for stacking hay in a way that caught fire, even though he sincerely believed that there was no such risk. The defendant's intelligence was not taken into account.

### 4.3.2 An Amalgum Subjective/Objective Test

(a) Under certain circumstances, a person will be held to an amalgam subjective/objective test that looks to a reasonable prudent person *in that person's position.*

(b) For example, in emergency situations, an actor is held to the standard of a reasonable prudent person *in an emergency situation;* the actor must exercise reasonable care *under the circumstances.*

(i) *See Cordas v. Peerless Transportation Co.* (N.Y. City Ct. 1941), where the defendant jumped out of his cab while it was still running, injuring a woman and her children, after a robber came into the car and, with a gun pointed at his head, commanded him to drive. Held: the defendant is not negligent, since a reasonable prudent person would have acted similarly in like circumstances and quick decision-making was necessary.

(c) The disabled are held to a "reasonable prudent person of like disability" standard. *Roberts v. State of La.* (La. Ct. App. 1981) (applying the standard of a "reasonable prudent blind person").

(d) Those with a diagnosable impairment (*e.g.*, retardation) are generally held to a subjective standard.

(e) Similarly, those who are subjected to a sudden and unforeseeable mental illness will be held to a subjective standard, as long as he has no prior history of the potential impairment that would make injury to third persons a foreseeable risk.

---

[12] Although custom may provide evidence as to what the reasonable prudent person standard is, custom is *not* dispositive, since an entire society can breach its duty of care.

(i) If an actor has a history of mental illness or some other warning of a potentially dangerous mental condition, he will be held to an objective, reasonable prudent person standard in most states.

(ii) *See Breunig v. American Family Ins. Co.* (Wisc. 1970), where the plaintiff sued the tortfeasor's insurance company for negligence when the tortfeasor, in a psychotic episode, believed God had been driving her car and slammed into the plaintiff's truck. The tortfeasor was held to a reasonable prudent person standard, and, given her history of mental illness, she failed.

(f) Children are held to a subjective standard that looks not only at the "reasonable prudent child," but rather, to a reasonable prudent child of "similar age, ability and intelligence."

(i) Some states have established a minimum age (*e.g.*, seven years old) under which children are not capable of negligence.

(ii) However, if the child, regardless of his age, is engaged in some highly dangerous (adult) activity, he will in most states be held to the reasonable prudent person standard as though he were an adult.

(1) *See Robinson v. Lindsay* (Wash. 1979), where the plaintiff brought suit against the defendant, a child who was operating a snowmobile when the plaintiff was injured. The defendant argued that a subjective standard based on a reasonable child of like age, ability, and intelligence should be applied. However, the court held that when a child is engaged in adult activities, the reasonable prudent adult standard is applied.

4.3.3 The Standard for Professionals

(a) Introduction

(i) With respect to professionals, a standard that looks to the reasonable prudent *professional*, not *person*, is applied.

(ii) A doctor or a lawyer is therefore not held to a duty commensurate with that of ordinary reasonable persons, or even a duty according to his own experience and training.

(iii) Rather, he is held to an industry-wide standard, a duty commensurate with that of *other professionals within his profession. Heath v. Swift Wings* (N.C. Ct. App. 1979) (applying a standard of care based on a reasonable prudent pilot).

(iv) While custom normally serves as *evidence* of a standard of care, it is generally dispositive in establishing malpractice in cases involving professionals.

(v) The plaintiff does not, however, need to prove breach of a standard of care based on custom when an act or omission is so negligent that the duty of care is considered to be breached as a matter of law (*prima facie* negligence, *e.g.*, a scalpel left in a patient's wound).

(b) Standard of Care in the Legal Profession

(i) A lawyer has the duty perform services with the care, diligence, and prudence of an ordinary and reasonable attorney under similar circumstances.

(1) *See Hodges v. Carter* (N.C. 1954), where the plaintiff sued his attorney, who served an insurance company improperly the first time and then failed to serve the company the second time before the SL expired. The court ruled for the defendant, since he performed his services with the care, diligence and prudence of an ordinary lawyer, who similarly would have concluded that the service was proper, given the statute in the case and a twenty-year custom.

(2) *N.B.*: if the court held that the defendant failed to meet the reasonable prudent attorney standard, he would have had a second defense if he had proven that there was less than a fifty percent chance that the plaintiff would have won the case.

(c) Standard of Care in the Medical Profession

(i) The standard of care in the medical profession is that of an ordinary and reasonable doctor *from within the community* under similar circumstances.

(1) *See Boyce v. Brown* (Ariz. 1938), where the defendant performed surgery on the plaintiff many years earlier. When the plaintiff later returned to the defendant and complained of pain, the defendant did nothing. The plaintiff went to another doctor, who took X-rays and found and removed a screw that had been causing the plaintiff's pain. The plaintiff sued for malpractice, alleging that the defendant should have taken an X-ray. Held: the standard to be used is not that another doctor would have taken steps contrary to those of the defendant, but rather, that the defendant's actions were contrary to the standard of medical practice *within the community*. Judgment for the defendant.

(ii) The rule that a doctor be held to the standard of the care, diligence, and prudence of a doctor *from within the community* is not strictly applied. Sometimes, the courts hold a doctor to a standard of acting with the care of a doctor from *outside* of the community.

(1) *See Morrison v. MacNamara* (D.C. Ct. App. 1979), where the plaintiff brought suit against the defendant for negligently requiring the plaintiff to stand during a urethral smear test, leading to the plaintiff's dizziness and fainting. The plaintiff brought in an out-of-state expert who testified that the standard in the medical community was to allow patients to sit or lie down during such tests. The trial court held that the testimony was inadmissible, since the expert was not from *within the community*. The appeals court reversed, holding that the origins of the locality rule are outdated in an age of greater mobility and communication. A national standard was adopted.

(iii) Today, most jurisdictions require doctors to perform services with the care of an ordinary and reasonable physician from a similar community under similar circumstances.

(1) Thus, a doctor from in a small, rural town in Ohio may testify in an action against a doctor in a small, rural town in Indiana, as to what he would do in similar circumstances.

(2) The benefit is that a doctor from a small, rural town will not be held to the standard of a doctor from an urban teaching hospital. Furthermore, plaintiffs are not limited in their selection of experts to bring in.

(iv) Some states have gone as far as adopting a national custom standard.

(v) In some cases, however, custom—within the community or otherwise—has not been dispositive. Although it is rare, risk-utility analysis has been applied in a malpractice cases.

(1) *See Helling v. Carey* (Wash. 1974), where the plaintiff sued the defendant for failing to screen the plaintiff for glaucoma. The defendant argued that it was not custom within the community to screen patients under forty years of age for glaucoma. Held: the defendant is liable, since the magnitude of the potential harm far outweighs the slight burden of the screening.

## 4.4 Causes of Action Based on Negligence

### 4.4.1 Informed Consent

(a) Introduction

(i) Informed consent, despite its misleading name, is not a defense to negligence, but rather, a cause of action relating to medical malpractice.

(ii) The tort arises when a physician fails to disclose the ***risks***, ***benefits***, and ***alternatives*** to a procedure, drug, etc.

(b) Elements

(i) Duty

(1) The duty is to disclose the ***material risks, benefits and alternatives*** to a procedure, a drug, or other medically-related practice.

(2) Generally, the standard for malpractice is custom (what other doctors do); here, the standard is based on what *other reasonable patients would expect and wish to know.*

(aa) *See Scott v. Bradford* (Okla. 1979), where the plaintiff Scott was not informed of the risks associated with a hysterectomy that a *reasonable patient* would wish to know. She would not have gone forward with the procedure had she known of the risks, which materialized and led to further surgeries. The defendant was liable for failing to disclose these risks.

(3) "Material" information includes a doctor's personal interests.

(aa) *See Moore v. The Regents of the University of California* (Cal. 1990), where the court held that a doctor breached his fiduciary duty and his duty to disclose material information by not disclosing to a patient that he would profit from a strain of cells he would create from cells removed from the plaintiff during surgery.

(ii) Breach

(1) Failure to disclose material information constitutes breach of the duty.

(2) As exceptions, failure to disclose material information does not constitute breach of the duty when:

(aa) The disclosure would cause an overly sensitive patient ***undue alarm***;

(bb) The risks are widely known and of ***common knowledge***; or

(cc) The patient's judgment is impaired by an ***emergency***.

(iii) Causation

(1) There are two approaches to causation in informed consent:

(aa) The *subjective* approach:

(I) The plaintiff must testify that he would have acted differently if informed of the risks;

(II) The plaintiff's credibility is subject to jury's scrutiny.

(bb) The *subjective/objective* combined approach:

(I) The plaintiff must testify that he would have acted differently if informed of the risks;

(II) The plaintiff's credibility is subject to jury's scrutiny; and

(III) The jury must conclude that a reasonable prudent patient would not have gone forward with the procedure if properly informed.

(iv) Damages

(1) With respect to the injuries, the plaintiff must testify that he suffered injuries whose risks he did not know of.

4.4.2 Negligent Infliction of Emotional Distress

(a) Evolution

(i) Under the common law, the negligent infliction of emotional distress (NIED) was a cause of action when there was a physical impact as well as an injury (***parasitic damages***).

(ii) Under the intermediate impact rule, any ***impact*** was both sufficient and required.

(iii) Under the modern approach in many states, an impact is no longer required, but some states require a physical manifestation of the emotional distress (ED).

(1) *See Daley v. LaCroix* (Mich. 1970), where the defendant's airborne car caused an explosion in the plaintiff's home. Because the crash caused the plaintiff to suffer nervousness and weight loss, there was enough evidence to support a jury finding for NIED, even though the plaintiff was neither physically impacted nor injured.

(b) The Three Approaches

(i) ***Zone of danger rule***: one can recover for the NIED only if:

(1) He was so close to the danger that he could have been injured; and

(2) He witnessed the accident.

(ii) ***Rule of Dillon v. Legg*** (Cal. 1968): one can recover for the NIED according to the following *factors*:

(1) Proximity to the scene of the accident;

(2) The witnessing of the accident; and

(3) A close relation to the victim.

(iii) ***Heightened requirements rule*** (used in California): one can recover for the NIED if the following *elements* are met:

(1) *Presence* at the scene of accident;

(2) Awareness that it is causing injury to victim; and

(3) A close relation to victim;

(aa) *See Thing v. La Chusa* (Cal. 1989), where the plaintiff, who was later informed of the accident by a third party, could not recover for NIED because she was not present at the scene of the accident and did not have awareness of the accident as it was happening.

# 5 The Duty of Care

## 5.1 Statutory Standards of Care

### 5.1.1 Introduction

(a) As we have seen, in establishing a defendant's duties owed, plaintiffs often look to custom (especially in cases involving professionals) or risk-utility analysis.

(b) A third tool that plaintiffs may use in establishing the duty owed is the violation of statutes (negligence *per se*), including civil, criminal, and regulatory statutes.

(c) The violation of a statute often establishes negligence *per se*, or negligence as a matter of law, without the need to prove to a jury the duty owed and the breach of that duty.

### 5.1.2 Statutes Establishing Negligence *Per Se*

(a) The violation of a statute may give rise to: (i) *negligence per se* (a dispositive finding of negligence, regardless of the care taken); (ii) a *rebuttable inference* of negligence; or (iii) mere *evidence* of negligence.

(b) State vary widely in how they treat statutes for the purpose of establishing a duty. One important factor that is considered is whether the statute is civil, criminal, or regulatory in nature.

(c) Plaintiffs may combine various classes of statutes when establishing a duty.

(i) *See Stachniewicz v. Mar-Cam Corp.* (Or. 1971), where the plaintiff sued the defendant for breach of a duty based on (i) a statute prohibiting giving alcohol to those visibly intoxicated; and (ii) a regulation prohibiting allowing disorderly or intoxicated persons to remain on the premises. The first theory failed because it was virtually impossible to prove that the plaintiff would have not been injured but for the extra drinks served to the already intoxicated the defendants; the second theory succeeded since, but for the violation of the regulation, the plaintiff would not have been injured.

### 5.1.3 Classes of Statutes

(a) Civil Statutes

(i) Civil tort statutes create a duty and a cause of action. The violation of such a statute establishes *negligence per se*.

(1) Because negligence is established as a matter of law, breach of duty is not a jury question.

(2) Example: a state adopts a statute requiring all people to sweep their driveways after a snowstorm. The legislature expresses in the statute that reasonable people would do so in order to avoid the hazard of a slippery driveway. If A slips on B's driveway as a result of B's failure to sweep his driveway, A will have a cause of action for negligence and will not need to establish duty or breach.

(ii) However, if a legislature adopts a civil statute without explicitly creating a cause of action or defining a reasonable person as one who would abide by that statute, most courts would adopt the statute as establishing a *rebuttable presumption* or *mere evidence* of negligence.

(b) Criminal Statutes

(i) Most states, based on the rationale that the purpose of criminal statutes is to punish wrongdoers, not to restitute victims, have not instituted the violation of a statute as negligence *per se*.

(ii) Some of these states have deemed the violation of a criminal statute to constitute a *rebuttable presumption* of negligence that can be rebutted with a valid excuse.

(iii) In other states, the violation of a criminal statute constitutes *mere evidence* of negligence.

(iv) In still other states, the violation of a criminal statute is considered negligence *per se*; it is dispositive in establishing negligence.

(c) Regulatory Statutes

(i) Regulatory statutes are passed not by legislatures, but by legislatively created agencies (*e.g.*, the FCC).

(ii) Regulatory laws, unlike civil laws, do not restitute victims, and unlike criminal laws, do not punish wrongdoers. They may, however, *revoke licenses*.

(iii) Violation of regulatory statutes, like custom, is ***evidence of negligence***, but it is *not dispositive*.

5.1.4 The Applicability of a Statute

(a) Courts only adopt statutes for the purpose of establishing a duty and breach when doing so is "fair, workable and wise." The following factors are considered:

(i) Whether the ***duty*** was recognized in the common law;

(1) When a statute creates a new duty that did not exist in the common law, courts will rarely hold non-compliant citizens liable for tort damages, unless it is a tort statute allowing for such recovery.

(2) Courts tend only to adopt regulatory or criminal statutes as standards of care when these statutes *clarify* already existing common law duties.

(ii) Whether the statute is clear as to what constitutes a ***breach*** or violation;

(iii) Whether the ***causal*** link between the violation and the injury is clear; and

(iv) Whether ***damages*** for the tort liability eclipse the civil fine.

(1) *See Perry v. S.N. and S.N.* (Tex. 1998), where the defendants (Perry) did not report the Kellers' sexual abuse of the plaintiffs' children. They were held not to be liable because: (i) the common law recognizes no duty to rescue (*see infra.*); (ii) the statute is not clear in defining the forbidden behavior, since it does not state at which point in their suspicions must the defendants report the abuse; (iii) the non-reporting of the abuse and the actual harm in this case are very indirect; and (iv) adopting the statute as a tort duty of care could lead to significantly higher civil liability than envisioned by the statute.

(b) If a court decides that adopting a statute as a duty of care is fair, the statute will only be applied to a case in particular if the party establishing negligence proves that:

(i) The *victim* is part of the class that the *legislature intended to protect* through the statute; and

(ii) The *injury* is of the kind that the *legislature wanted to prevent*.

5.1.5 Effects of Statutes Adopted as Standards of Care

(a) Statutes imposing a duty on citizens may be ***used by defendants*** in the affirmative defense of ***contributory negligence***.

(b) Defendants must show that (i) the plaintiff violated a statute that represents a duty of care owed to the defendant; and (ii) violation of the statute contributed to the plaintiff's injury.

(i) *See Martin v. Herzog* (N.Y. 1920), where the plaintiff sued for negligence when the defendant Herzog violated a statute by crossing the white line while turning in his car, hitting the plaintiff's buggy and causing the plaintiff's husband's death. The defendant argued and the court agreed that the plaintiff was contributorily negligent *per se* by violating a statute that required him to keep his lights on.

(ii) *N.B.*: the court expressed the need to show that the violation of the statute was what caused the injury: had it not been for the plaintiff's not having lights on, the accident would not have occurred.

(c) When the violation of a statute creates a rebuttable presumption of negligence, the presumption may be rebutted by the following valid excuses (§ 288A Restatement):

(i) The actor *lacks capacity* (*e.g.*, he is an infant, is mentally insane, etc.);

(ii) The actor has *no knowledge of the violation*;

(iii) The *impracticability* of compliance (*e.g.*, violation would be safer than compliance);

(1) *See Zeni v. Anderson* (Mich. 1976), where the plaintiff Zeni was held not to be contributorily negligent for violating a statute requiring pedestrians to walk on the sidewalk facing traffic, since the sidewalk was covered in snow and it would have been more dangerous for the plaintiff to walk on it than on the highway.

(iv) The *impossibility* of compliance; or

(v) An *emergency* renders compliance outside of the actor's control.

**5.2** Duty to Rescue

5.2.1 The Common Law Approach

(a) The common law never recognized a duty to intervene or to rescue.

(i) *See Hegel v. Langsam* (Ohio Ct. Com. Pl. 1971), where the court held that universities have no duty to monitor the lives of their students, and the defendant was accordingly not liable when the plaintiff Hegel's child became involved with drug criminals and missed classes.

(b) Rather, the common law imposed liability on a rescuer who undertook to act and exacerbated a victim's condition through his negligence or other torts.

(c) Naturally, this creates a disincentive to rescue. To offset the disincentive of potential liability, many states have passed ***Good Samaritan statutes*** that protect rescuers from liability.

(i) What is protected:

(1) *Majority approach*: negligence only.

(2) *Minority approach* (*e.g.*, California): *all* torts.

(ii) Who is protected:

(1) *Majority approach*: any rescuer.

(2) *Minority approach*: licensees (*e.g.*, doctors) only.

5.2.2 Exceptions to the Common Law "No Duty to Rescue" Rule

(a) The general common law rule is that there is no duty to intervene or to rescue.

(b) However, under certain circumstances, the common law imposed liability on a defendant for an omission to act. The duty to rescue was recognized by the common law when:

(i) The defendant undertook to act by: (i) promising to act; or (ii) beginning to undertake a rescue by giving assistance.

(ii) The defendant caused the victim's peril or left him in greater peril than he found him, whether or not he acted with intent or negligence.

(iii) The instrumentality is within the defendant's control (especially when the plaintiff is an invitee).

(1) *See L.S. Ayres and Co. v. Hicks* (Ind. 1942), where a child was injured when his fingers were caught in the defendant L.S. Ayres and Co.'s escalator. Since the escalator was an instrumentality within the defendant's control, the defendant had a duty to rescue. Because he was not being attentive in shutting it down rapidly enough, the defendant is liable for the aggravation of the injury resulting from the delay.

(iv) There is a special relationship with the victim (*e.g.*, relationships between spouses; employers and employees; parents and children; inviters and invitees; innkeepers and guests; common carriers and passengers, etc.).

(v) Other circumstances based on: (i) the *foreseeability* of the harm; (ii) the *societal interest* in recognizing the duty; and (iii) the *opportunity to avoid risk*.

(1) *See Tarasoff v. Regents of University of California* (Cal. 1976), where the defendant was liable for failure to rescue when it was *foreseeable* that the a patient of the defendant university's psychologist would murder another patient, since the former confessed his intention to do so. The defendant's duty was to do more than merely temporarily detain the patient.

(2) *See also J.S. and M.S. v. R.T.H* (N.J. 1998), where the defendant was sued for not reporting her husband's sexual abuse of the plaintiffs' children, who frequented the defendant's home to play with the defendant's horses. Held:

because the defendant had known or should have known about her husband's propensities, she owed a duty to rescue the children.

(aa) *N.B.*: because the defendant was the abuser's spouse, the foreseeability of sexual abuse was much higher, causing the court to impose a duty to rescue.

**5.3** Premises Liability

5.3.1 In the majority of states, the duty owed in premises liability varies according to whether the person on one's land is an invitee (highest duty of care owed), a licensee, or a trespasser (lowest duty of care owed).

(a) Invitees

(i) An invitee is a person who is conferring a business or pecuniary benefit on the owner or occupier of the premises.

(ii) The standard of care owed to invitees is one of ***reasonable care*** in all circumstances. This includes the duty to ***inspect*** the property at reasonable intervals, to ***warn*** invitees of potential hazards, and possibly to ***repair*** such hazards.

(iii) The pecuniary benefit may have been conferred at regular intervals in the past; the fact that the invitee did not confer a pecuniary benefit on the day that the negligence arose does not change his status.

(1) *See Campbell v. Weathers* (Kan. 1941), where the plaintiff Campbell fell through a trap door in the defendant's restaurant's toilet facility. The defendant argued that the plaintiff was not an invitee, since the plaintiff had only loitered at the counter and did not purchase food on that day. Held: because the plaintiff was a regular customer who intended to purchase something on that day or in the future, he is considered an invitee, and a *standard duty of care* is imposed on the defendant. Judgment for the defendant reversed.

(b) Licensees

(i) When a person is on the owner's premises with the owner's permission, but is not conferring a pecuniary benefit to the owner (*e.g.*, an invited social guest), he is a licensee.

(ii) States are divided on the duty of care owed to licensees.

(1) Under the majority approach, which is the approach adopted by the Restatement, there is a duty to warn licensees of *dangers known* by the owner and *dangers that should be known* by the owner.

(aa) *See Barmore v. Elmore* (Ill. App. Ct. 1980), where the plaintiff sued the defendant Elmore for failing to protect him when the defendant's son stabbed him while he was in the defendant's home. Held: since the plaintiff was not on the premises to discuss business directly benefiting the defendant, he was a mere licensee. Therefore, the defendant owed him *only a duty to warn of reasonable dangers*. Since the defendant had *no reasonable basis* to suspect his son was a threat, he did not breach this duty.

(2) Under the minority approach, the duty is to warn licensees only of *dangers known* by the owner.

(iii) However, an owner has no duty to warn licensees of dangers that are:

(1) Open and in the obvious; or

(2) The cause of natural weather patterns.

(iv) A person's status from invitee to licensee (and vice versa) may change under the circumstances.

(1) *See Whelan v. Van Natta* (Ky. Ct. App. 1964), where an invitee who bought cigarettes from a store became a licensee when he went into a back room to retrieve a box.

(c) Trespassers

(i) Trespassers constitute the last category in premises liability.

(ii) Owners owe ***no duty of care*** to unknown trespassers.

(iii) However, owners have a duty to warn ***known trespassers*** of *hidden dangers* on the property of which the owner is aware or has reason to be aware (under the majority approach) or, under the minority approach, only of which he *knows*.

(1) *See Sheehan v. St. Paul and Duluth Railway Co.* (7th Cir. 1896), where the plaintiff Sheehan's foot was run over by a train when he was trespassing near train tracks and got stuck when a train was passing. Held: since the defendant did not know of the trespasser's presence, no duty of care was owed.

(iv) A trespasser is known by the owner if he directly eye witnesses the trespasser if he becomes aware of the trespasser through an indirect third source.

(v) If the owner knows or reasonably should know that part of his property is frequently trespassed, an unknown trespasser using that part of the land will be treated as a known trespasser.

5.3.2 Distinction merged

(a) California has led a minority of states in merging the distinction between invitees, licensees, and trespassers.

(b) In such states, juries are instructed that the defendant owed the plaintiff a *duty of reasonable care under the circumstances* (informed by foreseeability).

(c) The jury may consider whether the plaintiff was a trespasser, licensee or invitee in determining whether there was a breach of duty.

(d) Other states have merged the difference between licensees and invitees only, but have continued imposing no duty of care towards unknown trespassers.

## 6 Proving Breach

### 6.1 Introduction

6.1.1 In examining standards of care, we have reviewed the three tests that are used in establishing duties owed: (i) the reasonable prudent person test; (ii) custom; and (iii) statutory standards of care.

6.1.2 Now, we move on to breach, which, unlike duty, is always ***heavily factual***.

6.1.3 It is generally obvious when a duty has been breached, but when direct evidence does not prove the breach, the analysis can be complex.

6.1.4 In such cases, fact finders are permitted to draw inferences based on circumstantial evidence.

6.1.5 The following is a general framework for analyzing breach:

(a) Look to direct evidence (99% of breach analyses end here);

(b) If there is no direct evidence, use ***circumstantial evidence*** – secondary facts and other evidence that lead to primary fact inferences;

(c) If there is no probative evidence, ***res ipsa loquitur*** may be used (*see infra.*).

6.2 Circumstantial evidence

6.2.1 In making a *prima facie* case for negligence, the burden is on the plaintiff to produce evidence that proves the defendant's negligence by a ***preponderance of the evidence***.

6.2.2 When the plaintiff fails to meet this burden, a directed verdict is ordered in favor of the defendant.

(a) *See Goddard v. Boston and Maine R.R. Co.* (Mass. 1901), where the plaintiff Goddard introduced neither direct nor indirect evidence of the defendant's ***actual notice*** or ***constructive notice*** (legal notice derived from the circumstances) of a banana peel's being on the ground. Failing to prove breach, the plaintiff's *prima facie* case was not made. The directed verdict for the defendant was affirmed.

(b) *Compare Anjou v. Boston Elevated Railray Co.* (Mass. 1911), where the plaintiff proved ***constructive notice*** by a preponderance of the evidence. Using circumstantial evidence, the plaintiff showed that a peel had been on the ground for a substantial period, since it was black, dry, and gritty.

6.2.3 This burden may be met through the use of either circumstantial or direct evidence. Circumstantial evidence is often used in establishing constructive notice of an unreasonable harm from which the defendant has a duty to protect third parties.

(a) *See Joye v. Great Atlantic and Pacific Tea Co.* (4th Cir. 1968), where the plaintiff introduced evidence in court showing that the defendant should have known about the banana peel on the ground, since it had been there for thirty five minutes or more. The plaintiff won and the defendant made a motion for a judgment *non obstante veredicto*. Held: the plaintiff failed to bring in clear evidence that established whether the banana peel had been on the ground for three minutes or three days. The defendant's motion for a judgment *non obstante veredicto* is granted.

6.2.4 Normally, there is a burden on the plaintiff to produce evidence that gives rise to either a ***conclusion***, or, when there is no direct evidence, an ***inference of negligence*** (*exception*: when the facts so strongly create an inference of negligence that probative evidence is not required—see *res ipsa loquitur*, *infra.*).

(a) In either case, the burden is on the plaintiff to prove the breach.

(b) However, some courts have been sloppy about this and have ruled for the plaintiff *even when he has failed* to furnish the evidence that proves breach as a part of his *prima facie* case.

(i) *See Ortega v. Kmart Corp.* (Cal. 2001), where the plaintiff Ortega failed to show with a preponderance of the evidence that Kmart had either actual or constructive notice of a puddle of milk that the plaintiff slipped on. Furthermore, the defendant testified that it was highly unlikely that milk would be on floor for more than fifteen to thirty minutes, and the plaintiff did not establish that it was on the floor for longer. The court nevertheless ruled in favor of the plaintiff

6.2.5 However, for certain activities, the plaintiff is not required to introduce evidence of the defendant's breach. Rather, certain activities ("mode of operation") are given strict liability treatment.

(a) *See Jasko v. F.W. Woolworth Co.* (Colo. 1972), where the defendant was liable to the plaintiff Jasko for a slip on a slice of pizza because of the *mode of operation* (a self service pizza parlor with pizza served on wax paper). Thus, despite the defendant's normal precautions (regular sweepers, etc.), he is on constant constructive notice of hazards and is liable for injuries.

### ***6.3*** *Res Ipsa Loquitur*

6.3.1 Introduction

(a) *Res ipsa loquitur* (RIL) is a negligence circumstantial evidence doctrine.

(b) It is invoked when the facts create such a strong presumption of negligence that "the thing speaks for itself" (*Lat.*). The plaintiff is not required to introduce evidence.

(i) *See Byrne v. Boadle* (Ct. of Exchequer 1863), where the plaintiff was walking when a barrel rolled out of the defendant's warehouse, striking him. The plaintiff sued for negligence, but had no evidence to prove a breach of duty. Held: it would be preposterous to require the plaintiff to produce evidence proving breach. The accident *would not have happened* but for the defendant's negligence. Judgment for the plaintiff.

(c) Two elements must be satisfied before RIL may be successfully invoked:

(i) The instrument must be in the defendant's exclusive control; and

(ii) The event must normally not occur absent someone's negligence.

(1) *See Larson v. St. Francis Hotel* (Cal. Ct. App. 1948), where the plaintiff was injured by a chair that was thrown out of the defendant's hotel window. The threshold test was not met when the plaintiff failed to show that: (i) the defendant had exclusive control over the instrumentality, since guests at the defendant's hotel could have thrown the chair out of the window; and (ii) that absent the defendant's negligence, the event normally would not occur, since the event could occur even if the defendant did everything in his power short of posting a security guard in each room.

(d) In meeting the threshold test, the plaintiff may invoke common sense and experience.

(i) *See McDougald v. Perry* (Fla. 1998), where common sense dictated that but for the defendant's negligence, a tire from his truck would not have come loose, striking the plaintiff McDougald's windshield.

(e) Once successfully invoked, the plaintiff's burden of proving breach is significantly lightened. However, the defendant may still rebut the presumption of negligence.

6.3.2 The Three Approaches to RIL

(a) *Permissive inference approach:* the jury may accept or reject the RIL inference.

(b) *Presumption and shift of the ultimate burden of proof approach:* this approach requires the defendant to prove by a preponderance of all of the evidence that the injury was not caused by his negligence.

(c) *Mandatory presumption approach:* raises a presumption that a jury *must accept*, unless the defendant proves otherwise.

6.3.3 Group *Res Ipsa Loquitur*

(a) In some jurisdictions, where group RIL is accepted, when the plaintiff knows that one of a group of the defendants was responsible for an injury, but is not certain which one, the plaintiff may sue all the defendants jointly.

(b) *See Ybarra v. Spangard* (Cal. 1944), where the plaintiff, unaware of who caused an injury during surgery that lead to pain in the plaintiff's shoulder upon his awaking, sued all of the doctors. The plaintiff invoked RIL and the defendants plead that RIL may not be applied, since the harm could not have arisen from the act of any single the defendant. Held: RIL applies because the injury was in the defendants' *exclusive collective control* and such injury does not normally arise absent negligence.

### *6.4* Summary for Proving Breach

6.4.1 The plaintiff must:

(a) Offer *direct evidence;*

(b) If direct evidence is lacking, offer *indirect (circumstantial) evidence;*

(c) If there is no probative evidence, *res ipsa loquitur* may be invoked in certain cases (*see infra.*).

6.4.2 In *slip and fall cases*, there are four ways of proving breach:

(a) By proving that *the defendant's employee caused the hazard*;

(b) By showing that the defendant had *actual notice* of a hazard (usually with direct evidence);

(c) By show that the defendant had *constructive notice* (usually with circumstantial evidence); or

(d) By proving a dangerous *mode of operation*.

## 7 Causation

### 7.1 Cause-in-Fact

7.1.1 *Sine Qua Non*

(a) In order for a defendant to be held liable in tort, the plaintiff must prove causation.

(b) First, cause-in-fact (*sine qua non* causation) must be established. The test is whether the plaintiff would have been injured had the defendant not done the negligent act.

(i) *See Perkins v. Texas and New Orleans Railway Co.* (La. 1962), where the plaintiff was unable to recover for her husband's death, since she was unable to prove that: (i) the train's violation of the speed limit was the *sine qua non* cause of his death; (ii) the train's speeding prevented it from stopping in time, because even if it had been going twelve miles per hour slower, the 1,250 foot long train still would have been unable to stop; and (iii) the train's speeding deprived the defendant's car from the extra moment to cross the tracks, since the car may have been going anywhere between three to twenty five miles per hour, rendering this theory pure speculation.

7.1.2 Proof of Causation

(a) Causation must be proven with the ***preponderance of the evidence***.

(i) *See Reynolds v. Texas and Pac. Railway Co.* (La. Ct. App. 1885), where the plaintiff Reynolds was injured while rushing up the stairs of the defendant's unlit railroad platform. Held: the defendant was liable for not having the stairs lit at the platform, even though the plaintiff's negligence in rushing up the stairs could have been the but-for cause of the injury, since not having the stairs lit greatly multiplied the chances of injury. The defendant's negligence was more than fifty percent likely to have caused the plaintiff's injury.

(b) The subsequent timing between one factor and another is not enough to establish the requisite proof of causation.

(i) *See Kramer Service, Inc. v. Wilkins* (Miss. 1939), where the fact that cancer subsequently appeared in an area cut by glass due to the defendant Kramer Service's negligence was too attenuated to prove causation, particularly since even the plaintiff's experts said that the chances that a cut could cause cancer were one in one hundred.

7.1.3 Concurrent Causes

(a) When there is more than one cause of an injury, the agent of either cause is fully responsible for the injury.

(b) This is true even when the defendant's actions on their own would not have passed the "but-for" test. *See Hill v. Edmonds* (N.Y. App. 1966) (plaintiff's contributory negligence does not bar him from recovery).

(c) When the defendant's breach of duty was a concurrent cause of the plaintiff's harm, and when this cause fails the *but-for test*, courts may find causation-in-fact satisfied if the factor was a ***substantial and material cause***.

(i) *See Anderson v. Minneapolis R.R.* (Minn. 1920), where a fire that was sparked by the defendant Minneapolis R.R.'s breach of duty merged with another fire of unknown cause, damaging the plaintiff's home. The plaintiff sued for negligence and the defendant argued that because the other fire would have burned down the plaintiff's home anyway, but-for cause was not satisfied. Held: because the defendant's breach of duty was a ***substantive factor*** in bringing about the plaintiff's harm, the cause-in-fact test is satisfied.

(ii) *N.B.*: the *substantial factor test* would release a defendant from liability when his act only slightly contributes to the damage (*e.g.*, throwing a lit match into an already raging forest fire).

**7.2** Proximate Cause

7.2.1 Unforeseeable Consequences

(a) Because so many causes may be considered causes-in-fact, public policy must draw a line somewhere. *Atlantic Coast Line Railroad Co. v. Daniels* (Ga. App. 1911).

(b) Thus, even when the defendant is negligent, he is not liable for damages caused to another's property when those damages were ***unforeseeable***.

(i) *See Ryan v. New York Central R.R. Co.* (N.Y. 1866), where the defendant's negligence led to a fire on his property that eventually spread to and damaged the plaintiff's property. Because the wind, heat, and other circumstances leading to the spreading were so unusual, the defendant was not liable for negligence.

(ii) *N.B.*: today, plaintiffs in NY have a cause of action when the damage comes from neighboring property.

(c) Under the ***thin skull rule***, a defendant is liable for *all* personal bodily injuries resulting from his negligence, including injuries due to a plaintiff's *unforeseeable sensitivity*, when at least *some* of that injury was foreseeable.

(d) Some jurisdictions apply the ***thin skull property rule***, or the Polemis *rule*, where the defendant is liable not only for all bodily injuries, but also, for all damages to property, when (i) at least some damage was *foreseeable;* and (ii) there was a *direct chain of events*, without superseding causes.

(i) *See In re Arbitration Between Polemis and Furness Withy and Co., Ltd.* (Eng. Ct. App. 1921), where the defendants were held liable for *all damages* directly resulting from the defendants' dropping of a plank on a ship, including the damages resulting when a spark *unforeseeably* ignited a fire due to petrol vapors, since (i) there was some foreseeable damage (*i.e.*, a broken plank) and (ii) the unforeseeable damages resulted from an uninterrupted chain of events.

(e) Other jurisdictions have repudiated the Polemis *approach*, and have adopted the "*Wagon Mound* approach," which allows for liability for *foreseeable property damage only*.

(i) *See Overseas Tankship (U.K.) Ltd. v. Morts Dock and Engineering Co., Ltd.* ("Wagon Mound No. 1") (Privy Council 1961), where the plaintiff Overseas Tankship's wharf was ***foreseeably and nominally damaged*** by the defendant's freighter's oil discharge and later ***unforeseeably destroyed*** when cotton floating in the water caught fire. Under *Polemis*, the foreseeable initial damage would be enough to establish liability for the later unforeseen damages. Held: the *Polemis* rule is "inherently unjust" and the defendant is not liable; judgment for the plaintiff is reversed.

(f) Under the *Palsgraf* foreseeable plaintiff rule, foreseeability also factors into *who* may sue.

(i) *See Palsgraf v. Long Island R.R. Co.* (N.Y. 1928) (Cardozo, J.) where the defendant's employees, helping a passenger onto a train, caused a package to fall, leading to the explosion of fireworks. This caused a scale to fall on and injure the plaintiff Palsgraf, who was standing at the other end of a platform. Held: because the employees had no way of knowing that the package contained explosives, the explosion was unforeseeable. Furthermore, the plaintiff was an unforeseeable plaintiff, since no risk of injuring her was foreseeable. The defendant could not have had a duty to prevent an unforeseeable injury to an unforeseeable plaintiff. Judgment for the plaintiff is reversed.

(ii) *Andrews dissent*: all people have a duty to protect all other people all of the time. Here, the defendant had a duty to protect the plaintiff and all of the passengers. Thus, the duty element is met, and it was breached. In analyzing proximate cause, the following factors must be considered: foreseeability, proximity in time and space, attenuation, the directness of cause and effect, the possibility of too many intervening acts, and superseding causes.

(g) Today, the defendants are held liable for injuries and damages that are proximately caused by their negligence, and the main factor used in determining proximate cause is ***foreseeability***: defendants are liable for *foreseeable risks* when the burden of eliminating the risk is outweighed by the risk and its magnitude.

7.2.2 Intervening Acts and Superseding Causes

(a) An ***intervening act*** is an act that falls in the line of events between an event and an injury, altering the chain of events that might have connected wrongful conduct to an injury.

(b) When an intervening act is sufficiently unusual and unforeseeable, it becomes a ***superseding cause***. When intervening acts, such as the plaintiff's own conduct, become superseding causes, the defendant is exonerated of liability. *See Yun v. Ford Motor Co.* (N.J. App. Div. 1994)

(c) However, when an intervening act is foreseeable, is it not a superseding cause and the actor is liable.

(d) One relatively dispositive test in measuring whether an intervening act is foreseeable is when rules and customs are established to prevent the act from occurring.

(i) *See Derdiarian v. Felix Contracting Corp.* (N.Y. 1980), where the defendant, a general contractor, was liable for injuries to the plaintiff Derdiarian, his employee, when the defendant failed to erect a safety barricade around the plaintiff's work station to protect him from oncoming traffic. When a nearby driver had an epileptic seizure, his car hit the site, causing sealing material to burn the plaintiff. The defendant's defense—the driver's epileptic seizure was an unforeseeable superseding cause—was without merit, since the barricades, as *required by custom*, were designed to protect against this very kind of car accident.

(e) Generally, because criminal and malicious acts are considered to be unforeseeable, intervening malicious acts are superseding causes.

(i) *See Watson v. Kentucky and Indiana Bridge and R.R. Co.* (Ky. Ct. App. 1910), where the court held that maliciously dropping a match over gas spilled when a train derailed would be a superseding act that would render the defendant Kentucky and Indiana Bridge and R.R. Co. not liable.

7.2.3 Rescue Doctrine

(a) Under the rescue doctrine, a party that negligently places another in peril is deemed to owe a duty of care to anyone who may attempt to rescue the imperiled party.

(b) The doctrine lightens rescuers' burden of proving negligence.

(c) For an actor to fit within the categories covered by the "rescue doctrine," he must show the following elements:

(i) Negligence *caused peril* to the person rescued;

(ii) The peril was *imminent;*

(iii) A reasonable prudent person would have concluded that there was *danger present;* and

(iv) The rescuer was *not grossly negligent.*

(d) Once these elements are met, the rescue doctrine applies and the following occurs:

(i) The plaintiff rescuer is permitted to sue the defendant whose breach of duty towards the injured party is transferred to the plaintiff;

(ii) The defendant may not raise A/R; and

(iii) The defendant may not argue that the rescue was a superseding cause. Rather, it is considered foreseeable.[13]

(e) Once the rescue doctrine applies, the plaintiff must prove:

---

[13] According to Justice Cardozo, "Danger invites rescue."

(i) Duty towards the original party;

(ii) Breach of that duty;

(iii) Causation (proving the rescue doctrine substitutes here); and

(iv) Damages.

(f) *See McCoy v. American Suzuki Motor Corp.* (Wash. 1998), where a car manufactured by the defendant flipped over on a highway and the plaintiff McCoy, while rescuing the driver, was struck and injured by a car. The plaintiff sued the defendant for negligence, invoking the duty to rescue. The defendant argued that the duty to rescue may not be invoked in products liability law, since that area of the law has been codified by statute, which has not included the doctrine. Held: even when the rescue doctrine is invoked, proximate cause must be proved. Since the plaintiff could prove that a rescuer's injury while rescuing the driver of a car that flipped over was foreseeable, this question needs to go to a jury. Reversed and remanded.

(i) *N.B.*: note the similar underlying public policy in the ***rescue doctrine*** and the ***Good Samaritan doctrine***. In the rescue doctrine, the defendant is unable to invoke assumption of the risk as a defense to his injury to a rescuer; in the Good Samaritan doctrine, the injured cannot sue the rescuer for negligence.

7.2.4 Public Policy: the Dram Shop Acts

(a) Many states have passed Dram Shop Acts, which make a host liable for injuries caused by his guests if the host serves alcohol to the guests when the guest is visibly intoxicated.

(i) Some Dram Shop Acts limit the liability of the host to only when the host knows that the guest will be driving.

(ii) Others allow for liability for *any* injury caused by a guest's intoxication.

(b) *Majority approach*: commercial hosts are liable for serving alcohol to *all guests*; social hosts are liable for serving alcohol *only to minors*.

(c) *Minority approach*: both social and commercial hosts are liable for serving alcohol to all guests.

(i) This is the approach adopted in NJ.

(ii) *See Kelly v. Gwinnell* (N.J. 1984), where the court held that social hosts are henceforth liable to parties injured by their visibly intoxicated guests, whether they are majors or minors, when the host served the guest alcohol knowing that the guest would be driving.

# 8 Damages

## 8.1 Damages from Personal Injuries and Mitigation

8.1.1 Introduction

(a) To win a judgment, the plaintiffs must prove both ***damage*** (some kind of injury or harm) and ***damages*** (the amount of money they are entitled to receive from the defendant).

(b) There are two kinds of damages that accrue both before and after trial:

(i) ***General damages***: physical pain and emotional suffering.

(ii) ***Special (consequential) damages***: lost wages and medical bills.

(c) In the appropriate case, there is also ***property damage***.

(d) Because plaintiffs must prove future damages in order to receive them, they often wait until just before the SL expires before filing suit in order to have more evidence for determining damages with certainty.

8.1.2 Personal Injuries

(a) ***Remittitur*** is the power of the judge to force the plaintiff to accept an award less than that awarded by the jury when the judge considers the jury award to be excessive.

(b) Remittitur is not necessary when the jury awards damages within what it is permitted to find, even when those damages may seem excessive.

(i) *See Anderson v. Sears, Roebuck and Co.* (E.D. La. 1974), where the defendant. Sears, Roebuck and Co.'s heater malfunctioned, injuring the plaintiffs and burning their home. The jury awarded over $2 million to husband, wife and daughter. The defendant moved for remittitur. Held: because the damages were within what the jury was allowed to find, and because the injuries, especially those sustained by the daughter, were severe, leading to emotional and physical pain for the rest of her life, the damages were not excessive. Motion for remittitur denied.

8.1.3 Collateral Source Rule

(a) When the plaintiff receives collateral sources to cover his costs or damages, the damages awarded are not to be reduced.

(b) Rationale: the defendant should not benefit from the plaintiff's foresight and industry.

(i) *See Montgomery Ward and Co., Inc. v. Anderson* (Ark. 1998), where the plaintiff Anderson received a 50 % discount from the hospital following her injury. Nevertheless, her damages were not reduced: collateral sources do not affect the judgment awarded.

(c) The collateral source rule is the majority approach today.

8.1.4 Mitigation of Damages

(a) Mitigation of damages is required when an ordinary, prudent person would mitigate in like circumstances.

(b) This does not always mean undergoing surgery to mitigate otherwise permanent injuries, especially when the surgery implicates high risks or costs. *Zimmerman v. Ausland* (Or. 1973).

(c) If a party fails to mitigate, he may not recover the difference between the present injury and its mitigation (through having either avoided aggravation or reduced overall injury).

## 8.2 Punitive Damages

### 8.2.1 Introduction

(a) The purposes of punitive damages are as follow:

(i) The ***punishment of the tortfeasor***;

(ii) ***Specific deterrence*** (deterrence of the particular tortfeasor); and

(iii) ***General deterrence*** (deterrence of other potential tortfeasors).

(b) Punitive damages are applied to aggravated forms of misconduct. The plaintiff must prove ***recklessness*** or ***intent.***

(i) Generally, gross negligence does not warrant punitive damages.

(ii) Thus, some lawyers will deliberately frame causes of action as based on intentional torts, rather than on negligence.

(c) Punitive damages are usually paid directly to plaintiffs. However, some states require all or a portion of punitive damages to be paid directly to the state or to some fund.

(i) *See Cheatham v. Pohle*, where the court held that funneling 75 % of punitive damages to a state fund was not unconstitutional, since the purpose of punitive damages was to punish the defendant, not to compensate the plaintiff.

### 8.2.2 Due Process

(a) Punitive damages are often criticized for having the same effects of criminal statutory fines, but without having the same safeguards.

(b) The Supreme Court, in *BMW v. Gore* (U.S. 1996), has therefore developed a three-prong test that assures the constitutionality of punitives, which must not significantly eclipse:

(i) Civil fines imposed in like circumstances;

(ii) The reprehensibility of the defendant's act; and

(iii) Compensatory damages.

(c) The Supreme Court has refined this test by holding that no more than a nine-to-one ratio of punitive to compensatory damages may be awarded.

(i) *See State Farm Mutual Automobile Ins. Co. v. Campbell* (U.S. 2003), where the Court held that the ratio of $145 million punitive damages to $2.6 million compensatory damages (reduced to $1 million) against State Farm was unconstitutionally excessive. Reversed and remanded.

# 9 Defenses

## 9.1 Contributory and Comparative Negligence

### 9.1.1 Introduction

(a) As we have already examined, the defenses to the IT's include consent and the non-consensual privileges (self-defense, defense of others, and the defense and recovery of property.

(b) The defenses to negligence include: contributory and comparative negligence and the assumption of the risk (A/R).

### 9.1.2 Contributory Negligence

(a) Contributory negligence refers to a plaintiff's failure to exercise ordinary care over himself. The same negligence elements against the defendant are applied to the plaintiff.

(b) If the defendant successfully proves all of the elements of contributory negligence, then this affirmative defense bars the plaintiff from recovery.

(i) *See Butterfield v. Forrester* (K.B. 1809), where the plaintiff, by riding his horse too fast, was contributorily negligent when trying to go around an obstruction negligently left in the road by the defendant. Held: because the plaintiff's contributory negligence was a factor bringing about his harm, he may not recover.

(c) Over the years, the courts have become more flexible and have developed the following tests:

(i) ***Substantial factor test***: the jury will not find contributory negligence if it finds that the plaintiff's negligence was not a substantial factor in bringing about his harm.

(ii) ***Last clear chance doctrine***: the plaintiff may recover, even when he was contributorily negligent, when he can show that the defendant: (i) had the *last clear chance*, or opportunity to prevent the harm from coming about; but he (ii) failed to use reasonable care in doing so.

(1) *See Davies v. Mann* (Ct. of Exchequer 1842), where the plaintiff, steering his fettered donkey onto a road, was struck by the defendant's wagon, killing the donkey. Held: because the defendant could have avoided the accident upon seeing the plaintiff, he had the *last clear chance* and the plaintiff may therefore recover.

### 9.1.3 Comparative Negligence

(a) Many states have completely replaced contributory negligence with comparative negligence, which allows the plaintiff to recover proportionately according to the degree of his negligence.

(b) There are two approaches to comparative negligence against a single the defendant:

(i) ***Pure comparative negligence***. The plaintiff may always recover the percentage of his damages corresponding to the defendant's fault.

(ii) ***Modified comparative negligence***

(1) There are two approaches to modified comparative damages:

(aa) The plaintiff may only recover when the defendant's fault was greater than or equal to the plaintiff's fault (*i.e.*, when the defendant's share of the fault was 50 % or more);

(bb) The plaintiff may only recover when the defendant's fault was greater than the plaintiff's fault (*i.e.*, when the defendant's share of the fault was *greater* than 50%).

(2) Unless the defendant's fault is greater than (or equal to) 50 %, the plaintiff may recover nothing (it has the same effect as contributory negligence).

(c) Similarly, there are two approaches to comparative negligence against multiple the defendants:

(i) ***Pure comparative negligence*** states

(1) The plaintiff may always recover the percentage of his damages that corresponds to the defendants' fault, even if that percentage is less than 50 %.

(2) Example: if the plaintiff was 40 % at fault, and the first defendant and his codefendant were each 30 % at fault, the plaintiff may collect 60 % of his damages.

(ii) ***Modified comparative negligence*** states

(1) Cumulative approach:

(aa) The plaintiff may only recover if his negligence was less than (or, in some states, less than or equal to) the defendants' combined negligence (*i.e.*, less than (or less than or equal to) 50 %).

(bb) Example: if the plaintiff was 40 % at fault, and the first defendant and his codefendant were each 30 % at fault, the plaintiff may collect 60 % of his damages, since his 40 % fault is less than that of the cumulative 60 % of the defendants. .

(2) Non-cumulative approach:

(aa) The plaintiff may only recover against defendants whose negligence is greater than (or, in some states, greater than or equal to) the plaintiff's negligence.

(bb) Example: if the plaintiff was 40 % at fault, and the first defendant and his codefendant were each 30 % at fault, the plaintiff would collect nothing, since his 40 % share of the fault is greater than either defendant's 30 % share.

(d) Forty six states have replaced contributory negligence with comparative negligence through statutes and through judicial decisions. *See, e.g., McIntyre v. Balentine* (Tenn. 1992) (adopting comparative negligence and abandoning the last clear chance doctrine and J/SL for Tennessee).

(e) Effects of the Adoption of Comparative Negligence on Other Doctrines

(i) Last Clear Chance Doctrine

(1) Since this rebuttal to contributory negligence is no longer needed, the last clear doctrine has been abolished in many states.

(2) However, the tests used in determining whether the defendant had the last clear chance continue to be used in apportioning his degree of fault.

(ii) Joint and Several Liability (J/SL)

(1) Many states that have adopted comparative negligence have abolished J/SL.

(2) Instead, they use the same tests in determining the plaintiff's comparative negligence in also determining each defendant's particular share of the fault.

**9.2** Assumption of Risk (A/R)

9.2.1 Express Assumption of the Risk

(a) When a party assumes the risk through signing a contract, he is precluded from later suing a defendant if the risk materializes, *unless*:

(i) The contract where he assumed the risk resulted from ***unequal bargaining power***;

(ii) The defendant acted with ***wanton*** or ***reckless negligence***; or

(iii) An area of the ***public interest*** (common carriers, hospitals, and other essential services) was involved.

(b) *See Seigneur v. National Fitness Institute, Inc.* (Md. Sp. App. 2000), where the plaintiff was unable to recover against the defendant National Fitness Institute when her shoulder muscle was torn at the defendant's fitness facility, since (i) her exculpatory clause was not the result of unequal bargaining power; (ii) the defendant was not grossly, wantonly, or recklessly negligent; and (iii) fitness institutes are not core institutions of the public interest.

9.2.2 Implied Assumption of the Risk

(a) A/R may be implied when the following three-part test is met:

(i) The plaintiff ***knew of the risk*** involved;

(1) This is a subjective element that is not concerned with the reasonable, prudent person; the plaintiff must have *actually known* of the risk.

(2) The best way to establish this is through the plaintiff's *admission*.

(ii) The plaintiff ***appreciated the magnitude*** of the risk; and

(iii) The plaintiff ***voluntarily assumed the risk***.

(1) *See Rush v. Commercial Realty Co.* (N.J. 1929), where the A/R defense failed, since the plaintiff did not "voluntarily assume the risk" when going to a privy used as a restroom; he was forced to use the privy when "nature called."

9.2.3 The effect of the A/R on the plaintiffs in states that have abolished contributory negligence varies.

(a) State statutes and judicial decisions that have adopted comparative negligence usually address how A/R will be dealt will in the state.

(b) Some states treat A/R as though it were contributory negligence, thus *barring the plaintiff from recovery*.

(c) Other states treat A/R in the same way as comparative negligence

(i) *See Blackburn v. Dorta* (Fl. 1977), where the Fl. Supreme Court held that express and implied A/R was to henceforth have the same effect as comparative negligence: it would mitigate the defendant's recovery.

9.2.4 The Different Kinds of Assumption of the Risk in Florida and in Other States

(a) Express Assumption of the Risk

(i) The A/R is express in releases and other contractual provisions where the potential plaintiff expressly agrees to assume the risks.

(b) Implied Assumption of the Risk

(i) Primary Assumption of the Risk

(1) The primary assumption of the risk applies to when there is no duty.

(2) Example: a party assumes the risk of being jostled about in an aircraft by winds. The A/R is no defense because the airline never had a duty of preventing the jostling about to begin with.

(ii) Secondary Assumption of the Risk

(1) Pure Assumption of the Risk

(aa) Pure A/R applies when the plaintiff goes into a situation knowing, appreciating, and voluntarily assuming a risk in a way that is *reasonable*.

(bb) Example: running into a burning building to save a child.

(cc) In these cases, the A/R is no defense.

(2) Qualified Assumption of the Risk

(aa) Qualified A/R applies when the plaintiff goes into a situation knowing, appreciating, and voluntarily assuming a risk in a way that is *unreasonable*.

(bb) Ex.: running into a burning building to save a book or some other object.

(cc) In these cases, A/R *is* a defense.

## 10 Parties that May be Held Liable

### 10.1 Joint Tortfeasors: Liability and Joinder of Defendants

#### 10.1.1 When Joint and Several Liability Applies

(a) Introduction

(i) We previously saw that joint and several liability (J/SL) applied when *res ipsa loquitur* was invoked, but the plaintiff could not prove which of multiple defendants caused the harm. *Ybarra v. Spangard*.

(ii) In this section, we will explore four other situations under which J/SL may apply.

(b) Determining Which Party Caused the Harm

(i) When it is clear that one of a group of the defendants caused harm, but it is not clear which one, all may be ***jointly and severally liable*** (J/SL).

(1) *See Summers v. Tice* (Cal. 1948), where the defendants (Tice) argued that, because the plaintiff could not prove which defendant's shot caused the plaintiff's eye injury, neither was liable because the plaintiff did not prove but-for cause. Held: since it is clear that one of the defendants was the cause of the injury, one or both are liable; the burden is on each the defendant to show that he was not the cause; otherwise, they are J/SL. The burden shifts to the defendants, who may untangle the facts.

(ii) Carried to its logical conclusion, *Summers* allows an entire industry to be held liable to the plaintiff, when it is clear that some member of that industry caused the plaintiff's injury, but when it is not clear as to which one.

(1) *See Sindell v. Abbott Laboratories* (Cal. 1980), where each company marketing the drug that caused the plaintiff's health problems was liable for its market share of the drug, even though only 90% of the companies that could have sold the drug to the plaintiff's mother were in the suit, and it was thus possible that none of them caused the plaintiff's injury.

(c) Common Acts of Negligence

(i) J/SL also applies when several actors are engaged in a *common act of negligence*.

(ii) *See Bierczynski v. Rogers* (Del. 1968), where the defendant argued that he should not be liable for the plaintiff Rogers's injuries, since it was Race, not the defendant, who had collided with and injured the plaintiff. Held: because both the defendant and Race were engaged in a common act of negligence (racing on a public way), both are jointly and severally liable to the plaintiff. But for the defendant's negligence, the plaintiff would not have been injured.

(d) In addition, J/SL may be used in cases involving employer/employee and master/servant relationships.

10.1.2 Joint and Several Liability in Comparative Negligence States

(a) Some states that have adopted comparative negligence still apply J/SL.

(i) *See Coney v. J.L.G. Industries, Inc.* (Ill. 1983), where the defendant was held J/SL for injuries caused to the plaintiff Coney when the plaintiff fell from the defendant's platform: comparative negligence is used to determine the plaintiff's comparative fault, not each the defendant's comparative fault.

(ii) *N.B.*: however, the first defendant may recover against the codefendant in a ***contribution and indemnity suit*** (*see infra.*), unless the codefendant is insolvent.

(b) In other states, the adoption of comparative negligence eliminates J/SL.

(i) Rationale: since these states have already become accustomed to apportioning the plaintiff's fault, they apply the same calculus to each of the defendants.

(ii) *See Barlett v. New Mexico Welding Supply, Inc.* (N.M. Ct. App. 1982), where the plaintiff Barlett was unable to collect the entire judgment against the defendant, who was only 30 % at fault, because NM abolished J/SL upon adopting comparative negligence. Since the codefendant, who was principally responsible for the accident, was "nowhere to be found," the plaintiff was able to recover only 30 %.

**10.2** Vicarious Liability

10.2.1 Introduction

(a) Vicarious liability is the liability of a supervisory party for the acts of a subordinate. Employers, for example, are said to be vicariously liable for the acts of their employees.

(b) The doctrine of *respondeat superior* (*Lat.*, "let the superior answer") holds that a master or principal is *vicariously liable* for the negligence of his employees or agents, even when he was not himself negligent.

(c) *Respondeat superior* is thus in many ways like SL: an employer is held liable, *regardless of his faultlessness*.

(d) There are two elements to *respondeat superior* vicarious liability:

(i) The damage was *actually and proximately caused* by an employee's negligence; and

(ii) The employee was working *within the scope of his employment or agency*, which includes both:

(1) *Work done for the employer* by the employee; and

(2) *Personal work* interconnected with the work done for the employer.

10.2.2 The Going and Coming Rule

(a) The "going and coming rule" is an exception to the scope of employment rule.

(b) When an employee is going and coming to work, he is not considered to be *within the scope of employment* (and the employer thus cannot be held liable for damages caused), *unless:*

(i) The negligence is triggered by a work incident and it is foreseeable that the employee will cause damage while coming or going to work.

(1) *See Bussard v. Minimed, Inc.* (Cal. Ct. App. 2003), where the defendant Minimed, Inc.'s employee, having left work while dizzy from insecticide sprayed at the work place, later collided with the plaintiff's car. Because the damage was foreseeable, the defendant employer was liable to the plaintiff for the injuries caused.

(ii) The employee is going or coming to work while on a company errand for the employer, even if the employee is on a *detour.*

(1) There is, however, a limit as to certain detours that take an employee *out of the scope of employment. O'Shea v. Welch* (10th Cir. 2003).

(2) Such detours are known as ***frolics***.

(3) The factors considered in determining whether a detour is a frolic include: (i) how long the diversion took; and (ii) whether it was related to work or was of purely personal interest.

10.2.3 Independent Contractors

(a) Unlike employees, independent contractors are not given specific directions on how to do their work.

(b) Rather, they are asked to achieve a certain result, *regardless of how they go about doing it*.

(c) Employers of independent contractors are not liable for the negligence of those contractors.

(i) *See Murrell v. Goertz* (Okla. Ct. App. 1979), where the employer of a newspaper carrier was not liable for the negligence of the carrier towards a plaintiff that was struck by the carrier, because the carrier operated under broad guidelines outside of the control of the employer.

(d) The justification of this rule: to hold an employer liable for the acts or omissions of one over whom he had no control would be a *miscarriage of justice*.

(e) However, employers of independent contractors *can be held liable for their* ***direct negligence*** over acts and omissions that they control.

(i) Example: hiring a contractor that the employer should have reasonably known to be negligent.

(f) In addition, employers could be held vicariously liable for ***non-delegable duties***, such as assuring safety in one's car.

(i) *See Maloney v. Rath* (Cal. 1968), where an employer is held vicariously liable for the negligence of her independent mechanic contractor. The general rule that employers are *not vicariously liable* for the negligence of their contractors does not apply when the question involves a non-delegable duty, such as the duty to maintain safe brakes.

## **10.3** Contribution and Indemnity

### 10.3.1 Contribution

(a) Under the old common law, a defendant was not entitled to contribution from a codefendant, even if the codefendant was simultaneously responsible for the plaintiff's injury.

(b) Under the intermediate common law, a defendant could recover 50 % of damages from his codefendant.

(c) Under the modern law, especially in states that have grown comfortable in allocating percentages of fault through comparative negligence, a defendant may recover whatever a codefendant's proportional share in damages was.

(i) However, in states that have not adopted comparative negligence, the *per capita* ("by the head") system is used.

(d) Contribution is allowed in forty nine states, and is generally allowed only in negligence cases (intentional torts are barred).

(e) Elements of contribution:

(i) Both the defendants are held liable through either:

(1) The plaintiff's proving both parties' negligence in a single lawsuit;

(2) A defendant's impleading of a codefendant; or

(3) A defendant's suing a codefendant in a separate action.

(ii) One defendant paid more than his proportionate share of the judgment.

(f) There are three approaches as to who pays the price of an insolvent defendant:

(i) One defendant takes the full brunt of a codefendant's insolvency (J/SL approach);

(ii) The plaintiff takes the full brunt of a codefendant's insolvency (the approach when J/SL is abolished);

(iii) One defendant pays a codefendant's share in proportion to his percent of liability in comparison with that of the plaintiff.

(1) Example: suppose the plaintiff was 20 % at fault, the defendant was 40 % at fault, and the codefendant was 40 % at fault.

(2) The defendant, in addition to paying his own 40 % share of the plaintiff's damages, will pay two thirds of the codefendant's share of the damages; the plaintiff will pay the remaining one third.

10.3.2 Indemnity

(a) Indemnity is a contract ***shifting liability from a defendant to another party*** who is legally responsible to the defendant.

(b) The common law recognized the right of indemnity in several relationships, such as that of an employer with his employees.

(c) When the right of indemnity is recognized, then when one member of the relationship who did not act tortiously is held liable for the tortious conduct of the other member of the relationship, the former has the right to collect the entire judgment from the latter.

(i) For example, if a non-negligent employer is held *vicariously liable* for a negligent employee's torts, the employer has a *right of indemnity* against the employee.

(ii) Similarly, if a seller or a service agent, through no negligence of his own, sells or installs a *defective product* and is sued by an injured purchaser, he has a *right of indemnity* against the manufacturer.

(1) Example: an electrician installs a light switch that later sparks and injures the plaintiff. If the electrician is held liable for negligence, he has a *right of indemnity* against the manufacturer.

# REVIEW CHARTS

## INTENTIONAL TORTS SUMMARY

<table>
<tr><td rowspan="2">Introduction and Background</td><td colspan="2">ITs are unique in that they always require a volitional act as well as intent that a particular result come about.</td></tr>
<tr><td colspan="2">Elements: volition, intent, a resulting tortious act.</td></tr>
<tr><td rowspan="7">The Seven Intentional Torts: elements</td><td>Assault</td><td>Volition, intent to cause fear of harmful contact, resulting fear.</td></tr>
<tr><td>Battery</td><td>Volition, intent to cause harmful contact, resulting contact.</td></tr>
<tr><td>False imprisonment</td><td>Volition, intent to confine, resulting confinement</td></tr>
<tr><td>IIED</td><td>Outrageous act, intent or recklessness, proximate cause, severe ED</td></tr>
<tr><td>Trespass to land</td><td>Volition, intent to enter land, resulting trespass</td></tr>
<tr><td>Trespass to chattels</td><td>Volition, intent to interfere with chattel, resulting interference</td></tr>
<tr><td>Conversion</td><td>Volition, intent to exercise dominion, resulting serious interference</td></tr>
<tr><td rowspan="5">Privileges</td><td>Consensual privilege</td><td>Actual or implied consent (implied-in-law, implied-in-fact).</td></tr>
<tr><td rowspan="4">Non-consensual privilege</td><td>Self-defense</td></tr>
<tr><td>Defense of others</td></tr>
<tr><td>Defense of property</td></tr>
<tr><td>Recovery of property</td></tr>
</table>

## CULPABILITY SUMMARY CHART

**← Culpability / fault →**

| ←<br>***Strict liability*** | ←<br>***Unforeseeable (no tort)*** | →<br>***Foreseeable (negligence)*** | →<br>***Recklessness*** | →<br>***Intentional torts*** |
|---|---|---|---|---|
| The defendant is liable, regardless of fault. | On this side of negligence, the behavior was reasonable or the event unforeseeable. | On this side of negligence, a reasonable person would have taken steps to avoid the danger. | IIED. | Assault, battery, FI, IIED, trespass to land, trespass to chattels, conversion. |
| The defendant is liable. | The defendant is not liable. | The defendant is liable. | The defendant is liable. | The defendant is liable. |
| Does not require fault. | There is no fault. | The defendant is at fault. | The defendant is at fault. | The defendant is at fault. |
| Blasting, fireworks displays, oil drilling, etc. | Leaving one's golf clubs in a backyard. *Lubitz v. Wells.* | Failing to have an attendee on board a barge, thus causing it to sink. *Carroll Towing Co.* | Threats of physical injury and the destruction of one's business. *Siliznoff.* | Intentional harm to a person or to his land or property. |

## SUMMARY CHART OF SPECIAL RELATIONSHIPS

| Duty to Rescue | J/SL | Indemnity | Vicarious liability |
|---|---|---|---|
| Employer/employee | Employer/employee | Employer against an employee | *Respondeat superior* (employer for employee) |
| Invitor/invitee (common carriers, innkeepers, etc.) | When it is not clear which one in a group of the defendants caused an injury | Seller or service agent against a manufacturer | General contractors for non-delegable duties |
| Husband/wife, parent/child | Joint tortfeasors engaged in a common act of negligence | The insured against his insurer | A parent for his child's torts (if established by statute) |

## Chapter IV. Civil Procedure

# 1 Introduction

## 1.1 Introduction to the Law of Civil Procedure

### 1.1.1 Defining Civil Procedure

(a) Civil procedure refers to the methods and practices within litigation between private parties.

(b) It can be contrasted to the domain governing the substance or content of the law. It can similarly be contrasted to criminal procedure, which governs cases prosecuted on behalf of the public against a criminal defendant.

### 1.1.2 Alternatives to Civil Litigation

(a) Alternative dispute resolution (ADR);

(b) Negotiation between parties coming to their own settlements;

(c) Mediation under the guidance of a third party; and

(d) Arbitration – dispute resolution "without the law" by a third party that usually has the power to make binding decisions.

### 1.1.3 Getting into Federal Court

(a) There are three ways to get into federal district courts:

(i) The United States as a party (plaintiff or defendant);

(ii) Federal question jurisdiction;

(1) This includes: (i) federal courts' exclusive jurisdiction (*e.g.*, on patent and copyright law, bankruptcy law, etc.), and (ii) federal courts' concurrent jurisdiction (*e.g.*, on the interpretation of the Constitution).

(2) The subject matter may involve, for example, questions of diversity, including cases involving admiralty and maritime jurisdiction, public ministers, ambassadors or aliens.

(iii) Diversity of citizenship of the parties.

(b) In addition, a case involving a question over which the federal courts hold concurrent jurisdiction can be appealed to the U.S. Supreme Court if it has exhausted the state court appeals process.

## 1.2 The hierarchy of Sources of Civil Procedural Law

### 1.2.1 The U.S. Constitution

(a) Art. VI, cl. 2 (Supremacy Clause): "This Constitution, and the Laws of the United States . . . and all Treaties made . . . under the Authority of the United States . . . shall be the supreme Law of the Land."

(b) By "Laws," the Constitution is referring to federal laws. Thus, the Constitution and federal laws trump state laws and municipal ordinances.

1.2.2 Federal Statutes

(a) These are passed by Congress and are contained in 28 USC, which deals with the Judiciary and Judicial Proceedings.

(b) In addition, they cover federal question jurisdiction (§ 1331); diversity jurisdiction (§ 1332); removal jurisdiction (§1441); supplemental jurisdiction (§ 1367); venue (§ 1391) and the FRCP.

1.2.3 Federal Rules of Civil Procedure (FRCP)

(a) These rules govern civil actions in the United States district courts (in contrast, the Federal Rules of Appellate Procedure deal with the appeals courts).

(b) Over half of the states have adopted the FRCP, either in their entirety or with some changes.

(c) The courts are not given ***the discretion to disregard the federal rules***, even if doing so would be in the interests of justice.

(i) *See Carlisle v. United States* (U.S. 1872), where Carlisle was declared guilty and sentenced for possession with intention to distribute marijuana. The court granted a motion for judgment of acquittal, even though it was filed by Carlisle's attorney one day late, because disregarding the motion would have been a "miscarriage of justice." The Sixth Circuit declared that the District Court did not have the authority to disregard Federal Rule of Criminal Procedure 29, even though Carlisle may have been innocent, and even if the error was due to attorney negligence. On appeal, the Supreme Court affirmed the Circuit Court decision.

1.2.4 Local Rules

(a) FRCP 83(a) states that each district court, "acting by a *majority of its district judges*, may, after giving appropriate public notice and an opportunity for comment, *make and amend rules* governing its practice."

(b) When the FRCP are silent on a matter, the local rules fill in the gaps.

(c) The numbering scheme in the FRCP must be used in the local rules.

(d) Failing to observe a local rule, such as a deadline for submitting a legal brief, can cause a party to lose rights.

(e) However, the failure to comply with a requirement of form (*e.g.*, the spacing between paragraphs in a legal brief) will not be enforced in a way that causes a party to lose rights when the non-compliance is not willful (FRCP 83(b)).

1.2.5 Standing Orders (FRCP 83b)

(a) Standing orders look forward to and apply to all cases pending before a court.

(b) Some judges issue standing orders on a subject when there is no applicable local rule.

(c) Standing orders are binding only on parties appearing before the judge who wrote them.

(d) One often must contact the clerk of the court to obtain them.

(e) The non-willful non-compliance of standing orders, unlike that of local rules, the FRCP, and statutes, cannot cause the breaching party to lose rights; ignorance is an excuse.

1.2.6 Orders

(a) An order is a written direction or command that may be interlocutory or final that is delivered by a court or judge.

(b) Parties apply to the court or judge for an order by making motions which, unless made during a hearing or trial, must be made in writing (FRCP 7(b)).

## 1.3 The Structure of the Federal Court System

1.3.1 The U.S. Judicial branch

(a) U.S. district courts may decide the following cases:

(i) Cases where the U.S. is a party;

(ii) Cases involving the Constitution, federal laws and treaties ("federal question jurisdiction"). This includes cases involving admiralty and maritime jurisdiction, public ministers, ambassadors or aliens.

(iii) Questions of diversity.

(b) The Supreme Court has jurisdiction over:

(i) Exclusive jurisdiction:

(1) Conflicts between two or more states

(ii) Original jurisdiction:

(1) The Supreme Court has original jurisdiction over:

(aa) Conflicts between two or more states;

(bb) Conflicts involving ambassadors, public ministers, or consults of foreign states;

(cc) Conflicts between the U.S. and a state;

(dd) Actions or proceedings by a state against citizens of another state or against aliens.

(2) These involve a very small number of cases, usually less than one dozen per year.

1.3.2 The Three Tiers of the Federal Courts

| | **Supreme Court** | **Circuit Courts** | **District Courts** |
|---|---|---|---|
| **Who created it?** | Constitution | Congress | Congress |
| **How many are there?** | One | Thirteen | About one hundred |
| **Jurisdiction discretionary or mandatory?** | Discretionary | Mandatory | Mandatory |
| **Oral argument allowed?** | Always | Usually (ct. decides) | Maybe |

1.3.3 *En Banc* Decisions

(a) Whereas one judge decides cases in the district courts, decisions are made *en banc* in the Supreme Court and in panels of three in the circuit courts.

(b) More judges participate in the decision-making in the higher courts because of the importance of higher court decisions, which apply over a greater geographic range.

1.3.4 Oral Argument

(a) Always allowed in the Supreme Court (one half of an hour is given to each side).

(b) Usually allowed in circuit courts (FRAP 34), depending on whether:

(i) The appeal is frivolous;

(ii) The law has been authoritatively decided; and

(iii) The facts and legal arguments are adequately presented in the briefs.

## 2 Subject Matter Jurisdiction

### 2.1 Introduction

2.1.1 There is a presumption against jurisdiction in the federal courts.

2.1.2 If the Constitution or USC does not specifically grant subject matter jurisdiction (SMJ) to the federal courts, the case must go to state court.

| Federal Courts | State Courts |
|---|---|
| Federal Courts are courts of *limited* jurisdiction | The primary state courts are courts of *general* jurisdiction |
| They can *only* hear cases that the Constitution *or* Congress say they may hear. Their SMJ is defined entirely by these two entities. | They can hear any case unless Congress *or* the state legislature states otherwise. |

2.1.3 The lack of SMJ in a court may be raised as a defense anytime, including on appeal.

**2.2 Federal Jurisdiction I: the U.S. as a Party**

2.2.1 The district courts have original, concurrent jurisdiction over any actions commenced by the U.S. (28 USC § 1345).

(a) These cases account for 4.3% of cases initiated in federal courts.

(b) Is knowing that U.S. is your client enough to establish that you may commence this case in federal court? Generally, yes, although Congress could create exceptions.

2.2.2 The district courts similarly have original jurisdiction over actions commenced against the U.S. (§ 1346).

(a) Cases with the U.S. as a defendant account for 15 % of cases initiated in federal courts.

(b) Is knowing that you are filing a case against the U.S. enough to establish that the federal courts have jurisdiction over your case?

(i) There are times when the district courts have original, exclusive jurisdiction over claims against U.S. (such as for money damages accruing after 1945 for injury or loss of property).

(ii) However, § 1346 limits jurisdiction to a number of cases. For example, a claim arising under the Constitution or congressional acts must not exceed $10,000 in order to be heard in the federal district courts.

(iii) Such cases may, however, be heard in state courts, but only if a statute permits state courts to hear cases against the U.S.

**2.3 Federal Jurisdiction II: Federal Question**

2.3.1 Introduction

(a) Federal courts are given SMJ over federal question cases because federal judges have expertise over the Constitution, federal laws and treaties.

(b) USC § 1331 grants district courts original jurisdiction over cases arising under the Constitution, laws, or treaties of the United States. This jurisdiction is concurrent with the state courts.

2.3.2 The Well-Pleaded Complaint

(a) A well-pleaded complaint is one that sufficiently sets forth: (i) a claim for relief, including grounds for a court's jurisdiction; (ii) a basis for the relief claimed; and (iii) a demand for judgment in a way that allows the defendant to respond to each of the issues presented.

(b) In federal court, when the plaintiff is seeking federal question jurisdiction, the well-pleaded complaint must raise the *controlling issue of federal law.*

(c) The claim stated in the complaint must arise under federal law; the defenses raised are irrelevant to determining whether the district court has federal question jurisdiction.

(i) *See Louisville and Nashville Railroad Co. v. Mottley* (U.S. 1908), where the plaintiff sued the defendant for breach of contract for having rescinded the plaintiff's railroad passes. In the complaint, the plaintiff anticipated the defendant's affirmative defense: a federal statute required the defendant to rescind the passes. Since the only questions to be litigated—whether rescinding the passes violated a federal statute and whether the statute was unconstitutional—were federal, the plaintiff filed the case in federal court. The Supreme Court held, however, that the relevant question was the claim made by the plaintiff in the complaint, which in this case was a breach of contract claim over which the state courts had exclusive jurisdiction.

2.3.3 Centrality of the Federal Question

(a) When an issue arises under federal law, but other issues arise under state law, the district courts have federal question jurisdiction *only if the federal issue is central to the claim*.

(i) *See Merrell Dow Pharm., Inc. v. Thompson* (U.S. 1986), where the plaintiff filed in state court a complaint invoking a federal statute and five other counts involving state law against a company whose drug caused birth defects. When the defendant removed the case to federal court, the plaintiff filed a motion to remand the case back to state court, which was denied. The Supreme Court held that, although a federal question was involved, there was no basis for federal jurisdiction over the matter, since Congress, in passing the law that was invoked, never intended for private actions for violations of the statute.

(b) If the plaintiff files a complaint in federal court in which two claims arise under state law and only one claim arises under federal law, the court could dismiss the state law claims and hear only the federal claim.

2.3.4 Jurisdiction of the Supreme Court

(a) The Supreme Court has original, *exclusive* jurisdiction over litigation between two or more states (28 USC § 1251(a)).

(b) The Supreme Court has original, *non-exclusive* jurisdiction over:

(i) Actions in which ambassadors, other public ministers, or consuls are parties;

(ii) Controversies between the U.S. and a state;

(iii) Actions by a state against citizens of another state or against aliens (28 USC § 1251(b)).

2.3.5 Jurisdiction of the District Courts

(a) The district courts have both *original* and *exclusive* jurisdiction over:

(i) Admiralty, maritime and prize cases (28 USC § 1333);

(ii) Bankruptcy cases (28 USC §1334);

(iii) Patent, plant variety and copyright cases (28 USC § 1338);

(iv) Federal antitrust cases (15 USC §§ 15-26).

(b) The district courts have *original*, *concurrent* jurisdiction over:

(i) Cases in which ambassadors, other public ministers and consuls are parties (over which the Supreme Court also has original, non-exclusive jurisdiction);

(ii) Cases between in which a state is a party (over which the Supreme Court has original, non-exclusive jurisdiction);

(iii) Interpleader cases ("suits to determine a right to property held by a stakeholder [usually a disinterested third party] who is in doubt about ownership and who therefore deposits the property with the court to permit interested parties to litigate ownership").

(iv) Commerce and antitrust cases;

(v) Unfair competition;

(vi) Postal matters;

(vii) Internal revenue;

(viii) Civil rights actions;

(ix) Election disputes;

(x) Actions to compel an officer of the U.S. to perform a duty owned to a plaintiff;

(xi) All civil actions brought by an Indian tribe arising under the Constitution, laws or treaties of U.S. (§ 1362)

(c) It appears that some of these statutes, such as § 1362, are redundant with § 1331, which states generally that the district courts have original jurisdiction of civil actions arising under federal laws.

(i) However, in § 1331's original form, the district courts had jurisdiction only over claims demanding more than $10,000 in remedies.

(ii) Thus, these other statutes, which do not set a minimum amount in controversy, are not redundant with the original wording of § 1331.

## 2.4 Federal Jurisdiction III: Federal Diversity

### 2.4.1 Diversity Jurisdiction in Lawsuits Between Individuals

(a) Diversity jurisdiction cases comprise 20 % of the federal docket.

(b) The district courts have *original* and *concurrent* jurisdiction when *more than $75,000* is sought in a controversy between citizens of different states (this is the majority of cases). 28 USC § 1332(a)(1).

(c) The courts also have jurisdiction when the conflict is between: (i) citizens of a state and citizens of a foreign state; (ii) citizens of different states and in which citizens of a foreign state are additional parties; or (iii) a foreign state, as plaintiff, and citizens of a state or of different states (28 USC § 1332(a)(1)-(4)).

(d) However, even if the case involves claims of more than $75,000 and diversity among the parties, the case cannot go to federal court if it involves domestic relations or probate claims.

(e) The Rules of Federal Diversity Jurisdiction

(i) The parties must be from different states, without regard to the citizenship or location of the judge or his court.

(ii) Specifically, they must be *citizens*, not *residents*, of different states;

(1) The key is *citizenship*, or *domicile*, that is, the state in which the subject has or once had a physical presence and in which he intends to remain indefinitely.

(2) Contrast this to *residency*, which refers to the state in which the subject has occasionally resided or is temporarily living without the intent to remain there indefinitely.

(aa) *See Mas v. Perry* (5th Cir. 1978), where the court accepted Mrs. Mas's contention that her domicile was not in Louisiana, since she did not intend to remain there indefinitely.

(iii) There must be *complete diversity* between the parties.

(1) Federal diversity jurisdiction requires *all of the plaintiffs* to be *completely diverse* from *all of the defendants.*

(2) Thus, a citizen of a state will be unable to bring a case under diversity jurisdiction if any single one of the defendants named in the complaint is a citizen of that same state, unless the plaintiff drops that defendant from the complaint.

(aa) The source of this rule is *Strawbridge v. Curtis* (U.S. 1806), a case that was dismissed from federal court because all of the plaintiffs were not diverse from all of the defendants.

(3) However, an exception is established with respect to class action lawsuits, where complete diversity is not required (28 USC § 1332(d)).

(aa) Rather, minimal diversity suffices. However, if greater than one-third of the members of all plaintiff classes and the primary defendants are citizens of the state in which the action was originally filed, the district court may decline to exercise jurisdiction.

(bb) Other differences include amount of money in controversy.

(4) Realignment

(aa) If a plaintiff puts other plaintiffs on the defendant side in order to establish federal diversity, the court may "realign" the parties and only afterwards decide if there is truly diversity.

(bb) For example, if a New York plaintiff sues a New Jersey plaintiff and places a New Jersey co-plaintiff on the defendant side in order to keep complete diversity, the court may realign the parties.

(iv) The court must determine citizenship and complete diversity *at the time the complaint was filed*.

(1) For example, if a plaintiff from California sued a defendant in Texas and, after filing the complaint, moved to Texas, the requirements for diversity would be met.

(2) However, if it can be shown that on the day that the plaintiff filed the complaint, he did not intend to remain in California, the court will conclude that he was not a California citizen at the time the complaint was filed and therefore, the requirements for diversity were not met.

(v) The amount in controversy must exceed $75,000.

(1) The amount in controversy is what the plaintiff states in the complaint, but it must be possible "to a legal certainty" that the plaintiff can get over $75,000.

(2) The defendant may thus raise several defenses against federal diversity jurisdiction (e.g., a statute caps the amount recoverable to less than $75,000).

(3) A judge may dismiss the complaint if it is virtually impossible that a jury would award more than $75,000 (e.g., in a case in which the plaintiff sues for a minor insult).

(4) However, if there is even the slightest chance that the plaintiff would be awarded more than $75,000, judge must exercise jurisdiction.

(5) The Amount in Controversy for Preventing Frivolous Cases

(aa) The general rule in the United States is that each party pays its own attorneys' fees,[14] but the loser pays the winner's costs (docket fees, court reporters, court appointed experts, interpreters, etc.).

---

[14] The policy behind this rule is to allow more the plaintiffs access to the courts. If the losing side were always obliged to pay the winner's attorneys' fees, then due to the often exorbitant costs of such fees in the United States, far fewer potential

(bb) Furthermore, in order to dissuade plaintiffs from asserting federal diversity jurisdiction by exaggerating the amount in controversy, federal courts *may deny costs* to the winning plaintiff and may even *impose the costs* of the losing defendant on the plaintiff if he wins the case but is awarded a judgment of $75,000 or less (28 USC § 1332(b)).

| **Jury's Verdict** | **What the Plaintiff Must Pay** |
|---|---|
| No award | His own attorneys' fees; all costs. |
| Award of $75,000 or less | His own attorneys' fees; possibly, his own costs and those of the defendant. |
| Award of over $75,000 | His own attorneys' fees. No costs. |

(6) Aggregate Claims

(aa) Plaintiffs will sometimes try to add up individual claims in order to reach the required $75,000 amount in controversy.

(bb) It is not clear as to when various claims may be added together, but it appears that the plaintiff can add up *all claims* (even transactionally unrelated claims) to reach the required amount if all of the claims are *against the same defendant*.

(I) For example, if the plaintiff injured the defendant in a $30,000 negligence claim, he can add an unrelated $50,000 breach of contract claim in order to exceed the $75,000 amount in controversy requirement.

(cc) However, if there are multiple parties on either side, aggregation of different claims generally is not allowed, even if the claims are transactionally related.

(I) For example, if co-plaintiffs hold claims of $50,000 each against a common defendant for two different injuries, the amount in controversy requirement is not met.

(dd) Nevertheless, if multiple parties share a common claim, aggregation is permitted.

(I) For example, if the plaintiff is injured by two co-defendants who cause him damages that exceed $75,000, the amount in controversy requirement is satisfied, since there is only one claim.

---

plaintiffs would exercise their legal rights. It is worth noting that in many European countries, where attorneys' fees are generally lower, the losing party pays both parties' attorneys' fees.
The American rule has many exceptions. For example, some states, as a penalty for bringing frivolous cases to court, or as a punishment for egregious violations, require the losing party to pay the attorneys' fees of both parties.

(ee) It is always easier to bring in additional claims to reach the amount in controversy requirement, provided they do not bring in additional parties.

2.4.2 Diversity Jurisdiction in Lawsuits Involving Legal Entities

(a) Corporations

(i) A corporation is an entity that acts as a person distinct from the shareholders who own it. It may issue stock, pay taxes and is liable for its own torts.

(ii) For the purposes of 28 USC §§ 1332 (diversity) and § 1441 (removal), a corporation has citizenship in both:

(1) The state of its *principal place of business* (which may be the location of either: (i) the headquarters, or "brain" of the corporation; or (ii) the main manufacturing center); and

(2) The state where it is *legally incorporated*. USC § 1332(c)(1).

(aa) *See Randozzo*, where the judge dismissed a case with prejudice after the plaintiff failed to mention *both* the state of incorporation *and* the state of the primary place of business when alleging diversity.

(3) (For insurers, it is the state where any of their insured are citizens).

(iii) The location of a corporation's principal place of business is not necessarily that of its corporate headquarters; it may be that of a major manufacturing plant.

(1) *See J.A. Olson Co. v. City of Winona* (5th Cir. 1987), where the plaintiff sued in Mississippi federal court based on diversity jurisdiction. The court dismissed the case, holding that the plaintiff was in fact a citizen of Mississippi, even though its corporate headquarters were in Chicago, since the plaintiff's only manufacturing plant was in Mississippi, many decisions were made in Mississippi, and most of its employees were Mississippians.

(2) If a plaintiff sues a defendant whose *headquarters* or *main manufacturing center* are located in the same state as the plaintiff, it would be safest to file the case in state court, since the defendant's citizenship is not clear.

(b) Non-Incorporated Businesses

(i) Limited liability partnerships (LLP)

(1) An LLP has citizenship in all of the states in which its members are citizens.

(ii) Limited liability companies (LLC)

(1) LLC's are hybrids between LLP's and corporations.

(2) They are statutorily authorized in many states.

(3) Under the majority rule, their citizenship is determined like that of LLPs; it is based on the citizenship of their members.

(aa) *See Belleville Catering Co. v. Champaign Market Place LLC* (7th Cir. 2003), where the plaintiff, calculating the defendant LLC's citizenship based on what it would have been had the defendant been a corporation, concluding that there was complete diversity. The court, calculating the defendant's citizenship based on the citizenship of all of its partners, held that the complete diversity requirement was not met.

2.4.3 The Exception for Domestic Relations and Probate Cases

(a) Perhaps rooted in the English tradition where ordinary courts of law or equity did not handle family matters (these were handled by the ecclesiastical courts), American federal courts may refuse to hear family matters. Federal courts will also not take cases that seem to interfere with state probate claims.

(b) This may be appropriate, since state courts tend to be in better touch with the local agencies that deal with probate and family issues (divorce, alimony and child custody).

(c) The origins of this rule are not found in 28 USC § 1332, which governs diversity, but rather, in *Barber v. Barber* (U.S. 1859), which held that Congress did not intend for the federal courts to handle these cases.

(i) Later, *Ankenbrandt v. Richards* (U.S. 1992), acknowledging that *Barber* may have been wrong, stated that since Congress did not annul *Barber* over for the last one hundred years, Congress has tacitly endorsed the decision.

(d) Note that there is nothing in the domestic relations and probate exceptions that would prevent a plaintiff from bringing tort suit in federal court against, for example, a father who abuses a child he has custody over. Although family issues are related, the central tort claim can be brought into federal court.

**2.5 Supplemental Jurisdiction in Federal Question Cases**

2.5.1 Introduction

(a) Supplemental Jurisdiction

(i) Also known as ancillary or pendent jurisdiction, supplemental jurisdiction is codified under 28 USC § 1367.

(ii) Whenever a district court has original jurisdiction over a claim (federal question or diversity jurisdiction), all other claims arising under the same § 1367(a) "case or controversy" as the original claim can be heard in the district court, even if they do not have an independent basis for subject matter jurisdiction.

(1) *See United Mine Workers v. Gibbs* (U.S. 1966), where the plaintiff Gibbs accused the defendant of intentional interference with the plaintiff's contracts and of a concerted union plan against him. The plaintiff sued the defendant for violation of Labor Management Relations Act and included a state law claim for

the defendant's malicious harm to the plaintiff's contracts. Because the state contract claim arose from the same core facts, or "case or controversy," as the federal claim, the Court allowed both to be tried in the federal courts.

(b) Pendent Parties Jurisdiction

(i) Pendent parties jurisdiction is jurisdiction to adjudicate a claim against a party who is otherwise not within court's jurisdiction, because the claim by or against that party arises from the same core facts of another claim that is properly before the court.

(ii) Pendent parties jurisdiction was limited in *Finley v. United States* (U.S. 1989), where Finley was barred from bringing a state torts action against new defendants (from which there was no diversity), even though this new claim arose under the same common core of facts of the original claim, which arose under a federal claim (the Federal Torts Claim Act) over which the District Courts had original, exclusive jurisdiction. The Court held that the District Courts did not have jurisdiction over the state claims, since there was no independent basis for jurisdiction (there was neither diversity nor a federal question). Pendant party jurisdiction was not allowed when only the federal question, not the additional claim, arose under federal law.

(iii) Congress overruled *Finley* with USC § 1367, which allows pendent parties jurisdiction *unless otherwise banned by statute*. "Such supplemental jurisdiction shall include claims that involve the joinder or intervention of additional parties."

(iv) However, with respect to federal diversity, § 1367(b) places several limits on pendent parties jurisdiction. Neither supplemental jurisdiction nor pendent parties jurisdiction may be used to circumvent the complete diversity requirement in cases founded on diversity jurisdiction.

**When Supplemental Jurisdiction is Permitted**

| | ***In a Federal Question Case*** | ***In a Diversity Case*** |
|---|---|---|
| *To Join a New Claim* | Permitted. This is the most compelling reason to join claims. Ex: codifying *Gibbs*. | There is no need, since in a diversity case, another claim against the same defendant will also be diverse and thus can be aggregated. |
| *To Join a New Party* | Permitted.<br>Ex: *Finley* overruled by Congress. | Maybe; see § 1367<br>Example: the court may have PJ over the defendant, but not over the codefendant. |

2.5.2 Courts have the discretion to decline jurisdiction over the state claim when:

(a) It raises a novel or complex issue of State law;

(b) It substantially predominates over the federal claim;

(c) The district court has dismissed all claims over which it has original jurisdiction; or

(d) For other compelling reasons. USC § 1367(c).

2.5.3 USC § 1367(d) deals with gifts to plaintiffs. If a plaintiff mistakenly believes that a case falls under supplemental jurisdiction, the statute of limitations is tolled.

(a) Rationale: unlike cases dismissed from federal court under federal question jurisdiction or federal diversity jurisdiction, here, the courts have a degree of discretion that plaintiffs cannot predict. Thus, it would not be their own fault if the case was dismissed.

2.5.4 Original Jurisdiction Distinguished

(a) Supplemental jurisdiction is different from original jurisdiction in that it provides a way for a federal court to hear a ***claim*** (a cause of action), not a ***case*** (a civil action). The case must still enter the federal court through federal question jurisdiction, diversity of citizenship, or the United States as a party.

(b) While the federal courts generally do not have discretion in hearing cases under their original jurisdiction,[15] they may exercise some discretion in exercising supplemental jurisdiction.

2.6 Supplemental Jurisdiction in Diversity Cases

2.6.1 USC § 1367(b) limits when the district courts may exercise supplemental jurisdiction when they have original jurisdiction founded solely on 28 USC § 1332.

2.6.2 This sub-rule is for benefit of defendants, since it makes bringing them into federal court much more difficult.

2.6.3 Claims (causes of action) within a case with § 1332 diversity jurisdiction may not enter federal court if they are made by plaintiffs against defendants who were made parties under:

(a) Rule 14 (when the defendant or the plaintiff may bring in a third party);

(b) Rule 19 (joinder of persons needed for just adjudication);

(c) Rule 20 (permissive joinder of parties);

(d) Rule 24 (intervention);

(e) Or under anyone claiming to be joined to the action through Rule 19 or seeking to intervene as the plaintiff through Rule 24, when exercising such supplemental jurisdiction conflicts with § 1332 diversity requirements by destroying complete diversity.

2.6.4 Example: Alice, Betty, and Carol have a three-way collision. A's damages are $90,000 and B's are $25,000. A and B join as co-plaintiffs against Carol and their citizenship presents no problem for diversity jurisdiction. A's claim meets § 1332's amount in controversy requirement, but B's does not. Under the rules of aggregation, they cannot be added up. Can they be added together through §1367?

(a) Under § 1367(a), this is possible, but under § 1367(b), there is no supplemental jurisdiction over diversity cases when parties are joined through Rule 20, but 20 is about prohibiting federal jurisdiction when defendants, not plaintiffs, are added to the claim.

---

[15] Exceptions: 28 USC § 1332(d) allows for the exercise of discretion in diversity jurisdiction in class action lawsuits.

(i) Courts have disagreed, and the Supreme Court is looking at this issue. But if it allows it the claims to be aggregated, isn't it overruling the complete diversity rule?

(ii) Example: suppose B and C are from the same state. There would not be complete diversity, even though § 1367 would allow it.

(iii) In such a situation, would a judge not be required not to hear the case, since *Strawbridge v. Curtis*(U.S. 1806) requires complete diversity?

(b) The Supreme Court has held that a federal court in a diversity case may exercise supplemental jurisdiction over additional plaintiffs whose claims *do not satisfy the amount-in-controversy requirement*, provided the claims are part of the same case as the claims of plaintiffs who do satisfy the requirement.

(i) *See Exxon Mobil Corp. v. Allapattah Services, Inc.* (U.S. 2005), where the Court ruled that if the other elements of jurisdiction are present, and at least one plaintiff satisfies the amount in controversy requirement, 28 USC § 1367 permits supplemental jurisdiction over *all of the other plaintiffs' claims*, even if they are for less than the required amt in controversy.

(c) However, in order to join a co-plaintiff with a claim that does not exceed $75,000 under supplemental jurisdiction where jurisdiction of the original claim is based on diversity, the original claim must ***exceed $75,000*** and ***complete diversity must not be destroyed***. *Ortega v. Star-Kist Foods* (1st Cir. 2004).

(d) Thus, a non-diverse party may *not* be joined. The *Exxon Mobil Corp. v. Allapattah Services, Inc.* (U.S. 2005) Court went to great lengths to explain that it was not overruling *Strawbridge v. Curtis* (U.S. 1806).

## 2.7 Removal Jurisdiction

2.7.1 Removal jurisdiction allows defendants to remove from state to federal court.

(a) It must be a case that could have been brought to federal court in the first place.

(b) Under the majority rule, a case may be removed no later than thirty days after receipt of the initial pleading by the first defendant.

(i) It can be thirty days from the original pleading, or from an amended pleading that now has jurisdiction in federal cts when original pleading did not (for example, non-diverse defendants are dropped out)

(ii) Exception: after one year has passed, a diversity action cannot be removed, even if the defendant receives a pleading that allows for diversity jurisdiction .

(c) In some minority jurisdictions, later defendants may remove if they can get former defendants to agree, even if former defendants did not originally file for removal.

2.7.2 Generally, those cases over which the district courts have original jurisdiction may be removed.

2.7.3 Removal Procedures

(a) Removal must take place within thirty days of when the defendant receives the complaint, or when the defendant receives the pleading that allows for removal (through creating federal SMJ).

(b) The defendant may remove by filing a ***notice to remove*** and delivering all of the pleadings to the district court.

(c) If the property procedures are followed and the district court has SMJ, then the remand is automatically granted. There are no pleadings or hearings.

(d) However, if the courts lacks SMJ, any party or the court may then seek to have the case remanded to state court.

(e) If the plaintiff seeks a remand for any other reason (*e.g.*, for a defect in the removal procedure, because it is a case that may not be removed, etc.), he has thirty days to file a ***motion for remand***.

(f) Remanding, unlike removing, involves the judge, pleadings, and a court decision to determine a disputed issue of law.

2.7.4 There are some cases over which the federal courts do *not* have original jurisdiction, but which may nonetheless be removed to federal court:

(a) 28 USC § 1442 cases against federal officers or agencies; and

(b) 28 USC § 1443 civil rights cases (where the defendant feels that because of his race, he will not receive a fair trial in state court).

2.7.5 There are other cases over which district courts *do have jurisdiction*, but which nonetheless may not be removed to federal court:

(a) 28 USC § 1445 provides a list of these cases, which include cases brought under the Violence Against Women Act, workmen's compensation actions, etc.

(b) In these cases, the plaintiff has the advantage of not only being able to choose the court, but also being able to keep the case there.

(c) Furthermore, when the defendant in a diversity case is a citizen of the forum state, he may not remove to federal court, since the rationale of avoiding the jury prejudice against out-of-state parties would not apply to a defendant who is a citizen of the forum state.

## 3 Personal Jurisdiction and Venue

### 3.1 Introduction

3.1.1 The Limits on Personal Jurisdiction

(a) Constitutional Limitations

(i) In order for a court to hear cases before it, the Constitution requires both ***adequate notice*** and ***nexus*** between the defendant and the forum state (see *infra.*, "Constitutional Limitations on *In Personam* Jurisdiction").

(b) Statutory Limitations

(i) If no statute grants the court the power to hear cases involving the parties in the case, there is no personal jurisdiction (PJ).

(ii) However, a statute does not create valid PJ unless it is within the limitations of the Constitution.

(c) Personal Jurisdiction in the Federal Courts

(i) Under FRCP 4(k), a federal court must analyze personal jurisdiction with all of the same rules that the courts of the state in which the federal court is located must follow.

3.1.2 Three Kinds of Personal Jurisdiction

(a) *In Personam* Jurisdiction

(i) Also termed "personal jurisdiction," *in personam* jurisdiction refers to a court's power to bring a person (as opposed to property) into its adjudicative process.

(ii) Judgments are entitled to full faith and credit in all fifty states (art. IV, Constitution).

(iii) Thus, if the forum state abided by the statutory and constitutional limitations on PJ and the plaintiff is awarded a judgment, the plaintiff can enforce the judgment against the defendant's property in all fifty states.

(b) *In Rem* Jurisdiction

(i) This refers to a court's ability to adjudicate the rights of *all the world* with respect to property located within the borders of the state in which the court is located.

(ii) The state can bind *all persons* regarding the property's ownership in, for example, a forfeiture proceeding.

(c) *Quasi in Rem* Jurisdiction

(i) *Quasi in rem* jurisdiction is jurisdiction over the person that is based on the presence of the person's *property* within the forum state, as opposed to the *presence or contacts* of that person with the forum state.

## 3.2 Constitutional Limitations on Personal Jurisdiction

3.2.1 Constitutional Limitations on In Personam Jurisdiction

(a) Introduction

(i) The Due Process Clause of the Fourteenth Amendment limits states' jurisdiction over nonresident defendants.

(ii) If a state has a statute giving its courts personal jurisdiction over the defendant, the statute must recognize two constitutional conditions: ***notice*** and ***nexus*** (sufficient contacts).

(b) Sufficient Notice under the Constitution

(i) Constitutional due process requires that the parties before the court receive ***adequate notice*** of the action.

(ii) Some ways of satisfying the due process notice requirements include:

(1) Personal service;

(2) Leaving service with a responsible person at the defendant's home; and

(3) Delivering service to the defendant's agent.

(iii) When an agent is appointed to the defendant by law (*e.g.*, state motor vehicle agencies under state long-arm motor vehicle statutes that bring nonresidents into state court PJ), the agent must notify the defendant of the charge.

(iv) When the defendant's address is unknown, making mailing of the notice impossible, publication is a viable alternative.

(c) The Constitutional Requirement of Nexus

(i) Overview

(1) Nexus requires both ***reasonableness*** and ***minimum contacts*** between the defendant and the forum state.

(2) This is the limit to which state long arm statutes may reach.

(ii) Physical Presence Test

(1) Traditionally, the state where the defendant is a resident or where he was served with process has sufficient nexus.

(aa) *See Pennoyer v. Neff* (U.S. 1877), where the plaintiff Neff brought an action against Pennoyer for taking his land, which was sold to Pennoyer in a default judgment. The Court held that a state holds exclusive jurisdiction over persons and property within its borders. The plaintiff, who was not a resident of Oregon, could not therefore have had a judgment against him by an Oregon court, *unless* it was with his consent. He also was not properly notified. Service within the state is not only sufficient, but also necessary to establish PJ. Therefore, the only ways to achieve personal jurisdiction over a defendant are to sue him in his resident state, to serve him with process in a state in which he is not a resident, or to sue him in a state in which he is not a resident if he consents.

(2) *Pennoyer v. Neff* has created the following rules:

(aa) A state has PJ over a non-resident defendant *only* if he is served within its borders or if he consents.

(I) This rule has been greatly expanded in the modern era.

(bb) Serving a defendant within a state's borders is *sufficient* grounds for establishing PJ.

(I) This rule continues today (see below, "Transient Jurisdiction").

(cc) *PJ is statewide*; if any judge in a state has PJ over a defendant, then any judge in that state also has PJ.

(I) This rule continues today.

(iii) Minimum Contacts and Reasonableness

(1) In the Modern Era, the due process standard is fairness. The requirement of consent or being served in-state under *Pennoyer v. Neff* was largely expanded to the requirements of only *minimum contacts* and *reasonableness*.

(aa) *See International Shoe v. Washington* (U.S. 1945), which held that personal jurisdiction applies even when a defendant is neither present nor served in-state, as long as certain "*minimum contacts*" are met and jurisdiction is "*reasonable*." In *Shoe*, the State of Washington sued to require the defendant International Shoe to conform with a statute requiring the defendant to pay unemployment benefits to its employees in Washington. The defendant argued that Washington did not have jurisdiction over it, since it was a Delaware corporation with its principal place of business in Missouri, with no offices in Washington. The court held that the company's employees, being located in Washington, established systematic and continuous contacts sufficient to establish PJ. The key issue is whether the exercise of personal jurisdiction offends "traditional notions of fair play and substantial justice."

(2) Reasonableness

(aa) A court can use its discretion in deciding whether it is reasonable for a state to hold jurisdiction over a defendant.

(bb) Many factors may be considered, including the burden over the defendant in defending himself in the forum state and the interest of the state in holding defendants within their jurisdiction for certain claims.

(cc) In some cases, the court might decide that although the defendant has minimum contacts with the forum state, it would be unreasonable to exercise PJ over him and that the case should be heard in another state.

(I) *See Asahi Metal Industry Co. v. Superior Ct.* (U.S. 1987), where Asahi, a Taiwanese Co., had minimum contacts with California, since it knew that its tires would wind up there, but PJ in California was unreasonable, given the interest of Asahi and California in litigating in California and the burden of having the defendant litigate in a foreign legal system. The defendant's knowledge that some of its products might end up in California was not enough to give California PJ.

(II) *Compare World-Wide Volkswagen Corp. v. Woodson* (U.S. 1980). Although it was reasonable to adjudicate a claim in Oklahoma (the claim arose there, all of the witnesses were there, and it was more convenient for the parties to litigate there), the Court held that Oklahoma did not have PJ because the defendant did not have the requisite minimum contacts with the state.

(iv) Three Kinds of Minimum Contacts

(1) General Jurisdiction

(aa) If the defendant engages in ***systematic and continuous activity***, the court will have "general jurisdiction" over him in any cause of action arising against him, even those that occur outside of the state.

(bb) Examples of systematic and continuous activity include presence, domicile, or having a business or employees in the state.

(cc) Regular visits to a state or substantial purchases made from the state do *not* constitute systematic and continuous activity.

(I) *See Helicopteros Nacionales de Colombia, S.A. v. Hall* (U.S. 1984), where the defendant had trained, negotiated a contract, accepted checks from, and purchased helicopters in Texas, yet the court held that such contacts were insufficient in order to establish the "systematic and continuous contacts" required to establish general jurisdiction, since the claim did not arise in Texas.

(II) *Compare International Shoe v. Washington* (U.S. 1945), where having employee in Washington *did* constitute systematic and continuous contacts.

(2) Specific Jurisdiction

(aa) The state may exercise "specific jurisdiction" over the defendant if the claim arose from activities within the state.

(bb) Example: if a California citizen, while visiting New York for the first time, got into a car accident, New York may exercise specific jurisdiction over him.

(I) *See McGee v. Int'l Life Insurance* (U.S. 1957), where the California courts had PJ over a Texas Co. whose only contact with California was limited to its one customer in California.

(II) *See Burger King Corp. v. Rudzewicz* (U.S. 1985), where the defendant enters into a franchise agreement with Burger King, which is incorporated in Fla. The agreement required the defendant, a Mich. resident, to send fees to franchisor's home office in Fla. Court held that Fla. courts had PJ over the defendant because he purposefully directed his activities toward Fla.

(3) Purposeful Availment

(aa) A state may exercise PJ over a defendant when he *purposefully avails* himself of the state's legal system.

(bb) The defendant's contacts with the forum state may not be casual, isolated, or accidental.

(cc) It is possible for a court to have PJ over the defendant even if the defendant has never entered the state, as long as the defendant knows that his activities would have a consequence in the state.

(I) *See Keeton v. Hustler Magazine* (U.S. 1984), where a magazine should have known that it would have damaged the plaintiff's reputation through libel in the forum where the plaintiff brought suit, since the magazine was distributed there.

(dd) However, the plaintiff's unilateral activity cannot satisfy the defendant's requirement with forum state; the defendant must ***purposefully avail*** himself of the privilege of conducting activities in the forum State.

(I) *See Hanson v. Denkla* (U.S. 1958), where the question arose as to whether a Florida court could have jurisdiction over a Delaware bank over a trust. The trust holder was a Pennsylvania resident who established the trust in Delaware, and then later moved to Florida. Since the bank had no connection with Florida when the trust was created, the Supreme Court held that Florida did not have PJ.

(ee) Where the defendant is not purposefully availing himself of the laws of a state, simply knowing of the possibility of a claim arising in the state does not establish sufficient nexus.

(I) *See World-Wide Volkswagen Corp. v. Woodson* (U.S. 1980), where the corporation's awareness that its sales in New York could have resulted in injuries in Oklahoma was not enough to establish "purposeful availment," since one's products could end up *anywhere* in the world without creating sufficiently minimal contacts.

(ff) Even where there are minimum contacts, a court may dismiss a claim for lack of PJ when there is a large burden on the defendant or the state has no interest in the case.

(I) For example, in *Kulko v. Superior Ct.* (U.S. 1978), a father's compliance with the request of his children to live with his ex-wife in California and his purchase of a one-way ticket for one child to go there (while the mother sent the other ticket) is not sufficient grounds to bring him within California's PJ. The father did not act to benefit himself of the laws of California, but rather, he acted in the interests of his family. He did not thus avail himself of the laws of California.

3.2.2 Constitutional Limitations on *In Rem* Jurisdiction

(a) Defined

(i) *In rem* jurisdiction refers to a court's power to adjudicate the rights of *all parties* to property within the state.

(b) Nexus

(i) The property's presence within a state is sufficient grounds for granting a court *in rem* jurisdiction, since states have a strong interest in adjudicating the rights of property within their borders.

(c) Notice

(i) Notice requires that the defendant be notified of an action through the best methods available.

(ii) Publication is insufficient process when the addresses of defendants are known. However, when personal notification of each defendant is cost-prohibitive, the plaintiff has a duty only to use the best methods available. *Mullane v. Central Hanover Bank and Trust Co.* (U.S. 1950).

3.2.3 Constitutional Limitations on *Quasi in Rem* Jurisdiction

(a) Defined

(i) *Quasi in rem* jurisdiction is *in personam* jurisdiction based on a defendant's property in a state.

(b) Nexus

(i) Traditionally, under *quasi in rem* jurisdiction, any plaintiff could sue any defendant in any state as long as the defendant owned property within that state.

(ii) A court could grant judgment up to the value of the property.

(iii) The Supreme Court later applied the "minimum contacts" test for establishing *in personam* jurisdiction to all actions, including those based on *in rem* and *quasi in rem* jurisdiction.

(1) *See Shaffer v. Heitner* (U.S. 1977), where the plaintiff, a stock holder, brought suit in Delaware against the officer defendants of Greyhound through *quasi in rem* jurisdiction by sequestering defendants' stock, which was located in Delaware, since the stock was deemed to be in the state of incorporation of the

organization (Greyhound was a Delaware corporation). Although traditionally, the defendant's ownership of property in the forum state was a sufficient nexus for personal jurisdiction in the forum state, after *Shaffer*, the ownership of such property was only *evidence* of jurisdiction. If the claim is related to the defendant's property, the state would have jurisdiction; if the claim is unrelated, then minimum contacts were not met by a mere showing of in-state property ownership.

(c) Notice

(i) The best available method is required for notice.

**3.3 Statutory Limitations on Personal Jurisdiction**

3.3.1 Statutory Limitations on *In Personam* Jurisdiction

(a) Federal Courts

(i) In federal court, the FRCP govern the requirements for notice.

(ii) Rule 4 leaves several possibilities for service of process, including:

(1) Those methods allowed under state law;

(2) Personal service;

(3) Leaving process with an agent; or

(4) Leaving service at one's home with a person of suitable age and discretion.

(aa) In an age where many people own multiple abodes, service of process can be met at any one of the defendant's homes.

(bb) *See National Dev. Co. v. Triad Holding Corp* (2d Cir. 1991)., where the court held that the defendant's Manhattan apartment was his "house" for the purposes of FRCP 4(e)(2), even though the defendant had multiple homes throughout the world and his permanent residence was in Saudi Arabia.

(iii) Rule 4(d) Requests to waive service

(1) From the defendant's perspective, the only time to allow it is when (i) you are immobile and can't just take off; or (ii) there is a long time before the 120 day service period ends.

(2) But if there is very little time before the time window runs out, and you are not immobile (like a corporation that can't go off and hide), the defendant should not allow a waiver of service and should instead disappear.

(iv) Rule 4(k) defines the territorial limits of effective service. It explains that a court has jurisdiction over *any* defendant who receives a summons and meets general jurisdiction or other conditions.

(v) Rule 12(b) defines two errors that can be made with respect to notice:

(1) Insufficiency of process (Rule 12(b)(4)), which is hardly ever is an error; and

(2) Insufficiency of service of process (Rule 12(b)(4)) which often is an error.

(aa) The issue with service of process is deciding how to serve a summons on a defendant in a way that will bring him within the court's jurisdiction.

(bb) "Actual notice" is not enough for proper service. For example, one may receive a summons that was left on his porch, but this will not constitute proper service.

(3) It may seem that if a defendant makes a motion to dismiss for improper service of process, the plaintiff can personally serve the defendant when the plaintiff arrives to court to argue.

(aa) However, the defendant does not always show up in court, and even if he did, he would have immunity from service.

(bb) Furthermore, the defendant's lawyer may not be an agent appointed to receive service of process on behalf of the defendant, so serving the defendant's lawyer would not solve this issue.

(b) State Long-Arm Statutes

(i) States do not have the power to hear all cases; they only have jurisdiction over cases when their legislatures have granted them powers to hear them.

(ii) All states have long-arm statutes that specify the scope of cases that can be brought within their courts.

(iii) All state long-arm statutes granted state courts PJ over:

(1) The state's domiciliaries; and

(2) Those served with process within the state (see "Transient Jurisdiction," *infra.*)

(iv) States generally also grant their courts *in personam* jurisdiction over defendants when the defendant commits a certain act within the state, whether or not the defendant is served within the state.

(v) All states also appear to have nonresident motor vehicle statutes, which have been held to be constitutional.

(1) *See Hess v. Pawloski* (U.S. 1927), where the defendant Hess, a resident of Pennsylvania that was allegedly driving recklessly in Massachusetts injured the plaintiff. Under a Massachusetts statute, drivers in Massachusetts give implied consent to Massachusetts Motor Vehicles to be their agent. The Court held that this statute did not violate the Fourteenth Amendment, which does not preclude

states from enforcing statutes to bring safety to their roads, even if such statutes are enforced against nonresident drivers.

(vi) Beyond these elements, which all states have in common, the states vary in their long-arm statutes.

(1) Some states, such as California, have "unlimited long arm statutes," which grant their courts PJ to the extent allowed under the Constitution's nexus and notice requirements.

(2) Other courts have limited long arm statutes, permitting only certain defined actions to be within the state's jurisdiction.

3.3.2 Statutory Limitations on *In Rem* Jurisdiction

(a) Many states have statutes granting *in rem* jurisdiction allowing the state to adjudicate the rights of all parties regarding property, as long as the property is in-state.

(b) *In rem* jurisdiction relates to condemnation proceedings, forfeiture proceedings of property to the state, settlement of decedents' estates, etc.

3.3.3 Statutory Limitations on *Quasi in Rem* Jurisdiction

(a) Most states have statutes that allow two kinds of *quasi in rem* jurisdiction:

(i) Claims arising out of the property within the state.

(1) The minimum contacts requirement is fulfilled when the claim relates specifically to the property.

(ii) Claims unrelated to property within the state.

(1) Since the constitutional requirements for *quasi in rem* jurisdiction have been so significantly limited by *Shaffer v. Heitner* (U.S. 1977), and since plaintiffs still have the burden of proving the defendant's minimum contacts with the state (even though he owns property in the state), plaintiffs will usually opt for *in personam* jurisdiction in order not to be limited by the value of the in-state property.

### 3.4 Transient Jurisdiction and the Internet

3.4.1 Transient Presence

(a) If the defendant does not have minimum contacts in the forum state, does not fall within the state's long arm statutes, and does not consent, a state will nevertheless have jurisdiction over him if he is ***served*** *while in the forum state.*

(b) Where the claim arose is irrelevant for the purpose of transient jurisdiction; all that is necessary is that the defendant *purposefully avail himself of the laws* of the state by voluntarily going there (vacationing there, driving his car through the state, etc.).

(c) Minimum contacts between the defendant and the forum state are considered satisfied when the defendant avails himself of the laws of the state.

(i) *See Burnham v. Superior Ct. Cal.* (U.S. 1990), where the defendant, passing through California to do some business and to visit his children who were with his ex-wife, was served by her in California for divorce. The court held that the California courts had PJ over the defendant because his presence in the state was voluntary.

(d) Exceptions

(i) There is no PJ when the defendant is served while in the foreign state because he was subpoenaed there as a witness to another case.

(ii) Similarly, there is no jurisdiction over the defendant who is served while forced into the forum state (*e.g.*, beat up and dragged over state lines) or deceived into the forum state (*e.g.*, defendant's ex-wife tells the defendant he must come see their sick son, who really is not sick).

3.4.2 The Internet

(a) Just as increased mobility has lead to an expansion of *Pennoyer*, some commentators have stated that PJ will be changed with respect to the Internet, which poses many challenges to PJ.

(b) However, this is not yet clear.

(i) *See Revell v. Lidov* (5th Cir. 2002), where the plaintiff sued the defendant and Columbia University in Texas for defamation for an article written by him and posted on Columbia University's website. The defendant had no systematic and continuous contacts with Texas and he did not know that the plaintiff even lived there. The court held that there was no PJ because the web site and Columbia University did not have sufficient contact with Texas to lead to them anticipate the possibility of being haled into court there.

3.5 Venue and Transfer of Actions

3.5.1 Introduction

(a) Venue and transfer are additional limits on the plaintiff's selection of a forum.

(b) If a plaintiff brings a case in an improper venue, the remedy is either dismissal or transfer.

(c) If the judge choose to transfer a case in a state court, it will be transferred to a proper venue within the same state; if the case is in a federal court, it will be transferred to a proper venue *anywhere in the country*.

(d) The law of venue has both similarities and differences with PJ.

**Differences Between Personal Jurisdiction and Venue**

| ***Fora that have PJ over the defendant*** | ***Districts that Have PJ*** | ***Districts that Have Proper Venue*** |
|---|---|---|
| Virginia (his domicile) | Eastern District | *Eastern District* |

| | | |
|---|---|---|
| | Western District | Western District |
| Indiana (where the cause of action arose) | Northern District<br>Soutern District | Northern District<br>*Soutern District* |
| Alabama (where he is on vacation now) | Northern District<br>Middle District<br>Southern District | Northern District<br>*Middle District*<br>Southern District |

3.5.2 Determining Where Venue Is Proper

(a) In local actions, venue is where the property is located. However, these are a small minority of cases.

(b) The vast majority of cases are transitory cases, and state and federal statutes prescribe where they can be brought.

(c) Proper Venue in State Court

(i) When the defendant is a natural persona, states generally have statutes that allow venue in a ***county***, ***parish*** or other ***subdivision*** *where the defendants reside* or have *systematic and continuous contact* or where the *claim arose*.

(ii) When the defendant is a corporation, it can generally be sued in the county of its principle place of business.

(iii) In certain actions, such as divorce, states allow venue in the county where the plaintiff resides.

(d) Proper Venue in Federal Court

(i) If a case is being removed from state court, then in the judicial district corresponding to the forum where the case was originally brought in state court will have proper venue.

(ii) If the case is originally brought in federal court, then the following federal districts will have venue:

(1) If all the defendants reside in the same state, then a district where *any* of the defendant resides;

(2) Otherwise, in a district in which a substantial part of the events occurred;

(3) If there is no district in which the action may otherwise be brought:

(aa) When it is founded on diversity only, it should be brought in a district where any defendant is subject to PJ;

(bb) When it is not founded only on diversity, it should be brought in any district where any defendant may be found.

(iii) Corporations are considered to reside in any district that has PJ over it (apply *International Shoe v. Washington's* minimum contacts test as if it were a natural person).

(1) When a state has more than one district, each district can be examined and analyzed as though it were a state in order to determine whether that district would have had PJ over the corporation.

3.5.3 Venue Mistakes

(a) If the plaintiff files a case to an improper venue, the defendant may move to dismiss.

(i) The motion must be made within twenty days.

(ii) The court in its discretion may dismiss the case or transfer the case to a proper venue.

(b) If the plaintiff files a case in a permissible but inconvenient forum, the defendant may move to transfer.

(i) No time limit is imposed on the defendant for the purpose of filing this motion.

(ii) The court will transfer the case to another venue if that venue is also proper and if it is more convenient for the parties, witnesses, or is in the interest of justice.

3.5.4 Transfer and Forum *Non Conveniens*

(a) Transfer and forum *non conveniens* are similar in that both can get a case moved to a better place for trial.

(b) However, forum *non conveniens* is used when the case belongs somewhere where the judge's transfer powers do not reach.

(i) Thus, in state courts, it is invoked when the proper forum is outside the state.

(ii) In federal court, it is only invoked when the proper forum is outside the United States.

(c) Forum *non conveniens* is a dismissal, but unlike other dismissals, the judge makes dismissal contingent on the defendant's waiving any defenses that would make it harder for the plaintiff to start over (statute of limitations; lack of PJ; venue, etc.).

**Summary of the Mistakes a Plaintiff May Make**

| ***Plaintiff's mistake*** | ***Can the mistake be fixed by transfer?*** |
|---|---|
| *Subject Matter Jurisdiction* | No, never (except, for example, if it was filed in one federal court, such as a bankruptcy court, when it needed to be filed in a federal district court). |
| *Personal Jurisdiction* | In state court, it can never be fixed by transfer, since a state court can only transfer a case to other courts within that state, but if the original court did not have PJ, then none of the other state courts would.<br>In federal court, one court may transfer the case to another |

| | |
|---|---|
| | court in the country that has PJ. |
| *Venue* | Always, if PJ is correct.<br>However, a court may choose instead to dismiss the case. |

# 4 State Law in Federal Court

## 4.1 The Evolution of the Doctrine for Determining what Law Applies

### 4.1.1 Historical Approach

(a) Historically, the federal courts, assuming that there was no federal law on point, were to apply state local laws (statutes and laws inherently local in character, such as state real property principles), but not general laws (state case law).

(b) *See Swift v. Tyson* (U.S. 1842), which held that under the Federal Rules of Decisions Act, the federal courts were to apply state law only when there was applicable statue ("local law") on point; otherwise, the federal courts could create the law (a federal common law).

### 4.1.2 *Erie* Approach

(a) The *Erie* doctrine, applying to both state local laws and general law, overruled *Swift v. Tyson* (U.S. 1842), and held the ***federal common law to be unconstitutional***.

(b) In *Erie Railroad Co. v. Tompkins* (U.S. 1938), the plaintiff sued to recover injuries sustained while on a footpath on railroad's right of way. The plaintiff argued to apply the federal common law, which recognized him as a licensee, but the defendant argued to apply the Pennsylvania state law, which would have held the plaintiff to be a trespasser. Held: the state common law should be applied.

(i) *N.B.*: despite *Erie*, which essentially held that there is to be no federal common law, many urge the federal courts to create a new federal common law based on international law and on the law of nations, and many consider customary international law to be a part of the federal common law that survived the holding of *Erie*.

### 4.1.3 Substantive v. Procedural Approach

(a) In his concurrence in *Erie Railroad Co. v. Tompkins*, Justice Reed articulated for the first time the *substantive v. procedural approach* to determining what law applies in federal court.

(b) Under this approach, the federal courts should apply state substantive law and federal procedural law ("no one doubts federal power over procedure").

### 4.1.4 The *Guaranty Trust Co.* Approach versus the *York* Outcome Determinative Approach

(a) Under *Guaranty Trust Co. v. York* (U.S. 1945), the test is not whether the law in question is substantive or procedural, but rather, whether applying a federal law over a state law would lead to a different outcome.

(b) If it would, then the state law should be applied.

4.1.5 *Byrd* Countervailing Federal Interest Approach

(a) Finally, under *Byrd v. Blue Ridge Rural Electrical Cooperative, Inc.* (U.S. 1958), the Court held that the *York* outcome determinative test should be applied, unless there is a ***countervailing federal interest***, in which case the Federal Rule or practice should be applied.

(b) In *Byrd*, the federal practice of allowing trials by jury conflicted with a South Carolina practice that would have required a bench trial. The federal practice was applied because of the countervailing federal interest in allowing trials by jury.

**4.2** *Hanna's* Modern Approach

4.2.1 The Rules Enabling Act Prong (*Hanna II*)

(a) When there is a Federal Rule on point, the Rules Enabling Act prong of *Hanna v. Plumer* (U.S. 1965) (see *infra.*) applies and the following must be determined:

(i) Whether the Federal Rule is valid.

(1) The validity turns on whether it is constitutional. A Federal Rule is constitutional if it was within Congress's power to legislate over federal procedure.

(2) The test looks to whether the Rule is arguably procedural; if it is, then it is valid and constitutional.

(ii) Whether the Federal Rule abridges, enlarges, or modifies any state substantive rights (the 28 USC § 2072(b) inquiry).

(1) The purpose of a substantive law is to abridge, enlarge, or modify any legal right.

(2) There are two ways that a law may be substantive:

(aa) It may primarily deal with areas of human conduct (*e.g.*, a tort law); or

(bb) It may appear to be procedural, but when applied, is outcome determinative in a way that undermines the twin aims of *Erie* (discouraging forum shopping and avoiding the inequitable distribution of justice).

(b) If the Federal Rule is valid and does not abridge, enlarge, or modify any state substantive rights (this is almost always the case), then the Federal Rule trumps the state law and should be applied.

(c) If the Federal Rule is invalid, or if it is valid but it abridges, enlarges, or modifies state substantive rights, then the state procedural rule should be applied.

4.2.2 The Rules of Decision Act Prong (*Hanna I*)

(a) When no Federal Rule is on point, the Rule of Decision Act prong of *Hanna v. Plumer* applies and a modified outcome determinative test should be applied by first determining:

(i) Whether applying the federal practice will lead to forum shopping; and

(ii) Whether the federal practice will lead to an inequitable distribution of justice.

(b) If following the federal practice undermines the twin aims of *Erie*, then the state rule should be applied, *unless* there is a *Byrd* countervailing federal interest, in which case the federal practice should be followed.

(c) *N.B.*: this analysis only applies to procedural questions. When there is a substantive question, the federal courts are required to apply *state law* when no Federal Rule is on point.

(i) *See Gasperini v. Center for Humanities, Inc.* (U.S. 1996), where the court followed the New York "materially deviates" standard for reviewing jury verdicts over the federal double jeopardy provision of the Seventh Amendment. Since the question was substantive, the federal court was obligated to apply the state law under *Erie*. The Seventh Amendment "shocking to the conscience" requirement does not apply to state courts, so no federal law on point applies. Between a state substantive law and an inapplicable federal practice, the state law must be followed.

4.2.3 Summary

(a) Thus, there are two situations in which a federal procedural practice or law would be applied over a state law or practice:

(i) There is no *valid* Federal Rule on point, but there is a countervailing federal interest; or

(ii) There is a valid Federal Rule on point;

(1) *See Hanna v. Plumer* (U.S. 1965), where the defendant argued for application of a Massachusetts state law, since under *York*, there was an outcome determinative difference between Rule 4 service of process requirements and the Massachusetts rule requiring process to be personally served. Held: where there is a Federal Rule on point, it is to be applied when it is (i) valid (arguably procedural) and (ii) does not abridge, enlarge, or modify any state substantive rights (§ 2072(b)). Rule 4, passing these tests, is a valid federal law and therefore trumps the state rule.

(b) This is true even when there is an outcome determinative difference that compromises the twin aims of *Erie*.

### 4.3 Determining the State Law to Apply

4.3.1 Once a federal court decides that it should apply state law, it has the obligation of deciding *which* state's laws to apply.

(a) As a general rule, the federal courts are required to apply the laws of the state in which the action was brought (the forum state), which states which laws to apply. When there are no laws on point, the court is to do what it believed the state supreme court would have done.

(i) Example: if a complaint was filed in a Massachusetts federal court, then that court would apply the Massachusetts rules as to the applicable laws. Thus, if in a diversity suit, the Massachusetts state courts would apply New York state laws in a given case, then a Massachusetts federal court must also apply the New York state laws.

(b) This is true even if a case is transferred.

(i) If the case in the above hypothetical were then transferred to Ohio, the Massachusetts choice of law rules would still govern and the New York state laws would apply.

(ii) Rationale: the plaintiff should have the benefit of the laws of the venue where he originally ***properly*** sued.

(iii) However, when the plaintiff originally sues in a wrong venue, and it is transferred under 28 USC § 1406, this rule does not apply, since the plaintiff should not benefit of the choice of law rules of a venue where he improperly originally sued.

(c) This can lead to gamesmanship among the plaintiffs

(i) *See Ferens v. John Deere* (U.S. 1990), where the Court allowed the plaintiff to adjudicate a claim in Pennsylvania even though he originally properly brought the claim in Mississippi merely to later transfer it without being subject to the Pennsylvania statute of limitations.

(ii) *N.B.*: a defense that the defendant could have raised was that this transfer was against the interests of justice, which are recognized by 28 USC §1404(a).

### 4.4 Federal Law in State Court

4.4.1 When adjudicating ***non-exclusive federal question claims***, state courts must apply only those federal procedural laws "essential to effectuate" the purposes behind the federal law.

## 5 Pleadings and Motions

### 5.1 An Overview of Pleadings

5.1.1 Introduction

(a) Pleadings are documents filed by a litigant that set forth the material facts and legal arguments of his claims or defenses.

(b) The purposes of pleadings are to: (i) give notice of the suit; (ii) give factual and legal information about the nature of the claim; (iii) establish jurisdiction; and (iv) narrow the issues.

(c) The plaintiff initiates suit by filing what most jurisdictions call a "complaint."

(d) The defendant may respond to the complaint by:

(i) Filing her own pleading, called the "answer," and raising any affirmative defenses;

(ii) The plaintiff may then respond to any affirmative defenses in his "reply."

5.1.2 Pleadings Allowed; Form of Motions

(a) Under Rule 7, the following pleadings are required in an action:

(i) A ***complaint*** and ***answer***;

(ii) A ***reply***, if there is a ***counterclaim*** (an independent cause of action made by the defendant against the plaintiff in order to defeat the plaintiff's claim) denominated as such;

(iii) An answer if there is a ***cross-claim*** (a claim under FRCP 13(g) by one party against a co-party);

(iv) A ***third party complaint***;

(v) A ***third party answer***.

(b) No other pleadings are permitted, except that the court may order a reply to an answer or a third-party answer. Rule 7(a).

(c) The deadline for service of all of these pleadings is twenty days from the date of receipt.

5.1.3 Computing (Counting) Days (Rule 6)

(a) In computing any period of time in the FRCP, the following rules apply:

(i) The day of the act, event, or default from which the designated period of time begins to run is not be included in computing the designated period of time;

(ii) The last day of the period is included when computing the period.

(1) However, if the last day is a *Saturday, a Sunday or a legal holiday*, the last day is *not* included in the computation.

(2) Moreover, when the act to be done is the filing of a paper in court, a day on which weather or other conditions have made the office of the district court clerk inaccessible is *not* included in the computation.

(iii) When the period of time prescribed or allowed is less than eleven days, intermediate Saturdays, Sundays, and legal holidays are excluded in the computation of the period.

(iv) When the period of time prescribed or allowed is eleven days or more, intermediate Saturdays, Sundays, and legal holidays are included in the computation of the period. Rule 6(a).

(b) Service is effectuated by the Mailbox Rule: the day the pleading is dropped in the mailbox is the day that it is served.

(c) When by the FRCPs, a notice given thereunder, or order of court, an act is required or allowed to be done within a specified time, the court for cause shown may at any time in its discretion order the period enlarged.

(i) It may do so with or without a motion, if a request is made before the expiration of the period originally prescribed

(ii) It may do so upon motion if a request is made after the expiration of the specified period, where the failure to act was the result of excusable neglect

(iii) However, it may not extend the time for taking any action relating to motions for a JNOV (Rule 50(b)), for a court to amend its findings (Rule 52(b)), to alter or amend a judgment (Rule 59(e)), to set aside a judgment (Rule 60(b) and for a new trial (Rule 50(c)(2), 59(b)), including when a new trial is ordered on the court's initiative (Rule 59(d)). Rule 6(b).

(d) Additional Time after Service

(i) Whenever a party has the right or is required to do some act or take some proceedings within a prescribed period *after the service of a notice or other paper* upon the party and the notice or paper is served upon the party under Rule 5(b)(2)(B) (service by mail), Rule 5(b)(2)(C) (service by leaving a copy with the clerk of the court), or Rule 5(b)(2)(D) (service by other means), three days are added to the prescribed period. Rule 6(e).

5.1.4 General Rules of Pleading

(a) Under Rule 8(a), all pleadings setting forth a claim for relief against another party (original claim, counterclaim, cross-claim, third-party claim) must contain:

(i) A short, plain statement of the court's jurisdiction;

(ii) A short, plain statement of the claim showing that the pleader is entitled to relief; and

(iii) A demand for judgment.

5.1.5 Pleading Inconsistent Facts and Alternative Theories

(a) Under Rule 8(e)(2), the plaintiff may plead inconsistent facts or theories in a complaint when the plaintiff has insufficient knowledge.

(i) *See McCormick v. Kopmann* (U.S. 1959), where the plaintiff McCormick was permitted to claim that the defendant negligently drove his truck and the plaintiff's husband was not contributorily negligent or, in the alternative, a co-defendant's serving him liquor caused his death.

(b) There are two limitations on pleading inconsistent facts:

(i) Ethical considerations: one may not plead what he knows to be untrue. Rule 11.

(ii) Tactical considerations: pleading inconsistent facts may negatively affect the jury's perception of the case.

5.1.6 Form of Pleadings.

(a) All pleadings require a ***caption*** containing: the name of the court, the file number, the title of the action (*e.g.*, "Smith v. Jones"), and the name of the pleading. Rule 10(a).

(b) Each set of circumstances must be set forth in separate, enumerated paragraphs. Rule 10(b).

(c) Statements in a pleading may be adopted by reference to exhibits, which become part of the pleading. Rule 10(c).

## 5.2 Requirements of the Complaint

### 5.2.1 General Requirements

(a) The complaint, like claims made in other pleadings, must contain a short and plain statement of the court's *jurisdiction*, a claim entitling the plaintiff to *relief*, and a statement of the *relief sought*.

(b) The complaint requires legal sufficiency in that the case must state a valid claim.

### 5.2.2 Factual (or "Formal") Sufficiency

(a) Rule 8(f) reflects a policy that places substantive justice over rigid, technical procedural rules.

(b) Within this context, the Court has taken a relaxed view as to factual, or formal sufficiency, by interpreting the Federal Rules as moving away from the rigid requirements of code pleading.

(c) The plaintiff need only plead with specificity sufficient to put the defendant on notice of any claims against him.

(i) *See Dioguardi v. Durning* (2d Cir. 1944), where the plaintiff Dioguardi sued the defendant for conversion. The defendant moved to dismiss for failure to state facts sufficient to constitute a claim. Held: stating facts is not necessary; rather, stating a claim upon which relief may be granted is required and sufficient. Judgment for the plaintiff.

### 5.2.3 Heightened Specificity Requirements in Certain Cases. Rule 9.

(a) There are two exceptions to the liberal pleading requirements in federal courts:

(i) When the Federal Rules require heightened specificity (Rule 9(b) fraud or mistake; Rule 9(g) special damages); and

(ii) When Congress requires it.

(b) In all other cases outside of these exceptions, the federal courts do not have authority to impose heightened standards. *See Leatherman v. Tarrant County* (U.S. 1993) (lower courts were not permitted to require heightened specificity for actions alleging municipal liability).

(c) When heightened specificity is required, six questions must be pleaded in the complaint: who, where, what, when, why and how.

### 5.2.4 Rule 41(a) Voluntary Dismissals

(a) By the Plaintiff

(i) The plaintiff may file a *notice* to dismiss his own action at any time between his filing of an action and the defendant's filing of an answer or motion for summary judgment (SJ), whichever comes first.

(ii) The dismissal is without prejudice, unless the plaintiff formerly brought and dismissed the same action in any other federal or state court in the United States.

(b) By Stipulation of the Parties

(i) The plaintiff may stipulate dismissal with the signatures of all other parties to the action.

(ii) The dismissal is without prejudice, unless the parties stipulate otherwise.

(c) By Court Order

(i) If the plaintiff wishes to dismiss his action *after* the defendant files an answer or a motion for SJ, the court may order such a dismissal without prejudice, unless prejudice is specified in the order.

5.2.5 Rule 41(b) Involuntary Dismissal

(a) The defendant may have an action dismissed if the plaintiff violates *any court order* or for his *failure to prosecute*.

(i) *N.B.*: these are different from Rule 12(b) motions, which are raised by the defendant before he serves his answer, and thus, before the defendant has the opportunity to move to dismiss against the plaintiff for failure to prosecute, for violating court orders, etc.

(b) Such a dismissal is considered to be with prejudice, unless otherwise specified by the court.

(c) An action may also be involuntarily dismissed by the initiative of the court.

(i) *See Link v. Wabash* (U.S. 1962), which established that a court may make an involuntary dismissal *sua sponte* (by order of the court "of its own will" (Lat.), without motions by either party**)**.

(d) Courts will consider several factors in granting involuntary dismissals, such as whether a lawyer intentionally violated a judge's order.

5.3 Veracity in Pleading

5.3.1 Introduction

(a) Attorneys and unrepresented parties must sign their pleadings, written motions, and other papers. Rule 11 (a).

(b) By presenting a document to the court, they are representing that to the best of their knowledge (a subjective element), formed after reasonable inquiry (an objective element):

(i) It is not being presented for any improper purpose;

(ii) The claims and defenses are warranted by existing law or there are non-frivolous arguments for the extension, modification, or reversal of existing law;

(iii) The allegations have evidentiary support, or if so indicated, the party believes they will likely have evidentiary support; and

(iv) The denials have evidentiary support, or if so indicated, the party does not have enough knowledge. Rule 11(b).

(c) The violation of Rule 11(b) can be through *signing, filing, submitting, or later advocating* such positions. Thus, more than one lawyer could be sanctioned under Rule 11(b) (*e.g.*, the one who signed and the one who filed).

(d) Rule 11(b) may be violated by attorneys, unrepresented parties, represented parties, and law firms. Rule 11(c).

(i) Thus, if a party makes false representations to his lawyers, *the party himself*, and not his lawyers, may have sanctions ordered against him.

(ii) Furthermore, if an attorney violates Rule 11(b), then the whole firm may be sanctioned.

5.3.2 The Twenty One Day "Safe Window"

(a) When a party moves for sanctions, he is obligated to abide by the twenty one day "safe window."

(b) This gives the party receiving the motion twenty one days from the day that he is served with the motion to correct his conduct. If he fails to do so, the motion may be filed with the court.

(c) This safe window is *mandatory*, but not *jurisdictional*. The party raising Rule 11 must provide the other party with notice, but this requirement may be waived.

(i) *See Rector v. Approved Federal Savings Bank* (4th Cir. 2001), where the court held that the safe window rule was like a statute of limitations; it was mandatory but could be waived if not raised as an affirmative defense in the trial court.

(ii) *N.B.*: not all courts would accept this court's reasoning; some would see the safe window as jurisdictional (*e.g.*, like SMJ).

(d) The safe window provision provides protection for lawyers who do not disclose contrary authority.

(i) Thus, if a lawyer fails to cite a case that is against his position, he may withdraw the paper within the safe window period and not be required to pay monetary sanctions.

(ii) However, failing to disclose such authority may not be ethical.

5.3.3 The Nature of Sanctions

(a) Monetary sanctions include attorneys' fees and court costs.

(b) Non-monetary sanctions include admonition, the suspension of practice before a court, and the publication of an opinion criticizing an attorney by name.

(c) Attorneys' fees and other expenses may only be rewarded by motion, not by the court's initiative (even if the court issues an order to show cause).

(i) Thus, while both fines and attorneys' fees may be requested by motion, only fines may be ordered by court's initiative.

(ii) As a limitation, monetary sanctions may not be imposed on a represented party for violations of Rule 11(b)(2), which requires that the representations made to a court are warranted by existing law or by a nonfrivolous argument for the modification of existing law or the establishment of new law. Rule 11(c)(2)(A).

(1) Example 1: Party pressures Lawyer into filing a frivolous claim. Lawyer tells Party that he has no case, but Party insists that he file the case anyway. May Party be monetarily sanctioned?

(aa) No, since this would be a violation of Rule 11(b)(2).

(2) Example 2: same as above, only Party knows that the claim is frivolous, but wants to harass the other Party. Can Party be sanctioned?

(aa) Yes, for the violation of Rule 11(b)(1), which deals with bringing a pleading for an improper purpose.

(3) Example 3: Party pressures Lawyer into filing a frivolous claim. Lawyer says Party has no case, but Party convinces him to file it anyway. May Party be non-monetarily sanctioned?

(aa) Yes; Rule 11(c)(2)(A) does *not* state that a party may not receive a *non-monetary* sanction; it applis only to monetary sanctions.

(d) For monetary sanctions to be imposed, one of the following must occur:

(i) A party must make a motion for attorneys' fees or other costs; or

(ii) A court must enter an order describing the problematic conduct, give the party a chance to show cause, and then impose a penalty while describing the conduct determined to constitute a violation of Rule 11.

**5.4** Defendant's Options in Response **to the Complaint**

5.4.1 Motions

(a) Rule 12(b) Motions

(i) The defendant may make motions to dismiss under Rule 12(b) based on the following causes: (i) lack of SMJ, (ii) lack of PJ, (iii) improper venue, (iv) failure to state a claim, (v) insufficiency of process, (vi) insufficiency of service of process, or (vii) failure to join a party under Rule 19.

(ii) The defendant has only one chance to make such a motion, and that is before serving his answer or motion for SJ.

(iii) Alternatively, the defendant may raise these defenses in his answer, but if he does, he may lose the defenses that require express invocation (PJ, venue, process, service of process), unless he amends his responsive pleading under Rule 15(a).

(iv) Once a Rule 12(b) motion is raised, it cannot be amended or raised another time.

(b) Other Motions

(i) The defendant may also make any of the following motions:

(1) A Rule 12(e) motion for a more definite statement (this may also be made by the plaintiff if the defendant serves a pleading requiring a reply).

(2) A Rule 12(f) motion to *strike* (this may also be made by the plaintiff).

(3) A Rule 56 motion for SJ, if the defendant introduces evidence outside of the complaint (this may also be raised by the plaintiff after receiving the defendant's answer);

(4) Rule 12(c) motions for judgment on the pleadings are *not* permitted by the defendant in response to the complaint. Such motions can only be made after all the pleadings are made and are closed. The defendant must file an answer before he may later move for a Rule 12(c) judgment on the pleadings.

5.4.2 File an Answer

(a) Introduction

(i) The defendant must file his answer within twenty days of being served or, if the defendant waives service of process, within sixty days.

(ii) In his answer, the defendant may raise Rule 12(b) defenses and also respond to the plaintiff's allegations, raise affirmative defenses, and make counterclaims.

(b) Responses to the Plaintiff's Allegations

(i) The defendant has three options as to what he may do in response to each of the plaintiff's allegations:

(1) Admissions

(aa) The defendant may admit some or all of the plaintiff's allegations.

(bb) If the defendant knows that some or all of the plaintiff's allegations are true, the defendant is ethically required to admit this in the answer.[16]

(cc) If an averment is not explicitly denied, it will be treated as admitted.[17]

(2) Denials

(aa) In a *general denial*, the defendant denies *everything* in the complaint.

(I) This is generally what one should do when ethically possible.

(II) If the defendant denies all of a claim, but fails to admit one part that is true, that can have serious consequences later on.

---

[16] This does not apply to criminal defendants.

[17] However, the amount in damages is not considered waived if not denied by the defendant.

(III) If it prejudices the plaintiff, it is possible for a court to require the defendant to proceed as though the entire claim were true.

(bb) *Specific denials* deal with each averment separately, admitting some and denying others.

(3) Denials for Lack of Knowledge or Information

(aa) When the defendant lacks knowledge or sufficient information, he may deny make a denial based on the same.

(c) Rule 8(c) Affirmative Defenses

(i) In his answer, the defendant may raise an affirmative defense, which is based on the notion that, even if everything that the plaintiff claims is true, the defendant is still entitled to a judgment in his favor.

(ii) These defenses vary by state. For example, some states require the plaintiff to plead lack of contributory negligence as part of his *prima facie* case; other states require it as an affirmative defense.

(iii) In federal court, regardless of what states require, affirmative defenses including the nineteen mentioned in Rule 8(c) must be included in the defendant's answer.

(iv) If they are not included, the defendant may not raise them. However, courts give liberally leave to amend.

(v) Nevertheless, the defendants should err on the side of caution and raise anything that may seem to be an affirmative defense in the answer.

(vi) How does one know if something is an affirmative defense?

(1) If it is included in the Rule 8(c) list of defenses (accord and satisfaction, arbitration and award, assumption of risk, contributory negligence, discharge in bankruptcy, duress, estoppel, failure of consideration, fraud, illegality, injury by fellow servant, laches, license, payment, release, *res judicata*, statute of frauds, statute of limitations, waiver), it is automatically an affirmative defense.

(2) If it is not, one of the following three tests should be used:

(aa) If the defendant's defense is based on some fact that the plaintiff did not have to prove to win the case, then it is an affirmative defense;

(bb) If the defendant's defense substantially resembles one of the other defenses listed in Rule 8(c), then it is an affirmative defense;

(cc) If the defendant's defense would catch the plaintiff off-guard if raised for the first time in trial, then it is an affirmative defense under the "Surprise Test."

(d) Counterclaims or Cross-Claims

(i) The defendant may raise counterclaims against the plaintiff.

(1) A counterclaim is an independent cause of action made by the defendant in order to defeat the plaintiff's claim.

(2) It does not need to be transactionally related and requires the plaintiff's reply.

(ii) The defendant may also raise a cross-claim against a co-party.

(1) Cross-claims must be transactionally related.

5.4.3 Failure to Respond: Default and Default Judgment

(a) Rule 55(a) Entry of Default

(i) Either party may file an affidavit for and obtain an entry of default when the other party fails to respond to its claims (*e.g.*, a defendant's failure to answer a complaint; the plaintiff's failure to reply to a counterclaim, etc.).

(ii) It is even possible for a party to get an entry of default when the other party defends a case on the merits.

(1) Example: the plaintiff files complaint against the defendant; the defendant files a motion for SJ arguing on the merits; the court rejects the defendant's motion; the defendant never serves an answer; the plaintiff files an affidavit with the court for entry of default, which the court grants.

(iii) The court has no discretion on this matter.

(b) Rule 55(b) Judgment of Default

(i) There are two possibilities regarding what the plaintiff may do in order to obtain a default judgment.

(1) When the defendant *has neither appeared nor responded* and the plaintiff's claim is for a *sum certain* (or for a sum that can be calculated into a sum certain), the plaintiff must file an affidavit with the clerk, and the clerk is obligated to grant the plaintiff the exact amount requested.

(2) When the defendant has *appeared but has not responded*, or has neither responded nor appeared, but the plaintiff's damages are *not for a sum certain*, the plaintiff must make an application to the court explaining why the plaintiff is entitled to a default judgment, and there must be a hearing on the matter.

(aa) This hearing may be as simple as the plaintiff's stating the damages and the court's granting it or it may as complicated as a full evidentiary hearing on the matter.

(bb) If the defendant ***has appeared*** (*e.g.*, through a motion made by the defendant, a letter to the court from a lawyer saying he will represent the defendant, etc.), he must be served with written notice of the application for a default judgment at least three days prior to the hearing on the application.

(cc) If the defendant ***has not appeared***, the plaintiff is not required to serve the defendant with written notice of the hearing on the application for default judgment.

(ii) Both plaintiffs and defendants may ask the court for an entry of default and may make application to the court for a default judgment.

(iii) However, only plaintiffs may obtain a default judgment by the clerk. Rule 55(b)(1).

**5.5 Defending for Lack of Personal and Subject Matter Jurisdiction**

5.5.1 Two Ways of Defending for Lack of Personal Jurisdiction

(a) Collateral Attacks

(i) A collateral attack on personal jurisdiction takes place outside of the original proceeding (after a default judgment has been handed down).

(ii) The advantage to a collateral attack is that the hearing for PJ takes place in the defendant's home state (unless the plaintiff goes to collect judgment in a foreign state where the defendant holds property). Thus, the defendant does not have to show up in a distant court.

(iii) The disadvantage, however, is that the defendant loses his right to defend the case on the merits and waives all other defenses.

(iv) Once a case is adjudicated, a collateral attack cannot be made.

(b) Direct Attack

(i) A direct attack is made *before* a case becomes final in all courts.

(ii) The advantage to a direct attack is that the defendant does not waive his right to defend the case on the merits.

(iii) The disadvantage is that the defendant may be forced to undergo the inconvenience of traveling to a distant forum and finding local counsel.

(1) In some PJ motions, this may include the added expense of discovery and moving evidence to the forum state, as well as the defendant's psychological discomfort of being in foreign territory.

(2) If the defendant loses, he is often required to litigate in the distant forum before having the chance to appeal for lack of jurisdiction.

(3) This is even true when he is right and the distant forum has no PJ over him.

5.5.2 Defending for Lack of Subject Matter Jurisdiction

(a) Under Rule 12h(3), lack of SMJ can be raised as a defense at any time, even after the case is decided, so long as it is through a direct attack in the trial court, on appeal, or in the Supreme Court.

(b) Although the defendant can raise lack of SMJ on appeal, it appears that the defendant may *not* raise lack of SMJ in a collateral suit. *See Chicot County Drainage Distr. v. Baxter State Bank* (U.S. 1940). SMJ challenges must be made in the suit in which they are being asserted, since courts have jurisdiction to decide their own jurisdiction.

(c) Regarding default judgments, the Restatement (Second) on Judgments allows collateral attacks for lack of SMJ on default judgments. Very few courts, however, have actually allowed for collateral attacks on SMJ on their own.

## **5.6** Impleader (Third-Party Practice) (Rule 14**)**

### 5.6.1 Procedural Aspects

(a) Impleader allows a defendant to join a person not a party to the action in limited circumstances.

(b) To invoke impleader, the defendant becomes a third-party plaintiff claiming that a third party would be liable to him for part or all of his liability to the plaintiff.

(c) Generally, impleader is allowed against one who owed the third party plaintiff contribution and indemnity.

(i) Example: the plaintiff sues the defendant for crashing into her with the defendant's car. The defendant claims mistaken identity as his defense, and claims that a thief who stole his car is liable. May the defendant implead the thief?

(ii) Here, the defendant's theory is based on his *not being liable*, not on indemnity or contribution. Therefore, impleader is not available.

(d) Impleader allows a court to determine all liabilities, including the liability of third-party defendants to third party plaintiffs, in one action.

(i) *See Markvicka v. Brodhead-Garrett Co.* (D. Neb. 1977), where the third party plaintiff Brodhead-Garrett Co. successfully brought a school district third party defendant into an action to determine whether it (the school district) was liable to the plaintiff Markvicka, who was injured while using a jointer machine manufactured by Brodhead. Brodhead proceeded on the theory that if it was liable to the plaintiff, then the school district was liable to Brodhead for failure to properly maintain the machine and supervise children.

(e) To bring in a third party, the defendant (third party plaintiff) must serve a summons and complaint. He may do so within ten days of filing the original answer. Otherwise, he must seek leave of court.

(f) The third party defendant may make defenses against the third party plaintiff's direct claims against him as well as defenses against the plaintiff's claims against the third party plaintiff.

(g) The plaintiff and the third party defendant may make additional claims against one another when such claims arise out of same "transaction or occurrence." Rule 14(a).

5.6.2 Jurisdictional Aspects

(a) To determine whether there is jurisdiction, first look for an independent basis for SMJ.

(i) Example: the plaintiff, a New York citizen, sues the defendant, a California citizen, in a claim that exceeds $75,000. The defendant impleads a Florida third party defendant for indemnity claims of over $75,000, and the third party defendant brings a claim against the plaintiff of under $75,000. Which of these claims has no independent basis for SMJ?

(ii) The third party defendant's claim against the plaintiff.

(b) If there is no independent basis for SMJ, there will always be supplemental jurisdiction in the third party plaintiff's case against the third party defendant for indemnity or contribution.

(i) Since it operates under the third party defendant's liability to the third party plaintiff for the plaintiff's claim against the third party plaintiff, it always involves a common case or controversy for the purpose of article III of the Constitution.

(c) Similarly, the third party defendant's case against the plaintiff and the plaintiff's case against the third party defendant always involves a common "case or controversy," under § 1367(a), since it must arise from same "transaction or occurrence" as the underlying dispute.[18]

(d) However, if the original claim is based *only* on diversity, this claim may not destroy that diversity. *Owen Equipment and Erection Co. v. Kroger* (U.S. 1978).

5.7 Amended Pleadings (Rule 15)

5.7.1 Rule 15(a) Guidelines for Determining When Pleadings May be Amended

(a) Amending pleadings is permitted once as a matter of course without the consent of the parties or of the court under the following guidelines:

(i) When the original pleading is one that ***requires a responsive pleading***, an amended pleading may be filed anytime *before the other party serves its responsive pleading*;

(ii) When the original pleading is one that ***does not require a responsive pleading***, an amended pleading may be filed within either of the following periods, whichever is shorter:

(1) Within twenty days of serving the original pleading; or

(2) Before the action is placed on the trial calendar.

(b) Otherwise, each party must amend the pleading with either:

(i) The ***written consent*** of the other party; or

---

[18] Most courts consider the § 1367(a) "same case or controversy" standard to be equivalent to the Federal Rules' common "transaction or occurrence" standard. Some Circuits, however, such as the Second Circuit, consider the former to be broader than the latter. Even in the Second Circuit, then, all impleaded cases fall under federal supplemental jurisdiction, since they will necessarily involve the "same case or controversy" as the original claim.

(ii) ***Leave of court***, which is freely given when in the interests of justice.

(1) When deciding whether to grant leave to amend, courts consider the following factors: the good or bad faith of the requesting party, the utility or futility of amending, whether leave would engender undue delay or undue prejudice, the repeated failure of the requesting party to cure deficiency, and how close the parties are to trial (amendments on the eve of trial are discouraged).

5.7.2 The Problem of Variance under Rule 15(b)

(a) There has been a debate over specificity and the need for correlation between what is pleaded in a complaint and what the judge or jury may decide.

(b) ***Variance*** refers to the plaintiff's introducing evidence in trial proving a legal theory different from that which he pleaded in his complaint (*e.g.*, the plaintiff claims fraud in the complaint, but proves negligence).

(c) Under the common law, this was fatal; but under the Federal Rules, which elevate substance over form, this is permitted.

(d) Under Rule 15(b), the plaintiff is not required to amend the complaint when the issue of variance arises, as long as the defendant expressly or impliedly consents (by not objecting).

(e) However, a party may object to evidence not within issues raised in pleadings. A court will then freely allow pleadings to be amended, unless the objecting party can show prejudice.

(i) *N.B.*: prejudice means more than mere general detriment; it must be detriment *inherently unfair* to a party (*e.g.*, evidence is suddenly sprung on the defendant in such a way that he lacks opportunity to respond).

(ii) Often, in such cases, the judge may cure prejudice by granting the disadvantaged party a continuance in order to conduct the requisite discovery to respond to the additional claims and evidence.

(iii) However, judges have the discretion to deny such continuances, and may do so if such a continuance will affect other cases on the trial calendar.

(f) The final determination of the issues to be tried is definitively decided at the final pretrial conference. Rule 16(d).

(g) After this conference, a ***pretrial order*** stating the issues to be tried is made. It *may only be modified if it is shown to lead to manifest injustice*.

(h) Thus, if after a pretrial order, a party brings in evidence relating to separate legal claims, the opposing party may object on two bases:

(i) The *new claim* was not in the original pleadings (in which case the court will freely grant leave to the first party to amend, unless the opposing party shows that such an amendment would prejudice him); or

(ii) Such a legal claim introduces *new issues* that are not within the scope of the pretrial order (in which case the judge will not allow the amendment, unless refusing the same would lead to manifest injustice).

5.7.3 Amendment and the Statute of Limitations under Rule 15(c)

(a) ***Amendments to claims or defenses*** are treated as though they had been in the original pleadings for the purpose of statutes of limitations and thus relate back to the time of the complaint when one of the following elements are met:

(i) The state law allows them to relate back. Rule 15(c)(1).

(ii) The new claim arises out of the same transaction or occurrence as the claims set forth in the original pleading. Rule 15(c)(2).

(1) Policy rationale: the purpose behind a statute of limitation is to put parties on notice. In a case where a transaction is tried before a court under one legal theory, it is reasonable to expect parties to be on notice for liability under other potential legal theories linked to the same transaction.

(2) The question of whether a new legal claim is based on the same transaction or occurrence is a subjective one over which courts will differ.

(aa) *See Marsh v. Coleman Company* (D. Kan. 1991), where the plaintiff Marsh sued the defendant for wrongful discharge when the defendant in 1988 allegedly fired the plaintiff due to the plaintiff's age, in violation of federal law. Later, the plaintiff brought another, related action, for fraud that occurred in 1985. The defendant raised the statute of limitations defense and the plaintiff argued that it was the same transaction and that the new claim would relate back. Held: because the two events are not based on the same events in time or space, the fraud claim does not relate back.

(bb) *N.B.*: some courts would have read the Rule more openly than this Court and would have allowed the fraud claims to relate back, since they were intimately connected with the plaintiff's termination case.

(iii) The amendment changes a party or the naming of a party against whom a claim is asserted. Rule 15(c)(3). Such amendments relate back only when the following elements are met:

(1) The new claim arises out of the same transaction or occurrence as the claims set forth in the original pleading; *and*

(2) Within Rule 4(m) for service of summons and complaint, the party to be brought in by amendment has:

(aa) Received notice of the lawsuit under Rule 15(c)(3)(A); and (bb) Knows that but for the other party's mistake with respect to the identity of the proper party, the action would have been brought against him. Rule 15(c)(3)(B).

5.7.4 Rule 15(d) Supplemental Pleadings

(a) A supplemental pleading is a pleading that sets forth *all events* that occurred ***after the pleading was filed*** that a ***party could not have included*** in the original pleading.

(b) It is therefore different from an amended pleading, which includes facts or legal theories that ***a party could have included*** in the original pleading, but did not.

(c) Permission for a supplemental pleading may be granted even though the original pleading is defective in its statement of a claim for relief or defense. If the court deems it advisable that the adverse party plead to the supplemental pleading, it will order such pleading. Rule 15(d).

# 6 Parties, Joinder, and Supplemental Jurisdiction

## 6.1 Introduction

6.1.1 Background

(a) ***Joinder*** is the uniting of distinct claims or parties in an action. SMJ, venue and PJ all may affect the possibility of joinder.

(b) Joinder is possible when: (i) the FRCP's permit it; and (ii) the court has power (SMJ) to hear the case.

6.1.2 Rule 17 Real Party in Interest and Capacity

(a) Real Party in Interest

(i) A suit may generally only be brought if a party has suffered injury.

(ii) However, the person suing is not always the person who will receive the benefit of a favorable judgment. Examples when the two do not align include:

(1) When a trustee sues on behalf of a real party in interest;

(2) When a claim is assigned by *subrogation*, by operation of law, as often occurs in insurance cases.

(b) Capacity to Sue or Be Sued

(i) The capacity to sue or be sued is determined by the state law of the individual's domicile.

(ii) In all other cases, it is to be determined by the law of the state in which the district court held, except that: (i) partnerships may be sued in their common name to enforce rights they have under the Constitution; and (ii) Title 28 governs receivers appointed by U.S. courts.

(iii) *N.B.*: generally, all states include infants and incompetent persons among those who lack capacity to sue or be sued.

**6.2** Claim Joinder by Plaintiffs and Defendants (Rule 18**)**

6.2.1 Procedural Aspects

(a) Under Rule 18(a), a party may join "as many claims … as the party has against an opposing party." They do not need to be transactionally related.

(b) Since claims may be joined to "an original claim, counterclaim, cross-claim, or third-party claim," any party, including the defendant, may use joinder.

(c) The standard is permissive in that parties are not *required* to join claims.

(d) When a claim is cognizable only after another has been prosecuted to a conclusion, the two claims may be joined. Rule 18(b).

(e) This applies not only to the original plaintiff, but also to any party seeking relief against another party, whether it is through a counterclaim, a cross-claim, or a third-party claim.

(f) However, an unrelated cross-claim may not be asserted under Rule 18(a) unless it is being added to a valid, related cross-claim under Rule 13(g).

6.2.2 Jurisdictional Aspects

(a) A claim must first have SMJ before being joined.

(b) When there is no independent basis for an additional claim, there may be a basis for SMJ through supplemental jurisdiction.

(i) In any civil action over which the district courts have original jurisdiction, they will also have supplemental jurisdiction over all other claims that arise from the same case or controversy under article III of Constitution

(1) Such supplemental jurisdiction will include claims that involve joinder or intervention of additional parties.

(2) However, even when an additional claim or party arises from the same claim, 28 USC § 1367(b)-(c) limit supplemental jurisdiction.

(ii) Yet when jurisdiction is based only on diversity, there is no supplemental jurisdiction when diversity is destroyed by additional claims by the plaintiffs (but not third party plaintiffs, etc.) against persons made parties under Rules 14, 19, 20, 24.

(1) But when a claim is brought by the defendant as a cross-claim against a second the defendant, there is supplemental jurisdiction even if it destroys diversity in an action based solely on 28 USC § 1332, as long as the additional claim arises from the same transaction or occurrence as the original claim.

(2) *N.B.*: 28 USC § 1367(b) makes efforts to protect diversity only when:

(aa) The original claim is brought *only* under § 1332 diversity; *and*

(bb) The joined claim is one brought by a plaintiff. Thus, claims brought by the defendants may destroy diversity, yet still be joined.

(iii) The district courts may decline supplemental jurisdiction over claims under § 1367(a) in certain circumstances, such as when the additional claim is one that involves a novel state law question.

**6.3** Compulsory Joinder (Necessary and Indispensable Parties) (Rule 19)

6.3.1 Procedural Aspects

(a) Rule 19 applies when a party *must* be joined.

(b) A party is considered *necessary* in an action when:

(i) Complete relief cannot be accorded absent the party; or

(ii) It is a person with an interest in the subject matter of the action such that his absence may (i) impede his ability to protect that interest; or (ii) leave those parties that are already named subject to substantial risks.

(1) A joint tortfeasor is not considered to be a "necessary" party under Rule 19(a).

(2) *See Temple v. Synthes Corp.* (U.S. 1990), where the plaintiff's claim was dismissed for failure to join a joint tortfeasor. On appeal, the court held that jointly and severally liable defendants are not indispensable under Rule 19; the plaintiff *may* join any or all of them, but is not required to do so. Reversed and remanded.

(c) A *necessary* party *must* be joined when it is *feasible* to join him: he can be found and served with process, is subject to PJ, and does not affect diversity jurisdiction.

(d) If it is *not* feasible to join him, the court must determine whether it should proceed in equity and good conscience without him or whether there is a way to get around the problem (*e.g.*, by transferring the case to a court in another state).

6.3.2 Jurisdictional Aspects

(a) Under Rule 19, there is always a common case or controversy; 28 USC § 1367(a) is met as a matter of course.

(b) Jurisdiction may, however, be limited by § 1367(b), which requires that parties joined under Rule 19 by plaintiffs *not destroy diversity*.

(c) In such an event, the plaintiffs may sometimes align the parties to preserve diversity. Courts may react to this by "realigning" parties to where they should have been.

**6.4 Permissive Party Joinder by Plaintiffs (Rule 20)**

6.4.1 Procedural Aspects

(a) Rule 20 allows additional parties to be joined.

(i) Permissive joinder

(1) All persons may join in one action as plaintiffs if:

(aa) As plaintiffs, they assert any right to ***relief jointly, severally, or in the alternative***, or, as defendants, there is asserted against them any right to relief jointly, severally, or in the alternative;

(bb) Arising out of the same ***transaction or occurrence***; and

(cc) A ***common question of law or fact*** to all these persons will arise in the action. Rule 20(a).[19]

(2) The plaintiff or the defendant need not be interested in obtaining or defending against all the relief demanded.

(3) Judgment may be given for one or more plaintiffs or defendants, according to their respective rights and liabilities.

(ii) Under Rule 20(b), the court may order ***separate trials*** and make other orders to:

(1) Prevent a party from being embarrassed, delayed, or put to expense by the inclusion of a party against whom the party asserts no claim and who asserts no claim against the party; or

(2) Prevent delays or prejudice.

(iii) Usually, it is not difficult to determine whether a right to relief arises out of the same transaction or occurrence.

(1) However, some ambiguous situations may arise.

(2) *See Schwartz v. Swan* (Ill. Ct. App. 1965), where Swan and Brey injured the plaintiff Schwartz in an auto accident, and on a separate occasion, Polivick exacerbated the plaintiff's injuries in a second accident. The plaintiff sued Swan and Brey, and joined Polivick under Rule 20. The trial court severed the joinder, holding that the two incidents were not the same transaction or occurrence. On appeal, the court held that the claims could be joined because the accident with Polivick had an effect on the injuries caused by the accident with Swan and Brey. It would be impossible for Schwartz to prove who caused which injuries, since the two were so closely intertwined.

(iv) Rule 42 (Consolidation; Separate Trials) parallels Rule 20 in that it allows for actions involving a common question of law or fact to be joined for hearing or trial.

[19] This element will generally be met if the right asserted arises out of the same occurrence or transaction.

(1) The standard for Rule 42 is more lax than that of Rule 20; Rule 42 merely requires a ***common question of law or fact***; it does not require a common transaction or occurrence.

(2) The difference between Rule 20(a) and Rule 42(a) is that the former is invoked by the parties; the latter is used by the court.

(3) Both Rules 20(b) and 42(b) allow a court to *order separate trials* within the same action.

(b) Rule 21 Misjoinder and Non-Joinder of Parties

(i) Courts are not to dismiss a case because of a misjoinder.

(ii) Rather, they may "sever" parties, dropping or adding them by court order on motion of any party or *sua sponte* at any stage of the action and on such terms as are just.

(iii) Any claim against a party may be severed and proceeded with separately.[20]

6.4.2 Jurisdictional Aspects

(a) Although Rule 20 allows additional parties to be joined whenever they assert any right to relief arising out of the same occurrence or transaction, the joinder of new parties is still subject to SMJ in federal courts.

(b) Additional parties may be joined even if they do not have their own, independent basis for SMJ, since under 28 USC § 1367(a), supplemental jurisdiction includes "claims that involve the joinder or intervention of additional parties."

(c) Thus, there will be supplemental jurisdiction as a matter of course for parties joined under Rule 20, since those parties are joined in when there is a common transaction or occurrence, which necessarily means that the case passes the § 1367(a) common case or controversy.

(d) However, in a case of which the district courts have jurisdiction founded soley on diversity, the complete diversity and jurisdictional amount in controversy requirements apply over claims made by plaintiffs against persons made parties under Rule 14, 19, 20, or 24. 28 USC § 1367(b).

(e) The jurisdiction of the federal courts over additional parties is also limited when the claims raises a novel issue of state law or falls into the other enumerated exceptions of 28 USC § 1367(c).

6.5 Claim Joinder by Defendants

6.5.1 Counterclaims

(a) Introduction

(i) Counterclaims may exceed the plaintiff's claims and may even be added with leave of court if the defendant leaves them out negligently.

(ii) Counterclaims may be *compulsory* or *permissive*.

---

[20] Severance is not the same as a Rule 20(b) order of separate trial.

(b) Compulsory Counterclaims (Rule 13(a))

(i) Procedural Aspects

(1) Compulsory counterclaims arise out of the same occurrence or transaction as the original claim.

(2) When a counterclaim is compulsory, the defendant *must raise it in his answer.*

(3) Rationale: plaintiffs have an interest in having any claims that will ever be brought regarding a specific transaction or occurrence tried all at one time.

(4) Generally, compulsory counterclaims not raised in a case are considered waived, *even when the case is settled.*

(aa) *See Dindo v. Whitney* (1st Cir. 1971), where the defendant Whitney originally sued the plaintiff for injuries sustained while the plaintiff driving. Through later consulting independent counsel, the plaintiff learned that he could have asserted a counterclaim for the defendant's putting hands on the wheel. Rather, however, the case was settled. Held: the plaintiff's failure to raise a compulsory counterclaim and the settling of the case constitute a waiver of the right to later raise the counterclaims, *if the plaintiff was aware of the his right to raise the claim* at the time that he waived them. Remanded to a jury to determine if the plaintiff knew.

(5) Many courts consider compulsory counterclaims waived, *even when not raised due to a default.*

(aa) *See Carteret Savings and Loan Assn. v. Jackson* (1st Cir. 1987), where the defendant Jackson was barred from bringing counterclaims in an action because he failed to raise them in a separate action where they would have been compulsory. He failed to raise them in the first action because he defaulted.

(ii) Jurisdiction Aspects

(1) Compulsory counterclaims must be supported by SMJ.

(2) There will often be an independent basis for SMJ, such as federal question or diversity.

(3) However, if there is not, there is generally SMJ over the counterclaim through supplemental jurisdiction.

(4) If, however, the counterclaim has an independent basis for SMJ, but the original claim does not, then under the ***well-pleaded complaint rule***, supplemental jurisdiction does not bring the original claim under the jurisdiction of the court, since the claims of the *complaint*, not of any other pleading, must fall within federal SMJ in order to be heard in federal court.

(c) Permissive Counterclaims (Rule 13(b))

(i) Procedural Aspects

(1) Permissive counterclaims do *not* arise from the same transaction or occurrence as those of the original claim.

(2) At his option, the defendant *may* make permissive counterclaims in the same case in which the plaintiff sues the defendant. Alternatively, he may do so in a different proceeding.

(ii) Jurisdictional Aspects

(1) Each claim must be assessed separately to determine whether it has SMJ.

(2) First, one should inquire whether there is an ***independent basis*** for SMJ.

(3) If there is not, one should inquire whether the case would fall within ***supplemental jurisdiction***.

(aa) To have supplemental jurisdiction, a case must arise from the same case or controversy.

(bb) Thus, for the majority of courts, supplemental jurisdiction does not apply, since permissive counterclaims do not arise from a common transaction or occurrence (if they did, they would be compulsory).

(cc) Since most courts consider a common "transaction or occurrence" to be the same as a § 1367(a) common "case or controversy," a permissive counterclaim automatically does not qualify.

(dd) However, for those few circuits (such as the Second Circuit) that consider the § 1367 "common case or controversy" standard to be broader than the Federal Rules' common "transaction or occurrence" standard, there are some cases that may arise from a common case or controversy, but not from a common occurrence or transaction. Such permissive counterclaims may fall within supplemental jurisdiction.

6.5.2 Cross-Claims (Rule 13(g))

(a) Procedural aspects

(i) Cross-claims are not compulsory; the defendant *may* make them against a co-party in the action.

(ii) Rule 13(g), which implicitly permits the defendants to seek contribution and indemnity, requires cross-claims to arise under *same transaction or occurrence* as:

(1) The original action;

(2) A counterclaim; or

(3) Property that is the subject matter of the original action.

(b) Jurisdictional aspects

(i) For there to be a cross-claim, the cross-claim must arise under the same transaction or occurrence. Therefore, it will automatically be of the same case or controversy.

(ii) There will always therefore be at least supplemental jurisdiction as long as the original claim had supplemental jurisdiction.

6.5.3 Intervention (Rule 24)

(a) Introduction

(i) Intervention implies that a third party initiates a joinder in an action already in progress.

(b) Procedural Aspects

(i) ***Intervention by right*** allows an applicant who is not a party to an action to become a party upon *timely application* when:

(1) A U.S. *statute* confers an unconditional right to intervene. Rule 24(a)(1); or

(2) The applicant claims an *interest* in an action that risks being *impaired* and the applicant is not adequately *represented* by existing parties. Rule 24(a)(2).

(ii) ***Permissive intervention*** allows an applicant who is not a party to an action to become a party upon *timely application* when:

(1) A U.S. *statute* confers an unconditional right to intervene. Rule 24(b)(2); or

(2) The claim or defense shares a *common question of law or fact* with the main action. Rule 24(b)(2).

(iii) No duty to intervene

(1) If a party having an interest in the subject matter of a case fails to intervene, and a judgment negatively impacts his interest, the failure to intervene does *not* waive his defense to that judgment, which he may later challenge in a separate suit.

(2) One is never legally bound by a judgment in a case in which he was not a formal party.

(c) Jurisdictional Aspects

(i) To assure that the claim of an applicant falls within the SMJ of the court, one should first check for an independent basis for SMJ (federal question or diversity between the plaintiff-intervener and all of the defendants or the defendant-intervener and all of the plaintiffs).

(ii) Otherwise, there may be a basis for SMJ under supplemental jurisdiction.

(1) Traditionally, 28 USC § 1367(a) supplemental jurisdiction is met with respect to *interventions by right*, since the joined claim is so closely related to the

controversy that the third party's interest may be impaired absent the intervention.

(2) There is, however, a tendency to exclude *permissive interventions* from § 1367(a) supplemental jurisdiction, since a "common question of law or fact" is broader than the same "case or controversy." When, however, the "common question of law or fact" is substantially related to the original claim, supplemental jurisdiction will apply.

## 7 Depositions and Discovery

### 7.1 Introduction

7.1.1 Detailed factual allegations come not in the pleadings, but in *discovery*, which serves the following purposes:

(a) To allow parties to narrow their issues;

(b) To facilitate settlements by allowing each side to know how much its case is worth; and

(c) To give each party more comprehensive information on the claims that will be raised at trial.

7.1.2 Other methods for obtaining information include the following:

(a) Interviews with voluntary witnesses;

(b) Visiting the scene of a crime; and

(c) Hiring private investigators.

**7.2** Overview of Discovery Devices

7.2.1 Required Disclosures

(a) Parties are required to turn over any information that is useful to that party's claims or defenses.

(b) This does not, however, include information that is harmful to those claims or defenses that aid the other side.

(i) *N.B.*: contrast this to criminal cases, where prosecution must turn over exculpatory information to the defense.

(c) There are three kinds of required disclosures:

(i) *Initial disclosures*, which are disclosed at a very early stage in the case. Rule 26(a)(1);

(ii) Disclosures of *expert testimony* of those expected to testify at trial. Rule 26(a)(2); and

(iii) *Pretrial disclosures*, which refer to what will be done at the trial. Rule26(a)(3).

7.2.2 Depositions

(a) Oral Depositions (Rule 30)

(i) Oral depositions are conducted as though the witness were testifying at trial, but no judge is present.

(ii) They may be done without leave of court.

(iii) They can be quite expensive, with $1,000 expended for a court reporter to transcribe a day-long deposition.

(iv) There is a presumptive limit of ten depositions per side.

(v) One may depose:

(1) *Parties*, with a Rule 30(b)(1) notice of deposition; or

(2) *Non-parties* (some of whom are not under the court's jurisdiction), with a court order.

(b) Written Depositions (Rule 31)

(i) Written depositions, or depositions "upon written questions," allow parties to serve a set of questions to be asked to a witness.

(ii) A court officer asks the questions and the lawyer need not be present.

(iii) Disadvantages to written depositions include the inability to:

(1) Ask follow up questions; and

(2) Watch how the witness reacts to certain questions.

7.2.3 Interrogatories to Parties

(a) Rule 33 interrogatories to parties are like depositions, except that in interrogatories, it is the parties that are required to give answers reflecting what they actually know and information available to them.

(b) There is a presumptive limit of twenty five interrogatories to each party. This limit may be modified by stipulation or court order.

(c) Usually, a party will begin with interrogatories to develop the follow up questions needing to be later asked in depositions.

(d) Upon receiving an interrogatory, a party may answer or object (privilege, irrelevance, undue burden, etc.). If a party does not object, the objection is waived.

7.2.4 Productions and Entry Upon Land for Inspection and Other Purposes

(a) Rule 34 requires a party to produce documents and other data compilations to the other side for inspection; or

(b) To permit entry upon land or property for inspection, surveying, photographing, testing, etc.

7.2.5 Physical and Mental Examinations of Persons

(a) Rule 35 requires a party that causes a physical or mental examination to be made to deliver a copy of a detailed written report of the examination, if requested.

(b) The examined party waives the privilege that he may have in requesting and obtaining a report of examination.

(c) This applies to examinations made by agreement of the parties, unless otherwise provided.

7.2.6 Requests for Admission

(a) Parties may use Rule 36 requests for admission to determine the undisputed facts.

(b) Admissions save resources by requiring each side to make direct admissions.

(c) Admissions are considered *conclusive*, unless the court permits their withdrawal or amendment. Rule 36(b).

**7.3** Scope of Discovery (Rule 26(b))

7.3.1 General Scope

(a) Parties may obtain discovery regarding any non-privileged matter that (i) is ***relevant*** to claim of any party; (ii) may ***lead to discovery*** of admissible evidence; (iii) is requested in ***good faith***; and (iv) is ***not prejudicial*** to other party.

(b) *See Anderson v. Hale* (N.D. Ill. 2001), where an African American sued the defendant Hale, a member of a racist church, while the defendant was on a shooting spree. The plaintiff demanded a document production from the state bar in the hope to getting insight into the defendant's character and fitness. The defendant objected on basis that information was irrelevant and that its purpose was to harass him. Held: if information seems reasonably calculated to lead to other evidence that will be used to prove a case, such information is discoverable. The defendant's motion is denied.

7.3.2 Relation to the Rules of Evidence

(a) Rule 26(b)(1) does not require that information be admissible to trial in order to be discoverable; it requires only that information reasonably lead to evidence that *would be admissible in trial*.

(b) ***Hearsay*** may be considered sufficiently relevant for discovery, but not sufficiently relevant for admission to trial.

(i) Thus, although hearsay may not be admissible in trial, it is discoverable if ***reasonably calculated to lead to discovery*** of admissible evidence.

(ii) Example: Mrs. Smith heard brakes making a screeching sound. Is her testimony admissible in trial? Yes.

(1) What if it was her husband who told her that he heard brakes screech?

(2) This would not be admissible in trial, since it was hearsay, but it would be within the scope of a deposition, since it appears *reasonably aimed at leading to discovery of other evidence*.

(c) Additionally, evidence of other similar incidents that would be prejudicial to a party would not admissible in trial but would be discoverable if it would reasonably lead to relevant information.

7.3.3 Privileged Material (Rule 26(b)(5))

(a) Overview

(i) The scope of privileged communications is generally determined by state law.

(ii) Among the categories of communications classified by state laws as privileged are those between an attorney and his client, a physician and his patient, a priest and his parishioner, and a husband and his wife.

(iii) Rule 26(b)(1) limits discovery to ***non-privileged materials***. A communication is *not* privileged merely because its disclosure would be embarrassing or detrimental.

(1) *See Coca-Cola Bottling Co. v. Coca-Cola Co.* (D.Del.1986) , where the plaintiff Coca-Cola Bottling Co. sought discovery of the defendant's secret formula in order to prove that Diet Coke and Coke were indeed the same product. When the defendant refused to disclose the formula due to potential detriment, the court held that the plaintiff was entitled to non-rebuttable factual finding in its favor.

(b) Waivers of Privilege

(i) Failure to claim a privilege may be viewed as a waiver.

(1) Example: The client, while being deposed, admits privileged information without his attorney's objecting. The privilege will be considered waived.

(ii) Revelation of the privileged information to another non-privileged party (someone other than a priest, spouse, etc.) destroys the confidentiality of the communication and also constitutes a waiver.

7.3.4 Work Product (Rule 26(b)(3))

(a) Work product is different from privileged material in that it is not *absolutely protected.*

(b) However, work product has some protections. It is not discoverable on mere demand; rather, the other party must show that (i) it has substantial need of the materials in the preparation of the party's case; and (ii) that the party is unable without undue hardship to obtain the equivalent of the materials by other means. Rule 26(b)(3).

(i) *See Hickman v. Taylor* (U.S. 1947), where the plaintiff Hickman, a representative of a crew member who drowned when a boat sank, sent interrogatories asking the defendant to produce all records of memoranda, statements, records, and reports from the crew members. The defendant refused. Held: in order for a party to obtain another party's work product, it must show why that work product is substantially significant to its arguments and why it cannot otherwise acquire the required information without undue hardship. Here, the plaintiff failed to make such showings, and the information and witnesses are easily available to the plaintiff. Judgment for the defendant affirmed.

(1) *N.B.*: the work product doctrine was first recognized in this case.

(ii) *Compare Holmgren v. State Farm Mutual Insurance Co.* (9th Cir. 1992), where handwritten notes written by the defendant State Farm's adjuster estimating the value of the plaintiff's claims was held to be discoverable, due to substantial need.

(c) Material that will gain the most protection as work product is that which reveals an attorney's thoughts, legal strategies, and mental impressions.

7.3.5 Experts

(a) Introduction

(i) An expert is someone with special knowledge or skill that will assist the trier of fact in a case to determine evidence pertaining to an issue.

(ii) Experts may *testify in court* ("testifying experts") or they may *consult and educate* the lawyers on the issues ("non-testifying experts").

(b) Testifying Experts

(i) The parties generally pick the testifying experts that bolster their arguments for trial.

(ii) The parties must disclose their testifying witnesses' identities. Rule 26(a)(2)(A).

(iii) Additionally, they must disclose a written report containing all testifying experts' opinions, reasons therefore, list of publications, other cases where testified, and other matters. Rule 26(a)(2)(B).

(c) Non-Testifying Experts

(i) The work and opinions of non-testifying experts are generally treated and protected to the extent of work product.

(ii) A party may depose or serve non-testifying experts with interrogatories only with a showing of *exceptional circumstances* under which it is impracticable for the party seeking discovery to obtain facts or opinions on the same subject by other means. Rule 26(b)(4)(B).

(iii) Some courts consider *only* the experts' work products to be protected, but not their names and identities. Other courts consider experts' work products as well as their names and identities to be protected.

(1) *See Ager v. Jane C. Stormont Hospital and Training School for Nurses* (10th Cir. 1980), where the plaintiff Ager's lawyer refused to reveal information regarding his non-testifying witnesses, in contempt of court. On appeal, the Court held that since information by one party regarding experts who will not testify is work-

product, it is not to be disclosed absent *extraordinary* circumstances. Order vacated and remanded.

**7.4** Timing and Pretrial Disclosures, Conferences, and Orders

7.4.1 Timing

(a) Rule 26(f) deals with the time limits for discovery.

(b) It requires the parties to confer to make arrangements for discovery and to make proposals regarding the subjects for which discovery will be needed and the limitations that should be made by the court as to what is discoverable.

7.4.2 Pretrial Disclosures

(a) Rule 26(a)(3) requires that a party disclose, in addition to those disclosures required by subsections (1)-(2), the documents, exhibits, and names of witnesses to be called on or used in trial.

(b) These disclosures generally must be made thirty days before trial.

7.4.3 Pretrial Conferences and Orders

(a) Rule 16 sets out the rules for pretrial conferences to expedite the case.

(b) Rule 16(b) allows the courts to hold a scheduling conference in order to create a scheduling order and as many pretrial conferences as necessary.

(c) Rule 16(d) deals with the final pretrial conference.

(i) The judge enters the "final pretrial conference order" reciting what happened in the conference.

(ii) The statement of issues to be tried, etc., trumps over the parties' pleadings.

(iii) The final order is only modified to prevent "manifest injustice."

7.5 Sanctions (Rule 37)

7.5.1 Introduction

(a) Rule 37 allows parties to make motions to *compel discovery* (Rule 37(a)) and *provides sanctions* for failure to comply with court orders (Rule 37(b)) and for failure to disclose information required by Rule 26 (Rule 37(c)).

7.5.2 Mechanics of the Rule

(a) If a party fails to produce materials requested by the other side, the other side may move the court for a Rule 37(a) Order Compelling Discovery.

(b) If the party disobeys the court order as well, the court may *find him **in contempt***; *presume that the **evidence stands against him***; ***dismiss** the case*, or ***grant judgment by default*** against him under to 37(b).

(c) Factors to be considered are whether the party's actions were done intentionally or negligently and in good faith or in bad faith.

(d) Under Rule 26(g), all discovery requests, responses, and objections must be signed by an attorney of a represented party or by an unrepresented party certifying that, to the best of the signor's knowledge formed after reasonable inquiry, the paper is (i) consistent with the federal rules; and (ii) not interposed for any improper purpose.

(e) Otherwise, sanctions may be imposed.

(i) *See Washington State Physicians Ins. Exchange and Association v. Fisons Corp.* (Wash. 1993), where during discovery, the defendant Fisons Corp. failed to turn over self-incriminating documents that pointed to the defendant's recklessness in continuing to market harmful drugs. Held: sanctions are warranted because in the defendant's stating that all relevant documents were disclosed, the defendant was being dishonest in artificially narrowing the scope of the requests being made.

(f) A party failing to abide by Rule 36(a) requests for admission by refusing to admit certain facts may be punished under Rule 37(c)(2), for failure to admit. *See Holmgren v. State Farm Mutual Automobile Ins. Co.* (9th Cir. 1992).

# 8 Trials and Adjudication

## 8.1 The Right to a Jury (Rule 38)

### 8.1.1 Scope of the Constitutional Right

(a) Assuming that a case passes the initial hurdles of PJ, SMJ, and venue, two questions must be asked: (i) will the case proceed to trial? and if so, (ii) will it be a trial by a judge or a jury?

(b) The Seventh Amendment "preserves" the right to trial by jury in cases at common law.[21] Rule 38(a) employs this same language.

(c) Thus, courts must look to the state of the law at the time that the Seventh Amendment was passed to determine the nature of the right that is to be preserved.

(d) At that time, the right to a trial by jury applied only to cases at law, not to cases at equity.

(e) Today, however, the question is complicated by the fact that: (i) the federal courts have ***merged law and equity***; and (ii) ***new causes of action*** that did not exist at the time of the drafting of the Bill of Rights cannot be neatly classified as either law or equity.

### 8.1.2 The Complications of Merger and the Federal Rules

[21] The Sixth Amendment, in contrast, grants the right to a speedy and public trial by jury in *criminal* proceedings.

(a) Ever since the federal courts merged actions at law and actions in equity, the rules governing when trials by jury are available have become more complicated.

(b) Generally, actions involving an equitable issue and an issue at-law may have a jury decide the issue at-law.

(c) Usually, the issue at-law will be decided first, since trials by juries are constitutional and since, through preclusion, whatever facts are found in the first issue tried will be binding facts on the second issue to be tried.

(d) When, however, the court tries an equity issue before an issue at-law, the court's factual findings in the equity issue will not be binding on the jury for the issue at-law because of claim preclusion (since doing so would abridge parties' right to trial by jury).

8.1.3 New Causes of Action

(a) As a result of the merger of law and equity, a two-prong historical test has been adopted that allows a court to examine (i) the closest historical claim at the time that the Seventh Amendment was passed and (ii) the remedy sought, in order to establish whether the current case more closely resembles law or equity.

(b) When the closest historical claim and remedy sought differ as to whether they resemble a remedy at law or at equity, the remedy sought has more sway.

(i) *See Chauffeurs, Teamsters, and Helpers Local 391 v. Terry* (U.S. 1990), where the plaintiffs sued the defendant Teamsters Union, Local 391 for not fairly representing them in a back pay action. The plaintiffs requested a trial by jury and the defendant claimed that the plaintiffs had no such right, since the cause of action more closely resembled what would have been an equity action at the time of the ratification of the Seventh Amendment. However, since the remedy sought (damages) more closely resembled a remedy at-law, and since this factor held more weight than the closest historical claim, the claim was recognized as a legal claim entitled to a trial by jury.

8.1.4 Juries in State Courts

(a) Although the Seventh Amendment does not require trials by jury in actions at-law in state courts, most states provide for the right of trials by jury in at least *some* causes of action.

**8.2** Summary Judgment (Rule 56)

8.2.1 Requirements for Summary Judgment

(a) Summary judgment (SJ) is granted when there is "***no genuine issue of material fact***." Under such circumstances, "the moving party is entitled to a ***judgment as a matter of law***." Rule 56(c).

(b) There is a ***genuine issue*** of material fact when a record contains evidence from which a reasonable jury could find either way on an issue. A genuine issue would exist even if there was only one witness against twenty, even if that one witness was the plaintiff.

(c) A ***material fact*** is one whose outcome affects the outcome of the case.

(d) SJ may be invoked in the following cases:

(i) There is no factual dispute (*e.g.*, the parties stipulate the facts and disagree only on the law); or

(ii) There is a factual dispute, but it is not genuine (*e.g.*, one side has so little evidence that the other side wins as a matter of law).

(e) The court interprets the evidence in a light most favorable to the non-moving party.

8.2.2 Summary Judgment Contrasted with Rule 12(b)(6) and 12(c) Motions.

(a) There are three kinds of motions that permit decisions without adjudication:

(i) Rule 12(b)(6) (and 12(b) generally) motions for dismissal for failure to state a claim;

(ii) Rule 12(c) motions for judgment on the pleadings; and

(iii) Rule 56 motions for summary judgment.

(b) In the Rule 12 motions, the court *only* considers the pleadings.

(c) In contrast, in SJ, the court may consider outside evidence. SJ is thus essentially a Rule 12(c) motion with additional evidence.

(d) SJ is similar to directed verdicts, which have the same standard. However, while in SJ, the court makes a ruling based on affidavits, a Rule 50 directed verdict is granted on basis of evidence presented at trial.

8.2.3 Questions Requiring a Heightened Summary Judgment Standard

(a) Some issues require a party to plead a case under heightened standards of evidence.

(b) In these cases, the same heightened standard used in trial applies to the standard required for SJ.

(i) *See Anderson v. Liberty Lobby, Inc.* (U.S. 1986), applying a heightened standard for malice in a libel case in the SJ proceeding, just as would have been applied had the case gone to trial. SJ cannot be determined without considering the underlying standard that the fact finder would ultimately apply to determine if there was liability.

8.2.4 Procedural Considerations

(a) There are two ways that a defendant can obtain SJ against a plaintiff:

(i) Present affirmative evidence showing that there is no way that the plaintiff can prove an element; or

(ii) Point out that the plaintiff has not and cannot produce evidence proving an element.

(1) *See Celotex Corp. v. Catrett* (U.S. 1986), where the plaintiff Catrett sued asbestos product manufacturers on the theory that her husband's exposure to

their products caused his death. The defendant moved for SJ, arguing that the plaintiff *did not and could not prove that her husband had the requisite exposure* to the defendant's products. The defendant pointed to the plaintiff's not having responded to the defendant's interrogatory asking the plaintiff to identify witnesses who could testify that her husband was exposed to the defendant's products. This created the presumption that the plaintiff had not in fact had such witnesses or other proof. SJ for the defendant.

(2) *N.B.*: had the plaintiff responded to the defendant's motion by submitting an affidavit or other evidence proving the plaintiff's husband's exposure to the asbestos, the defendant would not have been granted SJ.

(b) If the defendant successfully meets his burden, the burden shifts on the plaintiff to produce evidence to the contrary.

(i) The plaintiff may meet the burden of proof through affidavits or further testimony. Rule 56(e).

(ii) If the plaintiff is unable to do so, he must move the court to grant more time. Rule 56(f).

(iii) The court will only grant more time if it believes that there is a reasonable chance that the plaintiff will be able to do so.

(iv) Factors a court will look at include:

(1) How long it has been since the start of the case; and

(2) How much time the plaintiff has already had to produce the requisite evidence.

**8.3** Second-Guessing Juries (Rules 50, 59)

8.3.1 Judgments as a Matter of Law (Direct Verdict)

(a) Under Rule 50(a), a court may enter a directed verdict without a trial by jury when it concludes that no reasonable jury could find for one side.

(b) In the alternative, a court may under Rule 50(b) submit a case to a jury and if a jury returns a verdict that is not reasonably supported by evidence, the court may enter a judgment *non obstante veredicto* (JNOV).

(c) The standard for granting SJ, a directed verdict, or a JNOV considers whether a reasonable jury could return a verdict in favor of one of the parties on the presented evidence.

(d) Rule 50 controls directed verdicts and refers to them as, "judgments as a matter of law" (JMOL). JNOV's are now known as "renewed motions for judgment as a matter of law" under Rule 50(b).

(e) If a party's motion for a JMOL is denied and an issue is submitted to a jury and the moving party loses, that party may move for a renewed JMOL.

(f) A JMOL is similar to SJ, except that SJ motions are made outside of the context of trial.

(g) As with SJ, a court may grant a JMOL on some but not all issues.

(h) The timing for JMOL motions in trial is as follows:

(i) Opening statements;

(ii) The plaintiff introduces evidence and closes his case in chief;

(iii) The defendant may move for JMOL, or alternatively, may introduce evidence and close his case in chief;

(iv) The plaintiff or the defendant may move for JMOL;

(v) Closing arguments;

(vi) The judge instructs the jury, the jury deliberates, and gives its verdict; the judge enters a judgment on the verdict;

(vii) Within ten days, either party may renew its JMOL motion, but only if it had formerly moved for a JMOL during the trial, or may move for a new trial.

(viii) Whether a party makes a Rule 50(b) renewed motion for a JMOL or a Rule 59 motion for a new trial affects the amount of time that that party has to appeal.

(1) The thirty day limit time to appeal is no longer based on when the entry of judgment on the verdict was made.

(2) Rather, it is based on when the entry of judgment for the renewed motion was made (provided that the motion was made in a timely manner).

(i) The standard for granting a renewed JMOL (JNOV) requires that the jury's findings be clearly erroneous. A verdict is not considered to be clearly erroneous merely because it involved some degree of speculation.

(i) *See Lavender v. Kurn* (U.S. 1946), where the court denied a renewed JMOL because, although there was some speculation on the part of the jury, the verdict was *not* clearly erroneous. When a case goes to a jury, it usually means that there is some uncertainty. In such cases, it is best to allow the jury decide the facts, even if it involves some level of speculation.

8.3.2 New Trial (Rule 59)

(a) Sometimes, there is sufficient evidence such that a JMOL would not be permitted or warranted.

(b) Nevertheless, under Rule 59, a court may be able to exercise influence over the verdict when the court finds that the verdict is not supported by the *preponderance* of the evidence. In such cases, new trials are allowed, in both actions at law and actions in equity.

(c) Thus, it may be possible for a party's case to survive the adverse party's motion for a JMOL, but *not* its motion for a new trial.

(i) *See Dadurian v. Underwriters at Lloyd's of London* (1st Cir. 1986), where the jury found for the plaintiff Dadurian, a jewelry buyer, even though there was substantial evidence that the plaintiff had been misleading on several of the facts, including how he purchased the jewelry. Held: since the preponderance of the evidence is against the plaintiff, a new trial is ordered.

(d) New trials may be granted for both trial error (*e.g.*, errors in the jury instructions or in the evidence admitted) as well as error in a verdict that finds contrary to the overwhelming weight of the evidence.

(e) As with renewed JMOL's, parties have ten days to make motions for a new trial.

8.3.3 Bench Trial

(a) When the judge is the trier of fact (through parties' waiver of trial or when the action is in equity), the judge must record his fact findings and legal conclusions in a written opinion.

(b) This opinion is not a Rule 58 separate document.

(c) According to Rule 52(b), the parties may move for the court to amend its findings.

8.3.4 Motion to Set Aside the Judgment (Rule 60)

(a) Rule 60 allows parties to move to set aside the judgment.

(b) A motion to set aside the judgment (MSAJ) is not an appeal. Rather, it is made directly to the trial court.

(c) A judge's granting of a MSAJ is very rare. There are two kinds:

(i) Rule 60(a) MSAJ's for clerical error; and

(ii) Rule 60(b) MSAJ's for jury error, due to mistakes, inadvertence, excusable neglect, newly discovered evidence, fraud, etc (extremely rare).

## 8.4 Enforcing Judgments

8.4.1 Overview[22]

(a) Winning a judgment does not necessarily mean that the plaintiff collects. After a judgment is issued, the court sends a Notice of Judgment to the parties. Unless the debtor has filed an appeal or stayed the judgment, the debtor has 30 days to pay the judgment.

(b) If the debtor fails to pay the judgment within 30 days, the creditor should contact the debtor to attempt to collect. If this fails, the creditor may take the following steps to enforce the judgment.

(c) However, if the debtor files for bankruptcy, the collection efforts will cease. If the Bankruptcy Court does not discharge the debt, then the creditor may once again collect when the debtor is released from Bankruptcy Court.

---

[22] Note: this is a multistate review of enforcing judgments and does not necessarily correspond to the Federal Rules of Civil Procedure in all instances.

(d) If a ***Transcript of Judgment*** has been filed with the county clerk as provided below, the creditor has a duty to prepare and sign a ***Satisfaction of Judgment*** for the benefit of the Debtor, once the debt has been collected.

8.4.2 Seizing personal property or assets

(a) An execution issued from a court may be levied against and used to seize the debtor's personalty or assets. The enforcement officer at the state level is generally the county sheriff.

(b) Before a county sheriff may seize the debtor's personalty or assets, the creditor must first identify the debtor's property. To do so, the creditor may request the court to issue an ***Information Subpoena***, which directs the debtor or another person, company or institution to answer questions regarding the existence of the debtor's wages, assets and personalty as well as its location.

(c) Upon filing the request for an Information Subpoena, the court will issue the Information Subpoena, which the creditor is to mail to the debtor or other person, company or institution. The recipient of the Information Subpoena must generally answer the questions within 7 days. Otherwise, the creditor may commence a contempt proceeding.

(d) Once the creditor obtains knowledge of the whereabouts of the debtor's personalty, he may execute the judgment. The levy against and seizure of the debtor's personalty by the use of a ***property execution*** is the most common method for enforcing a judgment. Before proceeding to the sheriff to execute the judgment, the creditor must file a ***Transcript of Judgment*** with the court and provide the sheriff with instructions to identify the property in order to seize it and the names and addresses of other people who must be served with the notice that the property is being seized. The sheriff can then seize assets, sell them, and apply the proceeds to satisfy the judgment.

(e) However, there are certain exemptions as to the property that may be seized. These vary from state to state but generally exempt the first $30,000 worth of the debtor's personalty.

8.4.3 Filing an income execution

(a) A creditor may also file an ***income execution*** to obtain a portion of the debtor's wages to satisfy the judgment.

(b) The creditor must inform the sheriff of the debtor's employer's name and address and of the debtor's wages. The creditor may ascertain this information by requesting an ***Information Subpoena*** from the court.

(c) A ***Transcript of Judgment*** must be filed with the court before the sheriff will enforce the judgment by income execution.

8.4.4 Filing a lien against realty

(a) Finally, the creditor may obtain a lien against the debtor's real property. The creditor must obtain a ***Transcript of Judgment*** from the court and then file the Transcript of Judgment in the County Clerk's office.

(b) At this point, there is a public record of the Judgment against the debtor which impacts his credit rating and ability to borrow money.

## 9 Preclusion Doctrines

### 9.1 Collateral Estoppel (Issue Preclusion)

9.1.1 Introduction

(a) Collateral estoppel, which is sometimes referred to as "issue preclusion" or "estoppel by judgment," is the doctrine that prohibits a factual issue from being litigated in any lawsuit if it was litigated and decided in a previous proceeding.

9.1.2 For collateral estoppel to apply, the following elements must be met:

(a) The same issue must have been ***previously litigated***;

(b) The issue must have been ***actually litigated*** in the previous suit;

(c) The issue must have been ***decided*** in the first suit;

(d) The decision must have been ***necessary to the court's judgment*** in the first suit.

9.1.3 Mutual Collateral Estoppel

(a) Mutual collateral estoppel is the use of collateral estoppel by someone who was not a party in the first action to prevent a person who was a party in the first action from bringing a suit against him.

(i) Example: A sues B for a transaction. B successfully raises contributory negligence. Later, A sues C under the same transaction. C is not required to re-litigate contributory negligence; it automatically applies as a defense.

(b) In the above example, if in litigating the issue of A's contributory negligence, A was *not* contributorily negligent, C would not be estopped from a contributory negligence defense

(c) This is because one is not bound by a judgment from a lawsuit to which he was not a party.

### 9.2 *Res Judicata* (Claim Preclusion)

9.2.1 Under the doctrine of "*res judicata*" (Lat., the "the thing already adjudicated"), or "claim preclusion," a party *may not litigate claims* that he raised or could have raised in a previous suit that reached a final judgment.

9.2.2 Claim preclusion applies when the following elements are met:

(a) Two lawsuits must involve the same claims.

(i) Under the federal standard of *res judicata*, for federal courts, a "same claim" means any claim that arises out of the ***same transaction or occurrence***.

(ii) However, defining the scope of a claim is often difficult, since a "cause of action" has never been precisely defined.

(iii) Under the majority view, any claim that ***could have been brought*** but were not brought in a former suit is precluded from being re-litigated.

(iv) Under the minority approach, the plaintiff is precluded only from bringing claims that were actually brought in a previous suit. Claims that could have been brought but were not are not precluded.

(1) *See Carter v. Hinkle* (Va. 1949), where the plaintiff Hinkle was permitted to bring a personal injury claim arising out of the same occurrence from which a property damage claim that he had formerly adjudicated, even though he brought it in a separate, second action.

(b) The parties to the two suits must be the same or in privity.

(c) The first lawsuit must have ended in a final valid judgment.

(i) Majority view: whether a party can appeal is irrelevant for this calculus;

(ii) Minority view: the case must have been appealed or the time frame for appeals must have run and expired.

(d) The final judgment must have been on the merits.

(i) Examples of judgments on the merits: a case that went to trial and was decided; SJ; and Rule 12(b)(6) dismissals for failure to state a claim when they are amended and again dismissed.

(ii) Examples of judgments *not* on the merits: dismissal for lack of SMJ, PJ, or venue; and Rule 12(b)(6) dismissals for failure to state a claim.

# Chapter V. Constitutional Law

# 1 Separation of Powers

## 1.1 Justiciability in the Federal Courts

### 1.1.1 Overview

(a) A case is justiciable when it is properly brought before a court with subject matter jurisdiction and *is capable of being disposed of* judicially.

(b) This requires separate analyses of the distinct questions of nonjusticiability of political questions, standing to sue, ripeness, and mootness.

### 1.1.2 Nonjusticiable Political Questions

(a) A nonjusticiable political question is one that involves the exercise of ***discretionary power*** by either the Legislative or the Executive Branch; it does not involve a *judicial* question to be decided by the judiciary.

(b) A question is a nonjusticiable political question when there is "a textually demonstrable constitutional commitment of the issue to a coordinate political department; or a lack of judicially discoverable and manageable standards for resolving it." *Baker v. Carr* (U.S. 1962).

(c) Nonjusticiable political questions include, for example, claims that the President's is mishandling foreign affairs.

### 1.1.3 Standing

(a) To be justiciable, the parties to a case must have standing (*standing to sue*) before the court.

- (i) This refers to a party's judicial right to make a claim or enforce a duty or right before a court.
- (ii) There are two kinds—constitutional standing and prudential standing, both of which are necessary in any case in federal court (state courts have established their own standing rules).

(b) Constitutional Standing

- (i) Constitutional standing is based on the Article III Case or Controversy requirement. It is therefore not subject to congressional modification.
- (ii) In order to have constitutional standing, the following elements must be met:
  - (1) ***Injury***: the plaintiff must have been directly injured in the past or in the imminent future.
    - (aa) The injury may be economically or otherwise, but may not be excessively indeterminate; it must be more substantial on the plaintiff than on citizens at large.

(bb) However, a court may hear a case even if the plaintiff himself has not been injured if: (i) the party that is injured is unable to represent himself; and (ii) the plaintiff has a close relationship or substantial contact with the injured party, who has allowed the plaintiff to represent him.

(cc) In addition, actual injury need not be shown in cases involving the Establishment Clause, since the protection of fundamental freedoms is too important to limit to injured parties;

(2) ***Causation***: the injury must be traceable to the defendant's conduct; and

(3) ***Remedy***: a favorable court outcome must be able to redress the plaintiff's injury.

(c) Prudential Standing

(i) The common law rules are discretionary and are not dictated by article III of the Constitution. Congress may therefore change them by statute.

(ii) A plaintiff has prudential standing when he does *not*:

(1) Assert the claims of a ***third party***. Exceptions:

(aa) When the injured party lacks competence or faces exceptional obstacles and the party bringing the action will effectively represent him; or

(bb) The party bringing the action bears a close relationship to the affected party (*e.g.*, a liquor seller sues on behalf of women wanting to be able to purchase alcohol).

(2) Sue as a ***taxpayer*** with a common grievance with all other taxpayers;

(aa) Rationale: the injury is deemed to be too remote.

(bb) Exception: the plaintiff may bring a tax action if it involves the First Amendment Establishment Clause.

(cc) The Commerce Clause is *not* a part of this exception.

(I) *See Daimler-Chrysler Corp. v. Cuno* (U.S. 2006), where the plaintiff Cuno and other taxpayers sued when City of Toledo offered the defendant tax benefits. The plaintiffs claimed that the tax breaks increased their own tax burdens. Held: the alleged injury is indefinite and general. If the plaintiffs were granted standing, the separation of powers guaranteed by the Constitution would be eroded as courts begin to redress political and policy questions such as this one. The plaintiffs argue that the Establishment Clause exception to this rule should be extended to the Commerce clause. The Court refuses to extend this exception.

(3) Raise a claim ***outside of the zone of interests*** meant to be regulated by the statutory or constitutional guarantee in question.

1.1.4 Ripeness

(a) A case is ripe, or ready to be heard, when a claimant can make a showing of a ***direct injury*** resulting from the challenged action.

(b) However, courts do not always impose this rule strictly; a case may be considered ripe, even if actual injury has not occurred, when the following two elements are met:

(i) Great ***hardship*** would result if denied judicial review; and

(ii) The ***issues*** and ***record*** are ready for judicial review (*i.e.*, they have been sufficiently developed to allow the court a thorough review).

(c) Generally, a claimant must be prosecuted for the violation of a law before he may challenge such a law.

(d) However, in the following situations, because waiting for ripeness would incur a great hardship, pre-enforcement review is considered justified:

(i) When the enforcement of a statute against the plaintiff has not actually begun but is imminent;

(ii) When the plaintiff wishes to act, but does not want to risk violating the law; and

(iii) When collateral injury is possible (*e.g.*, plaintiffs may challenge a statute limiting the liability of nuclear power plants in the event of a nuclear accident, even though it has not occurred).

1.1.5 Mootness

(a) The mootness doctrine requires the plaintiff to have a personal interest from the beginning to the end of the litigation.

(b) If an intervening event removes the plaintiff's interest in the case (*e.g.*, a statute being challenged is repealed), the case becomes moot and is no longer justiciable.

(c) Exceptions:

(i) Wrongs "capable of repetition yet evading review" (*e.g.*, a pregnant woman claims that an anti-abortion statute is unconstitutional, but before the litigation is completed, she gives birth).

(ii) The defendant ceases the challenged conduct but can resume it at anytime (*e.g.*, the defendant ceases production at a factory, but may resume) or the government repeals a problematic statute, but can reinstate it at any time;

(iii) Collateral injuries (*e.g.*, a criminal who completes a prison sentence can challenge his conviction for collateral injuries, such as lost voting rights).

(iv) Class actions: even if the plaintiff's case becomes moot, the action may go forward for the rest of the class.

## 1.2 The Judicial Power

### 1.2.1 The Question of Lower Federal Courts

(a) After much controversy, the Constitutional Convention decided to leave the question of establishing lower federal courts (the district and circuit courts) to Congress: "The judicial Power of the United States, shall be vested in one supreme Court, and in such inferior Courts as the Congress may from time to time ordain and establish."

(b) The federal district and circuit courts are thus creatures of Congress, not of the Constitution, that can be abolished at the will of Congress.

### 1.2.2 Subject Matter Jurisdiction of the Federal Courts

(a) Article III § 2 of the Constitution establishes federal subject matter jurisdiction (SMJ) over:

(i) Cases arising under the Constitution and the laws and treaties of the U.S.;

(ii) Cases affecting ambassadors, other public ministers and consuls;

(iii) Cases of admiralty or maritime jurisdiction;

(iv) Cases in which the U.S. is a party;

(v) Cases in which a state is a party;

(vi) Cases between citizens of different states;

(1) This is known as "diversity jurisdiction";

(2) Congress has limited diversity jurisdiction to those cases involving amounts in controversy of more than $75,000 (28 USC § 1332).

(3) Diversity jurisdiction has further been limited to only those cases in which *all of the plaintiffs* are diverse from *all of the defendants* (*Strawbridge v. Curtis)*.

(vii) Cases between citizens of the same state claiming lands under grants of different states;

(viii) Cases between a state, or the citizens thereof, and foreign states or citizens.

### 1.2.3 Jurisdiction of the Supreme Court

(a) Original Jurisdiction

(i) Under the Constitution, the Supreme Court has *original jurisdiction* over cases involving ambassadors, other public ministers and consuls, or states.[23]

(ii) Congress has added by statute the following provisions:

[23] U.S. Const. art. III, § 2, cl. 2.

(1) The Supreme Court's original jurisdiction is ***exclusive*** in cases involving two or more states;[24] and

(2) The Supreme Court's original jurisdiction is ***concurrent*** in cases involving:

(aa) An ambassador, consul, or public minister of a foreign state; or

(bb) A state against the U.S., citizens of another state, or aliens.[25]

(iii) Congress ***may not restrict*** the Supreme Court's original jurisdiction.

(iv) Furthermore, according to a marjority of sources, Congress also ***may not expand*** the Supreme Court's original jurisdiction (there is some disagreement on this rule; *see Marbury v. Madison*, *infra.*).

(b) Appellate Jurisdiction

(i) Article III of the Constitution states that, "In all the other Cases before mentioned, the Supreme Court shall have appellate Jurisdiction, both as to Law and Fact, ***with such Exceptions, and under such Regulations as the Congress shall make***."[26]

(ii) Accordingly, the Supreme Court's appellate jurisdiction, unlike its original jurisdiction, ***may be restricted by Congress***.

(1) *See Ex Parte McCardle* (U.S. 1868), where McCardle, a southerner opposed to the presence of union troops in control of southern states, was arrested and locked up by a military court. When his writ for *habeas corpus* was denied, he appealed to the United States Supreme Court. While the case was pending, Congress abrogated the Supreme Court's appellate jurisdiction over the case, and the Supreme Court held that it was obligated to dismiss the case, regardless of the merits of McCardle's case, because it lacked jurisdiction.

1.2.4 Judicial Review

(a) According to *Federalist* No. 78, written by Alexander Hamilton, the judiciary, not controlling the nation's purse or military, is best suited to interpret the Constitution.

(b) Passively waiting for parties to bring their cases before them, the courts have ***neither force nor will*** and are therefore less biased than the other branches of government in interpreting the Constitution.

(c) However, when the text of the Constitution contradicts any branch's actions, the former trumps. The Supreme Court thus has a duty to not apply congressional statutes when it believes they violate the Constitution.

(i) *See Marbury v. Madison* (U.S. 1803) (Marshall, C.J.), where John Marshall, while Secretary of State, failed to deliver to the plaintiff Marbury his commission to become a justice of the peace in D.C. At the time, Congress passed the Judiciary Act of 1789,

---

[24] 28 USC § 1251(a). Original Jurisdiction.
[25] 28 USC § 1251(b). Original Jurisdiction.
[26] U.S. Const. art. III, § 2, cl. 2

which allowed parties to go to the Supreme Court to demand writs of mandamus that order a government official to fulfill his duty. Marbury went to the Supreme Court to demand the writ, but the Court refused, holding that the Act *impermissibly expanded the original jurisdiction of the Court*, which was constitutionally limited to cases involving ambassadors, other public ministers and consuls, and states.

(ii) *N.B.*: *Marbury* has been the object of much criticism. Many have argued the following against the decision:

(1) The Constitution, article III, § 2, cl. 2, was misread as stating that the Supreme Court *only* had original jurisdiction in the enumerated cases (ambassadors, consuls, ministers, states). However, the "exceptions" mentioned in the second sentence may be referring to exceptions to the rule that the Supreme Court has appellate jurisdiction—Congress may instead grant the Court original jurisdiction in those cases.

(2) The Judiciary Act did not actually grant original jurisdiction to the Supreme Court. Rather, it allowed Supreme Court to grant a mandamus remedy to cases already falling within the Supreme Court's original jurisdiction.

(d) The Scope of *Marbury v. Madison*

(i) *Marbury* held that the Supreme Court must go to the Constitution on its own when interpreting it, and not rely on interpretations of other branches of government.

(ii) When the Supreme Court finds contradictions between what the Constitution and other branches of government say, the Court is obliged by the text itself.

(iii) However, the meaning of *Marbury* has come to be interpreted in modern times as stating that the Supreme Court is the ultimate authority on what the Constitution says.

(iv) Yet nothing in *Marbury* suggests that the Judicial Branch can do any better a job than any of the other branches in interpreting the Constitution.

(v) One may similarly argue that each branch of government is obligated to read and abide by the Constitution. If the President reads the Constitution and concludes that it means something different than what the Supreme Court says, he is obliged to follow his own thinking.

(vi) The Court has disagreed, holding that the President and state courts and governors are obliged to follow the Court's interpretations of the Constitution over their own:

(1) ***The President.*** Many Presidents, including Lincoln, Franklin D. Roosevelt, and Reagan, have disagreed that the Supreme Court's reading of the Constitution trumps their own.

(2) ***State courts.*** *See Martin v. Hunter's Lessee* (U.S. 1816) (Story, J.), where the Virginia Supreme Court refused to comply with a U.S. Supreme Court order to enter a judgment pursuant to the federal Judiciary Act of 1789. The Court held that the Article VI Supremacy Clause binds all state courts to the U.S. Constitution, federal laws and treaties, and that the Supreme Court is the

*ultimate arbiter of constitutional questions* under article III. This ensures uniformity of decisions across the United States.

(3) ***State Governors.*** *See, e.g., Cooper v. Aaron* (U.S. 1958), where the Court held that an Arkansas Governor was bound by a federal court order to desegregate Arkansas public schools. The Governor argued that the state was not bound by the Court's interpretation of the Fourteenth Amendment. Held: every state officer is bound by the Supremacy Clause of the U.S. Constitution, and *the Supreme Court is the sole and ultimate arbiter of the same*.

### 1.3 The Legislative Power

1.3.1 In order for a bill to become a law, article I § 7 of the Constitution requires:

(a) The bill to be passed by both Houses; and

(b) The bill to be presented to the President and:

(i) Approved and signed; or

(ii) Opposed and returned to the House from which it originated and reconsidered by that House and the other House and approved by 2/3 of both Houses.

1.3.2 Congress may not depart from this process of ***bicameral approval*** and ***presentation***, even in processes by which Congress oversees the execution of authority that Congress constitutionally delegated to other parties.

(a) *See Immigration and Naturalization Service v. Chadha* (U.S. 1983), where Congress passed legislation delegating its power to decide deportation cases to the Executive Branch for the sake of efficiency. In the law, Congress reserved for itself the right to review the Executive decisions through a veto that did not go through the normal legislative process (bicameral ratification and presentation to the President). When the U.S. Attorney General upheld an immigration court's suspension of the deportation of the defendant Chadha, an alien, the House cancelled the suspension while consulting neither the Senate nor the President, as permitted by the resolution. When the defendant challenged this resolution, the Court held that when Congress takes action that alters the rights and relations of those outside of the legislative branch, since such action is legislation, it must be passed according to the Constitutional requirements of ***bicameralism*** and ***presentation to the President***. A law may not permit one House to unilaterally decide on an issue. Judgment for the plaintiff affirmed.

(i) Dissent (White, J.): Congress *was* acting in accordance with the constitutional requirements of *bicameralism and presentation to the President* when it passed the deportation legislation. It simply set up a system that delegated to the executive a question it had authority to act on while reserving a veto power to itself. The legislation was established through the normal legislative process, even if the actual veto was not.

(ii) *N.B.*: *Chadha* invalidated some 200 statutes, more statutes in one day than all others combined.

(b) *Compare Nixon v. United States* (U.S. 1993), where the Court held that the Senate has the ***authority to delegate the impeachment trial of a federal judge to a committee***, since under the Constitution, the Senate has the "sole Power to try all Impeachments." The issue as to whether the Senate's actions were right or wrong is a *nonjusticiable political question*: the Senate is free on the political question as to how it will handle its constitutional authority over impeachment trials. The word "sole" simply commits the issue to the Senate and the word "try" is not a judicially manageable term on which the Court can impose its own definition.

1.3.3 Not only is Congress prohibited from directly assuming an executive function, but it is also prohibited from delegating an executive function to an officer under its control.

(a) *See Bowsher v. Synar* (U.S. 1986), where Congress delegated deficit reduction legislation enforcement powers to a Comptroller General who exercises executive powers and tells the President to act. Held: this act violates the separation of powers, since the Comproller is controlled by and removable by Congress.

1.3.4 The President has the constitutional authority to sign bills into law ***as they come directly from Congress***. The president may not therefore approve some parts of a bill while rejecting others.

(a) *See Clinton v. New York* (U.S. 1998), where the Court held that the Line Item Veto Act of 1996, which permits the President to approve parts of a bill presented by Congress while rejecting others, is unconstitutional because it permits the President to "create" a new law that was never voted on by either House.

1.3.5 However, the Supreme Court may declare some parts of a law to be unconstitutional and uphold other parts under the following circumstances, which define when the law is severable:

(a) ***Congress includes a severability provision*** in the statute, which states that if any particular provision of the Act is invalid, the entire Act is not to be affected; or

(b) When the Court determines that Congress would have passed the Act in the absence of the invalid provision.

## 1.4 The Executive Power

1.4.1 The Source of Domestic Authority

(a) The president's powers must come from the Constitution or from Congress. He may not independently create laws, even in the interests of national security.

(b) *See Youngstown Sheet & Tube Co. v. Sawyer* (U.S. 1952) (Black, J.), where President Truman seized and gave control of the steel mills to Sawyer, his Secretary of Commerce who was the defendant in the case. The plaintiff challenged the constitutionality of the seizure. Held: the President is not a law maker, but he took actions that Congress specifically debated and decided not to grant to him. The defendant's actions are therefore unconstitutional.

(i) Concurrent opinion (Jackson, J.): a President's actions may fall into one of the three following categories:

(1) Cases in which the President's acts are *supported by Congress*. In this situation, his acts will come under the least amount of scrutiny by this Court;

(2) Cases in which Congress has *neither authorized nor denied the power of the President to undertake a certain action*. In cases where the President is acting by his own power alone, his actions will be subject to more scrutiny.

(3) Cases in which the President acts in *direct opposition of Congress*. Cautious scrutiny applies, as in this case, which Truman does not pass.

(ii) Concurrent opinion (Frankfurter, J.): since past Presidents have not used this kind of power in the past, the defendant's actions were unconstitutional.

1.4.2 The President's Appointment and Removal Powers

(a) Power of Appointment

(i) Introduction

(1) The Constitution requires the President to "***nominate***, and by and with the ***Advice and Consent of the Senate*** ... ***appoint*** Ambassadors, other public Ministers and Consuls, Judges of the supreme Court, and all other Officers of the United States, whose Appointments are not herein otherwise provided for, and which shall be established by Law: but the Congress may by Law vest the Appointment of such inferior Officers, as they think proper, in the President alone, in the Courts of Law, or in the Heads of Departments."[27]

(2) The default rule is that the President nominates and appoints *all* Ambassadors, Ministers and Consuls, Judges, and Officers of the United States *with the advice and consent of the Senate*. This includes both upper level and inferior offices.

(3) However, Congress may vest the full appointment power *of inferior officers* to either the President alone, to the Courts of Law, or to the Heads of Departments.

(ii) Those Working for the Federal Government Distinguished

(1) Principal Officers

(aa) Principal officers must *always* be nominated by the President and approved by the Senate.

(bb) *See Buckley v. Valeo* (U.S. 1976), where the Court held that Federal Election Commissioners, who *had rulemaking power and significant duties under public law*, including the duty to file civil enforcement suits, were not employees and thus were not exempted from the requirement that they be appointed by the President, subject to the advice and consent of the Senate. The appointment of some of these Commissioners by Congress violates the Constitution.

(2) Inferior Officers

[27] U.S. Const. art. II, § 2, cl. 2.

(aa) Inferior officers must be nominated by the President and approved by the Senate by default, but Congress may vest their appointment solely with the President, the Courts, or Heads of Departments.

(bb) If Congress vests the appointment power of an inferior officer to the President alone, then he may appoint the officer *without* the advice and consent of the Senate.

(3) Federal Employees

(aa) Federal employees are not officers and need not be nominated, approved, or appointed.

(b) Power of Removal

(i) Although the President requires Congress's advice and consent for the appointment of all principal officers, this requirement does not extend to his decision *to* ***remove officers***. He may do so unilaterally.

(1) *See Myers v. United States* (U.S. 1926), where the President removed the plaintiff Myers, a postmaster of the first class at Portland, from office, without the advice and consent of the Senate. The plaintiff sued for lost salary, on the basis that the President violated a congressional statute that stated that the President must appoint and remove postmasters with the advice and consent of the Senate. Held: the statute is unconstitutional. The Constitution requires the President to consult with the Senate *only in the appointment of United States officers*, not in their removal. The Constitution vests the executive power in the President (article II, § 1, cl. 1). Thus, unless the Constitution *specifically delegates executive power to Congress*, it is unconstitutional for Congress to carve out any part of the President's power, such as the power to fire his subordinates.

(ii) According to *Meyers*, Congress may not assume the President's executive power to remove his subordinate officers. However, Congress may limit the President's power to dismiss officers of *independent agencies created by Congress*.

(1) These agencies create regulations that have the power of law, but they are independent from the Executive and Legislative Branches.

(2) Most of the independent agencies that Congress has created fall within the Executive Branch.

(3) However, the Library of Congress and the Congressional Budget Office are independent agencies that are administered directly by Congress and are thus Legislative, not Executive Branch, agencies.

(4) Among the independent agencies that fall within the Executive Branch (Central Intelligence Agency (CIA), Environmental Protection Agency (EPA), Federal Communications Commision (FCC), Federal Election Commission (FEC), Securities and Exchange Commission (SEC), United States Agency for International Development (USAID), etc.), the President usually has the power to

appoint the heads of the agencies, but his power to remove them is usually limited by Congress.

(5) Independent agencies regulate a wide range of material, including communications (Federal Communications Commission) and the stock market (Securities and Exchange Commission).

(6) Independent agencies are distinct from executive agencies, which are wholly under the President's appointing and removal powers. For example, the Internal Revenue Service (IRS) is an agency that falls under the Department of the Treasury, whose secretary belongs to the President's cabinet.

(7) Thus, while the President has complete authority to remove officers in executive agencies, he does not have such authority in independent agencies, whether or not they fall within the Executive Branch.

(iii) Presidents are obligated to comply with the rules that Congress creates for the appointment and removal of the officers of independent agencies.

(1) *See Shurtleff v. United States* (U.S. 1903), where the President removed the plaintiff Shurtleff, a general appraiser of merchandise appointed under the Act of June 10, 1890, without showing the cause required by the statute (inefficiency, neglect of duty, or malfeasance). The plaintiff sued to recover salary, arguing *expressio unius est exclusio alterius* (the expression of one thing is the exclusion of others). Held: although the expression is valid in some circumstances, this reading would be to alter the general practice of the federal government, since only judicial officers have life tenure. The plaintiff's interpretation revolutionizes tenure of office by effectively extending it to appraisers unless cause is shown.

(2) *Compare with Humphrey's Executor v. United States* (U.S. 1935), where FDR removed Humphrey, a member of the Federal Trade Commission, for purely political reasons. Humphrey claimed that he was entitled to keep the post and salary, since the relevant Act specified the term of the office and the specific causes for removal. Held: this case is different from *Shurtleff*, since here, there is a term limit. To require the President to show cause in removing an officer would not be to alter federal practices. The statute is clear enough to indicate that Congress wanted Presidents to be able to remove federal officers *only if cause is shown*. Judgment for the plaintiff.

1.4.3 Executive Privilege

(a) In order to assure that the President can freely make difficult decisions, executive privilege grants him ***absolute immunity*** for all actions within ***the scope of his official duty***. *Nixon v. Fitzgerald* (U.S. 1982).

(b) This immunity does not apply to unofficial conduct.

(i) *See Clinton v. Jones* (U.S. 1997), where the Court held that immunity did not apply to a charge against defendant former President Clinton for sexual harassment.

(c) ***Absolute immunity does not equate absolute privilege.*** A balancing act is used to determine whether the President must turn over confidential incriminating information.

(i) *See United States v. Nixon* (U.S. 1974), where the court discovered that the defendant (former President Nixon) had been recording relevant conversations with his advisors in his office and required him to produce the tapes. Nixon tried to quash the subpoena by employing several arguments, one of which was a privilege argument: there is a need to protect confidential information because of privilege and the separation of powers. Held: there may be a privilege, but it is not absolute, and consulting the materials in camera will not destroy it.

1.4.4 The Independent Counsel

(a) As we have seen, Congress may vest in the courts the full appointment power of inferior officers.[28]

(b) Thus, a statute that enables an Article III Special Division to appoint an independent counsel to investigate the president is not unconstitutional.

(i) *See Morrison v. Olson* (U.S. 1988), where Congress passed the Ethics in Government Act of 1978, which allowed the *U.S. Attorney General* to *seek the appointment of an independent counsel* to conduct investigations if he finds grounds for them. The Act created the Special Division, an article III court composed of federal judges who appoint the independent counsel. When convicted by a grand jury, the plaintiff Olson challenged the constitutionality of the Act, arguing that it wrested powers from the President and allowed the judiciary to appoint the special counsel, a principal executive officer, thereby violating the Appointment Clause. Held: the special counsel is not a principal officer because the duties are limited to the case at hand (after which point the office disappears) and the tenure and jurisdiction are limited.

(ii) Dissent (Scalia, J.): this Act is unconstitutional because the independent counsel is a principal officer with significant power to topple an administration. The President must therefore have full control over appointment and removing him. Furthermore, this Act violates the separation of powers: only the President has the power to enforce law and prosecute. Congress improperly took this power form the Executive.

(iii) *N.B.*: the majority deals with the separation of power argument by stating that it is not concerned, since Congress is appropriating executive power not to itself, but rather, to the Judiciary. Doing so is proper, because to vest the power of the independent prosecutor in the Executive Branch would defeat the purpose behind an officer who investigates and prosecutes executive officials. Furthermore, the power being taken from the Executive is so minor that it in no way interferes with the Executive functions.

### 1.5 The President and Foreign Policy

1.5.1 The President's Foreign Powers

(a) There is a great tension in the issue of how much power to grant the President in foreign affairs.

---

[28] U.S. Const. art. II, § 2, cl. 2.

(b) On the one hand, the nation needs an authority that can acts quickly and decisively in international crises; on the other hand, the Congress is the principal source of legislative power.

(c) Some cases, looking beyond the Constitution, have concluded that power over foreign affairs is vested in the President because (i) an unbroken legislative history gives credence to this theory; and (ii) it is in the interests in the nation to allow a President alone to negotiate treaties and engage in other foreign activities that require secrecy.

(i) *See United States v. Curtiss-Wright Export Corp.* (U.S. 1936) (Sutherland, J.), where President Franklin D. Roosevelt, under authority of Congress, declared an embargo against arms sales to Bolivia and Paraguay. The defendant Curtiss-Wright Export Corp. was charged with violating the embargo and challenged the delegation of embargo-making power to the President as an unconstitutional delegation of legislative power to the President. *Held*: this was not an unconstitutional delegation of its domestic power, since it involved not domestic, but foreign power. Although the Constitution does not expressly address this question, based on the law of nations, the President has inherent power over foreign affairs rooted in the nation's security and well-being. This power is vested in the President because secrecy and national security will better be preserved in one man speaking for the nation. In international relations, the President is the sole organ of the federal government.

(ii) *N.B.*: if this case involved a domestic matter, the delegation of authority to the President probably would have been declared unconstitutional, since Congress must make decisions through bicameralism and presentation. *Immigration and Naturalization Service v. Chadha* (U.S. 1983) . The non-delegation doctrine, which was alive and well at the time, allowed Congress to delegate its powers only when it passes an Act enunciating clear principles to which the delegated party must conform. *J.W. Hampton & Co. v. United States* (U.S. 1928). Thus, the Court would not have been able to defend the United States by arguing that Congress was merely delegating its legislative powers. Today, however, the ***intelligible principle doctrine*** of Justice White in his *Chadha* dissent has granted Congress a lot more room to delegate authority. The doctrine allows agencies to gain power based on what is just, reasonable, and in the public interest. Independent agencies today have more rule-making power than the *J.W. Hampton* Court suggested was constitutional.

1.5.2 The Interpretation of International Treaties

(a) The Supreme Court is divided on how much influence foreign courts should have in the interpretation of international treaties of which the U.S. is a party.

(b) Because some of these courts, such as the International Court of Justice, often pronounce opinions binding on inquisitorial states, the U.S., an adversarial state, should only give these cases respectful consideration.

(i) *See Sanchez-Llamas v. Oregon* (U.S. 2006) (Part II[29]), where two cases were consolidated before the Supreme Court, both of which related to the interpretation of article 36 of the Vienna Convention, which addresses the right of communication between an individual detained in a foreign state and his consular officers. ICJ case law, which supports the second defendant Bustillo's *habeas corpus* arguments, does not take

[29] This is a division of the author, not of the Supreme Court.

into account the fundamental ***procedural default rules*** of the adversarial system; rather, they deal with Germany and Mexico, inquisitorial states, and thus should be of limited application. Furthermore, the U.S. is not bound by these interpretations because the U.S. had already withdrawn from the Optional Protocol that gave the ICJ authority to interpret the Vienna Convention. Because the ***American procedural rules of domestic law govern the implementation of international treaties***, the procedural default rules apply in this case and Bustillo's *habeas corpus* petition is denied because he raised his *habeas corpus* defense for the first time after he was convicted, *not at trial*. Judgment for the plaintiff is affirmed.

(c) The constitutional guarantees of due process, protection against self-incrimination, and unreasonable searches and seizures, as well as their domestic protections (*e.g.*, the exclusionary rule) apply to foreign nationals as well as to United States citizens.

(d) When treaties such as the Vienna Convention are adopted by the United States, they too may guarantee certain protections. When those protections are violated or ignored, it is not necessary to extend remedies reserved for violations of the statutory and constitutional domestic protections, since these latter remedies are already in place for the domestic protections, which are more than adequate.

(i) *See Sanchez-Llamas v. Oregon* (U.S. 2006) (Part I[30]), where the defendant Shanchez-Llamas, a Mexican national in the U.S., was convicted of murder after making self-incriminating statements. Sanchez was not informed of article 36 of the Vienna Convention, ***which would have entitled him to consult with his consular officers***. Sanchez thus argues that the self-incriminating evidence should be suppressed: since the Vienna Convention requires implementation of the treaty through domestic law, the proper remedy would be the exclusionary rule. Held: the exclusionary rule applies only to unconstitutional searches or seizures that violate the Fourth Amendment and interrogations that violate the Fifth Amendment protection against self-incrimination. The Court would not expand the exclusionary rule to encompass violations of foreign treaties.

1.5.3 Executive Agreements

(a) Executive agreements have the force of law and are thus treated as statutes.

(b) They fall within the President's executive power in foreign affairs. The President may thus enter into them without Senate approval.

(c) There are three kinds of executive agreements: (i) those based on a treaty; (ii) those invited by legislation; and (iii) those undertaken pursuant to the President's unilateral authority.

1.5.4 Military Commissions

(a) The Executive may prosecute cases by *military commissions* in only the following circumstances:

(i) As a substitute for civilian courts when *martial law* is declared;

(ii) To try civilians as part of a *temporary military government* over occupied territory; or

---

[30] This is a division of the author, not of the Supreme Court.

(iii) When enemies have violated the law of war.

(b) Otherwise, a trial by a military commission is unconstitutional.

(i) *See Hamdan v. Rumsfeld* (U.S. 2006), where the defendant Hamdan, a Yemeni national being detained at Guantanamo Bay, was captured by militia forces, turned over to the U.S. government, and tried by a military commission for conspiracy. The defendant challenged the trial by a military commission. *Held*: the military commission lacks power to try the defendant because its structure violates the Uniform Code of Military Justice and no statute provides that a military commission may try such a defendant or offense. Furthermore, the defendant has not been accused of a war crime. Judgment for the defendant.

(ii) Dissent (Scalia, J.): This Court does not have jurisdiction, since Congress's Detainee Treatment Act clearly and unambiguously removes this case, and all *habeas corpus* petitions of Guantanamo Bay detainees, from the jurisdiction of this court, and of every "court, justice, or judge."

## 2 A Government of Limited and Enumerated Powers

### 2.1 Background

2.1.1 Today, much of constitutional law scholarship and debate is focused around a divide of two fundamental worldviews.

2.1.2 The first view is held by those who see the United States as ***one nation*** that needs to be able to act as a united force in the world.

(a) According to this view, the unity of the nation as a force in world affairs trumps the independence and sovereignty of the states.

(b) State sovereignty should thus be submitted to this national interest.

2.1.3 The second view is held by those who see the principles of ***dual sovereignty and federalism*** as fundamental protections for individual rights. For those who hold this view, the right of states to govern is inalienable and indispensable.

### 2.2 Enumerated Powers of the Federal Government

2.2.1 There was always a great debate as to the tension between state and federal power during the early foundation of our nation.

2.2.2 Many anti-federalists feared a large national government, and suspected that the Constitution would eventually lead to a government of unlimited power.

2.2.3 Some feared that the ***Necessary and Proper Clause***, which allowed Congress to "make all Laws which shall be necessary and proper" for carrying out Congress's powers,[31] coupled with the ***Supremacy***

[31] U.S. Const. art. I, § 8, cl. 18.

***Clause***, which established the supremacy of the Constitution and federal laws and treaties,[32] would grant the government unlimited power.

2.2.4 In *The Federalist No. 33* (Hamilton) counters this view. In it, Hamilton argued that the Necessary and Proper Clause granted the federal government not unlimited power, but that power necessary to execute its *enumerated powers*.

**2.3 Implied Powers of the Federal Government**

2.3.1 The powers of Congress implied in the Necessary and Proper Clause and the Supremacy Clause have been the center of much controversy.

2.3.2 Among them was the debate over whether there ought to be a national bank. Hamilton argued that it was implied by the Necessary and Proper Clause; Jefferson argued that there should be no national power not specifically enumerated in the Constitution.

2.3.3 Hamilton's argument prevailed when a national bank was formed based on the implied powers not enumerated in the Constitution.

(a) *See McCulloch v. Maryland* (U.S. 1819) (C.J. Marshall), where the plaintiff, like many states that opposed the Bank of the United States, tried to tax the bank's presence in Maryland. When McCulloch, the defendant cashier of the National Bank in Maryland, refused to pay, the plaintiff sought to impose penalties on the defendant. Held: (i) ***Congress has implied powers to incorporate a bank***; just because a power is not enumerated in the Constitution does not make its exercise unconstitutional: *"Let the end be legitimate, let it be within the scope of the constitution, and all means which are appropriate … are constitutional."* (ii) ***Such a bank is immune from state taxation***, for the states, which only act to benefit their own citizens, have no right to control the federal government, which acts to the benefit of all citizens of all states.

(b) *N.B.*: Marshall took a broad approach to federal power by defining as "necessary and proper" not only what was necessary in order for Congress to accomplish the enumerated powers, but also ***whatever was useful*** to reach this same end. Congress is prohibited from doing only that which is prohibited by the Constitution.

2.3.4 A Federal Common Law

(a) A question that has arisen is whether the federal courts have the power to *only* interpret the Constitution and federal law or whether they may create a "federal common law" to enact judge-made law to create new rights and causes of action.

(b) The historical approach held that the federal courts may create a federal common law when state court claims were in federal court and no relevant state or federal statutes exist.

(i) *See Swift v. Tyson* (U.S. 1842) (Story, J.), holding that the Federal Rules of Decisions Act required federal courts to apply state law only when there was applicable local law (statutes). Otherwise, the federal courts could create the law.

[32] U.S. Const. art. VI, cl. 2.

(c) However, *Swift* was overruled by *Erie Railroad Co. v. Tompkins* (U.S. 1938), which held that a ***federal common law is unconstitutional***. The court must apply the relevant state common law *even when a case was in federal court* and no applicable statutes exist.

(i) *N.B.*: despite *Erie*, many continue to urge the federal courts to create a new federal common law based on international law and the law of nations.

(ii) Furthermore, many Supreme Court justices have deliberately left the door open for a federal common law.

## 2.4 The Power to Regulate Interstate Commerce

### 2.4.1 Defining "Commerce"

(a) The Commerce Clause permits Congress to "regulate Commerce with foreign Nations, and among the several States, and with the Indian Tribes."[33]

(b) Historically, this power encompassed the right to regulate only ***trade***. It later came to regulate **navigation** as well.

(i) *See Gibbons v. Ogden* (U.S. 1824) (C.J. Marshall), where a NY navigation statute contradicted the federal Coasting Act. Held: there exists a federal power to regulate navigation based on the commerce clause; it would be virtually impossible to regulate commerce without regulating navigation. *Some argue for a narrow interpretation of the Constitution*, yet there are no words in the Constitution directing it. Furthermore, the Constitution deals with Congress's power to regulate navigation when it states that no preference "shall be given by any Regulation of Commerce or Revenue to the *Ports of one State over those of another*: nor shall *Vessels bound to, or from, one State, be obliged to enter, clear, or pay Duties in another*."[34] Since Congress has the power to regulate navigation, and since the NY statute contradicts the federal statute, the federal rule trumps.

(ii) *N.B.*: Marshall's expansive reading of the Commerce Clause allows for very few exceptions and may violate the Tenth Amendment, which reserves all powers not delegated to the federal government to the states and to the people.

(c) Today, three categories of activities that Congress may regulate under its commerce power have been established:

(i) The use of ***channels*** of interstate commerce (roads, canals, waterways, etc.);

(ii) The ***instrumentalities*** of interstate commerce (the people and things being moved); and

(iii) The activities having a ***substantial*** relation to and impacting interstate commerce.[35]

---

[33] U.S. Const. art. I, § 8, cl. 3.

[34] U.S. Const. art. I, § 9, cl. 6.

[35] This leg has consistently and virulently been opposed by Justice Thomas.

(d) Traditionally, commerce did not extend to manufacturing and production. However, even this restriction has been overcome by later cases expanding the commerce power. *See National Labor Relations Board (NLRB) v. Jones & Laughlin Steel Corp.* (U.S. 1937), *infra*.

2.4.2 The Scope of Congress's Commerce Power

(a) Congress may regulate that which is within commerce. That which is outside of commerce is within the states' police power, which serves to regulate for the common good and "suppress evils."

(i) *See U.S. v. E.C. Knight Co.* (U.S. 1895), where the Court held that Congress could regulate combinations, contracts, and conspiracies to monopolize trade *among the several states or with foreign nations*, but since the present case was not about trade or conspiracies across state lines, but about manufacturing within a single state, the breakup of the intrastate manufacturing monopoly falls within Pennsylvania's *police power, not within Congress's power.* Judgment for the defendant E.C. Knight Co.

(ii) *N.B.*: this case takes a narrow view of the Commerce Clause: Congress can only regulate that which directly impacts commerce. The Commerce Clause has since been ***widely expanded***. *See National Labor Relations Board (NLRB) v. Jones & Laughlin Steel Corp.* (U.S. 1937), *infra*.

(b) However, when the regulation of some aspect of trade involves interstate commerce, ***Congress may regulate it****, even if its primary purpose is to suppress evils.*

(i) *See Champion v. Ames* (the "Lottery Case") (U.S. 1903), where Congress passed the federal Anti-Lottery Act of 1864, punishing anyone engaged in or transferring lottery tickets with prison and fines. When the defendant is convicted and imprisoned for violating the statute, he files a writ of *habeas corpus*. Held: lottery tickets transferred across state powers are subjects of traffic and are therefore subjects of Congress's commerce power. *Even if this activity falls within the police power,* ***Congress may legislate against the "pestilence"*** of state to state lotteries. Judgment for the plaintiff affirmed.

(ii) Fuller dissent: the power to restrict lottery tickets belongs to the states, not to Congress.

(1) *N.B.*: the implication of this case is that Congress may now regulate "interstate evils," such as products manufactured by child labor when they are shipped across state borders.

(c) *Knight* and *Champion* were further expanded as the Court came to include within the commerce power the ability to regulate ***streams*** and ***currents of commerce***.

(i) *See Swift & Co. v. United States* (U.S. 1905), where the regulation of an intrastate slaughterhouse was held to be within Congress's commerce power, since slaughterhouses were a factor in a ***national industry*** of ranches and retail.

(d) By 1914, the Court held that Congress's commerce power *transcended actual interstate commerce;* activities that merely ***have an effect on interstate commerce*** fall within the power. *See Streveport Rate Cases*, where Congress was permitted to regulate Texas traffic because of its effect on other states.

(e) However, the Court later pulled back from this decision in *A.L.A. Schechter Poultry Corp. v. United States* (U.S. 1935), where the Court held that Congress may not regulate a New York poultry slaughterhouse whose only customers were New Yorkers, even though there might be an effect of its activities on interstate commerce, since the effect would be at best indirect.

(f) The commerce power was once again expanded in the "Switch in Time that Saved Nine" (referring to the change in Supreme Court decision making that allowed Franklin D. Roosevelt to pass controversial New Deal legislation). In *National Labor Relations Board (NLRB) v. Jones & Laughlin Steel Corp.* (U.S. 1937), the Court held that Congress could regulate ***management and union activity*** at manufacturing plants. The Court rejected the direct/indirect test as well as the notion that manufacturing did not fall within commerce.

(g) By 1942, the Supreme Court had gone as far as establishing the "substantial effects" test: Congress could regulate activities that "substantially effect" interstate commerce.

(i) *See Wickard v. Filburn* (U.S. 1942), where Filburn, a farmer, grew more wheat on his land than permitted by the congressional Agricultural Adjustment Act. Although Filburn intended only to consume the wheat with his family and not to trade it, the Court held that he nevertheless violated the Act. Congress has jurisdiction because the activity, though not interstate, *could have a substantial* ***effect on interstate commerce***, not because of Filburn's limited activities, but because, ***in the aggregate***, the activity of thousands of Farmer Filburns would substantially affect interstate commerce.

2.4.3 The Height of the Commerce Power: the Rational Basis Test

(a) The "substantial effect" test is *almost* the high point of commerce clause power, but the Court went even further.

(i) In *Heart of Atlanta Hotel, Inc. v. United States* (U.S. 1964), the Court held that Congress may prohibit discrimination by hotels and motels under its commerce power because it impedes interstate commerce by blocking the channels of interstate movement.

(ii) In *Katzenbach v. McClung* (U.S. 1964), the Court held that Congress may prohibit racial discrimination by a restaurant under its commerce power when half the meat products were out of state. All Congress needs for an activity to fall within its commerce power is a ***rational basis to believe that the activity would affect interstate commerce.*** A rational basis without an actual effect is a sufficient basis for the commerce power.

(b) To the shock of many observers, the rational basis test was revoked in 1995 when the Court pulled back from the *Heart of Atlanta Motel* and *Katzenbach* rational basis test in cases in which Congress was exercising only a police power.

(i) *See United States v. Lopez* (U.S. 1995), where the defendant Lopez, charged with violating the Gun Free School Zone Act of 1993, argued that the Act was an unconstitutional exercise of congressional power falling outside of the Commerce Clause. Held: this is a case not about interstate commerce, but about police power, since violation of the Act requires neither the purchase of a gun nor transport across state lines. The plaintiff's arguments that possession of firearms could affect interstate commerce through affecting society's productivity are so attenuated that accepting them would give Congress power to regulate anything. Congress may not adopt such measures. Judgment for the defendant.

(c) Some believed that *Lopez* was simply an anomaly, or read it to mean that Congress had to include in its fact-finding that interstate commerce was affected by the regulated activity.

(d) Just a few years later, Congress made it clear that this was not the case: restrictions on the rational basis test were around to stay.

(i) *See United States v. Morrison* (U.S. 2000), where the Court invalidated a key section of the federal Violence Against Women Act (VAWA), even though it had *specific congressional findings* that *gender-based violence substantially affected commerce*, because the invalidated section did not fall within the Commerce Power and intruded on state police power. Even *expansive findings* by Congress that violence against women substantially affected interstate commerce were not enough to trigger the commerce power if there was in fact no substantial effect on interstate commerce.

(e) However, just a few years after *Lopez* and *Morrison*, the Court once again resurrected rational basis.

(i) In *Gonzales v. Raich* (U.S. 2005) (Stevens, J.), several plaintiffs sued for an injunction and for declaratory relief from prosecution of the federal Controlled Substances Act (CSA), on the basis that it prevented medical use of cannabis. The issue before the Court was whether Commerce Clause regulations encompass drugs grown and consumed locally when such drugs are neither purchased and sold nor transported across state borders. Held: because of the difficulty and uncertainty of determining whether marijuana originated in another state or was grown locally, Congress may regulate the intrastate manufacture and possession of marijuana. The Court does not need to "determine whether respondents' activities, taken in the aggregate, substantially affect interstate commerce in fact, but only ***whether a 'rational basis' exists*** for so concluding." Congress need not predict with "scientific exactitude" whether activities will affect interstate commerce; since Congress rationally believed that cannabis, even if grown and consumed locally, would have such an effect. Judgment for the plaintiff.

(ii) Scalia, J. (concurring in the judgment): a substantial effect on interstate commerce is not enough to root an activity in the Commerce Clause. However, this intrastate activity can be regulated by Congress based on the ***Necessary and Proper Clause*** of article I, § 8 of the Constitution.

(iii) Dissent (O'Connor joined by Rehnquist and Thomas): the majority tries to distinguish this case from *Lopez* and *Morrison* through arguing that this Act is a part of a ***large regulatory scheme***, and that if it was just a stand-alone statute, it would have been struck down as unconstitutional. But this gives Congress a perverse incentive to legislate expansively in order to fall within the Commerce Clause.

### 2.5 Negative Commerce Power

2.5.1 Within the Commerce Clause, there is a hidden, "dormant" power that Congress has not yet exercised.

2.5.2 This power allows Congress to authorize the states to regulate certain aspects interstate commerce or to prohibit them from doing so.

2.5.3 However, when a commercial activity requires national uniformity, the regulation of the activity falls within the ***exclusive control*** of Congress.

2.5.4 In contrast, when the activity *would* ***allow for differences in local results****,* Congress may permit the states to regulate it.

(a) *See Cooley v. Board of Wardens* (U.S. 1851), where a Pennsylvania statute required all vessels in the Port of Philadelphia to accept local pilots while in the Delaware River. Those who opted not to were required to pay one half of the pilotage fee into a special fund. The plaintiff Board of Wardens sued the defendant under the Act, relying on the Act of 1789, which conferred on states the authority to regulate local pilots. The defendant challenged the law by arguing that Congress did not have the right to delegate its interstate commerce lawmaking authority, since the power is exclusive to Congress. Held: this activity falls within Congress's commerce power because it is part of a larger scheme of interstate transport. However, it does *not* fall into Congress's *exclusive* commerce power, since it allows for differences in local results. Congress may therefore allow the states to regulate local aspects of the activity, which it did in this case. Judgment for the plaintiff affirmed.

2.5.5 As a general rule, when regulating local commerce, the states may not impose taxes or fees on commerce in a way that discriminates against interstate commerce. To determine whether a law is discriminatory, it must be determined whether the law is:

(a) Merely an *incidental burden*.

(i) An example of an incidental burden is a blanket law that burdens out-of-state interests more than in-state interests.

(ii) For an incidental burden to be valid, the *putative benefit to the state must outweigh the burden* on interstate commerce and there must be *no less restrictive alternative means of regulation*

(b) Real discrimination.

(i) A discriminatory tax is *virtually per se invalid*.

(ii) However, the state may raise the defense that the tax is imposed to ***compensate*** *for other real expenses*.

(1) *See Oregon Waste Systems, Inc. v. Dept. of Environmental Quality* (U.S. 1994) (Thomas, J.), where the plaintiffs Oregon Waste Systems, Inc. challenged an Oregon law that allowed the defendant to impose an additional fee on waste originating out of state. Held: the Commerce Clause includes a "*negative commerce power*" (dormant commerce power) that prohibits the states from passing discriminatory laws that interfere with free flow of commerce between states. The law involves real discrimination, not an incidental burden on insterstate commerce. It is therefore *virtually per se invalid*, but the defendant may raise the defense that *the tax is imposed to compensate for other real expenses*, which Oregon failed to persuasively show. Judgment for the defendant reversed.

(2) *N.B.*: Thomas later changed sides and came to write that the negative commerce power "has no basis in the text of the Constitution, makes little sense, and has proved virtually unworkable in application."

2.5.6 However, there are exceptions to this rule. The states may regulate local commerce in a discriminatory way when:

(a) Congress has ***authorized*** the states to discriminate against interstate commerce;

(b) The discrimination is the least restrictive means to an important health or safety interest; or

(c) The state is acting as a ***market participant***, as opposed to a mere ***market regulator***.

(i) *See South-Central Timber Development, Inc. v. Wunnicke* (U.S. 1984), where the Court held that Alaska violated a statute by imposing "downstream regulations" on who could purchase timber that it was selling. The act of selling the state-owned timber to state consumers did not violate the commerce power because the state was a participant. However, requiring the purchasers to then process the wood in-state did violate the negative commerce power because it put a burden on interstate commerce in an area where the defendant (Wunnicke) was a mere regulator.

## 3 Federalism, Term Limits and Traditional State Functions

### 3.1 Federalism and "Commandeering"

3.1.1 The states are not sub-agencies of the federal government. Congress may not therefore pass federal legislation and then require enforcement by the states.

3.1.2 Doing so would be to commandeer state powers and to violate dual sovereignty.

3.1.3 It is for the federal Executive Branch, not state chief law enforcement officers (CLEO's), to enforce federal legislation.

(a) *See New York v. United States* (U.S. 1992), where New York challenged a federal law requiring the states either to legislate according to Congress's directions or to implement an administrative solution towards the disposal of radioactive waste. Held: Congress may not "compel the states to enact or administer a federal regulatory program."

(b) *See also Printz v. United States* (U.S. 1997) (Scalia, J.), where Congress passed the amendments to the Gun Control Act of 1968 on gun distribution by imposing waiting periods and other restrictions. The amendments required implementation and enforcement by state CLEO's. The plaintiff CLEO's (Printz) challenged the amendments. Held: Congress may not require state enforcement officials to implement or enforce federal laws; doing so equates a usurpation of power that violates the separation of powers and dual sovereignty by dictating to the states *the policies that they must adopt*. Judgment for the defendant reversed.

(i) Dissent (Stevens, J.): In *Garcia v. San Antonio Metropolitan Transit Authority* (U.S. 1985) (*see infra.*), the Court held that Congress could impose labor regulations on state agencies. If the states disagree with Congress's regulations, they can make their voices heard through their representatives in Washington.

3.1.4 Although Congress may not tell the states how to govern, *it may regulate what the states do*.

(a) In *Garcia v. San Antonio Metropolitan Transit Authority* (U.S. 1985) (*see infra.*), Congress was permitted to regulate how the states compensate public workers.

(b) In *Reno v. Condon* (U.S. 2000), Congress was permitted to pass federal legislation regulating the disclosure of personal information obtained by state DMVs. Such regulation is not commandeering because *the provisions applied not only to states, but also to private entities* that obtained the personal information from DMV sales. This case was different from *Printz* because Congress was *not seeking to control or influence state regulation of private parties*. Rather, Congress was regulating state activities themselves.

### 3.2 Federalism and the Spending Power

3.2.1 Congress has no inherent police power to regulate for health, safety, and welfare on a national basis.[36]

3.2.2 The only reference to "general welfare" among Congress's enumerated powers in the Constitution is to be found in the first clause of section 8 of article I, within the context of Congress's spending power: "Congress shall have Power to lay and collect Taxes, Duties, Imposts and Excises, to pay the Debts and provide for the common Defence and general Welfare of the United States."

3.2.3 Although Congress may not directly regulate for the general welfare, it may choose how to tax or spend federal funding on a national basis.

3.2.4 Thus, while the Supreme Court held in *Printz v. United States* (U.S. 1997) that Congress may not require the states to adopt federal policies, Congress may use its spending power as a "carrot" in influencing the states to adopt federal policies or to enforce federal legislation by imposing conditions on the distribution of federal funding.

3.2.5 Congress may legitimately use its spending power in this way under the following limitations (a factor test):

(a) Congress's spending power must provide for the general welfare;

(b) The conditions must be unambiguous;

(c) The conditions must be related to federal interests in other programs; and

(d) The conditions must not be prohibited by other constitutional considerations.

3.2.6 If all of these limitations are met, and the amount that Congress is using is not so substantial that it effectively coerces the states into implementing the legislation, then Congress's use of its spending power is legitimate.

(a) *See South Dakota v. Dole* (U.S. 1987), where Congress passed a statute that put pressure on each state to either raise its drinking age to twenty one or otherwise to have 5 % of congressional transportation funding withheld if it did not comply. The plaintiff (South Dakota) challenged the statute in light of Congress's article I spending power and the Twenty First Amendment (repealing the Eighteenth Amendment). Held: Congress may influence the state distribution of alcohol by imposing conditions on the distribution of federal funding under its spending power. Here, the incentive provided to the states, 5% of transportation funding, is not unreasonable. Furthermore, Congress is using its spending power in accordance with all four of the limitations: (i) the first

[36] Congress may, however, under its "property power," exercise general police power over the District of Columbia and over other federal territories and property. U.S. Const. art. IV, § 3, cl. 2. This includes a general power to regulate both the realty (*e.g.*, federal parklands) and personalty (*e.g.*, wild animals on federal parklands) on federal property.

prong is met because the general welfare and common good is served by Congress's trying to prevent drunk driving among young people; (ii) the condition is unambiguous; (iii) the condition is related to the federal interest of interstate highway safety by reducing driving while intoxicated; and (iv) the condition does not violate other constitutional considerations (a complete ban on alcohol, not merely raising the drinking age, would violate the Twenty First Amendment). Judgment for the defendant Secretary of the Treasury affirmed.

(b) Dissent (O'Connor, J.): the majority's test and analysis is correct, with the exception of prong three: the condition is not related to a federal interest in other programs. The majority is reading this as stating that any condition that relates to any other federal interest will be legitimately restricted. Using this interpretation, any restriction would pass muster. Rather, the rule should mean that *only a condition reasonably related to spending federal funds on highways* (*e.g.*, conditions that night lamps be installed or speed limits imposed), would qualify. A condition based on the age for legal drinking is not related to federal highways funding. The causal connection is too remote.

**3.3 State Law and Federal Term Limits**

3.3.1 The U.S. Constitution's article I, §§ 2-3 eligibility requirements for holding office were not intended as *minimums* that could later be modified; rather, they were intended by the framers of the Constitution to be fixed.

(a) *See Powell v. McCormick* (U.S. 1969), where plaintiff U.S. Congressman Adam Powell, Jr. was excluded from his seat when it was found that he had wrongfully diverted funds. Held: the article I, § 2 age, citizenship, and residency requirements are the *fixed and unalterable requirements* for membership in the House of Representatives. This is apparent from both post-convention ratification debates and the exercise of Congress during its early existence, where it "limited its power to judge the qualification of its members to those enumerated in the Constitution." The Court ruled in favor of Powell.

3.3.2 The Court has gone even further, holding that the states may neither add to the constitutional minimum requirements nor impose certain regulations on whose names may appear on the ballots.

(a) *See U.S. Term Limits, Inc. v. Thornton* (U.S. 1995), where the Court held an Arkansas statute that prohibited the names of three-term Congressmen or two-term Senators to appear on the ballots (although they could still run) as unconstitutional. The dissent argues that the power to add to or take away from the qualifications has been reserved to the states through the Tenth Amendment. However, the states *may not reserve that which they never had*. The argument that this does not really limit anyone from running, but only limits whose name may appear on the ballot, is misleading and is attempting to allow the states to do indirectly what they may not do directly.

(b) Dissent (Thomas, J.): the qualifications listed are intended as minimums, not maximums. One can reserve things he does not have or has not had in the past, such as when one reserves a room. Over 60% of the people voted for this amendment, and it is their right to choose who may be qualified to serve as their congressional representative.

**3.4 The Rise and Fall of Traditional State Functions**

3.4.1 Historically, Congress could not infringe on state policies that determine how the states deliver services. Congressional legislation could not displace traditional state functions.

3.4.2 In the 1970s, for example, the Supreme Court held that Congress could *not* impose minimum wage and maximum hour requirements over the states under the federal Fair Labor Standards Act (FLSA).

(a) *See National League of Cities v. Usery* (U.S. 1976), where Congress passed amendments to the FLSA that eliminated minimum wage and maximum hour exemptions for public employees, thus requiring states to abide by these requirements. The plaintiff cities and statess sued for an injunction against the amendments, arguing that the Commerce Clause was being violated. Held: the amendments are unconstitutional because they ***displace state policies on how the states should deliver services***. Congress may not impose policies on how state and city decisions ought to be made. Judgment for the defendant reversed.

3.4.3 However, just nine years later, *Usery* was overruled and the Court abolished the "traditional state function test" as unworkable. The new test looks only to whether there is an affirmative limit on congressional power.

(a) In *Garcia v. San Antonio Metropolitan Transit Authority* (U.S. 1985), the Court held that the Fair Labor Standards Act (FLSA) could be extended to employees of the Metropolitan Transit Authority: Congress *may* regulate state minimum wages and other labor requirements. Although the defendant San Antonio Metropolitan Transit Authority, relying on *National League of Cities v. Usery*, told its employees that the FLSA did not apply to them, they sued anyway for overtime pay under the FLSA. The issue was whether the transit authority was a traditional state function that may not be regulated by Congress. Held: ***the "traditional state function test" is abolished***. There are no traditional state functions that deserve more protection from congressional regulation than others. Rather, this Court will ask ***whether the act goes beyond an affirmative limit on congressional power***, *i.e.*, if there is a limit on Congress articulated in the Bill of Rights, then Congress may not act. If the states are unhappy with Congress's regulations, they may change the Congress through their Senate representatives in Washington, D.C.

## 3.5 Individual Rights Limitations on State Power

3.5.1 One of the areas of controversy and debate in American constitutional law deals with individual rights limitations on state power. As we have seen under *Printz v. United States* (U.S. 1997) and other cases, the principles of dual sovereignty prohibit Congress from imposing regulatory schemes on the states.

3.5.2 A second area of controversy involves whether the U.S. Constitution applies to the states, and if so, to what extent it applies.

3.5.3 Some constitutional restrictions, such as those enumerated in article I, § 10, clearly apply limitations on state power ("No State shall ...").

3.5.4 However, it is not clear whether other restrictions, such as the Bill of Rights, apply to the states. Three views are possible with respect to the Bill of Rights:

(a) The Bill of Rights is intended only against Congress

(i) Since the Bill of Rights, with the exception of the First Amendment, does not specify who is being limited, some argue that it is intended *only* against Congress.

(b) The Bill of Rights applies to the states unless it states otherwise

(i) A second argument is that, because the First Amendment clearly limits itself to Congress, the rest of the Bill of Rights could not have been intended to apply only to Congress.

(ii) If the other Amendments were intended to limit *only Congress*, then they would have been as explicit as the First Amendment.

(c) The Bill of Rights applies to both the states and Congress

(i) A third argument is that, where the Constitution is silent, the limitation is intended for both the states and the federal government.

(ii) An example of this would be the several provisions of article I, § 9, which do not explicitly refer to Congress. These restrictions, according to this argument, are therefore intended for both Congress and the states.

(iii) However, if this were the case, many parts of article I, § 10, such as clause 1 prohibiting the states from passing *ex post facto* laws, would be rendered redundant by parts of § 9, such as clause 3, which lists the same prohibition.

(iv) Therefore, it would only make sense to interpret the vague language of article I, § 9 as applying *only to Congress*, and thus interpreting that same vague language throughout the Bill of Rights as applying only to Congress as well.

3.5.5 Before passage of the Fourteenth Amendment in 1866 (ratified in 1868, at the conclusion of the Civil War), there was an understanding that the Bill of Rights limited *only the federal government*.

3.5.6 For example, the Fifth Amendment (trial and punishment, just compensation for takings) applied only to the federal government.

(a) *See Barron v. Mayor and City Council of Baltimore* (U.S. 1833), holding that the Fifth Amendment did not apply to city level officials that the plaintiff Barron claimed owed him just compensation for permitting street construction that made his wharf inaccessible.

3.5.7 After ratification of the Fourteenth Amendment in 1868, this changed. Some of the provisions of the Fourteenth Amendment were incorporated.

3.5.8 The Supreme Court's original view was that the Fourteenth Amendment incorporated only fundamental rights: those that, if abolished, would violate a "*principle of justice so rooted in the traditions and conscience of our people to be ranked as fundamental*." Such rights must be "***implicit in the concept of ordered liberty***" (*Palko v. Connecticut* (U.S. 1937)).

3.5.9 The Fifth Amendment right against being "twice put in jeopardy of life or limb" was originally *not* held to be one of these fundamental rights. *Palko v. Connecticut* (U.S. 1937).

3.5.10 This later changed in *Benton v. Maryland* (U.S. 1969), which overruled *Palko v. Connecticut* (U.S. 1937) and incorporated the Fifth Amendment Double Jeopardy Clause.

3.5.11 The Supreme Court has since incorporated most of the Bill of Rights, applying it to the several States.

(a) The First Amendment, for example, was incorporated in 1925 in *Gitlow v. New York* (U.S. 1925), where the Court held that through the Fourteenth Amendment, the Free Speech and Free Press Clauses of the First Amendment applied to the States.

(b) In *Cantwell v. Connecticut* (U.S. 1940), this doctrine was extended to the religious freedom clauses of the First Amendment, thus prohibiting State Churches and other impediments to the free exercise of religion at the State level

3.5.12 However, the Court has neither incorporated the Fifth Amendment ***Grand Jury Indictment Clause*** nor the Seventh Amendment ***Right to a Trial by Jury*** in civil cases.

3.5.13 The Court originally held that the Fifth Amendment right against ***self-incrimination*** was *not* a fundamental right applying against the states.

(a) *See Adamson v. California* (U.S. 1947) (Reed, J.), where under a California statute, if a defendant did not testify, the prosecutor could comment on this to the jury, implying the defendant's guilt. The defendant Adamson challenged the statute, arguing for the incorporation of the Fifth Amendment ***Self-Incrimination Clause***. Held: due process does not require states to protect criminal defendants from self-incrimination. The right against self-incrimination is not one of those fundamental rights that apply to the states. Judgment for the state.

(i) Dissent (Black, Douglas, JJ.): the original intent of the Fourteenth Amendment was to incorporate *all of the first eight amendments of the Bill of Rights.*

(ii) *NB*: Black's argument for **total incorporation** never won the day. Even today, some of the Bill of Rights remains unincorporated.

3.5.14 However, *Adamson v. California* (U.S. 1947) was later overruled by *Malloy v. Hogan* (U.S. 1964), which incorporated the Self-Incrimination Clause against the states.

3.5.15 Today, through incorporation, the Constitution's limitations on state sovereignty are far broader than those envisioned by the *Palko* and *Adamson* Courts.

3.5.16 In fact, some cases have held that Congress may impose rules and regulations on the states that effectively tell the states what they may or may not do.

3.5.17 Under the authority of the Enforcement Clause ("Congress shall have power to enforce this article by appropriate legislation" Fourteenth Amendment, § 5), some of these cases have gone as far as invalidating state laws previously held to be valid by the Supreme Court.

(a) *See Katzenbach v. Morgan* (U.S. 1966) (Brennan, J.), where a N.Y. state statute required English language literacy as a prerequisite to voting in New York, to the detriment of Puerto Rican voters in New York who were educated in Spanish-speaking government schools in Puerto Rico and did not speak English. A previous case held that laws requiring citizens to read and write English were not unconstitutional. Nevertheless, Congress passed § 4(e) of the ***Voting Rights Act of 1965***, which allowed any person who had successfully completed the sixth grade in any accredited Puerto Rican school to vote regardless of English language proficiency. In this way, Congress granted the voters more rights than the Constitution did. The plaintiff voter challenged this law, arguing that it prevents enforcement of the N.Y. election laws. Held: under § 5 of the Fourteenth Amendment, Congress may prohibit the states from doing that which the Court has already deemed not to be unconstitutional. The congressional statute is therefore legitimate.

Congress may act independently of the courts in determining the constitutionality of a particular question and it may create more rights than the Constitution requires. Judgment for the plaintiff is reversed.

(i) Dissent (Harlan, J.): it is the job of the judiciary to decide when an act is unconstitutional. If Congress could expand rights beyond the Constitution, then it could also contract them.

(ii) *N.B.*: Justice Brennan replied to Justice Harlan's dissent in *Footnote 10*, where he articulated the "one-way ratchet theory": *Congress may ratchet out protections of individual liberty, but may not contract them.*

3.5.18 This view, granting Congress such power over the states, has not been uniformly upheld by the Court. Congress's attempt to impose individual rights limitations on the power of the states by statute has been limited by other cases, such as *City of Boerne v. Flores* (U.S. 1997), which modifies *Katzenbach v. Morgan* (U.S. 1966) . Background:

(a) Originally, any law restricting the First Amendment Free Exercise of Religion was invalid unless it withstood the strict scrutiny test.

(b) However, in *Employment Division, Department of Human Resources of Oregon v. Smith* (U.S. 1990), the Court held that state laws that only *incidentally burden* the free exercise of religion do not violate the First Amendment.

(c) Only laws that targeted religion were unconstitutional.

(i) Example → alcohol is banned. Under the pre-*Employment Division* test, the Catholic Church would likely prevail in a lawsuit, since strict scrutiny of the law would apply.

(ii) Under *Employment Division*, however, the law would more likely be upheld, since it does not target religion.

(d) After *Employment Division*, diverse groups joined together to lobby Congress to pass a statute to expand religious freedom to the pre-*Employment Division* era.

(e) The result was the ***Religious Freedom Restoration Act of 1993*** (RFRA), which once again imposed strict scrutiny on state infringements of religious liberty. The RFRA implemented the one-way ratchet theory of *Katzenbach v. Morgan* (U.S. 1966), whereby Congress could expand the constitutional protection of basic rights.

3.5.19 However, the RFRA was later held to unconstitutionally attempt "a substantive change in constitutional provisions."

(a) *See City of Boerne v. Flores* (U.S. 1997) (Kennedy, J.), where the plaintiff, the Catholic Archbishop of San Antonio, applied for a building permit to expand a church when it grew bigger than the building that housed it. Because the church was in the historic district, and the façade imitated Spanish mission architecture, the permit was denied. The plaintiff sued for unconstitutional denial under the RFRA. Held: the RFRA is unconstitutional because it "***attempts a substantive change in constitutional provisions***." Congress may expand constitutional substantive rights by statute only when the new rights are ***congruent and proportional to the rights as they are protected in the Constitution***. To protect those rights, Congress must point to a history of state violations of the rights and adopt remedies that are ***congruent and***

***proportional to the injury to be prevented or redressed***. Here, the statute does not remedy unconstitutional state actions; rather, it substantively changes the law, creating new rights, and is therefore unconstitutional.

(i) *N.B.*: both *City of Boerne v. Flores* and *Katzenbach v. Morgan* present a one-way ratchet theory fact pattern. In *Katzenbach*, the Court permits Congress to expand the rights of minority voters; in *Boerne*, it denies Congress the right to expand the free exercise of religion. They may seem inconsistent, but the difference is that in *Boerne*, the ratchet is a great deal larger than that in *Katzenbach*. The majority states that, unlike the Voting Rights Act, the RFRA does not attempt to remedy an injury. Rather than protect constitutional rights, the RFRA creates them.

### 3.6 State Sovereign Immunity

3.6.1 Under the common law, there were two aspects of state immunity: (i) the King's laws did not bind the King; and (ii) the courts, belonging to the King, could not be used against him.

3.6.2 This was the founders' frame of mind in the early republic, but the United States would take on a different nature than the government they were used to: the states would have sovereignty, as would the federal government. There would be dual sovereignty.

3.6.3 This would mean that a citizen could not sue his state in a state court. But it leaves open the question of whether he could sue the state in a district court within his state or in a federal court within his state or in a different state.

3.6.4 Article III, § 2 of the Constitution appears to indicate that a state *could be sued in a district court of another state*: "The judicial Power shall extend to *all Cases* ... ***between a State and Citizens of another State***."

(a) In *Chisholm v. Georgia* (U.S. 1793) (Jay, C.J.), the Court supported this reading, holding that sovereign immunity was waived when states were sued in federal court by citizens of other states.

3.6.5 However, the Constitution was thereafter amended and the Eleventh Amendment, ratified in 1798, removed this possibility when a citizen of another state is the plaintiff: "The Judicial power of the United States shall not be construed to extend to any suit in law or equity, ***commenced or prosecuted against one of the United States by Citizens of another State***, or by Citizens or Subjects of any Foreign State."

3.6.6 Still, the Eleventh Amendment does not leave clear whether it is limiting *only federal diversity jurisdiction* or if it is limiting *any private case* against states in federal court, even when there is, for example, federal question jurisdiction in a case brought against a state by a citizen of that state.

3.6.7 The Court later held that the Eleventh Amendment bans *any* action against a state commenced in federal court by citizens of that state, of another state, or of a foreign state, absent the state's consent.

(a) *See Seminole Tribe v. Florida* (U.S. 1996) (Rehnquist, C.J.), where the plaintiff Seminole Tribe brought suit in federal court under the Indian Gambling Regulatory Act, which required states to negotiate in good faith with Indian tribes towards setting up gambling compacts and authorized tribes to sue in federal court to compel negotiations. The defendant moved for dismissal based on sovereign immunity. Held: although the text of the Eleventh Amendment only bans suits against states by citizens of other States or of foreign states, ***the presupposition that it confirms***

***prohibits suits against states by any individuals***. The confirmed presupposition has two parts: (i) the states are sovereign; and (ii) sovereigns may not be sued without their consent. *Chisholm* broke with this tradition, but the Eleventh Amendment restored it. Sovereign immunity ***may not be abrogated by Congress*** *unless*: (i) *Congress's intent to abrogate is clear* (there is a presumption towards immunity); and (ii) *the abrogation must be done as a valid exercise of federal power* (generally, under § 5 of the Fourteenth Amendment). In this case, the Fourteenth Amendment does not justify abrogation of state immunity. Here, abrogation can only be based in the commerce power, but abrogation of state sovereign immunity may no longer be based on the commerce power. Furthermore, the plaintiff's remedy does not lie in an *Ex Parte Young* action against an individual of the state acting *ultra vires*, since the Gambling Act's remedial scheme is so complicated that a simple *Ex Parte Young* suit could not have been Congress's intended remedy. Judgment for the defendant is affirmed.

(i) Dissent (Souter, Ginsburg, Breyer, JJ.): the idea of sovereign immunity is based not on the Constitution, but on the common law. Therefore, Congress *may change it by statute*. Here, there was a statute with a clear abrogation of state immunity based on the commerce power, a valid federal power. This Court should uphold the plaintiff's right to sue under the Act.

(ii) *N.B.*: the Court has not extended sovereign immunity to ***counties***, *Northern Insurance Company of New York v. Chatham*, or to (U.S. 2006) cities and municipalities.

3.6.8 The Court has gone one step further: not only are private citizens prohibited from suing States in federal court, but they are also prohibited from suing States in state court.

(a) *See Alden v. Maine* (U.S. 1999), where the plaintiff Alden's case, pending in federal court during *Seminole Tribe*, was dismissed after the *Seminole* holding. When the plaintiff refiled in state court, the Court (Kennedy, J. for the majority) held that sovereignty immunity also prohibits private citizens from suing non-consenting states in state court: "the powers delegated to the Congress under Article I of the United States do not include the power to subject non-consenting States to private suits for damages in *state* courts." The arguments for sovereign immunity are even stronger when it is the sovereign's own courts being used to sue the sovereign.

3.6.9 Thus, in the absence of abrogation, the remedial schemes that Congress may pass are limited to federal enforcement channels. Generally, abrogation will be permitted under § 5 of the Fourteenth Amendment.

3.6.10 Congress may allow private citizens to sue states under the Fourteenth Amendment only when doing so is being used to enforce constitutional rights protected by the Fourteenth Amendment, ***not when it is being used to redefine or create new rights***.

3.6.11 To determine whether rights are being enforced or redefined, the *Boerne* "proportional and congruent" test is to be used: ***a statute may expand a constitutional right*** via the one-way ratchet, but the expanded right must be ***proportional and congruent*** to the constitutional right.

3.6.12 Furthermore, the ***remedy offered by a congressional statute must be congruent and proportional to state violations of the protected right***. Statutes protecting against suspect or quasi-suspect classifications will generally be held to be congruent and proportional; statutes protecting against non-suspect classifications will generally not be held to be congruent and proportional.

**Guideline Chart for Analyzing Abrogation Questions**

| | SUSPECT CLASSIFICATIONS | QUASI-SUSPECT CLASSIFICATIONS | NON-SUSPECT CLASSIFICATIONS |
|---|---|---|---|
| Standard of scrutiny: | ***Strict Scrutiny*** | ***Intermediate Scrutiny*** | ***Rational Basis Scrutiny*** |
| Discriminatory state statutes: | ***Burden on the state*** to show that the challenged measure is necessary (the least restrictive means) to protect a *compelling state interest*. | ***Burden on the state*** to show that the challenged measure is substantially related to an *important/substantial governmental objective*. | ***Burden on the plaintiff*** to show that the challenged measure is not rationally related to a *legitimate state interest*. |
| Examples of classifications: | Race; national origin; alienage. | Gender; children of illegal aliens; illegitimacy. | Sexual conduct; age; handicap; mental retardation; poverty. |
| The remedy of abrogation is: | Virtually always ***congruent and proportional*** | Usually ***congruent and proportional*** | Usually ***not congruent and proportional*** |

(a) *See Kimel v. Florida Board of Regents* (U.S. 2000), where the Court analyzed whether the remedy of private suits via abrogation of state immunity for the Age Discrimination in Employment Act was valid under § 5 of the Fourteenth Amendment. Under the equal protection clause, there are three standards: ***strict scrutiny*** (the government almost always wins); ***intermediate scrutiny*** (the government is likely to win); and ***rational basis*** (the government is likely to lose). Congress may not abrogate state immunity under § 5 of the Fourteenth Amendment based on the Age Discrimination Act because age is not a suspect or quasi suspect class and the remedy of allowing private suits for age discrimination is not proportional and congruent to any *systemic pattern of age discrimination*.

(b) *See also Board of Trustees v. Garrett* (U.S. 2001), where the majority held that ***disability is not a suspect or quasi suspect class***, since Congress presented very little evidence of systemic state discrimination. Because there is little evidence of constitutional violations, the remedy of federal monetary damages against states is not congruent and proportional to demonstrated discrimination.

(c) Although disability is not a suspect classification meriting § 5 private causes of action, the effects of disability may limit other rights that comprise suspect classifications.

(i) *See Tennessee v. Lane* (U.S. 2004), where the plaintiff paraplegic Lane sued the state for not making the court room accessible. Held: although *Garrett* held that disability and handicaps are not a suspect classifications, here, a more fundamental right is threatened: due process and the right to access the courts. This suspect classification merits broad protections and will be held to the standard of strict scrutiny. Here, permitting the plaintiff to sue in federal court is a congruent and proportional remedy.

(ii) Dissent (Scalia, J.): the "congruence and proportionality" standard should be abolished. The Court should give little protections to legislation outside of the race context, since it was race that was intended to be protected by the Fourteenth Amendment.

(d) *See also Nevada Dept. of Natural Resources v. Hibbs* (U.S. 2003) (Rehnquist, C.J.), where the plaintiff former employee Hibbs sued under the Family and Medical Leave Act (FMLA) of 1993, seeking damages and an injunction when, after the plaintiff sought take leave to care for his sick wife, he was fired. Held: this statute seeks to protect the workplace from sexual discrimination, a quasi-suspect class, and therefore the statutory classification requires intermediate scrutiny.[37] The rights protected under the FMLA must be ***congruent and proportional*** to the rights under the Constitution. The ***remedies*** offered must also be congruent and proportional to existing state practices threatening the rights. Here, there is a broad history of sexual discrimination in the workplace and of state laws applied in discriminatory ways. The FMLA is congruent and proportional to the constitutional rights affected and to the remedies required. Therefore, § 5 of the Fourteenth Amendment allows a private cause of action.

(i) Dissent (Kennedy, J.): the FMLA does *not* seek to remedy sexual discrimination in the workplace; rather, it is a benefit program.

3.6.13 Abrogation of state immunity will be more readily permitted when it is the Constitution itself, as opposed to only a statute, that has been violated.

(a) *See United States v. Georgia* (U.S. 2006), where the plaintiff, an imprisoned paraplegic, sued the state under Title II and 42 U.S.C. § 1983 civil rights, for housing him in a narrow cell and depriving him of assistance to the point that he was forced to spend periods of time in his own waste. Held: because the state's conduct, if proven, would violate not only the statutes, but also the Eighth Amendment of the Constitution, state immunity is properly abrogated. When the Constitution itself is being protected under § 5 of the Fourteenth Amendment, the case for abrogation is more compelling, and the congruence and proportionality test between the *rights protected* and the *constitutional rights* is unnecessary, since the two are the same.

## 4 The Protection of Contracts and Property

### 4.1 The Protection of Contracts against State Impairment

4.1.1 Article I, § 10 of the Constitution enumerates the powers prohibited of the states. Among these prohibitions is the adoption of any law "impairing the Obligation of Contracts."

4.1.2 The Contracts Clause ***applies only to the states;*** the federal government may pass laws impairing contracts.

4.1.3 The main purpose behind the Contracts Clause is to prevent retroactive state legislation that alters or modifies substantive contractual rights.

(a) *See Sturges v. Crowninshield* (U.S. 1819) (Marshall, C.J.), where a NY law that liberated debtors from their debts was held to be invalid because it attempted to discharge contractual obligations. Creditors who entered into a contract, expecting to have their loans repaid, would be prejudiced.

[37] Sometimes referred to as "heightened scrutiny," although this term may also refer to strict scrutiny and may be applied anytime the Court wishes to be vague.

(b) *N.B.*: just a few years later, in *Ogden v. Saunders* (U.S. 1827), the Court answered the question that *Sturges* left open: may a state pass only a bankruptcy law that prospectively alters contracts? The Court held that it could. The parties from the time of the bankruptcy act onward would have notice of its existence and the terms of the bankruptcy act would become incorporated into the contract.

4.1.4 The Court has therefore applied the Contract Clause to prevent governments from altering contracts that retrospectively relieve debtors.

4.1.5 Later, the issue arose as to whether this rule applied only between private parties or whether it extended to public contracts, where the state itself was a party. The Court held that the Contract Clause applied to both.

(a) *See Fletcher v. Peck* (U.S. 1810), where a later Georgia legislature rescinded a deal that the former legislature had entered into granting lands, because the deal was corrupt. The Court held that the legislature could not interfere with the earlier contract, which was protected by the Contracts Clause.

4.1.6 *Exception*: state laws rescinding state contracts that undermine morals are valid. States may not contract away their police power.

(a) *See Stone v. Mississippi* (U.S. 1879) (Waite, C.J.), where the defendant contractually granted the plaintiff lottery company Stone a charter to conduct state lotteries. One year later, in 1868, the new Constitution prohibited state lotteries. The plaintiff sued, arguing that the state was required to honor the charter. Held: one who accepts a lottery charter does so with the understanding that it may be revoked at any time, even if paid for. This is an exception to the rule that the Contract Clause applies to public contracts.

4.1.7 In addition, states may alter contractual obligations where an emergency, such as an economic crisis, warrants state action.

(a) *See Home Building & Loan Ass'n v. Blaisdell* (U.S. 1934), where the plaintiff challenged a Minnesota law that permitted the extension of redemption periods and imposed a moratorium on foreclosures and sales of mortgaged property, as an emergency measure in the Great Depression. Held: the Contract Clause *only prohibits the states from unreasonably modifying the obligations of contracts*. Here, the defendant's act was reasonable for the following reasons:

(i) A *crisis* justified use of the reserved powers;

(ii) The legislation protected a *basic public interest*;

(iii) The relief was *tailored* to the emergency;

(iv) The conditions are reasonable; and

(v) The debts were only temporarily suspended.

(b) *Compare Allied Structural Steel Company v. Spannaus* (U.S. 1978), where a pension funding change was held to fail the *Blaisdell* five-factor test: the importance to a public interest was low and the impairment on contracts was severe.

## 4.2 The Protection of Property Under the Takings Clause

### 4.2.1 Introduction

(a) The Takings Clause of the Fifth Amendment states that private property shall not be "taken for public use, without just compensation."[38]

(b) The government may only therefore take private property if: (i) it is for public use; and (ii) the owner is justly compensated.

(c) Historically, this restricted only the federal government. *Barron v. Mayor and City Council of Baltimore* (U.S. 1833). However, after the Bill of Rights was incorporated through the Due Process Clause of the Fourteenth Amendment, the Takings Clause came to apply against the states as well.

(d) Three issues arise in Takings Clause cases:

(i) Whether property has been taken;

(ii) How much is just compensation (a question not within the scope of the present text); and

(iii) Whether there has been a public use.

### 4.2.2 What is a Taking?

(a) Introduction

(i) Most government takings are actual appropriations.

(ii) However, state regulations may become so unduly burdensome that they become Fifth Amendment "takings" as well.

(b) Government Appropriations (Actual Takings)

(i) Actual government appropriations may take on two forms: (i) actual takings of property; or (ii) permanent physical invasions of the property.

(ii) In both cases, the act is a taking that requires just compensation.

(c) Government Regulations

(i) A three-part balancing test is implemented for determining whether a restriction is merely a ***regulation*** that decreases economic value or a ***taking*** requiring just compensation:

(1) The economic impact on the owner;

(2) The extent of interference with investment-backed expectations; and

(3) The character of the government action. *Penn Central Transportation Company v. City of New York* (U.S. 1978).

---

[38] U.S. Const. amend. V.

(ii) An example of a *mere regulation* would be a *landmark preservation project*. It is a valid exercise of police power that does not require just compensation.

(1) *See Penn Central Transportation Company v. City of New York* (U.S. 1978) (Brennan, J.), where the plaintiff owner Penn Central Transportation Company was prohibited from constructing an office building over an historic landmark and argued that its constitutional right to property was violated. Held: landmark preservation regulations are legitimate exercises of *state police power* that do not require compensation.

(2) Dissent (Rehnquist J.): if this regulation is for the public good, then it should be the general public, not the plaintiff, that takes the brunt of the decision.

(iii) However, if the regulation *unduly* ***burdens contractual obligations***, it will be considered a taking.

(1) *See Pennsylvania Coal Co. v. Mahon* (U.S. 1922) (Holmes, J.), where the plaintiff Mahon, while purchasing land, recognized that there might be subsidence, but waived all rights to recover damages. The Pennsylvania legislature then passed an act prohibiting such sales. Held: the subsidence law *so severely interferes with contractual obligations that it is virtually an appropriation*. It therefore requires just compensation.

(2) Dissent (Brandeis, J.): the state law is a valid exercise of the *state police power* prohibiting a noxious use. The restriction is a temporary one not requiring just compensation.

(iv) Similarly, if the regulation denies the property all ***economically viable use*** it will be a taking.

(1) *See Lucas v. South Carolina Coastal Council* (U.S. 1992) (Scalia, J.), where a zoning law prohibited the plaintiff from building any habitable structure on lots he recently purchased. Held: the law is so burdensome that it is effectively a taking requiring just compensation.

(2) Dissent (Blackmun, J.): this regulation did not deny the plaintiff *all economic utility*: he could use, possess, or sell the lots.

4.2.3 Public Use

(a) There are three situations in which the government effects a taking:

(i) *The government becomes the owner*. This is the traditional case, in which the government appropriates private property in order to build roads, public schools, etc.

(ii) *The government transfers ownership to private hands for* ***public use***. The government could transfer ownership of private property to private entities, such as railroad companies, common carriers, or hospitals.

(iii) The government transfers ownership to private hands for a ***public purpose***. This is the most controversial of the categories.

(1) The Court headed down a slippery slope as it embraced this third category.

(2) First, it permitted the transferring of private property from one private owner to another for *addressing blighted areas*.

(aa) *See Berman v. Parker* (U.S. 1954), where Congress appropriated property from landowners in a blighted area in Washington, D.C., to give to private owners as part of a redevelopment plan to build apartments and generate revenues. Held: although the appropriation of the property was not aimed at a public use, there was a *public purpose* of developing a blighted area, which justifies the taking.

(3) Then the Court permitted takings in order to remedy land oligarchy structures.

(aa) *See Hawaii Housing Authority v. Midkiff* (U.S. 1984) (O'Connor, J.), where the Court held that the taking of property in Hawaii that was predominantly held by a small oligarchy for the redistribution of title was constitutional, since it was a *legitimate public purpose* affecting health, safety, and welfare.

(4) Finally, the Court has gone as far as permitting government takings for economic revitalization, even in *non-blighted areas*. Such a purpose was held sufficient under the Takings Clause.

(aa) *See Kelo v. City of New London* (U.S. 2005) (Stevens, J.), where the Court held that Connecticut could transfer private property to a private development agency in order to build hotels, restaurants, and office buildings to create jobs in the city. Held: when a taking is *rationally related to an important state interest*, it is constitutional. Here, the state pursued the valid interests of economic development and the creation of jobs.

(bb) Dissent (Thomas, J.): this Court should apply only an original understanding of the Constitution. The Takings Clause originally meant that only takings for *public use*, not *public purposes*, were valid. *Berman v. Parker* was wrongly decided.

## 5 Economic Liberty

### 5.1 The Protection of Economic Liberty

5.1.1 There are principally three ways in which economic liberty is protected in the United States:

(a) Substantive Economic Due Process.

(b) The ***Privileges and Immunities Clause*** of article IV of the Constitution; and

(c) The Privileges or Immunities Clause of the Fourteenth Amendment.

## 5.2 Substantive Economic Due Process

5.2.1 Under the principle of substantive due process, a statute may be procedurally valid (properly passed through the legislative channels), and yet substantively invalid. This would be the case if citizens were being taxed in order to benfit private, not public interests.

(a) *See Loan Association v. Topeka* (U.S. 1874), where the Court struck down a scheme where bonds funded by taxes aided private enterprises to support the building of bridges and other internal improvement programs, since it was not for a public purpose.

5.2.2 In 1905, in a controversial and maligned case, the Court held that states *may not prohibit private agreements* to work for *more than a set number of hours* unless the state, pursuant to its police powers, is pursuing special protections for material dangers. Strict scrutiny was to be applied.

(a) *See Lochner v. New York* (U.S. 1905) (Peckham, J.), where the defendant Lochner challenged a New York law that prohibited employees of bakeries from working more than sixty hours per week. The Court held that the right to contract, which is protected by the Fourteenth Amendment, is subject to the state police power. However, the New York law never mentioned the ***health, safety, and welfare*** of the bakers that it purported to protect, and was therefore invalid.

(b) Dissent (Holmes, J.): the regulation, which is related to public health, is valid. The defendant has not been denied due process under the Fourteenth Amendment.

5.2.3 In the 1930s, however, Holmes' *Lochner* dissent became the norm. A deferential standard was applied to economic legislation: ***rational basis*** scrutiny, based on a reasonableness standard, was to be applied.

5.2.4 This was largely due to the Great Depression and a new spirit that government regulation was necessary during economic crisis. Considerations of substantive economic due process were to be deferred until major problems were first solved.

(a) *See Nebbia v. New York* (U.S. 1934) (Roberts, J.), where the defendant challenged a NY law regulating the prices of milk as a violation of economic due process. Held: as long as the law is *rationally related to a legitimate state purpose* and the means are reasonably related to the end sought, the Court is to defer to legislative judgment.

(b) *See also United States v. Carolene Products Co.* (U.S. 1938), where the defendant challenged a statute banning filled milk. Held: the "Filled Milk Act," which regulates the interstate commerce of skimmed milk compounded with any fat or oil, does not infringe on Fifth Amendment Due Process. This federal statute passes rational basis. The *famous Footnote 4*: although here, rational basis applies, heightened[39] scrutiny applies when (i) the Bill of Rights is offended; (ii) the government does something making it more difficult for people to use the political processes; or (iii) there is discrimination of religious, national, or racial minorities.

5.2.5 The principle of economic due process rose and fell. Today, its force has died down, being replaced with social due process, primarily involving abortion and homosexuality.

---

[39] This term generally refers to intermediate scrutiny, although it may also refer to strict scrutiny and may be applied anytime the Court wishes to be vague.

## 5.3 Privileges and Immunities Clause (Article IV)

5.3.1 The Privileges *and* Immunities Clause states that the "Citizens of each State shall be entitled to all Privileges and Immunities of Citizens in the several States."[40]

5.3.2 It prohibits States from ***discriminating against nonresidents*** as to ***rights fundamental to national unity***, including the following rights:

(a) To life and liberty;

(b) To earn a living;

(c) To reside in any other state; and

(d) To interstate travel.

5.3.3 However, a state may legitimately discriminate when doing so is ***the least restrictive means*** to protect a ***substantial state interest*** (similar to intermediate scrutiny).

(a) *See Corfield v. Coryell* (C.C.E.D. Pa. 1823) (Washington, J.), where a NJ law required those taking and harvesting oysters to be state inhabitants or to be on a vessel owned by a state inhabitant. The law was held to be valid because the state had a substantial interest in preserving its natural resources that trumps the privileges and immunities of non-state residents.

(b) *Compare Supreme Court of New Hampshire v. Piper* (U.S. 1985), where the plaintiff Piper challenged a New Hampshire state bar requirement that applicants establish a home address in New Hampshire prior to being admitted to the bar. Held: the right to practice law is among the ***rights fundamental to national unity***. Therefore, the statute excluding non-residents from the practice of law in New Hampshire is invalid. Although the state interest in having attorneys close to the state courts is legitimate, it can be achieved with a ***less restrictive means*** (*e.g.*, assigning local counsel).

5.3.4 Laws requiring employers to prefer state residents over non state-residents are unconstitutional when they are not ***closely related to a substantial state interest***, as they discriminate against nonresidents in the pursuit of a livelihood. *Hicklin v. Orbeck* (U.S. 1978).

5.3.5 The Privileges and Immunities Clause does not protect corporations and aliens from state discrimination.

(a) When a law discriminates against out-of-state corporations, it must be analyzed under the Commerce Clause, which permits an exception for state discrimination of out of state commerce when the state is a ***market participant***.

## 5.4 Privileges or Immunities Clause (Fourteenth Amendment)

5.4.1 The Fourteenth Amendment Privileges *or* Immunities Clause provides that "[n]o State shall make or enforce any law which shall abridge the privileges or immunities of citizens of the United States."

5.4.2 The Privileges or Immunities Clause has been used with less consistency than the Privideges and Immunities Clause.

---

[40] U.S. Const. art. IV, § 2.

5.4.3 Ever since the *Slaughter-House Cases* (U.S. 1873), where it was held to protect only a narrow set of ***national citizenship rights***, the Privileges or Immunities Clause has been rendered ineffective in protecting fundamental rights under the Fourteenth Amendment.

(a) *See the Slaughter-House Cases* (U.S. 1873), where a state law effectively created a monopoly and prevented the plaintiffs from operating slaughter houses. Held: the state's exercise of authority was constitutional under its police power. The Privileges or Immunities Clause applies only to "the privileges or immunities of citizens of the United States," which do not include the right to operate slaughter houses.

(b) *N.B.*: today, the rights asserted by the plaintiffs are covered by the Fourteenth Amendment *Equal Protection Clause* and *Due Process Clause*.

5.4.4 Although it was once widely invoked, its use disappeared in the 1930s.

5.4.5 Today, the Privilege or Immunities Clause does very little. It voids only state laws that infringe on the privileges of ***national citizenship***, such as the following rights:

(a) To *vote* for federal officers;

(b) To *petition Congress* for redress of grievances;

(c) To *travel* between the states and to Washington D.C. and other public lands.

(d) To *enter federal lands*;

(e) To access the *public waterways* not owned by any of the states; and

(f) To be *protected* while on the high seas.

5.4.6 The Right to Travel

(a) The right to travel between states, which is protected by the Fourteenth Amendment Privileges or Immunities Clause, also includes the right of the newly arrived resident to the same privileges and immunities of long-settled citizens of the same State.

(b) Strict scrutiny applies when a state limits the right to travel and the rights deriving from it, such as the right of newly arrived residents to the payment of welfare benefits.

(i) *See Shapiro v. Thompson* (U.S. 1969), where a Connecticut statute denied new residents welfare benefits during their first year of residency. Held: because ***welfare is a classification that touches on fundamental rights,*** the statute is subject to strict scrutiny and fails.

(ii) *See also Saenz v. Roe* (U.S. 1999), where a California welfare law limited new residents' welfare benefits to what they were receiving in the state where they were previously living. There are three rights to travel: (i) the right to travel from state to state; (ii) the right to be treated like a welcomed visitor (Article IV Privileges and Immunity), barring discrimination (appears to be intermediate scrutiny); and (iii) access to the same rights as others of the state when arriving in a new state (under both article IV and the Fourteenth Amendment Privileges and Immunities Clause) (strict scrutiny). The statute failed strict scrutiny. Although one of the reasons behind the statute was to prevent forum shopping, not enough evidence was raised to support it. Temporary restraining order affirmed.

(1) Dissent (Rehnquist, C.J.): the right to vote and other rights that have been upheld even though they infringe on privileges and immunities are just as important as welfare.

(2) Dissent (Thomas, J.): this Court must revisit the scope of the Privileges or Immunities Clause to put some content into it.

(c) However, in other contexts (*e.g.*, filing for divorce, in-state tuition rates, and voting, the Court has upheld the residency requirements.

(i) *N.B.*: the Privileges or Immunities Clause extends only to "citizens of the United States." Corporations and aliens are not protected.

(ii) *Compare* the Fourteenth Amendment Due Process and Equal Protection Clauses, which employ the word "person," which includes corporations.

**Summary Chart of the Privileges and Immunities Clauses**

| | ***Privileges and Immunities Clause (Art. IV)*** | ***Privileges or Immunities Clause (Fourteenth Amd.)*** |
|---|---|---|
| *History* | Consistent, but not generally used, since the Equal Protection Clause provides similar but broader protections. | The *Slaughterhouse Cases* limited protections to national citizenship rights. Its use disappeared in the 1930s, but there was a revival in 1999. |
| *Rights Protected* | State discrimination against nonresidents as to *rights fundamental to national unity*. | Very little: *national citizenship rights* only. |
| *Examples of rights protected* | The right to life and liberty; to earn a living; to reside in any other state; to interstate travel (probably also to acquire and own property). | The right to vote for federal officers; to petition Congress for redress of grievances; to travel between the states and public lands; to enter federal lands; to be protected while on the high seas. |

## 6 Religious Freedom

### 6.1 The Public Affirmation of God and the Importance of Religion

6.1.1 Early Establishment Clause Interpretation

(a) Early on, the Supreme Court did not view the First Amendment as erecting a wall of separation between church and state.

(b) Rather, the church was in many ways permitted to receive public funding and to cooperate with the state in providing basic social services, such as healthcare.

(i) *See Bradfield v. Roberts* (U.S. 1899), where the government provided public support to Providence Hospital, a private hospital run by the Catholic Church to support the poor. The Court held that it was not unconstitutional for the hospital to receive public aid; it is immaterial that it was run under the auspices of a religious body, since no one was forced to attend that hospital.

(ii) *N.B.*: this case dealt with the federal government because the city was Washington, D.C. Had it been a city in a State, there would not have been an issue because at the time, the Establishment Clause was not incorporated against the states.

(c) Even until the middle of the Twentieth Century, liberal, secularist justices continued to affirm the religious character of the American people and the Supreme Being presupposed by the American institutions.

(i) *See Zorach v. Clauson* (U.S. 1952) (Douglas, J.), where the court held that public schools may allow a recess during school hours when students could participate in religious services or activities ("release time education"). This case was not like *McCollum v. Board of Education* (U.S. 1948), where a school's bringing religious instructors to the premises was unconstitutional, since here, no school money or resources is being expended in the promotion of religion. Although there is a "separation of Church and State," the First Amendment did "not say that in every and all respects there shall be a separation," for if this were the case, municipalities would even be prohibited from providing police services to churches or other religious groups.

(ii) *N.B.*: at his time, Douglas was one of the most liberal, secularist justices on the Court.

6.1.2 Incorporation of the Religion Clauses against the states

(a) Some have argued that it makes no sense to incorporate the Establishment Clause against the states: it is not aimed at individual rights, but rather, at the government, and more specifically, at Congress.

(b) Today, however, the ***Establishment Clause has been incorporated*** by the Due Process Clause of the Fourteenth Amendment: no state may deny any person religious liberty without due process of law.

## 6.2 The Establishment Clause

6.2.1 The Four Establishment Views

(a) The Non-Coercion View

(i) This is the view of Justice Scalia and Thomas (perhaps even Roberts and Alito).

(ii) The government may not:

(1) ***Establish*** a national church;

(2) Use its coercive power to ***promote religion***;

(3) ***Prohibit*** the free exercise of religion; or

(4) ***Show favoritism*** towards any group.

(iii) Public school sponsorship of prayer at a graduation ceremony has been held to be a form of religious coercion.

(1) *See Lee v. Weisman* (U.S. 1992) (Kennedy, J.), where a Rabbi was invited to give non-sectarian theistic prayer at a graduation ceremony. The plaintiff Weisman challenged the prayer as unconstitutional. Held: the Establishment Clause was violated through the coercion of religion. Those present at the ceremony were pressured into standing silently and listening to the prayer.

(2) Dissent (Scalia, J.): this Court is trying to get into the minds of the graduation participants and conduct a psychological assessment of whether they were coerced. This is nonsense.

(3) *N.B.*: in some ways, this case has twisted the meaning of "coercion." First, no one was required to be at the ceremony; second, those who were present were not required to affirm or agree with the Rabbi's prayer.

(b) The Exclusionary View

(i) According to this view, the government may not:

(1) ***Establish*** a national church;

(2) Use its coercive power to ***promote religion***;

(3) ***Prohibit*** the free exercise of religion;

(4) ***Show favoritism*** towards any group; or

(5) Support religion in ***purpose***, ***effect***, or ***entanglement***.

(ii) The government may not give any benefits to religious institutions.

(iii) This rule's leading case did not fully apply it. Instead, it upheld a state law giving religious institutions the same benefits as those given to public schools.

(1) *See Everson v. Board of Education* (U.S. 1947) (Black, J.), where the plaintiff Everson challenged NJ's reimbursement of parents for the costs of transporting their children to parochial schools. Held: the Establishment Clause "was intended to erect 'a wall of separation between church and State.'" Here, however, the Establishment Clause does not apply because the purpose and effect of the law is not to promote or support religion, but rather, to help students get to school.

(2) *N.B.*: the court used strong rhetoric, laying the ground work for the exclusionary rule, but then failed to apply it. If the exclusionary rule were truly enforced, the law would have probably been struck down, since a strong argument can be made that religion was supported in effect.

(c) The No Endorsement Speculation

(i) According to this view, the government may not:

(1) ***Establish*** a national church;

(2) Use its coercive power to ***promote religion***;

(3) ***Prohibit*** the free exercise of religion;

(4) ***Show favoritism*** towards any group; or

(5) Act in a way that a ***reasonable observer*** might construe as government endorsement of a religion.

(ii) This has been endorsed by Justice O'Connor, and it is not clear whether it will last, now that she has left the Court.

(iii) Under the no endorsement view, a government may set up a religious display when it would not be seen as an *endorsement of religion* by a reasonable observer.

(1) *See Lynch v. Donnelly* (U.S. 1984) (Burger, C.J.), where the Court held that a manger scene erected by a Rhode Island city was not an establishment of religion because it was surrounded by a variety of other decorations, including a *Santa Clause, two reindeer, a Season's Greetings sign, and Christmas lights*. The display emphasized the historical, rather than the religious, facets of the holiday and therefore did not violate the Establishment Clause.

(aa) *N.B.*: in her concurrence, O'Connor found *no endorsement.*

(2) *Compare Allegheny County v. Greater Pittsburgh ACLU* (U.S. 1989) (Blackmun, J., referencing O'Connor's no endorsement view), where the Court held that a ***nativity*** *scene* set up on the main staircase of a court house violated the Establishment Clause because it was not accompanied by other symbols and decorations. However, a *menorah with an evergreen tree and a sign of liberty* set up at a nearby display did not violate the Establishment Clause because it was not explicitly religious.

(aa) Dissent (Kennedy, Rehnquist, Scalia, and White, JJ.): the non-coercion view, not the no endorsement speculation, is the proper test to apply.

(iv) Justice O'Connor continued to promote the no endorsement speculation throughout the 1990s (see her concurrence, *infra.*).

(1) In *Capitol Square Review and Advisory Board v. Pinette* (U.S. 1995) (Scalia, J.), where the KKK sued for an injunction requiring the defendant to permit a cross on the defendant's public square, which was initially denied on the basis that such a cross would be an establishment of religion. Held: the Establishment Clause does not prohibit a city from allowing a group to erect a religious symbol in a public forum that the government leaves open for a variety of groups to put up displays. Since it is not the government, but private citizens putting up the cross, the Establishment Clause does not apply. Judgment for the plaintiff affirmed.

(2) Concurrence (O'Connor, J.): because the KKK cross was surrounded by a variety of symbols, the display passes the no endorsement speculation.

(d) The Equal Protection Idea

(i) This view allows religion equal access to public forums, places, and funds.

(ii) In *Rosenberger v. Rector* (U.S. 1995) (Kennedy, J.), the University of Virginia refused to reimburse a student publication for printing costs, arguing that being a public university, it could not support a publication espousing a religious viewpoint. Held: the publication was private student speech, not the government establishment of religion. The ***government must treat religious groups in the same way that it treats nonreligious groups***. *Allowing religious groups equal access to public facilities does not violate the Establishment Clause.*

(1) Concurrence (O'Connor, J.): endorsement is the proper test. The university comes close to failing the test, but passes.

(iii) In *Good News Club v. Milford Central School District* (U.S. 2001) (Thomas, J.), the defendant Milford Central School District refused to allow the plaintiff, a private Christian organization, access to its facilities after hours on the basis that the plaintiff was a religious organization. Held: the plaintiff's due process rights were violated. If the government is ***creating a limited open forum,*** it is not establishing religion by allowing religious groups access. Here, the Club met after hours and was not sponsored by the school. ***No one was coerced to attend.***

6.2.2 The Special Context of Private, Religious Schools

(a) Direct Funding of Religious Schools

(i) For direct funding of religious schools, the three-prong *Lemon* test has been established for determining the constitutionality of statutes: "First, the statute must have a secular legislative purpose; second, its principal or primary effect must be one that neither advances nor inhibits religion … finally, the statute must not foster 'an excessive government entanglement with religion.'"

(1) *See Lemon v. Kurtzman* (U.S. 1971) (Burger, C.J.), where Pennsylvania and Rhode Island statutes provided aid to non-public schools, including church-related schools. The statutes' *purpose was to provide better education for children* (prong 1); and the primary effect or *purpose was not to advance or inhibit religion* (prong 2). However, because an elaborate monitoring scheme was necessary in order to assure the aid given was spent only on secular, not religious, educational materials, the government was excessively entangled with religion (prong 3). The statutes therefore failed.

(2) *N.B.*: if we were looking at this question from an equal-protection/non-coercion perspective, there would have been no problem with these schemes, which treat secular private schools in the same way that they treat religious private schools.

(ii) Providing public funds to religious colleges and universities for non-religious educational purposes and construction projects is not considered to be excessive government entanglements in religion. *Roemer v. Maryland Public Works Board* (U.S. 1976).

(1) Rationale: post-secondary education is primarily secular in nature and government oversight is generally not needed.

(b) School Vouchers or the Equivalent

(i) School vouchers are different from direct aid in that they are further removed from ultimate decisions supporting religion, since they give parents the right to make private choices.

(ii) State programs allowing tax deductions for parents who send their children to parochial schools are not unconstitutional if they are available to all parents, including those sending their children to public and non-parochial private schools.

(1) *See Mueller v. Allen* (U.S. 1983), where the Court rejected a challenge to a Minnesota program allowing tax deductions for private school expenses, even though parents of children in religious schools received 96 % of the benefits, since (i) the program was based on private choice; (ii) it was not limited to religious schools; and (iii) the primary purpose of the program was not to promote religion.

(iii) In *Witters v. Wash. Dept.of Services for the Blind* (U.S. 1986), the Court rejected a challenge to a students' using a state vocational scholarship program to pursue religious studies in seminary.

(iv) Public funds may be used to pay for interpreters for deaf children at private religious schools when they are also available to children at non-sectarian schools.

(1) *See Zobrest v. Catalina Foothills School District* (U.S. 1993), where a program that provided a translator to a hearing-impaired student in a Catholic school was challenged. Held: the program is upheld, since it is *neutral* and *does not discriminate* between religious and non-sectarian schools.

(v) In *Mitchell v. Helms* (U.S. 2000) (Thomas, J., writing for a four member plurality), the Court upheld a Louisiana provision providing books, computers, and other equipment to religious schools in the same way that it provided them to public schools.

(vi) In *Zelman v. Simmons-Harris* (U.S. 2002) (Rehnquist, C.J.), the Court upheld an Ohio statute allowing for school vouchers to attend religious or secular private schools, even though 96 % of participating students opted for religious schools. Under *Mueller*, *Witters*, and *Zobrest*, neutral government aid programs that empower citizens to make private choices do not violate the Establishment Clause, even when those citizens chose private institutions and thereby indirectly benefit them.

(1) Dissent (Souter, J., joined by Stevens, Ginsburg, and Breyer, JJ.): the majority's holding is inconsistent with the exclusionary view of the *Everson* holding. Furthermore, the statute probably is not neutral, given its *effect*: 96% of participants opt for religious schools.

(2) Dissent (Breyers, J.): (adopting a living constitutionalist approach) although we were primarily a homogenously Protestant society at our founding,, today, we are heterogenous. This ruling risks causing conflict in our nation's social fabric.

(vii) The Constitution thus permits tax deductions for private school expenses; students' using a state vocational scholarship program to pursue religious studies in seminaries; the provision of translators to hearing-impaired students in religious schools; the provision of books, computers, and other equipment to religious schools; and vouchers to attend religious schools.

(viii) However, although the Constitution permits these state provisions, it does not require them.

(1) *See Locke v. Davey* (U.S. 2004), where the Court upheld a Washington scholarship provision excepting devotional theology from qualifying courses of study available under the scholarship, because recipients could always study general theology without studying it in a way that prepares them for the ministry.

6.2.3 School Prayer

(a) Religious activities in public schools have generally been held to violate the Constitution by establishing religion.

(b) Two cases that set this rule in motion are *Engel v. Vitale* (U.S. 1962) and *School District of Abington v. Schempp* (U.S. 1963).

(c) Both are seen as the cases that excluded God and religion from the public square and are vilified by religious conservatives.

(i) In *Engel v. Vitale* (U.S. 1962), a New York Board of Regents non-denominational prayer, which stated, "Almighty God, we acknowledge our dependence upon Thee, and we beg Thy blessings upon us, our parents, our teachers and our Country," was to be recited each day in New York. The Court held for the first time that the Constitution prohibited a prayer selected by public officials to be recited in public schools.

(1) *N.B.*: this case extended *Everson's* exclusionary principle (tbe government may not support religion in purpose, effect, or entanglement).

(ii) In *School District of Abington v. Schempp* (U.S. 1963), the Court invalidated a Pennsylvania law requiring Bible verses to be read daily at the opening of public school.

(d) The Establishment Clause prohibits the government from favoring religion over non-religion.

(i) *See Wallace v. Jaffree* (U.S. 1985) (Stevens, J.), where the Court held that an Alabama statute providing a silent moment for "meditation or voluntary prayer" in public schools violated the Establishment Clause. The Constitution does not permit the encouragement of prayer in public schools.

(1) Dissent (Rehnquist, J.): the separation standard articulated by the majority lacks historical support and "proved all but useless as a guide to sound constitutional adjudication." It has led to very bizarre results in our jurisprudence: we can

support religious schools by providing them geography books with maps of the U.S. inside, for example, but it is unconstitutional to provide the maps themselves. Jefferson's "separation of church and State" has been misunderstood and misapplied.

(2) *N.B.*: Stevens' opinion is heavily exclusionary and imbued with the desire to keep religion outside of the public square.

(ii) *See also Santa Fe Independent School District v. Doe* (U.S. 2000) (Stevens, J.), where the Court held that a prayer before a public high school's varsity football games was unconstitutional, even though it was student-initiated.

(e) Under *Lemon*, government action lacking a secular purpose was held to be unconstitutional.

(f) When a secular purpose is but a façade covering a religious purpose, the government action is similarly unconstitutional.

(i) *See McCreary County v. ACLU of Kentucky* (U.S. 2005), where the Court held that a display of the Ten Commandments at a county courthouse was unconstitutional, even though it was surrounded by other décor, because this other décor was merely an attempt to cover up the true religious purpose of the display, and was only added when the display was held to be unconstitutional.

(ii) *Compare Van Orden v. Perry* (U.S. 2005) (Rehnquist, C.J.) where the Court held that a Ten Commandments display at a courthouse in Texas was constitutional, because the décor surrounding it had been there since the display's origin and thus showed that the primary purpose was secular, not religious.

### 6.3 The Free Exercise Clause

6.3.1 The government may inquire into the *sincerity*, not the *validity* or *reasonableness*, of religious belief.

(a) *See United States v. Ballard* (U.S. 1944), where the defendants (Ballard) were held guilty of fraud based only on the fact that they *did not believe their claims* on being able to heal incurable diseases—not on the fact that their claims were true or false.

6.3.2 The Scope of Religion Protected

(a) The Court has held that the object of the Free Exercise Clause is not only religion in the traditional sense, but any belief system that plays a comparable role to religion for a given individual.

(i) In *United States v. Seeger* (U.S. 1965) (Burger, J.), the defendants challenged § 6(j) of the Universal Military Training and Service Act, which permitted conscientious objectors from combatant training and service for their "religious training and belief," defined as "an individual's belief in a relation to a Supreme Being." The Court took a liberal view in interpreting the meaning of "religion," holding that the test for religious belief regarding a Supreme Being is "whether a given *belief that is sincere and meaningful* occupies a place in the life of its possessor parallel to that filled by the orthodox belief in God of one who clearly qualified for the exemption."

(ii) Furthermore, in *Corporation of the Presiding Bishop of the Church of Jesus Christ of Latter Day Saints v. Amos* (U.S. 1987), the Court upheld an *exception to discrimination* under Title VII of the Civil Rights Act of 1964. Although the Civil Rights Act prohibits discrimination generally, the Court permitted employers to discriminate on the basis of religious belief, not only for those in *positions involving thought and speech* (*e.g.*, faculty at a religious school), but also for support staff (*e.g.*, secretaries). The Court held that the statute was not offensive to the First Amendment.

(b) The Free Exercise Clause protects religious belief, not conduct.

(i) *See Reynolds v. United States* (U.S. 1878), where the Court upheld an anti-bigamy law, stating that the defendant, a Mormon, was free to believe as he wished, but was not permitted to act on such beliefs when doing so was contrary to the rule of law.

6.3.3 While Congress may not ***prohibit*** religious belief, it may ***indirectly burden*** it without violating the Free Exercise Clause.

(a) *See Braunfeld v. Brown* (U.S. 1961), where Pennsylvania blue laws prohibiting businesses from being open on Sundays burdened defendants' businesses by causing them to be closed on Sundays, since they were already closed on Saturdays because of their Orthodox Jewish faith. Held: ***general laws that do not target religion***, but are enacted "to advance the state's secular goals" are *valid even if they indirectly burden certain religions.* Here, the laws further the state's interest in providing a common day of rest.

(b) *N.B.*: this case could have also been brought under the Establishment Clause.

(c) *N.B.*: the Free Exercise Clause was read narrowly in this case.

6.3.4 By 1963, however, the Court reached a high point of constitutional protection of religious free exercise.

(a) In *Sherbert v. Verner* (U.S. 1963) (Brennan, J.), the plaintiff Sherbert lost her job because of her Adventist religious beliefs that prevented her from working on Saturdays. Unable to find suitable work because of the Saturday restriction, she applied for unemployment benefits. The benefits were denied because she failed to accept other reasonable suitable work. The plaintiff sued under the Free Exercise Clause. Because the denial of unemployment benefits imposes a burden on the plaintiff's free exercise of religion, the state law was subjected to the ***strict scrutiny***, which requires it to be the *least restrictive means* (LRM) of promoting a *compelling state interest* (CSI), which the law failed.

(i) Concurrence (Stewart, J.): this case is inconsistent with *Braunfeld*, a case that sadly fails to protect one of our most important freedoms.

(ii) *N.B.*: under the *Sherbert v. Verner* scrict scrutiny test, rights are granted the highest level of constitutional protection and the government will usually lose.[41]

---

[41] *N.B.*: where strict scrutiny applies to a government act that restricts a fundamental right or that discriminates against a suspect class, the government will usually lose. However, when strict scrutiny applies to a government act that favors a fundamental right or that favors or protects a suspect class, the government will generally win. This is why in cases involving the abrogation of state immunity under § 5 of the Fourteenth Amendment, when a suspect class is being protected, the government usually wins, but when abrogation is for a non-suspect class, the government will usually lose. This is because

(b) *See also Wisconsin v. Yoder* (U.S. 1972) where the defendants, practitioners of the Amish faith, were convicted for refusing to comply with a Wisconsin law requiring all students under age sixteen to attend school, since their religious values conflicted with those of the public school system. The Court again required the government to show a ***compelling state interest*** in burdening the free exercise of religion. Held: the laws are invalid under strict scrutiny. Reversal of the conviction is affirmed.

(i) *N.B.*: note how this case's holding contrasts with that of *Reynolds v. United States*, which did not protect conduct dictated by one's religious beliefs.

## 6.4 The Decline in the Protection of the Free Exercise Clause

6.4.1 In the 1980s, a series of cases began to undermine constitutional protection of the free exercise of religion.

(a) *See Goldman v. Weinberger* (U.S. 1986), where an Orthodox Jew wanting to wear his yarmulke in the military challenged a uniform dress requirement. The Court denied him an exemption because of the *state interest in uniformity in the military*.

6.4.2 The nadir of constitutional protection was *Employment Division, Department of Human Resources of Oregon v. Smith* (U.S. 1990), where the ***strict scrutiny test*** pronounced in *Sherbert* and *Yoder* was replaced by the ***neutral law of general applicability standard***.

6.4.3 When a law is neutral and generally applicable, strict scrutiny does not apply and the law is generally upheld.

(a) In *Employment Division, Department of Human Resources of Oregon v. Smith* (U.S. 1990) (Scalia, J.), Smith (plaintiff) was fired from his job for ingesting peyote as part of a ritual of the Native American Church, of which he was a member. When he was denied unemployment benefits, he sued, arguing that he was protected under the Free Exercise Clause. Held: the strict scrutiny test for free exercise cases "contradicts both constitutional tradition and common sense." The government may burden the free exercise of religion through ***neutral, generally applicable laws.*** Here, the law prohibiting peyote is generally applicable and does not target religion. Therefore, it is valid.

(i) *N.B.*: the concurrence (O'Connor) and three dissenters (JJ. Blackmun, Brennan, Marshall) all agreed that the strict scrutiny test should have been applied.

(ii) *N.B.*: the Court was in some ways disingenuous in reaching this result. The Court's attempt to distinguish *Sherbert* as an unemployment benefits case, for example, is not credible, since *Smith* also was an unemployment benefits case.

6.4.4 The post-*Smith* era saw the continued application of the neutral law of general applicability standard.

(a) *See Church of the Lukumi Babalu Aye, Inc. v. City of Hialeah* (U.S. 1993), where a law of the City of Hialeah permitted the killing of animals, *except for the purpose of religious sacrifice*. Held: the

---

statutes protecting against suspect or quasi-suspect classifications will generally be held to be congruent and proportional, whereas statutes protecting against non-suspect classifications will generally *not* be held to be congruent and proportional.

law purposefully interferes with the Lukumis' religious practice of animal sacrifice. It is neither neutral nor generally applicable and is therefore unconstitutional.

### 6.5 Legislative Action in Response to *Smith*

6.5.1 Diverse groups committed to civil and religious liberty, from the ACLU to the Christian Legal Society, later joined forces to get Congress to pass the ***Religious Freedom Restoration Act of 1993*** (RFRA), which sought to statutorily restore religious freedom to the pre-*Employment Division v. Smith* standard.

6.5.2 The RFRA was later held to be unconstitutional because it "attempts a substantive change in constitutional provisions."

(a) *See City of Boerne v. Flores* (U.S. 1997) (Kennedy, J.), where the Court held that Congress invalidly imposed regulations on the states, exceeding § 5 of the Fourteenth Amendment.

6.5.3 The religious coalition tried once again coming together, but experienced tensions along the way.

6.5.4 In 2000, however, the Religious Land and Institutionalized Persons Act (RLUIPA) of 2000 was successfully passed. In *Cutter v. Wilkonson* (U.S. 2005) (Ginsburg, J.), the Court upheld the RLUIPA's imposition of strict scrutiny on government restrictions on prisoners' free exercise of religion.

6.5.5 Although the federal RFRA was overruled, state RFRAs continue to pass. Furthermore, *only the RFRA's application to the states was held unconstitutional*. The RFRA continues to apply against the federal government.

(a) In *Gonzales v. O Centro Espirita Beneficiente Uniao do Vegetal* (U.S. 2006) (Roberts, C.J.), the plaintiff spiritist Christian sect O Centro Espirita Beneficiente Uniao do Vegetal was threatened with prosecution for the ritualistic use of a controlled substance. When the plaintiff sued to challenge the Controlled Substances Act, the Court held that *Boerne v. Flores* invalidated the RFRA only as applied against the states; it was valid against the federal government and strict scrutiny therefore applied.

(b) *Comment*: although the Court held that the RFRA was unconstitutional against the states based on § 5 of the Fourteenth Amendment, Congress was able to limit its own lawmaking authority by passing the RFRA against itself. In this respect, the RFRA was nothing more than Congress's passing an amendment to all of its own legislation.

### 6.6 Applying Free Exercise Today

6.6.1 First Amendment Protections (under *Smith*).

(a) Strict scrutiny (LRM/CSI test) applies in the following three situations:

(i) The case involves a ***hybrid right*** (as in *Wisconsin v. Yoder*), where one right is combined with others.

(ii) The case involves ***unemployment compensation*** restricted by religious beliefs (as in *Sherbert v. Verner*) or another case involving "individualized assessments" where the government must analyze different claims.

(iii) The case is ***not*** one involving a neutral law of general applicability (as in *Church of the Lukumi Babalu Aye, Inc. v. City of Hialeah*, where the law targeted religious practices). If it is a neutral law of general applicability, the government wins.

6.6.2 Federal Statutory Protections

(a) RFRA requires the CSI/LRM test to be applied in all cases against the federal government (*not* against states).

(b) RLUIPA requires the CSI/LRM in all cases against states involving:

(i) Land use decisions; and

(ii) Prisoners.

6.6.3 State Law

(a) Some state constitutions have free exercise clauses requiring the CSI/LRM test.

(b) Some states have adopted state RFRAs.

## 7 First Amendment Speech

### 7.1 Prior Restraint and Criticism of the Government

7.1.1 A ***prior restraint*** is an administrative requirement or judicial order that suppresses speech *before it is published* or otherwise made.

7.1.2 There is a strong presumption against prior restraints, which the government generally may not issue, because they put too much power into the hands of officials granting licenses.

7.1.3 In order to prevent the publication of materials that it considers threatening to national security, the government must meet a ***heavy burden of justification*** (similar to strict scrutiny).

(a) *See New York Times Co. v. United States* (U.S. 1971) (*per curiam*), where the government sued to enjoin the New York Times from publishing a classified study on U.S. policy in Vietnam (the Pentagon Papers). Held: the proposed government action must be a narrowly tailored means (similar to LRM) to pursuing a compelling state interest, which the government failed. The government has failed to meet its heavy burden of justification.

(b) Concurrence (White, J.): there was no clear showing of an emergency and no statute supports the plaintiff's position.

(c) Dissent (Burger, C.J.): this Court is deciding too hastefully a case whose facts require more time for analysis.

### 7.2 Public Forums: the Three Categories of Government-Owned Property

7.2.1 Traditional Public Forums

(a) These forums have traditionally been used for public expression.

(b) Examples include sidewalks, streets, and public spaces in front of city halls.

(c) If the government imposes a ***time, place, and manner restriction*** that is ***content neutral*** (does not regulate the subjects to be addressed) and ***viewpoint neutral*** (does not regulate the perspectives advocated),[42] intermediate scrutiny applies.

(i) Example: a regulation prohibiting the use of amplifiers after 9 p.m.

(d) If a restriction is content-based, it is subject to ***strict scrutiny***.

7.2.2 Designated Public Forums

(a) These forums are opened up by the government for the *specific purpose of allowing for public expression* (*e.g.*, an auditorium opened up to the public).

(b) Like traditional public forums, the ***strict scrutiny*** test (LRM to a CSI) is applied. However, in contrast to traditional public forums, designated public forums may be closed down completely.

(c) Time, place, and manner restrictions are subject to intermediate scrutiny.

(d) Limited Designated Public Forums

(i) A designated public forum may be opened by the government for a limited purpose (*e.g.*, a public forum at a public school for school groups only).

(ii) The restrictions must be ***content*** and ***viewpoint neutral***.

(iii) A school may not, for example, discriminate against a school group because it is religious.

7.2.3 All Remaining Government Property

(a) Remaining government property includes the Houses of the Senate and Congress, the Oval Office, naval bases, and the like.

(b) When the government restricts speech in these places, the ***rational basis test*** is applied and the ban needs only to be rationally related to a legitimate state interest.

(c) The restrictions must be reasonable and not viewpoint-based.

(i) *See International Society for Krishna Consciousness, Inc. ("ISKCON") v. Lee* (U.S. 1992) (Rehnquist, J.), where the plaintiffs "ISKCON" challenged a regulation prohibiting the distribution of literature and the solicitation of money in airports. Held: airports have not been historically available for the expression of free speech and are ***neither traditional nor designated public forums***. The government thus only needs a ***rational basis*** to restrict speech. Since solicitation in airports may cause disruptions and delays, it may be prohibited. However, *the distribution of literature is permitted*.

(ii) Dissent (Souter, J.): airports fit the archetype of traditional public forums. Strict scrutiny should have therefore applied.

---

[42] A restriction based on the viewpoints expressed is never permitted.

## 7.3 Government Speech

7.3.1 Government must allow all viewpoints equal access when it creates a forum, *not when the government undertakes speech*.

7.3.2 The government may endorse and express certain viewpoints without expressing alternate viewpoints.

7.3.3 When government undertakes speech by subsidizing one constitutionally-protected category of programs, it is not required to equally fund other related constitutionally-protected programs.

(a) *See Rust v. Sullivan* (U.S. 1991) (Rehnquist, C.J.), where a federal statute *subsidized family planning clinics*, but prohibited doctors of the clinics from even discussing abortion with clients. The statute was held to be constitutional, even though abortion is constitutionally protected: the government need not subsidize every constitutionally protected program just because it subsidizes one.

7.3.4 Thus, citizens may be compelled to fund government speech. However, government may not compel citizens to carry, support, or adopt its speech.

(a) *See Wooley v. Maynard* (U.S. 1977), where the motto “Live Free or Die” on N.H. license plates was held to be an impermissible compulsion of expression.

7.3.5 Furthermore, private law schools may be compelled by the government to allow military recruiters onto their campuses even if the law schools disagree with the policies of the government and of the recruiters.

(a) *See Rumsfeld v. Forum for Academic and Institutional Rights, Inc. (“FAIR”)* (U.S. 2006), where Congress, in passing the Solomon Act, required law schools to give military recruiters the same rights that other recruiters had on their campuses, despite many law schools’ opposition to the military’s homosexuality policy. The law schools challenged the act and the Court held that: (i) the statute did *not* require the plaintiff to engage in speech; (ii) the fact that schools were letting recruiters on campus to speak with students did *not* mean that the schools were being compelled to support the government speech; and (iii) Congress was *not* prohibiting expressive conduct, since exclusion of the recruiters could be interpreted to mean, *inter alia*, the recruiters decided not to come that year.

## 7.4 Termination of Public Employees as a Result of Speech

7.4.1 Private employers have free reign in telling their employees what they may and may not talk about on the job. Normally, such employees have no legal recourse.

7.4.2 The government, however, is *bound by the First and Fourteenth Amendments* when dealing with employees.

7.4.3 The government may not restrict the speech of its employees when they speak as citizens on matters of public concern. The speech, when balanced against the interests of employers, must not be very harmful.

7.4.4 However, there is *no constitutional protection* for the speech of govnerment employees undertaken within the scope of their employment.

(a) *See Garcetti v. Ceballos* (U.S. 2006), where the plaintiff Ceballos, a deputy district attorney, questioned via intra-office memorandum an affidavit used to obtain of a warrant. Claiming that his employer retaliated by firing him, the plaintiff sued. Held: the plaintiff is not protected under the First Amendment, because his speech was made pursuant to his official capacity: he was speaking not as a citizen, but as an employee. Factors to consider: the conversations occurred inside the office rather than in the public (not dispositive); it concerned his employment (not dispositive); and the expression was made pursuant to his duty as a deputy (controlling factor).

(b) *N.B.*: this case gives employees incentive to go to the newspapers and outside channels, where their speech will be protected under the First Amendment. They will then be within the realm of citizens speaking on matters of public concern.

**7.5 The Impermissibility of Government Content and Viewpoint Discrimination**

7.5.1 When a statute is merely a time, place, and manner restriction on free speech, *intermediate scrutiny applies*.

(a) *See Hill v. Colorado* (U.S. 2000) (Stevens, J.), where the Court upheld a Colorado statute restricting speech made within one hundred feet of entrances to health care facilities and prohibiting protesters from approaching within eight feet of persons entering such facilities. Because the restriction addressed not the content of speech but rather, its location and manner, ***intermediate scrutiny*** applies: the restriction must be substantially related to an important government objective and it must *leave open alternative means of communication*. Here, the statute serves the important governmental objective of protecting the right to be left alone and protestors have an alternative means of communication (*e.g.*, holding placards from across the street).

(i) Dissent (Scalia, J.): these restrictions are not content-neutral; they clearly target pro-life advocates. Strict scrutiny should have therefore been applied. Furthermore, the government interest cited by the Court is not legitimate; the right to be left alone was only declared in a dissent by Justice Brandeis and it was referring to the people's rights to be left alone *from the government*, not from private protesters.

(ii) *Comment:* the Court failed to see through the nature of this statute, which, like that of *Church of the Lukumi Babalu Aye, Inc. v. City of Hialeah*, was facially neutral but targeted anti-abortion groups, the only groups that generally protest outside of health care facilities.

7.5.2 Content-based regulations of speech are subject to strict scrutiny.

7.5.3 Viewpoint-based regulations of speech are not permitted.

(a) Example: a public university excludes a student publication from receiving funds for printing, on the grounds that the publication endorses a religious viewpoint (*Rosenberger v. Rector* (U.S. 1995)). This is impermissible viewpoint discrimination.

**7.6 Commercial Speech**

7.6.1 Commercial speech is speech proposing a commercial transaction.

7.6.2 The Court considers the First Amendment to offer less protection for commercial speech than for non-commercial speech.

7.6.3 General rule: commercial speech is protected *unless* it: (i) is *false or misleading*; or (ii) *supports illegal activities*.

7.6.4 There is a four-part analysis for determining whether the regulation of commercial speech is constitutional:

(a) The expression must be ***protected*** (it may not be untruthful or misleading or support unlawful activities);

(b) There must be a ***substantial asserted government interest***;

(c) The regulation must ***directly advance*** the government interest;

(d) The regulation must ***not be overbroad***.

(i) *See Central Hudson Gas & Electric Corp. v. Public Service Commission of New York* (U.S. 1980), where the defendant Public Service Commission's regulation prohibiting electric utilities from advertising in a way that would increase electricity consumption was held to be unconstitutional. Although there was an energy shortage, the ban prohibited the defendant from providing information on electric devices that would not affect overall energy consumption. ***The regulation was overbroad***. Judgment for the defendant is reversed.

### 7.7 Words versus Conduct

7.7.1 An act becomes ***symbolic speech*** when it conveys a message.

7.7.2 When an act involves both speech and conduct, the conduct element may be regulated even if it burdens free speech, as long as the regulation furthers an ***important government interest***.

7.7.3 The following *O'Brien* four-prong test is to be used:

(a) The regulation is within ***constitutional authority;***

(b) It furthers an ***important government interest;***

(c) The interest is ***unrelated to suppressing free expression*** (regulations may incidentally burden speech, but must be content-neutral).

(d) The incidental burden on free expression is ***no greater than necessary***[43] to further the government interest.

(i) *See United States v. O'Brien* (U.S. 1968), where the Court upheld a congressional statute prohibiting the knowing ***burning of draft cards,*** even when doing so was meant primarily as a means of expression. The regulation was (i) within Congress's authority; (ii) furthered an important government interest of operating a draft system and knowing who was eligible; (iii) this interest was unrelated to free expression; and (iv) the incidental burden on free expression is no greater than necessary to further the government interest. Conviction affirmed.

---

[43] "Narrow tailored" has also been language employed by the Court.

(ii) *Compare Texas v. Johnson* (U.S. 1989) (Brennan, J.), where the Court held that a Texas statute prohibiting ***flag burning*** was unconstitutional. The state argued that preserving peace and national unity were state interests furthered by the statute. However, preserving the peace was not implicated and establishing national unity shows that the statute attempts to regulate the content of speech. Therefore, ***strict scrutiny***, not the *O'Brien* test is to be applied, and the *statute fails*.

### 7.8 Adult Entertainment

7.8.1 Courts have traditionally applied the *O'Brien* test to statutes that regulate conduct and incidentally burden speech.

7.8.2 Narrowly-tailored anti-nudity statutes pass the test because they ***further the important government interest*** of preserving morality and are ***unrelated to suppressing speech.***

(a) *See Barnes v. Glen Theatre, Inc.* (U.S. 1991) (Rehnquist, C.J., O'Connor, Kennedy, JJ. plurality opinion), where the plaintiff Glen Theatre, wanting to employ completely nude dancers, challenged an Indiana anti-nudity statute on First Amendment grounds. Held: the statute passes the *O'Brien* test: (i) it is within the state of Indiana's constitutional authority (specifically, its police power); (ii) it furthers a legitimate government interest (preserving order and morality); (iii) it is unrelated to free expression; and (iv) its burden is no greater than needed to further the state interest (the dancers may continue to dance, but must wear pasties and g-strings).

(b) Concurrence (Souter, J.): the state ought not to regulate morality, but this statute would pass for another reason: the state may legislate to prevent the consequences of the regulated activity (crime, prostitution, etc.

(c) Dissent (White, Marshall, Blackmun, Stevens, JJ., etc.): this is not a neutral law of general applicability, as the materials from the records show. Since this is content-based, strict scrutiny should be applied.

7.8.3 However, ***obscenity*** receives *no protection* under the First Amendment. It is defined as material that:

(a) The average person, applying contemporary community standards, would find to appeal to the ***prurient interest*** (contemporary community standards are applied);

(b) In a ***patently offensive way,*** depicts or describes ***sexual conduct*** specifically defined by state law (contemporary community standards are applied); and

(c) Lacks ***serious*** literary, artistic, political, or scientific ***value*** (a national standard is applied). *Miller v. California* (U.S. 1973).

### 7.9 Expressions of Hate

7.9.1 Clear and Present Danger

(a) The First Amendment does not protect speech advocating illegal conduct when there is an ***imminent threat of lawless action.***

(i) *See Schenck v. United States* (U.S. 1919), where the Court, applying the *clear and present danger test*, upheld convictions for the distribution of leaflets against the draft during World War I.

(b) The test was refined in *Brandenburg v. Ohio* (U.S. 1969), which held that the constitutional protections of free speech do not extend to speech that:

(i) Aims to incite imminent unlawful conduct; and

(ii) Is likely to produce such conduct.

7.9.2 Fighting Words

(a) Words are not constitutionally protected when:

(i) They are ***directed*** at another;

(ii) They are ***calculated to provoke*** immediate violent retaliation; and

(iii) Their utterance ***inflicts injury*** or provokes a breach of the peace. *Chaplinsky v. New Hampshire* (U.S. 1942).

(b) Content-based hate crime statutes that punish only viewpoints based on race, gender, religion, or creed are unconstitutional. They must ban *all* fighting words.

(i) *See R.A.V. v. St. Paul* (U.S. 1992), where a statute prohibiting only the burning of crosses or swastikas was held to be unconstitutional.

(c) However, a state ban on cross-burning that is done with the intent to intimidate does not violate the First Amendment. *Virginia v. Black* (U.S. 2003).

7.9.3 Racial Motivation

(a) The First and Fourteenth Amendments do not prohibit the enhancement of penalties when the defendant picks a victim based on his race.

(b) *See Wisconsin v. Mitchell* (U.S. 1993) (Rehnquist, C.J., for a unanimous Court), where the Court upheld a statute enhancing penalties against defendant black youth whose assault of a white victim was racially motivated.

### 7.10 Free Speech Rights in Public Schools

7.10.1 Students' free speech rights continue to receive protection within "the schoolhouse gate."

(a) In *Tinker v. Des Moines Independent Community School District* (U.S. 1969), students were punished for wearing black armbands in school to protest the Vietnam War. The students challenged their punishment, arguing that their actions were speech. Held: students do not shed their First Amendment rights to free speech "at the schoolhouse gate." A public school may *not* punish students for symbolic acts that constitute First Amendment speech when such acts are passive and not disruptive.

7.10.2 If the acts would cause "substantial disruption" and interference with school activities, the school authorities may prohibit them.

### 7.11 Freedom of Speech and the Press

7.11.1 The First Amendment gives greater protection to speech about public officials or officers in their public capacities than it does to private individuals.

7.11.2 For example, although there is liability for ***negligent*** defamatory libel of a private person, the Constitution protects negligent defamatory libel made against a ***public figure*** in his official capacity.[44]

7.11.3 A state statute must therefore require public officials to show malice (***knowledge*** of the falsity of statements made or ***reckless disregard of their falsity***) when suing for defamatory libel.

(a) *See New York Times Co. v. Sullivan* (U.S. 1964), where a state law punishing negligently false defamatory assertions against public officials was held to violate the First and Fourteenth Amendments, which require that malice be shown. Since the plaintiff Montgomery commissioner Sullivan failed to show that the defendant published the statements either *knowing* or *recklessly disregarding their falsity*, judgment for the plaintiff was reversed

### 7.12 Speech within Private Associations

7.12.1 The right to associate is not explicitly mentioned in the Bill of Rights, but it has been held to be within the First Amendment Freedom of Speech Clause.

7.12.2 There are two categories of associations for determining free speech rights:

(a) Highly Personal Intimate Associations

(i) Factors include the size, purpose, and selectivity of the association.

(ii) These groups include families and small churches.

(iii) They receive protection as a *fundamental element* of personal liberty.

(iv) Infringements are subject to ***very strict scrutiny.***

(b) Expressive Associations

(i) In expressive associations, people come together to express their views and communicate a message.

(ii) They can be large, but they must be united around some kind of a message.

(iii) They also receive very high protection, but not as much as intimate associations.

7.12.3 Infringements on Expressive Associations

---

[44] The Constitution, however, protects neither knowing nor reckless defamatory libel made against public figures and private individuales.

(a) Infringements on expressive associations must "serve compelling state interests, unrelated to the suppression of ideas, that cannot be achieved through means significantly less restrictive of associational freedoms."

(b) This is a slightly less rigorous strict scrutiny test.

(c) An example of a compelling state interest that justifies infringing the freedom of association is *ending discrimination* on the basis of race, national origin, sex, or creed.

(d) States may limit freedom of association only when doing so does not compromise the group's ability to convey a First Amendment expressive message.

(i) *Compare Boy Scouts of America v. Dale* (U.S. 2000), where the defendant Boy Scouts of America excluded homosexuals from serving as leaders. A NJ antidiscrimination law sought to prevent the Boy Scouts from discriminating on the basis of sexual orientation. Held: because homosexuality is against the defendant's values, having a homosexual leader ***would comprise the defendant's message***. The First Amendment Freedom of Association therefore prohibits NJ from requiring the defendant to admit homosexuals within the ranks of its leaders. The First Amendment Freedom of Expressive Association protects the defendant's right to discriminate on the basis of sexual orientation.

## 8 Due Process

### 8.1 Introduction

8.1.1 The United States Constitution binds both federal and state governments to due process requirements; the Fifth Amendment Due Process Clause applies to the federal government; the Fourteenth Amendment Due Process Clause applies to the states.

8.1.2 There are two kinds of due process:

(a) Procedural Due Process

(i) Procedural due process guarantees that certain ***required processes*** are followed when depriving persons of fundamental rights, namely, life, liberty, and property.

(ii) The two main kinds of procedural due process are:

(1) Notice; and

(2) The opportunity to be heard.

(b) Substantive Due Process

(i) Substantive due process refers to the *substance* of historical fundamental rights.

(ii) It is rooted in ***history and tradition*** and, according to some Supreme Court jurisprudence, it must be *clearly defined.*

### 8.2 Procedural Due Process

8.2.1 What Constitutes State Action

(a) The Fourteenth Amendment prohibits ***state and local governments*** from depriving any person of life, liberty, or process without following proper legal procedures: "No *State* shall make or enforce any law which shall abridge the privileges or immunities of citizens of the United States; nor shall any State deprive any person of life, liberty, or property, without due process of law."

(b) Under the Enforcement Clause of the Fourteenth Amendment, Congress may prohibit states from discriminatory action.

(c) The Fourteenth Amendment does *not*, however, confer on Congress the ability to prohibit ***private discriminatory action***.[45]

(i) *See The Civil Rights Cases* (U.S. 1883), where the Congress passed the Civil Rights Act of 1875, which prohibited discrimination by common carriers, inns, etc. for discrimination in theatres, places of public accommodation, etc. When plaintiffs sued under the Civil Rights Act, the Court held that Congress had no authority to pass the Act. The Fourteenth Amendment gives Congress power to enforce its provisions against *only states, not private actors.*

(ii) Dissent (Harlan, J.): the Thirteenth Amendment is about more than just abolishing slavery and involuntary servitude; it is about eliminating the bades of slavery and bringing African Americans to *full equality.* Section 2 gives Congress the power to enforce the abolition of both slavery and discrimination.

(d) However, private action may become state action when the state offers a ***mantle of authority*** for private acts or is ***significantly involved*** *in the action.*

(e) Examples include *enforcing discriminatory covenants*, entering into *symbiotic relationships* with discriminatory actors, and permitting *race-based peremptory challenges* in the state court system.

(i) *See Shelley v. Kraemer* (U.S. 1948), where the plaintiffs (Kraemer) sued to enforce an equitable servitude preventing blacks from owning or occupying certain property. Held: private discriminatory *equitable servitudes become* ***state action*** *when enforced by the courts.* Although private actors may enter into such covenants (provided there are no applicable civil rights laws), the Equal Protection Clause prohibits state courts from enforcing them.

(ii) *See also Burton v. Wilmington Parking Authority* (U.S. 1961), where the plaintiff Burton challenged racial discrimination by a private restaurant that was located in a city-owned building. Held: there is a ***symbiotic relationship*** between the restaurant and the government, which owned the public building and depended on the restaurant's revenues. The discrimination is therefore state action.

(iii) *See also Edmonson v. Leesville Concrete Co., Inc.* (U.S. 1991), which held that private litigants could not use race for ***peremptory challenges***. Since private attorneys are acting under the public court system, their acts become state action.

---

[45] Note the distinction with the Thirteenth Amendment, which allows Congress to pass legislation to prohibit both *state and private action* in order to abolish slavery and involuntary servitude.

(iv) *Compare Jackson v. Metropolitan Edison Co.* (U.S. 1974), which held that private utilities cooperating with a state charter may terminate service for nonpayment without notice and a hearing.

(f) However, merely granting a ***license*** or ***essential services*** or ***heavily regulating an industry*** is not state action.

(g) The Fourteenth Amendment does not require states to affirmatively protect life, liberty, or property; it merely prohibits denial of these rights without due process of law.

(i) The Fourteenth Amendment does not therefore create a duty to act or to rescue.

(ii) ***Failure to act is not state action*** when the state has not taken someone into custody.

(1) *See DeShaney v. Winnebago County Dept. of Social Services* (U.S. 1989) (Rehnquist, C.J.) where the plaintiff son sued the defendant social workers and local officials for having deprived him of his due process rights for failing to protect him when they knew or should have known that his father was abusing him. Held: the Fourteenth Amendment prohibits the state from depriving a person of life or liberty, but it does not require state intervention to prevent abuse by private actors.

8.2.2 What Constitutes "Life, Liberty or Property"

(a) Procedural due process requires that a person have procedural safeguards (generally, ***notice*** and the opportunity to be ***heard***) before being deprived of life, liberty, or property.

(b) "Property" includes more than mere realty or chattels. It includes, for example, the right to ***continued welfare benefits.***

(i) *See Goldberg v. Kelly* (U.S. 1970), where plaintiff welfare recipients sued the state, arguing that they were entitled to a pre-termination hearing before welfare was cut off. Held: there is a property interest in continued welfare benefits. *Notice* and a *pre-termination evidence hearing* are therefore *required* before welfare is terminated., even if this means that the state must bear the cost of continued benefits to non *bona fide* welfare recipients in the interim until *after* hearings are held.

(ii) Dissent (Black, J.): the plaintiffs are not being deprived of any property, but rather, of a government handout. This handout is not protected under the Constitution.

(c) However, "property" does not include the right to continued ***Social Security disability insurance benefits.***

(i) *See Mathews v. Eldridge* (U.S. 1976), where the Court held that the same concerns for *bona fide* welfare recipients to not extend to those receiving Social Security disability insurance benefits. *A pre-termination evidentiary hearing is not required.* Determination as to whether there is a constitutionally protected liberty or property interest requires a balancing test based on the following factors:

(1) The *importance* of the property or liberty interest involved;

(2) The *value* of the procedural safeguard to protecting the interest; and

(3) The *government interest* in fiscal and administrative efficiency.

(d) The right to liberty and property does not include the right of an employee to ***continued government employment.*** Therefore, no hearing is necessary when such employment is terminated.

(i) *See Board of Regents v. Roth* (U.S. 1972), where the Court held that a state university was not required to give a hearing and explanation to the plaintiff when he was not hired back after one year, since he had neither a liberty nor property interest in maintaining the job.

(ii) Dissent (Marshall, J.): every citizen who *applies* for a government job is entitled to it unless the government can establish a reason for denying the employment.

(e) Constitutional procedural and substantive due process put a limit on the amount of ***punitive damages*** a plaintiff may win.

(i) In *Pacific Mutual Life Ins. Co. v. Haslip* (U.S. 1991), the Court hinted that there was such a limit, but did not state that a punitive damages award that was more than four times the amount in compensatory damages was excessive in light of the Due Process Clause of the Fourteenth Amendment.

(1) Concurrence (Scalia, J.): our Constitution is silent on the issue of punitive damages and our history and traditions leave them for the jury to decide.

(ii) In *BMW v. Gore* (U.S. 1996), a $2 million punitive damages award for $4,000 damages (a multiplier of 500) was unconstitutional. The Court held that the following three factors were to be considered:

(1) The *reprehensibility of the conduct*;

(2) The *disparity* between the *actual harm suffered* and the *punitive damages*; and

(3) The *difference* between *punitive damages awarded by the jury* and the *civil penalties* authorized or imposed in comparable cases.

(iii) In *State Farm Mutual Automobile Ins. Co. v. Campbell* (U.S. 2003) (Kennedy, J.), the Court further refined this rule by holding that no more than a single digit (1 to 9) ratio of punitive to compensatory damages should be awarded. Thus, a judgment for $145 million in punitive damages against State Farm for $2.6 million in compensatory damages was unconstitutional.

(1) Dissent (Scalia, Thomas, JJ.): punitive damages have traditionally been dealt with *by the states and legislatures*. Nothing in the Constitution limits them.

### 8.3 Substantive Due Process: the Protection of Unenumerated Rights

#### 8.3.1 Introduction

(a) Congress and the states may not violate the rights contained in the Constitution and in the Bill of Rights.

(b) However, the Ninth Amendment states that there are fundamental rights that the people have retained that are not enumerated in the Constitution: "The enumeration in the Constitution, of certain rights, shall not be construed to deny or disparage others retained by the people."

(c) One method in the sometimes difficult task of ascertaining which unemuerated rights merit protection is to look at history: if the right is deeply rooted in our ***history and traditions***, then it is a fundamental right.

(d) In recent cases, the Court has begun looking to "emerging traditions" in addition to history. *See, e.g., Romer v. Evans* (U.S. 1996).

(e) Another method is to look to the natural law. However, many prominent scholars, such as Robert Bork, and Supreme Court Justices, such as Justice Scalia, argue that natural law thinking is best left to the legislature, not to the judiciary.

(f) This section deals with the question of which unenumerated rights are entitled to constitutional protection.

8.3.2 Parental and Family Rights

(a) The Right to Marry

(i) The right to marry is a fundamental right strongly rooted in our ***history and traditions***.

(ii) Statutes that limit the right to marry based on race violate this right.

(1) *See Loving v. Virginia* (U.S. 1967), where Loving, a white man who was indicted and sentenced to jail for marrying a black woman, challenged a Virginia statute that banned interracial marriage on the basis that it violated ***equal protection***. The State argued that it was not a violation of equal protection, since the law applied equally to white people as it did to African Americans. Held: equal protection requires more than equal application. The statutes unduly burden the defendant's liberty without due process of law by creating classifications. Strict scrutiny applies. Since there is no state interest for preventing interracial marriage, judgment is granted to the defendant.

(2) Comment: the Court tries very hard to root the right in the common law and history.

(b) The Right to Procreation

(i) The right to procreation is a fundamental right. The state may not therefore arbitrarily discriminate against similarly situated classes when this right is involved.

(ii) *See Skinner v. Oklahoma* (U.S. 1942), where a law allows the state to *sterilize criminals* who have committed several crimes in order to prevent them from passing their genes on. Because the statute ***discriminates arbitrarily***, applying to the defendant

Skinner, a chicken thief, but not to acts of embezzlement or revenue acts, it is unconstitutional.

(1) *N.B.*: here, the classification of white-collared crimes versus other felonies falls into *rational basis scrutiny.* However, the Court applies strict scrutiny.

(2) *N.B.*: strict scrutiny can be triggered in Equal Protection cases if (i) if it is a suspect class; or, if a non-suspect line is drawn; (ii) if there is a fundamental right involved.

(3) *N.B.*: here, the Court could have analyzed this as a *substantive due process case* by arguing that procreation is a fundamental right. It probably did not because it was just 5 years after the 1937 "switch in time that saved 9," where FDR pressured the Court to abandon its substantive due process argumentation.

(c) Extended Family Living Relationships

(i) The extended family and the fundamental right of extended family members to live together are deeply rooted in our history.

(ii) Ordinances narrowly defining which family members may live together are subject to strict scrutiny.

(1) In *Moore v. City of East Cleveland* (U.S. 1977) (Powell, J.), a housing ordinance that did not permit the defendant Moore to live with her grandsons in a single household was challenged. Held: the ordinance violates the defendant's Fourteenth Amendment *Due Process* and her right to live together in privacy. Our Constitution protects the family because it is *deeply rooted in the nation's history and tradition.* If we are to find a non-textual fundamental right, it must be historically rooted.

(2) *Compare Village of Belle Terre v. Boraas* (U.S. 1974), where the Court held that the fundamental right to live together *does not apply to unrelated individuals.* A municipality may thus pass an ordinance under its police powers that prohibits unrelated individuals from living with one another in a single household.

(d) Presumed Paternity

(i) The Constitution does not prohibit state statutes that conclusively presume a mother's husband to be her child's father when the father is neither impotent nor sterile. In this case, an adulterer has no fundamental right to the paternity rights of his children when they were born to a married woman.

(ii) *See Michael H. v. Gerald D.* (U.S. 1989) (Scalia, J.), where Carol, the defendant husband's (Gerald D.) wife, was living with the plaintiff adulterer (Michael H.), with the defendant husband, and with Scott at different times. A California marriage law allowed a presumption that children born to a married woman are legitimate. The presumption could be rebutted by blood tests if requested by the father within two years. When genetic tests showed with 98% probability that the plaintiff was Victoria's father, he sued to establish paternity, arguing that he had a substantive due process right as the adulterer who allegedly conceived Victoria. He sought visitation rights with his daughter, who was living with her recently reconciled mother and her mother's husband. Held: the California law, which bans the plaintiff from having visitation rights with his daughter, is not unconstitutional. Prior cases have not allowed unmarried men to assert rights against an intact family. There is no fundamental liberty that allows adulterers visitation rights of their children. Judgment for the defendant affirmed.

(1) *Comment*: ***footnote 6*** is the famous part of this case. Scalia says that the main area of disagreement with the dissent is the definition of parenthood. His definition is based on history and tradition. If the dissent's generalist approach is adopted, any human relationship can be used in defining parentage. Scalia is not taking the absolute textualist position ("if it is not in the Constitution, it is not a right"); rather, he searches for the narrowest right that fits the facts and then asks if that right is fundamental. Here, the facts deal with the rights of an adulterer to visitation rights of his children. There is no such fundamental right.

(2) Justices O'Connor and Kennedy concur with the exception of footnote 6.

(3) Dissent (Brennan, Marshall, Blackmun, JJ.): the plurality squashes the right not to conform by "requiring specific approval from history before protecting anything in the name of liberty." The Constitution interpreted by the plurality as an unchanging document that is unfamiliar to me. The Constitution must be permitted to live and flow.

8.3.3 Privacy

(a) Introduction

(i) Among the fundamental rights deeply ingrained in traditions and history is the ***right of privacy***, which is protected in the Due Process Clause of the Fourteenth Amendment.

(b) Contraception

(i) The Court held in 1965 that the right to privacy extends to the use of contraception by married persons. The Court based this on the "***penumbras***," or peripheral rights, of those enumerated in the Bill of Rights.

(1) *See Griswold v. Connecticut* (U.S. 1965) (Douglas, J.), where a state statute prohibited contraceptives when used to prevent pregnancy (but not to prevent disease). The defendant (Planned Parenthood Executive Director Griswold) and the codefendant (a doctor) appealed their convictions for giving advice on using contraceptives, arguing that the law violates marital privacy. Held: statutes forbidding the use of contraceptives or the assistance to third parties for the use of contraceptives unconstitutionally violate the Constitution. There is a fundamental right of married couples in their private life based on the *penumbras* of those rights enumerated in the Bill of Rights. Judgments reversed.

(2) Concurrence (Harlan, J.): this is a fundamental right simply based on substantive due process; we do not have to fish around for the right in the Bill of Rights.

(3) Dissent (Black, Stewart, JJ.): there are no penumbras in the Constitution. If it is not written in the Constitution, it should not be enforced.

(ii) Just seven years later, the Court extended to ***all people*** (including single persons) the *marital privacy right* to use contraception.

(iii) The right of privacy was held to mean "the right of the individual, married or single, to be free from unwarranted governmental intrusion into matters so fundamentally affecting a person as the decision whether to bear or beget a child."

(1) *See Eisenstadt v. Baird* (U.S. 1972), where the state, wanting to restrict contraceptive use after *Griswold*, passed a statute limiting the distribution of contraceptives to married people only. The defendant Baird, a professor, was convicted for exhibiting contraceptive articles at a lecture and of handing out vaginal foam to a student, in violation of the statute. Held: the right to privacy should not be limited to married people. If distribution to married people cannot be prohibited under *Griswold*, then distribution to unmarried people cannot be prohibited under equal protection. Judgment for the defendant.

(iv) This right extends to all people; statutes that have excluded minors from the right to use contraception have accordingly been struck down as unconstitutional. *See Carey v. Population Services International* (U.S. 1977).

(c) Abortion

(i) A law banning a woman's right to an abortion in all cases except when necessary to preserve her life unconstitutionally violates women's personal liberty rights.

(1) *See Roe v. Wade* (U.S. 1973) (Blackmun, J.), where the plaintiff Roe, a pregnant unmarried woman, sought an abortion in Texas, where abortion was illegal except when necessary to save the mother's life. The plaintiff challenged the law, which the Court held unconstitutionally violated the right to privacy. Although the Constitution is not explicit about a right to privacy, this right is found in the Liberty Clause of the Fourteenth Amendment. Statutes infringing the right to privacy are ***subject to strict scrutiny*** – they must be necessary to protect a compelling state interest. Some argue that abortion procedures protect the woman from invasive, unsafe procedures, but these procedures are much safer today. Some argue that they protect against illicit sexual relations, but this relationship is attenuated; some argue that they protect fetal life, but the Fourteenth Amendment protects only post-natal life. ***The following scheme is to be applied:*** (i) in the *first trimester*, the state may not ban abortion; (ii) in the *second trimester*, it may regulate abortion procedures (but not the decision to have an abortion); and (iii) in the *third trimester*, it may regulate procedures and even prohibit abortion when viability of the fetus (at 28 weeks). However, such a ban must make exceptions for abortions that are necessary to protect the *life or health* of the mother.

(2) Dissent (Rehnquist, J.): the right to abortion is not in our Constitution and there is nothing in American or legal history that acknowledges a fundamental right to abortion.

(3) *N.B.*: J. Blackmun, whose daughter secured an illegal abortion shortly before this case, believed that by writing what he considered to be his *magnum opus*, the abortion controversy would come to an end.

(ii) In *Doe v. Bolton* (U.S. 1973), the Court expanded health under *Roe* to include *psychological health*, as determined by the abortionist. The woman's age as well as physical, emotional, psychological, and familial factors must be taken into account when determining whether her health is threatened.

(iii) Today, however, after the holding in *Planned Parenthood of Southeastern Pennsylvania v. Casey* (U.S. 1992), it appears that the Court has rejected trimester approach of *Roe* and the holding that abortion is a ***"fundamental right"*** whose restrictions merit strict scrutiny.

(iv) The test used in determining whether a State's regulation of abortion is constitutional is the ***undue burden test*** under *Casey.* States may not prohibit women from choosing abortion prior to quickening. However, they may regulate (but not prohibit) the right to choose an abortion as long as the regulations do not impose an *undue burden* on the right to choose.

(v) Permissible restrictions include the imposition of informed consent (with a twenty four hour waiting period) and parental consent requirements (unless judicial bypass, where the girl is permitted to persuade the judge that the abortion is in her best interest, is granted).

(vi) Post-viability abortions, however, may be completely prohibited by the states, as long as exceptions are left for the life or health of the mother.

(1) *See Planned Parenthood of Southeastern Pennsylvania v. Casey* (U.S. 1992) (O'Connor, Kennedy, Souter, JJ.), where the Court partially overruled the *Roe* ***trimester approach,*** replacing it with the ***undue burden test.*** The plaintiffs sued for an injunction and declaratory relief from provisions of the Pennsylvania Abortion Control Act of 1982, which (i) required a woman to give her informed consent prior to an abortion procedure; (ii) specified that she receive certain information twenty four hours before the procedure; (iii) required parental consent for minors; and (iv) obliged married women to notify their husbands, with some exceptions. The Court granted *certiorari* to determine when the Act was unconstitutional. Held (O'Connor): "Liberty finds no refuge in a jurisprudence of doubt ... At the heart of liberty is the right to define one's own concept of existence, of meaning, of the universe, and of the mystery of human life. Beliefs about these matters could not define the attributes of personhood were they formed under compulsion of the state." ***The Fourteenth Amendment protects fundamental rights*** such as the right to procreate and the right to privacy. The right is defined as among the choices central to personal dignity and autonomy. All of the regulations, except for the husband notification requirement, are constitutional. The husband notification requirement puts an undue burden on women's ability to have an abortion. Affirmed in part and remanded.

(aa) *N.B.*: O'Connor writes the majority opinion from realist perspective that embraces relativism. "There are reasonable people and views on both sides; the government must not impose its views."

(bb) *N.B.*: the Court abandons the strict scrutiny test and the trimester approach.

(2) Dissent (Scalia, J.): the Pennsylvania law was constitutional in its entirety, since the neither the text nor the history of the Constitution mentions or protects abortion, which has been proscribed since our early history. The majority throws around adjectives and expressions, such as "highly personal" and "necessary freedoms," that can be used to support any idea, from sodomy to slavery. The states can and should handle this question on their own: in a healthy democracy, citizens should be able to persuade one another and then vote.

(vii) Bans on abortion in the third trimester must include exceptions for the life and health of the mother.

(1) *See Stenberg v. Carhart* (U.S. 2000) (Breyer, J.), where the plaintiff physician Carhart challenged a Nebraska statute that criminalized partial-birth (D&X) abortions and allowed no exceptions for ***the health*** of the mother. Issue: is banning D&X abortions an undue burden under *Casey*, since D&X may be the only safe way to have an abortion in the last trimester? Held: the statute is unconstitutional because it does not have an exception for the life or health of the mother. This statute could be read to ban not only D&X abortions, but also D&E abortions. If it were read that way, it would ban the majority of abortions and it would constitute an undue burden. This statute imposes an ***undue burden.***

(2) Dissent (Kennedy, J.) (switching sides): the people of Nebraska chose to enact a law that reflected their high regard for the dignity of life. It does not impose a *Casey* undue burden on a woman's right to choose.

(3) Dissent (Scalia, J.): once this court gave itself power in *Casey* to arbitrate what restrictions a state may place on abortions, a case such as this one, where the court prevents the people from democratically electing to ban a gruesome procedure, will result. Both the Constitution and tradition are fully silent on the issue. The people must be free to choose; *Casey* must be overruled.

(viii) The Court later held that when part of a statute is unconstitutional, the correct remedy is not to invalidate it entirely.

(1) In *Ayotte v. Planned Parenthood of Northern New England* (U.S. 2006) (O'Connor, J.), a New Hampshire statute prohibited minors from obtaining abortions unless there had been forty eight hours of prior notice delivered to their parents or legal guardians. The lower courts declared the act to be unconstitutional because *no exceptions were made for situations where delays would endanger a minor's health*. They invalidated the statute entirely and enjoined its enforcement. Held: when part of a statute is unconstitutional, the correct remedy is not to invalidate it entirely, but rather, to prohibit only the unconstitutional provisions.

(2) *N.B.*: this opinion has a different tone than most abortion cases in that it was deferential to the legislature.

(d) Assisted Suicide and the Refusal of Medical Treatment

(i) The *liberty interest* protected by the Due Process Clause requires that a person not be forced to accept unwanted medical treatment. When a patient is not competent, the family must show clear and convincing evidence that termination of life support is what the patient would have wanted. *Cruzan v. Missouri Department of Health* (U.S. 1990).

(ii) However, this right does not carry over to commit suicide; there is no right to commit suicide that is firmly rooted in the Constitution or in the history and traditions of the nation, and ***the Court is hesitant to expand protected rights.***

(iii) At common law, there was no fundamental right to end one's life. Rather, suicide was a crime often referred to as "self murder."

(iv) Thus, a state acting in its interest in preserving life may ban assisted suicide. A law that denies suffering people the right to assisted suicide is not unconstitutional.

(1) *See Washington v. Glucksberg* (Rehnquist, C.J.) (U.S. 1997), where the plaintiff patients and doctors (Glucksberg) challenged a Washington ban on assisted suicide as unconstitutionally infringing on a fundamental right. Held: we have held that there is a right under due process to refuse medical treatment. Extending this constitutional protection to assisted suicide takes the issue outside the arena of public debate and legislative action. We must be reluctant to declare non-textual rights to be within the Constitution. *We will not expand these rights to include the right to assisted suicide.* It is not a right *based on history and tradition.* Second, in substantive due process cases, we have required a clear description. Furthermore, this ban is justified in that it is interrelated with the state's interest in preventing assisted suicide from becoming voluntary or involuntary euthanasia, which can threaten the poor, weak, and vulnerable.

(aa) *N.B.*: in his concurrence, Justice Souter is critical of limiting substantive due process to history and tradition.

(bb) *N.B.*: the Court must deal with *Casey's* fundamental right to define one's values and the meaning of the universe. The Court gets around *Casey* by stating that it did not mean a *broad, sweeping right* to define one's universe, but rather, a right within the context of fundamental rights rooted in history and tradition.

(cc) *N.B.*: if assisted suicide is not a fundamental right, government restrictions need only to pass rational basis scrutiny.

(2) *See also Vacco v. Quill* (U.S. 1997) (Rehnquist, C.J.), where the plaintiffs (Quill) assert that NY's law against assisted suicide unconstitutionally *violates equal protection.* The line drawn by the statute is between those who want assistance in committing suicide (who otherwise will not die) and those who need

life-saving treatments. Held: there is no suspect class targeted and, under *Glucksberg*, there is no fundamental right. Therefore, under the Equal Protection Clause, the statute has a *strong presumption of validity* under rational basis scrutiny. The Equal Protection Clause guarantees that ***similarly situated cases will be treated similarly***. It does not create substantive rights. This is not about denying those seeking assisted suicide the right held by those who voluntarily removed life-sustaining treatment. In the former, we are dealing with suicide; in the latter, it is the illness that causes death. Therefore, the two are not similarly situated. Judgment for the defendant: the statute passes rational basis scrutiny and does not violate equal protection.

(aa) *N.B.*: this case was decided on EP grounds.

(e) Homosexual Conduct

(i) There is no fundamental right to engage in homosexual sodomy, which is not protected under substantive due process.

(1) In *Bowers v. Hardwick* (U.S. 1986), two men engaged in consensual homosexual conduct were charged with violation of a Georgia statute criminalizing sodomy. The plaintiff challenged the constitutionality of the statute as a violation of privacy rights. Held: there is no fundamental right to homosexual sodomy based on history and tradition. Rather, the history was generally marked by criminal sanctions. If there is no textual right and no history and tradition, then there is no fundamental right. Thus, ***rational basis applies.*** The promotion of morality is a legitimate state interest based in the police power, which seeks to further the welfare and morality of the state. The fact that two adults engage in a criminal act in private does not exonerate them from having violated the law. Judgment for the plaintiff reversed.

(2) Dissent (Blackmun, J.): this is not about a fundamental right to engage in homosexual sodomy, but rather, it is about "the right to be let alone."

(ii) The privacy rights of *Griswold* and *Eisenstadt* were vastly expanded by later Courts, ultimately leading to the establishment of a privacy right of consenting adult homosexuals to engage in sodomy.

(1) *See Lawrence v. Texas* (U.S. 2003) (Kennedy, J.), where police again arrested two men who had been violating a sodomy statute. The plaintiffs challenged the statute based on due process and equal protection. This statute is not like the *Bowers* statute because here, *only the homosexuals are prohibited from sodomy* (this is relevant for equal protection but not for due process). Under *Casey*, there is a right to privacy in sexual matters. Under *Bowers*, history does not support a fundamental right to homosexual activity, which has been marked by criminal sanctions. However, over the centuries, homosexual sodomy was not always targeted by criminal statutes; sometimes, it was a part of broader bans on sodomy. Held: there is an ***"emerging awareness"*** that adults have liberty to conduct their private lives in matters relating to sex. The Texas statute furthers no legitimate state interest. The sodomy statutes are unconstitutional and *Bowers* must be overruled. Judgment for the plaintiffs.

(2) Concurrence (O'Connor, J.): there is no rational basis for Texas to permit heterosexual sodomy, but ban homosexual sodomy.

(3) Dissent (Scalia, J.): the majority contradicts itself by overruling *Bowers* and just a few years earlier, in *Planned Parenthood v. Casey*, arguing that *stare decisis* had to be followed and *Roe v. Wade* upheld.

# 9 Equal Protection

## 9.1 Introduction

9.1.1 The Equal Protection Clause of the Fourteenth Amendment prohibits any state from making or enforcing laws that "deny to any person within its jurisdiction the equal protection of the laws"—***similarly situated groups must be treated equially***.

9.1.2 The Fourteenth Amendment *applies only to the states,* but equal protection also applies to the federal government though *the Fifth Amendment Due Process Clause. Bolling v. Sharpe* (U.S. 1954) (companion case to *Brown v. Board of Education*, *infra.*).

9.1.3 Questions of equal protection are implicated whenever the government draws classifications (*e.g.*, the requirement that one be at least eighteen years old to vote).

9.1.4 The test used for the majority of classifications is rational basis, which the government usually passes.

9.1.5 However, when certain classes have been historically subjected to disadvantages and discrimination, a higher level of scrutiny will be applied.

9.1.6 Furthermore, undue burdens as to who may exercise ***fundamental rights*** are subject to strict scrutiny. These fundamental rights include:

(a) ***First Amendment Rights*** (free speech, religion, association, assembly, petition, press);

(b) ***Interstate travel*** (*e.g.*, residency requirements for in-state tuition benefits, etc.);

(c) ***Privacy*** (marriage, procreation, contraception, abortion, family living arrangements, death);

(d) ***Criminal due process*** (*Miranda* rights, right to counsel, etc.).

9.1.7 In analyzing equal protection cases, there are three question to be answered:

(a) What is the classification?

(b) If so, what is the appropriate level of scrutiny?

(i) Strict Scrutiny

(1) This applies to race, national origin, alienage, or when classifications are drawn that unduly burden some fundamental right.

(2) The law must be the least restrictive means to protect a compelling state interest.

(ii) Intermediate Scrutiny

(1) This applies to gender[46] and illegitimacy.

(2) The law must be substantially related to an important government interest; and

(iii) Rational Basis Scrutiny

(1) This applies to all other classes, including sexual conduct/homosexuality,[47] age, handicap, mental retardation, poverty, illegal alienage, children of illegal aliens, and state residency.

(2) The challenger must show that the government action is not rationally related to a legitimate state interest.

(c) Does the government's explanation for the classification meet the applicable level of scrutiny?

9.1.8 Proving Discriminatory Intent

(a) In order to violate the Equal Protection Clause, *government discrimination must be purposeful.*

(b) There are three ways in which a statute may purposefully discriminate:

(i) It may be discriminatory on its face (***prima facie discrimination***) (*e.g.*, a law that denies suffrage based on race);

(ii) It may have an impermissible ***motive*** or ***intent*** (proven through, for example, legislative debates);

(iii) It may be facially neutral but ***applied in a discriminatory way;***

(1) *See Yick Wo v. Hopkins* (U.S. 1886) (Mathews, J.), where a law required laundry facilities to be operated in brick or stone buildings only, unless a special permit was granted authorizing the operation in a wooden building. The law was facially neutral, but was applied in a discriminatory way against Chinese migrant workers in San Francisco. The defendant was denied a permit by the Board of Supervisors, which also turned down every Chinese laundry operator, while awarding them to white operators. Held: although the statute is facially neutral and serves a valid government interest (public safety for fires), the record shows that it is enforced in a discriminatory manner.

(c) However, ***de facto* discrimination,** on its own, does not violate the Equal Protection Clause, because it lacks *purpose*.

(i) In *Washington v. Davis* (U.S. 1976), the Court held that an employment examination does not necessarily violate the Equal Protection Clause simply because fewer blacks

---

[46] *N.B.*: in *United States v. Virginia* (1996), the Court held gender discrimination against women to an elevated standard between intermediate and strict scrutiny, requiring the government to show an "exceedingly persuasive justification" for the classification.

[47] *N.B.*: a rigorous version of rational basis scrutiny was applied for sexual orientation in *Romer v. Evans* (1996): the government was not given the typical deferential treatment of rational basis scrutiny.

than whites pass it. If there is no discriminatory motive behind the test, strict scrutiny will not apply.

## 9.2 Strict Scrutiny

### 9.2.1 Race

(a) Historical Overview

(i) In its early thinking, the Court held that although the founding fathers wrote in the Declaration of Independence that all men were created equal, they did not consider slaves included.

(ii) Early Supreme Court jurisprudence reflected this principle.

(1) *See Dred Scott v. Sandford* (U.S. 1857), where the Court held that a slave was mere property and had no right to bring an action in court.

(iii) The Court also later held that the state may permit separate railway carriages for blacks under the ***"separate but equal"*** doctrine.

(1) *See Plessy v. Ferguson* (U.S. 1896), holding segregation laws to be valid because they protected public peace and order.

(iv) The Court later changed course and held the "separate but equal" doctrine to be unconstitutional.

(1) *See Brown v. Board of Education* (U.S. 1954), a consolidated opinion, where plaintiffs who were denied admission to schools based on their race challenged the law. The Court held that separate is "inherently unequal" and declared the "separate but equal" doctrine unconstitutional. *Plessy v. Ferguson* was overruled.

(v) In 1955, the second *Brown v. Board of Education* case came down. This case dealt with the implementation of the first decision: the states had to desegregate "*with all deliberate speed.*"

(1) However, this could be interpreted in many different ways—it could mean tomorrow, next year, or never.

(2) Some states never did and never intended to segregate.

(vi) Fourteen years after the original *Brown* decision, the Court held that "the time for mere 'deliberate speed' has run out." *Green v. New Kent County* (U.S. 1968). Now was the time for desegregation—there was no freedom of choice.

(b) Affirmative Action

(i) Race may be considered a factor in college and university admissions decisions and legislation to aid minorities.

(ii) However, racial quotas are strongly disfavored and generally are not held to be necessary to protect a compelling state interest. *See Regents of University of California v. Bakke* (U.S. 1978).

(iii) The Court nevertheless allowed Congress to take race into consideration as early as 1980.

(1) *See Fullilove v. Klutznick* (U.S. 1980) (plurality), where the Court held that ***Congress may require a ten percent minority set-aside program*** as a condition to the receipt of federal grants.

(iv) Initially, the Supreme Court held that affirmative action by ***states and municipalities*** was subject to strict scrutiny (narrowly tailored to protect a compelling state interest).

(1) *See City of Richmond v. Croson* (U.S. 1989), where a state program set up to favor minority contractors for construction projects was subject o strict scrutiny. The Court held that the only way for state or local affirmative action to be valid is to react to the government's own systematic discrimination.

(v) However, the Court applied ***intermediate scrutiny*** for federal affirmative action programs in *Metro Broadcasting, Inc. v. FCC* (U.S. 1990).

(vi) The Court later concluded that scrict scrutiny was required of *all racial affirmative action programs*, whether they are *federal, state, or municipal.*

(1) *See Adarand Constructors, Inc. v. Pena* (U.S. 1995), where Gonzales Construction Co. got a bid over the plaintiff, even though the plaintiff's bid was cheaper, because Gonzales fit criteria for an affirmative action statute. The plaintiff sued, claiming that the Fourteenth Amendment Equal Protection Clause was violated. Held: all of the government's racial considerations should be looked on with skepticism; consistentency; congruence (federal and state programs should follow the same rules). All racial classifications *must be analyzed under strict scrutiny. Metro Broadcasting* and *Fullilove*, to the extent that they are inconsistent with this holding, are overruled.

(vii) Student diversity serves as a compelling state interest for the purposes of affirmative action.

(1) *See Grutter v. Bollinger* (U.S. 2003), where the University of Michigan Law School had an admissions plan looking at LSATs, GPAs, and multiple factors, including race, in order to achieve the *educational benefits of diversity.* Student diversity is a compelling state interest, at least within the context of an elite law school. The university passes strict scrutiny.

(2) *Compare Gratz v. Bollinger* (U.S. 2003), where the educational program at the *undergraduate* school of the University of Michigan was much more race-driven, using a *quota-like system* assigning race-based bonus points. Held: here, the role of race in admissions is more overt. The affirmative action program is unconstitutional.

(c) Race and Numerical Equality

(i) Before *Baker v. Carr* (U.S. 1962), the Court held that apportionment was a function to be delegated to the powers of the Legislative Branch. After *Baker*, however, the Court held that ***the judiciary could review apportionment*** to assure its constitutional conformity. Challenges of apportionment were held to be justiciable.

(ii) The Court has held that state redistricting plans may not be based on race alone.

(1) *See Shaw v. Reno* (U.S. 1993), which involved a NC voting redistricting scheme designed to get the largest amount of districts where minority groups would get the largest representation. Held: when a district is drawn in such a bizarre fashion, *strict scrutiny applies.* The federal Voting Rights Act requires that the proposed change not have the purpose or effect of abridging the right to vote on the basis of race. It is impermissible to consider only race when drawing lines, even in order to correct a history for discrimination.

(iii) When race is the ***primary factor*** in drawing up a district, ***strict scrutiny*** applies.

(1) *See Miller v. Johnson* (U.S. 1995), where a redistricting scheme using a narrow corridor to connect two black neighborhoods was challenged. Held: since the record shows that race was the primary factor used, rather than community interests or contiguity, strict scrutiny applies. Compliance with the Attorney General is not a compelling state interest, since the Attorney General was acting in a way prohibited by the Equal Protection Clause. The redistricting scheme is invalid.

(2) *Compare Hunt v. Cromartie* (U.S. 1999), where the Court held that party affiliation was an appropriate basis on which to draw redistricting lines.

(iv) Under the ***Equal Protection Clause***, the "one person, one vote" principle applies to the states.

(1) States basing their electoral system on the model of the U.S. Senate, where each state receives two Senators regardless of population, risk violating the "one person, one vote" principle when some districts are disproportionately more populated than others.

(2) When the "one person, one vote" principle is violated, citizens are denied the "equal protection of the laws" guaranteed by the Fourteenth Amendment. Strict scrutiny applies.

(aa) *See Reynolds v. Sims* (U.S. 1964), where the plaintiffs challenged the apportionment of the Alabama legislature, which was based on a 1900 federal census. The districts were badly disproportionate—some had ten times more voters than others. Held: the federal model may not be used as a guide for state apportionment of congressional districts. Rather, the Equal Protection Clause of the Fourteenth Amendment, requires that "the seats in both houses of a bicameral state legislature … be apportioned on a population basis." Judgment for the plaintiffs affirmed.

(bb) Dissent (Harlan, J.): the Fourteenth Amendment did not intend this result. When it was passed, many states based on their districting schemes off of the federal model and no one proposed that this practice be changed.

(v) Article II, § 1, cl. 2 states as follows: "Each State shall appoint, in such Manner as the Legislature thereof may direct, a Number of Electors, equal to the whole Number of Senators and Representatives to which the state may be entitled in the Congress." States are bound by this provision for presidential elections.

(vi) Furthermore, equal protection and due process require that all votes be granted the *same uniform standards when being counted* for choosing electors.

(1) *See Bush v. Gore* (U.S. 2000), where, after the Florida Secretary of State certified President Bush as the winner of Florida's electoral vote, Al Gore contested the election and demanded a recount. The Florida Supreme Court ordered a recount. Held: the recount procedures adopted are not consistent with the minimum requirement to secure the fundamental right of each voter in the instance of a statewide recount. The Florida Supreme Court decision ordering the manual recounts in some counties in Florida where it was believed that Gore would have received more votes, but not in other counties where Bush would have received more votes, violated the Equal Protection Clause. Furthermore, the record showed that inconsistent methodologies were being used, sometimes, even within the same county. Disparate standards may not be applied in different jurisdictions.

(2) Concurrence (Rehnquist, C.J.): there is an additional ground for the holding: the Constitution requires state legislatures, *not courts*, to direct the procedures for recounts.

9.2.2 Alienage

(a) The Federal Government

(i) If the federal government creates a classification based on alienage, ***rational basis*** scrutiny applies.

(ii) Rationale: the federal government has an interest in foreign affairs and immigration.

(iii) Furthermore, Congress has plenary power over immigration.

(b) The States

(i) If a state or any other government body creates a classification based on alienage, ***strict scrutiny*** generally applies, since aliens pay taxes and are entitled to the benefits rendered from those taxes.

(ii) However, when the classification relates to a matter at the "heart of representative democracy," ***rational basis*** scrutiny applies.

(1) Rationale: the states have an interest in maintaining the self-governance of citizens.

(2) Example: states may exclude aliens from and require citizenship for jobs at the "heart of representative democracy," such as public school teaching or serving as a police officer or probation officer. However, States may not exclude aliens from the practice of law or from becoming notary publics.

## 9.3 Intermediate Scrutiny

### 9.3.1 Gender

(a) In the nineteenth century, the Court affirmed lower courts that denied women the right to vote.

(i) *See Minor v. Happersett* (U.S. 1874), where the plaintiff sued when the defendant Happersett registrar refused to extend the suffrage to her because she was a woman. Held: the Constitution does not guarantee women the right to vote. If the Fourteenth Amendment Privileges and Immunities Clause were intended to extend the right to vote to all citizens, then the Fifteenth Amendment, guaranteeing the right to vote to African Americans, would have been superfluous. A state may choose to recognize the suffrage of women, but if it does not, this Court cannot intervene. Demurrer affirmed.

(b) Women were denied many other rights, including the right to practice law. *See Bradwell v. Illinois* (U.S. 1873) ("[t]he paramount destiny and mission of women are to fulfill the noble and benign offices of wife and mother").

(c) Much changed in 1920, when the Nineteenth Amendment was ratified, requiring the states to extend suffrage to women.

(d) Eventually, the Court changed course and held that classifications based on gender are subject to intermediate scrutiny. *Craig v. Boren* (U.S. 1976) (a law drawing classifications on the ages that men and women could legally begin to drink alcohol was struck down).

(i) Classifications based on gender had to be substantially related to an important government interest.

(ii) For example, Congress may require only men to register for the military draft because the very real differences between men and women are integrally connected to Congress's important interest in raising an army. *Rostker v. Goldberg* (U.S. 1981).

(e) In *United States v. Virginia* (U.S. 1996), the Court raised the standard, applying an even more ***rigorous test:*** intermediate scrutiny with an ***"exceedingly persuasive justification."***

(i) *See United States v. Virginia* (U.S. 1996), where the defendant's public school system established the Virginia Military Institute (VMI), which excluded women. It employed an adversative style of education in order to instill mental and physical discipline among its cadets via a high pressure environment lacking in privacy. The plaintiff sued, arguing that equal protection was violated. The defendant argued that the VMI's educational method would have to change if it admitted women and furthermore, it contributed to educational diversity within the state. Held: to prevail, the defendant must show that *its measures are substantially related* to an *important government interest* (however, the court *applied* a higher version of intermediate scrutiny, continually repeating the "exceedingly persuasive justification"). The defendant has failed to meet this burden. The state may not unilaterally deny the opportunity to attend the VMI to women simply because many women would not choose that kind of an environment. Furthermore, the women's version of VMI is not up to par.

(1) Dissent (Scalia, J.): the Court should not second guess the judgments of the trial court, which looked to the evidence in deciding that admitting women would in fact cause the VMI to change its educational approach. The Court has radically revised the standards under which gender-based classifications have historically been analyzed and has imposed its views on what should be the decision of the voters. As a result of this case, single-sex schools operated by the states are virtually *per se* unconstitutional. Traditionally, people could resolve differences in the political process. Yet this Court has undermined the political system by enshrining its views in the Constitution. The Supreme Court is imposing its own constitutional preferences on the people of Virginia.

(2) *N.B.*: although this was merely a gender discrimination case, the scrutiny applied was a hybrid between intermediate and strict scrutiny.

(f) Thus, laws that discriminate against women are subject to a high level of intermediate scrutiny.

(g) Laws that discriminate against men are subject to intermediate scrutiny.

(i) *See Michael M. v. Superior Court* (U.S. 1981), where a law that held only men to be criminally accountable to statutory rape was upheld, since (i) the consequences for women, such as pregnancy, are far harsher than those for men; and (ii) the states have an important government interest in preventing teen pregnancies.

(ii) *See also Mississippi University for Women v. Hogan* (U.S. 1982), where the Court found that an all-women nursing school operated by the state was unconstitutional because it violated the equal protection of men and reinforced stereotypes of nursing as an all-women field.

9.3.2 Illegitimacy

(a) Illegitimacy is a quasi-suspect class. Classifications based on illegitimacy are therefore subject to intermediate scrutiny: they must be substantially related to an important government interest.

(b) Such government interests include encouraging the acknowledgment of paternity and the just disposition of property upon a person's death by preventing fraudulent claims to such property.

### 9.4 Rational Basis Scrutiny

9.4.1 Sexual Orientation

(a) Sexual orientation is subject to rational basis scrutiny: the governmental classification must be rationally related to a legitimate state interest.

(b) Legislation creating classifications for its own sake will not withstand rational basis scrutiny: *some rational relationship to a legitimate state interest must exist.*

(c) A state statute that singles out and denies homosexuals state benefits simply because they are homosexuals is not rationally related to a legitimate state interest.

(i) *See Romer v. Evans* (U.S. 1996) (Kennedy, J.), where the plaintiff challenged a Colorado constitutional amendment prohibiting the adoption of protected status on or claims of discrimination by homosexuals based on their sexual orientation. Held: *when a statute neither burdens a fundamental right nor targets a suspect or quasi-suspect class, rational basis scrutiny applies.* Here, the statute has no rational relationship to a legitimate state interest. It creates a classification of homosexuals for its own sake and can only be based on animus towards homosexuals. This is not a legitimate state interest.

(ii) Dissent (Scalia, J., Rehnquist, C.J., Thomas, J.): this amendment is not about racial or religious discrimination, which is prohibited by the Constitution. Rather, it is about homosexuality, which is never mentioned in the Constitution. Resolution of this debate should be left to the people, not to this Court. This amendment is an effort by reasonable people to curb the power of a politically powerful minority.

(iii) *N.B.*: there is a difference of worldview between the majority and minority. The majority views homosexuals as a vulnerable minority like a racial minority; the dissent views homosexuality as conduct.

9.4.2 Illegal Alienage and Children of Illegal Aliens

(a) Classifications based on illegal alienage and the children of illegal aliens are subject to ***rational basis*** only.

(b) A state statute that denies illegal immigrants' children access to public schools fails rational basis.

(i) *See Plyler v. Doe* (U.S. 1982), where the Court held that a Texas statute denying illegal immigrant children access to public schools, when they did not reimburse the system, failed rational basis scrutiny: it was not rationally related to a legitimate state interest.

9.4.3 Other Classifications

(a) Other classifications that take on rational basis scrutiny include handicap, mental retardation, age, social and economic classes, poverty, state residency, and, as mentioned earlier, alienage (when Congress creates a classification or when states create a classification going to the "heart of representative democracy").

(b) However, in *City of Cleburne v. Cleburne Living Center, Inc.* (U.S. 1985), a classification based on mental retardation was held not to pass rational basis scrutiny. The Court struck down a special requirement permit for the mentally disabled, even though many would have believed that the requirement was rational.

# GUIDELINE CHART FOR DETERMINING STANDARDS OF SCRUTINY

| | STRICT SCRUTINY | INTERMEDIATE SCRUTINY | RATIONAL BASIS SCRUTINY |
|---|---|---|---|
| **Burdens:** | *The burden is on the state* to show that the challenged measure is ***necessary***[48] to protect a ***compelling state interest***. | *The burden is on the state* to show that the challenged measure is ***substantially related*** to an ***important state interest***. | *The burden is on the challenger* to show that the challenged measure is not ***rationally related*** to a ***legitimate state interest***. |
| **When the standard is used:** | *Discrimination based on* ***suspect classifications***: race[49]; national origin; alienage[50]; fundamental rights[51]; illegitimacy (sometimes). | *Discrimination based on* ***quasi-suspect classifications***: Gender (sometimes subject to a hybrid level of scrutiny between intermediate and strict scrutiny); illegitimacy (generally). | *Discrimination based on* ***all other classifications***: Homosexuality/ sexual conduct; illegal alienage and children of illegal aliens; handicap; mental retardation; age; social and economic classes; poverty; state residency; alienage.[52] |
| | ***Restrictions on express and implied fundamental rights***: First Amendment rights; interstate travel; privacy; criminal due process; voting. | ***Time, place, manner speech restrictions/ symbolic speech*** (the *O'Brien* "quasi intermediate scrutiny" test is used when the restrictions are content-neutral). | ***No fundamental rights burdened***: the right of illegal aliens to vote; the right to recreational hunting. |

[48] "Necessary" means it is a narrowly tailored means; in statutes, it is sometimes referred to as the "least restrictive means."

[49] Affirmative action is also subject to strict scrutiny.

[50] For state classifications not going to the "heart of representative democracy."

[51] When classifications are drawn that unduly burden some fundamental right.

[52] *N.B.*: alienage is subject to rational basis scrutiny when Congress creates the classification or when a state creates a classification going to the "heart of representative democracy."

## Chapter VI. Constitutional Criminal Procedure

## Pertinent Constitutional Amendments

### Fourth Amendment
### Searches and Seizures

The right of the people to be secure in their persons, houses, papers, and effects, against unreasonable searches and seizures, shall not be violated, and no Warrants shall issue, but upon probable cause, supported by Oath or affirmation, and particularly describing the place to be searched, and the persons or things to be seized.

### Fifth Amendment
### Grand Jury; Double Jeopardy; Self-Incrimination; Due Process

No person shall be held to answer for a capital, or otherwise infamous crime, unless on a presentment or indictment of a Grand Jury, except in cases arising in the land or naval forces, or in the Militia, when in actual service in time of War or public danger; nor shall any person be subject for the same offence to be twice put in jeopardy of life or limb; nor shall be compelled in any criminal case to be a witness against himself, nor be deprived of life, liberty, or property, without due process of law; nor shall private property be taken for public use, without just compensation.

### Sixth Amendment
### Speedy, Public Trial by an Impartial Jury; Right to Confront; Right to Counsel

In all criminal prosecutions, the accused shall enjoy the right to a speedy and public trial, by an impartial jury of the state and district wherein the crime shall have been committed, which district shall have been previously ascertained by law, and to be informed of the nature and cause of the accusation; to be confronted with the witnesses against him; to have compulsory process for obtaining witnesses in his favor, and to have the Assistance of Counsel for his defence.

### Eighth Amendment
### Excessive Bail or Fines; Cruel and Unusual punishment

Excessive bail shall not be required, nor excessive fines imposed, nor cruel and unusual punishments inflicted.

### Fourteenth Amendment
### Citizenship Rights

Section. 1. All persons born or naturalized in the United States and subject to the jurisdiction thereof, are citizens of the United States and of the state wherein they reside. No State shall make or enforce any law which shall abridge the privileges or immunities of citizens of the United States; nor shall any State deprive any person of life, liberty, or property, without due process of law; nor deny to any person within its jurisdiction the equal protection of the laws.

# 1 The Exclusionary Rule in Searches and Seizures

## 1.1 Individual Rights under the Constitution

1.1.1 Many of the founders did not support enumerating individual rights in the Constitution.

1.1.2 Many of them, including James Madison, the Constitution's principal author, instead supported enumerating rights in state constitutions.

1.1.3 The Bill of Rights was nonetheless included for political reasons. However, it originally applied only to the federal government—*not* to the states.

1.1.4 This was changed under the Fourteenth Amendment, which has in large part incorporated the Bill of Rights. Today, the following criminal procedural provisions have been incorporated:

(a) ***Fourth Amendment***: protection against illegal searches and seizures;

(b) ***Fifth Amendment***: right against self-incrimination; due process under the law; protection against double jeopardy;

(c) ***Sixth Amendment***: confrontation of witnesses; the right to counsel;

(d) ***Eighth Amendment***: right to be free of cruel or unusual punishment.

1.1.5 However, certain constitutional guarantees in federal court do not apply to the states, including:

(a) The right to a grand jury indictment for felonies (Fifth Amendment);

(b) The right to a jury trial in all criminal cases (Seventh Amendment).

## 1.2 The Exclusionary Rule and Other Remedies

1.2.1 The exclusionary rule requires a court to exclude evidence obtained in violation of the Constitution. *Boyd v. United States* (U.S. 1886) (the landmark exclusionary rule case).

1.2.2 The courts have long struggled with what to do with the excluded evidence. One potential solution was to return it to the defendant.

(a) *See Weeks v. United States* (U.S. 1914) (William Day, J.), where letters were seized unlawfully without a warrant. Held: in order to prevent the government from using the evidence on retrial, it should be returned.

(b) *N.B.*: this court's overbroad holding failed to take into account situations when the government seized drugs and other contraband.

1.2.3 Parties have tried to get around *Weeks* in various ways.

(a) *See Silverthorn Lumber Co. v. United States* (U.S. 1920) (Holmes, J.), where the plaintiff seized the defendant Silverthorn Lumber Co.'s originals, photocopied them, and returned them. Held: this act violates the intent of *Weeks*. The exclusionary rule applies not only to the original evidence, but also to the fruits (or in this case, copies) of the evidence.

1.2.4 Twenty nine years later, the Fourth Amendment was incorporated against the states in *Wolf v. People of the State of Colorado* (U.S. 1949) (Frankfurter, J.), since it was comprised of rights "implicit in the concept of ordered liberty."

1.2.5 However, the ***exclusionary rule*** was not incorporated against the states until *Mapp v. Ohio* (U.S. 1961) (Clark, J.), where police entered the defendant's home without a search warrant and found obscene materials that they used to convict her. Thus, in 1961 there came a bright line rule: the Fourth Amendment applied to the states through the Fourteenth Amendment. From that moment onward, if state law enforcement violated the defendant's constitutional rights, the judicially created exclusionary applied as a sanction, just as it would had the violation been at the hands of federal law enforcement.

**1.3 Limitations on the Exclusionary Rule**

1.3.1 The exclusionary rule does *not exclude all illegally obtained* evidence *for all purposes*.

1.3.2 Such illegally obtained evidence may be used, for example, to impeach the defendant if he testifies contrary to the excluded evidence.

1.3.3 The exclusionary rule applies to the person on trial, but if someone else's constitutional rights have been violated, the person on trial has no standing to exclude it.

1.3.4 In recent years, the Court has been limiting the scope of the exclusionary rule, holding that it acts to exclude evidence obtained *through* ***police misconduct only,*** not through the errors of others (*e.g.*, a magistrate who erroneously grants a warrant). *U.S. v. Leon* (U.S. 1984) (White, J.).

(a) Rationale: excluding evidence *when another party errs* will not have a deterrent effect on the police. *U.S. v. Leon* (U.S. 1984) (White, J.).

(b) The *"good faith" exception* to the exclusionary rule allows evidence to be admitted when police, acting with good faith, reasonably rely on the validity of a warrant, even if the warrant is invalid.

1.3.5 The Fourth Amendment is designed to protect citizens from illegal government searches. Thus, information obtained by a ***search conducted by a private or corporate person is admissible*** and does not need to be excluded when used by the government for prosecution (unless the person conducting the search is an agent of the government).

(a) *See Jacobsen*, where the Drug Enforcement Agency was permitted to use evidence obtained from FedEx, which broke open packages to be mailed, discovered cocaine, and turned them over to the government.

1.3.6 Traditionally, grand juries have been able to function without all of the same limits as those placed in trials.

(a) In *United States v. Calandra* (U.S. 1974) (Powell, J.), the Court limited the application of the exclusionary rule so as not to "seriously impede the grand jury."

(b) Illegally obtained evidence is thus admissible in grand jury proceedings.

1.3.7 The exclusionary rule applies only to criminal cases. In civil cases, the exclusionary rule does not apply because no liberty interest is jeopardized.

### 1.4 Technological Surveillance

1.4.1 Searches from the outside of a person's home using ***technological devices that are outside of ordinary public use*** are presumed to be unreasonable searches requiring a warrant under the Fourth Amendment.

(a) *See Kyllo v. United States* (U.S. 2001) (Scalia, J.), where the Court excluded evidence obtained with a thermal imaging device from a helicopter that showed that the defendant had been using heat lamps for growing marijuana plants in his home. Because the apparatus was not within the ordinary public use, the defendant had a reasonable expectation of privacy that was violated.

1.4.2 This rule does not extend to drug-sniffing canines.

(a) *See Illinois v. Caballes* (U.S. 2005) (Stevens, J.), where a narcotics dog sniffed drugs in the trunk of the defendant, who was stopped by a trooper. The defendant argued that just as evidence obtained with the heat imaging device was excluded, so too should the drugs be excluded. Held: the analogy cannot be drawn. Here, the only information that could be obtained is incriminating. A heat imaging device could, on the other hand, invade legitimate privacy rights, such as the hour that a resident enters her sauna.

### 1.5 "Fruit of the Poisonous Tree" and Purging the Taint

1.5.1 When police effect an illegal search or seizure, both illegally obtained primary evidence as well as all derivative evidence, including verbal statements, is to be excluded at trial as *"tainted fruit of the poisonous tree." Wong Sun v. United States* (U.S. 1963) (Brennan, J.).

1.5.2 However, the taint may be ***purged*** through the following:

(a) Inevitable Discovery

(i) If police can show that the evidence was to be inevitably discovered, it is admissible in trial.

(ii) *See Nix v. Williams* (U.S. 1984) (Warren Burger, C.J.), where a suspect was arrested by police when a ten year old girl went missing. In order to elicit an incriminating response from the defendant, a police officer said to another officer in the presence of the defendant that the least he could do is offer the girl's family a "Christian burial." The defendant then led the officers to the body of the victim, thus incriminating himself. However, although the defendant's constitutional rights were violated, the evidence was not excluded, since it was going to be inevitably discovered by independent sources in a matter of time.

(b) Intervening Voluntary Conduct

(i) Intervening voluntary conduct, such as a voluntary, subsequent confession by the defendant, purges the tainted fruit of the poisonous tree.

(ii) *See Wong Sun v. United States* (U.S. 1963) (Brennan, J.), where an unlawful arrest resulted in both a confession (primary evidence) and a witness lead (derivative evidence). The Court excluded both. Held: since the heroin would not have been seized but for the unlawful questioning of Toy, it is excluded. However, Sun's testimony is admissible because it has no connection to the arrest. Rather, it was voluntarily made.

**1.6 The Exclusionary Rule Applied to Fifth Amendment Violations**

1.6.1 If a party is unlawfully arrested or detained, the testimony obtained is ***automatically inadmissible*** if the party's *Miranda* rights are not read.

1.6.2 Yet reading the *Miranda* rights on its own is not sufficient to make the confession admissible.

1.6.3 Under *Brown v. Illinois* (U.S. 1975) (Blackmun, J.), the following factors are to be considered when determining whether the confession is admissible:

(a) The *presence of intervening events*;

(b) The *flagrancy of the police misconduct*; and

(c) The *amount of time elapsed* between the illegal act and the confession.

(i) Six hours is too little time to purge the taint of the confession. *Taylor v. Alabama* (U.S. 1982) (Marshall, J.).

1.6.4 The Court affirmed *Brown v. Illinois* in *Dunaway v. New York* (U.S. 1979) (Brennan, J.). Because the confession could not be separated from the initial illegality, it was excluded.

**1.7 Standing and Scope of the Fourth Amendment**

1.7.1 Traditional Rule: Standing Requires a Possessory Interest

(a) In *Olmstead v. United States* (U.S. 1928) (Taft, C.J.), the Court held that the Fourth Amendment did not apply to a *wiretap* on a telephone pole outside of the defendant's home, since the defendant ***did not have a possessory interest*** in the pole and conversations were not protected by the Fourth Amendment.

(b) Under the law as it existed shortly after WWII, the only way to make a motion to exclude evidence would be to admit ownership.

(c) This led to problems when the evidence was contraband. If the defendant admitted ownership, he would incriminate himself; but if he did not admit ownership, he would lack standing to challenge admission of the evidence.

(d) Thus, in *Jones v. United States* (U.S. 1960) (Frankfurter, J.), the Court resolved this problem by granting defendants ***automatic standing***. Without needing to admit ownership of contraband, defendants could challenge the admission of such contraband into evidence.

1.7.2 Modern Rule: Standing Requires a Reasonable Expectation of Privacy

(a) *Olmstead* (U.S. 1928) was later overruled, with a new rule pronounced in *Katz v. United States* (U.S. 1967) (Stewart, J.). Even if a defendant lacks a proprietary interest in a telephone booth, a wiretap infringes on a ***reasonable expectation of privacy*** that therefore requires that police obtain a search warrant.

(b) The reasonable expectation of privacy standard involves a two-prong test:

(i) Does the defendant assert a ***subjective interest*** in privacy?

(ii) If so, is ***society prepared to accept*** that subjective privacy expectation as an area that is private?

(c) *Rakas v. Illinois* (U.S. 1978) (Rehnquist, J.) modified *Jones*, holding that the *Jones* "legitimately on premises" test was overbroad. Just because the defendant is legitimately on the premises does not mean that he has standing to challenge the search or seizure.

(i) The new test is whether the defendant has a ***reasonable expectation of privacy*** based on *Katz v. United States* (U.S. 1967). The defendant ***has the burden of establishing both prongs.***

(ii) *The defendant* has standing to challenge evidence if he owns or has a right to possess the place or thing searched. A car passenger therefore has no standing to challenge a search of that car.

(d) Because Fourth Amendment rights are personal, a party may not demand that evidence be excluded when that party was not the direct victim of a constitutional violation. *United States v. Payner* (U.S. 1980).

(e) Ownership of items on its own does not give rise to standing to challenge a Fourth Amendment search or seizure.

(i) *See Rawlings v. Kentucky* (U.S. 1980) (Rehnquist), where the court did not apply the exclusionary rule against drugs seized from the defendant's companion's purse, because the defendant did not have a ***reasonable expectation of privacy*** *in the purse.*

### 1.8 Curtilage

1.8.1 Individuals have a reasonable expectation of privacy in their homes.

1.8.2 This privacy expectation encompasses the curtilage—the *dwelling* and *all buildings and property immediately surrounding it. Oliver v. United States* (U.S. 1984).

1.8.3 The privacy expectation does *not extend to distant fields* on the property. *Hester v. United States* (U.S. 1924).

1.8.4 The government must therefore have a warrant to search the dwelling and the curtilage, but not to the distant property outside of the curtilage. *Oliver v. United States* (U.S. 1984).

### 1.9 Arrest

1.9.1 Defining an Arrest

(a) An arrest occurs when a person is taken into custody for the purpose of a criminal action. *Dunaway v. New York* (U.S. 1979).

(b) Under *Henry v. United States* (U.S. 1959) (Douglas, J.), it is more precisely the ***restriction of movement*** of citizens by the police.

(c) In *California v. Hodari D.* (U.S. 1991) (Scalia, J.), the Court modified the definition pronounced in *Henry*: one is arrested if his movement is restricted when he: (i) is *touched*; (ii) is taken into the *physical custody* of the officer; or (iii) *submits to the authority* of the officer.

(i) *See California v. Hodari D.* (U.S. 1991), where a youth took note of police officers, panicked, and fled and the officers chased after him. While he was fleeing, the youth threw down a rock of crack cocaine, which was later seized by an officer. The defendant moved to suppress the crack cocaine as an illegal seizure. Held on *certiorari*: the defendant was not arrested at the time he fled and by extension, at the time the officer found the crack cocaine. Therefore, there was no illegal seizure. Judgment reversed.

1.9.2 Constitutional Requirements

(a) The Fourth Amendment requires that searches and seizures must be reasonable. An arrest, which is a "seizure" of a person, must fall into one of the following categories to be reasonable:

(i) Made with an ***arrest warrant*** (which is based on probable cause)*;* or

(ii) Based on ***probable cause*** *to arrest.*

(1) This is determined based on an ***objective standard.***

(2) *See Maryland v. Pringle* (U.S. 2003) (Rehnquist), where police stopped a car for speeding and received consent to search it and found cocaine. The lower court ruled that the defendant's being a front seat passenger of the car that held the cocaine was *insufficient probable cause to warrant an arrest*. On appeal, the Supreme Court (Rehnquist, J.) held that probable cause equates ***reasonable grounds*** *to believe someone is guilty*. In this case, there is sufficient probable cause that *someone* committed a crime.

1.9.3 Arrest Warrants

(a) Absent *exigent circumstances*, police must have a warrant to enter a defendant's home to arrest him. *Payton v. New York* (U.S. 1980) (Stevens, J.).

(b) Once an arrest warrant is issued, police have the implicit right to enter into the defendant's home to search for him.

(c) However, police with an arrest warrant do not have the implicit right to enter into the home of ***third parties*** to search for the defendant identified on the warrant. *Steagald v. United States* (U.S. 1981) (Marshall).

(d) Arrest warrants are *not required for felonies*.

## 2 Obtaining, Challenging, and Executing Search Warrants

### 2.1 Introduction

2.1.1 This section deals specifically with search warrants.

2.1.2 However, many of the requirements parallel those that apply to arrest warrants, which require:

(a) Probable cause;

(b) Support by oath or affirmation;

(c) A description with particularity of the person to be arrested; and

(d) Issuance by a neutral and detached magistrate.

2.1.3 Many of the rules articuled below are applicable to arrest warrants by analogy.

**2.2 The Requirements of a Valid Warrant**

2.2.1 Probable Cause

(a) Probable cause exists if, based on the facts presented to the magistrate, a reasonable person would conclude that *more likely than not*, contraband or other evidence will be at the place to be searched ***at the time the warrant is executed.***

(b) This may be at a ***future time;*** anticipatory warrants are constitutional.

(i) *See United States v. Grubbs* (U.S. 2006) (Scalia, J.), where a magistrate issued an anticipatory warrant to police who sought to intercept child pornography at a future delivery that, according to their sources, was to occur. The defendant moved to suppress because no crime was in progress when the warrant was issued. The Court held that probable cause may exist when evidence shows that a crime ***will take place***.

(c) However, probable cause dissipates when the facts presented to the magistrate are ***too remote in time.***

2.2.2 Supported by Oath or Affirmation

(a) The Fourth Amendment requires the warrant to be "supported by Oath or affirmation."

2.2.3 Particularity

(a) The warrant must describe *with specificity* the place to be searched and the persons or things to be seized.

(b) *See Groh v. Ramirez* (U.S. 2004) (Stevens, J.), where the Fourth Amendment was violated because the affidavit and warrant stated with particularity only what was to be searched, not what was to be seized.

2.2.4 A Neutral and Detached Magistrate

(a) A ***search warrant*** must be issued by a neutral and detached magistrate.

(b) A justice of the peace who is a state attorney would not qualify.

(i) *See Coolidge v. New Hampshire* (U.S. 1971) (Potter, J.), where a search warrant issued by a prosecutor failed because it was issued not by a neutral and detached magistrate of the Judicial Branch, but rather, by an Executive Branch official.

(c) The warrant itself must give a particular description of the things to be seized. The description may not be granted *after* the things are seized.

(i) *See Lo-Ji Sales Inc. v. New York* (U.S. 1979) (Burger, C.J.), where a warrant describing obscene materials *after they were seized* from an adult bookstore was deemed invalid.

**2.3 Probable Cause with Respect to Anonymous Informants**

2.3.1 An anonymous informant is known by the police, but not by the magistrate or the defense.

2.3.2 In the earlier days of the Court, no fixed rule was given on whether the identity of anonymous informants used in police affidavits needed to be revealed.

(a) In *Roviaro v. United States* (U.S. 1957) (Burton, J.), the defendant was convicted for possessing and transporting heroine across state lines. When the defendant attacked the evidence of an anonymous informant who he wanted disclosed, the Court applied a balancing test between the defendant's need of the information for his defense and the plaintiff's desire to protect the health, welfare, and safety of the informant.

2.3.3 In *Aguilar v. Texas* (U.S. 1964) (Goldberg, J.), the Court required magistrates to apply the following two-prong test on affidavits before issuing warrants:

(a) The Basis of Knowledge Prong

(i) There must be sufficient information showing how the informant arrived at his conclusions.

(ii) The magistrate may consider, for example, whether the informant was an eyewitness or whether his source is hearsay.

(b) The Veracity Prong

(i) Sufficient indicia must establish the informant's reliability. An undercover police officer, for example, would pass.

(ii) The affiant should also include whether the anonymous informant had been used in the past and if so, whether he was reliable.

2.3.4 Later, the ***Aguilar-Spinelli test*** was developed.

(a) In *Spinelli v. United States* (U.S. 1969), Justice Harlan fleshed out the first prong, resulting in the *Aguilar-Spinelli* test, applying *only to anonymous informants*.

(b) According to this test, insufficient knowledge on the part of the informant may be overcome if the informant gives *enough detail to show that he is not just engaging in gossip*.

2.3.5 This test was followed until 1983, when the much laxer ***totality of the circumstances*** standard was established by the Supreme Court.

(a) In *Illinois v. Gates* (U.S. 1983) (Rehnquist, C.J.), the Court held that probable cause should not be based on the two-prong test, but rather, on what a person's ***common sense would dictate to be probable cause*** (a "more likely than not" reasonable basis for belief) based on the totality of the circumstances. Corroboration from other sources and the informant's reliability are among the factors to be considered.

(i) *N.B.*: this case is the *majority rule*, which offers police a lower standard for their affidavits.

(ii) *N.B.*: probable cause based on the "totality of the circumstances" requires the alleged occurrence not to have taken place too remotely in the past. Otherwise, there will be no probable cause to justify that the evidence will still be present.

(iii) *N.B.*: although this case states the constitutional minimum, some states, wishing to grant the defendants greater protection, continue to use the *Aguilar-Spinelli test*, which remains the *minority rule* in 8 states.

### 2.4 Challenging the Warrant: the Four Corners Rule

2.4.1 In evaluating whether a warrant was supported by probable cause, the appeals court is limited to looking at *only the information* contained in the affidavit and warrant.

2.4.2 What was said to the magistrate is irrelevant if it was not in writing. *Franks v. Delaware* (U.S. 1978) (Blackmun, J.).

2.4.3 If the affidavit and warrant together do not give sufficient facts to form probable cause, the warrant is invalid.

2.4.4 Information given to the magistrate that is ***deliberately false*** or that ***recklessly disregards the truth*** voids the warrant.

2.4.5 The defendant has the burden of overcoming by a preponderance of the evidence a presumption that the warrant is valid.

### 2.5 Executing the Warrant

2.5.1 Time of Execution

(a) The Constitution requires execution of the warrant within reasonable time under the circumstances.

(b) Some states have statutes limiting this period even further, with some requiring execution in as little as ten days.

2.5.2 Notice

(a) Traditionally, police officers were not required to knock on the door and announce their presence.

(b) However, after *Wilson v. Arkansas* (U.S. 1995), a "reasonableness standard" requiring police to knock, identity themselves, and give a copy of the search warrant was imposed.

(i) However, the exclusionary rule does not apply to a knock and announce violation.

(ii) *See Hudson v. Michigan* (U.S. 2006), where the court held that although *Wilson* is still good law, the knock and announce provision is not required by the constitution. Other remedies are available, such as suing the police for damages.

(c) Police may apply for a ***no-knock warrant*** if they state, for example, that there is a high risk of danger or that the evidence may be destroyed if they knock and announce their presence.

2.5.3 Scope of the Search

(a) A warrant to search the house includes the right to search all of the curtilage (the dwelling and all buildings and property immediately surrounding it).

(b) If, while searching for something inside of a house, there are other people present, it is reasonable to segregate them for just long enough to ascertain their involvement in the potential crime and to prevent any interference with the search.

(c) Upon conclusion of the search, they may be arrested or let go.

## 3 Exceptions to the Invalidity of Warrantless Searches and Seizures

3.1.1 Under *Illinois v. Gates* (U.S. 1983), a search warrant is generally required and searches realized without a warrant are presumed to be invalid. *Mincey v. Arizona* (U.S. 1978).

3.1.2 However, as we will examine in this section, there are several notable exceptions to these general rules.

### 3.2 Search Incident to Lawful Arrest

3.2.1 If the defendant is already being arrested, *no additional search warrant is necessary*.

3.2.2 Under *Weeks v. United States* (U.S. 1914) (Day, J.), the probable cause for the arrest is imported as probable for the search; separate probable cause is not necessary.

3.2.3 If the arrest is invalid, then so too is the search, since both are based on the same probable cause.

3.2.4 There are two reasons justifying a search:

(a) The *officer's protection*; and

(b) To *secure evidence* before it is destroyed.

3.2.5 Under these circumstances, the officer does not need to actually fear for his safety or have any reasonable suspicion that illegal materials will be found; once a lawful arrest is effected, a search is permitted.

3.2.6 Police may search the ***arrestee's person*** and the area within his ***immediate control***.

(a) The rationale is to prevent the destruction of evidence within the defendant's ***"wingspan."***

(b) *See Chimel v. California* (U.S. 1969) (Stewart, J.), where a warrantless search of the defendant's entire house after his arrest was held unconstitutional. The permitted scope of a search incident to lawful arrest is the area under the defendant's immediate control, known as the ***"Chimel Perimeter."***

3.2.7 However, *when police have reasonable suspicion* and they arrest the defendant in his home for a violent crime, they may search his entire home. *Maryland v. Buie* (U.S. 1990).

3.2.8 If police arrest a criminal for one offense, and in the course of a search incident to lawful arrest, they find evidence of a separate, unrelated crime, that evidence is admissible. *United States v. Robinson* (U.S. 1973) (Rehnquist, J.) (heroin was recovered while an officer searched a man who was arrested for a traffic violation).

3.2.9 However, searches incident to lawful arrest apply *only when the defendant is arrested.* Police may not search the defendants during mere traffic stops.

(a) *See Knowles v. Iowa* (U.S. 1998) (Rehnquist), where the officer stopped the defendant, issued a summons, and sent him on his way. A search was not permitted because there was no full-blown arrest.

**3.3 The Carroll Doctrine/Automobile Exception**

3.3.1 A separate exception allowing for warrantless searches applies only to automobiles and other mobile vehicles (planes, boats, etc.).

3.3.2 Since these vehicles are mobile, requiring police to obtain a warrant before searching them gives rise to the risk that the evidence, along with the vehicles, will disappear.

3.3.3 This exception applies, even if there has been no arrest, when police have ***probable cause*** to believe a crime is being committed.

(a) *See Carroll v. United States* (U.S. 1925) (Taft, C.J.), where police were permitted to search the trunk of a car of a known bootlegger when they noticed the car heavily laden.

(b) *N.B.*: this case is the beginning of the ***exigent circumstances doctrine***.

3.3.4 After an automobile is seized, police are not required to obtain a search warrant, since they could have searched it at the time it was stopped.

3.3.5 This doctrine is justified by the fact that (i) cars and other mobile vehicles are primarily means of transportation; (ii) they are driven in plain view; and (iii) they are subject to heavy regulation. *Chambers v. Maroney* (U.S. 1970) (White, J.).

3.3.6 However, this rationale does not apply to closed objects, such as footlockers or trunks found within the car, since they are *not within plain view* and since they are intended for the *storage of personal effects.*

(a) Furthermore, since police may seize the objects before applying for a search warrant, the exigent circumstances inherent in automobiles does not apply.

(b) *See United States v. Chadwick* (U.S. 1977) (Burger, C.J.), where the Court excluded evidence obtained from a footlocker seized from a vehicle that was opened without a search warrant.

3.3.7 Although *Chadwick* gives heightened protection to suitcases and personal luggage, this protection does not apply to *containers* or *canisters* found inside the car when there is probable cause to warrant a search.

3.3.8 When police have probable cause to stop a car, they ***may search the entire car*** until they find the object of the probable cause. *United States v. Ross* (U.S. 1982) (Stevens, J.) (permitting police to search a film canister found in a vehicle, although they did not have a warrant).

### 3.4 Hot Pursuit

3.4.1 When pursuing a dangerous suspect and *time is of the essence*, police may conduct warrantless searches.

(a) *See* Warden v. Hayden (U.S. 1967) (Brennan, J.), where police were informed that the defendant Hayden had entered a house after a crime was committed. The police entered the house, searched it, and found clothing in the washing machine matching the description of the suspect. The defendant challenged the admission of the evidence, since it was obtained without a warrant. Held: because speed was essential, the warrantless search was justified. The Fourth Amendment is about reasonableness; it does not require police to obtain a warrant when doing so would allow the defendant to escape.

3.4.2 Hot pursuit justifies entry when:

(a) There is ***probable cause*** (always necessary for searches and seizures);

(b) Under ***exigent circumstances*** justifying the warrantless search;

(c) The pursuit begins from a place where the police have ***a lawful right to be;*** and

(d) The legal violation is ***serious*** enough to justify a warrantless search.

### 3.5 The Emergency Doctrine

3.5.1 In emergency situations, police are not required to obtain a warrant.

(a) *See Michigan v. Tyler* (U.S. 1978) (Stewart, J.), where a fire chief and detective discovered flammable liquid in plastic bags while the fire department responded to a fire in a department store. They went back shortly thereafter, while the fire was still being fought, and collected more evidence. Three weeks later, investigators again went of the scene of the crime. Held: no search warrant was necessary during the first two investigations because there was an emergency and the fire department was lawfully on the premises. However, the third investigation was unlawful because it took place three weeks after the emergency.

3.5.2 The emergency doctrine does not permit police to collect evidence of the crime scene if they do not obtain a warrant.

(a) In *Mincey v. Arizona* (U.S. 1978) (Stewart, J.), the Court struck down an Arizona statute that allowed police to conduct investigations at crime scenes without a warrant. Held: the statute is unconstitutional; there is ***no crime-scene exception.*** If police have probable cause, they must obtain a search warrant. If they do not have probable cause, they need consent.

### 3.6 Exigent Circumstances

3.6.1 The exigent circumstances exception arises when:

(a) Police have ***probable cause*** that a crime has been committed; and

(b) Absent immediate action, the evidence would be ***lost***.

(i) Standard: whether a reasonable person would expect the police to stop and obtain a warrant.

3.6.2 Body Searches

(a) If a defendant ingests drugs, the evidence of a crime, police may not ***pump his stomach***, not because of a Fourth Amendment prohibition, but rather, because Fourteenth Amendment Due Process would be offended. *Rochin v. California* (U.S. 1952) (Frankfurter, J.).

(b) ***Blood tests***, on the contrary, are not prohibited by the Fourteenth Amendment, since they are so commonplace that they do not offend ordinary sensibilities. *Breithaupt v. Abram* (U.S. 1957) (Clark, J.).

(c) Any body search, including blood samples and DNA tests, must meet the following three prong test:

(i) There is a ***"clear indication"*** that the search will result in the evidence being sought;

(ii) ***Exigent circumstances*** prevent the obtention of a warrant (*e.g.*, drugs in the blood will disappear); and

(iii) The search is done in a reasonable manner. *Schmerber v. California* (U.S. 1966) (Brennan, J.).

3.6.3 Border Searches and Airport Security Searches

(a) The Fourth Amendment applies only to searches and seizures *within the United States*. At the borders, with a reasonable suspicion on its own, a suspect may be detained and searched. Since the government has an interest in regulating who comes into the country, a search warrant is not necessary. *United States v. Montoya de Hernandez* (U.S. 1985) (Rehnquist, J.).

(b) Justification of this doctrine: at the borders, people have less expectation of privacy, there are exigent circumstances, and there is implied consent.

(c) Landlocked cities that have international flights landing in them, as well as cities with international shipping ports, are considered "borders" for the application of this rule.

3.6.4 Summary of Exigent Circumstances Exception

(a) There must be reason to believe (generally, probable cause, but in the case of border searches, a reasonable suspicion is sufficient) that an immediate search is necessary to prevent evidence from disappearing;

(b) The search is otherwise reasonable. For bodily intrusions, this means:

(i) The procedure is effective in obtaining the required evidence;

(ii) It does not cause significant pain or trauma; and

(iii) The medical procedures followed are appropriate and necessary.

### 3.7 Plain View Exception

3.7.1 The plain view doctrine is an exception to the rule that a warrant is necessary to effect *only a seizure* (this exception does not apply to warrantly searches).

3.7.2 Police may seize an object under the plain view doctrine when the following three elements are met:

(a) The object is in ***plain view***;

(b) The probable cause must be ***immediately apparent*** without the need for a further search.

(i) *See Arizona v. Hicks* (U.S. 1987) (Scalia, J.), where police, while investigating an apartment where gunshots went off, noticed a new radio that stood out from the squalor. Picking it up to obtain its serial number, they developed probable cause as to its being stolen. Held: the evidence of the stolen radio is inadmissible, since the probable cause was not immediately apparent, but rather, required that the radio first be manipulated. "No search no matter how cursory is allowed under the Fourth Amendment to determine whether probable cause exists."

(c) The police must be ***in a place where they have a lawful right to be*** (*e.g.*, they may not be trespassers);

(i) An object is always in plain view from some vantage point; the question is whether it is in plain view from a place where police may lawfully be.

(1) In *Coolidge v. New Hampshire* (U.S. 1971) (Stewart, J.) (the source of the "neutral and detached magistrate" rule), police were unable to rely on a warrant because it was issued by the state's attorney general (chief prosecutor). Thus, in order to admit incriminating evidence found in the vehicle, the police needed an exception to the warrant requirement. Because the car was parked, the *Carroll* doctrine did not apply. The State therefore argued the plain view doctrine: the car was in plain view from the public street. The Court rejected this argument, since the police were not in a place where they had lawful right to be.

(ii) Mere Pretext Doctrine

(1) Evidence in plain view is admissible even if a stop for one legal violation was a *mere pretext* to stop and search the defendant for other violations.

(2) *See Whren v. United States* (U.S. 1996) (Scalia, J.), where police, based on traffic law violations, stopped a defendant drug dealer and observed contraband in plain view. The defendants claimed that the stop was only a pretext to search if the defendant had drugs on him, but the Court admitted the evidence.

(3) Exceptions to the pretext doctrine:

(aa) When the pretext is based on race or other protected classes;

(bb) When there is no probable cause to stop the vehicle or no other basis; and (cc) Where the individual may be harmed (this would not occur in a traffic violation).

### 3.8 Frisk after Terry Stop

3.8.1 A person is arrested if his movement is restricted when he: (i) is *touched*; (ii) is taken into the *physical custody* of the officer; or (iii) *submits to the authority* of the officer. *California v. Hodari D.* (U.S. 1991).

3.8.2 A stop is a ***brief detention for questioning;*** it is somewhere between an encounter and an arrest. *Terry v. Ohio* (U.S. 1968).

3.8.3 To effect a stop, police do not need reasonable cause; all they require is a ***"reasonable suspicion"*** that "criminal activity is afoot."

(a) *See Terry v. Ohio* (U.S. 1968) (Warren, C.J.), where a police officer noticed three men acting suspiciously outside of a jewelry store at 3 a.m. He encountered them and asked them questions, but they did not respond. He patted them down and found two weapons. A conviction followed and the defendant attacked the stop and frisk on the grounds that there had been an arrest (restriction of movement), but ***no probable cause*** (no crime was committed). Held: a stop is to be distinguished from a full-blown arrest; probable cause is required for arrests, but is no longer required for stops, which are valid if there is a *reasonable suspicion* that criminal activity has happened, is happening, or will happen. The officer must *detain the suspect briefly for the purpose of investigation*.

3.8.4 If, after the stop, the police officer has a ***reasonable suspicion*** that the suspect is in ***possession of a weapon***, the officer ***may conduct a frisk*** of the suspect. This is limited to ***patting down the outer clothing*** to find a concealed weapon in order to provide for the protection of the police officer.

3.8.5 Under the ***plain feel doctrine,*** if, during the frisk, the officer feels something that he believes to be contraband, this may become independent probable cause for conducting a search.

3.8.6 The post-*Terry* categories of police-citizen contacts can be summarized as follow:

(a) Arrest and search incident to a lawful arrest (requiring probable cause);

(b) Stop and frisk limited to a search for weapons (requiring a reasonable suspicion); and

(c) Encounters, in which the defendant feels that he has the liberty to leave (determined by the totality of the circumstances). *United States v. Mendenhall* (U.S. 1980) (Stewart, J.).

3.8.7 Automobile Stop and Frisk

(a) Reasonable suspicion also permits a stop and frisk of the driver of a car. *Pennsylvania v. Mimms* (U.S. 1977). It is reasonable to demand that he exit and be subject to a frisk.

(b) If there is reasonable suspicion that other ***passengers*** are armed, they too may be frisked. *Maryland v. Wilson* (U.S. 1997).

### 3.9 Consent

3.9.1 One's Fourth Amendment privacy right may be fully or partially waived, regardless of whether the party waiving the right knows that he has a right to refuse to do so. *Schneckloth v. Bustamonte* (U.S. 1973) (Stewart, J.).

3.9.2 The consent may be revoked at any time.

3.9.3 If unrestricted consent is given to a police officer to search a house or a car, then the police officer has the right to search the entire house.

(a) However, even when an owner consents to a search without limitations, police are only permitted to search places where they could ***reasonably find*** the object sought. *Florida v. Jimeno* (U.S. 1991) (Rehnquist, C.J.).

(b) This means that ***police may only search where the object is likely to be found*** (*e.g.*, they may not pry open a jewelry box to find a sterio). Police may also manipulate objects.

(c) The scope of the search is limited to where a reasonable person would expect police to search.

3.9.4 The consent must be ***voluntary***.

(a) Courts are to look to the *totality of the circumstances* in determining whether consent was voluntary.

(b) The fact that the defendants who consented to a search were minorities does not on its own indicate that consent was coerced. *United States v. Mendenhall United States v. Mendenhall* (U.S. 1980) (Stewart, J.) (rejecting an exception based on race).

3.9.5 Third Party Consent

(a) If police enter a jointly occupied dwelling, either resident may consent to the police's search of any part of the dwelling where the other resident has no *Katz* reasonable expectation of privacy (*e.g.*, the common areas, a shared bedroom, etc.).

(i) The key to this consent is ***apparent authority*****:** police may rely on the consent of a third party who has apparent authority to consent to the search.

(ii) If police act reasonably in their belief that the party had authority to consent, the exclusionary rule will not apply, even if the police's judgment was erroneous.

(b) However, if either resident occupies his own separate bedroom or living space, his privacy to that space may not be waived by another resident, since he has a continued *Katz* reasonable expectation of privacy.

(c) Furthermore, if one resident consents to a search of the house, but another resident who is also physically present and who has an equal expectation of privacy objects to the search, police are not permitted to conduct the search. *Randolph v. Georgia* (U.S. 2006) (Souter, J.).

### 3.10 Regulatory Searches

3.10.1 Traditionally, it was thought that the Fourth Amendment applied only to criminal searches and seizures.

3.10.2 However, *Camara v. Municipal Court* (U.S. 1967) (White, J.) established that regulatory inspections, such as inspections for housing code violations, were also within the scope of the Fourth Amendment

3.10.3 Thus, regulatory searches also require warrants, but unlike criminal search warrants, regulatory search warrants do not require ***probable cause***, since it is impractical to expect the government to support an affidavit with probable cause, which usually only arises *after the warrant is issued* and the government is permitted to inspect the premises.

(a) *N.B.*: if there are exigent circumstances, no regulatory warrant is necessary.

3.10.4 Thus, although the regulatory purpose exception requires a warrant, it does not require probable cause to obtain the warrant.

**3.11 Special Needs Situations**

3.11.1 In the following situations, special needs justify not having to obtain a warrant.

3.11.2 Public Schools

(a) Because of the *special need* of keeping students safe in public schools, officials require neither a warrant nor probable cause to effect a search or seizure.

(b) *See New Jersey v. T.L.O.* (U.S. 1985) (White, J.), where the Court upheld the rights of public school officials to search students with neither warrants nor probable cause. Mere suspicion was sufficient. The Court drew a distinction between police officers and school officials, and held that the latter are not held to the same standards as the former, given the ***need to maintain the safety of the school environment***. Furthermore, when an educator suspects a student of possessing contraband, time is of the essence and it is not practical to expect the school official to obtain a warrant.

3.11.3 Parolees and Probationers

(a) Police may conduct unannounced searches and seizures of parolees (Executive Branch) and probationers (Judicial Branch) as a condition of their release.

(b) Parolees and probationers have a lessened expectation of privacy, since their freedom is conditional.

3.11.4 Drug Testing of Government Employees and Officials

(a) These drug tests may be conducted absent a warrant because of the special need of assuring society that its law enforcement and public officials are drug-free.

**3.12 Community Caretaker/Inventory Search**

3.12.1 This exception is different from other exceptions to the requirement for a warrant in that it is based not on a law enforcement purpose, but rather, on community care: the purpose is to protect the community.

(a) *See Cady v. Dombrowski* (U.S. 1973) (Rehnquist, C.J.), where police officers arrested the defendant, a corrupt Chicago cop, and towed his car to a private garage. When they later realized that his gun was likely in the car, they went to remove it and in the process, discovered incriminating evidence. Held: the evidence is admissible even though police did not have probable cause to search the car: care of the community permits officers to assure that guns are not left in unattended vehicles.

3.12.2 Once legally in their possession, police may inventory all effects without a search warrant.

(a) In *South Dakota v. Opperman* (U.S. 1976) (Burger, C.J.), the court extended the right to search impounded vehicles, regardless of whether dangerous objects were suspected to be in the car, in order to: (i) protect the belongings of the defendant from theft; and (ii) to protect police from liability accusations that the defendant's property was stolen.

### 3.13 Search and Seizure Analysis Sumary

3.13.1 When analyzing search and seizure questions, first ask if there was a search or seizure.

3.13.2 If there was, apply the following analysis:

(a) Does the Fourth Amendment apply (was the search/seizure unreasonable?)?

(b) Was a warrant necessary?

(c) If so, was there a search or seizure/arrest warrant?

(d) Was there probable cause?

(e) Was the warrant valid?

(f) Was the scope of the warrant exceeded?

(g) Did an exception to the warrant/probable cause requirements apply? (Search incident to lawful arrest; Carroll Doctrine/automobile exception; plain view; Frisk after *Terry* stop; consent; regulatory purpose).

(h) If not complied with, what is the remedy?

## 4 The Fifth Amendment Double Jeopardy Clause

### 4.1 Introduction

4.1.1 The Fifth Amendment requires that no person "be subject for the same offence to be twice put in jeopardy of life or limb."

4.1.2 Major issues surrounding the Double Jeopardy Clause include the following:

(a) Does it apply to only some or all criminal offenses?

(b) Does it apply only in the trial or also in the appeal?

(c) What if there is a guilty plea and there is no trial?

4.1.3 Under the common law, if a defendant has been acquitted or convicted of a crime, he cannot be retried. These principles are referred to as ***autre fois conviction*** and ***autre fois acquittal***, respectively.

4.1.4 Since *autre fois conviction* and *autre fois acquittal* were already prohibited under the common law, Madison believed that the Double Jeopardy Clause was unnecessary.

4.1.5 Today, however, the Double Jeopardy Clause also prevents the defendant from being *punished for the same offense* more than once.

4.1.6 The Double Jeopardy Clause applies to both the federal government and to the states through the Fourteenth Amendment Due Process Clause. *Benton v. Maryland* (U.S. 1969) (Marshall, J.).

**4.2 When Jeopardy Attaches**

4.2.1 Jeopardy attaches when the trial begins—which is when the ***jury is impaneled, takes the oath, and is sworn in***. *Crist v. Betz* (U.S. 1978) (Stewart, J.).

4.2.2 However, at a bench trial with no jury, jeopardy attaches when the first witness is ***sworn in*** and ***testifies***.

4.2.3 Anytime before then, jeopardy does not attach. The prosecutor may stop and start over again without implicating the Double Jeopardy Clause.

4.2.4 When there is no trial and the defendant pleads guilty, jeopardy attaches when the judge determines that the plea is entered knowingly and willingly and the judgment becomes final.

**4.3 When Jeopardy Applies**

4.3.1 Double jeopardy applies only to criminal cases whose sanctions threatan "life or limb."

4.3.2 The Legislative Branch defines when a case is criminal.

(a) *See Hudson v. United States* (U.S. 1997) (Rehnquist, C.J.), where the defendant had been charged and acquitted of a crime. The government then filed a forfeiture action for the defendant's ill-gotten gains. The defendant argued that he was being twice punished. Held: the legislature did indicate that this forfeiture case was criminal and the ***courts should not second guess legislature***, since there are no indicia showing the case to be criminal (*e.g.*, a "guilty beyond a reasonable doubt" evidentiary standard). The action is civil and the Double Jeopardy Clause does not apply.

**4.4 Special Contexts**

4.4.1 When the Double Jeopardy Clause Does Not Apply

(a) Under the doctrine of ***manifest necessity***, the Double Jeopardy Clause does not prohibit a retrial.

(b) Manifest necessity applies in two situations:

(i) A Mistrial is Caused by the Defendant's Conduct

(1) When a mistrial is caused by the misconduct of the defendant or that of his attorney, double jeopardy does not apply.

(2) The rationale of this rule is that the defendant should not be able to benefit from his causing a mistrial.

(ii) Hung Juries

(1) When the jury is unable to arrive at a unanimous verdict that is legally mandated in most states,[53] double jeopardy does not apply.

(2) The defendant may be retried, since neither a conviction nor an acquittal has been entered.

(3) The retrial is simply viewed as a continuation of the first trial.

(c) The founders intended the Double Jeopardy Clause to protect defendants when there has been a full and fair trial. Where there is a hung jury or a mistrial caused by the defendant's misconduct, there has been no full and fair trial. *Illinois v. Somerville* (U.S. 1973) (Rehnquist, J.).

4.4.2 When the Double Jeopardy Clause Does Apply

(a) The Double Jeopardy Clause does apply when a mistrial is caused by the prosecutor's misconduct.

(b) In this situation, the court must look at the nature of the misconduct.

(c) Merely negligent conduct causing a mistrial and a retrial does not offend double jeopardy.

(d) However, if the prosecution deliberately causes a mistrial or intentionally goads the defense into moving for a mistrial, double jeopardy would be implicated in a retrial. *Oregon v. Kennedy* (U.S. 1982) (Rehnquist, J.).

(e) If the prosecutor's own personal behavior is not the direct cause of a mistrial, it is not clear if double jeopardy will apply in a retrial.

(i) Example: a prosecutor's witness blurts out "the defendant confessed" with respect to an inadmissible confession. The court declares a mistrial.

(ii) Several factors will be considered as to whether a retrial can be heard (*e.g.*, whether whether the prosecutor put the witness up to making the statement).

## 4.5 Collateral Estoppel and Double Jeopardy

4.5.1 Introduction

(a) Collateral estoppel[54] (issue preclusion) prohibits an issue that has been judicially resolved between two parties from being relitigated.

(b) The earlier judgment is to be binding on the parties implicated in the original adjudication.

4.5.2 Lesser Included Offenses

[53] Colloquially referred to as a "hung jury."

[54] This idea is closely related to claim preclusion (*res judicata*, "the thing is adjudicated"), which deals not with relitigating the same issue, but rather, the same claim that was litigated or could have been litigated in a prior suit that reached a final judgment.

(a) Two offenses are considered the same offense for the purpose of jeopardy, *unless each of them contains an element not included in the other.*

(b) If they include the same elements or if one offense contains all of the elements of a lesser included offense, then double jeopardy bars relitigation of one after the other has reached a verdict (this includes trials for a lesser included offense if the defendant was already acquitted for the greater offense, *see infra.*).

(c) If, however, each offense has some unique element, then it is not the same offense for double jeopardy purposes. Since they are not the same offense, the defendant can be prosecuted separately for each offense without violating the Double Jeopardy Clause. *Blockburger v. United States* (U.S. 1932) (Sutherland, J.).

4.5.3 Examples Where Jeopardy Attaches

(a) The defendant is acquitted of second degree murder and is then tried for first degree murder.

(i) Since these offenses do not each contain some unique element (second degree murder is a lesser included offense within first degree murder), they are not separate offenses.

(ii) Therefore, once jeopardy attaches for second degree murder, the defendant cannot be prosecuted for first degree murder (this rule applies regardless of which offense is tried first).

(iii) This is because, once the defendant has been acquitted in the trial for second degree murder, it is implied that he is also acquitted for all lesser included crimes.

(iv) Bringing a later case for a lesser included crime would violate double jeopardy.

(b) The defendant is charged with first degree murder and is convicted of second degree murder. He cannot be again charged with first degree murder.

(i) Althought no verdict was entered with respect to the first degree murder, a conviction on the lesser included charge of second degree murder implies an acquittal on the greater offense.

(ii) Trying him again would be like trying him for an offense after a “verdict” of “not guilty” has already been entered. *Price v. Georgia* (U.S. 1970).

(c) The defendant is acquitted of felony murder and is later charged with the underlying felony.

(i) Except for in rare circumstances, the defendant cannot be tried separately for felony murder as well as for the underlying felony.

(ii) Since proving the felony does not require the plaintiff to prove any additional facts not already proved when the plaintiff shows the felony murder itself, the felony is a lesser included offense.

(iii) Therefore, reprosecuting the defendant for that offense would constitute double jeopardy.

4.5.4 Examples of Separate Offenses Where Jeopardy Does Not Attach

(a) DUI and involuntary manslaughter;

(b) Multiple robberies (each of which can be tried separately).

4.5.5 Modern Test

(a) *Brady v. Corbin* (U.S. 1990) overruled *Blockburger*, but Brady was then reversed by *United States v. Dixon* (U.S. 1993), which reinstituted the *Blockburger* test: ***unless each offense has one or more distinct elements, they are the same offense***.

(b) Today, the "same elements test" under *Blockburger* must be applied and it must be determined whether the legislature *clearly intended multiple punishments* for the same offense. If so, there is no double jeopardy problem.

(i) In *Missouri v. Hunter* (U.S. 1983) (Burger, C.J.), the defendant was convicted under one statute and then prosecuted and convicted under a second statute having the same elements. Held: under *Blockburger*, the two crimes are the same offense. However, it was clear from the record that the Missouri legislature intended for defendants to be prosecuted for both of them. Judgment for the defendant reversed.

## 4.6 Dual Sovereignty Doctrine

4.6.1 When a defendant's conduct violates both federal and state law, a double jeopardy problem will not arise if he is prosecuted by both the federal and state government.

4.6.2 Rationale: the federal government and every state is a separate sovereign, and the Double Jeopardy Clause is intended to prevent multiple prosecutions of a defendant for the same offense ***by the same sovereign.***

4.6.3 Where there is the ***same conduct***, a crime is not considered the "***same offense***" when punished by the state and federal governments separately.

(a) In *Bartkus v. Illinois* (U.S. 1959) (Frankfurter, J.), the defendant was charged with robbery and was acquitted in federal court. Later, the local state prosecutor indicted and convicted the defendant with the same facts and witnesses as those used in federal court. Held: every citizen may be liable to punishment for an infraction of the laws of both his state and federal government. By one act, he may be tried and punished for two offenses.

(b) *N.B.*: although the Constitution would not be offended by these double prosecutions, some states have imposed limitations on *state prosecutions brought after federal prosecutions*.

4.6.4 Double jeopardy does not prevent different states from trying the same offense.

(a) In *Heath v. Alabama* (U.S. 1985) (O'Connor, J.), the defendant hired two men to kill his wife. He was later charged in Georgia, where he received a life sentence, and later in Alabama by a prosecutor who believed he deserved the death penalty. Held: double jeopardy is not offended when a defendant is prosecuted by two states when he has violated the laws of both of them.

### 4.7 Appeals

4.7.1 Appeals, which are permitted in every state, are not constitutionally mandated. Nowhere in the Bill of Rights is the word "appeal" used. However, if the state is to give an appeal, it must honor due process.

4.7.2 Appeals by the Defendant

(a) When the defendant appeals his conviction and it is overturned, one of two things is possible:

(i) There was ***insufficient evidence*** as a matter of law, in which case double jeopardy attaches and retrial is prohibited. The trial court should have entered a verdict of acquittal; or

(ii) The ***trial court erred***, in which case a retrial is permitted, since the defendant, in appealing, waives his double jeopardy right and the jeopardy is simply continuing from the original trial. *Burks v. United States* (U.S. 1978) (Burger, C.J.).

(1) In *Green v. United States* (U.S. 1957) (Black, J.), the defendant appealed his conviction and the appeals court found that the trial court erred and remanded the case. The defendant appealed, arguing that the Double Jeopardy Clause was violated. Held: an appeal by a defendant either (i) constitutes a ***waiver of the double jeopardy right*** (the defendant is implying that he wants a new trial because the trial court erred); or (ii) is a ***continuation of the trial*** if it is sent back to trial on remand.

4.7.3 Appeals by the Prosecution

(a) Prosecutorial appeals are not constitutionally prohibited, but they are constrained by the Double Jeopardy Clause and Speedy Trial Clause.

(b) When the prosecution appeals pre-trial, there is no jeopardy issue.

(c) In states that allow post-trial appeals by the state, the Double Jeopardy Clause applies.

(i) A waiver theory would not apply, since it is not the defendant who is appealing.

(ii) There are two kinds of appeals:

(1) Stand-in Appeals

(aa) The prosecution notes an appeal, but the defendant can not be tried again.

(bb) The appeal goes up in his name but he has no risk, since the state is asking for an advisory opinion for future cases.

(cc) There is no effect on the defendant's acquittal or conviction.

(2) ***Interlocutory Appeal***

(aa) Interlocutory appeals apply only while the case is pending.

(d) Standard of Review for Constitutional Error

(i) An error is harmless only if it had minimal effect or did not not affect the jury. *Kotteakos v. United States* (U.S. 1946).

(ii) Proving harmless error is a high bar to overcome **requiring *proof beyond a reasonable doubt***.

(1) *See Chapman v. California* (U.S. 1967) (Black, J.), where the prosecution was required to show on appeal, beyond a reasonable doubt, that the error did not contribute to the verdict.

(iii) Error is never harmless when the following rights are violated:

(1) The Fifth Amendment right against double jeopardy; and

(2) The Sixth Amendment rights to a speedy trial by an impartial jury, and to the assistance of counsel.

### 4.8 Retroactivity

4.8.1 Traditionally, any new constitutional holding was to apply to any case active in the system (all cases on appeal or in habeas) at the time of the ruling.

4.8.2 This rule changed with *Linkletter v. Walker* (U.S. 1965) (Clark, J.), where the Court recognized that the traditional rule caused exorbitant costs and time expenditures on the parties. Under the new approach, a new rule is to be applied retroactively when the Court makes this clear when stating the rule; otherwise, the courts are to apply the rule retroactively when it is practical.

## 5 The Fifth Amendment Self-Incrimination Clause

### 5.1 Overview of The Privilege

5.1.1 The Fifth Amendment Self-Incrimination Clause guarantees that no person shall be compelled by the ***government*** in any criminal case to be a witness (must be ***testimonial*** in nature) against himself (it is strictly ***personal***).

5.1.2 There Must Be Testimony

(a) The privilege applies to evidence that is testimonial in nature, including the defendant's statements, documents and records, but does not apply to evidence that is ***real and demonstrable*** (*e.g.* hair, blood, fingerprints, photographs, signatures).

(b) The test: testimony must be ***an assertion of fact that is either true or false***, *Schmerber v. California* (U.S. 1966) (Brennan, J.), but one's ***name and identification*** is not considered to be testimonial, since there is nothing incriminating about it. *Hiibel v. Sixth Judicial District Court of Nevada* (U.S. 2004).

(c) Furthermore, the prosecution may generally obtain preexisting business records (*e.g.*, income tax statements, bank statements, etc.) that were voluntarily prepared by the defendant.

5.1.3 When the Privilege Applies

(a) Future Risk of Incrimination

(i) The privilege applies not only to criminal cases, but to any proceeding in which a future criminal prosecution may occur.

(1) *See Lefkowitz v. Turley* (U.S. 1973) (White, J.), where the Court held that requiring a defendant to testify when criminal charges could be made would be to subject him to a "cruel trilemna" of choosing between compelled testimony, perjury, or contempt of court.

(ii) In civil cases, when a witness faces no potential criminal charges (*e.g.*, he has already been tried and acquitted), he may be forced to testify. *Piemonte v. United States* (U.S. 1961).

(iii) It is not for the courts to determine whether charges are criminal or civil; rather, it is for the legislature.

(1) *See United States v. Ward* (U.S. 1980) (Rehnquist, J.), where the Court held that a penalty for polluting was not criminal because Congress had so expressed.

(iv) Several factors can be used to ascertain whether the legislature intended for a statute to be criminal or civil, including the penalties (prison versus a fine); and the burden of proof (beyond a reasonable doubt versus preponderance).

(b) State Action

(i) The constitutional protections apply only to government violations, not to violations by private actors.

(ii) Thus, if a defendant confesses to a friend who then gives the information to the police, there is no Fifth Amendment violation.

(iii) If, however, a "false friend" is planted by the police, that person becomes a police agent and the Fifth Amendment applies.

(c) Only Natural Persons Are Protected

(i) The privilege against self-incrimination applies only to natural, not legal persons.

(ii) *See Braswell v. United States* (U.S. 1988), holding that the Fifth Amendment is inapplicable to a closely-held corporation.

(d) Government Informants

(i) The privilege does not apply when a defendant assumes the risk of confiding to a "friend," who may be a government informant. *Hoffa v. United States* (U.S. 1966).

(e) Before a Subpoena Is Served

(i) When documents are prepared before a government subpoena is served, they are not protected under the Fifth Amendment. *See Fisher v. United States* (U.S. 1976) (White, J.) (overruling *Boyd v. United States*).

## 5.2 The *Miranda* Safeguards

5.2.1 The case *Miranda v. Arizona* (U.S. 1966) guarantees that defendants in police custody will be informed of the following four rights and warnings:

(a) The right to remain silent;

(b) The right to consult with an attorney and to have the attorney present during questioning;

(c) The right to court-appointed counsel if he is indigent; and

(d) That anything that defendants say can or will be used against them in court.

5.2.2 The Functions of the Warnings

(a) To enable suspects to make an "intelligent decision" regarding the exercise of constitutional rights.

(b) To make suspects "acutely aware" that they are "not in the presence of people acting in their sole interest."

5.2.3 Constructive Violations

(a) In closing arguments, prosecutors ***may not comment on the defendant's failure to testify.*** Doing so constructively violates the Fifth Amendment by compelling him to testify. Prosecutors may, however, state that evidence was uncontradicted. *Griffin v. California* (U.S. 1965).

(b) If, however, the defendant ***invites*** such comments, the privilege is waived.

(i) *See United States v. Robinson* (U.S. 1988) (Rehnquist, C.J.), where the defendant's attorney said that the government did not give the defendant the opportunity to present his side of the story. The prosecutor was permitted to respond that the defendant failed to avail himself of the opportunity to testify.

5.2.4 Deception and Misrepresentation

(a) The Fifth Amendment ***does not prohibit police from deceiving suspects*** by planting "false friends" in order to elicit confessions.

(i) *See Frazier v. Cupp* (U.S. 1969) (Marshall, J.), where the Court permitted police to lie in telling the defendant that a second defendant confessed. *There is nothing coercive about hearing that a friend confessed.*

(b) However, police may not trick the defendants into confessing by falsely offering to drop charges.

### 5.3 The Two-Prong Threshold Test

5.3.1 Determining *whether statements are admissible* under the Fifth Amendment Privilege against Self-Incrimination requires a threshold test.

5.3.2 First, *determine if the confession was voluntary*.

(a) There are three factors to consider when determining whether a confession is involuntary.

(i) **Police Conduct**. A confession is involuntary when it is the result of police torture, threats of violence, repeatedly denying requests for a lawyer, psychological coercion, or other acts that "overbear the will" of the suspect (*i.e.*, cause him to confess not because the confession is true, but because it is what the law enforcement officials wished to hear).

(ii) ***Characteristics of the suspect,*** such as his age, injuries, mental capacities, and mental state.

(iii) ***Surrounding circumstances***, including the length of an interrogation; the lack of food or rest; and the degree of isolation from family, friends, and counsel.

(b) If it is determined that a confession is involuntary, it is inadmissible under the Due Process Clause.

(i) *See Brown v. Mississippi* (U.S. 1936), where the defendants confessed only after brutal beatings by the police. The Court held that the confessions were not voluntary and were therefore inadmissible.

5.3.3 If it is determined that the confession was voluntary, move onto the *Miranda* prong: any statements given to the police will be excluded if the *Miranda* warnings were not first read when the statements are both:

(a) Made while the suspect was in ***police custody;***

(b) During a police ***interrogation***.

### 5.4 Custody and Interrogation

5.4.1 The Requirement of Custody

(a) The *Miranda* warnings apply only when the defendant is in police custody.

(b) A person is in custody when he *reasonably believes* that he is *not free to leave. Orozco v. Texas* (U.S. 1969).

(c) Although the test is objective, it considers what is reasonable from the perspective of a reasonable person in the defendant's circumstances.

(i) *See Berkemer v. McCarty* (U.S. 1984) (Marshall, J.), where the court held that *even if an officer planned on arresting a defendant* in a routine traffic stop, the defendant was not in custody if a reasonable person in his position would not have understood the traffic stop to have meant that he would be arrested. *It is measured from the reasonable suspect's perception* of the situation, not from the officer's reasoning and thinking.

(d) For the purposes of *Miranda*, questioning on the scene regarding the facts of a crime during fact-finding does not meet the requirement of custody.

5.4.2 The Requirement of an Interrogation

(a) Once it is shown that the defendant was in custody, the defense must also argue that an actual interrogation took place.

(b) A confession that is completely voluntary, without even a single interrogation by police, need not be excluded.

(i) *See Colorado v. Connelly* (U.S. 1986) (Rehnquist, C.J.), where the Court did not exclude evidence of a defendant who made incriminating statements while in a room with a video monitor even though police did not read him his *Miranda* rights, since there was no police interrogation. The police simply put the defendant in the room and video monitored him for his own safety, since he showed the symptoms of a mental disorder.

(c) The interrogation relates to testimonial information, not real and demonstrable evidence, such as name, social security number, and other identification information.

(d) It applies not only to the questioning of the defendant, but also to any words or actions by police other than those involved in ***booking***. *Illinois v. Perkins* (U.S. 1990) (Kennedy, J.) (affirming and amplifying *Rhode Island v. Innis* (U.S. 1980)).

(e) An interrogation may thus be comprised of police conduct without actual questioning as well as police statements seeking to ascertain information.

(i) For example, not only direct questions, but also statements such as "tell me more" are considered to be interrogation.

(ii) Furthermore, the statement by a police officer in the presence of the defendant that all he wanted to do was enable the family of a missing victim a "Christian burial" for their ten year old girl, because it was designed to elicit incriminating statements by the defendant, was held to be an interrogation requiring the *Miranda* warnings in *Nix v. Williams* (U.S. 1984).

(f) Volunteered Statements

(i) If the defendant offers incriminating testimony before there is ever an interrogation, the evidence will not be excluded on the basis of the *Miranda* rights having not been read.

(1) *See Pennsylvania v. Muniz* (U.S. 1990) (Brennan, J.), where the Court admitted confessions made by a drunk defendant, since there was never an actual police interrogation. The officer only asked for identifying information and then asked the defendant if he understood the officer's explanations as to taking a breathalyzer test.

(aa) *N.B.*: the dissent focused on the defendant's having been drunk as a strong factor against admissibility.

(2) *See also United States v. Patane* (U.S. 2004) (Thomas, J.), where the defendant interrupted police while they were advising him of his rights and and told them that he knew what his rights were. The Court did not exclude evidence of a gun because the defendant volunteered its whereabouts to the police.

(ii) Furthermore, statements that are not responsive to a question asked, are not to be excluded under *Miranda. Rhode Island v. Innis* (U.S. 1980).

## 5.5 The Exclusionary Remedy

### 5.5.1 The Prophylactic Remedy

(a) Before *Miranda v. Arizona* was decided in 1966, the ***McNabb-Mallory Rule*** requird that evidence violating the Fifth Amendment be excluded in federal court. *McNabb v. United States* (U.S. 1943); *Mallory v. United States* (U.S. 1957).

(b) Since the *McNabb-Mallory* Rule was not a constitutional doctrine, Congress had the power to overrule it, which it did in 18 USC § 3501.

(c) The Supreme Court later held that 18 USC § 3501 was unconstitutional because it failed to require police to adequately inform the defendants of their rights (*e.g.*, the right to counsel).

(d) *Miranda v. Arizona* (U.S. 1966) established a new test looking to the totality of the circumstances in determining whether a confession was voluntary. If a confession ***is not voluntary,*** or is voluntary but the defendant was not read the *Miranda* warnings during an interrogation in police custody, ***the confession must be excluded***.

(e) The rule is not constitutional; it is a ***prophylactic rule*** that carries the same remedies as constitutional rules.

(i) *See Miranda v. Arizona* (U.S. 1966) (Warren, C.J.), where the Court reversed the conviction of the defendant, who had been *interrogated* without being advised of his right to remain silent or have an attorney present. The Court held that once a defendant requests an attorney, the interrogation must cease until an attorney is present. Although this is *not a constitutional rule*, it is treated as one in order to *protect the constitutional right against self-incrimination*. It is to be applied until Congress and the states come up with a better rule.

(ii) Dissent (Harlan, J.): the required warnings will decrease confessions. There is no constitutional precedent for what the majority is doing and it is unwise as a matter of public policy.

(iii) *N.B.:* the dissents (JJ. Clark, Harlan, White, Stewart) disagreed as to what could be done as an alternative. Clark combined what they agreed upon and wrote it into a dissent. The chief disagreement was the *new right to counsel in the Fifth Amendment* that was created by the majority.

(iv) *N.B.:* after this decision, the states were incensed and many tried to impeach Chief Justice Warren. Congress tried to reverse the holding via statute, but the DOJ has rarely enforced it.

5.5.2 The Constitutional Rule

(a) Although originally, Chief Justice Warren made it clear that *Miranda* was not to be a constitutional rule, this later changed.

(b) In 2000, the Court held in *United States v. Dickerson* (U.S. 2000) (Rehnquist, C.J.) that because the states and Congress had not accepted the Court's prior invitation to come up with a better rule than that pronounced in *Miranda v. Arizona* (U.S. 1966), the ***Miranda Rule is now a constitutional rule.***

5.5.3 Reversible Error

(a) If a court errs by allowing an inadmissible confession into evidence, a conviction will be reversed and a new trial will be ordered ***if the error was material*** (*i.e.*, outcome determinative). *Arizona v. Fulminante* (U.S. 1991).

(b) If, however, the admission of an inadmissible confession was ***harmless error*** (*e.g.*, there was so much evidence that the defendant was inevitably going to be convicted), the conviction will stand.

5.5.4 Limited Uses of Excluded Confessions

(a) Although involuntary confessions are generally inadmissible, *they may be used to impeach* the defendant's testimony. *Harris v. New York* (U.S. 1971).

(b) Furthermore, confessions given *after the defendant has invoked his right to counsel*, even thought they are generally inadmissible, may be used to impeach the defendant's testimony. *Oregon v. Hass* (U.S. 1975).

**5.6 Public Safety Exception to Exclusion**

5.6.1 A court is not required to exclude evidence obtained without the *Miranda* warnings when ***"overriding considerations of public safety"*** warrant an interrogation without the *Miranda* safeguards.

5.6.2 A court is to weigh the following factors in a balancing test:

(a) *Public safety considerations* from the perspective of a reasonable police officer; against

(b) The *need for a prophylactic rule* designed to protect the Fifth Amendment right again self-incrimination.

5.6.3 *See New York v. Quarles* (U.S. 1984) (Rehnquist, J.), where police seize the defendant after he robbed a store. When they saw that he was wearing a gun belt but had no gun, they asked him where the abandoned gun was before they read him the *Miranda* warnings. Held: the *Miranda* warnings are not necessary under public safety emergencies. Here, there was a presumably loaded gun in a grocery store with small children who could access it. The public safety considerations outweigh the need for the warnings.

### 5.7 Purging an Illegal Confession Through a Repeat Confession

5.7.1 If police interrogate the defendant while he is in custody without reading him the *Miranda* warnings and obtain a confession, they may read the defendant his *Miranda* rights and interrogate him afresh in order to "purge" the confession from its taint.

5.7.2 If the defendant again confesses, the confession is admissible if it is ***knowing and voluntary.***

(a) *See Oregon v. Elstad* (U.S. 1985) (O'Connor), where the defendant made incriminating statements before police read him his *Miranda* warnings. When police later read him his *Miranda* rights, he waived them and again confessed. Held: *the voluntary and knowing waiver* cured any taint from the earlier confession.

### 5.8 The "Fruit of the Poisonous Tree" within the *Miranda* Context

5.8.1 The illegal fruit of confessions that violate *Miranda* is not required to be suppressed; the fruit of the poisonous tree doctrine does not apply to evidence obtained because of violations of *Miranda*.

(a) Originally, this holding was based on the theory that the *Miranda* warnings were merely prophylactic safeguards, not constitutional rights; therefore, the Court had the discretion to fashion the remedy as it wished.

(b) However, after *Dickerson* constitutionalized *Miranda*, the rationale for the admissibility of fruits of a *Miranda* violation is that the court has created an ***exception*** to the rule.

(c) Many police took advantage of this by illegally seeking confessions that would be suppressed in order to obtain new evidence that would not be suppressed as fruit of the poisonous tree.

5.8.2 Only Good Faith Error Permitted

(a) This eventually led to *Missouri v. Seibert* (U.S. 2004), which held that the fruit of a *Miranda* violation is admissible only if the *Miranda* error was made in good faith.

(b) Police may not in bad faith obtain an unlawful confession, then read the defendant his *Miranda* rights, obtain a lawful confession, and then offer the lawful confession as fruit of the poisonous tree.

### 5.9 The Right to Counsel in Interrogations

5.9.1 Under the Sixth Amendment Right to Counsel, defendants have a right to an attorney ***after adversarial proceedings*** have begun—when the defendant is formally charged with an offense.

5.9.2 Thus, pre-indictment interrogations are generally not protected under the Sixth Amendment. *Massiah v. United States* (U.S. 1964) (Stewart, J.). The Court held that the right to counsel does not apply in *Escobedo v. Illinois* (U.S. 1964).

5.9.3 However, this was overruled by *Miranda v. Arizona* (U.S. 1966), and *Kirby v. Illinois* (U.S. 1972) restated the *Miranda* holding that the Sixth Amendment right to counsel applies ***after "adversary judicial criminal proceedings"*** have begun. This includes the indictment.

5.9.4 The doctrine was expanded in *Brewer v. Williams* (U.S. 1977), where the Court held that a defendant's Sixth Amendment Right to Counsel applies ***whenever judicial proceedings are initiated against him,*** even if this occurs before indictment by a preliminary hearing, arraignment, etc.

## 5.10 The Requirement to Testify if Offered Immunity

5.10.1 The defendant is required to testify if offered either of the following forms of immunity:

(a) Transactional immunity

(i) Broad, full immunity for a specific crime.

(ii) The defendant is assured that he won't be prosecuted for ***any transaction*** implicated by the compelled testimony.

(b) Use/derivative-use immunity

(i) A narrower form of immunity.

(ii) The defendant is assured that ***his testimony and evidence deriving from it*** will not be used against him in a future prosecution.

(iii) However, the defendant may be prosecuted using outside, independent evidence.

5.10.2 The Fifth Amendment requires at least use immunity when compelling a witness to testify against himself.

5.10.3 When use immunity is offered, the Fifth Amendment Privilege against Self-Incrimination is not offended and the defendant cannot turn it down. The prosecution may, but is not required to, offer broad transactional immunity. *Kastigar v. United States* (U.S. 1972).

## 5.11 Invocation and Waiver of the *Miranda* Rights

5.11.1 The Requirement that Waivers Be Voluntary, Knowing, and Intelligent

(a) A defendant may waive his *Miranda* rights, provided that the waiver is ***voluntary, knowing, and intelligent,*** which the prosecution has the "heavy burden" of proving.

(b) Waiving the Right to Remain Silent

(i) If the defendant talks, he waives the right to remain silent.

(ii) If the defendant does not affirmatively invoke the right and remains silent, *the right is not waived.*

(1) Example: police take the defendant into custody where they read him his *Miranda* rights. The defendant says nothing. Police proceed to interrogate him and the defendant confesses. Has the defendant waived his rights?

(2) No; the waiver *may not be presumed* by the defendant's silence.

(iii) If the defendant waives the Fifth Amendment privilege against self-incrimination as to a subject matter, ***he waives it as to issues of the whole crime charged.*** However, the defendant may not be interrogated as to other, unrelated crimes.

5.11.2 Waiver Following Invocation

(a) If police read the defendant his *Miranda* rights and the defendant decides to exercise his rights and not to speak, the police may later return to him after a reasonable time has passed, reread his rights, and try to interrogate him anew. *Michigan v. Mosley* (U.S. 1975).

(b) However, multiple interrogations may get to the point of harassing the defendant into confessing. This is impermissible.

(c) Furthermore, *Miranda* Rights are offense-specific. Police may ask the defendant about one crime, and if the defendant refuses to speak, they can read the defendant's rights afresh for another offense and resume interrogation. The defendant may selectively waive some of his rights..

(d) Compare the right to counsel, which is not offense-specific. Once the defendant invokes his right to counsel, police must stop interrogation about *any* crime.

(i) *See Edwards v. Arizona* (U.S. 1981) by Justice White, where the defendant invoked his right to counsel and police stopped asking questions, but the next morning, resumed questioning him. Held: the right to counsel is different from the right to remain silent. Remaining silent is clear to the average person knowing his interests. But asking for a lawyer means that the defendant does not know what is in his best interests. Thus, once the defendant asks for counsel, police must stop questioning until the defendant has the opportunity to confer with a lawyer.

(e) The defendant's Right to Counsel is not offended, however, if he changes his mind and later initiates the contact.

(f) Thus, even if the defendant invokes the right against self-incrimination, police may later interrogate him, with or without rereading him his *Miranda* rights. Police may not, however, interrogate the defendant once he invokes his right to counsel, unless the defendant voluntarily initiates the communication.

5.11.3 Invocation of the Right to Counsel

(a) The right to counsel is invoked only if the defendant ***clearly and unequivocally*** requests counsel. *Davis v. United States* (U.S. 1994).

(b) The fact finder must find clear evidence that the defendant is asserting a constitutional right. Otherwise, police should not be penalized for asking the defendant questions.

(c) Examples:

(i) "I want a lawyer" → clear invocation meeting the test.

(ii) "Maybe I should talk to a lawyer" → does not meet the test.

5.11.4 Implied Waiver

(a) A waiver may be express (*e.g.*, through the signing of a waiver form; through the statement, "I waive my rights") or implied.

(b) When the defendant is aware of his rights but elects to talk anyway, his rights are impliedly waived, *even if he refuses to sign a written waiver form. North Carolina v. Butler* (U.S. 1979) (Stewart, J.).

(c) A waiver does not need to be absolute in order to be valid; it may be partial.

(d) However, silence does not imply a waiver of the Privilege against Self-Incrimination. The rights are still present, even if the defendant does not affirmatively invoke them. Although they can be affirmatively waived expressly or impliedly, they cannot be waived by silence.

(i) Compare the Right to Counsel, which is waived if not affirmatively invoked.

5.11.5 *Miranda* Summary

(a) Statements made while not in custody are admissible for any purpose.

(i) However, even these statements must be made voluntarily, since involuntary statements are *never admissible*.

(ii) Custodial statements in violation of *Miranda* are admissible for impeachment purposes if they are voluntary.

(b) Custodial statements are admissible for any purpose if there is a valid waiver of rights.

(i) Custodial interrogation may not begin until there has been an affirmative waiver of rights and may continue until there has been an unequivocal exercise of rights.

(ii) The waiver is not presumed by silence (however, the right to counsel must be affirmatively invoked).

(iii) If the defendant waives the right, he may revoke it at anytime. Police are then required to immediately stop.

# 6 Fifth Amendment Grand Juries, Due Process, and Charging

## 6.1 Grand Jury Indictments

6.1.1 Grand juries are investigative bodies with the power to issue subpoenas and grant immunity.

6.1.2 The proceedings of grand juries are held in secret, unless the court orders that grand jury transcripts be unsealed (*e.g.*, to impeach a witness who testifies differently in the trial).

6.1.3 The Fifth Amendment requires grand jury indictments in federal court ("[n]o person shall be held to answer for a capital, or otherwise infamous crime, unless on a presentment or indictment of a Grand Jury").

6.1.4 However, the Fifth Amendment Grand Jury Clause has not been incorporated against the states. The states are therefore not required to indict defendants through grand juries.[55]

## 6.2 Charging, Due Process and Equal Protection

6.2.1 Introduction

(a) The Fourteenth Amendment Equal Protection Clause and the Due Process Clause of the Fifth and Fourteenth Amendments may be violated by the manner in which a prosecutor decides to bring a charge.

(b) For example, the ***Equal Protection Clause*** would be violated if a prosecutor singles out one particular racial for a crime that is committed by a much wider group.

(c) ***Due Process*** would be violated if the prosecutor charges a defendant in response to the defendant's exercising of some constitutional right.

6.2.2 Due Process and Vindictive Prosecutions

(a) The Due Process Clauses does not permit prosecutors to vindictively punish defendants for exercising a statutory right to appeal.

(i) *See North Carolina v. Pearce* (U.S. 1969) (Stewart, J.), where the defendant was originally charged with a felony and under a plea bargain, pled guilty to a misdemeanor, but later appealed. The prosecutor was indignant and reacted by re-indicting him for the felony. Held: the prosecutor punished the defendant for exercising his statutory right to appeal. If the prosecutor had put into the agreement that the defendant would not appeal, he would have avoided this problem. Reversed.

(b) However, when two statutes overlap, the prosecutor may in his discretion charge the defendant with the statute carrying the greater penalty. *United States v. Batchelder* (U.S. 1979) (Marshall, J.). Such a charge is not considered to be vindictive.

6.2.3 Equal Protection

(a) When bringing charges, prosecutors may not single out and prosecute groups for reasons other than their participation in a crime; as doing so would violate the equal protection of citizens under the law. *See Yick Wo v. Hopkins* (U.S. 1886) (Mathews, J.).

(b) There is a three-part test for determining when enforcement violates equal protection. The burden is on the defendant to show the following:

(i) There is a failure to prosecute others similarly situated;

(ii) The failure is intentional and not accidental or inadvertent; and

(iii) There is an arbitrary (rather than a rational) reason for the discrimination. *Oyler v. Boles* (U.S. 1962).

---

[55] Most states charge the defendant using an "information," which is a written accusation presented by a public official (as opposed to a grand jury), on his oath. Some states, such as Virginia, nevertheless require indictments by grand juries.

(c) Discrimination in the Composition of the Grand Jury

(i) Grand jurors are summoned from community to investigate using summons, etc., returning bills of indictment if their investigation concludes with probable cause to show the defendant is guilty.

(ii) If the composition of a grand jury is tainted by discrimination, the indictment is invalid and a new one is required.

(1) In *Campbell v. Louisiana* (U.S. 1998), Justice Kennedy restated a former case holding that grand juries may not be discriminated against on the basis of race. When the grand jury is tainted by discrimination, the defendant suffers in fact. Louisiana argued that this should not matter: if the defendant was convicted, it doesn't matter whether the charging document was defective, since the jury was told not to consider the indictment. Held: this argument is rejected. Discrimination strikes at the fundamental trust in our jury system. This discrimination undermines confidence in our system and a new indictment is required. The original charge is constitutionally void.

# 7 Sixth Amendment Trial Rights

## 7.1 Introduction to the Sixth Amendment

7.1.1 The Sixth Amendment establishes rights that apply to both the trial and to pre-trial proceedings.

7.1.2 It establishes that, "In all criminal prosecutions, the accused shall enjoy the right to a speedy and public trial, by an impartial jury of the state and district wherein the crime shall have been committed, which district shall have been previously ascertained by law, and to be informed of the nature and cause of the accusation; to be confronted with the witnesses against him; to have compulsory process for obtaining witnesses in his favor, and to have the Assistance of Counsel for his defence."

7.1.3 It protects the rights to the following:

(a) A speedy trial;

(b) A public trial;

(c) An impartial jury;

(d) Confront one's accusers; and

(e) The assistance of counsel.

## 7.2 The Right to a Speedy Trial

7.2.1 The Sixth Amendment provides that in "all criminal prosecutions, the accused shall enjoy ***the right to a speedy and public trial***."

7.2.2 The Sixth Amendment protects the right to a *speedy trial*, not the right to a *speedy charge*. Thus, the clock does not begin ticking *until the defendant is actually charged* (post-accusation rule). *United States v. Marion* (U.S. 1971) (White, J.).

(a) However, Fourteenth Amendment Due Process is violated if the government's delay in filing charges is ***deliberate***, done in ***bad faith*** or with an ***improper purpose***, such as gaining a technical advantage over the accused.

(b) However, when the delay is due to the prosecution's completion of a thorough and proper investigation, there is no Due Process violation, even if the delay in some ways prejudices the defense.

(i) *See United States v. Lovasco* (U.S. 1977) (Marshall, J.), where before the indictment, two witnesses in the defendant's favor died. The defendant raised a novel due process argument: the eighteen month delay in indicting him violated his Fourteenth Amendment Due Process rights because he was prejudiced by the death of the two witnesses. Held: there is no violation of Due Process, since the apparent reason for the delay was a desire to obtain more evidence, which furthers an important government interest.

7.2.3 Once the defendant is indicted, if his right to a speedy trial is violated, the remedy is dismissal.

7.2.4 The defendant may waive the right to a speedy trial by his conduct (*e.g.*, by not raising this defense in a timely manner). *See Doggett v. United States* (U.S. 1992) (Souter, J.).

7.2.5 How Speedy is a Speedy Trial?

(a) Determining whether a trial was speedy involves a totality of the circumstances analysis that looks to factors such as whether the defendant was causing delays.

(b) Many states have also adopted speedy trial statutes. For example, Virginia requires triales within five months when the defendant is in custody and nine months when he is on bond.

**7.3 The Right to a Fair Trial, the Press, and Publicity**

7.3.1 The right to a public trial guarantees that the defendant's substantive and procedural due process rights can be scrutinized out in the open before the public and the press.

7.3.2 Any scandalous or corrupt acts will quickly be brought to light.

7.3.3 However, there are times when a public trial will actually act to the *detriment* of the defendant, as when, in a notorious case, the entire community is made aware of a case before a jury is even impaneled.

7.3.4 In such situations, where a pre-trial suppression hearing of a confession or an illegal seizure is made known to the public at large, the chances of impaneling an *impartial jury* will be substantially compromised.

7.3.5 The normally symbiotic relationship between the defendant's right to a public trial and the press's rights to free speech can be turned into a relationship of conflict.

7.3.6 The courts can sometimes resolve the tension through the sequestration of the jury and instructions that jury members not to speak to *anyone* outside of the court about the case.

7.3.7 Sometimes, however, such remedies will be inadequate. For example, if the defendant waives his right to a public trial, his waiver will enter into conflict with the First Amendment interests of the press.

7.3.8 The court will be forced into balancing the rights of one against the other in order to determine which one prevails.

7.3.9 The court will close the trial to the press and to the general public only under the following conditions:

(a) The state shows an *overwhelming interest* (*e.g.*, the need to protect a witness);

(b) The closure is *no broader than necessary* to further that interest;

(c) The court must consider *reasonable alternatives* (jury instructions, sequestration of the jury, etc.); and

(d) The court makes *findings on the record* adequate to support whatever decision it makes. *Waller v. Georgia* (U.S. 1984).

7.3.10 The court may find that the defendant's right to a future jury untainted by news from a preliminary hearing trumps the press's First Amendment rights. In such cases, it may enjoin the press from covering the hearing.

(a) *See Gannett Co., Inc. v. DePasquale* (U.S. 1979), where the defendant moved to suppress a confession and to exclude the media and public from the suppression hearing in order to prevent the media from finding out what he had said in the confession. Both parties agreed, but the press filed a writ of *mandamus* asserting a First Amendment right to hear it. Held: the defendant's right to a fair trial outweighs the freedom of the press. The Sixth Amendment ***right to a public trial is for the benefit of the defendant,*** not of the press. The Constitution mentions not the right of the public to a fair trial, but of the accused to a public trial. Furthermore, there is a difference between a trial and a pre-trial hearing; the requirement of a public trial does not apply pre-trial, as in this case. Here, the judge was taking steps with the agreement of the parties to minimize the risks of having a future jury tainted. The public's right of access does not necessarily apply to pre-trial hearings.

7.3.11 *Richmond Newspapers, Inc. v. Virginia* (U.S. 1980) discussed the need to balance the Sixth Amendment right to a public trial, which the defendant can waive, and First Amendment freedoms, but it gave little guidance.

7.3.12 The Sixth Amendment right to an impartial jury (which is intimately tied to the right to a public trial) does not require that a jury completely ignorant of the facts of the case be impanelled.

7.3.13 It requires simply that jurors be able to lay aside impressions acquired from pre-trial publicity in order to be able to give a verdict based only on that which is presented in the courtroom.

(a) *See Irvin v. Dowd* (U.S. 1961) (Clark, J.), where several egregious murders by a serial killer in 1954-55 created a great deal of publicity. When the prosecutor gave a press release stating that the defendant had confessed to all six murders, the widwspread publicity led the defendant sought a change of venue, which was granted in the adjoining county. The defendant moved for a change of venue outside of the media market, which was denied, and he was convicted. Held: in these days of swift communication, it is neither possible nor expected that jurors will be totally ignorant of the facts of a case. It is sufficient only that ***jurors be able to lay aside impressions and give a verdict based on only what they learn in the courtroom.*** Here, however, the prejudice was too strong, since the record shows that each juror knew that the defendant had already confessed. It would be very difficult to purge this from the jurors' minds. The refusal to allow a change of venue compromised the right to a fair trial.

7.3.14 When the press causes enough commotion to effect a probability of unfairness, the Fourteenth Amendment Due Process Clause becomes implicated.

(a) *See Sheppard v. Maxwell* (U.S. 1966) (Clark, J.), where a great deal of media attention was generated at the murder of the wife of the defendant, a doctor. The press immediately accused the defendant, with one front page story, among others, stating, "Why isn't Sam Sheppard in Jail?" The defendant was convicted and appealed on the basis of his due process rights. Held: the defendant ***was denied his Fourteenth Amendment Due Process rights*** when reporters took over the courtroom and hounded him. Twenty reporters were taking notes within the bar throughout the trial. The judge, assigning the places to the reporters, caused confusion and commotion that had a negative impact on the fairness of the trial, as it did here. There *must be a new trial.*

### 7.4 The Right to a Trial by an Impartial Jury

7.4.1 The Sixth Amendment provides that "[i]n all criminal prosecutions, the accused shall enjoy the right to a speedy and public trial, ***by an impartial jury*** of the state and district wherein the crime shall have been committed . . ."

7.4.2 A defendant has a right to a trial by jury whenever he is charged with a *crime*, which, unlike a *petty offense*, is any charge that carried ***more than a six month jail term***.

7.4.3 Thus, if *criminal imprisonment* for ***more than six months*** is possible, the state must provide the right to a trial by jury. *Baldwin v. New York* (U.S. 1970).

7.4.4 This constitutional requirement trumps any conflicting state constitutional provisions.

(a) *See Duncan v. Louisiana* (U.S. 1968) (White, J.), where the Court held that the Louisiana Constitution is subject to the Impartial Jury Clause of the Constitution. It is not relevant that Lousiana's legal system derived from the French civil law; once it joined the union, it was requird to conform to the federal Constitution.

7.4.5 The Constitution does not always require twelve jurors—this is just a "historical accident."

7.4.6 Many scholars believe that where there is a capital case, twelve jurors is required. However, as the law stands, six would be sufficient.

7.4.7 Unanimity among the jurors is not required by the Constitution. The Court has held that a ten-two supermajority is acceptable; in another case, a nine-three supermajority was permitted. However, most states require unanimous verdicts.

7.4.8 However, if there is a jury of less than twelve, a unanimous verdict is necessary whenever the defendant is charged with more than a petty offense.

7.4.9 The selection process must be about being fair and impartial and must not exclude anyone based on some improper motivation.

7.4.10 Lawyers may inquire as to the views of potential jurors on the issues of the case.

(a) *See Witherspoon v. Illinois* (U.S. 1968) (Stewart, J.), where the jurors were asked whether they were opposed to the death penalty. The prosecutor objected to the question and the judge allowed just the question with no further questioning. Held: the trial court erred because both the prosecution and the defense must be permitted to inquire jurors of their positions of issues "inextricably entwined" in the case in order to *unveil bias*. However, a lawyer may not automatically disqualify a juror unless it is clear that the juror is unable to render a fair verdict (*e.g.*, the juror states that under no circumstances will he be able to follow the law because he opposes capital punishment).

7.4.11 A fair cross section is a constitutional requirement guaranteed by the Sixth Amendment. *Taylor v. Louisiana* (U.S. 1975) (White, J.).

7.4.12 However, this does not necessarily mean that the defendant is entitled to a jury with an *exact representation* of the demographics of the community.

## 7.5 The Right to a Fair Trial: Jury Selection

7.5.1 *Voir dire* is the process in which attorneys examine prospective jurors to determine competency and potential bias. The process leads to the rejection or selection of those who will ultimately serve on the jury.

7.5.2 Peremptory challenges allow the parties to exclude prospective jurors from the jury without having to give a reason.

7.5.3 Peremptory challenges based on race alone are prohibited by the Equal Protection Clause.

7.5.4 A defendant who challenges a peremptory challenge on this basis has the burden of:

(a) Proving that he is a ***member of a protected class;***

(b) Making a *prima facie* showing that the prosecution has used peremptory challenges to ***systematically exclude jurors*** who are members of that protected class[56]; and

(c) Once these two prongs are met, an *inference is raised* that the prosecution's exclusion of jurors was based on race and the *burden then shifts to the prosecutor* to provide a neutral explanation for the exclusion based on something other than membership in the protected class. *Batson v. Kentucky* (U.S. 1986) (Powell, J.).

7.5.5 The Court has held that gender is a protected class, *J.E.B. v. Alabama* (U.S. 1994) (Blackmun, J.), and some scholars argue that religion is one as well.

7.5.6 In *Holland v. Illinois* (U.S. 1990) (Scalia, J.), the Court held that it has been going about this in the wrong way by focusing on the Sixth Amendment right to an impartial jury. Rather, the Fourteenth Amendment Due Process rights of jurors justify the *Batson v. Kentucky* and *J.E.B. v. Alabama* holdings. The jurors have a right to serve and the parties represent the jurors' interests.

(a) When the prosecution systematically excludes minorities from the jury, it is not the defendant's Sixth Amendment right to a fair trial that is offended, but rather, the juror's Due Process rights.

---

[56] This showing can be established solely on the prosecution's use of race in the defendant's trial in excluding jurors.

(b) Therefore, the criminal defendant is not the only party that has a right to challenge the exclusion of jurors; the prosecution may also challenge the defendant's exclusion of jurors based on the same Due Process rights of the jurors.

(c) Furthermore, since the right is rooted in the Fourteenth Amendment Due Process Clause, it applies not only in criminal cases, but in *civil cases* as well.

7.5.7 In *Johnson v. California* (U.S. 2005) (Stevens, J.), the *Batson* analysis changed and challenging a peremptory challenge requires two steps only:

(a) The defendant must make a *prima facie* showing that the prosecution has used peremptory challenges to ***systematically exclude jurors*** based on their membership of that protected class; and

(b) If the trial judge is satisfied that that is the case, ***the burden shifts to the prosecutor*** to provide a ***neutral explanation*** for the exclusion based on something other than membership in the protected class.

(c) Example:

(i) The prosecutor strikes three Hispanic Americans from the jury. The defendant argues that the prosecutor is excluding jurors based on their membership in a protected class. If the court holds that it is not satisfied that the prosecution is doing this, then that is the end of the analysis.

(ii) If, however, the court is satisfied that the prosecutor is using his peremptory challenges in a discriminatory manner, then the prosecutor must provide a neutral explanation.

(iii) If the prosecutor admits that he is discriminating based on race, then the excluded juror is brought back in.

(iv) If, however, he gives a neutral reason for the exclusion and the judge is convinced that those are the actual reasons, then the *Batson* challenge fails.

(d) The standard of review on appeal is abuse of discretion. If there is any evidence to sustain the trial court's decision, it will stand.

### 7.6 The Right to a Fair Trial: Exculpatory Evidence

7.6.1 Exculpatory evidence is evidence that tends to clear the defendant from criminal liability by, for example, proving his innocence, proving his guilt for a lesser crime, or mitigating his punishment.

7.6.2 Due process requires that prosecutors turn over *all **material** exculpatory evidence* to the defendant.

(a) *See Brady v. Maryland* (U.S. 1963) (Douglas, J.), where the witness gave a different statement in court than that given previously to law enforcement. The defendant asked for the statements that the witnesses made to police, but the prosecutor refused to disclose them. Held: due process requires the prosecutor to ***reveal material exculpatory evidence*** when requested by the defendant. Here, the prosecution failed to turn over material statements. Reversed.

7.6.3 However, when the exculpatory evidence is not material, the prosecutor will not be required to turn it over to the defense.

(a) *See United States v. Agurs* (U.S. 1976) (Stevens, J.), where although the defendant asked the prosecutor for any evidence that could have exculpated him, information that could have impacted a witness's credibility was not turned over. The lower courts overturned the conviction based on *Brady*. Held: the exculpatory information must be *material;* here, it was not. Furthermore, in *Brady*, we said that it is error for the prosecutor not to turn over exculpatory evidence when the defendant makes a *specific* request. Here, there was only a *general request, which is the functional equivalent of no request* at all.

7.6.4 If a *general request* or *no request* for exculpatory evidence is made, the prosecutor must turn over any material exculpatory information he may have.

7.6.5 If a *specific request* for material exculpatory information is made, the prosecutor must either:

(a) Turn over the requested information; or

(b) Let the judge review the record *in camera* if he disputes having exculpatory evidence. *United States v. Agurs* (U.S. 1976).

7.6.6 Defining the "Material" Element

(a) In *United States v. Bagley* (U.S. 1985), the Court held that evidence is "material" if there is a *"reasonable probability"* that had it been disclosed, the trial would have had a *different outcome*.

(b) Later, the Court refined this definition and held that the prosecution must turn over any evidence when there is a *reasonable probability* that it would be ***material to the defense***. There are four aspects of the reasonable probability:

(i) It requires not a preponderance of the evidence, but rather, a ***reasonable probability****;*

(ii) It does not require that the defendant show that he ***could not be convicted without the evidence***;

(iii) If a defendant has demonstrated a reasonable probability of the outcome, the court cannot find that the withholding did not cause injury (*the error may not be held harmless*); and

(iv) While the prosecutor is not required to show everything helpful to the defense, he must ***gauge the net effect*** and disclose when reasonable probability is reached. *Kyles v. Whitely* (U.S. 1995).

(c) When evidence that had a reasonable probability of being material to the defense is excluded, the defendant is entitled to a new trial.

## 7.7 The Right to a Fair Trial: an Impartial Judge

7.7.1 The Sixth Amendment guarantees the ***right to an impartial judge*** as part of a fair trial through the Due Process Clauses of the Fifth and Fourteenth Amendments.

7.7.2 The judge must be neutral and detached—he may be neither financially nor otherwise connected to the outcome of the case.

(a) *See Ward v. City of Monroeville* (U.S. 1972) (Brennan, J.), where the defendant was convicted of two traffic violations under an Ohio statute that allowed mayors to sit as judges in traffic offenses. Held: there is an *appearance of impropriety* and a *conflict of interest* because the mayor indirectly benefits every time somebody is convicted, since fines contribute to the town treasury. The right to an impartial judge has been violated.

7.7.3 Pre-Trial Rights

(a) The right to an impartial judge similarly applies before the actual trial: the custody and bail decision must be made before a neutral, detached judicial officer.

(b) In order to detain a defendant before trial, there must be a *Gerstein* hearing before a *neutral magistrate* to determine probable cause.

(i) *See Gerstein v. Pugh* (U.S. 1975), holding that when a person is arrested with no warrant or indictment, he is entitled to a hearing by a *neutral magistrate* to determine probable cause. The hearing should take place promptly after the arrest in order to avoid unconstitutional restraints on liberty.

## 8 The Sixth Amendment Confrontation Clause

### 8.1 The Incidental Rights to Be Present and Informed of the Accusation

8.1.1 The Confrontation Clause is established in the Sixth Amendment, which states that in all criminal prosecutions, the accused shall enjoy the right "to be confronted with the witnesses against him."

8.1.2 This right necessarily implies the ***right to be present*** at one's trial, since the defendant who is not present will not have the opportunity to confront those witnesses who testify against him.

(a) This right is not absolute; it may be waived by the defendant's disruptive behavior in the courtroom.

(b) After a warning, the court may remove the defendant from the courtroom, who thereby loses his right to confront witnesses against him.

(i) *See Illinois v. Allen* (U.S. 1970) (Black, J.), where the defendant, who represented himself, threatened the judge and destroyed a file in the courtroom. After an initial warning, which was to no avail, the trial judge removed the defendant from the courtroom and ordered the defendant's standby counsel to be present. The defendant challenged the decision. Held: if a defendant is warned of the consequences of his conduct, he can waive his right to be present if he persists in his misconduct. If the defendant later promises to behave, he may return.

8.1.3 If the defendant has a right to be physically present in the courtroom, by corollary, he also has a right to understand and "***be informed of the nature and cause of the accusation***."[57]

---

[57] U.S. Const. amend. VI.

(a) His presence in the courtroom is not meaningful unless he understands what is happening therein.

(b) Due process requires that *incompetent defendants not be tried* until they regain competence (through medical treatment, theraphy, etc.).

(c) When there is a reasonable doubt as to the defendant's competence, there is to be a competency hearing.

(i) *See Pate v. Robinson* (U.S. 1966) (Clark, J.), where the defendant claimed insanity and incompetence to stand trial. The state insisted that Robinson waived these rights. Held: when either party raises a *bona fide* doubt, due process requires that a hearing to determine competency be held. If an incompetent the defendant is tried, *the right to be present is rendered meaningless*.

**8.2 Introduction to the Confrontation Clause**

8.2.1 The Sixth Amendment Confrontation Clause gives the accused the right to confront all witnesses against him "in all criminal prosecutions."[58]

(a) *See Griffin v. California* (U.S. 1965) (Douglas, J.), where the Court held that the Confrontation Clause would be violated if a prosecutor, on closing argument, implied that the defendant was guilty because he did not take the stand, since the prosecutor could not be cross examined.

8.2.2 The Sixth Amendment Confrontation Clause is the right to cross-examine witnesses and to test evidence being used against the defendant.

8.2.3 The right to confront is to be read in the context of the drafting of the common law at the time of the ratification of the Constitution, which is what the founders had in mind.

**8.3 The History of the Confrontation Clause**

8.3.1 The Court has held that, where one codefendant gives a confession implicating another, the first codefendant's confession is admissible against the second codefendant only ***if the first codefendant takes the stand*** and submits himself to cross-examination.

(a) *See Bruton v. United States* (U.S. 1968) (Brennan, J.), where the prosecutor tried to convict one of the codefendants by using a statement that implicated a second codefendant. The defendant subpoenaed the second codefendant, but the second codefendant refused to testify under the Fifth Amendment, since she was on trial. Held: under these circumstances, the invocation of the Fifth Amendment made the second codefendant unavailable to the first, thereby infringing on his right to confront witnesses that testify against him. The cases can be tried separately, but this may not be practical and the courts cannot tell the Executive Branch how to bring charges.

8.3.2 Later, the Court held that the Confrontation Clause does not guarantee cross-examination, but rather, only ***the opportunity to cross-examine***.

(a) *See Ohio v. Roberts* (U.S. 1980) (Blackmun, J.), where evidence was presented at a preliminary hearing by a witness who later became unavailable. The prosecution offered the testimony of the

[58] U.S. Const. amend. VI.

witness from the preliminary hearing. The defendant objected on the basis of the Confrontation Clause. Held: the Confrontation Clause was not violated. At the preliminary hearing, the witness was presented and placed under oath, *but the defendant chose not to cross examine*. The Constitution guarantees only the opportunity to cross-examine. The state may therefore use the testimony in trial, even though the witness became unavailable.

(b) *N.B.*: this rule applies only to situations in which the witness becomes unavailable. If the witness is available, the prior testimony cannot be offered in lieu of the actual testimony.

8.3.3 In dicta, the *Ohio v. Roberts* Court held that *the FRE and the Sixth Amendment are largely congruent.* If the FRE are complied with, the Constitution is satisfied. An out of court statement against the defendant was admissible, even if the defendant did not have the opportunity to confront the witness, if it bore an ***"adequate indicia of reliability."***

8.3.4 This test was met if either of the following elements was satisfied:

(a) The evidence fell within a "firmly rooted hearsay exception"; or

(b) The evidence contained "particularized guarantees of trustworthiness."

8.3.5 The *Roberts* ruling worked well until 1999, when *Lilly v. Virginia* was handed down.

(a) In *Lilly v. Virginia* (U.S. 1999) (Stevens, J.), three codefendants, the defendant, his brother, and his roommate, broke into a home and stole guns, liquor, and a safe. They later kidnapped a passing motorist and committed robberies and murder. All were later taken into custody and questioned. The defendant did not mention the murder and explained that his brother and roommate forced him to participate in the robberies. The others stated that the defendant masterminded the incidents. The state charged the defendant with several offenses and offered his statements as declarations against penal interest as an exception to the hearsay rule. The lower courts held that since the FRE were satisfied, the statements were admissible under *Ohio v. Roberts*. The defendant appealed. Held: because the declaration against penal interest exception to the hearsay rule does not trace its way back to the time of the *ratification of the Bill of Rights*, it is not ***firmly rooted*** and is not what the framers had the mind. *Ohio v. Roberts* is good law, but ***in order for a FRE to be good under the Sixth Amendment, it must be firmly rooted.***

(b) *N.B.*: many commentators read this case as saying that a FRE must be rooted in the rules of evidence as they were at the time of the ratification.

## 8.4 The Confrontation Clause Today

8.4.1 Supreme Court jurisprudence based on *Roberts* was radically overturned in 2004, when the *Crawford* Court introduced the ***testimonial*** test:

(a) If the evidence is not testimonial in nature, the Constitution is not implicated; if it is, then the defendant must have the opportunity to confront his accuser.

(b) Evidence is testimonial when it is being used ***in furtherance of criminal prosecution***.

8.4.2 Evidence obtained in a 911 call whose primary purpose is to obtain emergency assistance is not testimonial in nature. The Confrontation Clause is therefore *not implicated.*

(a) *See Crawford v. Washington* (U.S. 2004) (Scalia, J.), where Michael Crawford stabbed Keneeth Lee, who he suspected of sexually assaulting his (Crawford's) wife. During the trial, the defendant's wife did not testify because of the marital privilege, but the prosecution played a recorded statement that she previously made to police and that contradicted Crawford's claim that he acted in self-defense. Crawford challenged the recording as violative of the Confrontation Clause. The state Supreme Court upheld his conviction, relying on the "adequate indicia of reliability" test of *Ohio v. Roberts* (U.S. 1980), which permits out of court statements against a defendant when such statements are reliable. Held: *Ohio v. Roberts* is overruled. The test for determining whether the Confrontation Clause was violated is no longer whether incriminating evidence that is admitted is reliable; rather, when the defendant does not have the opportunity to confront a witness, incriminating evidence is to be excluded when it is ***"testimonial" in nature***. Here, the wife's statements were testimonial and yet were admitted against the defendant, in violation of his right to confront witnesses. Judgment reversed.

(i) *N.B.:* Justice Scalia did not explicitly define "testimonial," but he said that affidavits are testimonial, while business records are not. Some courts began to define "testimonial" as that which is prepared specifically for court (a business record would thus not qualify).

(b) *See also Davis v. Washington* (U.S. 2006) (Scalia, J.), where the defendant was charged of assaulting his wife. At trial, the prosecutor offered his wife's 911 call into evidence against the defendant, pursuant to the excited utterance exception to the hearsay rules. The defendant objected. Held: 911 calls are not testimonial, since the circumstances behind them ***do not indicate that they are being used in furtherance of criminal prosecution.*** Rather, they are given in the hopes of securing immediate assistance. Here, unlike in *Crawford v. Washington*, the statements were given to police for the purpose of securing assistance in an emergency, not for preserving evidence for trial.

(c) *Compare Hammon v. Indiana* (U.S. 2006) (companion case to *Davis v. Washington*), where a witness's statements were inadmissible because they were made to police after an assault was already complete. Thus, there was no conceivable purpose to the interrogation other than preparation of prosecution. The statements were therefore testimonial and offering them into evidence violated the Confrontation Clause.

## 8.5 Limitations

8.5.1 The Confrontation Clause does not apply before a grand jury, which does not confer to defendants a right to cross examine witnesses presented against them.[59] *Jenkins v. McKeithen* (U.S. 1969).

8.5.2 Furthermore, the Confrontation Clause does not always guarantee the right of the defendant to be ***physically present*** before witnesses testifying against him; other prevailing interests may apply.

(a) *See Maryland v. Craig* (U.S. 1990), where a child was permitted to testify from another room via closed circuit television. Although the defendant, an alleged sexual abuser, was unable to directly confront the child, the Confrontation Clause was not offended because the defendant was able to communicate with his attorney in real time.

[59] Compare with preliminary hearings, which do permit the defendant to cross-examine witnesses presented against him.

## 9 The Sixth Amendment Right to Counsel

### 9.1 Introduction

9.1.1 Until 1963, the defendant got a lawyer if he so desired, but the state was not obligated to provide one.

9.1.2 Then, in 1963, the Court held that a defendant is *always entitled to the assistance of counsel* when there is a ***threat of imprisonment***, whether the prosecution is for a misdemeanor or felony.

(a) *See Gideon v. Wainwright* (U.S. 1963) (Black, J.), where a homeless defendant handwrote a petition to the Supreme Court, explaining that he could not afford a lawyer and asked for one to be appointed. Responding to one of the most articulate writings that the Supreme Court had seen, it held that ***if an offense carries the possibility of a jail sentence***, and if it is something ***more than a petty offense,*** the Constitution guarantees the right to an attorney of one's choosing. Otherwise, the court is to appoint an attorney of its choosing.

9.1.3 Defendants do not have a right to choose which lawyers are appointed to represent them.

(a) *See Morris v. Slappy* (U.S. 1983), where although the defendant did not like his attorney and refused to cooperate with him, the Court refused to appoint another one.

9.1.4 The Court later extended the *Gideon* right to counsel to *any offense* where imprisonment may be imposed, whether it is a ***petty offense***, a ***misdemeanor***, or a ***felony***. *Argersinger v. Hamlin* (U.S. 1972) (Douglas, J.).

(a) *N.B.*: states may avoid the requirement of appointing counsel for offenses that carry jail sentences by ***indicating in advance that they will ask not for imprisonment***, but rather, that only a fine be paid.

### 9.2 When the Right to Counsel Attaches

9.2.1 The right to counsel attaches at ***all critical stages*** affecting the defendant's right to a fair trial. This includes both trial and many pre-trial stages. *Massiah v. United States* (U.S. 1964); *Gilbert v. California* (U.S. 1967).

9.2.2 To qualify as a critical stage, the event must take place *after adversarial proceedings have begun,*[60] as determined from the perspective of the magistrate, such as when there is an indictment or information.

9.2.3 A critical stage is a ***"trial-like event"*** where the accused is confronted by a prosecutor and a procedural system where the result, without the presence of counsel, might *reduce the trial to a mere formality.*

9.2.4 ***Non-critical stages*** include the following:

(a) Photographic identification proceedings. *United States v. Ash* (U.S. 1973);

(b) Handwriting exemplar procedures. *Gilbert v. California* (U.S. 1967);

(c) Pre-indictment police lineups. *Kirby v. Illinois* (U.S. 1972);

(d) Detention hearings. *Gerstein v. Pugh* (U.S. 1975); and

---

[60] Adversarial proceedings are marked by lawyers and judges.

(e) The administrative detention of prison inmates. *United States v. Gouveia* (U.S. 1984).

9.2.5 ***Critical stages*** include the following:

(a) Police interrogations (based on the Fifth Amendment). *Miranda v. Arizona* (U.S. 1966);

(b) Preliminary hearings. *Coleman v. Alabama* (U.S. 1970)[61];

(c) Post-indictment police lineups. *United States v. Wade* (U.S. 1967);

(d) Guilty plea negotiations;

(e) Trials where imprisonment is imposed. *Argersinger v. Hamlin* (U.S. 1963); and

(f) Sentencing. *Mempa v. Rhay* (U.S. 1967).

## 9.3 The Right to Counsel During Identifications

9.3.1 Definitions

(a) A ***showup*** is where a crime has occurred and police seize a suspect, bring him to the victim, and ask the witness if that is the perpetrator. It usually occurs before an indictment when time is of the essence.

(b) A ***photographic lineup*** is where a witness identifies one suspect among others in a spread of photographs.

(c) A ***police lineup*** is where suspects are lined up at a police station.

(d) An ***in-court identification*** is when counsel asks a witness if she recognizes the perpetrator in court.

9.3.2 Pre-Indictment Identifications

(a) The Right to Counsel

(i) As already mentioned, the Sixth Amendment right to counsel attaches only in critical trial and pre-trial stages.

(ii) Within the context of identifications, this includes ***only post-indictment identifications***. *United States v. Wade* (U.S. 1967)

(iii) There is therefore no right to counsel at a police lineup that takes place before "adversary judicial criminal proceedings" have begun. *Kirby v. Illinois* (U.S. 1972).

(b) Due Process

(i) Although the Sixth Amendment Right to Counsel does not apply to pre-indictment identifications, the Fifth Amendment Due Process Clause continues to apply.

[61] Preliminary hearings, which otherwise are like grand jury proceedings, permit witnesses to be cross-examined.

(ii) The defendant's due process rights do not permit the admission of unnecessarily suggestive identifications against him.

(iii) Since showups are inherently suggestive, they are admissible *only under* ***exigent circumstances*** (*e.g.*, the witness will die before arranging a lineup is possible) when they are ***reliable*** under the circumstances (not overly suggestive). *Stovall v. Denno* (U.S. 1967) (Brennan, J.).

(iv) Shifting burdens under the *Stovall* Doctrine

(1) To exclude an identification (including a showup, a photographic lineup, or a police lineup), the defendant must meet the burden of proving that it was unreliably suggestive and unnecessary.

(aa) Example: the defendant shows that in a photographic lineup, he was the only black suspect.

(2) If he meets this burden, the burden of proof shifts to the prosecutor to show that under the totality of the circumstances, the identification is reliable.

(3) Factors that the prosecutor may use to meet his burden include the accuracy of the witness's description and the time elapsed between the crime and the identification.

(4) If the prosecutor meets his burden, the identification will be admitted. If the prosecutor fails to meet his burden, the evidence will be excluded and the witness will be prohibited from again identifying the suspect in court.

(c) Overview

(i) Thus, unlike the Sixth Amendment right to counsel, which applies only to post-indictment identifications, the *Stovall* doctrine applies to *pre-indictment identifications*.

(ii) Example: before he is indicted, the defendant is seized and brought to the victim, who is asked by police, "this is the guy, right?" Under what theory could the defendant suppress the identifation?

(1) The Sixth Amendment is inapplicable in a pre-indictment identification.

(2) However, under the *Stovall* Doctrine, the identification could be suppressed.

9.3.3 Post-Indictment Identifications

(a) Under the "*Wade-Gilbert* Rule," the suspect has an *absolute right* to counsel in all post-indictment critical stages, including ***all post-indictment showups*** and ***police lineups***, but not in photographic lineups, signature analyses, and other proceedings where there is no adversarial proceeding.

(i) *See United States v. Wade* (U.S. 1967) (Brennan, J.), where the defendant was charged with bank robbery. Employees were put on stand and said that the defendant was the robber. The defendant was indicted, after which a lineup took place. Both witnesses identified the defendant in an earlier lineup. The defendant argued that his Sixth Amendment Right to Counsel was violated. Held: a post-indictment ***lineup is a critical stage*** because it is a point where the defendant *would have benefited from access to counsel*. An attorney could have advised the defendant whether or not to have participated.

(b) The purpose behind extending the right to counsel to post-indictment identifications is to protect the defendants from potential prejudicial conditions to which they may not know to object.

(c) Thus, the right to an attorney does not apply in non-adversarial proceedings because the *presence of an attorney would not help to secure the defendant's rights*.

(d) Such proceedings include handwriting analyses and photographic lineups.

(i) *See Gilbert v. California* (U.S. 1967) (Brennan, J.) (companion case to *Wade*), where police took handwriting samples from a suspect and sent them off to a forensic lab. The defendant argued under *Wade* that he should have had an attorney present. Held: *Wade* involved a post-indictment lineup, which is a critical stage. However, ***a handwriting analysis is not a critical stage*** because the right to counsel would have been of no benefit.

(ii) *See also United States v. Ash* (U.S. 1973), holding that the right to counsel does not extend to ***photographic lineups,*** since police may go forward with the lineup even without the defendant's participation, if they have his photograph. Even if the defendant had an attorney, he would be of no help in protecting him from prejudicial conditions.

(e) Furthermore, the "adversary judicial criminal proceedings" under *Kirby v. Illinois* (U.S. 1972) have not yet begun in pre-indictment handwriting samples and photographic lineups. Therefore, such identifications cannot be critical stages and the right to counsel is not yet activated.

## 9.4 Restriction on Right to Retained Counsel

9.4.1 When there are conflicts between the interests of the state and the right to retain counsel, overriding state interests may prevent defendants from asserting an absolute right to counsel.

9.4.2 For example, defendants may not hire lawyers with illegal money that rightly belongs to the state; they must pay with their own money.

(a) *See Caplin & Drysdale, Chartered v. United States* (U.S. 1989) by Justice Byron R. White, where the state sought to seize retainers paid by the defendants for their lawyers because the defendants hired their lawyers with illegal money. The overriding state interest: the money belongs to the state, which filed a forfeiture proceeding.

## 9.5 Right to Counsel on Appeal

9.5.1 Overview

(a) There is a right to counsel on appeal based not on the Sixth Amendment, which applies only to the trial, but on the Fourteenth Amendment Due Process Clause.

(b) This due process right to counsel requires that states provide counsel to indigents on appeal. This right applies *only to the first appeal* (due process guarantees adequate, not perfect, access to the courts). *Douglas v. California* (U.S. 1963) (Douglas, J.).

(c) Although there is no constitutional right to counsel *after the first appeal*, some states grant defendants the assistance of counsel.

9.5.2 Obligation of Counsel in Meritless Appeal

(a) Defendants have a right to appeal under *Douglas*, even if their counsel believes that there was no reversible error to appeal.

(b) If the defendant's counsel truly believes that the appeal is frivolous, he must petition for the right to withdraw.

(c) He is nonetheless obligated to file an "*Anders* brief," arguing for argument that the client wants made that might support an appeal.

(d) If the court, after reading the brief, decides that there is any merit, then it must appoint new counsel. *Anders v. California* (U.S. 1967) (Clark, J.).

9.5.3 Right to Trial Transcripts in the Appeal

(a) A defendant cannot have a meaningful appeal without the trial transcripts.

(b) If the defendant is indigent, the state must pay for the transcripts on appeal (if he is not indigent, he must pay). *Griffen v. Illinois* (U.S. 1956) (Black, J.) (*N.B.*: this was decided before *Gideon* held in 1963 that there was a right to counsel).

### 9.6 Right to Experts

9.6.1 Indigent defendants have a right to the "basic tools" of an adequate trial, such as the right to counsel and transcripts on appeal.

9.6.2 This right includes the right to expert witnesses paid for by the state when they are needed by indigent defendants for an effective presentation of a case during the trial.

(a) *See Ake v. Oklahoma* (U.S. 1985) (Marshall, J.), where the defendant's lawyer wanted to raise the insanity defense and thus needed an expert to testify that the defendant was not guilty by reason of insanity. In a five to four decision, Justice Marshall held that he Sixth Amendment does not provide a right to experts; it supports the right to counsel. However, the Due Process Clause of the Fourteenth Amendment supports the right. An expert was required because the defendant's insanity was a *significant factor*.

(b) *N.B.*: the Court limited this right to experts *only for the advancement of affirmative defenses*, such as insanity. Furthermore, defendants are entitled to only those experts that the court is willing to appoint, not to those experts of the defendants' choosing.

## 9.7 Effective Assistance of Counsel

9.7.1 The Constitution requires not merely the right to counsel, but rather, the right to the *effective* assistance of counsel.

9.7.2 In *Strickland v. Washington* (U.S. 1984), the Court set out the following standard for determining whether the assistance of counsel was effective (both elements must be met):

(a) The defendant must overcome a presumption that his attorney was competent by showing that he made errors so serious that his "representation fell below an ***objective standard of reasonableness***"

(i) The defendant must thus provde that the representation did not fall within the range of competence demanded in criminal cases); and

(b) The defendant must also show that the counsel's incompetent representation prejudiced him.

(i) Standard for prejudice: whether there is a reasonable probability that, but for his attorney's unprofessional errors, ***the proceeding would have turned out differently*** (*i.e.*, the defendant would have been aquitted or convicted of a lesser offense).

9.7.3 Defendants rarely satisfy this test (especially the second prong).

(a) *See Strickland v. Washington* (U.S. 1984) (O'Connor, J.) where the defendant Washington planned and committed a host of crimes, including capital murder, robbery, and kidnapping. The defendant made several decisions against the advice of the public defender appointed to his case, including choosing a trial by jury (which was more likely to give the death sentence); and changing his plea to guilty to all charges (including three capital murder charges). After his attorney received the discovery, he became hopeless regarding the case, cut his efforts short by not pursuing all avenues, and did not present any evidence regarding his client's character and emotional state. In deciding whether the defendant received the effective assistance of counsel, the Court held that neither prong of the test was passed. ***First prong*:** although the lawyer could have done some things differently, he met the minimum requirements by advising his client (*e.g.*, not to speak to the police) and making all of the appropriate pre-trial motions. ***Second prong*:** the defendant, by going against his attorney's advice and confessing, made it impossible for the lawyer to defend him. The defendant could not have shown in any event how the result would have been different here.

9.7.4 Presumed Prejudice

(a) In limited circumstances, it is presumed that *no lawyer* can be effective in trial.

(b) In such circumstances, *there is no need to inquire* into the attorney's conduct at the trial.

(c) Courts will look to several factors in determining making a *per se* determination of ineffective counsel, including: (i) the time to prepare the case; (ii) the experience of the attorney; (iii) the gravity of charges; and (iv) the complexity of defenses.

(d) However, the case must pass a very high threshold in order for a court to make a *per se* determination of effective counsel. Such cases are limited to those characterized by only the most egregious circumstances.

(i) *See United States v. Cronic* (U.S. 1984) (Stevens, J.), where a young real estate lawyer trying his first case was appointed to represent the defendant. The attorney had only twenty five days to prepare his case against the government, which had years on its side. Yet despite these circumstances, this case did not pass the requisite threshold. The Court held that just because it was the attorney's first trial does not mean that the representation was ineffective. Furthermore, twenty five days is not so short that there is a presumption of ineffective assistance of counsel. Although there are some cases where prejudice can be presumed, this was not one of them.

### 9.8 Conflicts of Interest in Multiple Representation

9.8.1 There is a limited presumption of prejudice in cases of representation of multiple defendants by a single attorney.

9.8.2 Multiple representation may limit the ability of an attorney to act in the full interests of any single defendant, since he must balance the interests of each defendant against the interests of the defendants as a whole.

9.8.3 For example, in a gang or mafia prosecution, the government may not enter into deals with some criminals in order to convict others if the defendants are represented by the same lawyer.

9.8.4 These limitations may prejudice the interests of any single defendant, who may later move for reversal based on prejudice caused from the ineffective assistance of counsel based on the multiple representation.

9.8.5 If, however, the defendant waives his right to his own, separate attorney, there can be no later claim of ineffective assistance of counsel.

9.8.6 There is, however, no absolute right to a waiver. The court is not obligated to accept the defendant's wiaver and may even require an attorney that is representing several defendants to be removed from the case.

9.8.7 To avoid appeals based on the potential prejudice inherent in multiple representation and the limitation of its ability to enter into deals with individual defendants, the government prefers that each defendant have a separate lawyer.

(a) *See Cuyler v. Sullivan* (U.S. 1980) (Powell, J.), where the government asked the trial court to disqualify an attorney who was representing multiple defendants and to appoint multiple attorneys so that the government could separately offer them deals. Issue: is there a government interest in intervening that trumps the Sixth Amendment right to choose one's attorney? Held: there is an inherent risk of ineffective assistance of counsel in cases of multiple representation; the defendants would be entitled to a reversal in the case of prejudicial error. The trial court does not, however, have to assume that there is a conflict in the defendants' sharing the same attorney; it may assume that there is no conflict or that the defendant waived his right to have his own attorney. It is nonetheless wise to inquire if prejudice is likely to occur; otherwise, if the defendant is convicted, he may be able to appeal, claiming that his attorney did not effectively act in his interest. Thus, when the government protests multiple representations, the trial courts should ask whether the defendants understand the potential problem and waive it. If they do not, there may need to be a full retrial if the defendants show: (i) there was a conflict; and (ii) the lawyer acted adverse to their interests.

### 9.9 Self-Representation

9.9.1 The corollary of the right to counsel is the *right to not have counsel*. Like any constitutional rights, it may be waived.

9.9.2 The Court has characterized the waiver of counsel not as a waiver, but as a constitutional right—*i.e.*, there is an *affirmative right to self-representation* that courts must honor when invoked.

9.9.3 However, the Court treats the right as a waiver, since exercising it must be *knowing, intelligent, and voluntary*.

(a) *See Faretta v. California* (U.S. 1975) (Stewart, J.), where the defendant was charged with murder and was facing the death penalty. The defendant said that God would be his lawyer. The judge appointed a lawyer anyway. Although the lawyer did a good job, the defendant was convicted. There was no ineffective assistance of counsel claim, but the defendant alleged that the Sixth Amendment was violated when the judge refused to allow him to represent himself. Held: *a defendant has the right to make his own defense and must suffer the consequences if his defense fails*. There is an affirmative right to self-representation, as long as the defendant's giving up his right to counsel is knowing, intelligent, and voluntary. The defendant may waive his right to counsel if the consequences are explained to him and he is competent to make the decision.

9.9.4 If the defendant invokes the right to self-representation (waives his right to counsel) and does a poor job of representing himself, he may not make a claim claim for the ineffective assistance of counsel.

# REVIEW CHARTS AND SUMMARIES

## When Constitutional Rights Apply

| | |
|---|---|
| ***Fifth Amendment Right to a Trial by Jury*** | Anytime the defendant is charged with a crime that bears the possibility of a prison sentence of six or more months. |
| ***Sixth Amendment Right to Confront One's Accusers*** | When incriminating testimony offered against the defendant is *testimonial* (offered and used in furtherance of criminal prosecution). |
| ***Sixth Amendment Right to Counsel*** | Anytime the defendant is charged with *any offense* where prison may be imposed, whether it is a petty offense, misdemeanor, or felony.<br>The right applies to all trial and pre-trial *critical stages*, which take place after adversarial proceedings have begun. |

## Landmark Criminal Procedure Cases

1925 – ***Carroll v. United States*** – police are not required to obtain a warrant to effect a search of automobiles and other moving vehicles when they have ***probable cause*** that a crime is being committed, since the time required in obtaining a search would permit the mobile evidence to be lost or destroyed.

1961 – ***Mapp v. Ohio*** – the exclusionary rule for illegally searches and seizures applies in the states.

1963 – ***Gideon v. Wainwright*** – the state must provide an attorney to indigent defendants whenever there is the possibility of imprisonment.

1963 – ***Wong Sun v. United States*** – illegally obtained derivative evidence ("fruit of the poisonous tree") can be purged through voluntary conduct, such as a voluntary confession given after an improperly obtained confession.

1964 – ***Massiah v. United States*** – the right to counsel is activated at ***all critical stages*** of an adversarial proceeding. Cf. *Gilbert v. California*.

1966 – ***Miranda v. Arizona*** – (Warren, J.) police must read defendants the four warnings in interrogations of defendants in police custody. Otherwise, confessions are to be excluded.

1967 – ***Gilbert v. California*** – the right to counsel applies in all critical stages of an adversarial proceeding. Signature analyses are not critical stages, since the presence of an attorney would not in any way protect a defendant.

1967 – ***United States v. Wade*** – post-indictment police lineups are critical stages for purposes of the Sixth Amendment Right to Counsel.

1967 – ***Warden v. Hayden*** - when pursuing a dangerous suspect and time is of the essence, police may conduct warrantless searches. The following elements must be met: (i) there is ***probable cause*** (always necessary for searches and seizures); (ii) under ***exigent circumstances*** justifying the warrantless search; (iii) the pursuit begins from a place where the police have ***a lawful right to be;*** and (iv) the legal violation is ***serious*** enough to justify a warrantless search.

1968 – ***Terry v. Ohio*** – police do not need probable cause in order to effect a frisk of a defendant's body in order to assure officer safety. If police, while conducting a frisk, develop independent probable cause that a crime is being committed or that the defendant is in possession of contraband, they may search for and seize the contraband without a warrant. A police stop does not require probable cause, but rather, a reasonable and articulate suspicion that a crime is being committed.

1969 – ***Chimel v. California*** – police need neither a warrant nor probable cause in order to effect a search of a defendant's wingspan (the area within his immediate control) in order to assure officer protection (***search incident to lawful arrest*** exception to the need for a warrant).

1970 – ***Chambers v. Maroney*** – once police have seized a vehicle, they are not required to obtain a search warrant. They may search it as they would have at the time that it was stopped. Rationale: (i) cars and other mobile vehicles were primarily means of transportation; (ii) they are driven in plain view; and (iii) they are subject to heavy regulation.

1971 – ***Coolidge v. New Hampshire*** – when the incriminating nature of evidence is immediately apparent to police while they are in a place where they have a lawful right to be, they may seize it under the plain view doctrine.

1972 – ***Argersinger v. Hamlin*** – the state must provide an attorney to indigent defendants whenever imprisonment is imposed, for any offense, whether it is a felony, misdemeanor, or petty.

1972 – ***Kirby v. Illinois*** – there is no right to counsel under the Sixth Amendment during a pre-indictment police lineup, since adversarial judicial proceedings have not yet begun.

1973 – ***United States v. Ash*** – photographic lineups are not critical stages for the purposes of the Sixth Amendment Right and do not require the right of counsel.

1975 – ***Gerstein v. Pugh*** – a person who is arrested without a warrant is entitled to a hearing to determine whether there is probable cause to arrest him.

1975 – ***Michigan v. Mosley*** – if police read a defendant his *Miranda* rights and the defendant refuses to speak, the police may return to the defendant and interrogate him afresh without rereading the *Miranda* rights, provided it is done within a reasonable time.

1977 – ***United States v. Chadwick*** – police must first apply for a search warrant for small closed objects seized from a car before opening them. Since police may seize the objects before applying for a search warrant, the exigent circumstances inherent in mobile automobiles does not apply.

1980 – ***Ohio v. Roberts*** – when evidence is firmly rooted in exceptions at the time of ratification of the Constitution, it bears an adequate indicia of reliability and is not to be excluded by the Confrontation Clause. In dicta: the Confrontation Clause and the Federal Rules of Evidence are largely congruent: testimony that satisfies the rules of evidence is admissible under the Confrontation Clause.

1980 – ***Rhode Island v. Innis*** – courts are not required to suppress statements volunteered to the police or that are not responsive to a question, even when the *Miranda* warnings are not read.

1982 – ***United States v. Ross*** – when police have probable cause, they may search the entire vehicle until they find the object of the probable cause.

1984 – ***Nix v. Williams*** – evidence obtained through an illegal confession is not to be excluded when it would have been ***inevitably discovered.***

1984 – ***Berkemer v. McCarty*** – a person is in police custody when he believes that he is not free to leave from the perspective of the reasonable person (objective) in his situation (subjective).

1985 – ***United States v. Montoya de Hernandez*** – although probable cause is generally required for all Fourth Amendment Searches and Seizures, it is not required for border searches.

2000 – ***United States v. Dickerson*** – (Rehnquist, C.J.) since the states and Congress have not come up with an adequate alternative to *Miranda*, the *Miranda* rule is Constitutional.

2004 –***Crawford v. Washington*** – statements offered in court must be ***testimonial*** in order to trigger the Confrontation Clause protections.

## Chapter VII. Criminal Law

# 1 The Elements of a Crime

## 1.1 Elements that the Prosecution Must Prove

1.1.1 A voluntary act.

(a) *See Martin v. State* (Ala. App. 1944), where the defendant was found by police intoxicated in his home, was brought out to a public highway, and then charged and convicted of violating a statute prohibiting the appearance of intoxicated persons in public places. Held: the statute presupposes voluntary conduct, which here is not the case. Conviction reversed.

1.1.2 *Actus reus* – a criminal act (*see infra.*);

1.1.3 *Mens rea* – a guilty mind (*see infra.*);

1.1.4 The concurrence in time between the *actus reus* and the guilty mind.

(a) Example: an actor can only be guilty of larceny ***if at the time*** of the unlawful taking of the property of another (*actus reus*), he intended to permanently deprive him thereof.

1.1.5 Actual and proximate causation of the injury or harm suffered; and

1.1.6 An injury or harm suffered by the victim.

## 1.2 *Actus Reus*: a Criminal Act

1.2.1 The criminal law requires ***conduct*** before punishment can be made. *Mere thoughts* or *criminal propensity* is insufficient.

(a) *See Doe v. City of Lafayette* (7th Cir. 2003), where the plaintiff, who confessed to having entered into a public park to see small children at play and to contemplate having sexual contact with them, was banned by the City of Lafayette from entering private parks. The plaintiff sued to lift the ban. Held: the ban is unconstitutional because it punishes the plaintiff for mere thoughts and propensities, not actual conduct.

1.2.2 The Requirement that Offenses be Previously Defined

(a) An *ex post facto* law is a law that does any of the following retroactively: (i) makes conduct criminal; (ii) establishes a stricter punishment for a crime; or (iii) alters the procedural or evidentiary rules in favor of the prosecution.

(b) Such laws are unconstitutional; in order to hold a defendant criminally liable, the offense must be previously defined.

(i) *See Rex v. Manley* (K.B. 1933), where a defendant could be held guilty for making false statements to police if the offense was previously defined under the *common law of crimes.*

1.2.3 Omissions

(a) As a general rule, there is ***no legal duty to act at common law.***

(b) However, the common law recognizes a duty to act and imposes criminal liability for an omission under the following circumstances:[62]

(i) There is a duty based on ***statutes***.

(ii) There is a duty based on ***contract*** (*e.g.*, a lifeguard's employment contract);

(iii) The defendant ***undertook a rescue*** by: (i) promising to act; or (ii) voluntarily undertaking a rescue by giving assistance such that others are prevented from rendering assistance.

(iv) The defendant ***created the victim's peril*** or left him in greater peril than he found him, whether or not he acted with intent or negligence.

(v) The ***instrumentality*** is within the defendant's control (especially when the plaintiff is an invitee).

(vi) There is a ***special relationship*** with the victim (*e.g.*, relationships between spouses; employers and employees; parents and children; inviters and invitees; innkeepers and guests; common carriers and passengers; captain and crew).

(vii) ***Other circumstances*** based on: (i) the *foreseeability* of the harm; (ii) the *societal interest* in recognizing the duty; and (iii) the *opportunity to avoid risk*.

(c) A statute *may not criminalize an omission* unless another statute or source of law creates a duty to act.

(d) In some states, such as Texas, legal duties are based only on statute. Thus, a statute may not make it a crime not to render assistance in the absence of another statute creating an affirmative duty to act.

(i) *See Billingslea v. State* (Tex. 1989), where social services eventually found the defendant's mother who he left in a bed with rotting flesh and bed soars with live maggots in a pool of her own urine that caused her second degree burns. The defendant was charged with violating a Texas statute making it a crime to cause injury to an elderly person *by any reckless act or omission*, since he failed to obtain medical care for his mother. Held: in Texas, ***common law, factual, or familial duties are insufficient bases*** on which to predicate a legal duty to act. Such duties must be based on statutes. Here, there is no statute creating an affirmative duty to act; a statute criminalizing an omission without making the statutory duty to act known is unconstitutionally vague. The defendant had no notice of his duty.

(1) *N.B.*: if Texas had a more typical approach, the defendant would have been convicted under common law social and familial duties.

(e) In the majority of states, however, legal duties to act may be based on common law and social duties.

(i) *See Regina v. Instan* (Q.B. 1893), where the defendant was convicted of manslaughter for failure to provide sustenance to her aunt, who supported her. The legal duty was

[62] The civil tort law recognizes a duty to act imposes civil liability for omissions under these same circumstances.

based on the defendant's having taken on the care of her aunt and her duty to share the food brought into the home, based on the aunt's support.

(ii) *See also Jones v. United States* (U.S. 1960), where a defendant took on the care of a boy, who, left in her basement, died of malnutrition. The appeals court required the trial court to determine whether the defendant had a legal duty to care based on contract or based on her taking on the care of a boy to the exclusion of others before holding her guilty of involuntary manslaughter.

(f) Similarly, there is no duty to summon medical assistance for drug overdoses for those with whom one has no statutory, familial, or contractual relationship.

(i) *See People v. Beardsley* (Mich. 1907), where the defendant failed to provide reasonable care for a woman with whom he was drinking when she later took morphine and died. On appeal, the conviction was reversed: the fact that she was in his house did not create a legal duty to act.

(g) However, the contribution of one's actions to another person's state of peril gives rise to the legal duty to summon medical assistance.

(i) *See People v. Oliver* (Cal. Ct. App. 1989), where the defendant took the victim from a public place where he was drunk and where others could have provided assistance and brought him to her private home, where only she could provide assistance when he used narcotics and later collapsed. Her indictment was upheld for her her failing to summon medical assistance.

(h) With respect to the omission of life-sustaining treatment, doctors generally have no affirmative duty to continue to keep patients on life support when it has been determined that it will be ineffective.

(i) In *Barber v. Superior Court* (Ca. Ct. App. 1983), upon consultation with a patient's family, medical personnel removed life support equipment from a patient who they concluded would be in a permanent vegetative state. When the doctors were charged with murder and conspiracy to commit murder, the court of appeals dismissed the complaint, since the doctors had no legal duty to act.

1.2.4 Interpretation of Conduct Elements

(a) In order to hold a criminal defendant guilty of committing a crime, the prohibited conduct must be clearly defined.

(i) *See Keeler v. Superior Court of Amador County* (Cal. 1970), where the defendant, after kicking his former wife in the stomach and causing the birth of a still-born, was charged with murder. Held: the statute applies only when the victims of murder are born alive. Because the fetus died in uterus, the statute does not apply. Due process prevents us from reading the 1850 statute to have included unborn fetuses in the category of human beings, since the defendant would not have had notice. Judgment for the defendant.

(ii) Dissent: the specific classes of persons defined as "human beings" in the common law should change as science informs our understanding. Today, we know fetuses to be living, breathing human beings. They should therefore be covered under the statute. The defendant had adequate notice that his acts constituted homicide.

(b) However, some courts may modify preexisting laws based on common social duties.

(i) *See People v. Sobiek* (Cal. Ct. App. 1973), where the defendant was indicted for grand theft for allegedly embezzling partnership funds. The defendant moved to quash the indictment: since the laws define partnership assets as being all in common, one may not steal that which is his. Held: this theory is rejected based on a *common social duty informing the defendant of the offense*. Unlike in *Keeler*, here, the defendant had notice that nothing in the grand-theft statute excluded partnership property from the "property of another" being protected. Judgment for the defendant reversed.

### 1.3 *Mens Rea*: a Criminal Mind

#### 1.3.1 Historical Origins of *Mens Rea*

(a) The criminal law underwent the following stages of evolution:

(i) In the early common law, ***conduct*** on its own could be the object of criminal punishment (in a sense, tort and criminal law were treated as the same) (strict liability).

(ii) The canon law added to the development of the second stage, where ***general intent*** was required. General moral blameworthy was required in addition to the act.

(iii) The modern approach requires ***specific intent*** as to the offense: there must be *mens rea* with respect to the act charged.

(b) As judges' treatment of *mens rea* evolved, "intermediate categories" arose as the law moved from one stage to another.

(i) In *Regina v. Faulkner* (Ire. Cox C.C. 1877), the defendant sailor tried to steal rum from a ship and in so doing, negligently dropped a match burning the whole ship down. He was charged and convicted of larceny and arson. The prosecutor argued that the defendant had malice, which was true in the general sense of wickedness required to steal the rum (Sayre 2). The defendant appealed as to the jury instructions which required no showing of the defendant's intent *to set fire to the ship*, but allowed the malice of the larceny as sufficient for the arson. Held: the jury should have been instructed to find the defendant guilty of arson *only if the arson was the probable, foreseeable result of the larceny*. The conviction could not be sustained.

(c) Eventually, the courts came all the way around to embracing the doctrine of specific intent.

(i) In *Regina v. Cunningham* (Q.B. 1957), a statute punished anyone who "unlawfully and maliciously" caused a noxious thing to be administered to another person to endanger that person's life. The defendant, stealing a gas meter, allowed gas to escape, partially asphyxiating his mother-in-law next door. The jury was instructed that unlawful and malicious conduct (imputed from the larceny) on its own absent intent was a sufficient basis to convict the defendant. On appeal, the court quashed the conviction, arguing that general malice was not enough. Both ***foresight and consequence were required***. The court of appeals thus required a Sayre's third category of *mens rea* in order to achieve a conviction.

(d) In the modern law, depending on the crime, judges may impose one of the following standards of *mens rea*: negligence, recklessness, knowledge, or purpose.

(e) Distinguishing Specific Intent Crimes from General Intent Crimes

(i) Specific Intent Crimes

(1) Specific intent crimes require a certain state of mind in order to convict the defendant.

(2) There are three categories of specific intent crimes:

(aa) The defendant acts in a way harboring an ulterior intended ***result***. The state of mind is required by the definition of the offense (*e.g.*, *larceny*: the unlawful taking of the property of another with the *intent to permanently deprive him thereof*);

(bb) The defendant acts with the specific intent to commit another ***act in the future*** (*e.g.*, *burglary*: the (i) breaking and (ii) entering (iii) of a dwelling (iv) of another (v) at night (general intent elements) (vi) with intent to commit a felony therein (specific intent element));

(cc) The defendant acts with knowledge of certain ***circumstances*** (*e.g.*, she intentionally strikes a victim knowing that he is in a fragile physical state).

(3) Specific intent crimes include: assault, attempt, burglary, conspriracy, larceny, robbery, solicitation, intent to kill murder, and voluntary manslaughter.

(ii) General Intent Crimes

(1) All other crimes that do not fall into one of the categories of specific intent crimes are general intent crimes.

(2) General intent crimes include: arson, battery, rape, kidnapping, false imprisonment, involuntary manslaughter, depraved heart murder.

1.3.2 The Model Penal Code

(a) The Model Penal Code (MPC) of the American Law Institute analyzes *actus reus* based on the following terms:

(i) The nature of the conduct (the act);

(ii) The attendant circumstances (external facts, such as "property of another" for larceny); and

(iii) Results (the consequences of the conduct, such as death for murder).

(b) MPC Culpability Structure

(i) MPC § 2.02 requires culpability based on negligence (N), recklessness (R), knowledge (K), or purpose (P) for each element of the *actus reus*, unless § 2.05 puts the offense into a quasi "strict liability" category.

(1) ***Purpose*:** conscious objective or desire. MPC § 2.02(2)(a). Some enactments employ the word "intent."

(2) ***Knowledge*:** awareness. Under MPC § 2.02(2)(b), knowledge applies with respect to an element of the offense when one of the following elements is met:

> (i) if the element involves the nature of his conduct or the attendant circumstances, he is aware that his conduct is of that nature or that such circumstances exist; and
>
> (ii) if the element involves a result of his conduct, he is aware that it is practically certain that his conduct will cause such a result.

(3) ***Recklessness*:** "conscious disregard of a substantial and unjustifiable risk" that a material element "exists or will result from his conduct." MPC § 2.02(2)(c).

(aa) Recklessness in the criminal law is similar to recklessness in the civil law, except that, in the criminal law, it requires a *subjective conscious disregard of a risk*.

(bb) In some civil law jurisdictions, in contrast, recklessness is defined as "extreme negligence," which does not necessarily implicate a conscious disregard of a risk (though in other jurisdictions, it does, or encompasses both definitions).

(4) ***Negligence*:** like recklessness, it is based on *inattention to risk*, but does not implicate a conscious disregard of the risk.

(aa) Negligence in the criminal law is similar to gross negligence.

(bb) The actor should have been aware of a "substantial and justifiable risk" that a material element of an offense existed.

(cc) "The risk must be of such a nature and degree that the actor's failure to perceive it, considering the nature and purpose of his conduct and the circumstances known to him, involves a *gross deviation from the standard of care* that a reasonable person would observe in the actor's situation." MPC § 2.02(2)(d).

(ii) Where the requisite standard is lacking, presume that ***recklessness is sufficient*** (or knowledge or purpose, since the presence of either of these implies the presence of recklessness). MPC § 2.02(3).

(iii) Unless contrary purpose is clear, any one *mens rea* standard described in a statute ***carries over*** to every other *actus reus* of the statute. MPC § 2.04(4).

(1) Thus, if there is an ambiguity, apply the *mens rea* requirement of any other element.

(2) For example, if no *mens rea* standard is stated, then presume that all of the *actus reus* elements require recklessness (MPC § 202(3)).

(c) Examples with Explanations

(i) ***False Imprisonment***: "knowingly restrains another unlawfully so as to interfere substantially with his liberty." MPC § 212.3.

(1) *Actus reus* elements:

(aa) *Conduct*: restraining another;

(bb) *Circumstance*: unlawfully;

(cc) *Result*: interfering substantially with liberty.

(2) The *mens rea* required of all the *actus reus* elements is knowledge. This is evident from the modifier "knowingly."

(ii) ***Escape***: "unlawfully removes himself from official detention or fails to return to official detention following temporary leave granted for a specific purpose or limited period." MPC § 242.6(1).

(1) Since no *mens rea* standard is explicitly mentioned, recklessness is imported for all of the elements. MPC § 202(3).

(iii) ***Falsely Incriminating Another***: "knowingly gives false information to any law enforcement officer with purpose to implicate another." MPC § 241.5(1).

(1) Here, "purpose" refers not to any element of *actus reus* (conduct, circumstance, or consequence), but rather, speaks *only to mens rea*. It is a required element of the mental state of the defendant.

(2) Since implicating another is not an element of the crime, "purpose" to implicate another does not modify an *actus reus* element.

(3) Rather, the word "knowingly," which appears *before* the *actus reus* elements, modifies the conduct required to violate the statute.

(4) Suppose the statute read, "with purpose to implicate another, gives false information to any *known law enforcement officer*."

(aa) Here, "purpose" again refers only to a requisite *mens rea*, not *actus reus*.

(bb) The part that deals with *actus reus* is "gives false information" has no modifier. Thus, recklessness will be imported. MPC § 2.02(3).

(cc) Since "known" comes after "gives false information," it does not apply to that part of the sentence.

### 1.3.3 Application of the *Mens Rea* Structure

(a) Negligence

(i) Under the ***common law***, ordinary negligence is sufficient

(1) *See Regina v. Faulkner* (defendant sailor) (Cox C.C. 1877), where the Court held that a jury would only have to find that the arson was the probable, foreseeable result of the larceny.

(2) However, it is not the negligence on its own that causes criminal liability to arise. Rather, it is the *criminal liability coupled with an act aimed at a particular subject*.

(3) *See Director of Public Prosecutions v. Smith* (H.L. 1961), where the defendant was charged for capital murder when he accelerated his car in order to hide stolen goods when an officer stopped him. As he sped away, the officer grabbed the side of the car and the defendant swerved the car until the officer was hit by another car and killed. The defendant argued that he did not possess the *mens rea* for murder, since he did not intend to kill the officer. Held: since the unlawful and voluntary conduct was directed at the victim, *if a reasonable man would have contemplated that the conduct directed toward the officer would have subjected the officer to gross bodily harm*, then the defendant is guilty of capital murder. Otherwise, he is guilty of manslaughter.

(ii) The **MPC** gets rid of all of that and merely requires a higher legal of negligence—reckless or gross negligence.

(1) A person acts negligently under the MPC when he "should be aware of ***a substantial and unjustifiable risk*** that the material element exists or will result from his conduct. The risk must be of such a nature and degree that the actor's failure to perceive it, considering the nature and purpose of his conduct and the circumstances known to him, involves a ***gross deviation from the standard of care*** that a reasonable person would observe in the actor's situation." MPC § 2.02(2)(d).

(2) Civil law ordinary negligence will normally not pass the negligence threshold required in the MPC.

(b) Establishing the Appropriate *Mens Rea* Standard

(i) Unless a crime operates as a strict liability (SL) offense, there is a difference between a taking and a wrongful taking. Only the latter is punishable.

(1) Thus, in *Morissette v. United States* (U.S. 1952), the Court reversed the defendant's conviction for "knowingly" converting government property when he removed scrap metal from government property. The lower courts' reading of the statute as requiring no more than SL just because it failed to mention requisite intent was flawed.

(ii) For public welfare offenses, Specific Intent is not required.

(1) In *United States v. Freed* (U.S. 1971), a district court dismissed an indictment for possession of unregistered hand grenades because there was no allegation of *mens rea*. Although they knew that they possessed grenades, the defendants claimed that they did not know that possession was illegal. Held: the defendants are not required to know that possession of the unregistered grenades is illegal. A reasonable person would suspect that items as dangerous as grenades are heavily regulated and suspect to registration. Since the statute is regulatory, specific intent is not required. Knowledge of possession is sufficient.

(iii) Congress passed the Protection of Children Against Sexual Exploitation Act (PCASEA) of 1997, which punishes any person who "knowingly transports … any visual depiction, if … the producing of such visual depiction involves the use of a minor engaging in sexually explicit conduct; and … such visual depiction is of such conduct."

(1) In *United States v. X-Citement Video* (U.S. 1994) (Rehnquist, C.J.), the defendant was convicted under the PCASEA. The Court of Appeals interpreted "knowingly" in the statute to apply only to the transporting, shipping, receiving, or distribution of the pornography. Since knowledge that the pornography involved child performers was not necessary, the Court of Appeals held that the statute was unconstitutional and reversed the defendant's convictions. On appeal, the Supreme Court saved the statute by interpreting "knowingly" *mens rea* to carry all of the way through to the knowledge that the pornography involved child performers and reversed the Court of Appeals by holding that the statute was constitutional.

(2) Dissent (Scalia, J.): the majority's interpretation goes against the text of the statute. The statute is unconstitutionally broad.

# 2 Justification and Excuse

## 2.1 Introduction to the Three Forms of Defenses

### 2.1.1 Derivative Defenses

(a) Derivative defenses are based the plaintiff's failure *to prove all of the requisite elements*.

(b) Example: a crime requires the *mens rea* of recklessness, yet the plaintiff can only prove that the defendant acted with negligence.

### 2.1.2 Justification

(a) Justification is based on the notion that, although all of the requisite elements were met, there was "some good reason" that justified the act.

(b) Although normally the act is criminal, under the circumstances, it is not wrongful and ***possibly desirable***.

(c) Examples of justification (different texts vary as to where they categorize these defenses):

(i) Necessity;

(ii) Self-defense; and

(iii) Public authority (law enforcement).

2.1.3 Excuse

(a) Excuse applies when the defendant commits a crime for which that he *should not be held accountable*.

(b) Although the actor's conduct has been ***harmful and undesirable***, he should be ***neither blamed nor punished***.

(c) Rationale: society does not wish to encourage the behavior or condition, but it does not wish to punish it either.

(d) There are two kinds of excuse: (i) situational excuse (duress, entrapment); and (ii) excuse at the individual level (mental abnormality, intoxication, infancy).

## 2.2 Justification

2.2.1 Self-Defense

(a) General Rule

(i) A party may use force to defend himself against harm threatened by ***unlawful acts*** when the defendant ***reasonably believes*:**

(1) The harm threatened is imminent;

(2) The use of force is reasonably necessary (not excessive) to avoid the harm.

(ii) Self-defense only applies when there is a physical threat, not when there are only insults.

(iii) Similarly, it does not apply when the threat has disappeared and the subject is merely retaliating.

(b) Reasonable Person Standard

(i) Several formulations are possible under the common law:

(1) *State v. Leidholm* (N.D. 1983) ***purely objective standard*** (stated but not used in *Leidholm*): looks to an objective person without considering the defendant's personal history and characteristics;

(2) *State v. Leidholm* **subjective test**: looks to the reasonable battered woman; the reasonable courageous person, etc.

(3) *People v. Goetz* (N.Y. 1986) ***intermediate reasonable person standard:*** also takes into account in the personal history and physical characteristics of the defendant;

(aa) This third position is applied to a defendant who invokes defense as a justification for his acts: although the defendant's belief must be objectively reasonable, his *personal characteristics* are *not ignored*.

(bb) *See People v. Goetz* (NY 1986), where the court held that the standard for determining whether the defendant was justified in shooting four youths who solicited money from him on the subway was that of the reasonable person while ***taking into account the defendant's knowledge and experiences*** (such as his having previously been robbed).

(ii) The MPC Formulation

(1) Under the MPC, "the use of force upon or toward another person is justifiable when the actor believes that such force is immediately necessary for the purpose of protecting himself against the use of unlawful force by such other person on the present occasion." MPC § 3.04(1).

(2) Unlike the common law formulation, the MPC standard is purely subjective.

(c) Deadly Force in Defense of Self

(i) Deadly force is force likely to cause death or serious bodily harm.

(ii) Common Law Formulation

(1) ***Majority View***: in defending oneself against a deadly threat, one may use *deadly force* and stand his ground *in any situation*.

(2) ***Minority View***[63]: in defending oneself against a deadly threat, one may only use *deadly force* if he has first "fled to the wall," unless:

(aa) There is the slightest reason to believe that he cannot make a safe retreat (*e.g.*, he is threatened with a firearm at close range); or

(bb) He is in his own home (the "castle" exception).

(3) Because guns have made retreat impractical, the distinction between the majority and minority views has decreased, since defendants will not be required to retreat when threatened with a gun under either approach.

(iii) MPC Formulation

(1) Under MPC, a party may use deadly force to defend himself against the use of unlawful force when he ***believes*** the use of force is necessary to avoid death, serious bodily injury, kidnapping or sexual intercourse compelled by force or threat. MPC § 3.04(2)(b).

(2) The standard, like the MPC necessity standard, is purely subjective.

---

[63] This view is embraced by the MPC and Restatement (Second) of Torts.

(d) Effect of Mistake in Claims of Self-Defense

(i) The Common Law

(1) Reasonable Mistake

(aa) The common law and modern law agree that the defendant is justified in using deadly force, even if he is mistaken as to the need of deadly force, when the mistake is reasonable.

(2) Unreasonable Mistake

(aa) The justification of defense does not arise when the defendant makes an unreasonable mistake as to the need to employ deadly force.

(bb) However, the common law developed the doctrine of ***imperfect justification***, which can reduce the degrees of a crime.

(cc) Thus, under imperfect justification, an honest but unreasonable mistake can, for example, reduce murder to manslaughter.

(ii) Mistake and the MPC

(1) The MPC supports the ***imperfect justification doctrine*** by generalizing it.

(2) Under the MPC, an honest but unreasonable mistake can remove the *mens rea* for crimes that require ***purpose or knowledge.***

(3) However, for crimes requiring only recklessness or negligence, an unreasonable mistake, whether it is reckless or negligent, will not serve as a defense.

(aa) For a crime requiring recklessness, however, a negligent mistake will serve as a defense.

(bb) For a crime requiring negligence, only a reasonable mistake will serve as a defense.

(iii) Mistake within Battered Woman's Syndrome

(1) Battered woman's syndrome is relevant to a self-defense justification in cases of murder when evidence of the syndrome helps determine the credibility of the defendant's testimony as to the need to act immediately in self-defense.

(2) *See State v. Kelly* (NJ 1984), where evidence was admitted showing that a woman who murdered her husband acted with a reasonable belief that she was defending herself from him. Evidence of battered wife's syndrome was relevant in showing: (i) the reasonableness of her not having left her husband and her reasons for not having done so (an addiction is caused by the syndrome); and (ii) her honesty in believing that her husband was about to kill her (it would establish her perception at the time of the stabbing).

2.2.2 Defense of Others

(a) Majority View

(i) Under the majority view, the defendant is jusfitifed in defending another person if he *reasonably believes* that the person was being attacked and had the right to use such force.

(ii) This approach is to limit liability.

(iii) The defendant may use the *same amount of force* that the victim being rescued would be able to use (reasonable under the circumstances).

(iv) Reasonable mistake of fact applies to the defendant just as it would apply to the victim.

(1) *See People v. Young* (N.Y. S.Ct. 1961) (Breitel, J.), where the defendant's conviction for assault of a police officer was reversed, since his mistake that two plain-clothes police officers in the middle of making an arrest were assaulting a victim was reasonable.

(b) Minority View

(i) Under the minority view, the defendant may only use the *same amount of force* that the victim would have been able to use under the circumstances.

(ii) This approach is to expand liability.

(1) *See People v. Young* (N.Y. 1962) (Per Curiam), where rescuers go to the aid of others ***at their own risk***.

(iii) Some jurisdictions continue to apply the following common law rules:

(1) ***The alter ego rule:*** if the person being rescued did not have the right to use the force, then the rescuer did not either; and

(2) ***The relationship test:*** defense of others only justifies an actor when he has a special relationship with the victim that he rescues.

2.2.3 Defense of Property

(a) The ***reasonable force*** standard in self-defense and defense of others also applies to defense of property.

(b) The defense of property privilege does *not* permit the defendant to use ***deadly force*** in protecting a home that is not a dwelling.

(c) Under a traditional common law doctrine, the defendant may, however, use deadly force in his own home against trespassers based on the ***reasonable belief*** that such force is necessary to prevent certain felonies against himself or against others.

(d) A minority of jurisdictions have even gone as far as permitting defendants to use deadly force against trespassers who the occupant believes may use *even slight physical force* against the occupant (*see, e.g., Colorado Revised Statutes*).

(e) Other states have limited this use of deadly force, requiring, for example, that deadly force be used only against trespassers who threaten the occupant's *life or limb.*

2.2.4 Necessity

(a) Under the Common Law

(i) Necessity was a defense at common law for an act that was *unavoidable* and *compelled.*

(ii) Under the Common Law,[64] the defendant is justified when he makes a *clear offer of proof* that:

(1) He was faced with ***clear and imminent harm*** (not speculative);

(2) He could reasonably expect his actions to be ***effective in avoiding the* greater *harm;***

(3) ***No legal alternative*** could avoid the harm; and

(4) The legislature has not acted to ***preclude*** the defense with clear purpose.

(aa) *See Commonwealth v. Markum* (Pa. Sup. Ct. 1988), where the court held that the defendants were not justified in storming an abortion clinic and damaging its property because there were ***legal alternatives*** such as peaceful protesting and the legislature, by legalizing certain abortions, acted to preclude the defense (the actor may not avert conduct that the legislator has approved by legalizing it).

(bb) Dissent (Tamilia, J.): it is possible that the defendants, in storming the clinic, were acting to avoid illegal post-viability abortions, in which case the legislature would not have acted to preclude the defense. The defendants were not, however, permitted to present this evidence.

(iii) The defense of necessity was so rarely successful that it can hardly be called a justification. In addition, it was no justification for homicide.

(1) *See The Queen v. Dudley and Stephens* (Q.B. 1884), where the court did not accept Dudley and Stephens' necessity defense for the charge of murder and cannibalism on the high seas, even though evidence showed that it was highly improbable that they would have survived had they not murdered and cannibalized a starved boy on the boat. The court held that the defendants were guilty of murder, but it sentenced them to only six months of prison without hard labor, rather than the earlier death penalty sentence.

(2) *N.B.*: the discussion on whether necessity justified the homicide was likely dictum, since ***necessity was not a justification for homicide*** under the common law.

(b) Under the MPC

[64] These elements are taken from the Pa. common law as pronounced in *Commonwealth v. Markum.*

(i) Under the MPC, necessity is referred to as "justification" or "choice of evils."

(ii) Conduct is justifiable when the actor ***believes***[65] it to be necessary to avoid harm to himself or to others when:

(1) The harm to himself or to others to be avoided is ***greater*** than that of his illegal actions. MPC § 3.02(1)(a);

(2) The law provides ***no exceptions or defenses*** for the situation involved. MPC § 3.02(1)(b); and

(3) There is ***no clear legislative intent to exclude the justification*** of necessity (*e.g.*, no law was passed legalizing the harm that the actor is seeking to avoid). MPC § 3.02(1)(c).

(iii) Necessity Created by the Fault of the Actor

(1) The MPC does not allow a choice-of-evils defense when the necessity created is the defendant's own fault.

(2) When recklessness or negligence establishes the requisite *mens rea* of the offense, the justification of necessity is unavailable as a defense ***when the actor is reckless or negligent in bringing about the harm*** to be avoided. MPC § 3.02(2).

(3) Example: A, while intoxicated, strikes B, and then drives while intoxicated in order to rush him to the hospital. There is no necessity defense for driving while intoxicated, since A brought about the harm to be avoided.

(4) Compare: C strikes B, then A, while intoxicated, rushes B to the hospital. A has a defense for driving while intoxicated.

2.2.5 Public Authority

(a) The early common law recognized otherwise criminal acts as justifiable when committed as part of law enforcement.

(b) This does not, however, equate an absolute privilege. For example, public officials may not break into private property with no warrant, based on some implied executive authority.

(i) *See United States v. Ehrlichman* (D.C. Cir. 1976), where the defendant, an assistant to President Nixon, was assigned to investigate the leak of the Pentagon Papers to the press. He was later convicted of breaking and entering into property without a warrant.

(c) However, when a person acts reasonably and with *good faith reliance* on the apparent authority of a public official, he is not liable for breaking the criminal law. *See United States v. Barker* (D.C. Cir. 1976).

[65] The test is ***subjective***, since it requires only that the actor ***believe*** his conduct to be necessary, which makes it harder for a court to deny the defense.

### 2.3 Situational Excuse

2.3.1 Introduction

(a) Situational excuse focuses on situations that cause otherwise law-abiding citizens to break the law.

(b) Situational excuse excuses the defendant for the commission of an offense because his will is overcome by his circumstances.

2.3.2 Duress

(a) Introduction

(i) Duress applies when the defendant acts illegally as a result of another's ***unlawful threat*** of bodily harm.

(ii) Duress involves an ***objective*** standard: the defendant must *reasonably believe* that the only way to avoid the threatened harm is to undertaken the illegal conduct.

(iii) The rule for duress is succinctly summarized by the United States Court of Appeals for the Fifth Circuit in *United States v. Willis* (5th Cir. 1994). To successfully invoke the defense, the following elements must be met:

(1) The defendant must have been under an "*unlawful and present, imminent, and impending threat* of such a nature as to induce a **well-grounded apprehension** of death or serious bodily injury";

(2) The defendant must not have "recklessly or negligently ***placed herself in a situation*** in which it was probable that she would be forced to choose the criminal conduct";

(3) The defendant must have "no ***reasonable*** legal alternative to violating the law"; and

(4) A "direct causal relationship may be ***reasonably*** anticipated between the criminal action taken and the avoidance of the threatened harm."

(b) The MPC

(i) Under the MPC, duress is a defense whenever ***unlawful force is used or threatened*** against the actor. MPC § 2.09(1).

(ii) The defense is unavailable when the actor *recklessly* places himself in the situation where he would probably be subject to duress, or when he does so *negligently* and negligence is the requisite *mens rea*. MPC § 2.09(2).

(c) Some jurisdictions allow duress as a defense for third parties.

(i) *See United States v. Haney* (10th Cir. 2002), where Francis feared threats of African American prisoners when *America's Most Wanted* described him as a leader of the Aryan Brotherhood. The defendant, who was helping Francis to avoid the dangers by escaping, was convicted of possession of escape paraphernalia while in prison. The defendant appealed, arguing duress. Held: the defense of duress should apply even when the harm threatens a third party. The issue should have gone to the jury. Reversed and remanded.

(1) *N.B.*: this case takes a similar approach to the defense against aggression justification. There, the imminent threat of bodily harm need not be limited to the defendant. Rather, it applies to his family or to any third party (although some jurisdictions limit reasonable mistake of fact defenses with the ***alter ego rule*** and ***relationship test***).

(2) *N.B.*: whether a jurisdiction allows duress as a choice of evils justification or as an excuse has significant consequences on the results of the law. For example, a jurisdiction that treats it as excuse would allow the defendant to cut off five hands at the threat of having his hand cut off whereas the defense would not work in a jurisdiction using justification.

(d) Duress and Battered Woman Syndrome

(i) Generally, evidence of battered woman's syndrome is not allowed into evidence, since the prejudicial value outweighs its probative value.

(ii) Since in duress and excuse generally, the issue looks to the extent to which the defendant's will is overborne, evidence of battered woman's syndrome would gravely prejudice the state's case no matter how much the court tried to give limiting instructions.

(e) Inapplicable to Murder

(i) As with necessity, duress was no excuse for intentional homicide under the common law. However, under the MPC, duress can be a defense for intentional homicide and the threat does not have to be imminent or limited to threats of bodily harm.

2.3.3 Entrapment

(a) Entrapment occurs when police or other government officials induce the defendant to commit a crime that he is in no way predisposed to commit.

(b) Entrapment is used by law enforcement official in situations where, but for the entrapment, it would be very difficult to procure evidence.

(i) It therefore is generally used in crimes where no party would report the crime, since all of the engaged parties are guilty.

(ii) Example: in a jurisdiction where both the sale and solicitation of drugs is illegal, a police officer may pose as a drug dealer in order to obtain evidence that the defendant was soliciting drugs.

(c) Entrapment is used as an affirmative defense to show that, but for the inducement by the government officials, the defendant would not have committed the act.

(d) It is not, however, available as a defense when government officials merely provide the opportunity or the equipment for a crime without inducing the defendant to undertake the prohibited activity.

### 2.4 Excuse at the Individual Level

2.4.1 Introductory Notes

(a) With respect to the excuses that focus on the individual, it is not the situation, but rather, the individual himself that causes the law to excuse his conduct.

2.4.2 Mental Abnormality (Insanity): the Various Approaches and the Current Law

(a) *M'Naghten's* Test

(i) The modern insanity defense has its roots in the *M'Naghten's* case, which was pronounced by the House of Lords and is the majority approach.

(ii) According to the *M'Naghten* rule, the accused is excused from criminal punishment (but usually remitted to civil commitment) only if "at the time of committing the act, the party accused was laboring under such a defect of reason, from disease of the mind, as ***not to know the nature and quality of the act he was doing***, or if he did know it, that he ***did not know he was doing what was wrong***."

(iii) The M'Naghten approach uses a ***cognitive test*** (baed on knowledge): as a result of a defect of reason or disease of the mind, the defendant must not know either:

(1) The *nature and quality* of the thing being done;

(aa) Example: the defendant swings what he believes to be a disappearing baseball bat at victim's head, but the bat does not disappear and he kills her;

(2) That the thing being done was *wrong*.

(aa) Most cases fall under this prong.

(b) The Product Test

(i) Also known as the *Durham* test, the product test is used in a few states.

(ii) A defendant is exculpated for a crime when his conduct was the offspring and ***product*** of a mental illness.

(iii) Criticism: deterministic psychologists and psychiatrists tend to see *all conduct* as products.

(c) The Control Test

(i) Also known as the "volitional" or "irresistible impulse test," the control test is used in a few states.

(ii) It applies when the defendant is ***unable to resist an impulse*** (due to mental illness). The defendant is exculpated when his conduct results from an *irresistible impulse.*

(iii) A problem with this view: one is to ask the scientists if it was an irresistible impulse, but they tend to see everything as irresistible since most have a materialist, determinist worldview.

(iv) *M'Naghten's* cognitive test is different. Science *can* be approached to determine cognition.

(1) *N.B.*: the insanity defense is not available when a psychopath is garbling the moral code. When the heart is ill, the defendant is guilty; but when the heart's innocence is garbled by an ill mind, the defendant is innocent.

(d) Model Penal Code

(i) The MPC was the majority approach until the *Hinckley* case (*see infra.*).

(ii) The MPC responds to the criticism that the *M'Naghten* rule's exclusive focus on cognitive capacity is too narrow.

(iii) According to the MPC, a person is not responsible for criminal conduct if at the time of such conduct, as a result of mental disease or defect, he *lacks substantial capacity* either to:

(1) Appreciate the wrongfulness of his conduct (***cognitive prong*** based on knowledge); or

(2) Conform his conduct to the requirements of law (***control/volition prong***) MPC § 4.01(1).

(iv) This test is easier on the defendants in two ways:

(1) The defendant needs only to ***lack substantial capacity***; and

(2) The cognitive prong is satisfied even if the defendant does not *know* of the wrongfulness of his conduct; he only needs to not ***appreciate*** the wrongfulness of it.

(aa) *Compare the M'Naghten rule*, where the defense only applies when the defendant does not ***know*** of the wrongfulness; failure to appreciate the wrongfulness is insufficient.

(v) Regarding the cognitive prong, the MPC employs only the second ***knowledge of the wrongfulness*** prong of the *M'Naghten* cognitive test.

(1) This may be because the MPC views the first prong (knowledge of the ***nature and quality*** of the act) as superfluous: if the defendant does not realize that it is wrong, then he does not appreciate the nature and quality of the act.

(2) However, this could have adverse consequences.

(aa) Example: the defendant, while in a delusional state, kidnaps a girl, believing that he is stealing a doll. Verdict?

(bb) Under the *M'Naghten* test, the defendant is not guilty, since he did not know of the nature and quality of the act. Under the MPC cognitive prong, however, the defendant is guilty, if he recognizes that stealing even dolls is wrong.

(e) The *Hinckley* Case

(i) Up until this case, the *cognitive/volitional test* of the MPC was being applied by more and more courts over the *cognitive test* of the common law.

(ii) However, at the time of *United States v. Hinckley* (D.D.C. 1981), a case in which John Hinckley was indicted for the attempted assassination of President Reagan and then later acquitted, the trend was reversed, leading to more courts' returning to the common law cognitive test.

(iii) Congress and the states thereafter severely narrowed the insanity defense.

(f) Current Law

(i) Burdens of Proof

(1) Burden of Production

(aa) All states place the burden of producing sufficient evidence to raise the defense on the defendant.

(2) Burden of Persuasion

(aa) Two thirds of the states place the burden of persuasion on the defendant, who must generally prove the defense *by a preponderance of the evidence*.

(bb) One third of the states shift the burden of persuasion to the prosecutor, who must disprove the defense ***beyond a reasonable doubt*** once the defendant meets the burden of production.

(ii) The Federal Insanity Defense Statute

(1) 18 U.S.C. § 20 requires that the defendant be unable to "appreciate" the act. Both sub-prongs of M'Naghten are present.

(2) Unlike the MPC, where the prosecution has the burden of persuasion, the defendant must meet the burden of persuasion (and production) by clear and convincing evidence.

2.4.3 Intoxication

(a) Involuntary Intoxication

(i) Most American jurisdictions treat involuntary intoxication as a defense.

(ii) The MPC establishes this rule in § 2.08(4).

(b) Voluntary Intoxication

(i) The Common Law

(1) Specific Intent Crimes

(aa) For specific intent crimes, voluntary intoxication is generally a defense.

(bb) At least eleven states have, however, adopted a restrictive position, where voluntary intoxication is not a defense for most or all specific intent crimes.

(cc) In as many as half the states, voluntary intoxication serves as a defense only if the defendant proves *with the preponderance of the evidence* that *his intoxication was so severe that it negated the specific intent.* The burden on the defendant is much higher than that required to simply create a mere reasonable doubt as to the state's case.

(2) General Intent Crimes

(aa) For general intent crimes, however, voluntary intoxication was often seen to be irrelevant to or to aggravate the defendant's liability. *Director of Public Prosecutions v. Majewski* (H.L. 1976).

(bb) However, when voluntary intoxication leads to *lasting psychotic effects* that go *beyond the immediate effects of the intoxication*, there is a defense that functions in the same way as insanity.

(I) *See People v. Kelly* (Cal. 1973), where the defendant, after taking drugs, experienced lasting psychotic effects that lead her to stab and severely wound her mother. Held: by reason of insanity, the defendant is not guilty.

(II) *See also Beasley v. State* (Ala. 1874), where the defendant's conviction of second-degree murder was *reversed*, because the jury should have been instructed on insanity. He had an attack of delirium tremens, a withdrawal symptom that develops for people physiologically dependent on alcohol, several weeks before the killing.

(ii) The MPC

(1) Intoxication is a defense if it negates an element of a crime. MPC § 2.08(1).

(2) However, voluntary intoxication cannot be used to negate the *mens rea* of recklessness, even if his being intoxicated causes him to be unaware of a risk. MPC § 2.08(2).

(3) In addition, voluntary intoxication cannot negate the *mens rea* of negligence.

2.4.4 Infancy

(a) An infant is a person who has not yet reached the legal age of majority (generally, eighteen years of age).

(b) Under the traditional common law, infants under seven years of age cannot be held criminally liable for their acts. When a child is between seven to fourteen years old, a rebuttable presumption arises that he lacks criminal capacity.

(c) Many jurisdictions have abolished the common law approach through statutes that establish a minimum age after which a child may be held criminally liable.

2.4.5 Mistake

(a) Mistake of the Non-Criminal Law

(i) A mistake of the non-criminal law is the equivalent of a mistake of fact.

(1) Example: a subject's mistaken belief that he is divorced equates a mistaken belief that the divorce law considers him divorced.

(ii) Common Law Approach

(1) Specific Intent Crimes

(aa) A ***mistake of fact*** is a defense for specific intent crimes if it: (i) is honest; and (ii) removes the requisite intent.

(bb) Example: the defendant's honest mistake as to the ownership of hogs that he had captured and killed serves as a defense to the specific intent crime of larceny. *Green v. State* (1949).

(cc) This is true even if the mistake is unreasonable or negligent.

(2) General Intent Crimes

(aa) A mistake of fact is a defense for a general intent crime if it: (i) is *both subjectively* ***honest*** and *objectively* ***reasonable***; and (ii) negates the requisite *mens rea*.

(bb) Example: the defendant is charged with kidnapping a boy and girl. The former count was dismissed when the boy was shown to be his grandson, since the act was committed with the father's apparent consent. Regarding the girl, the defendant claims that he thought she was his granddaughter, and when he realized she was not, he let her go. Since kidnapping is a general intent crime, the jury must acquit the defendant if his mistake is *both honest and reasonable*. *State v. Walker* (1978).

(cc) *See People v. Bray* (Cal. 1975), where the court held that the defendant's mistake as to whether he was a felon was a *mistake of fact* that excused him of his offense.

(iii) MPC Approach

(1) Mistake of the non-criminal law serves as a defense if: (i) the ignorance or mistake negates the requisite *mens rea*; or (ii) the law provides that the state of mind established by such mistake constitutes a defense. MPC § 2.04(1).

(b) Mistake of the Criminal Law

(i) Under the *common law* and *MPC* § 2.04(3)(a), mistake of the criminal law is generally no defense. However, there are some exceptions.

(ii) The defendant is not liable when some element of the crime requires knowledge of some fact and he defendant is ignorant as to this fact.

(iii) The defendant is similarly not liable when he has no knowledge of the law and there is no reasonable way to inform himself of it.

(1) *See State v. Fox* (Idaho 1993), where the defendant was charged with possession of ephedrine, a controlled substance. On appeal, the defendant argued that the jury should have been instructed that he could only be found guilty if it was concluded that he possessed ephedrine *knowing that it was a controlled substance*. The court held that since this was a specific intent crime, only a mistake as to the non-criminal law could provide an excuse. Here, however, the mistake was of the criminal law (*i.e.*, the illegality of the ephedrine). Since ignorance of the criminal law is no excuse, the only intent required to violate this statute is the intent to knowingly do the forbidden act (not to knowingly violate the law), which the defendant did, regardless of whether he did not know that it was prohibited. Ignorance of the criminal law is no excuse, unless the defendant could not have been aware of the law, which here is not the case.

(iv) Furthermore, there is a defense when the defendant acts in reasonable reliance upon an official statement of the law that is afterward determined to be erroneous (this exception is codified in MPC § 2.04(3), but also applies in the common law).

(1) An official interpretation of the law must derive from the Judicial Branch, not from some executive officer.

(2) *See Hopkins v. State* (Md. 1950), where the court considered inconsequential the fact that the defendant relied on the state attorney general's interpretation of a signage statute before convicting him for violating it.

**Summary of Ignorance or Mistake**

<table>
<tr><td rowspan="3">Mistake of the Non-Criminal Law</td><td rowspan="2">Common law</td><td>Specific Intent</td><td>Serves as a defense if it: (i) is honest; and (ii) removes the requisite intent.</td></tr>
<tr><td>General Intent</td><td>Serves as a defense if it: (i) is both subjectively honest and objectively reasonable; and (ii) negates the requisite mens rea.</td></tr>
<tr><td>MPC</td><td colspan="2">Serves as a defense if: (i) the ignorance or mistake negates the requisite mens rea; or (ii) the law provides that the state of mind established by such mistake constitutes a defense. MPC § 2.04(1).</td></tr>
<tr><td>Mistake of the Criminal Law</td><td colspan="3">No defense, unless:<br>(i) some element of the crime requires knowledge of some fact and he defendant is ignorant as to this fact; or<br>(ii) the defendant has no reasonable way to inform himself of the law or he acts in reasonable reliance upon an official statement of the law that is afterward determined to be erroneous (these exceptions apply in the common law and MPC; the second prong is codified in MPC § 2.04(3)).</td></tr>
</table>

## 3 Complicity

### 3.1 Introduction

3.1.1 Complicity refers to the state of being an accomplice or partner in wrongdoing.

3.1.2 An accomplice must: (i) intend to facilitate the commission of a crime; and (ii) aid or fail to act on a legal duty.

### 3.2 Parties in a Crime at Common Law

3.2.1 Principal in the First Degree

(a) The principal in the first degree is the actor who performed the criminal act.

3.2.2 Principal in the Second Degree

(a) The principal in the second degree: (i) is ***present*** at the time of the crime; and (ii) "***aids and abets***" the principal in the first degree by counseling, directing, or encouraging him; with (iii) the ***specific intent*** that the crime be committed.

(i) Example: the driver of a getaway car in a bank robbery.

(b) Today, a principal in the second degree is referred to as an "accomplice" and can be punished to the same extent as the principal in the first degree.

3.2.3 Accessory Before the Fact

(a) An accessory before the fact: (i) is ***not present*** at the time of the crime; and (ii) "***aids and abets***" the principal in the first degree by counseling, commanding, or encouraging him; with (iii) the ***specific intent*** that the crime be committed.

(b) Under the MPC, an accessory is not liable when (i) he terminates his complicity *prior to the commission of the act*; and (ii) he either:

(i) Wholly deprives the act of its effectiveness; or

(ii) Gives timely warning to law enforcement officials or otherwise acts to prevent its commission. MPC § 2.06(6).

(c) Under the modern law, there is no distinction between *principals in the second degree* and *accessories before the act*.

(i) Today, both are considered *"accomplices"* and both can be *punished* to the same extent as the principal in the first degree.

(ii) However, under the common law, the accessory before the fact could only be convicted if the principal in the first degree was convicted (under the modern majority view, the accessory before the fact could be punished even if the principal in the first degree).

3.2.4 Accessory After the Fact

(a) An accessory after the fact commits the *obstruction of justice* by, for example, stopping the arrest of or harboring a felon or fugitive.

(b) The defendant is an accessory after the fact when:

(i) A felony was ***completed*** by another;

(ii) The accessory after the fact ***knew*** *that the felony had been committed*; and

(iii) The accessory ***assisted the felon*** by impeding his arrest or otherwise obstructing justice.

(c) Most jurisdictions recognize the acts of the *accessory after the fact* as a separate crime from that of the accomplices and thus do not punish them to the same extent as they punish the acts of the principal in the first degree and the acts of the accomplices.

**3.3 The Conduct Required for Complicity**

3.3.1 Rule: the defendant must be ***acting in preconcert*** with the principal and there must be some ***physical act*** (this is action-based).

3.3.2 Both of these elements have to do with aiding and abetting.

**3.4 The Culpability Required for Complicity**

3.4.1 Conduct

(a) Majority view: *purpose* is required for aiding and abetting.

(b) Minority view: mere *knowledge* is sufficient in supporting a conviction for aiding and abetting.

(i) *See Backun v. United States* (4th Cir. 1940), where the selling of stolen property with knowledge that it was to be illegally transported was enough to support a conviction for aiding and abetting the criminal transport of property in interstate commerce.

3.4.2 Circumstances

(a) Under both the common law and the MPC, *knowledge* is probably required, but this is not clear.

(b) Compare attempt, where the circumstance element carries over under the MPC and is probably boosted to knowledge under the common law.

3.4.3 Result

(a) Under the common law: purpose is required, but in the case of homicide, the requiste *mens rea* carries over.

(b) Under the MPC, it carries over. MPC § 2.06(4).

(i) *N.B.*: compare attempt, where there is a boosting to purpose (under the common law) or purpose or belief (under the MPC).

**3.5 Guilt of the Principal**

3.5.1 Under the common law, to convict an accessory, the principal must first be convicted.

3.5.2 Under the modern trend, a principal in the second degree can be convicted even if the principal in the first degree is not.

(a) *See Regina v. Cogan and Leak* (Q.B. 1975), where the defendant husband encouraged the codefendant to have sex with the defendant's wife, despite her refusal. After the act was completed, the defendant's wife called the police and both were arrested. The defendant confessed that he intended for his wife to be raped. The codefendant claimed that he thought that she consented. Both were convicted. The codefendant's conviction was quashed and the defendant appealed on the grounds that since the codefendant's conviction had been quashed, then the defendant could not be held guilty for aiding and abetting. Held: the defendant's argument is rejected. Just because a principal in the first degree is not found guilty does not mean that an accomplice cannot be. Here, the codefendant was not an innocent agent, even though he may have been partially duped.

**3.6 Renunciation**

3.6.1 Common Law

(a) Under the common law, withdrawal is a defense if the defendant (i) ***communicates*** his repudiation; and (ii) takes steps to ***neutralize any assistance*** he has provided through counseling, commanding, or encouraging the crime.

(b) The withdrawal must be because of a renunciation of the criminal intent to complete the crime, not because of outside circumstrances such as the fear of being caught or because of outside pressures.

3.6.2 MPC

(a) An accessory is not liable when he terminates his complicity prior to the commission of the act and either (i) wholly deprives the act of its effectiveness or (ii) gives timely warning to law enforcement officials or otherwise acts to prevent its commission. MPC § 2.06(6).

## 4 Inchoate Crimes

### 4.1 Attempt

4.1.1 Elements

(a) Attempt is an inchoate crime whose elements are as follow:

(i) The *specific intent* to cause an *ultimate, criminal offense* to occur (*mens rea*); and

(ii) A significant, overt act beyond mere preparation towards the commission of the *ultimate offense* (*actus reus*).

4.1.2 *Mens Rea*

(a) The Traditional View

(i) The traditional view of *mens rea* in the common law is that attempt requires specific intent: the defendant must ***intend to cause the ultimate offense*** to occur. This approach is followed in almost all jurisdictions.

(1) *See Thacker v. Commonwealth* (Va. 1922), where the defendant's conviction for attempted murder for shooting at Mrs. Ratrie's tent while he was intoxicated was reversed because he intended to shoot only the light, not Mrs. Ratrie.

(ii) According to this view, one cannot be held criminally liable for attempt of a crime whose requisite *mens rea* is mere negligence or recklessness.

(1) For example, one cannot be convicted of attempted manslaughter, since in manslaughter, a crime that lacks malice aforethought, one does not intend to cause the resulting homicide.

(b) Anomolous Cases

(i) Some *anomalous cases*, however, allow such prosecutions by applying the *mens rea* to only the actual conduct, not to the resulting consequences.

(ii) *See People v. Thomas* (Colo. 1986), where the defendant, who is charged with attempted reckless manslaughter, argued that there could be no such crime, since intent is an element of attempt and if the defendant intended to murder the alleged rapist of the defendant's girlfriend, then it would not be reckless manslaughter. Held: there is a cognizable crime of reckless manslaughter in Col. The specific intent did not carry over to the actual death of the victim, but rather, to only the act itself that lead to the death. Here, since the defendant had specific intent to fire his gun at the alleged rapist, the fact that the defendant did not intend for the man to die is immaterial, since he intended to fire the gun. The only *mens rea* required is purpose towards the risk-creating conduct.

(c) Comparing the *mens rea* of attempt to the *mens rea* of the ultimate offense:

(i) Under the Common Law:

(1) ***Conduct:*** it is boosted to *purpose* for attempt;

(2) ***Circumstance:*** it is probably boosted to *knowledge*, but it is unclear and it may be carry over.[66]

(3) ***Result:*** it is boosted to *purpose* for attempt (with the exception of some anomalous jurisdictions that do not require purpose for the result. *See People v. Thomas*).

(ii) Under the MPC § 5.01:

(1) ***Conduct:*** requires *purpose*;

(2) ***Circumstance:*** carries over from the underlying offense with no boosting;

(3) ***Result:*** *purpose* or *belief* (similar to knowledge) is required.

(d) The Moral Wrong and Legal Wrong Doctrines

(i) Moral Wrong Doctrine

(1) Under the ***moral wrong doctrine*** for both the common law and MPC, there is no exculpation when the defendant's behavior would be immoral even if the circumstances were as the defendant honestly and reasonably believed them to be.

(2) For example, in a jurisdiction that accepts the moral wrong doctrine, an honest and reasonable mistake as to the nighttime element in a case of burglary would be no defense, since the facts, as the defendant believed them to be, would be *morally wrong*. Although the *mens rea* as to the circumstances element is normally knowledge, the defendant's lack of knowledge is no excuse.

(3) Under common law attempt, in contrast, an honest and reasonable mistake would be a defense, if the *mens rea* with respect to the circumstance element is boosted to knowledge. If the defendant, in his mistake, did not know that it was night, he could not be guilty of attempted burglary.

---

[66] Note the difference in result: if the defendant is charged with attempted statutory rape and he does not know that victim is underage, if the *mens rea* for attempted is boosted to knowledge, the defendant will *not* be guilty of attempted statutory rape, since he had no knowledge; but if the *mens rea* is carried over from the underlying offense, he will be guilty of statutory rape.

(4) The MPC would lead to the same result as that of the moral wrong doctrine: since the *mens rea* with respect to the circumstance element carries over from the underlying offense, mistake with respect to nighttime would be no defense.

(ii) Legal Wrong Doctrine

(1) The moral doctrine is accepted in many American states, but jurisdictions are more likely to adopt the ***legal wrong doctrine***.

(2) Under this doctrine, if the defendant, because of his mistake, would normally be found not guilty of some offense because of a sincerely held but mistaken belief, a court may nevertheless hold him guilty of that offense ***if under circumstances as he believed them to be, he would have been guilty of some other offense.***

(3) Courts feel much more comfortable applying the legal wrong doctrine since they only have to look at statutes to see what is illegal, rather than impose their views of morality, which is required under the moral wrong doctrine.

### 4.1.3 *Actus Reus*

(a) The *actus reus* must manifest or be symbolic of the offense and unambiguously further the intended crime in a way that goes beyond mere preparation. *People v. Bowen and Rouse*, (Mich. Ct. App. 1968).

(b) There are three approaches for determining whether the defendant's acts meet attempt's *actus reus* requirement:

(i) Common Law Proximity Test

(1) The common law proximity test takes the ultimate offense as the starting point and examines its *proximity* to the completed act.

(2) If defendant's is close enough to reaching the *ultimate offense*, then it is worthy of punishment.

(3) Several tests have been offered for proximity based on dangerousness, closeness, and wickedness.

(ii) Common Law *Res Ipsa Loquitur* Test

(1) This test looks to the completed conduct and asks whether that conduct *unequivocally refers* to the ultimate offense as the natural and probable result of that conduct.

(iii) MPC "Strongly Corroborates" Test

(1) Under the MPC, the *actus reus* in attempt must be a ***substantial step*** toward the commission of the crime.

(2) The substantial step must "***strongly corroborate***" the ultimate offense.

(c) Example: the defendant waves his arms while in his home, believing that he will cause traffic to stop on a main thoroughfare, in violation of a local ordinance. Is the defendant guilty of attempt?

(i) Under the Common Law

(1) *Mens rea*: this is met, since the defendant intended to stop traffic;

(2) *Actus reus*: not met, since the step taken in furtherance of the crime was neither within proximity of the prohibited result nor unequivocally referred to the ultimate offense.

(ii) Under the MPC

(1) *Mens rea*:

(aa) Conduct: there is purpose to engage in the conduct;

(bb) Circumstance: this is met.

(cc) Result: there is purpose or belief that the result come about.

(2) *Actus reus*: most courts consider this to be just a carry-over element. The *actus reus*, or "substantial step" that "strongly corroborates" the *mens rea*, helps to show the *mens rea*, and is generally automatically met.

4.1.4 Impossibility

(a) Under the Common Law

(i) Traditionally, the courts distinguished between two kinds of impossibility:

(1) ***Factual impossibility***: where commission is impossible because of some underlying fact (*e.g.*, the defendant attempts to murder his victim, but the victim is already dead);

(2) ***Legal impossibility***: where commission of attempt is impossible because the attempted behavior does not constitute a crime (*e.g.*, the defendant attempts to take aspirin without a prescription).

(ii) Under the common law, *factual* impossibility was no defense, but legal impossibility was.

(iii) Courts, however, became bogged down in deciding what constituted factual impossibility and what constituted legal impossibility.

(iv) Just as mistake of the non-criminal law could be phrased as a mistake of fact, so too could legal impossibility be categorized as factual impossibility by the turning of a phrase.

(v) For example, although one could classify as factual impossibility the attempted murder of a person who is already dead, so too could it be considered legal impossibility, since firing at a corpse is no crime.

(vi) The tendency under the common law today is thus to treat both as legal impossibility, which offers a defense.

(b) Under the MPC

(i) The MPC abolishes the distinction between factual and legal impossibility and provides neither as a defense.

(ii) Thus, if the defendant intended to do an act proscribed by the law, then even if committing the act was impossible (*e.g.*, the person he was trying to murder was already dead), he could be convicted of attempted murder, provided that under the mistaken facts as the defendant believed them to be, he was committing a crime.

(1) *See People v. Dlugash* (N.Y. 1977), where the court held that a defendant may be convicted of attempt, even if the victim was already dead at the time that the defendant shot him in the head five times. What matters for attempt is what is in the defendant's mind, not the reality. Thus, if while acting, the defendant thought he was committing murder, this would be enough for attempted murder.

(c) "True" Legal Impossibility

(i) Under both the common law and MPC, ***"true" legal impossibility***, where the attempted conduct is not criminal (*e.g.*, the consumption of aspirin without a prescription), is always a defense.

(ii) Thus, if the victim of the defendant's battery was already dead before the defendant shot at him five times, and the defendant knew him to be dead, then the defendant could not be guilty of attempted murder, since shooting at a corpse constitutes no crime.

4.1.5 Renunciation

(a) The Common Law

(i) The traditional common law position on abandonment (the term often used in the common law for renunciation) is retributive: as long as the defendant's act went beyond mere preparation, it does not matter whether he later abandoned his criminal purpose.

(ii) The act insofar as it was committed was an evil act to be punished.

(iii) Since attempt is itself an offense, then abandonment is no defense once attempt is complete; the evil act can not be afterwards "undone."

(b) The MPC

(i) The MPC, embracing social control theories, allows renunciation (the MPC term) as a basis for acquittal.

(ii) If the defendant renounces the criminal conduct, then *it does not matter that he committed the act*, since he repented and was reformed.

(iii) The defense operates when the following elements are met:

(1) The defendant ***abandons*** or otherwise prevents the commission of the crime; and

(2) There is ***complete*** and ***voluntary*** renunciation of the defendant's criminal purpose.

(aa) Renunciation is not complete when "motivated by a decision to postpone the criminal conduct until a more advantageous time or to transfer the criminal effort to another but similar objective or victim." MPC § 5.01(4).

(bb) Renunciation is not voluntary when motivated by "circumstances, not present or apparent at the inception of the actor's course of conduct, that increase the probability of detection or apprehension or that make more difficult the accomplishment of the criminal purpose." MPC § 5.01(4).

(I) Renunciation is voluntary when the defendant is motivated solely by the defendant's conscience.

(II) *See Ross v. Mississippi* (Miss. 1992), where the defendant failed to consummate a rape not because of outside circumstances, but rather, because of his own conscience for the victim when he heard about her daughter. Under the Mississippi attempt statute, he could not be convicted of attempted rape.

### 4.2 Conspiracy

4.2.1 The elements of conspiracy are as follow:

(a) An agreement between two or more people;

(i) The agreement does not have to be express; it may be inferred through *conduct* or *circumstances*.

(ii) It must be a *bona fide* agreement between at least two competent people (an agreement between the defendant and an undercover police officer does not qualify);

(1) *See Regle v. State of Maryland* (Md. App. 1970), the defendant conspired with three others to commit an armed robbery. One of them was a police informant; another was an undercover police officer; and the third was insane. The court held that the defendant could not be held guilty of conspiracy to commit armed robbery because there had been no agreement with any of the others (the mentally ill partner lacked capacity to agree).

(b) With the specific intent to commit either: (i) an illegal act; or (ii) a legal act by illegal means;

(c) Accompanied by an overt act (in some states).

(i) Although the traditional common law does not require an overt act, about half of the states require an overt act for a conspiracy conviction.

(ii) The MPC has an overt act requirement for *less grave offenses only*.

(iii) Where required, the act does not have to be criminal. It needs to be no more than a step towards completion of the conspiracy, *however insignificant* and *innocent*.

(iv) The standard is much lower than that required for attempt under the common law proximity and "unequivocally refer to" tests and the MPC "strongly corroborates" test.

(v) For conspiracy, mere preparation meets the test.

(vi) The act answers a criticism that the agreement, which may be only *implicit*, does not satisfy the conduct required for a crime to be punished.

4.2.2 Conspiracy as an Inchoate Offense

(a) Those states that do require an overt act for the purpose of conspiracy do not require the act to be completed.

(b) Thus, like attempt and solicitation, conspiracy is an inchoate offense.

(c) Conspiracy as a Lesser Included Offense in Attempt

(i) The elements of conspiracy are the specific intent to commit an illegal act and the *actus reus* of an agreement and, in some jurisdictions, an overt act (no matter how insignificant).

(ii) Some jurisdictions consider the elements of conspiracy to be included in those of attempt, which requires the specific intent to commit an ultimate offense and a significant, overt act towards that end.

(1) In *People v. Burleson* (Ill. App. 1977), the defendants intended to rob a bank on September 13. The defendant was in charge of getting the shotgun and his codefendant of obtaining disguises. When they arrived, they decided to postpone the operation until September 16, since there were too many people. On the day of the robbery, their plan was frustrated and both defendants were caught. They were convicted for conspiracy on September 13 and for attempt on September 16. Issue: can conspiracy be vacated because of the conviction for the attempt? Held: attempt requires intent to commit the ultimate offense and a significant, overt act towards that end; conspiracy requires only intent for the target offense, an agreement, and an overt act, however insignificant (not required in all jurisdictions; under the traditional common law, it is not required). Conspiracy is therefore a lesser included offense of attempt. Therefore, the defendant cannot be convicted for conspiracy because he was convicted for attempt.

(iii) The MPC does not adopt this approach and does not consider conspiracy to be a lesser included offense of attempt. This seems reasonable, since attempt does not require an agreement.

(iv) The MPC nonetheless does not alow for a conviction of both conspiracy and attempt.

4.2.3 Impossibility

(a) Factual Impossibility

(i) Factual impossibility is no defense to conspiracy.

(b) Legal Impossibility

(i) Legal impossibility, which can easily be confused with factual responsibility, is no defense to conspiracy.

(ii) Legal impossibility is no defense to conspiracy.

(iii) Theoretically, then, a prosecutor could charge a defendant with conspiracy to rape, even if it were legally impossible to rape the victim.

(c) "True" Legal Impossibility

(i) "True" legal impossibility, where the underlying conduct does not constitute a crime, is a defense under the MPC and under the modern law.

(ii) Thus, if the conspiracy is to commit a target that is not a real crime (*e.g.*, conspiracy to consume aspirin without a prescription), the defendant cannot be held criminally liable.

(iii) However, under the common law, defendants have been convicted for conspiracy to commit that which is not a crime, when the defendants believed that they were conspiring to commit a crime.

4.2.4 Renunciation

(a) Common Law Approach

(i) Under the traditional common law, abandonment for conspiracy, like abandonment for attempt, was ***no defense***.

(ii) However, renucniation limits the actor's liability for acts committed after his withdrawal.

(b) MPC Approach

(i) Under MPC § 5.03(6), renunciation of criminal purpose is an affirmative defense when:

(1) The actor performs an affirmative act to ***thwart*** the success of the conspiracy; and

(2) The circumstances represent ***complete*** and ***voluntary*** renunciation of the actor's criminal purpose.

4.2.5 The Relation of Conspiracy to Complicity

(a) Conspiracy requires an agreement with others to commit an illegal act or a legal act by illegal means, with the intent to enter into the agreement and to commit the act.

(b) Complicity, on the other hand, does not necessarily require an agreement. An accomplice may aid and abet in the commission of a crime without outright agreement.

(c) Rather, complicity requires a ***complete act*** (which conspiracies do not necessarily require).

(d) However, generally speaking, accomplices are also conspirators.

(i) Under both the common law and the MPC, mere knowledge generally fulfills the *mens rea* circumstance requirement for conspiracy.

(ii) *N.B.*: if the offense were ***aggravated*** (*e.g.*, the defendant knew that he was selling the H-bomb to the codefendant, who would use it to blow up NY), it would be required that he purpose that the codefendant use it. In such a situation, a court would likely infer P from K.

(e) If the charge is conspiracy, each conspirator is liable for every target offense.

(f) Under the MPC, even if a co-conspirator is found not guilty, a conspirator can be found guilty, since under the MPC, conspiracy can be unilateral.

## 4.3 Solicitation

### 4.3.1 Introduction

(a) Solicitation is the act of entreating, imploring, inducing, encouraging, or promoting another person to engage in behavior that would constitute a crime. It is an inchoate crime that is punishable separately from the underlying solicited conduct.

(b) The soliciting party must have the *specific intent* that the solicited party commit the underlying offense.

(c) If the defendant communicates the solicitation in such a negligent way that a third party receives the communication and undertakes the solicited action, the defendant will not be guilty of solicitation because he never intended to solicit the third party.

(d) The common law limited solicitation to cases where the underlying crime was a felony or a breach of the peace. The MPC, in contrast, considers any crime or an attempt thereof as sufficient for solicitation.

(e) Like attempt, but unlike conspiracy, solicitation *merges* with the underlying offense.

### 4.3.2 Solicitation as an Inchoate Crime

(a) Since solicitation is an inchoate crime, it is not necessary that the underlying crime be completed or that the solicited party agree to engage in the prohibited behavior.

(i) Example: A solicits B to break into C's home and commit a felony therein. It turns out that B is a police officer who immediately arrests A for solicitation. Although B never agreed to the act, and the act never came about, A would be guilty of solicitation.

(b) Uncommunicated Solicitation

(i) The states are divided as to whether a solicitation that never reaches its intended recipient constitutes a completed or an attempted solicitation.

(ii) Some courts have held that the defendant is guilty if the communication is communicated, but never reaches the recipient, as long as the defendant *intended* to communicate it.

(1) The MPC takes this even further in holding the defendant criminally liable, even if he "fails to communicate with the person he solicits to commit a crime if his conduct was designed to effect such communication." MPC § 5.02(2).

(iii) Other courts, however, hold the defendant guilty only of *attempted solicitation* when the communication does not reach the intended recipient.

4.3.3 Defenses

(a) Impossibility

(i) Impossibility of the underlying offense is no defense to solicitation when the soliciting party believed that completion of the underlying offense was possible.

(ii) However, "true" legal impossibility is a defense, since the underlying offense must be a real crime.

(1) Example: a defendant cannot be held guilty of "the solicitation of purchasing aspirin with no prescription," even if he honeslty believes that such conduct constitutes a crime.

(b) Withdrawal

(i) At common law, ***withdrawal*** ("abandonment") is not a defense to solicitation once the solicitation is complete (it may, however, be a defense to the underlying crime).

(ii) In contrast, under the MPC, withdrawal ("renunciation") is an affirmative defense when the following elements are met:

(1) The actor persuades the solicited party not commit the solicited crime or otherwise prevents the commission of the crime; and

(2) The withdrawal is done under circumstances manifesting a *complete* and *voluntary renunciation* of the criminal purpose. MPC § 5.02(3).

## 5 Crimes Against the Person

### 5.1 Introduction to Homicide

5.1.1 The Common Law

(a) Murder

(i) Murder under the common law is defined as an unlawful killing having the following elements:

(1) *Conduct*: an act or an omission under a duty;

(2) *Mens rea*: "malice aforethought" (not intent) which may be: (i) intent to kill; (ii) intent to cause serious bodily harm; (iii) depraved heart/indifference; or (iv) intent to commit a serious or dangerous felony.

(3) *Causation* in-fact and proximate cause of the death of another;

(4) Within *one year and one day* of the act (the trend of the modern law is to abandon this common law rule).

(b) Voluntary Manslaughter

(i) Voluntary manslaughter is homicide that lacks malice aforethought.

(ii) It is an *intentional killing* mitigated by extenuating circumstances, such as *adequate provocation*, which tends to negate malice aforethought;

(iii) Adequate provocation thus reduces murder to voluntary manslaughter.

(c) Involuntary Manslaughter

(i) Involuntary manslaughter is also a form of homicide that lacks malice aforethought.

(ii) At common law, it has been typically defined as criminal negligence manslaughter or unlawful act / misdemeanor manslaughter.

(iii) The *mens rea* required was either recklessness or negligence.

5.1.2 Modern State Statutes

(a) First Degree Murder

(i) Under modern state statutes, all classes of murder (both first and second degree murder), *require malice aforethought.* In this way, murder is distinguished from manslaughter.

(ii) First degree murder, in addition to malice aforethought, requires *premeditation and deliberation.*

(b) Second Degree Murder

(i) Second degree murder includes all other forms of homicide having *malice aforethought* but lacking premediatation and deliberation.

(ii) Example: depraved heart murder (which does not require premeditation) or felony murder committed in tandem with one of the dangerous felonies not enumerated in first degree murder statutes.

(c) Manslaughter

(i) Manslaughter is homicide that lacks malice aforethought.

(ii) It is thus the equivalent of both common law voluntary and common law involuntary manslaughter.

(iii) Adequate provocation reduces murder to manslaughter.

5.1.3 The MPC

(a) Murder

(i) Murder in the MPC is defined as criminal homicide committed with P or K or with R showing indifference to the value of life.

(ii) R showing indifference to the valu of life is presumed when the actor was engaged in robbery, rape, deviate sexual intercourse, arson, burglary, kidnapping, or felonious escape. MPC § 210.2(1)(b).

(b) Manslaughter

(i) Mansaughter is criminal homicide committed through recklessness or some *extreme mental* or *emotional disturbance* having a reasonable explanation or excuse.

(ii) This is to be analyzed subjectively.

(c) Negligent Homicide

(i) Negligent homicide is criminal homicide committed with N.

## 5.2 Murder[67]

5.2.1 Common Law Murder: an Introduction

(a) Common Law Murder is defined as an unlawful killing having the following elements:

(i) *Conduct*: an act or omission under a duty;

(ii) *Mens rea*: "malice aforethought" (not necessarily intent), which can take on any of the following forms:

(1) *Intent to kill* – the actor intends to kill or knows that a death will result from his conduct;

(2) *Intent to cause serious bodily harm* – the actor intends to cause serious bodily harm or knows that it will result from his conduct.

(3) *Depraved heart* – the actor lacks the intent to murder, but acts with wanton or *reckless indifference* to human life that creates a very high risk of and results in death;

---

[67] Under both the common law as well as the modern statutory approach, murder requires malice aforethought. Provocation can negate malice aforethought such that murder is reduced to manslaughter.

(4) *Intent to commit a felony* – the actor lacks the intent to murder, but *proximately causes* the death of another while *intending to commit a serious or dangerous felony*.

(iii) *Causation*: the cause in-fact and proximate cause of the victim's death;

(iv) *Within one year and one day* of the act (in modern jurisdictions, the overwhelming trend is to abandon this common law rule).

5.2.2 Depraved Heart Murder

(a) Depraved heart murder is an unintentional killing resulting from conduct manifesting a wanton indifference to human life.

(b) It appears that a majority of the jurisdictions require, in addition to the *objective* unreasonableness of the risk, a *subjective* conscious disregard of a high risk of death or serious bodily injury.

(c) In other jurisdictions, the *mens rea* required for depraved heart murder is a purely objective standard based on gross negligence that, unlike recklessness, *does not require a subjective prong* that looks to the defendant's disregard of a risk.

(i) In *People v. Roe* (N.Y. 1989), the defendant was showing his friends his father's shotgun. He randomly loaded some live and dummy shells into the gun and, not knowing whether there was a live shell in the gun, pointed it at his friend Darrin, and stated, "Let's play Polish roulette. Who is first?" He then shot and killed Darrin. The defendant was convicted of depraved indifference murder and appealed, claiming that the gun slipped, went airborne, and discharged. Held: depraved indifference murder requires ***conduct that poses a substantial risk of death.*** The standard is objective. Neither the defendant's remorse after the act nor his ignorance as to whether the shell in the gun was live are irrelevant. The only question is, looking at the facts, whether this an outrageous threat to human life. Regardless of the defendant's thinking and motives, it was. The defendant is guilty of ***depraved indifference murder,*** not involuntary manslaughter.

(1) Dissent (Bellacosa, J.): this case's holding obliterates the distinction between depraved indifference murder and manslaughter. Acts that have constituted depraved indifference murder include firing a gun three times into a packed ballroom having boasted in advance of an intention to kill someone, driving a car at high speed on a crowded urban street and failing to apply the brakes after striking someone, or continuously beating a child over a five day period. We should look to the defendant's age and the remorse he showed after the act. The defendant ***would have to disregard a grave, enormous risk*** in a way that is irresponsible.

(2) *N.B.*: this approach is available in jurisdictions based largely on the common law approach.

(d) Voluntary Intoxication and Depraved Heart Murder

(i) Voluntary intoxication is no defense to depraved heart murder, a general intent crime.

(ii) Under the MPC, depraved heart murder is murder when "committed recklessly under circumstances manifesting extreme indifference to the value of human life." MPC § 210.2(1)(b). Voluntary intoxication is not allowed in to negate the indifference.

5.2.3 Felony Murder

(a) Traditionally, a person and *any of his accomplices* are guilty of felony murder if they:

(i) Commit or attempt to commit an ***inherently dangerous felony***; and

(ii) A death occurs (even if there was no intent to kill or to cause serious bodily harm) ***during the commission*** of the felony or while the defendant is fleeing.

(b) The following limitations apply:

(i) The defendant's conduct must be the cause in fact and ***proximate cause*** of the homicide.

(1) In the minority view, the felon starts a motion of events and is responsible for any deaths that follow.

(2) In the majority view, the death must be the *natural and probable result* of (proximately caused by) the felony.

(aa) *N.B.*: even in states that embrace this majority view, the courts interpret most deaths that occur during a felony to be foreseeable and thus proximately caused.

(ii) When states presume malice from the intent to commit a felony, the felony must be *serious* or ***inherently dangerous***.

(1) Examples of serious or inherently dangerous felonies include arson, burglary, rape, robbery, felonious escape, kidnapping, or deviate sexual intercourse.

(2) Examples of non-inherently dangerous felonies include securities fraud and conflict of interest.

(iii) Under the ***merger doctrine***, the felony must be *independent* from the homicide.

(1) Under the merger doctrine, certain crimes are said to "merge" into murder and are *not considered to be a sufficiently independent* basis on which to prosecute a defendant for felony murder.

(2) For example, because voluntary manslaughter is *not considered to be sufficiently independent of murder*, it cannot provide the basis for prosecuting a defendant for felony murder. Otherwise, every defendant guilty of involuntary manslaughter could be convicted of felony murder.

(3) Similarly, there is no felony murder committed during the course of involuntary manslaughter or aggravated battery.

(iv) Under ***agency theory*** (majority view), a defendant can only be convicted of murder *if it was committed by the defendant*, his accomplice, or some other party acting in *furtherance of the felony.*

(1) *See State v. Sophophone* (Kan. 2001), where a defendant and codefendant committed aggravated burglary. They were apprehended and while the defendant was in custody, the codefendant was lawfully killed by an officer acting in self-defense. The defendant was convicted for felony murder and appealed. Held: the defendant is not guilty of the codefendant's death, since it was caused by an officer's lawful act while the officer was within the scope of his duties. The purpose of Kansas's felony statute, adopting the *agency theory* of felony murder, is not to punish a defendant for justifiable homicides, such as those committed by police offices acting lawfully within the scope of their duties. Conviction reversed.

(c) Judicial Rejection of Felony Murder

(i) Some courts no longer recognize the *mens rea* requirements for murder to be met through the defendant's intent to commit a felony.

(ii) In *People v. Aaron* (Mich. 1980), for example, the Michigan Supreme Court held that in order for a person to be held guilty of murder, he must either have: (i) an intent to kill; (ii) an intent to cause serious bodily injury; or (iii) an intent to act with reckless indifference to human life. There is no rule in Michigan that allows for the malice requirement of murder to be met by the defendant's intent to commit a felony.

(d) The MPC and Modern Statutes

(i) Felony murder has largely been abolished and merged into the MPC homicide category of murder.

(ii) The MPC divides murder into two groups:

(1) Murder committed with *purpose* or *knowledge*. MPC § 210.2(1)(a); and

(2) Murder committed with *recklessness* under circumstances showing indifference to human life. MPC § 210.2(1)(b).

(iii) However, vestiges of common law felony murder can be found in § 210.2(1)(b), which states that the *mens rea* for murder is met when the actor commits or attempts to commit "robbery, rape or deviate sexual intercourse by force or threat of force, arson, burglary, kidnapping or felonious escape."

(e) Attempted Felony Murder

(i) Some states have recognized attempted felony murder to be a crime. *See, e.g., Amlotte v. Florida* (Fla.1984) (holding that attempted felony murder is a crime.

(ii) Elements:

(1) The commission or attempted commission of an enumerated felony; and

(2) An intentional overt act or aiding and abetting of an intentional overt act that could cause the death of another (even if it does not).

(f) Further Issues

(i) Homicide Committed by a Non-Participant

(1) There are two views as to whether the defendants should be liable for felony murder when the homicide is caused by a police officer or victim:

(aa) Under *State v. Canola* (N.J. Sup. A. D. 1975), the defendant is guilty of felony murder if it was foreseeable that a death would occur by even a police officer or victim (the holding was reversed by the N.J. S.Ct. two years later).

(bb) Under *Commonwealth v. Redline* (Pa. 1958), the defendant can be convicted only if the murder was done "by the defendant or by an accomplice or confederate or by one acting in furtherance of the felonious undertaking." However, the defendant is ***not liable for a justifiable killing of a willing participant***—such as when the victim kills his attacker in self-defense—in inherently dangerous crimes.

(I) *N.B.*: this is the prevailing view that is also embraced by the MPC.

(ii) Duration of the Felony

(1) The typical rule is that the felony murder doctrine applies from the time of attempt through the commission of the crime up to the flight from the crime.

(iii) Modern Statutes

(1) New York limits felony murder by providing an affirmative defense when the defendant: (i) did not commit or participate in any way in the homicide; (ii) was not armed with a deadly weapon; (iii) had no reasonable ground to believe that any other participate was armed with a deadly weapon; and (iv) had no reasonable ground to believe that another participant intended to engage in any conduct that would likely cause a serious bodily injury.

(2) In Florida, on the other hand, a defendant is guilty for felony murder whenever he or an accomplice cause a death during the commission of a felony.

5.2.4 Modern Statutory Approach

(a) First Degree Murder

(i) First degree murder is homicide having malice aforethought as well as premeditation and deliberation. The mind must be free from provocation and must be able to coolly rationalize.

(1) *Premeditation* requires a design to kill formed before the act. It can be developed over seconds.

(2) *Deliberation* requires cool purpose developed over time free from excitement or passion.

(ii) Jurisdictions having first and second degree murder statutes define first degree murder as murder committed:

(1) By means of a premeditated, deliberate intent-to-kill (willful) murder;

(2) By means of poison or lying in wait (in some jurisdictions);

(3) In the perpetration or attempted perpetration of any arson, burglary, rape, or robbery;

(aa) This rule is based on the Pennsylvania statute adopted in 1794 (the first to distinguish between degrees of murder);

(bb) Some state statutes also include the felonies of larceny, kidnapping, aircraft piracy, or the unlawful throwing, placing or discharging of a destructive device or bomb.

(iii) In some states, such as Virginia, all that is required to qualify as first degree murder is intent to kill. *Premeditation and deliberation* is not necessary. In these states, homicide with malice aforethought that lacks the intent to kill is classified as second degree murder.

(iv) Premeditation and Deliberation

(1) In *People v. Anderson* (Cal. 1968), the court held that in order for a crime to fall within the first degree murder classification, there must be premeditation and deliberation according to a "*deliberate* judgment or plan; carried on coolly and steadily, [especially] according to a *preconceived design*." Premeditation and deliberation falls into three categories: (i) evidence of planning activity; (ii) evidence of motive; and (iii) evidence of the manner of the killing.

(2) Repeated blows with a deadly weapon or repeated shots with a gun are not sufficient in and of themselves to establish ***premeditation and deliberation.***

(aa) *See State v. Brown* (Tenn. 1992), where one night, the neighbors of the defendant, the victim's father, heard a loud bang on the wall. The defendant was charged with first degree murder and child neglect of his 4 year old son. All that the defendant remembered from that night was his spanking Eddie. Held: while there is strong evidence of repeated blows in this case, there is no evidence of premeditation and deliberation. The defendant acted maliciously toward Eddie in the heat of passion and without adequate provocation which shows guilt for second-degree murder. *LaChance* held that a homicide from repeated blows alone is per se first-degree se murder. That doctrine is abandoned. Although there is circumstantial evidence that the defendant acted maliciously towards the victim, there is insufficient evidence for proving the requisite elements of premeditation and deliberation.

(b) Second Degree Murder

(i) Second degree murder is homicide having malice aforethought but lacking premeditation and deliberation.

(ii) Examples: intent to kill murder lacking premeditation; intent to cause serious bodily injury lacking premeditation; ***depraved heart murder*** (which does not require premeditation); and felony murder based on a felony not enumerated for first degree murder.

(iii) Common Law Background: all murder not falling within the first degree murder classification is considered second-degree murder.

(1) *Commonwealth v. Malone* involves a standard for recklessness that is even more objective that that cited in the majority opinion in *Roe*. Subjectiveness is never mentioned, unlike in the majority opinion.

(2) The MPC uses a subjective/objective standard. Part of the definition requires that the defendant consciously disregard a risk. "[H]e consciously disregards a substantial and unjustifiable risk that the material element exists or will result from his conduct." MPC § 2.02(2)(c).

### 5.3 Voluntary Manslaughter

5.3.1 Introduction

(a) Voluntary manslaughter is an intentional killing mitigated by provocation in the heat of passion or other circumstances that negate malice aforethought.

(i) Provocation

(1) Today, every jurisdiction, whether it uses the common law or a statutory approach, uses a provocation formula to distinguish murder from the lesser crime of manslaughter.

(2) Categories of provocation generally sufficient to establish the lesser charge include:

(aa) The sight of a man's wife engaged in adultery;

(bb) The sight of a friend or relative being beaten; and

(cc) Angry words followed by an assault.

**(I)** *N.B.*: some have commented that the rules surrounding provocation are only applicable to the behavior of men, not women. The rages mitigating murder to manslaughter typically occur only with men.

(ii) Other Circumstances

(1) Imperfect defenses also serve to reduce murder to voluntary manslaughter.

(2) An example is any "imperfect" defense, where the actor acts honestly but unreasonably under circumstances in which, had he been acting reasonably, would constitute a defense.

(b) Cooling Time

(i) Traditionally, the reduction to manslaughter required that the homicide occur *before a period sufficient for cooling down* has passed.

(ii) In *State v. Gounagias* (Wash. 1915), for example, the victim sodomized the defendant. As a result, the defendant was taunted, and this provoked him to murder the victim. The court held that the period between the original sodomy and the murder was too lengthy to support a finding of provocation.

(c) The Objective Standard

(i) One of the questions that has been posed is what the standard should be for the reasonable person against whom we test the defendant.

(ii) Is it the reasonable person who has been in a concentration camp? A man who has just returned from war and is being yelled at as a murderer?

(iii) Some have suggested an objective standard (*see Bedder*, where the defendant's impotence was not taken into account in a trial for his murder of a prostitute) and others have suggested a subjective standard.

(iv) In *People v. Maher* (Mich. 1862), the court held that the reasonable person standard *should* apply unless there is some peculiar weakness of mind "not arising from wickedness of heart or cruelty of disposition."

(v) All of the non-moral factors are allowed in (social history, medical history, height).

(d) The Relevance of Mistake

(i) It appears that a mistake as to whether there was in fact provocation must be ***both honest and reasonable***.

(ii) *See, e.g., State v. Yanz* (Conn. 1901), where the Connecticut Supreme Court held that if the defendant's offense should be reduced to *manslaughter*, even though he was mistaken as to his wife's adultery, if the mistake was reasonable.

5.3.2 Common Law Approach

(a) There are *three elements required for provocation* under the common law:

(i) The defendant is suddenly provoked (if the provocation is cumulative, this prong is not required);

(ii) The provocation is legally adequate; and

(iii) The provocation must have been sufficient to provoke a reasonable person.

(b) Under the common law, insults followed by an assault could qualify as provocation that reduces murder to manslaughter.

(c) However, angry words, on their own, do not constitute adequate provocation.

(i) *See Freddo v. State* (Tenn. 1913), where Higginbotham continually repeatedly verbally abused the defendant, despite the defendant's demands that Higginbotham to stop. At one point, the defendant seized a steel bar and hit Higginbotham on the head, claiming that he thought that the defendant was assaulting him. When he was convicted for second degree murder, the defendant appealed, ***arguing that he should have been guilty of only voluntary manslaughter.*** Held: voluntary manslaughter requires adequate provocation, such as verbal abuse accompanied by assault. Here, there was no assault, and words alone do not constitute provocation. The defendant struck Higginbotham from the back when he could not have been in a position to attack him. Therefore, the provocation was not legally adequate and the defendant failed the second prong.

(ii) *N.B.*: the standard for provocation is objective: a reasonable person would lose control.

(iii) *N.B.*: ***imperfect justification*** in many jurisdictions allows for an honest but unreasonable mistake to reduce murder to manslaughter. Perhaps here, the jury did not believe the defendant when he said that he needed to employ force for self-defense.

5.3.3 The Model Penal Code Approach

(a) Just as provocation reduces murder to manslaughter under the common law, "extreme mental or emotional disturbance" reduces murder to manslaughter under MPC § 210.3(1)(b) (recklessness similarly reduces murder to manslaughter under the MPC).

(b) The emotional disturbance must have "reasonable explanation or excuse."

(c) The reasonableness of such explanation or excuse "shall be determined from the viewpoint of a person in the actor's situation under the circumstances as he believes them to be." MPC § 210.3(1)(b).

(d) The defendant's subjective features, such as blindness, are taken into account, whereas moral depravity is not (*e.g.*, it is no defense that the defendant thought that killing was not morally wrong). As to the grey area in between, it is not clear if it will be taken into consideration.

(i) In *People v. Casassa* (N.Y. 1980), the defendant had a casual dating relationship with Ms. Lo Consolo, until she rejected him and he became obsessed with her. The relationship culminated in his murdering her. At the trial, a psychiatrist testified that the defendant's obsession, combined with peculiar personality attributes, caused the defendant to kill Consolo under extreme mental or emotional disturbance. The state argued that § 125.25(1)(a) of the New York Penal Law (which is identical to MPC § 210.3(1)(b)), should not apply, because the defendant's disturbed state was the result of stress created from within himself, not to of external factors. Held: the defendant must show that his reaction to the events triggering the distress ***must be reasonable.*** The standard is not based on the defendant's perspective alone. Here, the defendant's reaction to the events was so peculiar to him that it escapes reasonableness. ***The reasonableness is determined in view of the defendant's circumstances***, not

between .19 and .22. When the defendant was charged with first degree aggravated manslaughter, he moved to dismiss on the grounds that the removal of the victim's ventilator was an intervening act that was a superseding cause, since it was unforeseeable. Held: the victim's desire to be removed from life support is not an unforeseeable intervening act that removes the defendant's liability. Judgment for the defendant reversed: the jury should not even be instructed as to the independent intervening cause.

(i) *N.B.:* the NJ statute involved in this case is based on the MPC formulation of causation.

### 5.5.3 The MPC Approach to Causation

> § 2.03. Causal Relationship Between Conduct and Result; Divergence Between Result Designed or Contemplated and Actual Result or Between Probable and Actual Result.
>
> (1) Conduct is the cause of a result when:
>
> (a) it is an antecedent but for which the result in question would not have occurred; and
>
> (b) the relationship between the conduct and result satisfies any additional causal requirements imposed by the Code or by the law defining the offense.
>
> (2) When purposely or knowingly causing a particular result is an element of an offense, the element is not established if the actual result is not within the purpose or the contemplation of the actor unless:
>
> (a) the actual result differs from that designed or contemplated, as the case may be, only in the respect that a different person or different property is injured or affected or that the injury or harm designed or contemplated would have been more serious or more extensive than that caused; or
>
> (b) the actual result involves the same kind of injury or harm as that designed or contemplated and is not too remote or accidental in its occurrence to have a [just] bearing on the actor's liability or on the gravity of his offense.
>
> (3) When recklessly or negligently causing a particular result is an element of an offense, the element is not established if the actual result is not within the risk of which the actor is aware or, in the case of negligence, of which he should be aware unless:
>
> (a) the actual result differs from the probable result only in the respect that a different person or different property is injured or affected or that the probable injury or harm would have been more serious or more extensive than that caused; or
>
> (b) the actual result involves the same kind of injury or harm as the probable result and is not too remote or accidental in its occurrence to have a [just] bearing on the actor's liability or on the gravity of his offense.
>
> (4) When causing a particular result is a material element of an offense for which absolute liability is imposed by law, the element is not established unless the actual

> result is a probable consequence of the actor's conduct.

(a) There is one problem in the MPC with respect to concurrent causes.

(b) Under the current formulation of MPC § 2.03(1)(a), B would not be guilty of C's murder if D's assault was a concurrent but-for cause and C would have died even if B did not also assault him.

## 5.6 Rape

### 5.6.1 The Traditional Approach

(a) The common law defined rape as "the carnal knowledge of a woman forcibly and against her will" through the use of fear or force against the woman.

(b) The modern law has departed from this view by defining rape in gender-neutral terms. However, rape continues to be perpetrated predominantly by men against women, although cases of rape by men against other men are increasingly seen.

(c) Consent is normally a defense to a rape charge. However, a defendant cannot show the victim's consent through her submission to sexual intercourse because of a reasonable fear of imminent death or bodily harm.

(i) *See State v. Rusk* (Md. 1981), where Pat, the prosecutrix, met the defendant at a bar and gave him a ride home. Pat claimed that the defendant, threatened to use force and raped her. The defendant argued that Pat did not resist. Held: lack of consent is established when the victim can show that her submission was a result of fear of imminent death or bodily harm. The reasonableness of this fear is a factual question to be submitted to the jury. The defendant's acts had to have been reasonably calculated to induce this fear in the victim's mind. The fear must be reasonable, not, *e.g.*, the victim submitted to sex because she became terrified at being kissed. Here, there was enough evidence of the victim's fear to have been submitted to the jury.

(ii) Dissent: nothing in the evidence would support a jury finding that the victim could have had a reasonable basis to fear the defendant, even if the victim did actually fear the defendant.

### 5.6.2 Nonconsent and *Mens Rea*

(a) Rape is a general intent crime requiring only the general intent to perform the physical acts. *State v. Smith* (Vt. 1978).

(b) Although before the 1970s, rape cases routinely looked into the victim's prior sexual activity, this changed after the 1970s.

(i) *N.B.*: however, state laws based on Federal Rule of Evidence 412(b) allow evidence of the victim's past sexual conduct to be admitted under some circumstances (*e.g.*, to prove that a person other than the accused was the source of semen in an alleged rape case).

(c) Competence to Consent

(i) Many jurisdictions hold a defendant liable for rape if the victim does not understand the "nature and consequences" of sexual intercourse.

(ii) However, determining what the exact test for determining incompetence is still an unresolved issue, as is the question of whether strict liability should be imposed upon perpetrators when they have intercourse with incompetent victims.

(iii) The traditional approach to competence holds that when the victim is unconscious, intoxicated by drugs or alcohol, or, in some cases, mentally retarded or insane, she is unable to give effective consent. In these cases, sexual intercourse with hre constitutes rape.

(iv) Consent is similarly lacking, and sexual intercourse constitutes rape, when the victim is threatened into having intercourse or her consent is obtained through fraud.

5.6.3 Statutory Rape

(a) When a jurisdiction has passed a statutory rape statute, the defendant is guilty of rape when he has sexual intercourse with a female under the age of consent (generally, between sixteen to eighteen years old).

(b) Whether the female actually consented is irrelevant; she is held not to have consented as a matter of law.

(c) The defendant's mistake as to the victim's age is generally no defense. However, some jurisdictions allow for the defense if the victim deliberately misled the defendant into believing that she was of the age of consent.

## 6 Crimes Against Property

### 6.1 Larceny

6.1.1 Introduction

(a) Larceny is a specific intent crime consisting of the unlawful taking and carrying away of the property of another with the intent to permanently deprive him thereof.

(b) Only personalty, not real property or services, may be the object of larceny.

6.1.2 Custody and Possession Distinguished

(a) Larceny may occur when the defendant unlawfully and forcefully takes and carries away the property of another.

(b) This includes cases where the owner of the property gives the defendant ***custody*** of some particular item, without granting him *ownership* or *possession* (in which case there may be liability for embezzlement or false pretenses).

(i) If the owner grants him ***ownership***, there would be no criminal liability if the defendant, with the intent to permanently deprive the owner of the property, fails to return it.

(ii) If the owner grants him ***possession***, there may be liability for embezzlement or false pretenses if the defendant, with the intent to permanently deprive the owner of the property, fails to return it.

(c) Possession involves a much larger scope of authority to deal with the property than does mere custody and implies a certain relationship between the owner and the possessor that usually involves the posessor's fiduciary duties.

(i) Example: if an employer grants his employee a clock to take to a repair shop and return, the employee, given the limited scope of his authority over the clock, has mere custody, not possession. Thus, if he fails to return it with the intent of permantently depriving the employer of the clock, he will be guilty of larceny.

(d) Under some modern statutes, the scope of larceny has been broadened to include embezzlement and false pretenses.

**6.2 Embezzlement**

6.2.1 Embezzlement is a specific intent crime consisting of the ***fraudulent taking*** for one's own use the property of another by one who originally acquired it lawfully.

6.2.2 Embezzlement was statutorily developed in order to make provisions for a gap in the common law, which did not punish unlawful takings when the defendant originally acquired possession of the stolen property lawfully.

6.2.3 Embezzlement punishes the defendant when he comes to ***possess*** the money or property *through a fiduciary relationship* with the owner.

6.2.4 Criminal intent for embezzlement arises *after* the taking (not during or before the taking, as with larceny).

**6.3 False Pretenses**

6.3.1 False pretenses is a specific intent crime consisting of the: (i) acquiring of title; (ii) to the property of another; (iii) through making false statements or misrepresentations; (iv) with the intent of defrauding the owner.

6.3.2 Unlike the crime of ***larceny by trick***, in the case of false pretenses, the defendant obtains full title of the owner's property, not mere possession.

**6.4 Robbery**

6.4.1 Robbery is the specific intent crime that consists of the unlawful taking of property from another person or in the person's presence by the use of force or by threatening the imminent use of force.

6.4.2 Robbery is essentially larceny with force or intimidation. The force or intimidation may be directed towards the victim of the crime or towards his relative or any person in the victim's company.

6.4.3 The defendant need not have the present ability to carry out the threatened harm, as long as he has the *apparent ability* to do so.

6.4.4 Under the MPC, a robbery is defined as the commission of a theft in which the actor does any of the following:

(a) Inflicts serious bodily injury upon another;

(b) Threatens another with or purposely puts him in fear of immediate serious bodily injury; or

(c) Commits or threatens immediately to commit any felony of the first or second degree. MPC § 222.1(1).

## 7 Crimes Against the Habitation

### 7.1 Arson

7.1.1 Arson is a general intent crime that was defined at common law as the malicious, willful, and unlawful burning of the dwelling place of another.

7.1.2 Merely blackening or discoloring the walls or burning the contents of the dwelling without burning or at least charring the actual structure does not constitute arson at common law.

7.1.3 Under the modern law, the structure need not be the dwelling place of another; it may be any building or room.

(a) Example: A sets out to burn down B's office building. Although the act would not be arson at common law, most modern jurisdictions would hold A guilty of arson.

### 7.2 Burglary

7.2.1 At common law, burglary was a specific intent crime that consisted of the breaking and entering of the dwelling of another at night with the intent to commit a felony therein.

7.2.2 Most modern statutes have broadened the definition, such that the breaking and entering may be into any building or room and need not occur at night.

7.2.3 The MPC reflects this approach by defining burglary as the entering of a building or occupied structure, or separately secured or occupied portion thereof, with purpose to commit a crime therein, unless the premises are at the time open to the public or the actor is licensed or privileged to enter. MPC § 221.1(1).

# REVIEW CHARTS

## Classification of Crimes Based on Common Law Intent

| General Intent Crimes | Specific Intent Crimes |
|---|---|
| Arson | Assault |
| Battery | Attempt |
| Depraved heart murder | Burglary |
| False imprisonment | Conspiracy |
| Involuntary manslaughter | Embezzlement |
| Kidnapping | False pretenses |
| Rape | Intent to kill murder |
| | Larceny |
| | Robbery |
| | Solicitation |

## Summary Charts of Attempt, Complicity, and Conspiracy

**Elements**

| | Mens Rea | Actus Reus |
|---|---|---|
| *Complicity* | Intent to facilitate the commission of a crime. | Aiding or failing to act on a legal duty. |
| *Attempt* | Specific intent to commit the ultimate offense. | A significant, overt act (under the proximity test, *res ipsa loquitur* test or "strongly corroborates" test). |
| *Conspiracy* | Specific intent to commit an illegal act or a legal act by illegal means. | An agreement; and<br>An overt act (under the modern law and for less grave offenses in the MPC), however small.[68] |
| *Solicitation* | The specific intent that the solicited party commit the underlying offense. | Entreating, imploring, inducing, encouraging, or promoting another person to engage in behavior that would constitute a crime. |

[68] Mere preparation suffices.

**Impossibility**

| | *Common Law* | *MPC* |
|---|---|---|
| *Attempt* | Factual impossibility historically was no defense, but legal impossibility was. Under the modern view, however, either one offers a defense. In addition, "true" legal impossibility is a defense. | Neither legal nor factual impossibility is a defense. However, "true" legal impossibility is a defense. Thus, any attempt must be an attempt to commit a real offense. |
| *Conspiracy* | Factual and legal impossibility is no defense. However, "true" legal impossibility is a defense, since the target must be a real crime. | |
| *Solicitation* | Impossibility of the underlying offense is no defense. However, "true" legal impossibility is a defense, since the underlying offense must be a real crime. | |

**Renunciation**

| | *Common Law* | *Model Penal Code* |
|---|---|---|
| *Complicity* | An accomplice is not liable if he communicates his repudiation and takes steps to neutralize any assistance he has provided. | An accomplice is not liable when he terminates his complicity prior to the commission of the act and either (i) deprives the act of its effectiveness or (ii) gives timely warning to law enforcement officials or otherwise prevents its commission. MPC § 2.06(6). |
| *Attempt* | Abandonment (the common law term for renunciation) is no defense. | Renunciation is a defense when the defendant abandons the effort or prevents its commission and there is complete and voluntary renunciation. MPC § 5.01(4). |
| *Conspiracy* | Abandonment is no defense. However, renunciation limits liability for acts committed after the withdrawal. | *Renunciation* is a defense when it is complete and voluntary and the actor thwarts the conspiracy. MPC § 5.03(6). |
| *Solicitation* | Abandonment is no defense to solicitation once the solicitation is complete. | Renunciation is an affirmative defense when: (i) the actor persuades the solicited party not commit the solicited crime or prevents the crime; and (ii) the withdrawal is *complete* and *voluntary*. MPC § 5.02(3). |

## SUMMARY OF HOMICIDE CATEGORIES

| | *Common law* | *Modern Statutes* | *MPC* |
|---|---|---|---|

<table>
<tr><td>Homicide having malice aforethought</td><td>Murder (having malice aforethought)</td><td>First and second degree murder (having malice aforethought)</td><td>Murder (having P, K, or R showing indifference to the value of life). § 210.2.</td></tr>
<tr><td>Malice aforethought negated by circumstances</td><td>Voluntary manslaughter</td><td rowspan="2">Manslaughter</td><td>Manslaughter (“extreme mental or emotional disturbance”). § 210.3(b)</td></tr>
<tr><td>Homicide lacking malice aforethought</td><td>Involuntary manslaughter:<br>- criminal negligence manslaughter;<br>- misdemeanor manslaughter</td><td>- Manslaughter (recklessesly committed). § 210.3(a); or<br>- Negligent homicide. § 210.4.</td></tr>
</table>

## Chapter VIII. Evidence

# ARTICLE I. GENERAL PROVISIONS

## Rule 101. Scope

> These rules govern proceedings in the courts of the United States and before United States bankruptcy judges and United States magistrate judges, to the extent and with the exceptions stated in rule 1101.

1. The Federal Rules of Evidence (FRE) govern both criminal and civil proceedings in the federal courts.
2. Federal bankruptcy and magistrate judges are bound by the rules (see FRE 1101 for exceptions).

## Rule 102. Purpose and Construction

> These rules shall be construed to secure fairness in administration, elimination of unjustifiable expense and delay, and promotion of growth and development of the law of evidence to the end that the truth may be ascertained and proceedings justly determined.

1. This rule purports to support fairness and justice in the interpretation of the rules of evidence. In reality, however, it has little or no relevance.
2. First, this rule *only* applies when there is reasonable ambiguity in the meaning of a rule—it *never* allows the judge to replace the clear meaning of a rule with his own notions of justice and fairness.
3. Furthermore, even if a rule is slightly ambiguous, it is naturally presumed that judges will interpret such rules fairly and justly.

## Rule 103. Rulings on Evidence

> (a) Effect of erroneous ruling.
>
> Error may not be predicated upon a ruling which admits or excludes evidence unless a substantial right of the party is affected, and
>
> (1) Objection. - In case the ruling is one admitting evidence, a timely objection or motion to strike appears of record, stating the specific ground of objection, if the specific ground was not apparent from the context; or
>
> (2) Offer of proof. - In case the ruling is one excluding evidence, the substance of the evidence was made known to the court by offer or was apparent from the context within which questions were asked.
>
> Once the court makes a definitive ruling on the record admitting or excluding evidence, either at or before trial, a party need not renew an objection or offer of proof to preserve a claim of error for appeal.

1. In order for an appeals court to reverse a trial court, the following three elements *must* be met:
    a. There must be an ***error;***
    b. The error must be prejudicial by ***altering the case's outcome***.

i. A "substantial right of the party" must be affected.

ii. Factors for determining whether an error was prejudicial include: how long the jury took to return a verdict; how many counts of guilt the defendant received; and how many other exhibits were offered.

c. The error was ***preserved*** through either an *objection* or an *offer of proof.* Rule 103(a). An error will not be preserved when it is:

i. *Forfeited* – the attorney does nothing;

ii. *Waived* – the attorney affirmatively gives up the right (*e.g.*, "let it in, your honor."); or

iii. *Invited* – the error is admitted due to the attorney's own conduct.

2. Objections

a. Objections are made when the opposing counsel is trying to admit evidence and a ruling admits that evidence.

b. They may be either:

i. *Objections* that are made when the opposing counsel asks a question or seeks to admit evidence; or

ii. *Motions to strike* that are made *after* the opposing counsel asks a question and the respondent already responded.[69]

1) Every motion to strike is a late objection.

2) Sometimes, an attorney is forced to offer a motion to strike, such as when he has no notice of the content of unresponsive answers.

c. Objections must be:

i. Timely;

ii. Appearing of record with notice to the court and recorded by the court reporter; and

iii. Specific with the grounds for the objection, unless the specific grounds are "apparent from the context." Rule 103(a)(1).

3. Offers of Proof

a. Offers of proof are made by the attorney trying to introduce evidence when a ruling excludes that evidence.

b. Offers of proof must be:

i. Made with *notice to the court* and court reporter. Rule 103(a)(2);

ii. *Specific*, with the "substance of the evidence" made known to the court by offer (unless apparent from the context).[70] Rule 103(a)(2);

---

[69] These are also referred to as "motions to strike from the record."

iii. Made *outside of the hearing* of the jury. Rule 103(c).

1) *Note*: offers of proof do not need to be timely, since evidence omitted is not prejudicial (as opposed to when the evidence has already been admitted and no objection was made).

4. Motions *in Limine*

a. A motion *in limine* ("on the threshold"; "in the beginning") is one done outside of the hearing of the jury before the judge. They generally take place before trial.

b. The states are divided as to whether an attorney whose motion *in limine* was denied must renew his objection or offer of proof to preserve his claim of error when the court ruled against him in a motion *in limine*.

c. In federal court, however, a renewed objection or offer of proof is unnecessary. Rule 103(a) states that "a party need not renew an objection or offer of proof to preserve a claim of error for appeal" once the court has made a definitive ruling on the evidence.

> (b) Record of offer and ruling.
>
> The court may add any other or further statement which shows the character of the evidence, the form in which it was offered, the objection made, and the ruling thereon. It may direct the making of an offer in question and answer form.

5. Methods of offering proof:

a. *Attorney narrative*. This is an efficient way of offering proof, but it is less reliable, since it allows the attorney to put a "spin" on the narrative.

b. *Question and answer form*. The court calls the witness to the stand to verify for itself the proof being offered. This method is both more reliable and more time-consuming than an attorney narrative.

c. *In writing with an affidavit*. The writing could show, for example, what a witness would have testified if he were permitted.

> (c) Hearing of jury.
>
> In jury cases, proceedings shall be conducted, to the extent practicable, so as to prevent inadmissible evidence from being suggested to the jury by any means, such as making statements or offers of proof or asking questions in the hearing of the jury.
>
> (d) Plain error.
>
> Nothing in this rule precludes taking notice of plain errors affecting substantial rights although they were not brought to the attention of the court.

6. Plain Error

a. An exception to the requirement of preserving error is in circumstances where the error was ***plain***.

---

[70] This element is different from that required of objections: the evidence offered must be factually, not legally specific.

b. Nothing precludes a trial court from excluding evidence on its own, *even absent any objections from the attorneys*, when an error is so serious that its inadmissibility is clear.

c. Similarly, appeals courts may take notice when the error of a trial court is ***plain.***

d. This rule is meant to be a middle ground between *inflexible rules* and the *abandonment* of the preservation of error doctrine.

e. This narrow exception is usually granted in criminal cases when the defendant is trying to exclude admitted evidence.

f. The rule states that nothing in it "precludes" taking notice of plain errors. Thus, the court is not required to take notice of errors; it is within the ***discretionary power*** of the judge.

g. Thus, in order to guarantee that an *error* that *affects* a party's substantial rights is not given up to the whims of the court, it ***must be preserved*** (through making an objection or offer of proof) in order for the trial court's decision to be reversed.

7. The Rationale of Rule 103: because Rule 103 requires any error on trial to be preserved, many appeals are automatically dismissed. This in turn keeps the court dockets moving and avoids expense and delay (see Rule 102).

**Rule 104. Preliminary Questions**

> (a) Questions of admissibility generally.
>
> Preliminary questions concerning the qualification of a person to be a witness, the existence of a privilege, or the admissibility of evidence shall be determined by the court, subject to the provisions of subdivision (b). In making its determination it is not bound by the rules of evidence except those with respect to privileges.
>
> (b) Relevancy conditioned on fact.
>
> When the relevancy of evidence depends upon the fulfillment of a condition of fact, the court shall admit it upon, or subject to, the introduction of evidence sufficient to support a finding of the fulfillment of the condition.

1. Generally, the facts are decided by the jury and the law is decided by the judge.

2. However, the jury decides only ***ultimate factual questions*** (the charges in the indictment; the claims in the complaint; the defenses in the answer).

3. The ***judge decides preliminary factual questions*** that must be answered before the admissibility of evidence may be determined. These factual questions are ancillary to legal questions; they are foundational and serve as a springboard to other questions.

4. Two Kinds of Preliminary Factual Questions:

a. Questions Conditioned on *Admissibility*. Rule 104(a).

i. Examples: whether police read the suspect's *Miranda* rights, whether a marital privilege exists, whether an expert witness is qualified.

ii. These are determined by the judge because they are raised by rules of law that the jury is not qualified to answer.

iii. The trial judge's decisions are final; if a party disagrees with the judge's finding, he may not ask for the question to be reconsidered by the jury.

b. Questions Conditioned on *Credibility/Relevance*. Rule 104(b).

i. Examples: whether a confession was voluntary; whether the signature on the confession belongs to the defendant.

ii. These are questions of both *admissibility* and *credibility*.

iii. They are not decided by the judge with finality (Rule 104(a) does not apply).

iv. Thus, if a judge rules against the defendant's favor, the defendant may have the question heard by the jury.

v. They are decided by juries because they are raised by rules of logic to which we trust juries.

> (c) Hearing of jury.
>
> Hearings on the admissibility of confessions shall in all cases be conducted out of the hearing of the jury. Hearings on other preliminary matters shall be so conducted when the interests of justice require, or when an accused is a witness and so requests.

5. When a question of admissibility involves a confession, it must be done *outside of the hearing of the jury*.

6. When it involves the defendant as a witness, the defendant may decide whether or not the jury be present.

7. Otherwise, the question of the presence of the jury in hearings on preliminary matters is to be decided as justice requires. Rule 104(c).

> (d) Testimony by accused.
>
> The accused does not, by testifying upon a preliminary matter, become subject to cross-examination as to other issues in the case.

8. In preliminary matters, the defendant does not waive his privilege against self-incrimination by testifying on a preliminary matter.

> (e) Weight and credibility.
>
> This rule does not limit the right of a party to introduce before the jury evidence relevant to weight or credibility.

9. The judge may not insert his own judgment as to whether evidence conditioned on ***weight*** or ***credibility*** is true or false (and thereby admissible or inadmissible).

10. Otherwise, the judge would be submitting to the jury only that evidence that conforms to his own mind and thinking and would be undermining the jury system.

11. In this way, Rule 104(e) protects the rights of the defendants to introduce evidence conditioned on credibility.

**Rule 105. Limited Admissibility**

> When evidence which is admissible as to one party or for one purpose but not admissible as

> to another party or for another purpose is admitted, the court, upon request, shall restrict the evidence to its proper scope and instruct the jury accordingly.

1. If an attorney asks for limiting instructions, the judge must instruct the jury to limit the evidence to its purpose.
2. Even if an attorney does not ask for limiting instructions, the judge may give them anyway.
3. If limiting instructions are not given, then the jury can use the evidence for any purpose.
4. Attorneys do not always ask for limiting instructions; if a judge orders the jury not to consider evidence for a particular purpose, the jury may consider the evidence for that purpose even more strongly.
5. Yet asking for limiting instructions can give a party an advantage, since if a judge denies the request, the attorney may be able to get a reversal on appeal (unless the appeals court holds that the error was harmless).
6. If evidence that is offered is objected to, the attorney offering the evidence may reply that it is not being offered for the prohibited purpose, but for some permissible purpose.

### Rule 106. Remainder of or Related Writings or Recorded Statements

> When a writing or recorded statement or part thereof is introduced by a party, an adverse party may require the introduction at that time of any other part or any other writing or recorded statement which ought in fairness to be considered contemporaneously with it.

1. Rule 106 offers one of the exceptions to the normal rule that while one party is examining a witness, the other party may not interrupt (see discussion under Rule 611(a), *infra.*).
2. Under Rule 106, if one party offers into evidence a writing or recording, the other party may request that related writings or recordings be introduced *at that time* into evidence, in order to assure that the writing or recording offered does not mislead the trier of fact.

## ARTICLE II. JUDICIAL NOTICE

### Rule 201. Judicial Notice of Adjudicative Facts

> (a) Scope of rule.
>
> This rule governs only judicial notice of adjudicative facts.

1. Judicial notice is a court decision that recognizes the truth of a fact without requiring proof.
2. When a court takes judicial notice, a party is relieved of the burden of proving a fact to be true.

> (b) Kinds of facts.
>
> A judicially noticed fact must be one not subject to reasonable dispute in that it is either (1) generally known within the territorial jurisdiction of the trial court or (2) capable of accurate and ready determination by resort to sources whose accuracy cannot reasonably be questioned.

3. Judicial notice can be taken of either:
    a. A fact of common knowledge in the court's jurisdiction; or
    b. A fact capable of being verified in reliable sources.

> (c) When discretionary.
>
> A court may take judicial notice, whether requested or not.

4. Like a plain error under Rule 103(d), a judge may take judicial notice without a specific request by one of the parties.

> (d) When mandatory.
>
> A court shall take judicial notice if requested by a party and supplied with the necessary information.
>
> (e) Opportunity to be heard.
>
> A party is entitled upon timely request to an opportunity to be heard as to the propriety of taking judicial notice and the tenor of the matter noticed. In the absence of prior notification, the request may be made after judicial notice has been taken.
>
> (f) Time of taking notice.
>
> Judicial notice may be taken at any stage of the proceeding.

5. The judge may take judicial notice *at any stage.*

> (g) Instructing jury.
>
> In a civil action or proceeding, the court shall instruct the jury to accept as conclusive any fact judicially noticed. In a criminal case, the court shall instruct the jury that it may, but is not required to, accept as conclusive any fact judicially noticed.

6. Jury instructions:
    a. In civil cases, the judge may tell the jury to accept a judicially noticed fact as conclusive.
    b. In criminal cases, the judge may *not* tell the jury to accept a judicially noticed fact as conclusive. The judge must instruct the jury that it "may, but is not required" to accept a judicially noticed fact as conclusive.
7. Judicial notice is frequently a source of dispute, since when the parties already agree ona particular fact, they will stipulate it.

## ARTICLE III. PRESUMPTIONS IN CIVIL ACTIONS AND PROCEEDINGS

### Rule 301. Presumptions in General Civil Actions and Proceedings

> In all civil actions and proceedings not otherwise provided for by Act of Congress or by these rules, a presumption imposes on the party against whom it is directed the burden of going forward with evidence to rebut or meet the presumption, but does not shift to such party the burden of proof in the sense of the risk of nonpersuasion, which remains throughout the trial upon the party on whom it was originally cast.

1. In civil actions, presumptions are ***definitive legal inferences*** based on the rule of law.

2. They are different from ***permissive inferences***, which *may* be drawn by a jury.

3. Juries *must* accept presumptions as decided in civil cases if the opposing party fails to *produce evidence to the contrary.*

4. Base facts give way to presumptions. Typical examples include:

| Base Fact | Legal Presumption |
|---|---|
| A has not been seen in seven years. | A is dead. |
| The package was properly mailed. | The package was received. |
| B's parents were married at his birth. | B is legitimate. |
| The letter had a date on the corner. | The date is correct. |

5. The ***burden of persuasion*** refers to the obligation to provide sufficient evidence to establish a belief in the mind of the trier of fact.

   a. Examples of burdens of persuasion: the preponderance of the evidence; guilt beyond a reasonable doubt.

   b. The plaintiff carries the burden of persuasion for every element of his case. If he produces evidence to prove an affirmative element of his case, the defendant may attack the credibility of that evidence.

6. The ***burden of production*** refers to a party's obligation to provide sufficient evidence so that a reasonable jury can infer the fact alleged.

   a. The party against whom a presumption is made bears the burden of production. Thus, if a legal presumption is drawn against a party, the ***burden of production*** to rebut the presumption shifts to that party.

   b. The party may not attack the original party's evidence as he would be permitted to do if it were merely a permissive inference.

   c. Rather, he must meet his burden of production by offering evidence against the presumption.

   d. However, the burden of persuasion does not shift because of the presumption. Rule 301 does nothing to shift burdens of persuasion, which rest with the original party.

   e. If the party against whom the presumption is drawn meets his burden of production and yet the jury remains unconvinced by either party, it must find against the first party because *he failed to meet the burden of persuasion.*

7. Example:

   a. Suppose that the plaintiff claims that her husband is dead because he has not been seen or heard in ***seven months*** (not years). The defendant insurance company may defend itself by doing any of the following:

      i. Undermining the credibility of the testimony of the plaintiff or of any of the plaintiff's witnesses.

      ii. Introducing evidence showing that the husband has been seen or heard in seven months; or

iii. Doing nothing in the hope that the jury will not find that the plaintiff has met her burden of persuasion.

b. Now suppose that the plaintiff claims that her husband is dead because he has not been seen or heard from in ***seven years.*** This creates a *legal presumption* that the plaintiff's husband is dead.

i. If the defendant ***does not meet its burden of production***, the court will instruct the jury that if it believes the base fact (the plaintiff's husband has not been seen or heard from for seven years), it must accept the presumption that he is dead.

ii. If the defendant ***does meet its burden of production***, the presumption that the plaintiff's husband is dead "bursts," or is rebutted. The plaintiff must now meet the burden of persuasion on the question of her husband's death by either proving that he has not in fact been seen for seven years or by directly trying to prove that he is dead.

1) If the jury believes her, she wins.

2) If the jury does not believe her, she loses.

3) If it is a close call, she loses, because she has failed to meet her burden of persuasion.

c. Thus, when there is a presumption, the defendant may not defend the case by doing nothing, as he can when there is no presumption and he can simply hope that the jury will find that the plaintiff has not met her burden of persuasion.

d. If he does nothing, the jury must find for the plaintiff. Thus, he must first rebut ("burst") the presumption by meeting his burden of production ***by producing any evidence*** (including his own testimony) to the contrary.

e. His victory then becomes possible by his (i) attacking the plaintiff's evidence; (ii) introducing new, contrary evidence; or (iii) doing nothing and hoping that the jury will not be convinced that the plaintiff has met her burden of persuasion.

8. Legal presumptions apply only in civil cases. In criminal cases, while base facts may be introduced, the Constitution requires that the jury be free to reject the presumptions that follow from them. *Sandstrom v. Montana* (U.S. 1979).

**Rule 302. Applicability of State Law in Civil Actions and Proceedings**

> In civil actions and proceedings, the effect of a presumption respecting a fact which is an element of a claim or defense as to which State law supplies the rule of decision is determined in accordance with State law.

1. In cases where the rules of decision are supplied by state law (*i.e.*, diversity cases), the effect of presumptions is governed by state law.

2. The effect of presumptions is one of *three areas* of evidence law where state common law, not the FRE and the FRCP, applies when state law supplies the rule of decision. The other two areas are privileges (Rule 501) and witness competency (Rule 601).

3. Rationale: these exceptions are based on the logic that where procedural laws are based on substantive social policies, such laws should be based on the state's laws being applied. Presumptions involve the policies and weighty matters of human relationships. These are best left to the states to decide.

4. Thus, a federal court, in a case in which the rule of decision is determined by state law, would apply

5. Thus, in a case in which the rule of decision is determined by state law, if the plaintiff properly addressed and mailed a letter, a federal court would apply the presumption that the defendant received the letter ***if the state law imposes that presumption.***

    a. *N.B.*: case law generally supplies the rules for presumptions in federal law; in state law, presumptions are generally governed by statutes.

## ARTICLE IV. RELEVANCY AND ITS LIMITS

### Rule 401. Definition of "Relevant Evidence"

> "Relevant evidence" means evidence having any tendency to make the existence of any fact that is of consequence to the determination of the action more probable or less probable than it would be without the evidence.

1. To be relevant, evidence must have some tendency to make the existence of some fact that is ***material*** ("of consequence to the determination of the action") more or less probable.

2. Such evidence is said to be ***logically relevant.***

### Rule 402. Relevant Evidence Generally Admissible; Irrelevant Evidence Inadmissible

> All relevant evidence is admissible, except as otherwise provided by the Constitution of the United States, by Act of Congress, by these rules, or by other rules prescribed by the Supreme Court pursuant to statutory authority. Evidence which is not relevant is not admissible.

1. There is a presumption of admissibility of evidence, unless the Constitution, a federal statute, or a FRE provides otherwise.

### Rule 403. Exclusion of Relevant Evidence on Grounds of Prejudice, Confusion, or Waste of Time

> Although relevant, evidence may be excluded if its probative value is substantially outweighed by the danger of unfair prejudice, confusion of the issues, or misleading the jury, or by considerations of undue delay, waste of time, or needless presentation of cumulative evidence.

1. This rule is perhaps the most frequently invoked among objections for the admission of evidence.

2. It excludes evidence whose ***probative value*** is *substantially outweighed* by its tendency to:

    a. Cause unfair prejudice;

    b. To confuse the issues or mislead the jury; or

c. Cause undue delay, waste time, or needlessly cumulate evidence.

3. The ***probative value*** of evidence refers to its *logical force* and *relevance*. It does not refer to such questions as *truthfulness* or *credibility*.

4. Even if evidence has probative value, it may be ***excluded*** if it causes unfair prejudice, causes confusion, misleads the jury, wastes time (*e.g.*, asking questions that have already been asked and answered), or accumulates evidence (*i.e.*, needlessly tries to prove facts that have already been proven with other evidence).

5. Note that the Advisory Committee notes do not count the surprise inherent in the introduction of new evidence as a ground for excluding the evidence. Rather, the remedy would be to give the other party a postponement in order to respond to the new evidence.

6. Evidence may be directly probative (*e.g.*, the testimony of an eye witness) or circumstantially probative (*i.e.*, evidence that indirectly points to the fact being proven).

**Rule 404. Character Evidence Not Admissible To Prove Conduct; Exceptions; Other Crimes**

> (a) Character evidence generally
>
> Evidence of a person's character or a trait of character is not admissible for the purpose of proving action in conformity therewith on a particular occasion, except ...

1. Introduction

   a. Rules 404-412 reiterate Rule 403: when the prejudicial effect of evidence outweighs its probative value, it is to be excluded.

   b. However, unlike Rule 403, Rules 404-12 *give no discretion to the judge*.

   c. For example, whereas under Rule 403, a judge may admit prejudicial evidence when he determines that its probative value outweighs the danger of unfair prejudice, he may *never* admit, for example, evidence of subsequent remedial measures for proving liability, under Rule 407.

2. Defining Character

   a. Character deals with qualities that define how a person ***generally acts*** (*e.g.*, dishonestly, generously, selflessly). These traits are are inadmissible under Rules 403 - 412.

   b. Character does *not* deal with traits that do not describe conduct (*e.g.*, intelligence, skills and talents), which are admissible when relevant.

3. Application

   a. Note that Rule 404 refers to evidence of a "person's character." It thus refers only to *people*.

   b. Thus, character evidence may be introduced in proving the acts of animals (*e.g.*, evidence of a dog's history of biting passersby in order to prove a biting propensity) or machines (*e.g.*, twenty other air conditioning units similarly caused sparks when plugged in).

   c. The Rule does not limit itself to the parties. Thus, a defendant may not try to prove his innocence by introducing character evidence of another potential suspect who he argues was the true culprit.

> (1) Character of accused - In a criminal case, evidence of a pertinent trait of character offered by an accused, or by the prosecution to rebut the same, or if evidence of a trait of character of the alleged victim of the crime is offered by an accused and admitted under Rule 404 (a)(2), evidence of the same trait of character of the accused offered by the prosecution;

4. Character of the Accused: the "Mercy Rule"

   a. In criminal cases *only*, evidence of the defendant's character is admissible in proving his conduct.

   b. The defendant may bring in witnesses on behalf of himself in proving his own favorable character traits.

   c. The prosecution may offer evidence of the defendant's character to ***rebut*** the defendant's evidence. He may do this by:

      i. Cross-examining the defense witness about pertinent *specific acts* that the defendant committed.

      ii. *Call character witnesses* to testify to the same issue.

   ***d.*** The evidence must be of a "pertinent trait" to the crime charged.

      i. For example, a defendant in a criminal assault case may introduce witnesses as to his peacefulness, but not of his honesty (a trait that bears little relevance to assault).

      ii. The same defendant in a corresponding civil assault case may not introduce *any* character evidence, whether or not it is relevant.

      iii. In the criminal assault case, the prosecutor may *not* introduce character evidence, unless he is doing so to rebut character evidence introduced by the defendant.

   e. The purpose of this rule is to prevent the prosecutor from introducing evidence trying to prove that the defendant is the *kind* of person who would commit the crime charged in the indictment.

   f. It seeks to prevent jurors from reasoning that because he committed a particular act, the defendant has an evil character and is therefore be more likely to have committed the crime.

> (2) Character of alleged victim - In a criminal case, and subject to the limitations imposed by Rule 412, evidence of a pertinent trait of character of the alleged victim of the crime offered by an accused, or by the prosecution to rebut the same, or evidence of a character trait of peacefulness of the alleged victim offered by the prosecution in a homicide case to rebut evidence that the alleged victim was the first aggressor;

5. Character of an Alleged Victim

   a. *In criminal cases only*, evidence of the victim's character is admissible in the following circumstances:

      i. When offered by the ***defendant*** where it is pertinent and tends to prove the defendant's innocence; or

ii. When offered by the ***prosecutor***, if:

1) The defendant offers evidence of the victim's character, which the prosecutor is entitled to rebut; or

2) In a homicide case, the defendant offers evidence that he acted in self defense, which the prosecutor is entitled to rebut by offering evidence of the victim's peaceful character, *even if the defendant never raises the issue of the victim's character.*

b. *N.B.*: Rule 404(a)(2) is preempted by Rule 412, *infra.*, which generally prohibits character evidence of the alleged victim in criminal and civil sexual misconduct cases.

(3) Character of witness - Evidence of the character of a witness, as provided in rules 607, 608, and 609.

6. Character of the Witness

a. This rule deals with the admissibility of evidence of a witness's credibility (*e.g.*, evidence of a witness's *propensity to lie*).

b. It is used for the purpose of impeachment.

c. Note that this rule is different from Rule 404(a)(1)-(2) and Rules 412-415 because it deals only with *the time of the trial* and it does not limit itself to criminal cases; it applies to civil cases as well.

d. When a criminal defendant waives his Fifth Amendment privilege against self-incrimination and takes the stand, this rule overlaps with Rule 403(a)(1) and evidence of the defendant's character may be presented in order to impeach his credibility.

e. *See* Rules 607-609, *infra.*, for a more detailed treatment of the impeachment of witnesses.

(b) Other crimes, wrongs, or acts

Evidence of other crimes, wrongs, or acts is not admissible to prove the character of a person in order to show action in conformity therewith. It may, however, be admissible for other purposes, such as proof of motive, opportunity, intent, preparation, plan, knowledge, identity, or absence of mistake or accident, provided that upon request by the accused, the prosecution in a criminal case shall provide reasonable notice in advance of trial, or during trial if the court excuses pretrial notice on good cause shown, of the general nature of any such evidence it intends to introduce at trial.

7. Similar Crimes, Wrongs, or Acts

a. Evidence of other crimes, wrongs, or acts is inadmissible for proving character to show action in conformity therewith

i. Example: evidence of the defendant's having formerly stabbed a man would be inadmissible in proving the defendant's violent character and likelihood of guilt in a later crime.

b. However, evidence of similar happenings and wrongs is admissible for the following purposes: to prove motive, opportunity, intent, preparation, plan, knowledge, identity, or absence of mistake or accident. Character evidence may also be admissible for impeachment.

**Rule 405. Methods of Proving Character**

> (a) Reputation or opinion.
>
> In all cases in which evidence of character or a trait of character of a person is admissible, proof may be made by testimony as to reputation or by testimony in the form of an opinion. On cross-examination, inquiry is allowable into relevant specific instances of conduct.
>
> (b) Specific instances of conduct.
>
> In cases in which character or a trait of character of a person is an essential element of a charge, claim, or defense, proof may also be made of specific instances of that person's conduct.

1. Under Rule 405, two methods are available for proving character:
   a. Reputation or opinion; and
   b. Specific instances of conduct.
2. Reputation or Opinion
   a. Whenever character evidence is admissible, it may be proven with reputation or opinion evidence.
   b. *N.B.*: evidence of the reputation of a person is necessarily hearsay evidence, since it involves out of court statements offered for their truth. Under Rule 803(21), reputation is admissible as an exception to the hearsay rule.
3. Specific Instances of Conduct
   a. On Cross-Examination. Rule 405(a).
      i. When the defendant first raises the issue of character in his defense, he may only offer reputation or opinion evidence, not specific acts.
      ii. However, the prosecutor, in rebutting the defendant's character evidence on cross-examination, may offer evidence of specific acts in addition to opinion and reputation evidence. Rule 405(a).
   b. When Character is "In Issue." Rule 405(b).
      i. Furthermore, evidence of specific acts may be offered into evidence when character is "in issue." Rule 405(b).
      ii. Character is in issue whenever it is an ***essential element*** of a ***charge***, ***claim***, or ***defense***.
      iii. Examples:
         1) *Defamation:* evidence of the plaintiff's character is relevant as a defense in showing that the statements made about the plaintiff were true. The defendant may thus offer event-

specific instances of the plaintiff's conduct in defending himself.

2) *Felons*: when one of the elements of a crime requires that the crime be committed by a felon, the prosecution may introduced evidence that the defendant has been charged and convicted of a felony. Proving this specific instance of conduct is an essential element of the charge.

***3)*** *Entrapment*: if a defendant raises the defense of entrapment, the prosecution is required to show that the defendant was predisposed to commit the crime.

**Rule 406. Habit; Routine Practice**

> Evidence of the habit of a person or of the routine practice of an organization, whether corroborated or not and regardless of the presence of eyewitnesses, is relevant to prove that the conduct of the person or organization on a particular occasion was in conformity with the habit or routine practice.

1. Compare:

   a. Habit

      i. It refers to a party's regular ***responses to repeated, specific situations***—the things he does).

      ii. Traits of habit are usually defined by words such as "always," not "usually."

      iii. To prove habit, the conduct must be sufficiently frequent; one or two responses from the past will not suffice.

         1) Example: the *plaintiff* always stops at red lights.

      iv. Evidence of habit (and of an organization's routine practices) is admissible in showing conformity therewith.

   b. Character

      i. It refers to a party's generalized traits—what kind of a person he is.

         1) Example: the plaintiff is a safe driver.

      ii. Character evidence generally is *not* admissible in showing conformity therewith.

**Rule 404-406 Summary Chart**

| | ***Character Evidence*: *General Rule*:** | ***Exception 1*: *Character of the Accused*** | ***Exception 2*: *Character of an Alleged Victim*** | ***Exception 3*: *Character of a Witness*** | ***Evidence of Habit*** |
|---|---|---|---|---|---|
| ***Civil Cases*** | Character evidence is inadmissible in proving action in conformity therewith. | Inadmissible. | Inadmissible. | Admissible pursuant to Rules 607-609. | Admissible. |
| ***Criminal Cases*** | Character evidence is inadmissible in proving action in conformity therewith. | - the defendant may offer favorable opinion or reputation character evidence;<br>- the state may rebut with opinion or reputation character evidence or, on cross examination, with specific instances of conduct. | Subject to Rule 412 limitations,<br>- the defendant may offer opinion or reputation evidence;<br>- the state may rebut with opinion or reputation evidence, or specific instances of conduct on cross-examination.<br>- Where the defendant claims self-defense, the state may offer evidence of peaceful character. | Admissible pursuant to Rules 607-609. | Admissible. |

**Rule 407. Subsequent Remedial Measures**

> When, after an injury or harm allegedly caused by an event, measures are taken that, if taken previously, would have made the injury or harm less likely to occur, evidence of the subsequent measures is not admissible to prove negligence, culpable conduct, a defect in a product, a defect in a product's design, or a need for a warning or instruction. This rule does not require the exclusion of evidence of subsequent measures when offered for another purpose, such as proving ownership, control, or feasibility of precautionary measures, if controverted, or impeachment.

1. Rules 407-410 Generally

    a. Rules 407-410, like Rules generally 404-412 (but not 413-415), are reiterations of Rule 403: when the prejudicial effect of evidence outweighs its probative value, it is to be excluded. However, these rules give no discretion to a judge.

    b. *For the purpose of proving liability*, a judge may never admit evidence of the following:

        i. Subsequent remedial measures (Rule 407);

        ii. Compromise negotiations (Rule 408);

iii. The payment of medical expenses (Rule 409);

iv. Pleas and plea discussions (Rule 410); and

v. The existence of liability insurance (Rule 411).

c. Such evidence may, however, be admitted *for other purposes* (*i.e.*, impeachment) if it passes the Rule 403 test and other limitations imposed by the rules.

d. These Rules are based on a ***public policy*** consideration that seeks to encourage individuals to take remedial measures, compromise, assist one another and undertake other socially desirable measures.

2. Subsequent Remedial Measures. Rule 407

a. Evidence of remedial measures taken after harm was caused that would have mitigated the harm if taken earlier is inadmissible in proving negligence, culpable conduct, or a defect in a product or in a product's design.

b. However, evidence of measures taken after harm was caused is admissible for other purposes, "such as proving ownership, control, or feasibility of precautionary measures, if controverted, or impeachment."

**Rule 408. Compromise and Offers to Compromise**

> (a) Prohibited uses. Evidence of the following is not admissible on behalf of any party, when offered to prove liability for, invalidity of, or amount of a claim that was disputed as to validity or amount, or to impeach through a prior inconsistent statement or contradiction:
>
> (1) furnishing or offering or promising to furnish or accepting or offering or promising to accept a valuable consideration in compromising or attempting to compromise the claim; and
>
> (2) conduct or statements made in compromise negotiations regarding the claim, except when offered in a criminal case and the negotiations related to a claim by a public office or agency in the exercise of regulatory, investigative, or enforcement authority.

1. The following is inadmissible in establishing "liability for, invalidity of, or amount of a claim ***that was disputed*** as to validity or amount, or to impeach through a prior inconsistent statement or contradiction":

***a.*** Compromise negotiations/actual settlement in civil cases offered in either *civil or criminal cases;*

b. Conduct and statements in civil cases made ***in conjunction with*** compromise negotiations (such as admissions) offered in:

i. Civil cases: always inadmissible.

1) Conduct and statements made in conjunction with compromise negotiations, such as admissions, are ***not severable*** from the compromise negotiations.

ii. Criminal cases: sometimes admissible.

1) Conduct and statements made in conjunction with compromise negotiations, such as admissions, ***may be***

***severable*** from the compromise negotiations and therefore admissible.

2) To be severed, the negotiations must be:

a) Related to a claim by a public office or agency; and

b) The public office or agency must be in the exercise of its authority.

3) Compare Rule 409, where statements made in conjunction with offers to pay medical expenses, such as admissions, are severable and thus admissible.

c. It is implied that Rule 408 refers only to conduct or statements made in conjunction with compromise settlements in *civil* cases for the following reasons:

i. The word "claim" is a term of art referring only to civil cases

ii. Furthermore, Rule 408 covers negotiations made by a "public office or agency," and does not use the language "prosecuting authority" as does Rule 410, the corollary Rule that deals with plea bargains (compromise settlements in *criminal* cases).

d. Example: in a civil case to recover money obtained through alleged fraud, the defendant, in negotiating with the Assistant U.S. Attorney assigned to the case, apologizes for what he did and offers to pay $50,000 to settle out of court.

i. Is the offer to settle admissible against the defendant in proving his liability for the claim?

1) No. Under Rule 408, "furnishing or offering or promising to furnish or accepting or offering or promising to accept a valuable consideration in compromising or attempting to compromise the claim" is inadmissible against the defendant in proving his liability.

2) Although Rule 408 does not explicitly state that such evidence is also inadmissible in a parallel criminal case, a pending 2006 amendment to the rule clarifies that it applies both to civil and criminal cases against defendants.

ii. Is the apology admissible?

1) No, "except when offered in a criminal case and the negotiations related to a claim by a public office or agency in the exercise of regulatory, investigative, or enforcement authority."

e. This rule gives the parties an incentive to settle, since settlement offers may not be used to show a party's liability.

f. *See infra.*, Rule 408-409 Summary Chart.

(b) Permitted uses. This rule does not require exclusion if the evidence is offered for

> purposes not prohibited by subdivision (a). Examples of permissible purposes include proving a witness's bias or prejudice; negating a contention of undue delay; and proving an effort to obstruct a criminal investigation or prosecution.

2. Such evidence is, however, admissible for other purposes, such as "proving a witness's bias or prejudice; negating a contention of undue delay; and proving an effort to obstruct a criminal investigation or prosecution." Rule 408(b).

**Rule 409. Payment of Medical and Similar Expenses**

> Evidence of furnishing or offering or promising to pay medical, hospital, or similar expenses occasioned by an injury is not admissible to prove liability for the injury.

1. Evidence of offers to pay medical expenses or actual payment of medical expenses is inadmissible *for proving liability for an injury*.
2. This rule is based on a "humanitarian motive" to encourage people to help one another.
3. Nothing in the rule suggests that such evidence is inadmissible for proving ownership, control, identity, etc.
    a. Example: the plaintiff could prove that the defendant had control over an employee that delivered pizza, because the defendant immediately offered to pay the plaintiff for his medical expenses when he heard that the employee hit the plaintiff while delivering pizza.
4. Statements made in conjunction with offers to pay medical and similar expenses, such as admissions, ***are severable*** and thus admissible.
    a. Example → the defendant states, "I am so sorry, it was all my fault! I will pay all of your medical expenses."
    b. The statement "it was all my fault" *is* admissible against the defendant, even though the statement "I will pay all of your medical expenses" is inadmissible.

**Rule 408 and 409 Summary Chart:**
**When Evidence is Admissible to Prove Liability**

| | | | |
|---|---|---|---|
| ***Rule 408*** | Compromise negotiations, actual settlement | Offered in civil cases ⇨ | Inadmissible to prove liability |
| | | Offered in criminal cases ⇨ | Inadmissible to prove liability (according to a pending amendment) |
| | Conduct or statements made in conjunction | Offered in civil cases ⇨ | Inadmissible to prove liability |
| | | Offered in criminal cases ⇨ | Admissible when made in negotiations with a public office or agency in the exercise of its authority |
| ***Rule 409*** | Offers to pay expenses, actual payment | Inadmissible to prove liability | |
| | Conduct or statements made in conjunction | Admissible to prove liability | |

**Rule 410. Inadmissibility of Pleas, Plea Discussions, and Related Statements**

> Except as otherwise provided in this rule, evidence of the following is not, in any civil or criminal proceeding, admissible against the defendant who made the plea or was a participant in the plea discussions:
>
> (1) a plea of guilty which was later withdrawn;
>
> (2) a plea of nolo contendere;
>
> (3) any statement made in the course of any proceedings under Rule 11 of the Federal Rules of Criminal Procedure or comparable state procedure regarding either of the foregoing pleas; or
>
> (4) any statement made in the course of plea discussions with an attorney for the prosecuting authority which do not result in a plea of guilty or which result in a plea of guilty later withdrawn.
>
> However, such a statement is admissible (i) in any proceeding wherein another statement made in the course of the same plea or plea discussions has been introduced and the statement ought in fairness be considered contemporaneously with it, or (ii) in a criminal proceeding for perjury or false statement if the statement was made by the defendant under oath, on the record and in the presence of counsel.

1. Evidence of the following is inadmissible in any civil or criminal proceeding against the defendant who made the pleas or who participated in plea discussions:
    a. A plea of guilty later withdrawn;
    b. A plea of nolo contendere;
        i. Note that only pleas of *nolo contendere*, not guilty pleas, are listed as inadmissible.

ii. This is because, whereas guilty pleas have high probative value (the judge must assure that there is a factual basis for the plea and that the defendant understands the implications of the plea and that it is voluntary), pleas of *nolo contendere* indicate only that the defendant accepts the punishment, but not that he admits being guilty. They thus have little probative value and may not be used against the defendant in subsequent cases.

c. Any statement under FRCrP 11 (Pleas) proceedings regarding the foregoing pleas;

d. Any statement made in the course of plea discussions with an attorney for the prosecuting authority not resulting in a plea of guilty or resulting in one but later withdrawn.

i. *N.B.*: note that this refers only to statement made in the course of plea discussions when they do *not* result in a plea of guilty.

ii. Thus, when discussions result in a plea of guilty, a statement made by the defendant may be used against him in a subsequent civil trial.

2. Failed Plea Bargain Negotiations

a. Unsuccessful settlement offers by the defendant may not be used as evidence against him. Thus, if the prosecutor and the defendant are negotiating in a criminal case and the defendant offers to take a lower charge, this is not admissible in any criminal or civil proceeding if it does not result in a successful plea bargain.

b. Note that evidence of unsuccessful plea bargaining is only inadmissible if made with "an attorney for the prosecuting authority."

i. Thus, if the defendant attempts to negotiate with the witness who charged him, the defendant's offers to settle are admissible against him.

ii. The rationale of this rule is to encourage the defendants to settle their cases the proper way, with the authority who has the power to settle the case, not with witnesses in a way that may lead to improper solicitation or the obstruction of justice.

c. Unlike Rule 408, however, ***the charge does not need to be disputed;*** statements made in the course of plea discussions are inadmissible whether or not they are disputed.

d. Furthermore, *any statement made in conjunction* with such an offer is not admissible (unlike Rule 408, where the defendant's conduct or statements made in conjunction to compromise settlements in civil cases may be admissible in criminal prosecutions).

e. Two exceptions:

i. In any proceeding where another statement made in the course of the same plea or plea discussions has been introduced and the statement ought in ***fairness*** be considered contemporaneously with it;

1) Example: if the defendant offers to the jury parts of the conversation with the prosecutor taken out of context (*e.g.*, "the prosecutor offered to drop the murder charges"), the prosecutor may bring in the rest of the conversation *even if it was made in the course of please discussions.*

ii. Statements made in conjunction with offers to settle are admissible in separate cases for ***perjury*** or ***false statement*** if the statement was made by the defendant while under oath.

3. Example: while talking to an Assistant U.S. Attorney in a criminal fraud charge, the defendant says that he will plead guilty and offer the names of all of the conspirators if the attorney offers no jail time. The Assistant U.S. Attorney accepts the offer. Is a statement made in the course of plea discussions admissible against the defendant in a later suit?

a. Yes. Since rule 410 only excludes only statements made in the course of plea discussions which *do not result in a plea of guilty* or which result in a *plea of guilty later withdrawn*, a statement made in the course of plea discussions will be admissible.

b. Similarly, nothing in Rule 410 prohibits admission of the *plea itself* (not just statements made in the course of plea discussions) as evidence in a later case.

c. A plaintiff may thus tell the jury in a later case that the defendant pled guilty in a criminal case. This is the required result under collateral estoppel doctrine (issue preclusion); the same issue cannot be twice litigated.

**Rule 411. Liability Insurance**

> Evidence that a person was or was not insured against liability is not admissible upon the issue whether the person acted negligently or otherwise wrongfully. This rule does not require the exclusion of evidence of insurance against liability when offered for another purpose, such as proof of agency, ownership, or control, or bias or prejudice of a witness.

1. Evidence of insurance is inadmissible on the issue of whether a person was negligent.
2. This includes evidence that the defendant both ***had*** and ***did not have insurance***.
3. However, evidence that the defendant had or did not have insurance is admissible as to any other logically relevant issue, including: agency, ownership, control, or bias or prejudice of a witness.

**Summary of the Public Policy Rules:**
**Rules 407 - 411 Summary Chart**

<table>
<tr><td rowspan="2">Subsequent Remdial Measures (Rule 407 )</td><td>Subsequent Remdial Measures</td><td colspan="2">Inadmissible in proving liability</td></tr>
<tr><td>Conduct or statements made in conjunction</td><td colspan="2">Admissible in proving liability</td></tr>
<tr><td rowspan="4">Compro-mise in Civil Cases (Rule 408)</td><td rowspan="2">Compromise negotiations, actual settlement</td><td>Offered in civil cases ⇨</td><td>Inadmissible</td></tr>
<tr><td>Offered in criminal cases ⇨</td><td>Inadmissible in proving liability (according to a pending amendment)</td></tr>
<tr><td rowspan="2">Conduct or statements made in conjunction</td><td>Offered in civil cases ⇨</td><td>Inadmissible in proving liability</td></tr>
<tr><td>Offered in criminal cases ⇨</td><td>Inadmissible, unless made in negotiations with a public office or agency in the exercise of its authority</td></tr>
<tr><td rowspan="2">Payment of Medical Expenses (Rule 409)</td><td>Offers to pay expenses, actual payment</td><td colspan="2">Inadmissible in proving liability</td></tr>
<tr><td>Conduct or statements made in conjunction</td><td colspan="2">Admissible in proving liability</td></tr>
<tr><td rowspan="4">Compro-mise in Criminal Cases (Rule 410)</td><td rowspan="2">Plea of guilty later withdrawn or plea of nolo contendere</td><td>Offered in civil cases ⇨</td><td>Inadmissible in proving liability</td></tr>
<tr><td>Offered in criminal cases ⇨</td><td>Inadmissible in proving liability</td></tr>
<tr><td rowspan="2">Conduct or statements made in conjunction</td><td>Offered in civil cases ⇨</td><td>Inadmissible, subject to the requirements of fairness.</td></tr>
<tr><td>Offered in criminal cases ⇨</td><td>Inadmissible, subject to the requirements of fairness and separate perjury proceedings.</td></tr>
<tr><td rowspan="2">Liability Insurance (Rule 411)</td><td>Evidence of liability insurance</td><td colspan="2">Inadmissible in proving liability</td></tr>
<tr><td>Conduct or statements made in conjunction</td><td colspan="2">N/A</td></tr>
</table>

**Rule 412. Sex Offense Cases; Relevance of Alleged Victim's Past Sexual Behavior or Alleged Sexual Predisposition**

(a) Evidence generally inadmissible.

> The following evidence is not admissible in any civil or criminal proceeding involving alleged sexual misconduct except as provided in subdivisions (b) and (c):
>
> (1) Evidence offered to prove that any alleged victim engaged in other sexual behavior.
>
> (2) Evidence offered to prove any alleged victim's sexual predisposition.

1. General Rule

    ***a.*** In sexual misconduct cases, evidence of a victim's other alleged sexual behavior and predisposition is generally ***inadmissible.***

    b. Rationale: allowing evidence of past sexual conduct would discourage victim of sexual abuse from coming forward.

    c. Examples: the defendant offers evidence that at the time of the encounter, the victim was using contraceptives. This would be inadmissible under Rule 412(a)(2).

> (b) Exceptions.
>
> (1) In a criminal case, the following evidence is admissible, if otherwise admissible under these rules:
>
> (A) evidence of specific instances of sexual behavior by the alleged victim offered to prove that a person other than the accused was the source of semen, injury, or other physical evidence;
>
> (B) evidence of specific instances of sexual behavior by the alleged victim with respect to the person accused of the sexual misconduct offered by the accused to prove consent or by the prosecution; and
>
> (C) evidence the exclusion of which would violate the constitutional rights of the defendant.
>
> (2) In a civil case, evidence offered to prove the sexual behavior or sexual predisposition of any alleged victim is admissible if it is otherwise admissible under these rules and its probative value substantially outweighs the danger of harm to any victim and of unfair prejudice to any party. Evidence of an alleged victim's reputation is admissible only if it has been placed in controversy by the alleged victim.

2. In ***criminal cases***, evidence that is otherwise inadmissible is admissible under the following circumstances:

    a. It is used to show that the defendant *was not the source* of the semen, injury, or other physical evidence. Rule 412(b)(1)(A);

        i. Semen Exception

            1) Today, however, the advent of DNA testing renders meaningless the offering of the victim's past sexual behavior as evidence that the defendant was not the source of semen.

        ii. Injury and Other Physical Evidence Exception

            1) This exception allows evidence of other sexual encounters only if one of the other offenders might have been the source of the injuries or physical evidence.

2) *N.B.*: if the prosecutor does not bring in the evidence of the injuries and physical evidence, then the defendant will not have the opportunity to bring in evidence of the victim's other sexual encounters.

b. It is used to show the victim's consent or by the prosecution. Rule 412(b)(1)(B);

i. This exception allows the defendant to bring in evidence regarding the alleged victim's sexual conduct ***with respect to the defendant.***

ii. Example: the victim claims that briefly after meeting the defendant at a party, he brought her home and raped her. If the jury knew that the defendant and the victim were involved in a sexual relationship that had lasted years, it would put things in perspective.

c. It is admissible under the defendant's constitutional rights. Rule 412(b)(1)(C).

i. Example: "precocious sexual knowledge." A man is accused of sexually molesting a nine year old, who is able to recite the encounter with specificity. The defendant claims that the victim is lying and must explain to the jury how the victim would know of such things if he did not molest her. He may want to show evidence that the victim had a sexual history of being molested. In such a case, the Constitution requires that the defendant be able to offer such evidence, even though it involves sexual history.

3. Exceptions in Civil Cases

a. Evidence of a victim's previous sexual conduct or sexual disposition is generally inadmissible in civil proceedings involving alleged sexual misconduct, unless: (i) it is ***otherwise admissible*** under the FRE; and (ii) its ***probative value substantially outweighs the danger of harm*** to any victim and of unfair prejudice to any party.

b. However, evidence of an alleged victim's reputation is admissible "only if it has been placed in controversy by the alleged victim" (*e.g.*, the victim argues that she has a reputation for chastity). Rule 412(b)(2).

> (c) Procedure to determine admissibility.
>
> (1) A party intending to offer evidence under subdivision (b) must --
>
> (A) file a written motion at least 14 days before trial specifically describing the evidence and stating the purpose for which it is offered unless the court, for good cause requires a different time for filing or permits filing during trial; and
>
> (B) serve the motion on all parties and notify the alleged victim or, when appropriate, the alleged victim's guardian or representative.
>
> (2) Before admitting evidence under this rule the court must conduct a hearing in camera and afford the victim and parties a right to attend and be heard. The motion, related papers, and the record of the hearing must be sealed and remain under seal unless the court orders otherwise.

4. *N.B.*: in sex offense cases, Rule 412 preempts Rule 402(a)(2), which deals with circumstances in which the defendant may offer evidence of his victim's character in general.

**Rule 413. Evidence of Similar Crimes in Sexual Assault Cases**

(a) In a criminal case in which the defendant is accused of an offense of sexual assault, evidence of the defendant's commission of another offense or offenses of sexual assault is admissible, and may be considered for its bearing on any matter to which it is relevant.

(b) In a case in which the Government intends to offer evidence under this rule, the attorney for the Government shall disclose the evidence to the defendant, including statements of witnesses or a summary of the substance of any testimony that is expected to be offered, at least fifteen days before the scheduled date of trial or at such later time as the court may allow for good cause.

(c) This rule shall not be construed to limit the admission or consideration of evidence under any other rule.

(d) For purposes of this rule and Rule 415, "offense of sexual assault" means a crime under Federal law or the law of a State (as defined in section 513 of title 18, United States Code) that involved--

(1) any conduct proscribed by chapter 109A of title 18, United States Code;

(2) contact, without consent, between any part of the defendant's body or an object and the genitals or anus of another person;

(3) contact, without consent, between the genitals or anus of the defendant and any part of another person's body;

(4) deriving sexual pleasure or gratification from the infliction of death, bodily injury, or physical pain on another person; or

(5) an attempt or conspiracy to engage in conduct described in paragraphs (1)-(4).

1. Rules 413-415

    a. In summary, under Rules 413-415, in any civil or criminal case where the defendant is accused of sexual abuse or child molestation, evidence of the defendant's commission of similar crimes *is admissible* whenever it is relevant.

    b. These rules represent a radical departure from centuries of legal precedent.

    c. It is not clear why these Rules are limited to sexual abuse defined with such specificity (not sexual misconduct generally) and why they are split into three separate rules, which does not allow cross over (*e.g.*, if the defendant is accused of child molestation, the government may not offer evidence that the defendant molested an adult woman).

    d. Furthermore, there appears to be a double standard: under Rule 413(a), the prosecution may bring in witnesses to testify that they too were sexually assulated by the defendant, but under Rule 412(a), the defendant may not bring in witnesses to testify that she consented to sex with them.

2. Rule 413

    a. Under Rule 404(b), evidence of other crimes, wrongs, or acts is not admissible to prove the character of a person in order to show action in conformity therewith.

b. Rule 413, however, in order to protect society against sex offenders, expands the admissibility of evidence of similar crimes of the defendant in ***sexual assault cases***.

c. It allows for the admission of evidence of the defendant's commission of other sexual assault offenses, to be considered for its bearing on any matter to which it is relevant.

d. It seeks to facilitate proving that, if the defendant was previously convicted, he is probably guilty of the current offense.

e. The evidence is still under Rule 403, whereby such evidence is admissible only if its probative value outweighs the risk of unfair prejudice.

**Rule 414. Evidence of Similar Crimes in Child Molestation Cases**

(a) In a criminal case in which the defendant is accused of an offense of child molestation, evidence of the defendant's commission of another offense or offenses of child molestation is admissible, and may be considered for its bearing on any matter to which it is relevant.

(b) In a case in which the Government intends to offer evidence under this rule, the attorney for the Government shall disclose the evidence to the defendant, including statements of witnesses or a summary of the substance of any testimony that is expected to be offered, at least fifteen days before the scheduled date of trial or at such later time as the court may allow for good cause.

(c) This rule shall not be construed to limit the admission or consideration of evidence under any other rule.

(d) For purposes of this rule and Rule 415, "child" means a person below the age of fourteen, and "offense of child molestation" means a crime under Federal law or the law of a State (as defined in section 513 of title 18, United States Code) that involved--

(1) any conduct proscribed by chapter 109A of title 18, United States Code, that was committed in relation to a child;

(2) any conduct proscribed by chapter 110 of title 18, United States Code;

(3) contact between any part of the defendant's body or an object and the genitals or anus of a child;

(4) contact between the genitals or anus of the defendant and any part of the body of a child;

(5) deriving sexual pleasure or gratification from the infliction of death, bodily injury, or physical pain on a child; or

(6) an attempt or conspiracy to engage in conduct described in paragraphs (1)-(5).

1. Like Rule 413, this rule expands the admissibility of evidence of other crimes, wrongs or acts under Rule 404(b) in cases of child molestation.

2. It allows for evidence of the defendant's commission of another offense or offenses of child molestation to be admitted for consideration for its bearing *on any matter to which it is relevant*.

3. Under Rule 403, such evidence is admissible only when its probative value outweighs the danger of unfair prejudice.

4. Such evidence is not limited to convictions.

5. 415. Evidence of Similar Acts in Civil Cases Concerning Sexual Assault or Child Molestation

> (a) In a civil case in which a claim for damages or other relief is predicated on a party's alleged commission of conduct constituting an offense of sexual assault or child molestation, evidence of that party's commission of another offense or offenses of sexual assault or child molestation is admissible and may be considered as provided in Rule 413 and Rule 414 of these rules.
>
> (b) A party who intends to offer evidence under this Rule shall disclose the evidence to the party against whom it will be offered, including statements of witnesses or a summary of the substance of any testimony that is expected to be offered, at least fifteen days before the scheduled date of trial or at such later time as the court may allow for good cause.
>
> (c) This rule shall not be construed to limit the admission or consideration of evidence under any other rule.

6. Rule 415, which deals with ***civil cases*** involving sex offenses, did not come about through the typical Supreme Court promulgation followed by Congressional approval; rather, the rule was created as part of Congress's Violent Crime Control and Law Enforcement Act of 1994.
7. It may appear that this rule may lead to the defendant's liability in a civil case for past acts or reputation alone, but Rule 403 preempts this risk by allowing for evidence to be excluded when its probative value is substantially outweighed by the danger of unfair prejudice.

## ARTICLE V. PRIVILEGES

### Rule 501. General Rule

> Except as otherwise required by the Constitution of the United States or provided by Act of Congress or in rules prescribed by the Supreme Court pursuant to statutory authority, the privilege of a witness, person, government, State, or political subdivision thereof shall be governed by the principles of the common law as they may be interpreted by the courts of the United States in the light of reason and experience. However, in civil actions and proceedings, with respect to an element of a claim or defense as to which State law supplies the rule of decision, the privilege of a witness, person, government, State, or political subdivision thereof shall be determined in accordance with State law.

1. Under Rule 501, federal judges may develop the privilege law as they decide cases and ***interpret the common law "in the light of reason and experience"*** in criminal and federal question civil cases.
2. However, in cases where the rules of decision are supplied by state law (*i.e.*, diversity cases), the rule of privileges is ***governed by state law***.
3. Rule 501 is therefore one of the three Rules of the FRE that defers to state law (the other two being presumptions (Rule 302) and competency of witnesses (Rule 601)).
4. In criminal cases, due to the Fifth Amendment right against self-incrimination, prosecutors often are unable to directly examine defendants.

a. They often therefore rely on family and close friends of the defendant and offer evidence of what they say the defendant told them.

b. Privilege issues are likely to come up, since the content of these conversations may be within the scope of some privilege.

c. Since the Fifth Amendment right against self-incrimination applies only "in any criminal case,"[71] privilege issues are more likely to be litigated in criminal cases.

5. Examples of privileges include the attorney-client privilege, the spousal privileges, the priest-parishioner privilege, the physician-patient privilege.

6. To be privileged, an exchange must be:

a. A Communication

i. A communication is an exchange of information.

ii. Example: a patient's explaining to his doctor the circumstances behind a stab wound, *not* the doctor's finding a knife-stab in his patient.

b. That is Confidential

i. The privileged parties must have been alone when the communication was made, with no third party present, unless the third party was:

1) Present to further the purpose behind the communication (*e.g.*, an interpreter facilitating communication between an attorney and a non-English speaking client);

2) Unable to appreciate the content of the communication (*e.g.*, he or she was mentally insane, asleep, etc.); or

3) Present within the scope of the same or another privilege (*e.g.*, the privilege holder speaks to his doctor within the presence of his spouse. Since the spouse holds an independent privilege, the confidentiality of the statement is not affected).

ii. A communication cannot be confidential when made in a public place where it is possible that third parties will overhear.

iii. A document may be confidential in certain circumstances, but if it is shown or prepared for the purpose of sharing with third parties, it cannot be privileged.

1) Example: even if a party shares his income tax returns with his attorney, the attorney-client privilege does not apply, since these documents were prepared for the purpose of sharing with a third party (the government).

c. Made within the Privilege Holder's Official Capacity

---

[71] U.S. Const. amend. V.

i. Example: a communication to one's physician relating to marital problems does not fall within the privilege holder's capacity, since it is not related to medical treatment.

ii. between a client and his attorney must be made while the latter is serving as his attorney, not as his golf partner.

iii. *N.B.*: one's spouse is always acting within his or her capacity as a spouse.

7. The privileges rule "applies at all stages of all actions, cases, and proceedings." Rule 1101(c). As a corollary, parties may only obtain discovery that is *not privileged*. Under FRCP 26(b)(1).

8. Attorney-Client Privilege

a. The attorney-client privilege applies when confidential communications are made to an attorney for the purpose of obtaining legal services.

b. Preexisting documents (*e.g.*, income tax records) are not confidential between a client and his attorney and do *not* become privileged when they are turned over to an attorney.

c. The privilege attaches when the party making the statements ***reasonably believes*** that the party in whom he confides is an attorney, even if he is mistaken.

d. The privilege does not, however, apply to communications related to the commission or planning of a future illegal act.

9. Spousal Privileges

a. The federal courts recognize two spousal privileges: the adverse spousal testimony privilege and the confidential marital communications privilege.

b. Adverse Spousal Testimony Privilege

i. The adverse spousal testimony privilege permits one spouse to refuse to testify against the other when the other is the defendant in a criminal proceeding.

ii. The privilege is thus inapplicable when the parties divorce, since it is intended to allow the refusal to testify against one's ***spouse.***

iii. The adverse spousal testimony privilege allows the witness spouse to refuse to testify not only as to communications made during the course of the marriage, but also as to *any communications or occurrences* from *before and during the marriage*.

iv. The privilege is carried by the ***witness spouse***, not by the ***defendant***. The privilege can thus only be invoked or waived by the witness; if she chooses to waive it, the defendant can do nothing to stop her.

c. Confidential Marital Communications Privilege

i. The confidential marital communications privilege is carried by *both spouses.*

ii. According to the majority view, one spouse may testify *only with the consent of the other.*

iii. The privilege applies both during and after the marriage, in both civil and criminal proceedings, to confidential communications ***made during the marriage,*** not communications made before the marriage or after a divorce.

d. These privileges do *not* apply to communications made for the purpose of committing or planning a criminal or fraudulent act.

**Summary Chart of the Spousal Privileges**

| | ***Adverse Spousal Testimony Privilege*** | ***Confidential Marital Communications Privilege*** |
|---|---|---|
| *Who Carries It* | The witness spouse. | Both spouses. |
| *When It Applies* | In a criminal proceeding against one of the spouses *while the parties are married.* | In any civil or criminal proceeding, both during and after the marriage, whether or not one of the spouses is a party. |
| *What Is Covered* | *Testimony* as to *communications* and *occurrences* from before and during the marriage. | Testimony as to confidential communications made during the marriage. |

## ARTICLE VI. WITNESSES

### Rule 601. General Rule of Competency

> Every person is competent to be a witness except as otherwise provided in these rules. However, in civil actions and proceedings, with respect to an element of a claim or defense as to which State law supplies the rule of decision, the competency of a witness shall be determined in accordance with State law.

1. The law regarding the compency of a witness is one of the three areas of the federal evidence law that is determined by state law when the state law supplies the rule of decision (the other two being the law of presumptions (Rule 302) and the law of privilege (Rule 501)).

2. In cases where the rules of decision are *not* supplied by state law, the FRE establish who is competent to be a witness.

3. Under the common law, the following three groups may not testify:

a. Those whose ***trustworthiness*** is questionable (this is reflected in Rules 602-03);

b. Those rendered incompetent because of their ***roles*** in the trial (this is reflected in Rules 605-606(a)); and

c. Those made incompetent due to "***secret***" reasons: jurors testifying as to the validity of a verdict or indictment (reflected in Rule 606(b)).

4. The FRE in large part reflect the common law rules, but have adapted them substantially.

5. Example: Questionable Trustworthiness

   a. Under the common law, those whose trustworthiness is questionable, including infants, the insane, felons, and interested witnesses (such as a party's spouse), were excluded from testifying.

   b. Even atheists were not allowed to testify, given the presumed untrustworthiness of their testimony.

   c. In contrast, under the FRE, the default rule is that *anyone* may testify, with restrictions placed only with respect to those that lack adequate *mental* faculties (Rule 602) or adequate *moral* faculties (Rule 603).

   d. Other safeguards, such as impeachment, are designed to protect against unreliable testimony.

**Trustworthiness under the Common Law and FRE**

| ***Common law category*** | ***What remains today*** |
|---|---|
| *Infants, the insane, and felons* | - *Impeachment*, which brings these issues out on cross-examination. |
| *Interested witnesses* (parties, their spouses) | - *Impeachment.*<br>- *Dead Man's Acts*, which disqualify a party from testifying *against the estate* of the deceased because of the party's incentive to lie based on (i) his interest in the case; and (ii) the unavailability of the deceased to contradict him. |
| *Atheists* | *Nothing* remains under the FRE. |

**Rule 602. Lack of Personal Knowledge**

> A witness may not testify to a matter unless evidence is introduced sufficient to support a finding that the witness has personal knowledge of the matter. Evidence to prove personal knowledge may, but need not, consist of the witness' own testimony. This rule is subject to the provisions of rule 703, relating to opinion testimony by expert witnesses.

1. Rule 602 represents the first of two trustworthiness prongs required of a witness before he may testify.

2. It deals with *mental faculties* (the second prong deals with *moral faculties* under Rule 603, *infra.*).

3. In order to testify, a witness must have personal knowledge of the matter, which may either be:

   a. First hand knowledge (*i.e.*, he was an eye witness); or

   b. Expertise, under Article VII (Opinions and Expert Testimony), *infra*.

**Rule 603. Oath or Affirmation**

> Before testifying, every witness shall be required to declare that the witness will testify truthfully, by oath or affirmation administered in a form calculated to awaken the witness' conscience and impress the witness' mind with the duty to do so.

1. This Rule represents the second of the two prongs required of a witness before he may testify—*moral faculties* (the first prong deals with *mental faculties* under Rule 602, *supra*.).
2. The witness must declare by oath or affirmation so as to "awaken the witness' conscience" that he will testify truthfully.
3. Traditionally, the oath was administered with much formality and solemnity, sometimes with references to God (*e.g.*, "Do you solemnly swear that the testimony that you are about to give shall be the truth, the whole truth, and nothing but the truth, so help you God?"), and a requirement that the witness place his hand on the Bible.
4. Today, however, the oath has lost much of this solemnity.
5. Moreover, the oath today is not even required at all; under rule 603, an affirmation (*e.g.*, "I ***promise*** to tell the truth") may be used in its place.

**Rule 604. Interpreters**

> An interpreter is subject to the provisions of these rules relating to qualification as an expert and the administration of an oath or affirmation to make a true translation.

**Rule 605. Competency of Judge as Witness**

> The judge presiding at the trial may not testify in that trial as a witness. No objection need be made in order to preserve the point.

1. Incompetent Witnesses Based on Their Roles in the Trial.
    a. Rules 605-606(a) establish two categories of incompetency of witnesses based on their roles in the trial: judges (Rule 605) and jurors (Rule 606(a)).
2. Judges Incompetent as Witnesses
    a. Under Rule 605, judges may not testify as witnesses in ***trials in which they preside***.
    b. One of the first steps judges are required to undertake when they know the parties or the facts of a case assigned to them is to recuse themselves under the United States Code.
    c. If a judge takes on a case where he should have been recused, he could violate Rule 605 by serving as a witness.
        i. *N.B.*: he could violate the *spirit* of Rule 605 by simply taking judicial notice on a fact and instructing the jury to accept it according to his knowledge and experience.
    d. A judge could, however, avoid violating Rule 605, even if he takes a case, if he neither mentions nor applies his first hand knowledge in any way, shape, or form.

**Rule 606. Competency of Juror as Witness**

> (a) At the trial.
>
> A member of the jury may not testify as a witness before that jury in the trial of the case in which the juror is sitting. If the juror is called so to testify, the opposing party shall be afforded an opportunity to object out of the presence of the jury.

1. Jurors may not be called as witnesses.
2. If they were, then the attorneys on cross-examination may be perceived by the witness juror as being hostile towards him, and this in turn may cause the attorney to be prejudiced.
3. To prevent this from happening, one of the first questions asked of jurors in *voir dire* is whether they know any of the parties or whether they have any familiarity with the facts of the case.

> (b) Inquiry into validity of verdict or indictment.
>
> Upon an inquiry into the validity of a verdict or indictment, a juror may not testify as to any matter or statement occurring during the course of the jury's deliberations or to the effect of anything upon that or any other juror's mind or emotions as influencing the juror to assent to or dissent from the verdict or indictment or concerning the juror's mental processes in connection therewith. But a juror may testify about (1) whether extraneous prejudicial information was improperly brought to the jury's attention, (2) whether any outside influence was improperly brought to bear upon any juror, or (3) whether there was a mistake in entering the verdict onto the verdict form. A juror's affidavit or evidence of any statement by the juror may not be received on a matter about which the juror would be precluded from testifying.

4. The Sanctity of the Jury Room
   a. "Upon an inquiry as to the validity of a verdict or indictment," jurors may not testify as to what went on in the jury room. Rule 606(b).
   b. Note that this only applies *after* an indictment or verdict is reached and recorded.
      i. Thus, if the jury comes back from the jury room with a confused or self-contradictory verdict, the judge may make inquiry into it.
      ii. The judge may even order the jurors back into the jury room to deliberate anew.
   c. However, from the moment that a final verdict is entered, the jurors' deliberations become closed off from inquiry.
5. The Alleged Reasons for Rule 606(b)
   a. To protect the ***privacy*** of the jury.
      i. However, since Rule 606(b) applies only *after* a verdict is entered, jurors may still go to the judge, complaining about what is going on in the jury room *before* a verdict is entered.

ii. Furthermore, Rule 606(b) limits jurors from commenting only "upon an inquiry into the *validity* of a verdict or indictment." A juror may thus speak to the press or even write a book about the deliberations more generally.

iii. The fact that judges frequently quote juries' affidavits in their opinions further undermines the idea that Rule 606(b) is intended for privacy.

b. To protect former jurors from ***harassment*** after the case is over.

i. If Rule 606(b) were really about harassment, the law would give jurors a privilege, permitting them not to answer questions.

ii. Rather, the Rules make him incompetent to *testify* on those matters defined in Rule 606(b).

c. Finality.

i. This is the *real* reason behind Rule 606(b).

**Rule 607. Who May Impeach**

> The credibility of a witness may be attacked by any party, including the party calling the witness.

1. Rule 607 allows for any party, including the party calling a witness, to impeach that witness's credibility.

2. This rule therefore departs from the common law rule, which prohibited a party from impeaching his own witness.

3. Techniques used for impeaching a witness include:

a. Demonstrating defects in mental capacity;

b. Showing defects in perception; or

c. Using prior inconsistent statements.

**Rule 608. Evidence of Character and Conduct of Witness**

> (a) Opinion and reputation evidence of character.
>
> The credibility of a witness may be attacked or supported by evidence in the form of opinion or reputation, but subject to these limitations: (1) the evidence may refer only to character for truthfulness or untruthfulness, and (2) evidence of truthful character is admissible only after the character of the witness for truthfulness has been attacked by opinion or reputation evidence or otherwise.

1. Rule 608 deals with the use of character evidence of a witness in impeaching the witness for honesty. The rule applies to *both civil and criminal cases*.

2. Opinion and Reputation Evidence of Character

a. Rule 608(a) allows for character to be attacked by evidence in the form of opinion and reputation.

b. Such evidence is subject to the following limitations:

i. The evidence must refer only to character for truthfulness or untruthfulness;

ii. Evidence of truthful character may be offered only after the character of the witness for truthfulness has been attacked.[72]

> (b) Specific instances of conduct.
>
> Specific instances of the conduct of a witness, for the purpose of attacking or supporting the witness' character for truthfulness, other than conviction of crime as provided in rule 609, may not be proved by extrinsic evidence. They may, however, in the discretion of the court, if probative of truthfulness or untruthfulness, be inquired into on cross-examination of the witness (1) concerning the witness' character for truthfulness or untruthfulness, or (2) concerning the character for truthfulness or untruthfulness of another witness as to which character the witness being cross-examined has testified.
>
> The giving of testimony, whether by an accused or by any other witness, does not operate as a waiver of the accused's or the witness' privilege against self-incrimination when examined with respect to matters that relate only to character for truthfulness.

3. Specific Instances of Conduct

a. Rule 608(b) deals with the proper uses of a primary witness's specific acts when such acts are to be used to impeach the witness's credibility.

b. *If specific acts are probative of truthfulness or untruthfulness,* they may be inquired into of the witness only on cross-examination concerning:

i. The witness's character for truthfulness or untruthfulness; or

ii. The character for truthfulness or untruthfulness of another witness as to which character the witness being cross-examined has testified.

c. Such specific acts *may not be proved by extrinsic evidence;* they may be proved only by the witness's *direct admissions.* Thus, if the witness denies the alleged act, the cross-examiner has no other recourse in proving the act.[73]

d. Rationale: if the cross-examiner is permitted to bring in extrinsic evidence of the witness's past conduct, the parties would be moving too far away from the main issues of the trial by focusing their efforts on whether the witness did or did not commit a certain act in the past.

e. Rule 608(b) governs acts that have not resulted in conviction (for cases involving conviction, *see* Rule 609).

f. The giving of testimony by the accused does not amount to a waiver of his Fifth Amendment privilege against self-incrimination.

**Rule 609. Impeachment by Evidence of Conviction of Crime**

> (a) General rule.
>
> For the purpose of attacking the character for truthfulness of a witness,

---

[72] A party may not therefore try to *bolster* the credibility of his witness by introducing evidence of his truthful character. In this way, Rule 608 follows the common law.

[73] The cross examiner is not, however, precluded from introducing Rule 608(a) opinion and reputation evidence.

> (1) evidence that a witness other than an accused has been convicted of a crime shall be admitted, subject to Rule 403, if the crime was punishable by death or imprisonment in excess of one year under the law under which the witness was convicted, and evidence that an accused has been convicted of such a crime shall be admitted if the court determines that the probative value of admitting this evidence outweighs its prejudicial effect to the accused; and
>
> (2) evidence that any witness has been convicted of a crime shall be admitted regardless of the punishment, if it readily can be determined that establishing the elements of the crime required proof or admission of an act of dishonesty or false statement by the witness.

1. Under the FREs, a witness may be impeached with evidence of prior convictions of:
   a. A ***capital crime*** or one carrying a sentence greater than one year, subject to Rule 403. Rule 609(a)(1); or
   b. A crime involving ***dishonestly or false statement*** (*e.g.*, a conviction for false pretenses), regardless of the penalty. Rule 609(a)(2).
      i. This rule applies to "any witness," including the accused who has waived his Fifth Amendment privilege against self-incrimination and has taken the stand.
      ii. *N.B.*: subsection 609(a)(2), unlike 609(a)(1), is not subject to the requirements of Rule 403. Thus, evidence that a witness committed a crime involving a dishonest or false statement is always admissible for the purpose of impeaching him, regardless of the potential for unfair prejudice.
2. Given its low probative value and the presumption of innocence, evidence of a mere *arrest* or *indictment* is inadmissible for impeaching a witness.
3. Since ***extrinsic evidence*** is relevant, it is admissible under Rule 402.
4. To a certain extent, this rule reflects the common law rule where felons and defendants convicted of misdemeanors involving dishonesty were automatically considered incompetent.

> (b) Time limit.
>
> Evidence of a conviction under this rule is not admissible if a period of more than ten years has elapsed since the date of the conviction or of the release of the witness from the confinement imposed for that conviction, whichever is the later date, unless the court determines, in the interests of justice, that the probative value of the conviction supported by specific facts and circumstances substantially outweighs its prejudicial effect. However, evidence of a conviction more than 10 years old as calculated herein, is not admissible unless the proponent gives to the adverse party sufficient advance written notice of intent to use such evidence to provide the adverse party with a fair opportunity to contest the use of such evidence.

5. Rule 609(b) places a ten-year limit on evidence that may be admitted for attacking the character of a witness for truthfulness
6. However, exceptions may be granted at the ***discretion of the court*** if:
   a. The court determines that "the probative value of the conviction supported by specific facts and circumstances substantially outweighs its prejudicial effect" (the burden of proof is on the proponent of the evidence); and

b. The proponent of the evidence gives his opponent sufficient advance written notice of his intent to use the evidence.

> (c) Effect of pardon, annulment, or certificate of rehabilitation.
>
> Evidence of a conviction is not admissible under this rule if (1) the conviction has been the subject of a pardon, annulment, certificate of rehabilitation, or other equivalent procedure based on a finding of the rehabilitation of the person convicted, and that person has not been convicted of a subsequent crime which was punishable by death or imprisonment in excess of one year, or (2) the conviction has been the subject of a pardon, annulment, or other equivalent procedure based on a finding of innocence.

7. Evidence of a prior conviction is inadmissible against a witness when he later received a pardon or its equivalent and:

   a. The pardon was based on a finding of his innocence (rationale: any probative value that the conviction once had is now lost); or

   b. The pardon was based on a "finding of rehabilitation" and the person has not since been convicted of a capital crime or felony.

> (d) Juvenile adjudications.
>
> Evidence of juvenile adjudications is generally not admissible under this rule. The court may, however, in a criminal case allow evidence of a juvenile adjudication of a witness other than the accused if conviction of the offense would be admissible to attack the credibility of an adult and the court is satisfied that admission in evidence is necessary for a fair determination of the issue of guilt or innocence.

8. Juvenile adjudications are generally not admissible because of their low probative value.

9. Rationale: people change substantially and have the opportunity to reform as they grow older.

> (e) Pendency of appeal.
>
> The pendency of an appeal therefrom does not render evidence of a conviction inadmissible. Evidence of the pendency of an appeal is admissible.

**Rule 610. Religious Beliefs or Opinions**

> Evidence of the beliefs or opinions of a witness on matters of religion is not admissible for the purpose of showing that by reason of their nature the witness' credibility is impaired or enhanced.

1. A party may not use a witness's religious beliefs or opinions to attack his character for honesty.

2. However, a party may use the witness's religious beliefs or opinions for other purposes (*e.g.*, showing bias or motive).

3. This Rule, in conjunction with Rules 608-609, provides one of the methods of impeaching the character of witnesses. The four methods are as follow:

   a. Opinion and reputation evidence. Rule 608(a);

   b. Specific acts of dishonest conduct. Rule 608(b);

   c. Convictions for dishonest acts. Rule 609; and

d. Religious beliefs. Rule 610.

**Rule 611. Mode and Order of Interrogation and Presentation.**

(a) Control by court.

The court shall exercise reasonable control over the mode and order of interrogating witnesses and presenting evidence so as to (1) make the interrogation and presentation effective for the ascertainment of the truth, (2) avoid needless consumption of time, and (3) protect witnesses from harassment or undue embarrassment.

1. Cases begin with the plaintiff's opening statement followed by the defendant's opening statement. The plaintiff then calls his first witness and examines him, followed by the defendant's cross examination.
2. The plaintiff then calls his second witness, third witness, etc., until he rests his case.
3. The defendant repeats these same steps. The plaintiff then has a chance for rebuttal. The defendant then has a chance for rebuttal.
4. While one party is examining a witness, the other party normally may not interrupt.
5. However, there are some exceptions.
   a. For example, under Rule 106, when a writing or recording or part of a writing or recording is offered into evidence, the other party may request that related writings or recordings or other parts of the writing or recording be introduced *at that time* into evidence, in order to assure that the part of the writing or recording offered is put within its proper context and does not mislead the trier of fact.
   b. Similarly, under FRCP 32(a)(4), if only part of a deposition is offered in evidence by a party, the adverse party may require the offeror to introduce any other part which ought in fairness to be considered with the part introduced.
6. Rule 611 gives the judge much discretion in the mode and order of presentation and interrogation. Much of what cannot be objected to under the Rules (*e.g.*, an examining attorney's aggressive tone), can be objected to by appealing to the judge's discretion in exercising "reasonable control" over the proceeding.
7. A judge will always sustain an objection that a question is misleading, vague, or ambiguous (provided that he agrees that the question is indeed misleading, vague, or ambiguous).
8. However, he may not always sustain an objection of narration, even when he agrees with the objecting party.
   a. Questions calling for narration are generally not preferred by the courts. Unlike with directed questions, narration does not allow the opposite party to be on guard for objecting to inadmissible evidence before it is spoken and the jury hears it.
   b. However, narration tends to get to more of the truth than directed questions.
   c. Judges are more likely to permit narrative testimony when the parties are outside of the hearing of the jury or *when the witness is highly experienced* and is aware of what is and is not admissible.

(b) Scope of cross-examination.

Cross-examination should be limited to the subject matter of the direct examination and

> matters affecting the credibility of the witness. The court may, in the exercise of discretion, permit inquiry into additional matters as if on direct examination.

9. Questions Beyond the Scope
    a. Questions on cross-examination are limited to:
        i. The ***subject matter*** of the direct examination;
        ii. The ***credibility*** of the witness; and
        iii. Additional matters permitted by the ***discretion*** of the court (as if on direct examination).
    b. Some states, such as North Carolina, employ "wide open cross-examination," which permits an attorney to inquire into *any relevant issue* on cross examination.
    c. This rule works in tandem with the Fifth Amendment privilege against self-incrimination.
10. Under Rule 104(d), when the accused testifies on any preliminary matter, he is not subject to cross-examination on any other issue.
    a. However, under Rule 611(b), when the defendant testifies on an issue ***other than a preliminary matter***, a judge, in his discretion, may require the defendant to testify on issues that were not within the subject of the direct examination during cross-examination.
    b. If the judge permits such cross-examination, the attorney cross-examining the witness on matters outside of the subject matter covered in direct examination *must examine him as if on direct examination* (*see* "Leading Questions," *infra.*).

> (c) Leading questions.
>
> Leading questions should not be used on the direct examination of a witness except as may be necessary to develop the witness' testimony. Ordinarily leading questions should be permitted on cross-examination. When a party calls a hostile witness, an adverse party, or a witness identified with an adverse party, interrogation may be by leading questions.

11. Leading Questions
    a. Definition
        i. Leading questions are questions that tend to lead the witness towards the answer that the interrogator is seeking.
    b. On Direct Examination
        i. Leading questions on direct examination are discouraged by the courts and by Rule 611(c).
        ii. However, they are *always permitted* in three situations:
            1) When necessary to ***develop the testimony*** of the witness.
                a) Leading questions may be employed in situations where the witness is, for example, so young,

traumatized, or elderly and forgetful that without leading, he or she would be unable to testify.

b) Rationale: answers to leading questions are better than no answers at all.

c) The leading is only permitted to the extent necessary to develop the testimony (*i.e.*, progressively higher levels of leading as required).

2) When the party being interrogated is ***hostile***

a) A party is hostile when he or she demonstrates a propensity not to cooperate.

b) Leading questions are permitted because hostile parties are the least likely to be influenced by the leading of the examining attorney.

3) On ***preliminary undisputed matters***

a) Leading is permitted when the information solicited does not threaten to harm the other party's case.

b) For example, leading will be permitted as to the date that an accident took place, not whether the defendant ran a red light.

c. On Cross Examination

i. Leading questions are ***generally permitted*** on cross examination.

ii. Leading is always permitted on cross examination when *necessary to develop the testimony* of the witness; when the party being interrogated is *hostile*, and on *preliminary undisputed matters*.

iii. Leading is not permitted in cross-examination when:

1) The witness is the lawyer's own client; and

2) The cross-examination goes beyond the scope of the direct examination.

**Rule 612. Writing Used to Refresh Memory**

Except as otherwise provided in criminal proceedings by section 3500 of title 18, United States Code, if a witness uses a writing to refresh memory for the purpose of testifying, either--

(1) while testifying, or

(2) before testifying, if the court in its discretion determines it is necessary in the interests of justice,

an adverse party is entitled to have the writing produced at the hearing, to inspect it, to cross-examine the witness thereon, and to introduce in evidence those portions which relate to the testimony of the witness. If it is claimed that the writing contains matters not related to the subject matter of the testimony the court shall examine the writing in camera, excise any portions not so related, and order delivery of the remainder to the party entitled thereto. Any portion withheld over objections shall be preserved and made available to the appellate court in the event of an appeal. If a writing is not produced or delivered pursuant to order under this rule, the court shall make any order justice requires, except that in criminal cases when the prosecution elects not to comply, the order shall be one striking the testimony or, if the court in its discretion determines that the interests of justice so require, declaring a mistrial.

1. Rule 612 governs writings used in trial to jog the witness's memory when laying a proper foundation. It is sometimes referred to as "***present recollection refreshed***."
2. Whenever a witness uses a writing to refresh his memory, the other party *may have the writing produced* in order to inspect it, to cross examine the witness, and to introduce other relevant portions of the writing.
   a. *N.B.*: under the majority view, the material must be given up to the other side, even if it is privileged and non-discoverable.
3. The primary purpose of Rule 612 is to ***refresh the witness's memory***.
4. It may be constrasted with Rule 613, Prior Statements of Witnesses, which deals with offering the witness evidence in order to encourage him to change some aspect of his testimony. Rule 613 takes on the character of impeachment.
5. The use of such a statement is not hearsay because it is ***not offered into evidence*** and, in theory, is neither read nor shown to the jury. However, if the document is read aloud and the jury hears it, it would be prohibited as hearsay.

**Rule 613. Prior Statements of Witnesses**

(a) Examining witness concerning prior statement.

In examining a witness concerning a prior statement made by the witness, whether written or not, the statement need not be shown nor its contents disclosed to the witness at that time, but on request the same shall be shown or disclosed to opposing counsel.

1. If an attorney wants to undermine the testimony of a witness, he may bring up the witness's prior inconsistent statements.
2. In so doing, he is not required to disclose the statements to the witness if he is trying to get the witness to contradict himself.
3. However, the attorney must show it to opposing counsel upon his request.

(b) Extrinsic evidence of prior inconsistent statement of witness.

Extrinsic evidence of a prior inconsistent statement by a witness is not admissible unless the witness is afforded an opportunity to explain or deny the same and the opposite party is afforded an opportunity to interrogate the witness thereon, or the interests of justice otherwise require. This provision does not apply to admissions of a party-opponent as defined in rule 801(d)(2).

**Rule 614. Calling and Interrogation of Witnesses by Court**

(a) Calling by court.

The court may, on its own motion or at the suggestion of a party, call witnesses, and all parties are entitled to cross-examine witnesses thus called.

(b) Interrogation by court.

The court may interrogate witnesses, whether called by itself or by a party.

(c) Objections.

Objections to the calling of witnesses by the court or to interrogation by it may be made at the time or at the next available opportunity when the jury is not present.

**Rule 615. Exclusion of Witnesses**

At the request of a party the court shall order witnesses excluded so that they cannot hear the testimony of other witnesses, and it may make the order of its own motion. This rule does not authorize exclusion of (1) a party who is a natural person, or (2) an officer or employee of a party which is not a natural person designated as its representative by its attorney, or (3) a person whose presence is shown by a party to be essential to the presentation of the party's cause, or (4) a person authorized by statute to be present.

## ARTICLE VII. OPINIONS AND EXPERT TESTIMONY

**Rule 701. Opinion Testimony by Lay Witnesses**

If the witness is not testifying as an expert, the witness' testimony in the form of opinions or inferences is limited to those opinions or inferences which are (a) rationally based on the perception of the witness, and (b) helpful to a clear understanding of the witness' testimony or the determination of a fact in issue, and (c) not based on scientific, technical, or other specialized knowledge within the scope of Rule 702.

1. Witnesses generally can be divided into the following two groups:
    a. ***Lay witnesses*** (Rule 701), who must have some degree of first hand knowledge; and
    b. ***Expert witnesses*** (Rule 702), who may give opinion testimony even though they have no firsthand knowledge..
        i. *N.B.*: some witnesses, such as police officers who were at the scene of a crime, fall into the grey area between these two categories.
2. Under Rules 701 and 702, every witness must know more than the jury about either the facts of the case or the expertise involved.
3. Under Rule 701, a ***lay witness*** may only give testimony that meets all three of the following conditions:
    a. He had first hand knowledge (the testimony is "*rationally based*" on his perceptions);
    b. His opinions or inferences are *helpful to a clear understanding* of his testimony or of the facts in issue;
        i. The witness may not testify as to what is irrelevant, even if the testimony is based on first-hand knowledge.

ii. He may not give testimony on that which he believes if it gives no additional, helpful information to the jury.

1) Example: he may not give a "guess" or "speculate" as to the whereabouts of the defendant on the night of a crime.

iii. However, if the witness would give the jury helpful information in a ***guess*** or ***speculation*** based on some degree of first hand knowledge that any ordinary person would not be able to give, then it will be admissible.

1) Example: he may give a "guess" or "speculate" as to the whereabouts of the defendant on the night of a crime, if the defendant were his son who lived in the same home as him. Here, there would be some threshold of helpful information that the witness could provide that any ordinary witness would *not* be able to supply.

iv. If such speculation is not helpful to the jury, then it will be inadmissible under Rule 701(b).

c. His testimony is not expert testimony governed by Rule 702.

i. *See State of North Carolina v. Robert Kelly* (N.C. Ct. App. 1995), where the defendant's convictions for child sexual abuse were reversed on appeal because the trial court allowed the lay witnesses to testify on symptoms of the sexually abused, which are matters that should be reserved for experts.

ii. *Rationale*: if the parents were permitted to testify as to the symptoms of their children, the jury would lend more credence to the experts whose testimony was in agreement with that of the parents.

**Rule 702. Testimony by Experts**

> If scientific, technical, or other specialized knowledge will assist the trier of fact to understand the evidence or to determine a fact in issue, a witness qualified as an expert by knowledge, skill, experience, training, or education, may testify thereto in the form of an opinion or otherwise, if (1) the testimony is based upon sufficient facts or data, (2) the testimony is the product of reliable principles and methods, and (3) the witness has applied the principles and methods reliably to the facts of the case.

1. Reasons to Be Wary of Expert Witnesses

a. There is more of a risk of jury confusion than of providing helpful information to the jury; and

b. There is a great risk of bending the truth for money.

i. It is criminal to give anything of consideration to any normal lay witness.

ii. Nevertheless, expert witnesses are generally handsomely compensated.

2. Nothing under Rule 702 or any of the Rules requires tendering of the witnesses and getting court approval for an expert.

   a. If a party believes a witness is competent, he may simply offer him.

   b. The witness only needs to be defended if challenged.

3. However, Rule 702 requires the following conditions to be met before an opinion may become admissible as expert testimony:

   a. Scientific, technical, or other specialized knowledge will ***assist the jury***;

   b. The witness is ***qualified as an expert*** by knowledge, skill, experience, training, or education;[74] and

   c. The testimony is be based on ***sufficient facts*** or *data*, is the product of ***reliable principles*** and *methods;* and the witness has applied the principles and methods ***reliably***.

4. The expert and her opinions do not need to be generally accepted in the scientific community; they only need to be ***"reasonably reliable."*** If they are not, the court may exclude the expert and her testimony. *Daubert v. Merrell Dow Pharmaceuticals, Inc.* (U.S. 1993) (codified in Rule 702).

   a. *N.B.*: courts do not have this power with respect to lay witnesses.

**Rule 703. Bases of Opinion Testimony by Experts**

> The facts or data in the particular case upon which an expert bases an opinion or inference may be those perceived by or made known to the expert at or before the hearing. If of a type reasonably relied upon by experts in the particular field in forming opinions or inferences upon the subject, the facts or data need not be admissible in evidence in order for the opinion or inference to be admitted. Facts or data that are otherwise inadmissible shall not be disclosed to the jury by the proponent of the opinion or inference unless the court determines that their probative value in assisting the jury to evaluate the expert's opinion substantially outweighs their prejudicial effect.

1. The benefit of designating an expert as a witness is that he may testify *even though he was not an eye-witness.*

2. His testimony may be based on any of the following:

   a. Facts ***perceived*** by him or made known to him;

   b. ***At*** or ***before*** the hearing;[75]

   c. Whhich may be admissible in evidence or, if they are inadmissible, are of the type ***reasonably relied upon*** by experts in the particular field in forming opinions or inferences upon the subject.

3. When an opinion is based on inadmissible facts, they are not to be disclosed to the jury, unless the court determines that their probative value outweighs their prejudicial effect.

---

[74] Note that a witness may be qualified as an expert through skill or experience alone; formal education is not necessary.

[75] At the hearing, facts may be made known to him through hearing others' testimony or by way of summary by an attorney.

### Rule 704. Opinion on Ultimate Issue

> (a) Except as provided in subdivision (b), testimony in the form of an opinion or inference otherwise admissible is not objectionable because it embraces an ultimate issue to be decided by the trier of fact.
>
> (b) No expert witness testifying with respect to the mental state or condition of a defendant in a criminal case may state an opinion or inference as to whether the defendant did or did not have the mental state or condition constituting an element of the crime charged or of a defense thereto. Such ultimate issues are matters for the trier of fact alone.

1. The common law traditionally drew a line between what was a fact and what was an ultimate issue and permitted witnesses to testify ***only as to the facts***.
2. As witnesses got closer to the ultimate issue, they were more likely to approach the legal questions that would be less helpful to the jury, since the jury and witnesses would be less likely to be speaking the same language.
    a. For example, a lay witness might use the word "rape" without being aware of all of the elements on which the jury would later be instructed.
    b. Even though lawyers are experts who speak the same language as the jury, they are not permitted to give their opinions on the ultimate issues of the, since the judge, in his legal expertise, handles the legal questions.
3. This impractical distinction was abolished by Rule 704, which allows testimony even if it "embraces the ultimate issue to be decided by the trier of fact."
4. Rule 704(b), however, limits this rule by prohibiting experts from to testify as to the ultimate issue of whether a defendant in a criminal case had a mental state or condition constituting an element of a crime or a defense thereto.
5. This ultimate issue is left to the trier of fact alone.

### Rule 705. Disclosure of Facts or Data Underlying Expert Opinion

> The expert may testify in terms of opinion or inference and give reasons therefore without first testifying to the underlying facts or data, unless the court requires otherwise. The expert may in any event be required to disclose the underlying facts or data on cross-examination.

1. An expert may testify without first testifying to the facts and information on which he is basing his opinion.
2. Thus, in addition to being able to give testimony not based on first hand knowledge and base opinions on inadmissible evidence, experts may testify without disclosing the grounds of their opinions.
3. However, designating a witness as an expert requires the attorney to give the opponent ***extensive pretrial disclosure*** about the witness, including "work product."

### Rule 706. Court Appointed Experts

> (a) Appointment.
>
> The court may on its own motion or on the motion of any party enter an order to show cause why expert witnesses should not be appointed, and may request the parties to submit nominations. The court may appoint any expert witnesses agreed upon by the parties, and may appoint expert witnesses of its own selection. An expert witness shall not be appointed

> by the court unless the witness consents to act. A witness so appointed shall be informed of the witness' duties by the court in writing, a copy of which shall be filed with the clerk, or at a conference in which the parties shall have opportunity to participate. A witness so appointed shall advise the parties of the witness' findings, if any; the witness' deposition may be taken by any party; and the witness may be called to testify by the court or any party. The witness shall be subject to cross-examination by each party, including a party calling the witness.
>
> (b) Compensation.
>
> Expert witnesses so appointed are entitled to reasonable compensation in whatever sum the court may allow. The compensation thus fixed is payable from funds which may be provided by law in criminal cases and civil actions and proceedings involving just compensation under the fifth amendment. In other civil actions and proceedings the compensation shall be paid by the parties in such proportion and at such time as the court directs, and thereafter charged in like manner as other costs.
>
> (c) Disclosure of appointment.
>
> In the exercise of its discretion, the court may authorize disclosure to the jury of the fact that the court appointed the expert witness.
>
> (d) Parties' experts of own selection.
>
> Nothing in this rule limits the parties in calling expert witnesses of their own selection.

1. Rule 706 gives judges the power to resolve many of the issues that often arise with respect to experts, such as jury confusion.
2. Rarely, however, do judges exercise this power.

## ARTICLE VIII. HEARSAY

### Rule 801. Definitions

> The following definitions apply under this article:
>
> (a) Statement. A "statement" is (1) an oral or written assertion or (2) nonverbal conduct of a person, if it is intended by the person as an assertion.

1. For the purposes of hearsay, a ***"statement"*** may be either one of the following:
   a. An oral or written assertion;
      i. An assertion is generally a declaratory statement.
      ii. Commands, requests, instructions, and questions are generally not considered to be hearsay.
      iii. Example:
         1) A testifies that he heard the defendant say to the victim, "give me all of your money!"
         2) This would not be considered hearsay, since there is *no assertion*. Rather, it is a *command*.
   b. *Conduct* intended to be an assertion (*e.g.*, nodding, gesturing, etc.).
      i. Examples of conduct intended to be an assertion:

1) Nodding in response to a question; and

2) Pointing when asked where an object is located.

ii. Examples of conduct *not* intended to be an assertion:

1) Taking one's foot off the brake as an indication of whether a light turned green (although this indicates that the light turned green, it is not *intented* as such).

2) Walking into a room with a wet raincoat and umbrella (although this indicates that it was raining, it is not *intended* as such).

iii. Only conduct intended to be an assertion is included under the hearsay rule because there is generally no ***potential for deception*** when there is no intent to communicate.

(b) Declarant. A "declarant" is a person who makes a statement.

2. Only a person can make a statement, whether the statement is an oral or written assertion or conduct intended to be an assertion.

a. Thus, if B testifies that he look at the thermometer, and it indicated 99°, the indication of the temperature would *not* be hearsay, since the declarant must be a person, not a machine.

b. Similarly, if a police officer testifies that a canine detected drugs in C's luggage, the statement would not fall into hearsay, since the declarant must be a person, not an animal.

i. *N.B.*: Rule 801(a) parallels this rule when it defines conduct that comprises a statement as "nonverbal conduct *of a person*."

(c) Hearsay. "Hearsay" is a statement, other than one made by the declarant while testifying at the trial or hearing, offered in evidence to prove the truth of the matter asserted.

3. There are three elements required for evidence to be hearsay:

a. There must be a ***statement*** (see *supra.*, for details);

b. That is ***out of court*** (made by someone other than the declarant while testifying);

i. For the purposes of hearsay, a declarant is the person making an out of court statement that is later offered into evidence.

ii. To be hearsay, a statement must be "out of court," which simply means that it was *not made by the declarant* while testifying.

iii. Thus, even some in-court statements can be considered to be "out of court" for the purpose of hearsay.

c. Offered "***to prove the truth*** of the matter asserted."

i. A statement is hearsay when its relevance to the case is conditioned on *whether the statement is true.*

ii. However, when the a statement is offered not to prove that it is true, but rather, to prove motive, notice, effect on a listener, perception of danger, or *merely that it was said*, or when it is offered to show the feelings or state of mind of the person who made it, is not hearsay.

iii. Verbal Acts

1) "Verbal acts" (*i.e.*, "operative facts" or "legally operative" words) are not hearsay because the words have *legal consequences regardless of their truth.*

2) Examples of verbal acts include statements offered not to prove the truth of the matter asserted, but rather, the existence of:

a) Gifts, acceptance to a contract, consent, wills;

b) Apologies, warnings, slander.

3) Example:

a) The plaintiff sues for slander and calls witness A, who testifies that he heard the defendant say that the plaintiff was a liar and a thief. Is this testimony prohibited by the hearsay rule?

b) No: the statements are not offered to prove *the truth of the matter asserted* (that the plaintiff is a liar and a thief), but rather, to prove that the *statements were made.*

> (d) Statements which are not hearsay.
>
> A statement is not hearsay if--
>
> (1) *Prior statement by witness.* The declarant testifies at the trial or hearing and is subject to cross-examination concerning the statement, and the statement is (A) inconsistent with the declarant's testimony, and was given under oath subject to the penalty of perjury at a trial, hearing, or other proceeding, or in a deposition, or (B) consistent with the declarant's testimony and is offered to rebut an express or implied charge against the declarant of recent fabrication or improper influence or motive, or (C) one of identification of a person made after perceiving the person;

4. Rule 801(d)(1) removes the prior statement of a witness[76] from the definition of hearsay and thus permits a party to introduce such a statement to impeach the witness or to be used as substantive evidence,[77] when both of the following elements are met:

a. The declarant testifies at the trial or hearing and is subject to cross-examination regarding the prior statement[78]; and

[76] The reference to "witnesses" in this rule refers only to those who testify at a trial. It does not include all who "witness" some occurrence with his eyes.
[77] The majority of states do not follow this federal practice and admit prior statements of a witness for the limited purpose of impeaching the witness.
[78] This element obviously can only be met when the witness is *available*.

b. The prior statement is one of the following:

i. An *inconsistent statement* given *under oath* in a prior trial, hearing, or other proceeding, or in a deposition and subject to perjury;

1) *N.B.*: note that a prior inconsistent statement could be used for impeachment purposes *regardless of whether it was made under oath.*

(aa) In such a case, Pattern Criminal Jury Instruction[79] (PJI) 32 applies, where the judge tells the jury to use such statements *for impeachment only*, not as evidence in the case (unless it was under oath).

2) However, if it was under oath, it will be admissible for its truth as well. *See* PJI 33.

ii. A *prior consistent statement* offered to rebut a charge against the declarant of recent fabrication, bias, or improper motive;

1) Example: the defendant argues that the alleged victim of sexual abuse is lying about the defendant's molesting her. He states that the motive of her fabrication is a fight that she got into with him last summer.

2) The prosecutor may offer a prior consistent statement made by the victim from before last summer in order to show that the fight last summer did not motivate a fabrication.

iii. A *prior identification* of a person that is made after perceiving the person.

1) Example: the victim picked out the accused in a lineup. This is an out of court "statement" (in this case, non-verbal conduct) offered for its truth.

> (2) *Admission by party-opponent.* The statement is offered against a party and is (A) the party's own statement, in either an individual or a representative capacity or (B) a statement of which the party has manifested an adoption or belief in its truth, or (C) a statement by a person authorized by the party to make a statement concerning the subject, or (D) a statement by the party's agent or servant concerning a matter within the scope of the agency or employment, made during the existence of the relationship, or (E) a statement by a coconspirator of a party during the course and in furtherance of the conspiracy. The contents of the statement shall be considered but are not alone sufficient to establish the declarant's authority under subdivision (C), the agency or employment relationship and scope thereof under subdivision (D), or the existence of the conspiracy and the participation therein of the declarant and the party against whom the statement is offered under subdivision (E).

5. Rule 801(d)(2) removes ***admissions by party-opponents*** from hearsay.

---

[79] The Pattern Criminal Jury Instructions are put out by the Federal Judicial Center to federal judges as patterns to follow in criminal trials. Most of the details of the Pattern Criminal Jury Instructions also apply in civil cases.

a. To qualify as non hearsay under this section, statements must be offered against a party and must be one of the following:

i. The party's ***own statement.*** Rule 801(d)(2)(A).

1) This is perhaps the most important category of statements that seem like hearsay but that are excluded from the hearsay rule:

a) An admission is never hearsay if it is offered at the trial against the party-declarant.

2) However, this rule is imprecisely worded.

a) As it is worded, a judge would first have to make a finding that the party did in fact did say it.

b) However, such findings are not necessary: the fact that the witness may be mistaken or lying on the stand is not the concern of this rule.

c) Thus, when a witness claims that a party made the statement, it is admissible even if the party can prove that he did not in fact make it.

3) A party's statement can be an admission if it is made verbally (orally or written) or nonverbally, through nodding, gesturing, or even through silence ("*admission by silence*"), if a party fails to deny a statement that he would normally be expected to deny if it were not true.

a) *N.B.*: the defendant's silence in response to statements by the police is normally expected in order to avoid self-incrimination. Offering the defendant's silence into evidence as an admission would violate the Fifth Amendment.

4) Guilty pleas are considered admissions. *See* Rule 803(22) for further details.

ii. A statement in which the party has ***manifested belief*** (an "adoptive admission"). Rule 801(d)(2)(B).

1) Example: B makes a statement and C agrees. C has in effect adopted the statement, even though he did not say it.

2) Sometimes, silence can be used in adopting a statement as well ("*adoption by silence*").

iii. A statement made by a person with ***express or implied authority*** to speak for the party. Rule 801(d)(2)(C).

1) Example: a party's attorney, spokesperson, press secretary.

2) Thus, a person should always pick his representatives carefully, since anything they say can be used against him.

iv. A statement by the party's ***agent*** regarding a matter within the scope of the agency and during the agent's employment. Rule 801(d)(2)(D).

1) This is known as a "agency admission" or "vicarious admission."

2) It applies to one's secretaries and other employees.

3) The statement must be made: (i) within the scope of the agency; and (ii) during the existence of the agency.

v. A statement by a ***coconspirator*** of a party during the course and in furtherance of a conspiracy. Rule 801(d)(2)(E).

1) This subsection usually applies when the defendant is not present, since, if he were present, the statement would be admitted as an adoptive admission.

2) The statement must be made while the coconspirator at least *believes* that what he is saying is in ***furtherance*** of the conspiracy.

3) Thus, if the coconspirator makes statements after he has been recruited by the police for the purpose of arresting the defendant, the coconspirator's statements are inadmissible because they are not made in furtherance of the conspiracy.

4) Similarly, if the conspiracy has been completed, a coconspirator's statements cannot be used against the defendant.

5) The proponent of the statements must show:

i) There was a conspiracy involving the declarant and the defendant; and

ii) The declarant's statement was made by the declarant during and in furtherance of the conspiracy.

6) It does not matter that the listener was not a member of the conspiracy.

b. This rule departs from the common law, where admissions by party-opponents, in any of the five forms outlined by this rule, were considered hearsay.

c. There are two protections given to the defendants against whom admissions are offered:

i. The statements are not *judicial admissions*—which are binding and conclusive and waive the need for a trial (guilty plea, stipulation)—but rather, *evidentiary admissions*—which are admissible but not binding against the defendant and can be denied or revoked (*e.g.*, the party can argue that he made the statements because he was frightened or intoxicated).

**ii.** Also, Rule 806 allows the defendant to attack the credibility of the witnesses that is offering the defendant's admissions into evidence (see *infra.*).

**Rule 802. Hearsay Rule**

> Hearsay is not admissible except as provided by these rules or by other rules prescribed by the Supreme Court pursuant to statutory authority or by Act of Congress.

1. The general rule for hearsay evidence is that it is inadmissible, *unless* the proponent can show that the evidence falls into one of the hearsay exceptions.
2. There are three ways for a statement to be hearsay:
   a. Ask a *witness* what he or another person once said or wrote before taking the stand;
   b. Offer a document or a copy of a document that someone wrote; or
   c. Offer a tape or video *recording* of what someone said.
3. When hearsay is offered into evidence, consider:
   a. Has the evidence being offered been ***identified*** (also known as "authentication") (see Article IX)?
   b. Does the evidence violate the ***original evidence rule*** ("Best Evidence Rule") (see Article X)?
   c. Was the statement ***privileged*** (see Article V)?
   d. Is the hearsay inadmissible (see Article VIII)?
4. The Hearsay Doctrine and the Sixth Amendment Confrontation Clause
   a. Under the Confrontation Clause, "[i]n all criminal prosecutions, the accused shall enjoy the right . . . to be confronted with the witnesses against him."[80]
   b. Even if a statement is considered not to be hearsay or if it fits into a hearsay exception under the FRE, the statement still must pass the Sixth Amendment Confrontation Clause.
   c. There is generally a good deal of overlap. However, while the hearsay doctrine prohibits out of court statements offered for their truth in both civil and criminal cases, the Confrontation Clause applies in only criminal cases.
   d. In dicta in *Ohio v. Roberts* (U.S. 1980), the Court held that hearsay offered against a defendant does not violate the Confrontation Clause when it bears an *"adequate indicia of reliability,"* by either falling within a *"firmly rooted hearsay*

[80] U.S. Const. amend. VI.

*exception"* or containing *"particularized guarantees of trustworthiness."* Under this rule, the FRE and the Confrontation Clause were rendered largely congruent: if a statement was admissible under the FRE, then it would be admissible under the Confrontation Clause.

e. Supreme Court jurisprudence based on *Ohio v. Roberts* (U.S. 1980) was radically overturned in 2004, where the Suporeme Court replace the "adequate indicia of reliability" test with the ***testimonial test***.

i. *See Crawford v. Washington* (U.S. 2004) (Scalia, J.), where Michael Crawford stabbed Keneeth Lee, who he suspected of sexually assaulting his (Crawford's) wife. During the trial, the defendant's wife did not testify because of the marital privilege, but the prosecution played a recorded statement that she previously made to police and that contradicted Crawford's claim that he acted in self-defense. Crawford challenged the recording as violative of the Confrontation Clause. The state Supreme Court upheld his conviction, relying on the "adequate indicia of reliability" test of *Ohio v. Roberts* (U.S. 1980), which permits out of court statements against a defendant when such statements are reliable. Held: *Ohio v. Roberts* is overruled. The test for determining whether the Confrontation Clause was violated is no longer whether incriminating evidence that is admitted is reliable; rather, when the defendant does not have the opportunity to confront a witness, incriminating evidence is to be excluded when it is ***"testimonial" in nature***. Here, the wife's statements were testimonial and yet were admitted against the defendant, in violation of his right to confront witnesses. Judgment reversed.

1) *N.B.*: Justice Scalia did not explicitly define "testimonial," but he said that affidavits are testimonial, while business records are not. Some courts began to define "testimonial" as that which is prepared specifically for court (a business record would thus not qualify).

ii. *See also Davis v. Washington* (U.S. 2006) (Scalia, J.), where the defendant was charged of assaulting his wife. At trial, the prosecutor offered his wife's 911 call into evidence against the defendant, pursuant to the excited utterance exception to the hearsay rules. The defendant objected. Held: 911 calls are not testimonial, since the circumstances behind them ***do not indicate that they are being used in furtherance of criminal prosecution.*** Rather, they are given in the hopes of securing immediate assistance. Here, unlike in *Crawford v. Washington*, the statements were given to police for the purpose of securing assistance in an emergency, not for preserving evidence for trial.

iii. *Compare Hammon v. Indiana* (U.S. 206) (companion case to *Davis*), where a witness's statements were inadmissible because they were made to police after an assault was already complete. Thus, there was no conceivable purpose to the interrogation other than preparation of prosecution. The statements were therefore testimonial and offering them into evidence violated the Confrontation Clause.

f. The hearsay rules do one thing that the Confrontation Clause does not do: they ban some hearsay that is not testimonial.

g. The Confrontation Clause does two things that the hearsay rules do not do:

i. It bans some testimonial hearsay that may be admissible under one of the exceptions to the hearsay rules; and

ii. It applies to the states. *Pointer v. Texas* (U.S. 1965).

**Rule 803. Hearsay Exceptions; Availability of Declarant Immaterial**

> The following are not excluded by the hearsay rule, even though the declarant is available as a witness:

1. Rule 803 deals with hearsay that is admissible for its truth, even when the declarant is available (his availability is immaterial).

a. Because the evidence is so reliable, the normal requirement that the witness be present for cross-examination is waived.

b. *N.B.*: just because evidence is admissible under a hearsay exception does not mean that a judge cannot exclude it for some other reason (*e.g.*, privilege, substantial prejudice, etc.).

> (1) Present sense impression. A statement describing or explaining an event or condition made while the declarant was perceiving the event or condition, or immediately thereafter.

2. "Present Sense Impression"

a. A present sense impression is admissible as an exception to the hearsay doctrine when:

i. It describes or explains an event or condition; and

ii. It is made while or immediately after the declarant was perceiving the event or condition.

b. Rationale: statements made during or immediately after the declarant's perception are highly trustworthy, since the proximity in time between the statement and the perception allows little time for calculated misstatements.

c. Example: when the plaintiff is struck by the defendant's car, she states, "why didn't he stop at the stop sign?"

> (2) Excited utterance. A statement relating to a startling event or condition made while the declarant was under the stress of excitement caused by the event or condition.

3. "Excited Utterance"

a. A statement is admissible as an exception to the hearsay doctrine when the statement:

i. Relates to a startling event or condition; and

ii. Is made *while the declarant is under the stress* of excitement caused by the event or condition (the utterance must thus be made during or within close temporal proximity to the startling events).

b. The Advisory Committee notes require the event or the condition to bring the declarant into near hysteria.

c. Rationale: the stress of the excitement allows little opportunity for calculated misstatements and conscious fabrication.

d. However, any decrease in the likelihood of conscious fabrication is accompanied by an increase in inaccurate perception while a subject is in a state of excitement.

> (3) Then existing mental, emotional, or physical condition. A statement of the declarant's then existing state of mind, emotion, sensation, or physical condition (such as intent, plan, motive, design, mental feeling, pain, and bodily health), but not including a statement of memory or belief to prove the fact remembered or believed unless it relates to the execution, revocation, identification, or terms of declarant's will.

4. "Then Existing State of Mind"

a. Evidence of a declarant's then existing state of mind, including emotion, sensation, or physical condition (such as intent, plan, motive, design, mental feeling, pain, and bodily health), is admissible as an exception to the hearsay rule.

b. Evidence of the declarant's then existing state of mind may be used to prove:

i. The declarant's state of mind (*e.g.*, intent, motive, pain, etc.); or

ii. The declarant's later conduct (*e.g.*, that the defendant murdered the victim after stating, "I shall kill X").

c. Evidence of memory or belief is not admissible in proving the fact remembered or believed.

d. Example: A witness testifies that as the victim was dying, the victim stated, "I am an orphan." This statement is inadmissible under Rule 803(3), because it is a memory.

i. However, If the victim later stated, "I am tired," it would be admissible as a "then existing state of mind."

ii. Rationale: (i) the statement refers to the *then existing state of mind* and is thus reliable against memory defects; and (ii) the declarant has *first hand knowledge* of his perceptions.

> (4) Statements for purposes of medical diagnosis or treatment. Statements made for purposes of medical diagnosis or treatment and describing medical history, or past or present symptoms, pain, or sensations, or the inception or general character of the cause or external source thereof insofar as reasonably pertinent to diagnosis or treatment.

5. "Statements for Purposes of Medical Diagnosis or Treatment"

a. Elements:

i. The statement must be made for *purposes of medical diagnosis* or treatment;

ii. The statement must *describe* "medical history, or past or present symptoms, pain, or sensations, or the inception or general character of the cause or external source thereof"; and

iii. The statement must be *made to a doctor* or medical personnel.

b. This is broader than the other rules in that it applies to statements from the past.

c. Examples

i. Admissible: "Doctor, I have had this pain for five years!"

ii. Inadmissible: "Doctor, I have had this pain for five years because my boyfriend assaulted me!"

1) Rationale: the fact that Todd caused the injury is inadmissible because that portion of the statement is not relevant to the diagnosis or treatment.

d. Rationale: people are honest when they talk to their doctors because they do not want a misdiagnosis.

> (5) Recorded recollection. A memorandum or record concerning a matter about which a witness once had knowledge but now has insufficient recollection to enable the witness to testify fully and accurately, shown to have been made or adopted by the witness when the matter was fresh in the witness' memory and to reflect that knowledge correctly. If admitted, the memorandum or record may be read into evidence but may not itself be received as an exhibit unless offered by an adverse party.

6. "Past Recollection Recorded"

a. This exception works in tandem with Rule 612, Writing Used to Refresh Memory.

i. If a writing is used merely to refresh the witness's memory under Rule 612, it is not being offered into evidence and therefore is not hearsay.

ii. If, however, a writing is being used as substantive evidence (as opposed to merely as a way of refreshing the witness's memory), then it is hearsay and Article VIII applies.

b. A past recollection recorded is an exception to the hearsay rule when the following elements are met:

i. The witness had *first hand knowledge* of the matter in a writing;

ii. The witness *made or adopted the writing* when the matter was fresh in his mind;

iii. The witness now has *insufficient recollection* of the matter and his memory cannot be refreshed; and

iv. The witness verifies that the memorandum or record correctly *reflected his knowledge* when it was made.

c. *N.B.*: only the adverse party can offer the writing into evidence as an exhibit, but the other party can read it into evidence.

> (6) Records of regularly conducted activity. A memorandum, report, record, or data compilation, in any form, of acts, events, conditions, opinions, or diagnoses, made at or near the time by, or from information transmitted by, a person with knowledge, if kept in the course of a regularly conducted business activity, and if it was the regular practice of that business activity to make the memorandum, report, record or data compilation, all as shown by the testimony of the custodian or other qualified witness, or by certification that complies with Rule 902(11), Rule 902(12), or a statute permitting certification, unless the source of information or the method or circumstances of preparation indicate lack of trustworthiness. The term "business" as used in this paragraph includes business, institution, association, profession, occupation, and calling of every kind, whether or not conducted for profit.

7. "Business Records Exception"

a. Business records constitute an exception to the hearsay rule because workers have a self-interest in the accuracy of their records, since their jobs demand it. If records are not accurate, employyes could lose their jobs.

b. The business records exception does not apply to every document written while a subject is at work. To fall within the exception, the following elements must be met:

***i.*** The record or document must have been kept in the ***course*** of a ***business activity;***

ii. It must have been the ***regular practice*** of that business activity to make the record, memorandum, report, or data compilation (it was not, for example, prepared for court); and

iii. The source of information or the method or circumstances of preparation ***does not lack trustworthiness.***

c. The records must be ***authenticated*** by:

i. The *testimony* of the custodian or other qualified witness; or

ii. A ***certification*** that complies with Rule 902(11) (Certified domestic records of regularly conducted activity), Rule 902(12) (Certified foreign records of regularly conducted activity), or an applicable statute.

> (7) Absence of entry in records kept in accordance with the provisions of paragraph (6). Evidence that a matter is not included in the memoranda reports, records, or data compilations, in any form, kept in accordance with the provisions of paragraph (6), to prove the nonoccurrence or nonexistence of the matter, if the matter was of a kind of which a memorandum, report, record, or data compilation was regularly made and preserved, unless the sources of information or other circumstances indicate lack of trustworthiness.

8. "Absence of Entry in a Record"

a. The absence of an entry in a record is admissible to prove the nonoccurrence or nonexistence of the matter.

b. For example, if a car rental agency is trying to prove that the defendant stole a car, a log of the rentals that went out during that day is admissible in showing that the defendant did not rent the car that day.

c. *N.B.*: the enumeration of this as an exception to hearsay is not necessary because the failure to enter a record is not an assertion, and therefore is not hearsay.

> (8) Public records and reports. Records, reports, statements, or data compilations, in any form, of public offices or agencies, setting forth (A) the activities of the office or agency, or (B) matters observed pursuant to duty imposed by law as to which matters there was a duty to report, excluding, however, in criminal cases matters observed by police officers and other law enforcement personnel, or (C) in civil actions and proceedings and against the Government in criminal cases, factual findings resulting from an investigation made pursuant to authority granted by law, unless the sources of information or other circumstances indicate lack of trustworthiness.

9. "Public Records"

a. This exception applies to records, reports, statements, or data compilations *prepared by public offices* or agencies setting forth one:

i. The activities of the public offices or agencies;

ii. "Matters observed pursuant to duty imposed by law as to which matters there was a duty to report," with the exception of matters observed by police officers and other law enforcement personnel in criminal cases; or

iii. Factual findings resulting from an investigation (in civil actions and proceedings and against the government in criminal cases).

> (9) Records of vital statistics. Records or data compilations, in any form, of births, fetal deaths, deaths, or marriages, if the report thereof was made to a public office pursuant to requirements of law.
>
> (10) Absence of public record or entry. To prove the absence of a record, report, statement, or data compilation, in any form, or the nonoccurrence or nonexistence of a matter of which a record, report, statement, or data compilation, in any form, was regularly made and preserved by a public office or agency, evidence in the form of a certification in accordance with rule 902, or testimony, that diligent search failed to disclose the record, report, statement, or data compilation, or entry.

10. Exception 10 allows as a hearsay exception either a self-authenticating certification under Rule 902 or testimony that a search failed to disclose the record to prove the absence of a public record or entry.

> (11) Records of religious organizations. Statements of births, marriages, divorces, deaths, legitimacy, ancestry, relationship by blood or marriage, or other similar facts of personal or family history, contained in a regularly kept record of a religious organization.
>
> (12) Marriage, baptismal, and similar certificates. Statements of fact contained in a certificate that the maker performed a marriage or other ceremony or administered a

> sacrament, made by a clergyman, public official, or other person authorized by the rules or practices of a religious organization or by law to perform the act certified, and purporting to have been issued at the time of the act or within a reasonable time thereafter.
>
> (13) Family records. Statements of fact concerning personal or family history contained in family Bibles, genealogies, charts, engravings on rings, inscriptions on family portraits, engravings on urns, crypts, or tombstones, or the like.
>
> (14) Records of documents affecting an interest in property. The record of a document purporting to establish or affect an interest in property, as proof of the content of the original recorded document and its execution and delivery by each person by whom it purports to have been executed, if the record is a record of a public office and an applicable statute authorizes the recording of documents of that kind in that office.
>
> (15) Statements in documents affecting an interest in property. A statement contained in a document purporting to establish or affect an interest in property if the matter stated was relevant to the purpose of the document, unless dealings with the property since the document was made have been inconsistent with the truth of the statement or the purport of the document.
>
> (16) Statements in ancient documents. Statements in a document in existence twenty years or more the authenticity of which is established.

11. Once authenticated, all statements that have been in a document in existence for at least twenty years are admissible.

> (17) Market reports, commercial publications. Market quotations, tabulations, lists, directories, or other published compilations, generally used and relied upon by the public or by persons in particular occupations.

12. The rules permit the admission of market reports and commercial publications, since they are prepared with the expectation that the general public will rely on them and are therefore considered reliable.

> (18) Learned treatises. To the extent called to the attention of an expert witness upon cross-examination or relied upon by the expert witness in direct examination, statements contained in published treatises, periodicals, or pamphlets on a subject of history, medicine, or other science or art, established as a reliable authority by the testimony or admission of the witness or by other expert testimony or by judicial notice. If admitted, the statements may be read into evidence but may not be received as exhibits.
>
> (19) Reputation concerning personal or family history. Reputation among members of a person's family by blood, adoption, or marriage, or among a person's associates, or in the community, concerning a person's birth, adoption, marriage, divorce, death, legitimacy, relationship by blood, adoption, or marriage, ancestry, or other similar fact of personal or family history.

13. "Reputation Concerning Personal or Family History"

    a. This rule is limited only to reputation as to members of a family.

    b. To be reputation, several members of a family must believe a particular fact about a related family member.

    c. Example: W is asked where his mother was born, and he replies "I was told she was born in Nigeria." The opposing party objects. Is it hearsay?

        i. If W's only source is his mother, then it is inadmissible as hearsay.

ii. However, if several family members and neighbors tell him that, then this hearsay exception applies and the statement is admissible.

d. This rule is limited to questions of birth, adoption, marriage, and related questions.

> (20) Reputation concerning boundaries or general history. Reputation in a community, arising before the controversy, as to boundaries of or customs affecting lands in the community, and reputation as to events of general history important to the community or State or nation in which located.
>
> (21) Reputation as to character. Reputation of a person's character among associates or in the community.

14. "Reputation as to Character"

a. Rationale: since reputation is the assimilation of various different individual hearsay statements, it has a higher degree of reliability than any individual statement.

b. Thus, although Rule 404 prohibits the use of character in proving acts in conformity therewith,

c. This exception thus does not cover rumors that the witness may have heard from one person.

d. The reputation exception allows evidence of reputation to be offered in proving *character*,[81] and *not* conduct.

i. Example: everyone at the plant thinks that Bob killed his wife. Does the reputation exception apply?

ii. No; it is offered to prove Bob's conduct, not his character.

e. Reputation evidence is not always hearsay:

i. Case one: "I know Victor and he has a reputation for violence." This is hearsay because it is offered for its truth.

ii. Case two: the defendant claims that he perceived self-defense and calls a witness to testify that "the victims had a reputation for being violent." This is not hearsay because it is not offered for its truth; rather, it is offered to lend credibility to his self-defense argument.

> (22) Judgment of previous conviction. Evidence of a final judgment, entered after a trial or upon a plea of guilty (but not upon a plea of nolo contendere), adjudging a person guilty of a crime punishable by death or imprisonment in excess of one year, to prove any fact essential to sustain the judgment, but not including, when offered by the Government in a criminal prosecution for purposes other than impeachment, judgments against persons other than the accused. The pendency of an appeal may be shown but does not affect admissibility.

[81] This rule does not alter Rule 404, which does not permit character evidence to prove conduct (with some exceptions). Thus, although reputation may be used to prove character, character may *not* be used to prove conduct in conformity therewith.

15. "Judgment of Previous Conviction"

a. Final judgments resulting from trials or guilty pleas are admissible.

b. However, pleas of *nolo condendere*, guilty pleas later withdrawn, and guilty pleas to misdemeanor charges, minor charges, and infractions (*e.g.*, a traffic court violation) are inadmissible.

c. Rationale: unlike guilty pleas and convictions resulting from trial, they have low probative value in showing the defendant's guilt or even admission because the stakes are lower (*e.g.*, a guilty plea to a traffic court violation may only have been entered to avoid the time and expenses of litigation).

d. *Judgments in civil cases* and *acquittals in criminal cases* are not included in this hearsay exception, since both have low probative value.

e. When a conviction is not offered for its truth, it is not hearsay and therefore, this exception does not apply.

i. Example: under Rule 405(b), evidence that the defendant was convicted of armed robbery two years ago is offered by the prosecution in order to prove possession of a firearm by a convicted felon Is the conviction hearsay?

ii. Since it is not being offered to prove that the defendant actually committed armed robbery, but rather, that he was *convicted* of a felony, it is not hearsay.

iii. However, if it were offered to prove that the defendant committed armed robbery, it would be hearsay, but would be admissible under the Judgment of Previous Convcition exception to the hearsay rule.

> (23) Judgment as to personal, family or general history, or boundaries. Judgments as proof of matters of personal, family or general history, or boundaries, essential to the judgment, if the same would be provable by evidence of reputation.
>
> (24) [Other exceptions.][Transferred to Rule 807]

**Rule 804. Hearsay Exceptions; Declarant Unavailable**

> (a) Definition of unavailability.
>
> "Unavailability as a witness" includes situations in which the declarant--
>
> (1) is exempted by ruling of the court on the ground of privilege from testifying concerning the subject matter of the declarant's statement; or
>
> (2) persists in refusing to testify concerning the subject matter of the declarant's statement despite an order of the court to do so; or
>
> (3) testifies to a lack of memory of the subject matter of the declarant's statement; or
>
> (4) is unable to be present or to testify at the hearing because of death or then existing physical or mental illness or infirmity; or
>
> (5) is absent from the hearing and the proponent of a statement has been unable to procure the declarant's attendance (or in the case of a hearsay exception under subdivision (b)(2), (3), or (4), the declarant's attendance or testimony) by process or other reasonable means.

A declarant is not unavailable as a witness if exemption, refusal, claim of lack of memory, inability, or absence is due to the procurement or wrongdoing of the proponent of a statement for the purpose of preventing the witness from attending or testifying.

1. An Exception When the Declarant is Unavailable
   a. Normally, an out of court statement offered for its truth is inadmissible as hearsay.
   b. We have already seen exceptions where., because of the reliability of the statement being offered, the availability of the declarant is immaterial.
   c. Now we turn our attention to exceptions in which hearsay statements are admissible, despite the unavailability of the declarant.
   d. A witness is unavailable when he:
      i. Is exempted because of a privilege;
      ii. Persistently refuses to testify;
      iii. Testifies that he does not remember;
      iv. Is unable to testify because of death or illness; or
      v. Is absent from the hearing and the proponent was not able to procure the declarant "by process or other reasonable means."
   e. A declarant is *not considered unavailable* if his inability to testify is procured by the ***wrongdoing of the proponent*** of the testimony. Rational: no man should profit from his wrongdoing.
   f. Unavailability is to be determined by the court.

(b) Hearsay exceptions.

The following are not excluded by the hearsay rule if the declarant is unavailable as a witness:

(1) *Former testimony*. Testimony given as a witness at another hearing of the same or a different proceeding, or in a deposition taken in compliance with law in the course of the same or another proceeding, if the party against whom the testimony is now offered, or, in a civil action or proceeding, a predecessor in interest, had an opportunity and similar motive to develop the testimony by direct, cross, or redirect examination.

2. "Former Testimony"
   a. The former testimony of a declarant is admissible when the following elements are met:
      *i.* The witness is now ***unavailable****;*
      ii. The former testimony is made at a ***hearing or deposition;***
      iii. The defendant in a criminal case or the predecessor in interest in a civil case had an ***opportunity to examine*** the declarant; and
      iv. The defendant in a criminal case or the predecessor in interest in a civil case had a ***similar motive*** to develop the testimony.

1) *N.B.*: generally, this will mean that the same issue will be involved.

b. Example: B takes a deposition of C, who later dies. Is C's deposition admissible in trial as an exception to hearsay?

i. Yes. Although the deposition is hearsay, the declarant is now unavailable and the deposition falls within the Rule 804 exceptions as former testimony, since the opposing party could have cross examined C at the deposition.

> (2) *Statement under belief of impending death*. In a prosecution for homicide or in a civil action or proceeding, a statement made by a declarant while believing that the declarant's death was imminent, concerning the cause or circumstances of what the declarant believed to be impending death.

3. "Dying Declaration"

a. Dying declarations are admissible when the following elements are met:

i. The declarant must be ***unavailable*** (not necessarily dead);

ii. There must be ***a criminal homicide*** case or a civil case;

iii. The statement must be made by a declarant ***believing*** his death to be imminent; and

iv. The statement must concern the ***cause of the impending death***.

b. The rationale for this exception is that, where a witness's death is impending, there is little opportunity for fabricated calculations. It is also based on the religious notion that no man would want to die with a "lie on his lips."

c. A subjective standard is applied for the declarant's belief in his death.

d. As with all preliminary questions under Rule 104(a), ***the judge must determine*** whether the declarant believed his death to be impending.

> (3) *Statement against interest*. A statement which was at the time of its making so far contrary to the declarant's pecuniary or proprietary interest, or so far tended to subject the declarant to civil or criminal liability, or to render invalid a claim by the declarant against another, that a reasonable person in the declarant's position would not have made the statement unless believing it to be true. A statement tending to expose the declarant to criminal liability and offered to exculpate the accused is not admissible unless corroborating circumstances clearly indicate the trustworthiness of the statement.

4. "Statements against Interest"

a. This hearsay exception has been the most greatly reduced by *Crawford.*

b. A statement against interest is admissible when the following elements are met:

i. The declarant is unavailable;

ii. The statement was so far against his pecuniary or proprietary interest ***when made*** that the declarant would not have said it unless it was true; and

iii. Corroborating circumstances "clearly indicate the trustworthiness of the statement," when it is offered to exculpate the accused. Rule 804(b)(3).

c. A statement against interest may be ***pecuniary*** or ***proprietary***.

d. A statement against interest is an exception to the hearsay rule because it is extra reliable.

(4) *Statement of personal or family history.* (A) A statement concerning the declarant's own birth, adoption, marriage, divorce, legitimacy, relationship by blood, adoption, or marriage, ancestry, or other similar fact of personal or family history, even though declarant had no means of acquiring personal knowledge of the matter stated; or (B) a statement concerning the foregoing matters, and death also, of another person, if the declarant was related to the other by blood, adoption, or marriage or was so intimately associated with the other's family as to be likely to have accurate information concerning the matter declared.

5. "Family History/Pedigree"

a. This rule must be understood with Rule 803(19), which deals with statements of reputation that are admissible because they are based on the opinions of various members of a family.

b. Rule 804(4), on the contrary, applies to a statement of personal or family history when the following elements are met:

i. The declarant is unavailable; and

ii. One of the following:

1) The statement concerns the declarant's personal or family history (*e.g.*, birth, adoption, marriage, divorce, etc.); or

2) The statement concerns one of the foregoing matters or the death of another person if the declarant was a family member or otherwise was intimately associated with the family.

(5) [Other exceptions.][Transferred to Rule 807]

(6) Forfeiture by wrongdoing. A statement offered against a party that has engaged or acquiesced in wrongdoing that was intended to, and did, procure the unavailability of the declarant as a witness.

6. "Forfeiture by Wrongdoing"

a. A party would have to show the court that the reason that the witness is unavailable is because the opposing party has killed him or otherwise procured his unavailability.

b. Example: the defendant against whom testimony is offered threatens the witness and as a result, the witness refuses to testify, thereby becoming unavailable. The plaintiff may offer the witness's out of court statements against the defendant to prove the truth of the matter asserted.

c. This exception does not apply in every murder trial. It applies only if the defendant procured the unavailability of the victim ***as a witness***. The prosecution must therefore show that the defendant killed the victim for the purpose of preventing him from testifying.

**Rule 805. Hearsay Within Hearsay**

> Hearsay included within hearsay is not excluded under the hearsay rule if each part of the combined statements conforms with an exception to the hearsay rule provided in these rules.

1. Example: the prosecution offers a diary entry where the victim stated that the defendant threatened to kill her.

**Rule 806. Attacking and Supporting Credibility of Declarant**

> When a hearsay statement, or a statement defined in Rule 801(d)(2)(C), (D), or (E), has been admitted in evidence, the credibility of the declarant may be attacked, and if attacked may be supported, by any evidence which would be admissible for those purposes if declarant had testified as a witness. Evidence of a statement or conduct by the declarant at any time, inconsistent with the declarant's hearsay statement, is not subject to any requirement that the declarant may have been afforded an opportunity to deny or explain. If the party against whom a hearsay statement has been admitted calls the declarant as a witness, the party is entitled to examine the declarant on the statement as if under cross-examination.

1. This rule offers the defendant some protections against statements made against him under Rule 801(d)(2)(C), (D), or (E) ("(C) a statement by a person authorized by the party to make a statement concerning the subject, or (D) a statement by the party's agent or servant concerning a matter within the scope of the agency or employment, made during the existence of the relationship, or (E) a statement by a coconspirator of a party during the course and in furtherance of the conspiracy").
2. Ordinary, we never allow someone to impeach the character of a witness who has not testified.
3. However, under this rule, a party can impeach the character of the out of court declarant. The party can offer in any evidence against the character of the witness as though he had been in court.

**Rule 807. Residual Exception**

> A statement not specifically covered by Rule 803 or 804 but having equivalent circumstantial guarantees of trustworthiness, is not excluded by the hearsay rule, if the court determines that (A) the statement is offered as evidence of a material fact; (B) the statement is more probative on the point for which it is offered than any other evidence which the proponent can procure through reasonable efforts; and (C) the general purposes of these rules and the interests of justice will best be served by admission of the statement into evidence. However, a statement may not be admitted under this exception unless the proponent of it makes known to the adverse party sufficiently in advance of the trial or hearing to provide the adverse party with a fair opportunity to prepare to meet it, the proponent's intention to offer the statement and the particulars of it, including the name and address of the declarant.

1. Under this exception, statements that are otherwise hearsay may be admissible when accompanied by circumstantial guarantees of trustworthiness equivalent to those of the other hearsay exceptions.

2. A court must determine that the following elements are met:

   a. The statement is offered as evidence of a material fact;

   b. The statement is more probative on point than any other evidence that can be offered; and

   c. The general interests of justice as well as the purposes of the rules will be served by admitting the evidence.

3. The proponent must first give his opponent sufficient notice of his intention to admit the evidence.

## ARTICLE IX. AUTHENTICATION AND IDENTIFICATION

### Rule 901. Requirement of Authentication or Identification

> (a) General provision.
>
> The requirement of authentication or identification as a condition precedent to admissibility is satisfied by evidence sufficient to support a finding that the matter in question is what its proponent claims.

1. Once authenticated by ***laying a foundation,*** relevant evidence is admissible.

2. Until authentication, relevant evidence is inadmissible (with some exceptions under Rule 902).[82]

   a. Example: Party A offers evidence of a will allegedly written by B because it has B's name and signature on the bottom. Is the will admissible?

   b. No; there must first be some kind of evidence showing that the signature in fact belongs to B (*e.g.*, the identification of the document by a witness *with knowledge*. Rule 901(b)(1)).

3. If a party wishes to offer evidence, it must be "satisfied by evidence sufficient to support a finding that the matter in question is what its proponent claims."

> (b) Illustrations.
>
> By way of illustration only, and not by way of limitation, the following are examples of authentication or identification conforming with the requirements of this rule:
>
> (1) *Testimony of witness with knowledge*. Testimony that a matter is what it is claimed to be.
>
> (2) *Nonexpert opinion on handwriting*. Nonexpert opinion as to the genuineness of handwriting, based upon familiarity not acquired for purposes of the litigation.

[82] However, evidence need not be authenticated when proponent has made a request to admit under FRCP 36 (Requests for Admission) and the adverse party has agreed to stipulate some fact. For this reason, authentication is not as relevant in civil cases where the parties can send one another requests to admit. However, in criminal cases, where the defendant may assert a privilege against self-incrimination, authentication is far more relevant.

4. Example: B may testify that the signature on a contract is A's signature if he has personal familiarity with A's signature, even if he is not an expert.

   a. *N.B.*: B's familiarity must not have been acquired *for the purpose of litigation*.

> (3) *Comparison by trier or expert witness*. Comparison by the trier of fact or by expert witnesses with specimens which have been authenticated.
>
> (4) *Distinctive characteristics and the like*. Appearance, contents, substance, internal patterns, or other distinctive characteristics, taken in conjunction with circumstances.

5. Example: B may authenticate an object by showing its distinct characteristics, even without offering a witness to take the stand.

> (5) *Voice identification*. Identification of a voice, whether heard firsthand or through mechanical or electronic transmission or recording, by opinion based upon hearing the voice at any time under circumstances connecting it with the alleged speaker.

6. As with handwriting under Rule 901(b)(2), nonexperts may give opinion testimony as to the identification of a voice.

   a. Example: A receives a phone call and recognizes the voice of James W., who states, "hello, this is James W."

   b. The combination of the speaker's self-identification and the witness's recognition of the voice will serve as sufficient authentication that the voice was that of James W.

   c. *N.B.*: self-identification on its own is *not* sufficient in establishing authentication.

> (6) *Telephone conversations*. Telephone conversations, by evidence that a call was made to the number assigned at the time by the telephone company to a particular person or business, if (A) in the case of a person, circumstances, including self-identification, show the person answering to be the one called, or (B) in the case of a business, the call was made to a place of business and the conversation related to business reasonably transacted over the telephone.
>
> (7) *Public records or reports*. Evidence that a writing authorized by law to be recorded or filed and in fact recorded or filed in a public office, or a purported public record, report, statement, or data compilation, in any form, is from the public office where items of this nature are kept.
>
> (8) *Ancient documents or data compilation*. Evidence that a document or data compilation, in any form, (A) is in such condition as to create no suspicion concerning its authenticity, (B) was in a place where it, if authentic, would likely be, and (C) has been in existence 20 years or more at the time it is offered.

7. This Rule is related to Rule 803(16) (Statements in ancient documents), which establishes that all statements having existed for at least twenty years are admissible when authenticated.

   a. A document that has bee in existence for at least twenty years is authenticated when (i) it creates no suspicion concerning its authenticity; and (ii) it is in a place where it would be likely to be if authentic.

   b. Note, however, that this is not the *only* way of establishing the authenticity of a document that has been in existence for at least twenty years.

(9) *Process or system.* Evidence describing a process or system used to produce a result and showing that the process or system produces an accurate result.

(10) *Methods provided by statute or rule.* Any method of authentication or identification provided by Act of Congress or by other rules prescribed by the Supreme Court pursuant to statutory authority.

**Rule 902. Self-Authentication**

Extrinsic evidence of authenticity as a condition precedent to admissibility is not required with respect to the following:

(1) Domestic public documents under seal. A document bearing a seal purporting to be that of the United States, or of any State, district, Commonwealth, territory, or insular possession thereof, or the Panama Canal Zone, or the Trust Territory of the Pacific Islands, or of a political subdivision, department, officer, or agency thereof, and a signature purporting to be an attestation or execution.

(2) Domestic public documents not under seal. A document purporting to bear the signature in the official capacity of an officer or employee of any entity included in paragraph (1) hereof, having no seal, if a public officer having a seal and having official duties in the district or political subdivision of the officer or employee certifies under seal that the signer has the official capacity and that the signature is genuine.

(3) Foreign public documents. A document purporting to be executed or attested in an official capacity by a person authorized by the laws of a foreign country to make the execution or attestation, and accompanied by a final certification as to the genuineness of the signature and official position (A) of the executing or attesting person, or (B) of any foreign official whose certificate of genuineness of signature and official position relates to the execution or attestation or is in a chain of certificates of genuineness of signature and official position relating to the execution or attestation. A final certification may be made by a secretary of an embassy or legation, consul general, consul, vice consul, or consular agent of the United States, or a diplomatic or consular official of the foreign country assigned or accredited to the United States. If reasonable opportunity has been given to all parties to investigate the authenticity and accuracy of official documents, the court may, for good cause shown, order that they be treated as presumptively authentic without final certification or permit them to be evidenced by an attested summary with or without final certification.

(4) Certified copies of public records. A copy of an official record or report or entry therein, or of a document authorized by law to be recorded or filed and actually recorded or filed in a public office, including data compilations in any form, certified as correct by the custodian or other person authorized to make the certification, by certificate complying with paragraph (1), (2), or (3) of this rule or complying with any Act of Congress or rule prescribed by the Supreme Court pursuant to statutory authority.

(5) Official publications. Books, pamphlets, or other publications purporting to be issued by public authority.

(6) Newspapers and periodicals. Printed materials purporting to be newspapers or periodicals.

(7) Trade inscriptions and the like. Inscriptions, signs, tags, or labels purporting to have been affixed in the course of business and indicating ownership, control, or origin.

1. Example: a can with a Campbell's Soup label will be presumed to be a Campbell's Soup can.

(8) Acknowledged documents. Documents accompanied by a certificate of acknowledgment executed in the manner provided by law by a notary public or other officer authorized by law to take acknowledgments.

(9) Commercial paper and related documents. Commercial paper, signatures thereon, and documents relating thereto to the extent provided by general commercial law.

(10) Presumptions under Acts of Congress. Any signature, document, or other matter declared by Act of Congress to be presumptively or prima facie genuine or authentic.

(11) Certified domestic records of regularly conducted activity. The original or a duplicate of a domestic record of regularly conducted activity that would be admissible under Rule 803(6) if accompanied by a written declaration of its custodian or other qualified person, in a manner complying with any Act of Congress or rule prescribed by the Supreme Court pursuant to statutory authority, certifying that the record:

(A) was made at or near the time of the occurrence of the matters set forth by, or from information transmitted by, a person with knowledge of those matters;

(B) was kept in the course of the regularly conducted activity; and

(C) was made by the regularly conducted activity as a regular practice.

A party intending to offer a record into evidence under this paragraph must provide written notice of that intention to all adverse parties, and must make the record and declaration available for inspection sufficiently in advance of their offer into evidence to provide an adverse party with a fair opportunity to challenge them.

(12) Certified foreign records of regularly conducted activity. In a civil case, the original or a duplicate of a foreign record of regularly conducted activity that would be admissible under Rule 803(6) if accompanied by a written declaration by its custodian or other qualified person certifying that the record:

(A) was made at or near the time of the occurrence of the matters set forth by, or from information transmitted by, a person with knowledge of those matters;

(B) was kept in the course of the regularly conducted activity; and

(C) was made by the regularly conducted activity as a regular practice.

The declaration must be signed in a manner that, if falsely made, would subject the maker to criminal penalty under the laws of the country where the declaration is signed. A party intending to offer a record into evidence under this paragraph must provide written notice of that intention to all adverse parties, and must make the record and declaration available for inspection sufficiently in advance of their offer into evidence to provide an adverse party with a fair opportunity to challenge them.

2. Documents and other exhibits normally are not self-authenticating.

3. However, evidence falling within the categories of Rule 902 does not require extrinsic evidence for the purpose of authentication.

4. What these exceptions have in common: if anyone has a doubt as to the authenticity of these exceptions, he can simply look up the information. If, however, a party doubts the accuracy of a signed statement, he cannot verify its authenticity in this way.

**Rule 903. Subscribing Witness' Testimony Unnecessary**

The testimony of a subscribing witness is not necessary to authenticate a writing unless required by the laws of the jurisdiction whose laws govern the validity of the writing.

## ARTICLE X. CONTENTS OF WRITINGS, RECORDINGS, AND PHOTOGRAPHS

### Rule 1001. Definitions

For purposes of this article the following definitions are applicable:

(1) Writings and recordings. "Writings" and "recordings" consist of letters, words, or numbers, or their equivalent, set down by handwriting, typewriting, printing, photostating, photographing, magnetic impulse, mechanical or electronic recording, or other form of data compilation.

(2) Photographs. "Photographs" include still photographs, X-ray films, video tapes, and motion pictures.

(3) Original. An "original" of a writing or recording is the writing or recording itself or any counterpart intended to have the same effect by a person executing or issuing it. An "original" of a photograph includes the negative or any print therefrom. If data are stored in a computer or similar device, any printout or other output readable by sight, shown to reflect the data accurately, is an "original".

(4) Duplicate. A "duplicate" is a counterpart produced by the same impression as the original, or from the same matrix, or by means of photography, including enlargements and miniatures, or by mechanical or electronic re-recording, or by chemical reproduction, or by other equivalent techniques which accurately reproduces the original.

### Rule 1002. Requirement of Original

To prove the content of a writing, recording, or photograph, the original writing, recording, or photograph is required, except as otherwise provided in these rules or by Act of Congress.

1. This is known as the ***"Best Evidence Rule"*** (or "Original Document Rule").
2. General rule: an original is required when the proponent is trying to "prove the content of a writing."
3. The Best Evidence Rule applies when the ***contents of a writing are in issue***, not when the truth of what the evidence said is in issue.
    a. When the contents of a writing *are* in issue:
        i. The evidence is offered to ***prove an event;***
        ii. The contents have a ***legal effect*** and must be ***proven;***
        iii. A witness's testimony ***relies*** on the writing.
    b. When the contents of a writing are not in issue:
        i. An employment contract is offered by the defendant to prove that he was an employee of the plaintiff. Here, it is the mere existence of the contract, not its content, that is relevant. Therefore, the Best Evidence Rule does not apply.
4. There are two ways an opponent may violate the Best Evidence Rule:
    a. The original is available but the opponent offers secondary evidence (descriptions, oral testimony, imperfect duplicates) of what the original states.

i. Example; an attorney asks a witness about her recollection of the original contract.

ii. Note that the admission of exact duplicates (*e.g.*, photocopies) are *not* considered to be violations of the Best Evidence Rule.

b. The original is unavailable by the fault of the opponent.

i. Example: the attorney tells the judge, "your Honor, normally, I am required to produce the original, but I destroyed it. Therefore, I would like to ask my secretary to testify about it."

ii. The Best Evidence Rule would prohibit the secretary from testifying about the original.

iii. Rationale: an attorney should not benefit from his own wrongdoing.

**Rule 1003. Admissibility of Duplicates**

> A duplicate is admissible to the same extent as an original unless (1) a genuine question is raised as to the authenticity of the original or (2) in the circumstances it would be unfair to admit the duplicate in lieu of the original.

1. For the purpose of the Best Evidence Rule, duplicates are ordinarily treated like originals.
2. Modern photocopy technology has therefore rendered the Best Evidence Rule largely irrelevant today.
3. Today, when someone successfully objects under the Best Evidence Rule, it is usually because secondary evidence is offered in one of the following ways:

a. A description through ***oral testimony*** (example: an attorney offers to describe what an original contract states); or

b. A ***handmade written copy*** (this almost never happens anymore).

**Rule 1004. Admissibility of Other Evidence of Contents**

> The original is not required, and other evidence of the contents of a writing, recording, or photograph is admissible if—
>
> (1) Originals lost or destroyed. All originals are lost or have been destroyed, unless the proponent lost or destroyed them in bad faith; or
>
> (2) Original not obtainable. No original can be obtained by any available judicial process or procedure; or
>
> (3) Original in possession of opponent. At a time when an original was under the control of the party against whom offered, that party was put on notice, by the pleadings or otherwise, that the contents would be a subject of proof at the hearing, and that party does not produce the original at the hearing; or
>
> (4) Collateral matters. The writing, recording, or photograph is not closely related to a controlling issue.

1. Secondary evidence includes descriptions, oral testimony, imperfect duplicates, and written copies of an original.

2. Secondary evidence is admissible when:

   a. The original is unavailable for reasons other than the bad faith of the proponent of the evidence (a foundation must be laid accounting for the non-production); or

   b. No original is obtainable through any available judicial procedure; or

   c. The original is in the possession of the opponent; or

   d. The original relates only to non-material collateral matters.

**Rule 1005. Public Records**

> The contents of an official record, or of a document authorized to be recorded or filed and actually recorded or filed, including data compilations in any form, if otherwise admissible, may be proved by copy, certified as correct in accordance with rule 902 or testified to be correct by a witness who has compared it with the original. If a copy which complies with the foregoing cannot be obtained by the exercise of reasonable diligence, then other evidence of the contents may be given.

**Rule 1006. Summaries**

> The contents of voluminous writings, recordings, or photographs which cannot conveniently be examined in court may be presented in the form of a chart, summary, or calculation. The originals, or duplicates, shall be made available for examination or copying, or both, by other parties at reasonable time and place. The court may order that they be produced in court.

**Rule 1007. Testimony or Written Admission of Party**

> Contents of writings, recordings, or photographs may be proved by the testimony or deposition of the party against whom offered or by that party's written admission, without accounting for the nonproduction of the original.

1. When a party admits to the contents of a writing, the original does not need to be offered to prove its contents.

**Rule 1008. Functions of Court and Jury**

> When the admissibility of other evidence of contents of writings, recordings, or photographs under these rules depends upon the fulfillment of a condition of fact, the question whether the condition has been fulfilled is ordinarily for the court to determine in accordance with the provisions of rule 104. However, when an issue is raised (a) whether the asserted writing ever existed, or (b) whether another writing, recording, or photograph produced at the trial is the original, or (c) whether other evidence of contents correctly reflects the contents, the issue is for the trier of fact to determine as in the case of other issues of fact.

1. The jury determines whether an original document ever existed, whether a certain document is an original, and "whether other evidence of contents correctly reflects the contents."

# ARTICLE XI. MISCELLANEOUS RULES

**Rule 1101. Applicability of Rules**

(a) Courts and judges.

These rules apply to the United States district courts, the District Court of Guam, the District Court of the Virgin Islands, the Disrict Court for the Northern Mariana Islands, the United States courts of appeals, the United States Claims Court, and to the United States bankruptcy judges and United States magistrate judges, in the actions, cases, and proceedings and to the extent hereinafter set forth. The terms "judge" and "court" in these rules include United States bankruptcy judges and United States magistrate judges.

(b) Proceedings generally.

These rules apply generally to civil actions and proceedings, including admiralty and maritime cases, to criminal cases and proceedings, to contempt proceedings except those in which the court may act summarily, and to proceedings and cases under title 11, United States Code.

1. The rules apply to civil and criminal proceedings, but ***not to contempt proceedings*** where the court may act summarily, and to cases and proceedings under *USC 11.*

(c) Rule of privilege.

The rule with respect to privileges applies at all stages of all actions, cases, and proceedings.

2. In parallel with FRCP 26(b)(1), which allows for the discovery of any materials *not privileged*, FRE 1101(c) applies the rules of privilege to *all stages of all proceedings* (*i.e.*, privilege is not limited to only trials).

(d) Rules inapplicable.

The rules (other than with respect to privileges) do not apply in the following situations:

(1) *Preliminary questions of fact*. The determination of questions of fact preliminary to admissibility of evidence when the issue is to be determined by the court under rule 104.

(2) *Grand jury*. Proceedings before grand juries.

(3) *Miscellaneous proceedings*. Proceedings for extradition or rendition; preliminary examinations in criminal cases; sentencing, or granting or revoking probation; issuance of warrants for arrest, criminal summonses, and search warrants; and proceedings with respect to release on bail or otherwise.

(e) Rules applicable in part.

In the following proceedings these rules apply to the extent that matters of evidence are not provided for in the statutes which govern procedure therein or in other rules prescribed by the Supreme Court pursuant to statutory authority: the trial of misdemeanors and other petty offenses before United States magistrate judge; review of agency actions when the facts are subject to trail de novo under section 706(2)(F) of title 5, United States Code; review of orders of the Secretary of Agriculture under section 2 of the Act entitled "An Act to authorize association of producers of agricultural products" approved February 18, 1922 (7 U.S.C. 292), and under section 6 and 7(c) of the Perishable Agricultural Commodities Act, 1930 (7 U.S.C. 499f, 499g(c)); naturalization and revocation of naturalization under sections 310 - 318 of the Immigration and Nationality Act (8 U.S.C. 1421 - 1429); prize proceedings in admiralty under sections 7651 - 7681 of title 10, United States Code; review of orders of the

Secretary of the Interior under section 2 of the Act entitled "An Act authorizing associations of producers of aquatic products" approved June 25, 1934 (15 U.S.C. 522); review of orders of petroleum control boards under section 5 of the Act entitled "An act to regulate interstate and foreign commerce in petroleum and its products by prohibiting the shipment in such commerce of petroleum and its products produced in violation of State law, and for other purposes", approved February 22, 1935 (15 U.S.C. 715d); actions for fines, penalties, or forfeitures under part V of title IV of the Tariff Act of 1930 (19 U.S.C. 1581 - 1624), or under the Anti-Smuggling Act (19 U.S.C. 1701 - 1711); criminal libel for condemnation, exclusion of imports, or other proceedings under the Federal Food, Drug, and Cosmetic Act (21 U.S.C. 301 - 392); disputes between seamen under sections 4079, 4080, and 4081 of the Revised Statutes (22 U.S.C. 256 - 258); habeas corpus under sections 2241 - 2254 of title 28, United States Code; motions to vacate, set aside or correct sentence under section 2255 of title 28, United States Code; actions for penalties for refusal to transport destitute seamen under section 4578 of the Revised Statutes (46 U.S.C. 679); actions against the United States under the Act entitled "An Act authorizing suits against the United States in admiralty for damage caused by and salvage service rendered to public vessels belonging to the United States, and for other purposes", approved March 3, 1925 (46 U.S.C. 781 - 790), as implemented by section 7730 of title 10, United States Code.

3. In most proceedings in which there is no jury, the FRE do not apply.

    a. These include preliminary questions of fact, grand jury proceedings, and other miscellaneous proceedings, such as proceedings for the issuance of an arrest warrant. Rule 1101(d).

4. However, the FRE are not inapplicable in all proceedings in which a jury is absent. For example, they apply in bench trials.

# APPENDICES

# TABLE OF CASES

## *Cases*

# THEMATIC INDEX

### *F*

# GLOSSARY

## A

**Absolute majority** A majority consisting of at least half of the votes cast plus one or, stated in another form, more than half of the votes. An absolute majority requires more votes in favor than abstentions and votes against combined. *Compare* SIMPLE MAJORITY and QUALIFIED MAJORITY.

**Accord** Agreement that a debt obligation be settled for less than the creditor is entitled. *Compare* SATISFACTION.

**Accord and satisfaction** *See* ACCORD *and* SATISFACTION (separately).

***Ad coelum* doctrine** Under this doctrine, for the purpose of immovable minerals, "to whomever the soil belongs, he also owns to the sky and to the depths." It refers to the right of the owner of property to the space that extends vertically upward and downward from his property.

**Arson** The malicious, willful, and unlawful burning of a structure which, at common law, had to be the dwelling place of another.

**Assignment** A transfer of property that grants the possession of land for the *entire period of a lease*. By default, an assignment grants *all of the property* for the lease period. A *partial assignment* may however, be granted for only *part of the property* during the lease period. *Compare* SUBLEASE.

## B

**Bailment** A legally recognized property relationship between a bailor, who gives personalty to another to be held for a particular purpose, and a bailee, party that receives the property.

**Bill of attainder** An uconstitutional legislative action that singles out an individual or group for punishment without the benefit of a trial.

**Burglary** At common law, the specific intent crime that consisted of the breaking and entering of the dwelling of another at night with the intent to commit a felony therein.

## C

**Causation in fact** Actual causation that links an act with a result through implementing the "but-for" test (*i.e.*, "but for A, B would not have occurred"). *Compare* PROXIMATE CAUSE.

**Circumstantial evidence** Secondary facts and other evidence that lead to primary fact inferences.

**Chattel** An item of personal, as opposed to real property; any moveable object.

**Claim preclusion** *See RES JUDICATA*.

**Closing** (real property) The final meeting between the seller and the purchaser in a land sale contract, whereby the executory period is concluded and the payment and property are exchanged.

**Closing of escrow** *See* CLOSING.

**Collateral estoppel** Under the doctrine of collateral estoppel, a factual issue *may not be litigated* in any lawsuit if it was litigated and decided in a previous proceeding. Also referred to as ISSUE PRECLUSION.

**Consent decree** Final, binding judicial decree or judgment memorializing a voluntary agreement between parties to a lawsuit in return for withdrawal of a criminal charge or an end to a civil litigation. In a typical consent decree, the defendant has already ceased or agrees to cease the conduct alleged by the plaintiff to be illegal and consents to a court injunction barring the conduct in the future. Sometimes the defendant does not expressly admit fault, illegality or damages. Consent decrees are used most commonly in criminal and family law. They are frequently used by the US Securities and Exchange Commission. *Also known as* CONSENT ORDER or STIPULATED JUDGMENT or AGREED JUDGMENT.

**Consequential damages** Legal damages for a loss that are an indirect consequence of a breach of contract or other wrongful act. For example, if a courier failed to deliver a parcel, the dispatcher's lost revenues as a result of the non-delivery are the consequential damages. *Also known as* SPECIAL DAMAGES or INDIRECT DAMAGES. *Compare* DIRECT DAMAGES *and* INCIDENTAL DAMAGES.

**Consideration** The concept of legal value in connection with contracts. It can be anything of value, including money, services, or any action abstinence from a future action that is promised to another when making a contract. With some exceptions, in order for a promise to be enforceable, it must be supported by consideration.

**Constructive notice** Legal notice derived from the circumstances.

**Construction** The act of interpreting the sense or intention of a constitution, statute, contract, or some other text; the process of construing the meaning of a writing.

**Constructive possession doctrine** Doctrine by which control or dominion of property is granted to the owner of the *locus in quo*, in situations in which it would otherwise go to the finder (*e.g.*, in cases of treasure trove and findings generally). The doctrine is applied, for example, when an object is found in a private place of a store. The owner of the *locus in quo*, rather than the finder, obtains possession.

**Conversion** A tortious act of willful interference with the property of another without lawful justification, in a way that *deprives the owner of the use of his property*. Examples of conversion include illegal takings, the assumption of ownership, and the destruction of the property of another.

**Counterclaim** An independent cause of action made by the defendant against the plaintiff in order to defeat the plaintiff's claim.

**Criminal negligence** Extremely negligent conduct that creates a risk of death or serious bodily injury beyond that of mere civil negligence.

**Cross-claim** A claim under FRCP 13(g) by one party against a co-party arising out of the transaction or occurrence that is the subject matter either of the original action or of a counterclaim therein or relating to any property that is the subject matter of the original action

## D

**Dead Man's Act** A statute that disqualifies a party from testifying *against the estate* of the deceased because of the party's incentive to lie based on: (i) his interest in the case; and (ii) the unavailability of the deceased to contradict him.

**Detinue** An action at common law to recover PERSONALTY or its value when it is unlawfully held by another.

**Devise** To make a gift of real property by will. Property that can be given in such a gift is referred to as "devisable."

**Direct damages** Legal damages for a loss that are directly, immediately, naturally, and foreseeably related to a breach of contract or other wrongful act. *Compare* CONSEQUENTIAL DAMAGES *and* INCIDENTAL DAMAGES.

**Due process** *See* SUBSTANTIVE DUE PROCESS *and* PROCEDURAL DUE PROCESS.

**Duress** A defense that applies when the defendant acts illegally and against his own will as a result of another's *unlawful threat* of bodily harm. Duress excuses an actor from the legal effects of his actions (*e.g.*, a defendant is not guilty for a theft committed under duress).

## E

**Easement** The right to use part of land owned by another for a special purpose. *See* EASEMENT APPURTENANT and EASEMENT IN GROSS.

**Easement appurtenant** An easement that benefits the grantee's (dominant tenant) land. When there is an easement appurtenant, there are *both dominant* and *servient tenements*. *Compare* EASEMENT IN GROSS.

**Easement in gross** An easement that does not benefit the grantee's land. Although there is a servient estate, but there is no *dominant estate*. *Compare* EASEMENT APPURTENANT.

**Equitable servitude** Covenants restricting the use of land that run with the land at equity and thus offer remedies at equity (*e.g.*, injunctions). *Compare* REAL COVENANTS.

**Executory contract** Contract not yet been performed or executed by either side, such that failure to perform the contract by either side would constitute a breach of contract.

**Executory period** In a land sale contract, the period between the formation of the sale contract and the closing.

***Ex post facto* law** (Lat., a law "after the fact"). A law that does any of the following retroactively: (i) makes conduct criminal; (ii) establishes a stricter punishment for a crime; or (iii) alters the procedural or evidentiary rules in favor of the prosecution.

## F

**False pretenses** A specific intent crime consisting of the acquiring of title to the property of another through making false statements or misrepresentations with the intent of defrauding the owner.

**False swearing** Making a false statement under oath or equivalent affirmation, or swearing or affirming the truth of such a statement previously made, without believing the statement to be true.

**First degree murder** Under the modern statutory approach to murder, first degree murder is generally defined as all forms of murder having malic aforethought *and* premediation and deliberation. *Compare* SECOND DEGREE MURDER.

***Force majeure*** Extraordinary and compelling unforeseen event or circumstance, such as a war, riot, crime, or "act of God" (e.g., earthquake, flood), beyond the control of a party. A party that is unable to fulfill the terms of a contract due to *force majeure* is excused from performance.

**Freehold estate** An estate where the possessor is the owner of the property (at least for a temporary period of time).

## G

**Grand theft** The commission of LARCENY when the value of the property unlawfully taken exceeds some predetermined amount.

## H

***Habeas corpus*** Legal proceeding where a writ is brought to determine whether a person is being lawfully detained.

**Holdover tenant** A tenant who keeps possession of the property beyond the expiration of the lease.

**Homestead exemption** Legal regime designed to protect the value of the homes from property taxes, creditors, and circumstances arising from the death of the homeowner spouse. Homestead exemptions have been enacted by the laws or constitutions of several US states.

## I

**Implied easement by prior use** An easement that comes into being when an owner of two parcels of land uses one of them, the servient estate, to benefit the other in such a way that when he sells one of them, the purchaser can *reasonably expect* that the servient estate will continue to be used in a way that is consistent with its prior use.

**In-court identification** Modality of identification where an attorney asks a witness if she recognizes the perpetrator of a crime in court.

**Incidental damages** Legal damages for a loss generally arising out of breach of contract for commercially reasonable expenses, such as shipping or restocking or expenses reasonably associated with the resale of goods. *Compare* CONSEQUENTIAL DAMAGES *and* DIRECT DAMAGES.

**Indictment** Since a defendant may not cross-examine witnesses presented against him in a grand jury indictment, the Confrontation Clause does no apply. Compare RELIMINARY HEARING.

**Indirect damages** *See* CONSEQUENTIAL DAMAGES.

**Infant** A person who has not yet reached the legal age of majority (generally, eighteen years of age); a minor.

**Intent** (torts) The *mens rea* element for intentional torts, which is formed when the defendant possesses either: (i) purpose (a wanting or desiring) that a certain result come about; or (ii) knowledge to a substantial certainty that a result is substantially certain to come about as a result of his act (based on belief or knowledge).

**Intervening cause** An act that intervenes in the series of events after an act, such that it alters the resulting consequence. When intervening causes are strong enough to relieve wrongdoer of liability, they become SUPERSEDING CAUSES.

**Involuntary manslaughter** An *unintentional* killing lacking malice aforethought committed either with criminal negligence or during the commission of an unlawful act.

**Issue preclusion** *See* COLLATERAL ESTOPPEL.

## J

**Joinder** The uniting of distinct claims or parties in an action.

## K

**Knowledge to a substantial certainty** (torts) Knowledge of an extremely high risk that a particular consequence will materialize as a result of one's act. It may be based on knowledge or belief and, like purpose, satisfies the *mens rea* required in intentional torts.

## L

**Larceny** A specific intent crime consisting of the unlawful taking and carrying away of the property of another with the intent to permanently deprive him thereof.

**Leasehold estate** An estate where the possessor is not the owner of the property (*e.g.*, in the case of a rental property). Possession will spring back to the owner after the current possessor's lease or rental comes to a close.

**License** (property law) A right to use another's property that is terminable at the will of the possessor of the land.

## M

**Simple majority** A majority consisting of more votes in favor than votes against, or, stated in another way, more "yea's" than "nay's," not withstanding the number of abstentions or voters absent. *Also known as* ORDINARY MAJORITY. *Compare* ABSOLUTE MAJORITY and QUALIFIED MAJORITY.

***Malum in se*** (Lat., "a wrong in itself"). An inherently evil or immoral act, regardless of whether it is prohibited.

***Malum prohibitum*** (Lat., "a prohibited wrong"). An act or offense which is prohibited but is not inherently wrong (*e.g.*, failing to stop at a stop sign).

**Merchantable title** Title not subject to such reasonable doubt that it would create a just apprehension of its validity in the mind of a reasonable prudent person. Merchantable title is not necessarily good title; it may have *slight defects*.

**Mortgage** Security for a debt given by a mortgagor (a debtor) to a mortgagee (a creditor) to secure a loan given to the mortgagor, usually for the purpose of purchasing land or some other real estate.

**Mortgagee** In a mortgage, the creditor, loan company, or bank that lends to the debtor, or mortgagor.

**Mortgagor** In a mortgage, the party that borrows from a creditor, loan company, or bank; a debtor.

## N

**Negligence *per se*** Negligence established as a matter of law such that the plaintiff need not establish duty and breach. The violation of civil and criminal statutes gives rise to negligence *per se* in most states, such that the jury is instructed that the violation of a statute constitutes the breach of duty for the purposes of negligence.

**Nonjusticiable political question** A question that involves the exercise of *discretionary power* by either the Legislative or the Executive Branch; it does not involve a *judicial* question to be decided by the judiciary.

**Nuisance** A condition or activity on another's land that unreasonably affects the other's right to enjoy and use his land. The standard is one of a person of *ordinary sensibility*.

## O

**Ordinary majority** *See* SIMPLE MAJORITY.

**Order to show cause** Court order that requires one or more of the parties to justify, explain, or prove something to the court. They are commonly used when a judge needs more information before deciding whether or not to issue an order requested by a party.

## P

**Parol evidence** Oral or written evidence of a bargain that occurred before the final terms of the contract were laid down and that was not made part of the final contract.

**Parol evidence rule** Rule of substantive law that states that supplementary oral or written evidence of any agreement prior to or contemporaneous with the laying down of the final terms of the contract cannot be used to contradict or vary the final agreement.

**Partial-birth abortion** Any abortion where a physician partially induces a vaginal delivery of the fetus prior to destroying and delivering the fetus.

**Pendent parties jurisdiction** The jurisdiction to adjudicate a claim against a party who is not otherwise within court's jurisdiction, because the claim by or against that party arises from the same core facts of another claim that is properly before the court.

**Perjury** Knowingly making a false statement under oath during an official proceeding, such as a trial or a grand jury hearing. For a statement to rise to the level of perjury in most states, it must be "material" to the proceeding, meaning that the false information could have affected the outcome of the proceeding.

**Personalty** Personal property, which is moveable, as contrasted with REALTY (real property).

**Photographic lineup** Modality of identification where a witness identifies one suspect among others in a spread of photographs.

**Pleading** Documents filed by a litigant that set forth the material facts and legal arguments of his claims or defenses.

**Police lineup** Modality of identification in which suspects are lined up at a police station and a witness is asked if he recognizes the perpetrator among them.

**Preliminary hearing** Permits a defendant to cross-examine witnesses presented against him. Compare INDICTMENT.

***Prima facie case*** A case in which the plaintiff presents sufficient evidence "on its first appearance" (Lat.) supporting the cause of action. If no contrary or rebutting evidence is presented, the plaintiff is entitled to a decision in his favor.

**Privity of contract** Doctrine whereby a contract cannot confer rights or impose obligations arising under it on any person or agent except the parties to it. Horizontal privity occurs when the benefits of a contract are given to a third party. Vertical privity arises when one of the parties to a contract enters into a contract with a third party.

**Procedural due process** One of the modalities of DUE PROCESS (the other being SUBSTANTIVE DUE PROCESS) consisting of the constitutional guarantees of notice and a hearing.

***Profit à prendre*** An easement that grants the right to enter and remove timber, minerals, oil, gas, game, and other substances from another's land.

**Promissory note** Negotiable instrument where the issuer makes an unconditional promise in writing to pay a determined sum of money to a payee, either at a fixed or determinable future time or on demand of the payee, under specific terms. Regulated by the Convention Providing a Uniform Law for Bills of Exchange and Promissory Notes.

**Proximate cause** is legal causation that serves as a limitation on actual cause. The law limits those acts that are said to be "causes" of some consequence, requiring the acts to be related to the consequence through some foreseeable sequence of events. If an act is foreseeably related, it is said to be the proximate. Compare CAUSATION IN FACT.

## Q

**Qualified majority** A majority requiring more votes or other conditions than a SIMPLE MAJORITY. It may, for example, require the votes of at least two thirds of the eligible voters or a limit on the number of abstentions that would be allowed in order for a measure to be adopted. *Also known as* SPECIAL MAJORITY. *Compare* SIMPLE MAJORITY *and* ABSOLUTE MAJORITY.

***Quantum meruit*** A Latin expression meaning "as much as he deserves." This is a doctrine at equity that allows a party to recover for the value of the labor or materials delivered to another, even if there was no actual contract or if there was a contract and the party breached it, in order to prevent the other party's unjust enrichment.

## R

**Rape** Under the common law, rape was defined as "the carnal knowledge of a woman forcibly and against her will." The modern law has departed from this view by defining rape in gender-neutral terms.

***Ratione soli* doctrine** Under this doctrine, also known as the "*ad coelum* minor doctrine," the owner of the soil *is the first occupant* and owner of whatever is found on the soil, including minerals and *ferae naturae*, regardless of who the finder is.

**Real covenant** A promise relating to land use that runs with the land at law and is enforceable at law (offering monetary damages as remedies) between the original covenanting parties as a contract. Compare EQUITABLE SERVITUDE.

**Realty** Real property, which is immovable and fixed to the ground (*e.g.*, buildings, land), as contrasted with PERSONALTY.

**Recklessness** (torts) The purposeful disregard of a high probability of a resulting consequence (*e.g.*, of resulting emotional distress, in the case of the intentional infliction of emotional distress).

**Replevin** An action at common law to recover *the possession* of personalty wrongfully taken from the plaintiff. Compare TROVER.

**Replevy** To exercise the common law action of REPLEVIN.

***Res ipsa loquitur*** A negligence circumstantial evidence doctrine that is invoked when the facts create such a strong presumption of negligence that "the thing speaks for itself" (*Lat.*). The plaintiff is not required to introduce direct evidence.

***Res judicata*** Under the doctrine of *res judicata* (Lat., the "the thing already adjudicated"), a party *may not litigate* ***claims*** that he raised or could have raised in a previous suit that reached a final judgment. Also referred to as CLAIM PRECLUSION.

**Respondeat superior** (*Lat.*, "let the superior answer") The doctrine that a master or principal is *vicariously liable* for the negligence of his servants or agents, even when he was not himself negligent. This doctrine usually refers to the liability of employers for their employees.

**Restitution** Restoration of an original situation before an injury was caused, often in the form of repayment to the offended. In contract law, it puts the ***promisor*** back into the position that he would have been in had there been no contract.

**Robbery** The specific intent crime that consists of the unlawful taking of property from another person or in the person's presence by the use of force or by threatening the imminent use of force.

## S

**Satisfaction** Satisfactory fulfillment of a debt obligation through the rendering of an agreed-to lesser performance. *Compare* ACCORD.

**Second degree murder** Under the modern statutory approach to murder, second degree murder is generally defined as all forms of murder having malice aforethought, but, unlike FIRST DEGREE MURDER, lacks premeditation and deliberation (*e.g.*, depraved heart murder, felony murder committed in tandem with a non-inherently dangerous felony, etc.).

**Shelter principle** Under this principle, if a possessor of some chattel or other property became the legitimate owner of the property under some theory of ownership (*e.g.*, adverse possession, accession, etc.), then all subsequent possessors may claim that good title was also passed to them if they legitimately acquired the good.

**Showup** Modality of identification in which police seize a suspect, bring him to the victim of a crime, and ask the witness if the suspect is the perpetrator. A showup usually occurs before an indictment, when time is of the essence.

**Solicitation** The act of entreating, imploring, inducing, or encouraging another person to engage in some unlawful behavior.

**Special damages** *See* CONSEQUENTIAL DAMAGES.

**Special majority** *See* QUALIFIED MAJORITY.

**Statute of limitations** Statute that sets the maximum time after an event in which legal proceedings based on that event may commence.

***Sua sponte*** By order of the court, "of its own will" (Lat.), without motions by either party.

**Sublease** A transfer of property that grants possession of the land to a new tenant for *part of the duration of a lease period*, even if it is as little as one minute. Compare ASSIGNMENT.

**Subpoena** Writ issued by court authority to compel the attendance of a witness at a judicial proceeding; disobedience may be punishable as a contempt of court.

**Substantive due process** One of the modalities of DUE PROCESS (the other being PROCEDURAL DUE PROCESS) generally held to consist of unenumerated historical rights based on longstanding traditions.

**Suicide pact** An agreement whereby two or more people agree to kill one another.

**Superseding cause** An INTERVENING CAUSE that is strong enough to relieve a wrongdoer of liability.

**Supplemental jurisdiction** The jurisdiction that a court has over a claim that is *part of the same case or controversy* as another claim over which the court has *original jurisdiction*.

## T

**Tort** A civil wrong, other than a breach of contract, for which the law provides a remedy.

**Tortfeasor** A person who has committed a tort.

**Trover** A remedy that allows the rightful owner of property to recover possession or to recover damages for the wrongful taking of his property. Compare REPLEVIN.

## V

**Voidable title** Title that is fraudulently transferred or transferred through the owner's negligence. Although it is imperfect, it has the potential of becoming full title (if transferred to a *bona fide* purchasaer, for example). Compare VOID TITLE.

**Void Title** Fatally flawed title that no action can cure or transform into full title. Compare VOIDABLE TITLE.

***Voir Dire*** Judicial procedure in which attorneys examine prospective jurors to determine competency and potential bias. The process leads to the rejection or selection of those who will ultimately serve on the jury in a particular case.

**Voluntary manslaughter** An intentional killing mitigated by provocation in the heat of passion or other circumstances that negate malice aforethought.

## W

**Without prejudice** Without any loss or waiver of rights or privileges. When used in negotiations, statements "without prejudice" cannot be used as evidence in court, since they are made for the purpose of settlement and not as concessions for litigation. When a lawsuit is dismissed without prejudice, none of the rights or privileges of the defendant are considered lost or waived, and if the defendant is later retried, he cannot invoke the doctrine of *res judicata*.

www.ingramcontent.com/pod-product-compliance
Lightning Source LLC
LaVergne TN
LVHW082012200926
848481LV00010B/2841